THE POPES

John Julius Norwich is the author of histories of Norman Sicily, the Republic of Venice, the Byzantine Empire and, most recently, *The Middle Sea: A History of the Mediterranean*. He has also written on architecture, music and the history plays of Shakespeare, and has presented some thirty historical documentaries on BBC Television. Formerly Chairman of Colnaghi – the oldest fine art dealers in London – he is Honorary Chairman of Venice in Peril and Chairman Emeritus of the World Monuments Fund in Britain. For twenty-five years he was a member of the Executive Committee of the National Trust, and has also served on the Boards of English National Opera and the London Library. He is a regular lecturer on history, art history, architecture and music, and is an enthusiastic nightclub pianist.

JOHN JULIUS NORWICH

The Popes

A History

VINTAGE BOOKS
London

Published by Vintage 2012

8 10 9

First published in Great Britain in 2011 by
Chatto & Windus

Vintage
Random House, 20 Vauxhall Bridge Road,
London SW1V 2SA

www.vintage-books.co.uk

Addresses for companies within The Random House Group Limited
can be found at: www.randomhouse.co.uk/offices.htm

The Random House Group Limited Reg. No. 954009

A CIP catalogue record for this book
is available from the British Library

ISBN 9780099565871

The Random House Group Limited supports the Forest Stewardship
Council® (FSC®), the leading international forest-certification
organisation. Our books carrying the FSC label are printed on
FSC®-certified paper. FSC is the only forest-certification scheme
supported by the leading environmental organisations, including
Greenpeace. Our paper procurement policy can be found at
www.randomhouse.co.uk/environment

Typeset in Sabon by Palimpsest Book Production Limited,
Falkirk, Stirlingshire

Printed and bound by CPI Group (UK) Ltd, Croydon, CR0 4YY

For Allegra
who had the idea in the first place

Contents

CONTENTS

List of Illustrations

Section Two

Pope Pius II at Ancona. Pinturicchio, Piccolomini Library, Siena Cathedral © 2011. Photo Scala, Florence

Pope Leo X and his nephews. Raphael, Galleria degli Uffizi, Florence. © 2011. Photo Scala, Florence – courtesy of the Ministero Beni e Att. Culturali

Pope Clement VII. Sebastiano del Piombo, Museo di Capodimonte, Naples. Italy/ Giraudon/ The Bridgeman Art Library

Pope Paul III. Titian, Museo di Capodimonte, Naples © 2011. Photo Scala, Florence – courtesy of the Ministero Beni e Att. Culturali

Bust of Pope Paul V. Gianlorenzo Bernini, Statens Museum for Kunst, Copenhagen © AKG-images/Erich Lessing

Pope Innocent X. Velasquez, Galleria Doria Pamphilj, Rome © V&A Images/ Victoria and Albert Museum, London

Pope Pius VII. Jacques-Louis David, Musée du Louvre, Paris © RMN / Géard Blot

Coronation of the Emperor Napoleon and the Empress Josephine in Notre-Dame, 2 December 1804. Jacques-Louis David, Musée du Louvre, Paris © RMN / Hervé Lewandowski

Pope Pius IX and King Victor Emmanuel II. Popular Print © Mary Evans Picture Library

Pope Leo XIII. Mass-produced popular print, Museo del Risorgimento, Milan © 2011. Photo Scala, Florence

Pope Pius XII at his coronation in 1939 © Mary Evans Picture Library

Pope John Paul I, 1978 © Getty Images / Hulton Archive

Pope John Paul II, 1981 © Press Association

List of Maps

Maps by Reginald Piggott

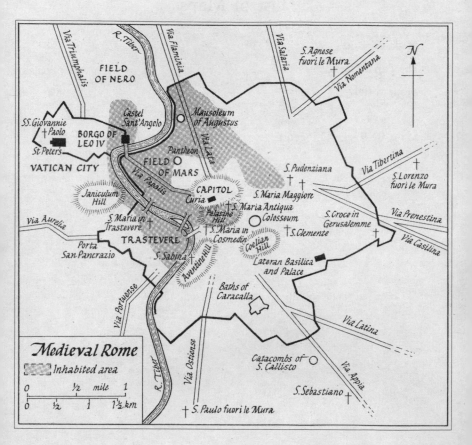

Medieval Rome

Inhabited area

0   ½   mile   1
0   ½   1   1½ km

N

FIELD OF NERO

Via Triumphalis

R. Tiber

Via Flaminia

Via Salaria

S. Agnese fuori le Mura

Via Nomentana

SS. Giovannie Paolo

St Peter's

VATICAN CITY

BORGO OF LEO IV

Castel Sant'Angelo

Mausoleum of Augustus

Via Lata

Pantheon

FIELD OF MARS

Via Papalis

Via Tiberina

S. Lorenzo fuori le Mura

S. Pudenziana

Via Prenestina

Janiculum Hill

CAPITOL

Curia

S. Maria Maggiore

Via Aurelia

S. Maria in Trastevere

Palatine Hill

S. Maria Antiqua

Colosseum

S. Croce in Gerusalemme

Via Casilina

Porta San Pancrazio

TRASTEVERE

S. Maria in Cosmedin

Coelian Hill

S. Clemente

S. Sabina

Aventine Hill

Lateran Basilica and Palace

Via Portuense

Baths of Caracalla

Via Latina

Via Ostiense

R. Tiber

Catacombs of S. Callisto

Via Appia

S. Sebastiano

S. Paulo fuori le Mura

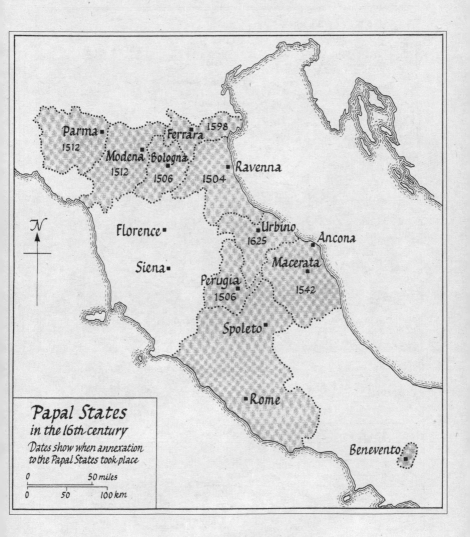

Parma
1512

Modena
1512

Ferrara 1598

Bologna
1506

Ravenna

1504

Florence

Siena

Urbino
1625

Ancona

Macerata
1542

Perugia
1506

Spoleto

Rome

Benevento

N

Papal States
in the 16th century
Dates show when annexation
to the Papal States took place

0   50 miles
0   50   100 km

Modern Italy

THE POPES

Introduction

After nearly 2,000 years of existence, the papacy is the oldest continuing absolute monarchy in the world. To millions, the Pope is the Vicar of Christ on Earth, the infallible interpreter of divine revelation. To millions more, he is the fulfilment of biblical prophecies of the Antichrist. What cannot be denied is that Roman Catholicism began with Christianity itself; all other Christian religions – and there are more than 22,000 of them – are offshoots or deviations from it.

This book is, essentially, a straightforward single-volume history of the papacy. It is an idea that I have had at the back of my mind for at least a quarter of a century, and I have been running up against various individual popes for a good deal longer than that. Several of them played a major part in my history of Norman Sicily, written forty years ago, and a good many more played equally important roles in my histories of Venice, Byzantium and – most recently – the Mediterranean. I can even claim some personal experience of the Vatican, having worked in its Library and having had two private audiences – with Pius XII and Paul VI – the latter when I was lucky enough to attend his coronation as dogsbody to the Duke of Norfolk, who was representing the Queen. In addition, I well remember the future John XXIII, who was Papal Nuncio in Paris while my father was ambassador there, and the future John Paul I, when he was Patriarch of Venice.

But we are talking about a history, not a personal memoir. As such, it clearly cannot hope to tell the whole story – which is far too long for one volume and all too often verging on the tedious. Many of the early popes are little more than names, and one of them – Pope Joan, to whom I have nevertheless been unable to resist devoting a short chapter – never existed at all. We naturally begin at the beginning, with St Peter; but after him, for the better part of the next millennium, the story will be episodic rather than continuous, concentrating on those pontiffs who made history: Leo the Great, for example, protecting Rome from the Huns and the Goths; Leo III, laying the imperial crown on the head of an astonished Charlemagne; Gregory the Great and his successors, manfully struggling with emperor after emperor for supremacy; and Innocent III and the calamitous Fourth

Crusade. Later chapters will deal with the 'Babylonian captivity' in Avignon; with the monstrous popes of the High Renaissance, notably the Borgia Alexander VI, Julius II and the Medici Leo X ('God has given us the Papacy, now let us enjoy it'); with those of the Counter-Reformation, above all Paul III; with the luckless Pius VII, who had to contend with Napoleon; and with his still more unfortunate name-sake Pius IX, who steered – or more often failed to steer – the papacy through the storm of the Risorgimento.

When we reach the start of the twentieth century we shall look particularly at the remarkable Leo XIII, and then at the popes of the two world wars, Benedict XV and the odiously anti-Semitic Pius XII, to whom the beloved Pope John XXIII came as such a welcome contrast. Then, after a brief glimpse of the unhappy Paul VI, we come to the greatest papal mystery of modern times, the death – after a pontificate lasting barely a month – of John Paul I. Was he murdered? At the start of my investigations it seemed to me more than likely that he was; now I am not so sure. Finally we shall discuss the aston-ishing phenomenon of John Paul II. As for Benedict XVI, we shall just have to wait and see.

Papal history can, like other varieties, be written from any number of points of view. This book is essentially political, cultural and, up to a point, social. There are moments, from time to time, when basic matters of doctrine cannot be avoided – in order to explain the Arian Heresy, the Great Schism with the Orthodox Church, the Albigensian Crusade, the Reformation, even Infallibility and the Immaculate Conception – but as far as possible I have tried to steer well clear of theology, on which I am in any case unqualified to pronounce. In doing so, I have followed in the footsteps of many of the popes themselves, a surprising number of whom seem to have been far more interested in their own temporal power than in their spiritual well-being.

Let me say once again what I have protested on countless occasions before: I am no scholar, and my books are not works of scholarship. This one probably contains no significant information that any self-respecting Church historian will not be perfectly well aware of already; but it is not designed for Church historians. It is intended, like every-thing else I have written, for the average intelligent reader, believer or unbeliever, who would simply like to know a little more about the background to what is, by any account, an astonishing story.

I have tried, as always, to maintain a certain lightness of touch. Historical accuracy must never, of course, be knowingly sacrificed in the cause of entertainment – even though, particularly in the early centuries, it is all too often impossible to guarantee – but there remain countless fascinating and well-authenticated stories and anecdotes that it would have been sad indeed to omit. Some of these are to the credit of the papacy, others not; I can only say that, as an agnostic Protestant, I have absolutely no axe to grind, still less any desire either to whitewash the papacy or to hold it up to ridicule. My job has been simply to look at what is perhaps the most astonishing social, political and spiritual institution ever created, and to give as honest, as objective and as accurate an account of it as I possibly can.

John Julius Norwich
London
October 2010

CHAPTER I

St Peter

(1–100 AD)

It all started, according to the generally accepted view, with St Peter. To most of us he is a familiar figure. We see his portrait in a thousand churches – painted, frescoed or chiselled in stone: curly grey hair, close-cropped beard, his keys dangling from his waist. Sometimes he stands beside, sometimes opposite, the black-bearded, balding St Paul, armed with book and sword. Together they represent the Church's joint mission: Peter to the Jews of the Diaspora, Paul to the Gentiles. Peter's original name was Simon, or perhaps Symeon. (Oddly enough, the two names are unrelated: the first is Greek, the second Hebrew, but both languages were current in Bethsaida in Galilee where he was born.) Profession: fisherman, and quite a successful one. Simon and his brother Andrew were in partnership with James and John, the sons of Zebedee; he seems to have had his own boat, and could certainly afford to employ a number of assistants. His brother Andrew is described by St John as having been a disciple of John the Baptist, and it may well have been through the Baptist that Simon first met Jesus. At any rate he soon became the first of the disciples, and then of the twelve Apostles whom Christ selected from them – seeing them, perhaps, as a symbol of the twelve tribes of Israel; and he had already reached this position of pre-eminence when, at Caesarea Philippi, St Matthew (XVI, 18–19) reports Jesus as saying to him: 'Thou art Peter, and on this rock I will build my church . . . I will give unto thee the keys of the Kingdom of Heaven.' On those few words – the Latin version of which is inscribed around the base of the dome of St Peter's Basilica – rests the entire structure of the Roman Catholic Church.

The name Peter is so familiar to us today that it comes as something of a surprise to learn that until those words were uttered it was not a name at all, but a perfectly ordinary noun: the Aramaic *kephas*, translated into the Greek *petros*, meaning a rock or stone. There seems little doubt that Jesus did indeed bestow it upon Simon; the fact is confirmed by St Mark, and also by St John, although John's version is rather later, and the two admittedly disagree about the actual occasion when the event occurred. Matthew's is, however, the only gospel that adds Jesus's stated reason for the choice of name, and it is this addition that has led scholars to suggest that the whole passage may be a later interpolation. The very fact that it does not appear in the other gospels has struck some of them as suspicious – though there are plenty of other incidents that are reported by only one of the evangelists and that have gone unquestioned. A stronger objection is that the word for 'church' – the Greek *ecclesia* – occurs only twice in all four gospels, its other appearance[1] being in a context that is suspect for other reasons. In any event, would Jesus really be thinking at this early stage of founding a Church?

If Jesus never uttered the words at all, then the Roman Catholic Church, far from being founded on a rock, rests on very shaky foundations indeed. But even if he did, another question remains: what precisely did he mean? Was Peter, having established the Church, to be followed by an infinite number of successors, each in turn inheriting Peter's own apostolic commission? And if so, in what capacity? Not, certainly, as Bishops of Rome, a city that Christ never mentioned – to him, Jerusalem was far more important. The evidence, such as it is, suggests that he meant nothing of the kind.

And what happened to Peter anyway? The New Testament tells us virtually nothing, either about him or about his colleague, St Paul. According to a very early tradition, they were both in Rome in the year AD 64, when a terrifying fire raged through the city. The Emperor Nero was accused of 'fiddling', or singing to his lute, during the conflagration, and was later rumoured to have started it himself. Tacitus tells us that:

> to be rid of this rumour, Nero fastened the guilt on a class hated for their abominations, which the populace called Christians. Mockery of every sort accompanied their deaths. Covered with the skins of beasts, they were torn apart by dogs and so perished. Others were nailed to crosses or consumed by the flames. Nero even threw open his garden for the spectacle and mounted a performance in the circus.

According to that same tradition, both Peter and Paul were among the victims. The Acts of the Apostles, however – written, almost

---

[1] Matthew XVIII, 17.

certainly after these persecutions, by St Luke, whom we know to have accompanied Paul to Rome – is once again maddeningly uninformative. It does not even mention Paul's martyrdom, merely remarking in its penultimate verse that he stayed in the city for two years; as for Peter, he fades out of the book for ever, halfway through Chapter XII, when we are told, quite simply, that 'he departed, and went to another place'. The spotlight then turns on Paul, and remains on him until the end.

There are so many questions that Luke could have answered. Was Peter indeed crucified head downwards, at his request? Was he even crucified at all? Did he ever actually travel to Rome? He certainly had good reason to, simply because to him was entrusted the mission to the Jews, and – with some 30,000–40,000 Jews living in Rome at that time – the embryonic Roman Church would have been very largely Jewish. But nowhere in the New Testament is there any evidence that he went to Rome at all. He certainly does not seem to have been there when Paul wrote his Epistle to the Romans, probably in AD 58. The final chapter of this Epistle gives a long list of names to whom the writer sends his greetings; the name of Peter is not among them. If, then, he did indeed meet his death in Rome, he could not have been there for very long – and certainly not long enough to found the Roman Church, which in any case had already begun to take shape. It is worth pointing out, too, that there is no contemporary or even near-contemporary reference to Peter having been a bishop; nor, according to all the indications, was there even a bishop in Rome before the second century AD.[1]

There are, however, two pieces of evidence that suggest Peter did indeed visit the capital and die there, though neither is conclusive. The first comes from his own First Epistle, the penultimate verse of which contains the words 'She [presumably the Church, such as it was] that is in Babylon . . . saluteth you.' This is at first sight nonsense, until we discover that Babylon was a recognised symbolic name for Rome, used in this sense no fewer than four times in the Book of Revelation. The second testimony comes in a letter from a certain Clement, a Roman presbyter or elder of the Church – he usually

---

[1] A treatise known as *The Shepherd of Hermas*, written in Rome at the beginning of the second century AD, always speaks of 'the rulers of the Church' or 'the elders that preside over the Church'. It is hard to say who was the first true Pope, or supreme bishop; but the process seems to have been complete by the time of Anicetus (*c*.155–66), though until well into the third century the Christian community in Rome remained dangerously fissile.

appears as third or fourth in the list of popes – who seems to have known St Peter personally.[1] It was written in about AD 96 to the Church at Corinth, where a serious dispute had arisen. The key passage here (in Chapter V) reads:

> Let us set before our eyes our good apostles: Peter, who because of unrighteous jealousy suffered not one or two but many trials, and having thus given his testimony went to the glorious place which was his due. Through jealousy and strife Paul demonstrated how to win the prize of patient endurance: seven times he was imprisoned; he was forced to leave and stoned; he preached in the East and the West; and, finally, he won the splendid renown which his faith had earned.

Why, we ask ourselves for the thousandth time, did the early fathers have to do quite so much beating about the bush? Why could they not say in so many words that people were martyred or crucified? But there: we know that Paul met his death during the persecutions under Nero (Tertullian tells us that he was beheaded) and the way Clement mentions the two in almost the same breath strongly suggests that Peter met a similar fate. All that can be said for sure is that by the middle of the second century – which could well be during the lifetime of the grandchildren of people who had actually known them – it was generally accepted that Peter and Paul had both been martyred in Rome. There were even two places associated with their martyrdom: and not specifically Christian burial places like the Catacombs, but non-denominational cemeteries, one on the Vatican Hill, the other outside the walls on the road to Ostia.

When, in about AD 320, the Roman Emperor Constantine the Great decided to build a basilica dedicated to St Peter on the Vatican Hill, he was clearly determined to build it on that precise spot and nowhere else. This caused him appalling difficulties. Instead of settling for the more or less level ground at the base of the hill, he chose a site on a steep slope – a decision that involved cutting away a vast mass of the hillside above and constructing three heavy parallel walls beneath, the spaces between them densely packed with earth. Moreover the chosen site was already a huge necropolis, teeming with burial places, and was still in use. Hundreds of tombs must have been destroyed, thou-

---

[1] Later, according at least to legend, Clement was exiled to the Crimea and martyred by being tied to an anchor and hurled into the sea.

sands of bodies desecrated. There was no time for demolition: the buildings simply had their roofs removed, after which they were filled with rubble to make a foundation for the new basilica – a practice, incidentally, that proved a blessing to twentieth-century archaeologists. The orientation of the Emperor's new building was also curious: the liturgical east end faced due west. For all this, there can only have been one reason: Constantine built directly over the spot where he believed the bones of St Peter to lie.

Was he right? Well, he may have been. We have one more piece of near-contemporary evidence. The historian Eusebius[1] quotes a Roman priest named Gaius, who wrote in about AD 200: 'If you go to the Vatican or to the Ostian Way, there you find the trophies (*tropaia*) of those who founded this Church.' The Ostian Way refers to St Paul and does not concern us here; but the Vatican reference surely suggests some sort of memorial – *tropaion* means a monument of victory or triumph – to St Peter that was clearly visible on the Vatican Hill, at that time an open cemetery.

Excavations undertaken in the *sacre grotte* (the crypt of the basilica, below the floor of the Constantinian church) during and immediately after the Second World War revealed a two-tiered, three-niched construction, usually known as the *aedicula* and datable to AD 160–70. In front of it are several earlier burial places – a fact that may well be more significant than initially appears. Since these contain no tombs or sarcophagi, we cannot be sure whether they are Christian or pagan; however, we know that in Rome, up to at least the middle of the second century, bodies were normally cremated; the absence of cremations from this particular corner of the old cemetery suggests that it may have been reserved for people holding special beliefs, in which case they were probably Christians. Moreover, the presence of a considerable number of votive coins – a few from as early as the first century – strongly suggests that here was a much-visited shrine.

For reasons too long and complicated to go into here,[2] the *aedicula* is now generally believed to be Gaius's 'trophy'. Pope Pius XII, however, went a good deal further when, in his 1950 Christmas Message, he confidently claimed it to be the burial place of St Peter. Such certainly seems to have been the generally held belief in Rome towards the end of the

---

[1] *Ecclesiastical History.*
[2] Readers wishing to know more are referred to J.M.C. Toynbee and J. Ward-Perkins, *The Shrine of St Peter and the Vatican Excavations.*

second century; but, perhaps inevitably, there have been objections. Peter was not, as Paul was, a highly sophisticated Roman citizen; he was an uneducated Galilean fisherman. If he had been executed – whether or not by crucifixion – his body would normally have been thrown into the River Tiber and would have been difficult indeed to recover. If he had met his death by fire among the countless other victims of Nero's persecutions, his remains are even less likely to have survived. Perhaps, then, it is more probable that the *aedicula* was intended as a sort of cenotaph, a memorial rather than a mausoleum.

We can speculate for ever; we shall never know for sure. Nor, on the other hand, is it really necessary that we should. Even if that enigmatic little construction has no connection with him at all, St Peter may still have come to Rome. If it does indeed mark his final resting place, it still gives no real support to the claims of all succeeding popes to have inherited from him their divine commission.

And here, surely, is the crux of the matter. Peter's function, if we are to accept the testimony of St Matthew, was to be a foundation stone for the Church; and foundation stones are, by definition, unique. The doctrine of the Apostolic Succession, which is accepted by both the Roman Catholic and the Orthodox Churches, holds that bishops represent a direct, uninterrupted line of spiritual descent from the Apostles, by virtue of which they possess certain special powers, including those of confirming church members, ordaining priests and consecrating other bishops. So far so good; but there is nothing in the New Testament to suggest that they may inherit the distinctive commission that was given to Peter alone.

So what conclusions, if any, are we to draw from all this? It seems more likely than not that St Peter did in fact come to Rome and was martyred there, probably somewhere on the Vatican Hill. There his remains may have been buried, the site being marked (with greater or lesser accuracy) by the shrine that grew up in the later second century; unfortunately there are still too many question marks for any confident deductions to be made. What Peter most certainly did not do was found the Roman Church. He seems to have been in the city for only a very short time before his martyrdom, and he could not possibly have been a diocesan bishop as we understand the term, and as the Pope is Bishop of Rome today. The obvious reason for his subsequent elevation is that when, in the course of the second century, the Church of Rome acquired an effective primacy over its fellow-churches – largely owing to the prestige of the imperial capital – it sought justification for its position; and there, lying ready to hand, was Matthew XVI, 18. It looked no further.

But let us return now to St Peter himself. What sort of a man was he? He certainly had his faults, which the gospels (except Luke's) make no attempt to conceal; his denial of Christ alone, had the Master been less forgiving, might have ended his career once and for all. He continued to be vacillating and unsure of himself; there is a curious passage in Paul's epistle to the Galatians telling of a row that the two had at Antioch, when Peter at first ate with the Gentiles and later – caving in, as he so often did, to the opposition, in this case the hard-line Jewish Christians concerned about the kosher laws – refused to do so.[1] He could be impulsive and violent, as when he drew his sword and struck off the ear of the high priest's servant.[2] And yet, from the very start, there can be little doubt that he was the generally acknowledged leader of Christ's disciples. Every time any one of the three synoptic evangelists[3] refers to a small group, Peter is one of them and is named first. Consistently, too, it is he who is spokesman for them all. He was certainly no more educated than his fellows – how could he have been? – and we know that in later life he had great difficulty in learning Greek; but he must have possessed certain innate and instantly recognisable qualities that singled him out from his fellows. Finally, he was the first of the disciples (if we are to believe St Paul) to whom the resurrected Christ appeared.[4]

By the time of his martyrdom – if martyred he was – Peter could look back on a relatively long and, by any standards, astonishing life. Beginning as a simple Galilean fisherman, he had been taken up by the most charismatic teacher the world has ever known and had almost immediately been selected as his right-hand man. Although his later mission was to the Jews, it was he, after the crucifixion, who first opened Christianity to the Gentiles, baptising them without requiring them to be first circumcised and converted to Judaism – a concession that doubtless came as a considerable relief to middle-aged males considering conversion, but which aroused the furious opposition of Jewish Christians and may have been at least partially responsible for

---

[1] Galatians II, 11–14.
[2] John XVIII, 10.
[3] Matthew, Mark and Luke, all of whose gospels share strong similarities. Mark's gospel was the first to be written, and was used as a framework for the other two. John, writing later, differed radically from them in content, style and general outlook.
[4] I Corinthians XV, 5. See also Luke XXIV, 34.

his imprisonment by Herod,[1] which has never been properly explained. After his escape he seems to have left the leadership of the Church to James ('the brother of the Lord') and to have embarked instead on missionary work in Asia Minor – accompanied, apparently, by his wife[2] – and then, at some date unknown between AD 60 and 65, to have settled in Rome, the only one of the original Apostles to have travelled to the West.

He was not, one suspects, a legend in his own lifetime. Over the next 200 years, however, he was gradually seen to be not just a hero of the early Church, but an essential part of its mystique. It is those twelve short words recorded in the Gospel of St Matthew (there are only ten of them in the Latin text inscribed around the dome of the Basilica) that, rather than Peter himself, were the true rock upon which the Church of Christ was to be built. And when, in the early fourth century AD, the first great basilica began to rise over the spot presumed to contain his bones, there was no doubt as to the name that it was to bear.

---

[1] Acts II, 4.
[2] I Corinthians IX, 5. It is worth remembering that all Christ's first disciples were married and remained so; Paul claims that he was an exception. Why then should the Catholic clergy be celibate?

CHAPTER II

Defenders of the City

(c.100–536)

Rome, the second century AD. The Christians were growing in numbers and developing their own organisation, but they still had a long way to go. Their composition, too, was changing. Their earliest communities were almost exclusively composed of Jews, but the Jewish population was now on the decline: many had emigrated from Jerusalem to Pella (in what is now the Kingdom of Jordan) in AD 66, after the execution of their leader, James. The Christian community in Rome was now overwhelmingly Gentile, and would become still more so with the passage of time.

How was it administered? Although St Irenaeus of Lyons gives us the list of the first thirteen 'popes', from St Peter down to his friend Eleutherius (c.175–89), it is important to remember that until at least the ninth century the title of Pope (which derives from the Greek *papas*, 'little father') was applied generally to any senior member of the community – Rome was far from being a diocese as we understand the word today. Nor was the Roman Church, such as it was, generally accepted, or even respected. The Roman Empire, after all, had its own official religion – though nobody much believed in it – and Christians everywhere were still well advised to keep a discreetly low profile. The Neronian nightmare was over, but outbreaks of persecution still could, and did, occur. There was, for example, a disagreeable period under the Emperor Domitian (ruled AD 81–96), who himself had delusions of divinity and insisted on being addressed as *dominus et deus*, 'master and god'; fortunately for the Christians, he was assassinated during a palace revolt, and they were quick to see his fate as a sign of heavenly displeasure.

The first half of the second century saw, if not a more benevolent, at least a more indifferent attitude on the part of the emperors towards their Christian subjects: Trajan, Hadrian and Antoninus Pius (who together ruled from 96 to 161) were all inclined to let them be. But the Empire by now covered a vast area, and not all its provincial governors took so enlightened a view. Excuses could always be found for the occasional bloodbath; besides, the public demanded its circuses, and the animals had to be fed. The two most brilliant churchmen of their day, St Ignatius, Bishop of Antioch (the first writer to use the Greek word for 'catholic', or 'universal', in its religious sense), and his friend St Polycarp, Bishop of Smyrna (champion of St Paul and suspected author of several of the Pauline Epistles), both met martyrs' deaths – the former being fed to the lions in the arena in c.110, the latter stabbed to death some half a century later at the age of about eighty-six, after the failure of an attempt to burn him at the stake.

Ignatius and Polycarp were both Levantines, and illustrate another problem for the early Church in Rome: the fact that Christianity was essentially a Levantine religion, the greater part of which was still firmly centred in the Greek-speaking world of the eastern Mediterranean. Considered from the perspective of history, the Churches that, thanks to St Paul and his successors, were springing up in Asia Minor, Egypt, Syria and Greece were far more important than the relatively small communities in Italy. Alexandria was by now the second city of the Empire, and Antioch – where the word 'Christian' was first used – the third. Intellectually, too, these cities were incomparably more distinguished than Rome. Despite the fact that Greek was (even in Rome itself) the first language of Christianity it would continue to be dominant in the liturgy until the middle of the fourth century – and that the first- and second-century popes in Rome were nearly all Greeks, none of them proved to be thinkers or theologians or even administrators of any real distinction. Certainly they were not in the same intellectual league as the Bishops of Antioch and Smyrna and their friends.

But this view, not altogether surprisingly, failed to appeal to the Church of Rome. For the first two centuries of their existence, the popes had their work cut out to establish their supremacy. Rome, as they were forever pointing out, was not only the imperial capital; it was also the burial place of Peter and Paul, the two towering giants of the early Church. Oddly enough, the most vocal and persuasive champion of the Roman cause was another Levantine, St Irenaeus, who as a boy had heard Polycarp preach and is therefore thought to have been, like him, a native of Smyrna. He had settled, however, in the West, becoming Bishop of Lyons immediately after the hideous persecutions that took place there in 177 (instituted by the violently anti-Christian Marcus Aurelius, a philosopher-emperor who should have known better). For Irenaeus, the Church of Rome was 'the great and illustrious Church, to which, by reason of its supreme status, every church, which is to say the faithful wherever they may be, must turn'.

The son and successor of Marcus Aurelius, Commodus, is generally considered one of the most vicious of the Roman emperors. Edward Gibbon, the first great historian to combine scholarship with a sense of humour, tells us that:

> his hours were spent in a seraglio of three hundred beautiful women, and as many boys, of every rank and of every province; and, whenever the arts of seduction proved ineffectual, the brutal lover had recourse to violence. The ancient historians have expatiated on these abandoned scenes of prostitution, which scorned every restraint of nature or modesty; but it would not be easy to translate their too faithful descriptions into the decency of a modern language.[1]

As he grew more and more unbalanced, the Emperor identified himself with Hercules and gave regular performances in the arena, slaughtering wild animals in prodigious numbers and even entering the lists as a gladiator. In this capacity he is said to have made no fewer than 735 appearances, all of them – it need hardly be said – victorious. Assassination, sooner or later, was inevitable, but it was somehow appropriate that the man who strangled him on 31 December 192 should have been a champion wrestler.

For the Christians, however, life under Commodus was a good deal easier than it had been under his father, to the point where a eunuch named Hyacinthus became the first (and almost certainly the last) man in history to combine the duties of controller of a 300-strong harem and a presbyter of the Christian Church. It was thanks to him and to Marcia, the Emperor's favourite concubine, that Pope Victor I (189–99) – in the intervals when he was not furiously quarrelling with all the churches outside Rome over the date of Easter – was able to infiltrate the imperial palace and so further the interests of his flock. On at least one occasion he was to do so with signal success, when he saved a company of Christians from the nightmare fate of forced labour in the Sardinian iron and copper mines.

* * *

---

[1] E. Gibbon, *The Decline and Fall of the Roman Empire*, ch. IV.

By the beginning of the third century the popes were still working to establish their authority over the Churches of Asia, and were making steady progress. Sporadic periods of persecution varied, according to the attitude and occasionally even the mood of the reigning emperor; but the reputation of the Christians was greatly increased by the fact that the two most hostile rulers, Decius[1] and Valerian, both came (as had Domitian) to unpleasant ends: the first massacred by the Goths in 249, the second captured eleven years later by the Persian King Shapur, who used him for the rest of his life as a mounting block. Fortunately Gallienus, Valerian's son and successor, very sensibly reversed his father's policies, allowing Christians throughout the Empire not only to worship in freedom but to proselytise. There were by this time several competing religions, including the cult of Mithras, that of *Sol Invictus* (the unconquered sun) and of course the old worship of the Olympian gods, which was kept going by an official priesthood more as an ancient tradition than as a living faith; but in Rome the Christians by now outnumbered them all.

There was one problem only: the fact that Rome itself was in rapid decline, becoming more and more out of touch with the new Hellenistic world. Throughout the Italian peninsula populations were dwindling; and the Empire's principal enemy, Persia, was several weeks', if not months', journey away. Even when in 293 the Emperor Diocletian split his empire into four, he made his capital at Nicomedia (now Izmit, in the north-eastern corner of the Sea of Marmara) and none of his other three tetrarchs (joint rulers) dreamed of living in what was still technically the imperial capital. The whole focus of the Empire had shifted to the east. Italy had become a backwater. In the absence of the Emperor, the Pope was the most important man in Rome; but Rome itself was now a sad and distinctly seedy city, decimated by malaria and showing little trace of its former splendour.

One more burst of persecution was still to come. For the first twenty years of his reign Diocletian, who had succeeded to the imperial throne in 284, seemed willing enough to tolerate his Christian subjects – both his wife and daughter were almost certainly baptised

---

[1] It was under Decius that the first head of the Church was martyred since St Peter: Pope Fabian (236–50), who died from the brutality of his treatment in prison. A few years later, under Valerian, he was followed by Pope Sixtus II (257–8), arrested in the catacombs and beheaded with his attendant deacons.

– but then, in 303 and 304, he suddenly published four separate edicts against them. By all accounts a normally humane and merciful man, he specifically laid down that there should be no bloodshed; but his second-in-command Gallienus and his brother-officers, unwilling to be deprived of their pleasures, went ahead regardless, and for two years a monstrous wave of violence surged across the Empire. It might have lasted longer; but to its victims' relief, the Emperor abdicated in 305 and retired to live in his palace on the Dalmatian coast and grow cabbages. And once again the pendulum swung.

It could hardly have swung faster, or further. In 306 a young general named Constantine was acclaimed by the army at York on the death of his father Constantius Chlorus, who had been reigning there as one of Diocletian's tetrarchs. Nowadays he is known to us as Constantine the Great, and with good reason: with the exceptions of Jesus Christ, the Prophet Mohammed and the Buddha, he was to be perhaps the most influential man who ever lived. It is given to few men to take a decision that changes the course of history; Constantine took two. The first was religious: his adoption, both personally and imperially, of Christianity. He needed a few years to establish his supreme authority – Diocletian's system of the four tetrarchs appealed to him not at all – but by 313 he and his co-regent Licinius were able to issue the Edict of Milan, which granted total freedom of religion to every imperial citizen. Two years later crucifixion was abolished, and in 321 Sunday was named a legal festival. By the time of Constantine's death in 337 (less than thirty-five years after Diocletian's persecutions) Christianity was the official religion of the Roman Empire.

The second decision was political. Constantine moved the imperial capital away from Rome, to a new eastern city built expressly for it on the shores of the Bosphorus, occupying the site of the ancient Greek city of Byzantium – a city that he originally intended should be named New Rome, but which from the start was always called after him, Constantinople. He inaugurated it on 11 May 330 – dedicating it, incidentally, to the Virgin – and on that day the Empire too acquired a new description, the Byzantine; but it is important to remember that neither he nor his subjects recognised any qualitative change or break in continuity. To them the Empire was what it had always been: the Roman Empire of Augustus and his successors; and they, regardless of the language they spoke – and, as time went on, Latin died out and Greek became universal – remained in their own eyes Romans through and through.

To Pope Sylvester I (314–35) and his flock in Rome, the news of the Emperor's second decision must have done a good deal to mitigate that of his first. Christianity might now be smiled upon, persecution a thing of the past; and on Constantine's only visit to Rome in 326 he had not only refused to take part in a pagan procession (causing considerable offence to the traditionalists), but had chosen the sites for several of the great basilicas that he intended to build – and lavishly endow – in and around the city. First among these was that which was to be dedicated to St Peter, above the saint's shrine on the Vatican Hill. Then there was to be a second cathedral and baptistery next to the palace on the Lateran, occupying the site of the old barracks of the imperial cavalry.[1] Next was the basilica of S. Croce in Gerusalemme, commemorating the finding of the True Cross by the Emperor's mother, St Helena; and finally the great church on the Appian Way, marking the traditional spot to which the bodies of St Peter and St Paul were transferred in 258, but now dedicated (somewhat unfairly, it may be thought) to St Sebastian.

All this was excellent news; on the other hand, as Sylvester was well aware, Constantine had almost simultaneously ordered the construction of the Church of the Holy Sepulchre at Jerusalem,[2] together with others at Trier, Aquileia, Nicomedia, Antioch, Alexandria and several other cities – to say nothing of the Great Church of St Sophia, the Holy Wisdom, in his new capital. How now was the Bishop of Rome to further his claim to supremacy over the whole Christian Church? It was not he, but his brother in Constantinople who would henceforth have the Emperor's ear. For well over 600 years it was firmly believed that Constantine, in gratitude for his miraculous healing by Sylvester from leprosy, had sugared the pill by handing over to the Pope and his successors 'Rome and all the provinces, districts and cities of Italy and the West as subject to the Roman Church for ever'. Alas for the papacy, he did no such thing. The so-called 'Donation of Constantine' is now known to have been a forgery

---

[1] It took its name from the old Roman family of the Laterani, who had originally built it.
[2] Constantine had initiated this project to celebrate the successful conclusion of the Council of Nicaea in 325, but it had been given new impetus by his mother St Helena, who had set off two years later at the age of seventy-two for Jerusalem, with the result described above.

– fabricated, probably during the eighth century, within the Roman Curia; it was however to prove of inestimable value to the territorial claims of the papacy until the fraud was finally exposed (by the Italian humanist Lorenzo Valla) in 1440.

It was Pope Sylvester's misfortune to witness, during his papacy, the appearance of the first of all the great heresies that were to split the Church in the centuries to come. This was first propagated by a certain Arius, Presbyter of Alexandria, a man of immense learning and splendid physical presence. His message was simple enough: that Jesus Christ was not coeternal and of one substance with God the Father, but had been created by him at a specific time and for a specific purpose, as his Instrument for the salvation of the world. Thus, although a perfect man, the Son must always be subordinate to the Father. Here, in the eyes of Arius's archbishop, Athanasius, was a dangerous doctrine indeed; and he took immediate measures to stamp it out. In 320 its propagator was arraigned before nearly a hundred bishops from Egypt, Libya and Tripolitania and excommunicated as a heretic.

The damage, however, was done: the teaching spread like wildfire. Those were the days, it must be remembered, when theological arguments were of passionate interest, not just to churchmen and scholars, but to the whole Greek-speaking world. Broadsheets were distributed; rabble-rousing speeches were made in the market place; slogans were chalked on walls. Everyone had an opinion: you were either for Arius or against him. He himself, unlike most theologians, was a brilliant publicist; the better to disseminate his views, he had actually written several popular songs and jingles – for sailors, travellers, carpenters and other trades – which were sung and whistled in the streets.[1] Then, a year or two later, Arius, who had hurriedly left Alexandria after his excommunication, returned in triumph. He had appeared before two further synods in Asia Minor, both of which had declared overwhelmingly in his favour, and now he demanded his old job back.

Finally, in 324, the Emperor intervened. There would be no more synods of local bishops; instead there would be a universal Council of the Church, to be attended by all the leading ecclesiastics from

---

[1] 'We do him too much honour when we hail him as the father of religious music in the Christian Church' (*Dictionnaire de théologie catholique*, article on 'Arianism'). We certainly do.

both East and West – an Ecumenical Council of such authority and distinction that both parties to the dispute would be bound to accept its rulings. It would be held in Nicaea during May and June 325, and he – Constantine – would participate himself. In the event he did rather more than that; effectively, he seems to have taken the chair, arguing, encouraging, assuaging ruffled feelings, forever urging the importance of unity and the virtues of compromise, and even on occasion switching from Latin into halting Greek in his efforts to convince his hearers.

It was Constantine, too, who proposed the insertion into the draft resolution of the key word that was to settle, at least temporarily, the fate of Arius and his doctrine. This was the word *homoousios* – meaning consubstantial, or 'of one substance', to describe the relation of the Son to the Father. Its inclusion in the draft was almost tantamount to a condemnation of Arianism, and it says much for the Emperor's powers of persuasion – and, it must be suspected, of intimidation – that he was able to secure its acceptance. And so the Council delivered its verdict: Arius, with his remaining adherents, was formally condemned, his writings placed under anathema and ordered to be burned.

The Emperor had hoped for a large attendance from the Western churches at the Council of Nicaea; but he was disappointed. As against some 300 or more bishops from the East, the West was represented by just five – plus two priests sent, more as observers than anything else, by Pope Sylvester from Rome. It was, on the Pope's part, an understandable decision; he probably considered that to make the journey would be demeaning both to himself and to his office. Besides, western churchmen lacked the insatiable intellectual curiosity of their eastern brethren; the Latin language, which had replaced Greek as the lingua franca of the Roman Church less than a century before, did not even possess the technical terms necessary to express the subtle shades of meaning that gave Orthodox theologians such delight. Nevertheless, he made a grave mistake. His attendance at the Council would have immensely strengthened his prestige. One claiming to be the supreme head of the universal Church should surely have been present at the drafting of the Nicene Creed, that Church's first official statement of belief, a revised version of which is still today regularly recited at both Catholic and Anglican eucharists.

And what of Arius himself? He was exiled to Illyricum – the Roman province running along the Dalmatian coast – and forbidden to return to Alexandria; but he was soon back in Nicomedia, where over the next ten years he gave the authorities no rest. At last, in 336, Constantine was forced to summon him to Constantinople for further investigation of his beliefs. It was during this last inquiry that:

> Arius, made bold by the protection of his followers, engaged in light-hearted and foolish conversation, until he was suddenly compelled by a call of nature to retire; and immediately, as it is written,[1] 'falling headlong, he burst asunder in the midst, and gave up the ghost'.

This version of the story, admittedly, comes from the pen of Arius's implacable enemy, Archbishop Athanasius of Alexandria; but the unattractive circumstances of his demise are too well attested by contemporary writers to be open to serious question. Inevitably they were interpreted by those who hated him as divine retribution: the Archbishop's biblical reference is to the somewhat similar fate that befell Judas Iscariot.

The death of its initiator did not, however, put an end to Arianism. It continued to flourish in many parts of the Empire, until in 381 a fanatically anti-Arian Spaniard, the Emperor Theodosius the Great, summoned the second Ecumenical Council, which was held at Constantinople and finally worked out a satisfactory solution to the problem. Indeed, it did more. It decreed a general ban on all pagan and heretical cults. Heresy – any heresy – would henceforth be a crime against the State. In less than a century a persecuted Church had become a persecuting Church. The Jews in particular came under heavy pressure; it was they, after all, who had crucified Christ. As for Arianism, it was virtually extinguished within the Empire, although it was to remain widespread among the Germanic barbarian tribes for at least another 300 years.

Pope Damasus (366–84) sent no representatives to this council, nor even were any Western bishops present; and he was horrified later to learn of its decree that 'the Bishop of Constantinople shall have the pre-eminence in honour after the Bishop of Rome, for Constantinople is the New Rome'. That pre-eminence, he thundered, was in no way due to Rome's past as the capital of the Empire; it was based exclusively on its Apostolic pedigree going back to St Peter and St Paul. Nor was Constantinople even second in seniority; not

---

[1] Acts I, 18.

even yet a patriarchate, it was outranked by both Alexandria and Antioch – the former having traditionally been founded on Peter's orders by St Mark, the latter because St Peter had been its first bishop before he went on to Rome.

Relations between Rome and Constantinople were deteriorating fast.

The Emperor Constantine had died on Whit Sunday, 337. Though for years a self-styled bishop of the Christian Church, he had received baptism only on his deathbed, from Bishop Eusebius of Caesarea – ironically enough, an Arian. Until the end of the century he and his successors reigned supreme over the whole Empire; but Theodosius the Great, dying in 395, divided it again – giving his elder son, Arcadius, the East, and his younger, Honorius, the West. It proved a disastrous decision. Under the sway of thirteen emperors, living for the most part not in Rome but in Ravenna, each more feckless than the last and all today virtually forgotten, the Western Empire now embarked on an inexorable eighty-year decline, prey to the Germanic and other tribes that progressively tightened their grip.

But by now the Bishops of Rome had developed a quasi-monarchical position of dominance in the West. The Emperor, as always involved in the East, had exempted them from taxes and granted them jurisdiction over matters of faith and civil law, and over the years they had steadily built up their authority. Bishop Damasus had claimed an 'apostolic' seat, deliberately using Christ's declaration in St Matthew to support his claims to power; he had further increased his reputation by commissioning the Vulgate – a new and vastly superior Latin translation of the Bible – from the Italian scholar St Jerome. His successor Bishop Siricius (384–99) had been the first to assume the title of 'Pope', giving it much of the significance that it bears today; Pope Innocent I (401–17) insisted that all important matters discussed at synods should be submitted to himself for a final decision. In the East such claims were never for a moment taken seriously; there, the Emperor alone – assisted, perhaps, by an Ecumenical Council, which only he could summon – remained the only supreme authority. Nonetheless, the Bishops of Rome could be said to have come of age: they were, at long last, effectively popes, using Latin, not Greek, for their liturgy; and it was as popes that they now found themselves with a new role: as defenders of Rome itself.

*   *   *

The fifth century began with a bang: in the early summer of 401 Alaric the Visigoth invaded Italy. Still no more than thirty years old, he had already spread terror from the walls of Constantinople to the southern Peloponnese. In fact, he was not fundamentally hostile to the Empire; his real objective was to establish a permanent home for his people within it. If only the Roman Senate and the dim-witted Western Emperor Honorius – whose only interest at the time seems to have been the raising of poultry – could have understood this, they might have averted the final catastrophe; by their lack of comprehension they made it inevitable. In September 408 Alaric was before the walls of Rome, and the first of his three sieges of the city began. It lasted for three months. The civic authorities were helpless, while Honorius cowered among the marshes of Ravenna; it was left to Pope Innocent I to negotiate with the conqueror and make what terms he could. Alaric demanded a huge ransom, of gold and silver and other precious materials, including 3,000 pounds of pepper; but, thanks entirely to the Pope, he respected Church property and there was no bloodbath.

The second of Alaric's sieges had one purpose only: to overthrow Honorius. The King of the Goths made it clear to the Romans that all they had to do was depose their idiotic emperor; he would then instantly withdraw. The Roman Senate, meeting in emergency session, did not take long to concur; but Honorius refused to go. He continued to make trouble until eventually, in the early summer of 410, Alaric marched on Rome and besieged it for the third time. With food already short, the city could not hold out for long. Some time towards the end of August the Goths burst in through the northern wall, just at the foot of the Pincian Hill.

After the capture there were the traditional three days of pillage; but this early sack of Rome seems to have been a good deal less savage than the school history books would have us believe – quite restrained, in fact, compared with the havoc wrought by the Normans in 1078 or the army of Charles V in 1527. Alaric himself, devout Christian that he was, had given orders that no churches or religious buildings were to be touched, and that the right of asylum was everywhere to be respected. Yet a sack, however decorously conducted, remains just that; the Goths were far from being saints and, despite occasional exaggerations, there is probably all too much truth in the pages that Gibbon devotes to the atrocities committed: the countless magnificent buildings consumed by the flames, the multitudes of innocents slain, the matrons ravished and the virgins deflowered.

When the three days were over, Alaric moved on to the south; but he had got no further than Cosenza when he was attacked by a sudden violent fever, and within a few days he was dead. He was still only forty. His followers carried his body to the River Busento, which they dammed and temporarily deflected from its usual channel. There, in the stream's dry bed, they buried their leader; then they broke the dam, and the waters came surging back and covered him.

Pope Innocent had done all he could, but had been unable to save his flock from the third and last siege. Arguably he was the first really great Pope. A man of vast ability, high resolution and impeccable morality, he stands out like a beacon after the scores of mediocrities who preceded him. Papal supremacy, he was determined, should be absolute; all major causes of dispute must be submitted to the judgement of the Holy See. He was surely gratified when, in 404, he received a respectful appeal from the Bishop of Constantinople, St John Chrysostom, that saintly but insufferable prelate whose scorching castigations of the Empress Eudoxia – who had by this time deserted her husband Arcadius in favour of an apparently interminable string of lovers – had resulted in his deposition by the Patriarch of Alexandria[1] and subsequent exile. John now demanded a formal trial at which he could confront his accusers – unmistakably implying that he recognised the Bishop of Rome as his superior. Innocent naturally leaped to his defence, summoning a synod of Latin bishops which duly called on Arcadius to restore Chrysostom at once to his see; then, when this was seen to have no effect, he despatched a delegation to Constantinople. Including as it did no fewer than four senior bishops, it could hardly be ignored; but Arcadius was unimpressed. The envoys were not even permitted to enter the city. Their letters of credence were snatched from them; they were then thrown into a Thracian castle, where they were subjected to what was almost certainly a painful interrogation. Only then, insulted and humiliated, were they allowed to return to Italy.

And so when in 407 St John Chrysostom died in a remote region of Pontus on the Black Sea – probably as a result of ill-treatment by his guards – he left the Church profoundly split; and Pope Innocent, who only three years before had good reason to believe that his supremacy was generally acknowledged in Constantinople, was now faced with all-too-convincing proof of his misapprehension. He

---

[1] Constantinople was to have no patriarch of its own until 451.

remained in power, however, for another decade, making important contributions in the fields of the liturgy and theology, and governing Rome with a firm hand. Whether or not he altogether deserved the sainthood that was subsequently bestowed on him is perhaps open to discussion; but he gave the papacy an international prestige of a kind that it had never before known, and he marks the first milestone on its road to greatness.

Just twenty-three years (and five popes) after Innocent's death in 417, the Tuscan lawyer and theologian Leo I (440–61) was elected to the papal throne. He was the first Bishop of Rome to adopt the title of the pagan chief priest, *pontifex maximus*, and the first of only two in all papal history to have been known as 'the Great'. In fact, he deserved the title no more than had Innocent, whose campaign to establish the supremacy of Rome he enthusiastically continued. Papal authority, he claimed, was the authority of St Peter himself; the Pope was Peter's unworthy spokesman. This is the overriding message of his vast correspondence with bishops and churchmen all over the Western world. He, and he alone, was the guardian of orthodoxy, which he did his utmost to spread also throughout the East – though such a task, as he well knew, required much diplomacy and tact.

Just how much became clear with the storm that was soon to burst over the head of Eutyches, an elderly archimandrite (head of a large monastery) of Constantinople. Already for a century and more the Church, and particularly the Eastern Church, had been deeply divided on the question of the nature – or natures – of Christ. Did he possess two separate natures, the human and the divine? Or only one? And if only one, which was it? The leading exponent of the dual nature was Nestorius, Bishop of Constantinople, who had been consequently deposed in 431 by the Council of Ephesus. It was possible, on the other hand, to go too far in the opposite direction; such was the mistake of Eutyches, who held that Christ had only one nature, the human nature being absorbed in the divine. This theory, known as the monophysite, was equally unacceptable to Nestorius's third successor, Bishop Flavian. Found guilty of heresy, condemned and degraded, Eutyches appealed to Pope Leo, to the Emperor Theodosius and to the monks of Constantinople, and in so doing unleashed a whirlwind of almost unimaginable ferocity. For three years the Church was in uproar, with councils summoned and discredited, bishops unseated and restored; with intrigues and conspiracies, violence and vituperation, curses and anathemas thundering between Rome and Constantinople, Ephesus and Alexandria. In the course of all this, Pope Leo sent to Flavian a copy of his celebrated *Tome*, which, he believed, established once and for all the doctrine that Christ possessed two natures coexisting. Its findings were upheld in 451 by the Council of Chalcedon, at which the papal delegates presided and which condemned monophysitism in all its forms. The doctrine of the dual nature has remained ever since an integral part of orthodox Christian dogma, though several monophysite Churches – including the Copts of Egypt, the Nestorians in Syria, the Armenians and the Georgians – broke away at Chalcedon and still continue in existence.[1]

By now, however, the whole Roman Empire of the West was crumbling. Britain, Spain and Africa were already gone; Italy was in rapid disintegration. The new enemy were the Huns, the most savage of all the barbarian tribes, most of whom still lived and slept in the open, disdaining all agriculture and even cooked foods – though they would soften raw meat by massaging it between their thighs and the flanks of their horses as they rode. For clothing they favoured tunics made, rather surprisingly, from the skins of field-mice crudely stitched together; these they wore continuously, without ever removing them, until they dropped off of their own accord. They practically lived on their horses: eating, trading, holding their councils, even sleeping in the saddle. Their leader Attila was typical of his race: short, swarthy and snub-nosed, with a thin, straggling beard and beady little eyes set in a head too big for his body. He was not a great ruler, or even a particularly able general; but so overmastering were his ambition, his pride and his lust for power that within the space of a few years he had made himself feared throughout the length and breadth of Europe: more feared, perhaps, than any other single man – with the possible exception of Napoleon – before or since.

But no sooner had Attila begun his march on Rome in 452 than he suddenly halted. Why he did so we do not know. Traditionally the credit has always been given to Pope Leo, who travelled to meet him on the banks of the Mincio river – probably at Peschiera, where the river issues from Lake Garda – and somehow persuaded him to advance no further; but the pagan Hun would not have obeyed the Pope out

---

[1] It was at Chalcedon, too, that the bishoprics of Constantinople and Jerusalem were raised to the status of patriarchates, joining those of Rome, Alexandria and Antioch. Constantinople was once again decreed to be second in precedence after Rome.

of mere respect for his office; so what arguments or inducements did Leo offer? A substantial tribute is the likeliest answer. But there is another possibility too: Attila, like all his race, was incorrigibly superstitious, and the Pope may well have reminded him of how Alaric had died almost immediately after his sack of Rome, pointing out that a similar fate was known to befall every invader who raised his hand against the Holy City. It is possible, too, that his subjects themselves were partially responsible for persuading their leader to retire; there is evidence to suggest that, after their devastation of all the surrounding countryside, they were beginning to suffer from a serious shortage of food, and that disease had broken out within their ranks. A final consideration was that troops from Constantinople were beginning to arrive to swell the imperial forces. A march on Rome, it began to appear, might not prove quite as straightforward as had at first been thought.

For some or all of these reasons, Attila decided to turn back. A year later, during the night following his marriage to yet another of his already innumerable wives, his exertions brought on a haemorrhage; and as his life-blood flowed away, all Europe breathed again. While the funeral feast was in progress, a specially selected group of captives encased his body in three coffins: one of gold, one of silver and one of iron. Then, when the body had been lowered into the grave and covered over, first with rich spoils of war and then with earth until the ground was level above it, all those involved in the burial ceremonies were put to death, so that the great king's last resting place might for ever remain secret and inviolate.

Pope Leo had saved Rome once; but when, only three years later, the Vandal King Gaiseric appeared at the walls, he was less successful. He persuaded Gaiseric not to put the city to the torch; but he could not prevent a hideous fourteen-day sack. The *Liber Pontificalis* tells us that when the nightmare was over and Leo found that the silver chalices and patens had been plundered from all the churches in Rome, he gave orders for the melting-down of the six great urns from St Peter's – dating from the time of Constantine – to provide replacements[1]. By now, after both the Goths and the Vandals had done their worst, there can have been little of the old Rome that was still worth plundering. Imperial Rome was already dead, and past recall; more

---

[1] It also reports his decree that 'a nun should not receive the blessing of a veil without having been tested in her virginity for sixty years' – by which time she should certainly have deserved it.

than a hundred years before, its spirit had passed to Constantinople. What mattered now was Christian, papal Rome – and that, fortunately, was proof against any number of barbarian atrocities.

CHAPTER III

Vigilius

(537–55)

Just fifteen years after the death of Leo the Great – who was the first Bishop of Rome to be buried in St Peter's – the Roman Empire of the West came to its end; but the abdication, on 4 September 476, of its last emperor, the pathetic, double-diminutived child-ruler Romulus Augustulus, was hardly noticed by most of his subjects and made little difference to their lives. For almost a century the Western Empire had been in a state of near-chaos, dominated by one barbarian general after another; the most recent of these, a Scyrian[1] named Odoacer, had made no claim to sovereignty for himself; all he asked was the title of Patrician, in which rank he proposed to take over the governance of Italy in the name of the Emperor Zeno, then reigning in Constantinople.

Zeno, however, had a better idea. Throughout his reign he had been plagued by Theodoric, leader of the Eastern Goths, who were widely scattered in the lands to the north of the Black Sea. The main purpose of Theodoric's early life was to find and secure a permanent home for his people. To this end he had spent the better part of twenty years fighting – sometimes for and sometimes against the Empire – arguing, bargaining, cajoling and threatening by turns. This constant vacillation between friendship and hostility was, in the long term, unprofitable to both parties; and probably some time towards the end of 487 it was agreed between Theodoric and Zeno that the former should lead his entire people into Italy, overthrow Odoacer and rule the land as an Ostrogothic Kingdom under imperial sovereignty. Early in 488 the great westward migration took place: men, women and children, with their horses and their pack-animals, their cattle and sheep, lumbering slowly across the plains of central Europe in search of greener and more peaceful pastures.

---

[1] The Scyrians were one of the many minor Germanic tribes, of minimal importance in this story.

On their arrival in Italy, Odoacer put up fierce resistance; but Theodoric steadily wore him down, before agreeing to what appeared to be remarkably generous terms: the two of them should rule jointly from Ravenna, where they would share the royal palace. It was ostensibly to seal this agreement that on 15 March 493 Theodoric invited Odoacer, with his brother, his son and his chief officers, to a banquet in his wing of the palace. As the Scyrian took his place in the seat of honour, Theodoric stepped forward and, with one tremendous stroke of his sword, clove the body of Odoacer from collarbone to thigh. The members of Odoacer's suite were quickly dealt with by the surrounding guards, while his brother was shot down by arrows as he fled through the palace gardens. His wife was thrown into prison, where she later died of hunger; his son was first sent off to Gaul, but later executed. Then, with the Scyrian line satisfactorily wiped out, Theodoric the Ostrogoth laid aside the skins and furs that were the traditional clothing of his race, robed himself in the imperial purple and settled down to rule.

After this unpromising beginning, his thirty-three years on the throne were prosperous and peaceful. One thing only made him unacceptable to Emperor and Pope alike – his uncompromising Arianism; and it was unfortunate that the end of his reign should have coincided with a campaign by the Emperor Justin to stamp out the heresy once and for all. It was as a reaction to this that in 524 Theodoric imprisoned one of Justin's chief advisers, the philosopher Boethius, whom he subsequently ordered to be garrotted; and two years later he sent Pope John I (523–6) at the head of a delegation to Constantinople to remonstrate. This journey – the first ever made by a Pope to the Bosphorus – was a tremendous success from John's point of view: the Emperor prostrated himself before him and accorded him a magnificent reception, at which the Pope was actually seated on a higher throne than the Patriarch. From Theodoric's, however, it was a failure, Justin having categorically refused to allow those Arians who had been forcibly converted to revert to their old heretical ways.

There can be no doubt that Theodoric was a giant; and the extraordinary mausoleum that he built – and which still stands in the northeastern suburbs of Ravenna – perfectly symbolises, in its half-classical, half-barbaric architectural strength, the colossus who himself bestrode two civilisations. No other Germanic ruler, setting up his throne on the ruins of the Western Empire, possessed a fraction of Theodoric's statesmanship and political vision; and when he died, on 30 August

526, Italy lost the greatest of her early medieval rulers, unequalled until the days of Charlemagne.

Just eleven months later, on 1 August 527, a ruler of similar stature ascended the throne at Constantinople. From the very first moment he came to power, Justinian had been determined to bring the entire Italian peninsula back into the imperial fold. A Roman Empire that did not include Rome was an obvious absurdity; an Ostrogothic Kingdom that did – and was heretical to boot – could never be anything but an abomination in his sight. Clearly it had to be destroyed, and equally clearly the man best able to destroy it was the greatest living Byzantine general, Belisarius.

In 535, with an army of 7,500 men, Belisarius sailed for Sicily, which he took with scarcely a struggle. Crossing the Straits of Messina to the mainland, he captured Naples and – after a disastrous year-long siege – Rome; finally, at Ravenna, the Gothic King Vitiges offered to surrender the city and deliver up his crown, on one condition: that Belisarius should then proclaim himself Emperor of the West. Many an ambitious imperial general would have seized such an opportunity; but Belisarius, utterly loyal to his Emperor, had no intention of doing anything of the kind. On the other hand, he saw the proposal as an ideal means of bringing the war to a quick and victorious end. He accepted; the gates of Ravenna were flung open, and the imperial army marched in.

As Vitiges, his family and the leading Gothic nobles were led off into captivity, they must have reflected bitterly indeed on the perfidy of the general who had betrayed them. But as Belisarius took ship back to Constantinople in May 540, there is no indication that his conscience gave him any trouble. Had the Goths' proposal not in itself been perfidious? And in any case, were the Goths not rebels against the lawful authority of the Emperor? In occupying Ravenna by trickery, he had saved untold bloodshed on both sides. Besides, he had now achieved his objective. Thanks to him, all Italy was now back in imperial hands.

Not, however, for long. The Goths re-established their monarchy and fought back; and a young Gothic King named Totila appealed to all his subjects, Goth and Italian alike, to unite and drive the Byzantines from Italian soil. In the early summer of 544 Belisarius found himself on his way back to Italy. But this time he was at a serious disadvantage. Justinian had always been jealous of his power and popularity – at one moment his accumulated treasure had been confiscated, though it was later returned – and on this occasion had allowed Belisarius only a handful of inexperienced troops, little authority and even fewer funds. Belisarius did his best, but was unable to prevent Totila from laying siege to Rome and, in December 546, capturing the city; and after a few more months of desultory fighting up and down the peninsula it became clear that the two sides had reached a stalemate, with neither strong enough to eliminate the other. Early in 549 Belisarius returned to Constantinople. After the glory of his first Italian campaign, his second had brought him five years of frustration and disappointment.

During Totila's siege of Rome a somewhat surprising event took place: the Pope was kidnapped. Pope Vigilius (537–55) was a noble Roman who, as deacon, had accompanied Pope Agapetus I (535–6) to Constantinople in 536 on an unsuccessful mission to persuade Justinian to call off his Italian campaign. They were still in the capital when Agapetus died suddenly; and Vigilius, who had confidently expected to succeed him, was horrified to receive news from Rome that a certain Silverius (536–7) had been elected in his stead. He had already been at some pains to ingratiate himself with the passionately monophysite Empress Theodora, and now made a secret agreement with her by which Belisarius, then in Italy, would depose Silverius and install him, Vigilius, in his stead. In return, he promised to denounce the principles laid down by the Council of Chalcedon[1] and proclaim his acceptance of the monophysite creed. Belisarius had done as he was bidden; Vigilius had then hurried back to Rome for his coronation, forcing Silverius into an Anatolian exile.

By the autumn of 545 the army of Totila was at the gates of Rome. Belisarius, with the limited means at his disposal, was doing everything he could to avoid a siege, but was receiving little or no support from his emperor. Justinian had other problems on his mind. The root of the trouble was that hoary old enigma, the identity of Christ. The orthodox view was that laid down almost a century before at Chalcedon: that the Saviour possessed, in his one person, two natures divided but inseparable, the human and the divine. This view, however, had never been accepted by the monophysites, according to whom the divine nature alone existed, and who consequently saw Christ as God rather than man; and these, heretics as they might be,

[1] See Chapter II, p.22.

were far too numerous and widespread to be eliminated. Egypt, for example, was monophysite through and through; in Syria and Palestine too the doctrine had taken a firm and potentially dangerous hold. In the West, on the other hand, such heresy as existed at all – which was to be found almost exclusively among the barbarians – championed the opposite, Arian view that Christ was essentially human. The Roman Church meanwhile remained staunchly orthodox and was predictably quick to protest at any deviation from the Chalcedonian path. Justinian therefore had a difficult and delicate course to steer. If he dealt too harshly with the monophysites, he risked rebellion and possible loss to the Empire of valuable provinces – Egypt was one of its chief sources of corn. If he treated them with too much consideration, he incurred the wrath of the orthodox and split his subjects more than ever. He was fully aware of his wife's own monophysite sympathies, and rather welcomed them: they enabled him on occasion to take an outwardly rigid line, in the knowledge that she would secretly be able to temper its severity.

Thanks to this highly disingenuous policy, the Emperor had managed to curb most of the monophysite communities – apart from those of Egypt, which he left firmly alone; but then, suddenly, there emerged a dangerously charismatic new troublemaker. Jacob Baradaeus ('the Ragged') was a monk from Mesopotamia who, having in 543 been consecrated Bishop of Edessa by the monophysite Patriarch of Alexandria, took it upon himself to revive monophysite sentiment throughout the East, travelling constantly and at prodigious speed the length and breadth of Syria and Palestine, consecrating some thirty bishops as he went and ordaining several thousand priests.

Unable to stamp out the flames of fanaticism that sprang up everywhere in the wake of Baradaeus, Justinian found himself in a quandary. The monophysites in their present mood needed more careful treatment than ever; at the same time he was already being criticised in the West for weakness and inertia in the face of the new threat. Some kind of positive action was clearly required; and so, for want of any better solution, he decided on a public condemnation – not of the monophysites, but of those who occupied the other end of the theological spectrum, professing the humanity rather than the divinity of Christ: the Nestorians. This by now half-forgotten sect had been condemned as early as 431 by the Council of Ephesus; afterwards the majority had fled eastwards, to Persia and beyond, and few – if any – Nestorians now remained within the imperial frontiers. It thus mattered little whether they were attacked again or not; but they had the advantage of being detested by the monophysites and orthodox alike, and an *ex cathedra* pronouncement of the kind the Emperor had in mind would, he hoped, do something to defuse the increasing hostility between the two. Early in 544 he published an edict, condemning not the heresy itself, but three particular manifestations of it, soon to become notorious as the 'Three Chapters': the person and writings of Nestorius's teacher, Theodore of Mopsuestia, and certain specific works of two other, still more obscure theologians, Theodoret of Cyrrhus and Ibas of Edessa.

It was an idiotic idea, which fully deserved the response it received. Only the orthodox clergy in the East agreed – in some cases a trifle unwillingly – to toe the imperial line. The monophysites, who had hoped for genuine concessions, were unappeased; in the West, the Roman bishops made no attempt to conceal their fury. Any attack on the Nestorians, they thundered, could only be a blow in favour of the monophysites. They refused absolutely to condemn the Three Chapters; and Stephen, the Papal Legate in Constantinople, made known his master's displeasure by pronouncing the ban of the Church on the Patriarch himself.

Justinian was at first surprised by these reactions, and then seriously alarmed. In Italy, during the four years that had passed since the first campaign of Belisarius, the Byzantine position had grown steadily worse; now, at a moment when he needed their support more than ever, he had managed to antagonise Pope Vigilius and the entire Church of Rome. The sooner the whole thing was forgotten, the better. He made no protest when the Pope refused to condemn the Three Chapters, but settled down quietly to repair relations.

For a year and a half he pursued this policy, and would presumably have continued to do so had circumstances allowed; but when Belisarius reported that Rome was threatened by siege, a new and alarming thought struck him: were Totila to capture the city, there was nothing to prevent his holding the Pope hostage, with consequences that could only add further fuel to the flames. Justinian acted quickly. On 22 November 545 an officer of the imperial guard with a company of soldiers arrived in Rome, seized Vigilius just as he was leaving the church of St Cecilia after Mass, loaded him on to a boat waiting in the Tiber and carried him off down the river.

The Pope, who had no particular wish to remain in Rome during what threatened to be an uncomfortable and protracted siege, made no complaint when told that he was being taken to Constantinople – though he may not altogether have relished the prospect of renewing his acquaintance with Theodora: his promise to declare in favour of monophysitism remained unfulfilled, and he would obviously have a certain amount of explaining to do. As things turned out, however, his meeting with the imperial couple did not occur as soon as he had expected; he remained for a whole year as their guest at Catania in Sicily, during which time he was able to despatch several ships, laden with grain, for the relief of Rome. Not until January 547 did he reach the Bosphorus.

At this stage Vigilius was still firm in his refusal to condemn the Three Chapters. Though Justinian had greeted him warmly on his arrival, the Pope lost no time in making his authority felt, immediately placing the Patriarch and all the bishops who had subscribed to the imperial edict under four months' further sentence of excommunication. Before long, however, the constant pressure exerted by the Emperor and Empress – who seemed to have forgotten her previous grievances, but who on this issue was every bit as zealous and determined as her husband – began to wear him down. On 29 June 547 Vigilius was formally reconciled with the Patriarch, and on the same day handed Justinian his signed condemnation of the Three Chapters, stipulating only that it should be kept secret until the end of an official inquiry by a committee of Western bishops – whose findings, he hinted, were a foregone conclusion; and on 11 April 548 he published his *Judicatum*, in which he solemnly anathematised the Chapters, while emphasising that his support for the doctrines of Chalcedon remained unshaken.

Thus, when the Empress died eleven weeks later, it might have been thought that she and her husband had triumphed, and had succeeded at last in restoring unity to the Church. In fact, the split was soon revealed to be deeper than ever. Theodora had always been more feared than her husband; while she lived, many distinguished churchmen had preferred to keep a low profile rather than incur her displeasure. After her death, they came out publicly in opposition to the imperial edict, and gradually others followed suit across Europe. Whatever Vigilius might have said to the contrary, it was generally accepted that his anathemas had dangerously undermined the authority of Chalcedon; and the Pope was now generally reviled throughout Western Christendom as a turncoat and an apostate. In Carthage, indeed, the bishops went further still and excommunicated him. Vigilius saw that he had gone too far. He had never wanted to condemn the Chapters in the first place, and had only done so as a result of the intolerable pressure put upon him by Justinian and Theodora. There was nothing for it but to retract, which – with what little dignity he could muster – he did.

For Justinian, this was the last straw. He now ordered his religious adviser, Theodore Ascidas, Bishop of Caesarea, to draft a second edict, which went considerably further than its predecessor, and summoned a General Council of the Church to endorse it. Supported, no doubt, by many of the Western churchmen in Constantinople, Virgilius protested that this document flew in the face of the principles of Chalcedon and demanded that it should be immediately withdrawn. Justinian predictably refused; whereupon the Pope summoned a meeting of all the bishops from both East and West who were present in the city. This assembly pronounced unanimously against the edict, solemnly forbidding any cleric to say Mass in any church in which it was exhibited. When, a few days later, two prelates ignored the decree, they were excommunicated on the spot – as was (for the third time) the Patriarch himself.

On hearing the news, Justinian flew into one of those terrible rages for which he was famous; and the Pope, fearing that he was no longer safe from arrest, sought refuge in the church of St Peter and St Paul, which the Emperor had recently built on the Marmara just to the south of St Sophia. Scarcely had he reached it, however, when there arrived a company of the imperial guard. According to a number of Italian churchmen, who were eyewitnesses to what took place and subsequently described it in detail to the Frankish ambassadors,[1] they burst into the church with swords drawn and bows ready-strung and advanced threateningly on the Pope – who made a dash for the high altar. Meanwhile the various priests and deacons surrounding him remonstrated with the guard and a scuffle ensued, during which several of them were injured, though none seriously. The soldiers then seized hold of the Pope himself, who was by this time clinging tightly to the columns supporting the altar, and tried to drag him – some by the legs, some by the hair and others by the beard – forcibly away. But the more they pulled, the tighter he clung, until at last the columns came loose and the whole altar crashed to the ground, narrowly missing his head.

---

[1] Their letter will be found in J.P. Migne, *Patrologia Latina*, vol. LXIX, cols 113–19.

By this time a considerable crowd, attracted by the commotion, had begun to protest vehemently against such treatment being accorded to the Vicar of Christ; and the soldiers, manifestly unhappy, wisely decided to withdraw, leaving a triumphant, though badly shaken Vigilius to survey the damage. The next day there arrived a high-powered delegation led by Belisarius himself, to express the Emperor's regret for what had occurred and to give the Pope a formal assurance that he could return to the palace that Justinian had put at his disposal without fear of apprehension.

Vigilius returned at once, but soon found that he was being kept under such close surveillance as to amount to something approaching house arrest. He realised, too, that if he were to break the present deadlock and maintain the prestige that he had striven so hard to recover among the Western Churches, he must once again take decisive action. Two nights before Christmas, in the late evening of 23 December 551, he squeezed his considerable bulk through a small window of the palace and took a boat across the Bosphorus to Chalcedon, where he made straight for the church of St Euphemia. It was a clever move, and a symbolic one in that he was deliberately associating himself with the scene of the Great Council of 451, distancing himself from the Emperor who was questioning its authority, and taking refuge from him in the very building in which its sessions had been held exactly a century before. Once again a delegation under Belisarius came to plead with him, but this time Vigilius stood firm; and when a detachment of soldiers called a few days later they were content to arrest some of his priests, and made no attempt to lay hands on the Pope himself. Vigilius meanwhile composed a long letter to Justinian, known as his *Encyclica*, in which he answered accusations made by the Emperor by giving his own account of the controversy as he saw it and once again proposing negotiations. In a less conciliatory mood, he also published his sentences of excommunication on the Patriarch and the two bishops who had incurred his wrath the previous August.

Negotiations were resumed in the spring, and in June 552 Justinian decided on a major tactical concession: the Patriarch and the other excommunicated bishops were despatched to St Euphemia to apologise and humble themselves before Vigilius, after which the Pope returned to his palace. It was also agreed to annul all recent statements on both sides covering the Three Chapters, including the Emperor's edict. To the papal supporters it must have seemed like victory; but Justinian was not yet beaten. He now summoned a new Ecumenical Council and invited Vigilius to preside.

In theory, an Ecumenical Council of the Church was a convocation of bishops from all over Christendom. When all were gathered together, it was believed that the Holy Spirit would descend on them, giving a sort of infallibility to their pronouncements. Their judgement was supreme, their decisions final. In practice, however, attendance was inevitably selective. If, therefore, the Church was split on any given issue, the outcome of the Council's deliberations would depend less on divine intervention than on the number of bishops from each side able to attend; and both Emperor and Pope knew full well that bishops were considerably thicker on the ground in the East than they were in the West, so that (particularly if the meetings were held in Constantinople) the Easterners would command a substantial majority. Vigilius accordingly suggested that the question should be put to a small committee composed of an equal number of representatives from both East and West, but Justinian refused; and after various other possibilities had been put forward and similarly rejected, the Pope decided that his only chance lay in boycotting the assembly altogether. In consequence, when the Fifth Ecumenical Council eventually met in St Sophia on 5 May 553, of the 168 bishops present, only eleven were from the West, and nine of those were from North Africa. Justinian too had elected to stay away, because, he explained, he did not wish to influence the assembly; but his letter to the delegates, read aloud at the opening session, reminded them that they had already anathematised the Three Chapters. None of those present could have had any doubt about what was expected of them.

For over a week the deliberations continued; then, on 14 May, after repeated invitations to attend, the Pope produced what he described as a *Constitutum*, signed by himself and nineteen other Western churchmen. It was to some degree a compromise, in that it allowed that there were indeed certain grave errors in the writings of Theodore of Mopsuestia; but, it pointed out, the other two writers who were accused had not been pronounced 'orthodox fathers' at Chalcedon. In any case, it was not proper to anathematise the dead. The present agitation over the Three Chapters was therefore unfounded and unnecessary, and was itself to be condemned. Vigilius concluded by forbidding – 'by the authority of the Apostolic See, over which by the Grace of God we preside' – any ecclesiastic to venture any further opinion on the matter.

It was not until 25 May that the Pope formally sent a copy of his paper to the imperial palace. He cannot have expected it to be well received; nor, however, had he reckoned with the changed situation in Italy. Totila was dead; the Goths were defeated; no longer was it necessary to woo the Roman citizens in Italy for their support. The Emperor had had more than enough of Vigilius, and now at last could afford to treat him as he deserved. He made no reply to the *Constitutum*; instead, he sent one of his secretaries to the Council with the text of the Pope's secret declaration of June 547, anathematising the Three Chapters, together with a decree that Vigilius's name should forthwith be struck from the diptychs[1] – though Justinian stressed that, in repudiating Vigilius personally, he was not severing communion with Rome. At its seventh session on 26 May the Council formally endorsed the Emperor's decree and condemned the Pope 'until he should repent his errors'.

For Vigilius, it was the end of the road. Disgraced and banished to an island in the Marmara, he was told that until he accepted the findings of the Council he would never be permitted to return to Rome. Not for another six months – by which time he was suffering agonies from gallstones – did he capitulate; but when at last he did so, his surrender was absolute. In a letter to the Patriarch of 8 December he admitted all his previous errors, and early in 554 – almost certainly at Justinian's insistence – he addressed to the Western Churches a second *Constitutum* in which he formally condemned the Three Chapters and all who dared uphold them; as for himself, 'whatever is brought forward or anywhere discovered in my name in their defence is hereby nullified'. He could not say more. By now too ill to travel, he remained for another year in Constantinople and only then, in a brief respite from pain, started for home. But the effort was too great. On the way his condition suddenly worsened. He was obliged to interrupt his journey at Syracuse; and there, broken alike in body and spirit, he died. For him there was to be no tomb in St Peter's.

The story of Vigilius did untold harm to the papacy; and when his successor Pelagius I (556–61) on his accession instantly added his voice to the condemnation, papal prestige lay in tatters. Several sees – including those of Milan and Aquileia – broke off communion with Rome; it was to be half a century before relations were restored with

---

[1] Diptychs were the two-leaved folders in which were inscribed the names of all those Christians, living and dead, for whom special prayers were to be made in the liturgies. The striking of a name could thus be taken as a sign of excommunication.

Milan, one and a half before Aquileia and Istria returned to the fold. Meanwhile, in 555 Justinian had decreed that in future the Emperor's personal *fiat* ('Let it be done') must be obtained for any election of a Bishop of Rome. But fewer than thirty years after the death of Pelagius in 561 there was to be consecrated a new pontiff who, while failing to heal these particular breaches, would utterly transform his office, giving it new energy and direction: Gregory the Great.

CHAPTER IV

Gregory the Great

(590–604)

Justinian's anxieties over the Three Chapters, though largely of his own making, had turned his mind away from his Italian problems. He always tended to underestimate the Goths; it may well be, too, that the recovery of Rome by the Byzantines in April 547, only four months after its capture by Totila, had confirmed him in his belief that, given only a little more time, the Gothic opposition would crumble of its own accord.

Alas, it had done no such thing. On 16 January 550, for the second time, a few disaffected members of the imperial garrison had opened the gates to Totila's men. But whereas in 546 the Goths had entered the city as invaders, now they showed every sign of staying. Many of them had appropriated empty houses and settled in with their families; the Senate was reopened; refugees were encouraged to return to their own homes; damaged buildings were repaired and restored. The following summer Totila had given still more conclusive evidence of his intentions: he had staged a full-scale revival of the Games in the Circus Maximus, personally presiding over them from the imperial box. Meanwhile his fleet was ravaging both Italy and Sicily, to return in 551 loaded to the gunwales with plunder. These two insults had finally stung Justinian into action. His initial choice of commander for the projected new expedition was his own first cousin, Germanus; but in the autumn of 550 Germanus died of a fever. Did the Emperor now turn, as he had turned twice before, to Belisarius? If so, Belisarius must have refused; for the man chosen for this last attempt to bring Italy back into the imperial fold was a eunuch named Narses, by now well into his seventies.

The choice was not as perverse as might have been thought. Although Narses had spent most of his life in the imperial palace, he was not without military experience, having fought with Belisarius in Italy during the former's first campaign. He was also a superb organiser, strong-willed and determined and, despite his age and his castration, he had lost none of his energy or decisiveness. He had no delusions about the magnitude of his task; by now only four cities in all Italy – Ravenna, Ancona, Otranto and Crotone – remained under Byzantine control. But he probably knew Justinian better than any man alive and easily persuaded him to make available at least 35,000 men. In the early summer of 552 Narses marched them into Italy; and towards the end of June, at Taginae near the modern town of Scheggia, the Roman and Gothic armies met for what was to prove the most decisive encounter of the entire war. The Gothic army, progressively outflanked and outfought, fled in panic as the sun was sinking. Totila himself, mortally wounded, took flight with the rest and died in the little village of Caprae (now Caprara) a few hours later. One more battle remained to be fought. Teia, the bravest of Totila's generals, was determined to continue the struggle; and at the end of October came the final encounter, just a mile or two from the long-forgotten Pompeii. It was that battle beneath Vesuvius that marked the final defeat of the Goths in Italy. Justinian's grandest ambition was realised at last.

But not for long: the war had ushered in a dark age. Italy was a scene of desolation; Milan in the north and Rome in the south lay in ruins. And now, within a few years of the Goths' departure, a new Germanic horde appeared on the scene: the Lombards, under their warlike King Alboin, crossing the Alps in 568, spreading relentlessly over northern Italy and the great plain that still bears their name, finally establishing their capital at Pavia. Within five years they had captured Milan, Verona and Florence; Byzantine rule over northern Italy, won at such a cost by Justinian, Belisarius and Narses, was ended almost as soon as it had begun. The Lombards' line of advance was finally checked by the Exarchate of Ravenna and by Rome itself, but two spearheads pressed on to set up the great independent duchies of Spoleto and Benevento. From here they might well have gone on to conquer the rest of the south, but never managed to unite quite firmly enough to do so. Apulia, Calabria and Sicily remained under Byzantine control – as, surprisingly, did much of the Italian coastline. The Lombards showed little interest in the sea; they were never really a Mediterranean people. That Rome itself did not succumb to the Lombard tide was a miracle hardly less extraordinary than that which had saved the city from Attila the preceding century. Once again it was wrought by a pope, one of the most formidable ever to occupy the throne of St Peter.

Gregory, son of Gordian, came from a rich and well-established Roman family, with strong connections to the papacy. He seems to have been related to Pope Agapetus I; he was certainly a direct descendant of Felix III (483–92). The precise year of his birth is uncertain; it must have been around 540. He at first preferred a civil career to one in the Church – by 573, while still in his early thirties, he had risen to be Prefect of the City of Rome – but in that year his father died and Gregory's life took a new direction. Resigning all his civic responsibilities, he turned the family palace on the Caelian Hill into a Benedictine monastery (simultaneously founding six more on his family estates in Sicily) and entered it himself as a simple brother.

Monasticism was something new in Italy. In the East it had long been part of the religious life, but it had only recently been introduced into the West – by St Benedict, who had founded his great monastery at Monte Cassino less than half a century before and had drawn up the monastic Rule that is still observed today. Once established, it had struck an immediate response. The West at this time was deeply pessimistic. The Roman Empire was gone, the barbarians were spreading across Europe; the world, as Gregory himself put it, 'was growing old and hoary, hastening to its approaching death'. In such a world, the call to a life of manual labour, contemplation and prayer was attractive indeed. Benedict had died while Gregory was still a child, but his influence on the future Pope had been deep and lasting. Long after Gregory had been obliged to abandon monastic life, he was to look back on his three years in his monastery as the happiest he had ever known.

All too soon, Pope Benedict I (575–9) nominated Gregory a *regionarius*, or deacon, in charge of one of Rome's seven ecclesiastical districts, responsible for local administration and the care of the poor; then, in around 580, Benedict's successor Pelagius II (579–90) sent him off to Constantinople as his Nuncio, in the vain hope of persuading the Emperor to send an army against the ever-advancing Lombards. Accommodated in the same palace that had been allotted to the luckless Vigilius, Gregory does not seem to have enjoyed his five years in the city much more than his predecessor – largely, one suspects, because of his mistrust of everything Greek, including even the language, which he resolutely refused to learn. But his time was not entirely wasted: he earned the respect of the two successive emperors to whom he was accredited, and returned in 585 with first-hand knowledge of the Byzantine court and its ways.

Although he had taken a number of his fellow-monks with him to Constantinople – where the atmosphere in his palace must have been a good deal more monastic than diplomatic – we can imagine the relief with which, on his return to Rome, Gregory re-entered his monastery. This time he had five years there instead of three; but on the death of Pelagius, stricken in 590 by the plague, he was the obvious choice for Pope. The first monk ever to achieve papal office, he accepted with genuine reluctance. He wrote to John, Patriarch of Constantinople, that he had inherited an old ship that was becoming ever more waterlogged, its rotten timbers warning of shipwreck. Italy had been devastated by floods, pestilence and famine; the Lombards, moreover, were virtually at the gates of Rome. 'How can I consider,' he wrote:

> the needs of my brethren, ensuring that the city is protected from the swords of the enemy and that the people are not destroyed by a sudden attack, and yet at the same time deliver the word of exhortation fully and effectively for the salvation of souls? To speak of God we need a mind thoroughly at peace and free from care.

His own mind was certainly nothing of the sort. And indeed Gregory was soon to discover that in those dark days the duties of Pope were much the same as those that he had already performed as Prefect of Rome. The city was swamped with refugees, including 3,000 nuns, who had fled from the Lombards. One of his first tasks was to bring in grain from Sicily and release considerable sums from Church funds to alleviate their misery. His difficulties were greatly increased by the attitude of Romanus, the Byzantine Exarch (effectively the provincial governor) of Ravenna. This man – who should have been his ally – was insanely jealous of papal power and prestige and refused to lift a finger in support of Gregory's efforts. 'His malice towards us,' the Pope complained, 'is worse than the swords of the Lombards.' In consequence, Gregory found himself acting as civil and military governor of virtually the whole of central Italy: organising supplies and directing troop movements, as well as paying wages (often from Church funds) and shouldering responsibility for the defence of both

Rome and Naples, now simultaneously under attack from the Lombard Dukes of Spoleto and Benevento, as well as from Alboin's successor, King Agilulf. On occasion this meant buying them all off, at hideous cost to the papal treasury; but the continued inertia and passive hostility of the Exarch – whose officials also demanded the occasional bribe – left him little choice, and the steady drain on the exchequer continued until, in 598, an uneasy peace was at last concluded.

Where did all the money come from? 'The Patrimony of Peter', as it was called, consisted of a vast number of landed estates extending throughout western Europe and even in limited areas of North Africa. These had gradually accumulated over the centuries, thanks largely to pious endowments and donations, but also, in more recent years, to the determination of their former owners to save them from falling into barbarian hands. The Church was by now the largest single landowner in the West. Efficient management of so heterogeneous and widely dispersed a heritage had until now scarcely even been attempted; Gregory at last took the task seriously in hand, dividing the Patrimony up into fifteen separate sections – two of them in Sicily alone – each to be administered by a Rector appointed personally by the Pope. Within his section each Rector was all-powerful, being responsible not only for the collection of rents, the transport and sale of produce and the rendering of exact accounts, but also for all charitable institutions and the maintenance of churches and monasteries.

This reorganisation necessitated a dramatic development of the papal chancery. When Gregory became Pope, it was effectively in the hands of nineteen deacons, seven of whom had charge of the seven regions of the city; it was from these deacons that the popes were normally elected. (They were occasionally given the unofficial title of Cardinal, but cardinals as we know them today were not to make their appearance for another hundred years.) Gregory not only increased their numbers several times over, but swelled them further by newly created ranks of sub-deacons, notaries, treasurers and senior executive officers known as *defensores*, together forming a civil service unparalleled in Europe outside Constantinople itself. By means of this, he also had to keep in touch with (and, when possible, in control of) his several hundred bishops, not all of whom were prepared to respect papal authority.

The new chancery was also responsible for foreign relations, and above all those with by far the most important state in the Christian world, the Byzantine Empire. Since 582 its emperor had been a

Cappadocian soldier named Maurice, with a long and distinguished military record. In normal circumstances he and the Pope might have got on well enough; but in 588, just two years before the start of Gregory's pontificate, the Patriarch of Constantinople, John the Faster, took it upon himself to adopt the title of 'Ecumenical' – thereby implying universal supremacy over all other prelates, including the Pope himself. John was in fact not the first Patriarch to make the claim; the title had been used at various times for the best part of a century, and until now had passed apparently unnoticed. This time, however, there had been angry expostulations from Pope Pelagius; and Gregory on his accession made his displeasure still more evident, firing off two letters to Constantinople. The first, addressed to the Emperor, demanded, for the sake of the peace of the Empire, that he call his recalcitrant Patriarch to order; the second, to the Empress Constantina, begged her to intervene with her husband. John's arrogance in assuming the Ecumenical title was, the Pope claimed, a clear indication that the age of Antichrist was at hand.

Whether Constantina ever replied we do not know; but her husband did, and he fully supported his Patriarch. From that time forward, Gregory's resentment was plain to see; when Emperor Maurice issued an edict forbidding serving soldiers to desert on the grounds that they wished to enter monasteries, Gregory – who had himself left public service for the monastic life – denounced it violently as a further blow struck against the Church. But the Byzantines were irritated too, and it may well have been as a result of the Pope's protests that the fatal title soon became an integral part of the Patriarchal style. Gregory's successors wisely decided to ignore it; but what both sides must have understood well enough was that the incident, trivial as it might seem in retrospect, marked another stage in the steadily growing rivalry between the Eastern and Western Churches.

This rivalry was also responsible for the most indelible stain on the Pope's reputation. In November 602 the reign of the Emperor Maurice came to an abrupt and premature end. His army, deployed against the barbarian Avars and Slavs in the Balkans and looking forward to returning for the winter to Constantinople, was suddenly ordered to sit it out in the inhospitable lands beyond the Danube. Rather than endure the intense cold and discomfort under canvas, living as best they could off the local populations and in constant danger from marauding barbarian clans, the soldiers mutinied, raising as their leader one of their own centurions, a brutal and bloodthirsty monster named

Phocas. Maurice and his five sons (the eldest of whom was the Pope's godson) were all murdered; Constantina and their three daughters were despatched to a nunnery; and Phocas was crowned Emperor of the Romans. Such an atrocity should have led to the most violent condemnation of which Gregory was capable; almost unbelievably, he sent the new Emperor a message of fulsome congratulation, and supported him for the remaining two years of his life. Had he lived to witness the reign of terror that was to follow for another six, the executions and the judicial murders, the blindings and the mutilations, the tortures and the burnings alive, until in 610 Phocas himself was seized and torn to pieces, one can only hope that Gregory would have changed his mind.

In northern and far western Europe the prospects for extending Christendom seemed a good deal more promising than in the south. Some of the former Roman provinces, now ruled by barbarian kings mostly of Frankish origin, were already nominally Christian, though probably of the Arian persuasion; others were still pagan. All were in need of guidance if they were to be brought into the Catholic fold. At the beginning of Gregory's pontificate the principal regions to be taken in hand seemed to be Visigothic Spain, Frankish Gaul and Anglo-Saxon Britain.

The challenge of Visigothic Spain solved itself. Around the turn of the century its Arian King Recared, encouraged by the Pope's friend Leander, Bishop of Seville, announced his conversion to Catholicism. The bulk of the population – being by origin Roman provincials – were Catholic already; now, the remaining Arian nobles and bishops followed their monarch's lead. As a sign of his pleasure (and perhaps relief) at the news, Gregory made the King a present of two relics of extreme holiness: a key made from the chains of St Peter, and a crucifix containing within it a fragment of the True Cross together with a few hairs from the severed head of John the Baptist.

The Kingdom (or, more accurately, the Kingdoms) of the Franks extended over modern France, Belgium, the Netherlands, north-west Germany and Switzerland. They were a Germanic people, theoretically Christian, their King Clovis having been baptised in 499; but with them the challenge was not Arianism: it was chaos, with a dozen petty states and kingdoms all warring and intriguing against each other, and the Church hierarchy – most of whose members had purchased their highly profitable offices – far gone in depravity. (When King Childebert – who ruled from 511 to 558, having murdered his nephews to acquire their lands – visited Soissons, the Bishop was so drunk that he was denied admission to his own city.)

In his attempts to restore a degree of order, Gregory had but one ally, though not perhaps an entirely satisfactory one: Queen Brunhilde of Austrasia, daughter of King Athenagild of Visigothic Spain, who had converted from Arianism on her marriage to Sigebert I.[1] In 575 Sigebert himself was assassinated, and Brunhilde was briefly imprisoned at Rouen; on her release she joined her young son Childebert II in his capital at Metz, and for the next thirty years struggled to establish a united Catholic kingdom, maintaining a long and lively correspondence with the Pope, who gave her all the support he could. Alas, they failed. Her objectives may have been praiseworthy, but her methods – which Gregory did his best to overlook – were no less violent than those of the rest of her family, and in 613, unable to bear her a moment longer, the Austrasian nobles seized her, tortured her for three days, tied her onto the back of a camel, paraded her for the mockery of the army and finally dragged her to death at a horse's tail.

In England the problem was somewhat different. The first missionaries had probably arrived during the third century AD – English bishops had been present at the Council of Arles as early as 314 – but with the coming of the largely pagan Anglo-Saxons, the Christians had been driven to the furthest west and the religion had suffered a temporary eclipse. Celtic missionaries from Ireland and Scotland had done something to reverse the trend, but their churches had always ploughed their own furrow. Celtic monasticism in particular, tending towards the Orthodox model, had little in common with that of the West; the Celts also had an individual system of calculating the date of Easter, which they celebrated on a different day. It remained a fact that no previous pope had given serious thought to missionary work beyond the imperial frontier, and Gregory himself had countless problems nearer home. What is interesting is the importance he attached to this remote island – which he himself regularly described as the end of the universe – and his determination not only that the Christian word should be spread, but that those Christians already existing there

---

[1] It was somehow typical of her time that her sister Galswintha, who had married Sigebert's half-brother Chilperic I, King of the Western Franks, was subsequently murdered by her husband at the instigation of his mistress.

should be brought under papal control and properly aligned with the ideas and practices of Rome.

All British children are (or used to be) brought up on the story, told by the Venerable Bede, of one of history's first (and worst) puns: of how, some years before, Gregory had been wandering through the Roman market and, noticing some beautiful blond boys being offered for sale as slaves, asked from which country they had come. He was told that they came from the island of England, and were called Angles. '"Right," said he, "for they have angelic faces, and it is meet that such should be co-heirs with the Angels in heaven."'[1] In 595 we find him writing to his Rector in Gaul with instructions to recruit young English slave-boys to be trained as monks, whom he may well have seen as potential interpreters; and in the following year he despatched a mission of about forty monks to England, under the leadership of Augustine, Prior of St Andrew's monastery in Rome – that same house in which he himself had been a brother. Warned, on his arrival in southern Gaul, of the dire perils that awaited him among the barbarian English, Augustine turned back to Rome with the suggestion that the mission be abandoned; but Gregory put new heart in him, gave him letters of recommendation and set him back on the road.

Still, presumably, in a state of some trepidation, Augustine and his monks finally landed on the Kentish coast in the spring of 597 – the same year, incidentally, that St Columba died on the island of Iona. They were politely received by King Ethelbert of Kent, at that time the chief ruler in the south of England; he is said by Bede to have extended his power to all England south of the Humber. His wife Bertha, daughter of the Frankish King Charibert and niece of Queen Brunhilde, was already a Christian and naturally gave Augustine her full support. Her husband at first remained cautious: 'I see,' he said to Augustine:

that you believe what you say, or you would not have come all this way to say it. But you must not expect me immediately to renounce the customs which I and the English have observed from one generation to another. So go on talking: no one will interfere with you and, if you convince us, of course it will follow that we will accept your message.

[1] Bede, *Ecclesiastical History of England*, tr. A.M. Sellar, vol. II, ch. 7. The hoary old quotation '*Non Angli sed Angeli*', despite being in Latin, is – alas – spurious. Still according to Bede, Gregory followed up this first pun with two more even worse ones, which the reader will be spared.

A few months later Ethelbert, together with his court and the majority of his subjects, accepted baptism. He thus became the first Christian English king – and a saint to boot.[1] St Augustine meanwhile established a monastery at Canterbury, which he dedicated to St Peter and St Paul (though it was later to become St Augustine's) and which was almost certainly the earliest Benedictine foundation outside Italy. Canterbury in turn became the headquarters of Christianity in England, as it remains today. Pope Gregory was delighted. 'By the shining miracles of his preachers,' he declared:

> God has brought even the ends of the earth to the faith. He has linked in one confession the limits of East and West. Behold, the tongue of Britain, which could formerly utter only barbaric sounds, has lately learned to make the Hebrew Alleluia resound in God's praise.

Gregory was an administrator of genius, an organiser and a missionary; he was not, and never could be, an abstract thinker or theologian, or even a politician. His faith was surprisingly simple: he was largely responsible for the growing belief in miracles and prophecies, as well as for the widespread veneration of saints and relics. Pious but practical, he intended the Patrimony of Peter to be a huge charitable fund, at the immediate disposal of the Church for the benefit of the poor – every day twelve paupers shared his table. In fact, by his work of consolidation, he unknowingly laid the foundations of what was later to be the Papal State, ensuring the temporal power of his successors, which was to endure for the next thirteen centuries. Had he ever realised this, it would have horrified him. For all his determination to uphold the ecclesiastical supremacy of the papal throne, he had no desire for worldly glory; it was enough for him to be, as he constantly maintained, *servus servorum Dei* – the Servant of the Servants of God.

As the greatest Pope of the early Middle Ages, Gregory's most important achievement was to implant ineradicably in men's minds the idea that the Roman Catholic Church was the most important institution in the world, and that the papacy was the supreme authority within it. He made important changes in the liturgy and showed a particular interest in church music: traditional plainsong is commonly known today as 'Gregorian chant' – even though in his time it remained

---

[1] Statues of Ethelbert and Bertha were unveiled on Lady Wootton's Green in Canterbury in 2006.

largely undeveloped – and the Roman *Schola Cantorum,* probably the first body of trained singers to take over from the clergy and congregation and, as such, the ancestor of the modern cathedral choir school, was his personal creation. He was also a compulsive writer. In the first year of his papacy he produced a book, the *Liber Regulae Pastoralis,* setting out directives for the pastoral life of a bishop, whom he saw primarily as a curator of souls. It was astonishingly widely read by the standards of the time, and was later to be translated by Alfred the Great. Then there were the *Dialogues,* dealing with the lives and miracles of Italian saints – including of course Benedict – a series of sermons on the gospels and a critical essay on the book of Job. Finally there are nearly a thousand letters, probably the principal source of what we know of Gregory's life and work. All these writings were, in the Middle Ages, to earn him a place – together with St Ambrose, St Augustine (of Hippo, not Canterbury) and St Jerome – among the four original 'Doctors of the Church'.

Of the four, Gregory was the latest and the last; and the fact is not surprising, because the ancient world was on the verge of collapse. In Rome, the barbarians had done their worst. During their siege in 537 the Goths had cut the aqueducts, dealing the city a blow from which it was not to recover for a thousand years. The history of the aqueducts stretched almost as far back into the past: it had been as early as 312 BC that the Romans, no longer prepared to make do with the murky insufficiency of the Tiber, built the first of those magnificent conduits; over the eight centuries that followed they were to construct ten more, the better to supply not only their domestic needs, but also the innumerable fountains and public baths for which the city was famous. And those aqueducts provided something else as well: the hydraulic power that drove, among much else, the mills on which the people depended for their bread. Their destruction was followed by famine and disease, together with a disastrous decline in popular morale.[1]

Amid the general *dégringolade,* the figure of Gregory the Great shone out like a beacon. He stood for integrity, for order, and for the Christian faith that alone offered hope for a better and happier world. At heart, nevertheless, he remained a humble monk, carrying on the traditions of his hero St Benedict in every way that he could. It was

---

[1] One pilgrim during the Dark Ages, a draper from Douai, was informed that the aqueducts 'were formerly used to bring oil, wine and water from Naples'.

perhaps because of this humility – for no man was ever less spoilt by power – that he was genuinely loved, so much so that immediately after his death his people demanded that he should be made a saint. The title of 'the Great' came later; both were abundantly deserved.

CHAPTER V

Leo III and Charlemagne

(622–816)

Early in the seventh century a new people and a new faith appeared on the world stage. Until the third decade of that century the land of Arabia was *terra incognita* to the Christian world. But in September 622 the Prophet Mohammed had fled from the hostile city of Mecca to friendly Medina: this was the *hegira*, the event that marks the beginning of the whole Muslim era. Just eleven years later, his followers burst out of Arabia. The following year an Arab army defeated the Byzantine Emperor Heraclius on the banks of the Yarmuk river; two years later still they had taken Damascus; after five, Jerusalem; after eight, they controlled all Syria, Palestine and Egypt. Within twenty years the whole Persian Empire as far as the Oxus had fallen to the Arab sword; within thirty, Afghanistan and most of the Punjab. Then the Muslims turned their attention to the West. Progress across North Africa was somewhat slower, but by the end of the seventh century they had reached the Atlantic, and by 732 – still less than a century after their eruption from their desert homeland – they had (according to tradition) made their way over the Pyrenees as far as Tours. There, just 150 miles from Paris, they were stopped at last by the Frankish leader Charles Martel.

For Christendom, the effect was cataclysmic. Three of the five historical patriarchates – Alexandria, Antioch and Jerusalem – now existed in little more than name; all the great Churches of North Africa disappeared, save only the Copts of Egypt, who managed to retain a tenuous foothold. The lands that had seen the origins of Christianity were all lost, never to be properly recovered. The Eastern Empire was hideously maimed. The political focus of necessity now shifted northwards and westwards. Perhaps, as the great Belgian historian Henri Pirenne suggested, it was Mohammed who made Charlemagne possible.

In Italy, all through the second half of the seventh century and the first half of the eighth, we see two opposing tendencies: on the one hand, a steady weakening of political and religious links with the Byzantine Empire; on the other, an equally steady increase in the power of the Lombards. In 653 Pope Martin I (649–55), though old and ill, was arrested on trumped-up charges and taken to Constantinople, where he was publicly stripped of his vestments, dragged in chains through the city, flogged and deported to the Crimea, dying there soon afterwards; and matters came to a head in 726, when the Emperor Leo III published his fateful edict imposing iconoclasm – a doctrine that, calling as it did for the wholesale destruction of all holy images, was received with horror in the West and caused revolts throughout Byzantine Italy. In retaliation, Leo confiscated the annual incomes from the churches of Sicily and Calabria, transferring their bishoprics, together with a considerable number of others in the Balkan penin-sula, from the see of Rome to that of Constantinople. It was the begin-ning of that long, slow process of estrangement that would end, 300 years later, in schism.

The Lombards, meanwhile, were steadily strengthening their hold. Under the greatest of their kings, Liutprand, they twice – successfully – laid siege to Rome. On the first occasion, in 729, Pope Gregory II (715–31) – at last a Roman-born pope after a long succession of Greeks – confronted Liutprand, who abandoned the siege, feeling guilty enough to leave his arms and armour in St Peter's as a votive offering; but on the second, ten years later, he and his men were in a very different mood. This time, rather than enriching the basilica, they looted it. Gregory's successor, Gregory III (731–41), powerless to stop them, looked about desperately for a new ally; and found him – or thought he had – beyond the Alps in Gaul, in the person of Charles Martel.

Charles was not himself a monarch. Technically, he was Mayor of the Palace at the court of the Merovingian king; but the Merovin-gians were nonentities, and it was in the hands of the Mayor that power effectively rested. Charles had already earned fame throughout Europe as the first man to check the advance of the Muslim army; if he could halt the Saracens, might he not do the same to the Lombards?

Perhaps; but he would not be hurried. He had his hands full in Gaul, and he remained there until his death. In 751, however, his son Pepin – the Short, as he was always called – managed to convince Pope Zachary (741–52) that the holder of the power should also be wearer of the crown. Thus, at the hands of the English Archbishop Boniface, Pepin received his coronation at Soissons, the feckless King

Childeric being packed off to end his days in a monastery. Henceforth Pepin was deeply in the Pope's debt: there was a good chance that any future appeal for aid might have a more sympathetic hearing. In any case the coronation came not a moment too soon; for in that very same year Ravenna was finally captured by the Lombard King Aistulf, and the Byzantine Empire's final foothold in northern Italy was lost for ever.

Zachary – the last of a long line of Greek popes[1] – died in the following year. His eleven-year pontificate had not been easy. He had worked hard to save papal–imperial relations from a complete breakdown – an objective to which his translation of Gregory the Great's *Dialogues* into Greek may or may not have contributed – but the fall of Ravenna had marked a further degree of rupture, and Aistulf was now busy mopping up what was left of Byzantine power in north and central Italy. For the papacy the situation was now desperate, and it was hardly surprising that a Roman aristocrat, Stephen II (752–7), was chosen – rather than yet another Greek – as Zachary's successor.[2]

Pope Stephen lost no time in travelling personally to Pepin's court at Ponthion near Châlons-sur-Marne, where he arrived in the first days of 754. On 6 January, the Feast of the Epiphany, he anointed the King, together with his wife and two sons Charles and Carloman, awarding to all three the title that he had just invented: Patrician of the Romans. Meetings between King and Pope continued sporadically over the next six months, and were a triumphant success. Pepin willingly undertook the role of defender of the papacy, promising to recover on behalf of the Pope all the Italian cities and territories that the Lombards had captured from the Empire; and in two major expeditions, in 754 and again in 756, he proved as good as his word, bringing King Aistulf to his knees, putting a client-king, Desiderius, on the Lombard throne and marrying his daughter. After the second campaign Pepin proclaimed the Pope sole ruler of the lands formerly composed of the imperial Exarchate, snaking across central Italy to embrace Ravenna, Perugia and Rome itself.

---

[1] It is ironical indeed that the steady breakdown of papal-Byzantine relations should have occurred under Greek popes. Of the twelve elected between John V in 685 and Stephen in 752, only Gregory II (715–31) was a Latin. At the Sixth Ecumenical Council of the Church, held at Constantinople in 680-1, the entire papal delegation was Greek.

[2] He is sometimes known as Stephen III. The numbering of the Stephens is a little confused, since the Stephen elected on 23 March 752 died two days later before he could be consecrated. He is therefore not normally counted. In this book the lesser figure will always be used.

His authority for this so-called 'Donation of Pepin' is, to say the least, doubtful; and in Constantinople the Emperor Constantine V predictably lodged a furious protest. It was at one time suggested that Pepin might have based his action on the so-called 'Donation of Constantine';[1] but recent evidence suggests that this shameless fabrication was not concocted for another half-century. Pepin himself justified it by claiming that his intervention had been for the love of St Peter, and that it was therefore to St Peter that the conquered lands would belong. It remains true that the Papal States which he thus brought into being, however shaky their legal foundation, were to endure for more than eleven centuries.

Pepin died in 768, leaving his kingdom – in accordance with the old Frankish custom – to be divided between his two sons, Charles and Carloman; but Carloman's sudden death in 771 enabled Charles, ignoring the rights of his young nephews, to make himself sole ruler. Only two months later a tough-minded Roman aristocrat assumed the papal throne under the name of Hadrian I (772–95). He and Charles together continued the work that had been begun by Pope Stephen II and Pepin, further cementing relations between the Frankish Kingdom and the papacy; and when in 773 the Lombard client-king Desiderius forgot his place to the point where he began besieging Rome, Hadrian turned immediately to Charles for help. The Patrician of the Romans lost no time. He marched into Italy, seized the Lombard capital at Pavia, packed Desiderius off to a monastery and – apart from adding 'King of the Lombards' to his own steadily growing list of titles – abolished the Lombard Kingdom once and for all. Then, at Easter 774, he decided to come to Rome.

The decision took Pope Hadrian by surprise; but he rose magnificently to the occasion, greeting his royal guest on the steps of St Peter's – which Charles is said to have climbed on his knees – and showing him every honour. In return Charles reconfirmed his father's Donation, adding considerably to the extent of the territory concerned, and expressed his intention of imposing unity and uniformity according to the Roman model on all the churches within his dominions. Returning to Germany, he next subdued the heathen Saxons, whom he converted en masse to Christianity before going on to annex already-Christian Bavaria. An invasion of Spain was less successful – though

---

[1] See Chapter II, p.14–15.

it provided the inspiration for the first great epic ballad of western Europe, the *Chanson de Roland* – but Charles's subsequent campaign against the Avars in Hungary and upper Austria resulted in the destruction of their kingdom as an independent state and its incorporation in turn within his own frontiers. Thus, in little more than a generation, he had raised the Kingdom of the Franks from just one of the many semi-tribal European states to a single political unit of vast extent, unparalleled since the days of imperial Rome.

And he had done so, for most of the time at least, with the enthusiastic support of the papacy. It was nearly half a century since Pope Stephen had struggled across the Alps to seek help from Pepin – an appeal that might more properly have been addressed to the Byzantine Emperor, and probably would have been, if the Emperor Constantine V could only have spared a few moments from his obsession with iconoclasm to turn his attention to Italy. Pepin and Charles, in effectively eliminating the Lombard Kingdom, had succeeded where Byzantium had failed; and Byzantium was to pay dearly for its failure.

The two did not, however, always see eye to eye: and a particular bone of contention was, rather surprisingly, iconoclasm. In 787, in an attempt to settle the issue, the Empress Irene (she was in fact the widow of the Emperor Leo IV, acting as regent for her seventeen-year-old son) summoned the Seventh Ecumenical Council, to be held (like the first) at Nicaea. Hadrian duly despatched his legates, carrying a long and closely argued defence of holy images; and the Council most gratifyingly declared in his favour. Charles, however, objected. This sudden rapprochement between Rome and Constantinople was not at all to his liking. Why, he demanded, had *he* not also been invited to send representatives to Nicaea? In what looks suspiciously like a fit of pique, he ordered his theologians to produce a defence of iconoclasm in the shape of what were called the *Libri Carolini*; and for a few years his relations with Pope Hadrian were seriously strained. But the cloud eventually passed. A mistake was fortunately discovered in the Latin version of the Council's findings – 'veneration' had been mistranslated as 'adoration' – and by the time of Hadrian's death on Christmas Day 795 the two were once more on excellent terms.

It was just as well that they were; for the climax to the story was now rapidly approaching. The new Pope, Leo III (795–816) – not to be confused with the Byzantine emperor of the same name – could boast neither the birth nor the breeding of his predecessor. There is a theory that he may even have been of Arab stock. From the moment of his elevation he was the victim of incessant intrigue on the part of Hadrian's family and friends, who had expected the papal throne to pass to one of them and were consequently determined to remove him. On 25 April 799 a group led by the late Pope's nephew actually attacked Leo in the course of a solemn procession from the Lateran to the church of St Lawrence. They failed in their original intention of blinding him and cutting out his tongue – mutilations that would have obliged him to resign the papacy – but left him unconscious in the street. Only by the greatest good fortune was he rescued by friends and removed for safety to Charles's court at Paderborn. Under the protection of Frankish agents he returned to Rome in November, only to find himself facing a number of serious charges levelled by his enemies, including simony, perjury and adultery.

Whether or not the Pope was guilty of these charges was almost immaterial – though Charles certainly had his suspicions. There was another question, infinitely more important: by whom could he possibly be tried? Who, after all, was qualified to pass judgement on the Vicar of Christ? In normal circumstances the answer given by some would have been the Emperor at Constantinople; but the imperial throne was at that time occupied by Irene. That Irene was notorious for having blinded and murdered her own son was, in the minds of both Leo and Charles, also immaterial; it was enough that she was a woman. The female sex was known to be incapable of governing, and by the old Salic tradition was debarred from even attempting to do so. As far as western Europe was concerned, the Throne of the Emperors was vacant; Irene's claim to it was merely an additional proof, if any were needed, of the degradation into which the so-called Roman Empire had fallen.

By the time he himself reached Rome in November 800, Charles had been firmly reminded by his chief adviser, the Englishman Alcuin of York, that he had no more authority than Irene to sit in judgement over the successor of St Peter; but he also knew that while the accusations remained unrefuted, Christendom lacked not only an Emperor but a Pope as well, and he was determined to clear Leo's name. Obviously anything resembling a trial was out of the question; but on 23 December, at the high altar, the Pope swore a solemn oath on the gospels that he was innocent of all the charges levelled against him – and the assembled synod accepted his word. Two days later, as Charles rose from his knees at the conclusion of the Christmas Mass, Leo laid the imperial crown upon his head.

*   *   *

Charles had received, as his enemies were quick to point out, only a title; the imperial crown brought with it not a single new subject or soldier, not an acre of new territory. But that title was of more lasting significance than any number of conquests; for it meant that, after more than 400 years, there was once again an emperor in western Europe. There remains the question of why the Pope acted as he did. Not, certainly, to engineer a deliberate split in the Roman Empire, still less to bring about two rival empires where one had been before. There was, so far as Leo was concerned, no living emperor at that time. Very well, he would create one; and because the Byzantines had proved so unsatisfactory from every point of view – political, military and doctrinal – he would select a Westerner: the one man who, by his wisdom and statesmanship and the vastness of his dominions as well as by his prodigious physical stature, stood head and shoulders above his contemporaries. But if Leo conferred a great honour on Charles that Christmas morning, he bestowed a still greater one on himself: the right to appoint, and to invest with crown and sceptre, the Emperor of the Romans. Here was something new, even revolutionary. No pontiff had ever before claimed for himself such a privilege – not only establishing the imperial crown as his own personal gift, but simultaneously granting himself implicit superiority over the Emperor whom he had created.

Historians have long argued whether the imperial coronation had been jointly planned by Leo and Charles or whether, as appeared at the time, the King of the Franks was taken completely by surprise. His first biographer, Einhard, quotes him as claiming that he would not have set foot in the basilica had he had any idea of the Pope's intentions. True, he had never shown the faintest interest in claiming imperial status, and for the rest of his life continued to style himself *Rex Francorum et Langobardorum* (King of the Franks and the Lombards). Nor, clearly, would he have wished to owe any obligation to the Pope. On the other hand, once the thought of the coronation had occurred to Leo, is it really conceivable that he would not have suggested it in advance to Charles, even if only as a simple courtesy? And for Charles himself, would not the advantages of the imperial title easily outweigh the drawbacks? We are forced to the conclusion that Pope and Emperor had already discussed the idea at length, probably at Paderborn, and that Einhard's statement – together with Charles's own later protestations – was disingenuously designed to deflect the criticism that he could not fail to incur.

Of one thing we can be virtually certain: neither Leo nor Charles would have touched the crown had there been at the time a male emperor of Byzantium. The concept of two simultaneous emperors would have been unthinkable; it was the presence of a woman on the Byzantine throne that put an utterly different complexion on the matter. At the same time, that very fact gave Charles a further important reason to accept the crown that he was offered: for now, at this one critical moment of history, he recognised an opportunity that might never be repeated. Irene, for all her faults, remained a marriageable widow – and, by all accounts, a remarkably attractive one. If he could but persuade her to become his wife, all the imperial territories of East and West would be reunited under a single crown: his own.

The reaction in Constantinople to the news of Charles's coronation can easily be imagined. To any right-thinking Greek it was an act not only of breathtaking arrogance, but also of sacrilege. The Byzantine Empire was built on a dual foundation: on the one hand, Roman power; on the other, the Christian faith. The two had first come together in the person of Constantine the Great, Emperor of Rome and 'Equal of the Apostles', and this mystical union had continued through all his legitimate successors. It followed that, just as there was only one God in heaven, so there could be but one supreme ruler here on Earth; all other claimants to such a title were impostors, and blasphemers as well.

Moreover, unlike the princes of the West, the Byzantines had no Salic law. However much they might detest their empress and even attempt to depose her, they never questioned her right to occupy the imperial throne. So much the greater, therefore, was their anxiety when, early in 802, Charles's ambassadors arrived in Constantinople; and so much the greater still when they realised that Irene, far from being insulted by the very idea of marriage with an illiterate barbarian – for Charles, though he could read a little, made no secret of his inability to write – appeared on the contrary to be intrigued, gratified and disposed, in principle, to accept.

Her reasons are not hard to understand. Her subjects loathed her, her exchequer was empty. She had reduced her empire to degradation and penury. Sooner or later – probably sooner – a *coup d'état* was inevitable. It mattered little to her that her suitor was a rival, an adventurer and a heretic; if he were as uneducated as reports suggested, she would probably be able to manipulate him as easily as she had manipulated her late husband and her unfortunate son. Meanwhile in marrying him she would preserve the unity of the Empire and – in her eyes far more important – her own skin.

There were other attractions too. The proposal offered an opportunity to escape from the stifling atmosphere of the imperial court. Though twenty-two years a widow – during which time she had lived surrounded by women and eunuchs – Irene was probably still in her early fifties, perhaps even younger: what could be more natural than that she should look favourably on the prospect of a new husband at last, particularly one rumoured to be tall and outstandingly handsome, a superb hunter with a fine singing voice and flashing blue eyes? But it was not to be. Her subjects had no intention of allowing the throne to be taken over by this boorish Frank, in his outlandish linen tunic and his ridiculously cross-gartered scarlet leggings, speaking an incomprehensible language and unable even to sign his name except by stencilling it through a gold plate – just as Theodoric the Ostrogoth had done three centuries before. On the last day of October 802 Irene was arrested, deposed and sent into exile; a year later she was dead.

If Charles had married Irene ... the speculation is irresistible, even though – like all such speculations – ultimately sterile. Would the West have taken over the East, or vice versa? Charles would certainly not for a second have considered living in Constantinople: in theory, at any rate, the capital would have moved back to the West. But would the Byzantines have accepted such a state of affairs? It seems most unlikely. A far more probable scenario is that they would have declared Irene deposed and would have crowned a new Emperor in her place – just as in fact they did – effectively challenging Charles to do something about it; and that he, much as he might have wished to retaliate, would have been unable to do so. The distances were too great, the lines of communication too long. He would have been in a humiliating position indeed, and powerless to extricate himself. He might never even have acquired the name of Charlemagne. And who in any case was to know that within a few years of his death his own, Western Empire would effectively crumble away? How lucky he was that the Byzantines took their strong line then rather than later, and that Frankish emperor and Greek empress never came together after all.

Pope Leo III was an unremarkable man: it is one of the ironies of history that he should have been responsible for one of the most momentous acts ever performed by a pope. He had worked his way up through the hierarchy from relatively humble beginnings, and remained essentially a simplistic one, for whom the coronation of Charlemagne meant a simple division of responsibilities. The Emperor would wield the sword: the Pope would fight for the faith, protecting it and extending it wherever possible, and would provide the spiritual guidance for his entire flock – the Emperor included.

All would have been well if Charles could only have seen things in the same way. He had already made a moderately disastrous intervention in the iconoclast debate; in 810 he involved himself yet again in theological matters, this time over another old warhorse, the *filioque* clause. The original Creed determined by the Councils of Nicaea and Constantinople had held that the Holy Ghost 'proceeded from the Father'; to this, from the sixth century on, the Western Church had added the word *filioque*, 'and the Son'. By Charles's time this addition was generally adopted throughout the Frankish Empire, and in 809 it was formally endorsed by the Council of Aachen, his own capital. Two years earlier the Frankish monks on the Mount of Olives in Jerusalem had introduced it into their services – arousing furious opposition from the Eastern community of the nearby monastery of St Saba, whereupon they had referred the question to the Pope for a definitive ruling.

Leo was in a quandary. As a devout Westerner, he was perfectly happy with the offending word, for which there was good scriptural authority. On the other hand, he was prepared to admit that the Western Church had had no right to tamper with a Creed that had been drafted by an Ecumenical Council, and relations with Constantinople were already quite difficult enough without sparking off another conflict. His solution was an attempt to have it both ways: to approve the doctrine while suppressing the word itself – which he did, not by means of any inflammatory edict, but by having the text of the Creed in its original form (that is without the *filioque*) engraved in Greek and Latin on two silver plaques that were fixed to the tombs of St Peter and St Paul. His endorsement of the unity of the two Churches in their joint authorship of the ancient Creed could hardly have been clearer.

Charlemagne, however, was predictably furious. He had grown up with the *filioque*; if the East refused to accept it, then the East was wrong. And who cared about the East anyway? He was the Emperor now; the Pope should nail his colours firmly to the Western mast and leave those heretics in Constantinople to their own devices. When

Leo ordered him to remove the word from his liturgies, he took no action, and sent no reply; and when in 813 he decided to make his son Louis co-Emperor, he pointedly failed to invite the Pope to perform the ceremony.

For centuries popes and emperors were to continue their struggle over the demarcation line between their two authorities, each trying to push it as far as possible into the territory of the other; in the short term, however, the bickering continued for only twenty-five years after Charlemagne's death in January 814 – when, on the death of Louis in 840, the Carolingian Empire fell apart. From then on, the power of the papacy grew steadily: and before long it was generally agreed that every new emperor must be anointed by the Pope personally, in Rome.

But the imperial disintegration meant that the popes must now assume responsibilities that could previously have been left to the Empire; and now a new and terrible enemy threatened southern Italy. In 827 the Arabs of North Africa had invaded Sicily in strength at the invitation of the Byzantine governor, Euthymius, who was rebelling against Constantinople in an effort to avoid the consequences of having eloped with a local nun. Four years later they took Palermo, and henceforth the peninsula was in constant danger. Brindisi fell, then Taranto, then Bari – which for thirty years was the seat of an Arab emirate – and in 846 it was the turn of Rome itself: an Arab fleet sailed up the Tiber and sacked the city, even going so far as to strip the silver plate from the doors of St Peter's. No help was to be expected from the Western Empire, which had effectively ceased to exist.

And once again the city was saved by its Pope. In 849, summoning the combined navies of his three maritime neighbours – Naples, Gaeta and Amalfi – and assuming the supreme command himself, Pope Leo IV (847–55) destroyed the Arab fleet off Ostia. The hundreds of captives were sent to join local workmen in building an immense rampart around the Vatican and down as far as the Castel Sant'Angelo: the forty-foot-high Leonine Wall, the most spectacular monument of early medieval Rome, sweeping up from the Tiber to the crest of the Vatican Hill and then down again to the river. It was completed in 852, and considerable sections of it still stand today.

CHAPTER VI

Pope Joan

(?855–7)

After Leo, John, an Englishman born at Mainz, was Pope for two years, seven months and four days, and died in Rome, after which there was a vacancy in the papacy of one month. It is claimed that this John was a woman, who as a girl had been brought to Athens in the clothes of a man by a certain lover of hers. There she became proficient in a diversity of branches of knowledge until she had no equal; and afterwards in Rome, she taught the liberal arts and had great masters among her students and audience. In the city the opinion of her life and learning grew ever higher, and she was the unanimous choice for Pope. While Pope, however, she became pregnant by her companion. Through ignorance of the exact time when the birth was expected, she was delivered of a child while in procession from St Peter's to the Lateran, in a narrow lane between the Colosseum and St Clement's church. After her death, it is said that she was buried in that same place. The Lord Pope always turns aside from this street and it is believed by many that this is done because of abhorrence of the event. Nor is she placed on the list of the holy pontiffs, both because of her female sex and on account of the shamefulness of the event.

So, in the year 1265, wrote a Dominican monk named Martin in his *Chronicon Pontificum et Imperatum*. Originally from Troppau in Poland, Martin had made his way to Rome, where he served as chaplain to Clement IV (1265–8). His book proved, by the standards of the time, immensely popular, with versions of it – all laboriously copied by hand – circulating throughout Europe. And it is largely thanks to him that the legend of Pope Joan, who is said to have reigned from 855 to 857, between Leo IV and Benedict III (855–8), has become one of the hoariest canards in papal history.

Martin is not the earliest chronicler in whose work the story occurs. Several of his predecessors are credited with it, the first of them being Anastasius, the papal librarian (there will be more about him in the next chapter), who, if Joan had existed, would have known her personally. But though their histories may have been written earlier, all the surviving copies of them comfortably post-date Martin. Some omit Joan altogether; some refer to her as John VII or VIII;[1] one – an early Vatican manuscript of Anastasius – includes her, but in an obvious insertion at the bottom of the page and in a later (fourteenth-century) script; and most of the rest echo Martin's words so closely as to leave no doubt that they are using him as their authority. A few lend additional glosses to the story: that Joan was killed by a furious populace and buried on the spot; that she ended her life in a convent; that her son became Bishop of Ostia. But the main lines remain intact: that in the mid-ninth century a certain Englishwoman became Pope, and that she reigned for some two and a half years until, by some unhappy miscalculation, she gave birth to a baby on the way to the Lateran.

One chronicler only gives a version of the story different enough to be worth quoting in full. He is Jean de Mailly, another thirteenth-century Dominican, who lived at Metz near the German border and was largely responsible for the *Chronica Universalis Metensis*, which first appeared some fifteen years earlier than Martin's history, but achieved nowhere near the same degree of acclaim. 'Query:' he writes:

> concerning a certain pope or rather female pope, who is not set down in the list of popes or bishops of Rome, because she was a woman who disguised herself as a man and became, by her character and talents, a curial secretary, then a cardinal and finally pope. One day, while mounting her horse, she gave birth to a child. Immediately, by Roman justice, she was bound by the feet to a horse's tail and dragged and stoned by the people for half a league. And where she died, there she was buried, and at the place is written, *Petre, Pater Patrum, Papisse Prodito Partum* ('Oh Peter, Father of Fathers, Betray the Childbirth of the Woman Pope'). At the same time, the four-day fast called 'the fast of the female pope' was first established.

A particularly curious feature of de Mailly's version is that he dates Joan's pontificate to nearly two and a half centuries later than Martin, to 1099 – the date usually attributed to Paschal II (1099–1118), whose accession he cheerfully postpones to 1106. Joan is thus allowed to

---

[1] Both these popes existed in their own right. As it was generally agreed that Joan was to be ignored, the numeration was not affected; but the reputation of the admirable John VIII (872–82) – a ruthless warrior pope who fortified Rome against the Saracens, founded a papal navy and came to a violent end, beaten to death after an attempt to poison him failed – regrettably suffered: a book was published in 1530 entitled *Puerperium Johannis Papae* (*The Childbirth of Pope John VIII*). He deserved better.

reign for no fewer than seven years – a long time indeed to maintain her deception. But this dating would in any case be manifestly impossible. During the middle of the ninth century, Rome, sacked by the Saracens in 846, was still going through her Dark Ages. All was confusion, records were few and untrustworthy, and the notion of a woman Pope was, perhaps, just conceivable. Three and a half centuries later, on the other hand, the times were thoroughly documented; the story of Pope Joan would have been as impossible then as it would be today.

Nevertheless, that story had by then been firmly established in the popular mind; and there for centuries it remained. Even Bartolomeo Platina, Prefect of the Vatican Library under Sixtus IV (1471–84), inserts 'John VIII' between Leo IV and Benedict III in his *Lives of the Popes*, and tells the story in considerable detail. 'These things which I relate,' he adds, 'are popular reports, but derived from uncertain and obscure authors, which I have therefore inserted briefly and baldly, lest I should seem obstinate and pertinacious by omitting what most people assert ... although,' he continues, 'what I have related may not be thought altogether incredible.'

At the time of the Reformation, Joan became an admirable stick with which to beat the Church of Rome. As early as the Council of Constance in 1414–15 the Bohemian reformer John Hus was only too pleased to use her as part of his evidence. Significantly, the Council did not deny it. As the French eighteenth-century historian Jacques Lenfant perceptively pointed out, 'if it had not been looked upon at that Time as an undeniable Fact, the Fathers of the Council wou'd not have fail'd either to correct John Hus with some Displeasure, or to have laugh'd and shook their Heads, as ... they did presently for less cause'. At the same time, the reference to Joan (Hus, like several other chroniclers of his time, actually calls her Agnes) cannot have endeared him to the Council; but he probably knew by then that he could not escape the stake, so felt that he had little to lose.

The Welshman Adam of Usk, who spent four years in Rome from 1402 to 1406, gives an account of the coronation procession from St Peter's to the Lateran of Pope Innocent VII (1404–6), in the course of which he confirms an interesting detail in Martin's version:

After turning aside out of abhorrence for Pope Agnes [*sic*], whose image in stone with her son stands in the straight road near St Clement's, the Pope, dismounting from his horse, enters the Lateran for his enthronement.

The Constantinian Basilica of St John Lateran was – as it had always been – the cathedral of the Pope in his capacity as Bishop of Rome. Since it stands at the opposite end of the city from St Peter's, there were frequent processions between one and the other, passing through the centre of Rome by way of the Colosseum and the church of S. Clemente. It was probably somewhere near the latter, on the Via S. Giovanni in Laterano, that the offending statue stood. We can have no doubt that it existed – it is mentioned in all the old handbooks for pilgrims – though there is a considerable difference of opinion as to the form it actually took. Theodoric of Niem, cofounder of the German College in Rome, reported in about 1414 that the image was of marble, and that it 'represented the fact as it occurred; that is to say, a woman who was delivered of a child'. Martin Luther, on the other hand, who was in the city towards the end of 1510 – and was surprised that the popes should have allowed such an embarrassment in a public place – writes of 'a woman wearing a papal cloak, holding a child and a sceptre'. We can take our choice. We shall never know, because the statue (together with the stone and its alliterative inscription) has long gone, almost certainly removed in about 1480 by Sixtus IV, who is said to have had it thrown into the Tiber.

Nor can there be any doubt that the place was regularly avoided by the popes. Johannes Burckhardt, Bishop of Strasbourg and papal Master of Ceremonies under Innocent VIII (1484–92) and his two successors, Alexander VI and Pius III, ruefully records how Innocent was brave enough to break tradition:

> In going as in returning, [Pope Innocent] came by way of the Colosseum, and that straight road where the image of the female pope is located, in token, it is said, that John VII [*sic*] gave birth there to a child. For that reason, many say that the Popes may never ride on horseback there. And so the Lord Archbishop of Florence ... reprimanded me.

But let us return to Adam of Usk:

> And there [in the Lateran] he is seated in a chair of porphyry, which is pierced beneath for this purpose, that one of the younger cardinals

may make proof of his sex; and then, while a *Te Deum* is chanted, he is borne to the high altar.

The fullest description of this *chaise percée*, by means of which the Church made sure that so embarrassing an occurrence should never be repeated, is that given by Felix Haemerlein, in *De Nobilitate et Rusticitate Dialogus* (*c*.1490):

> ... up to the present day the seat is still in the same place and is used at the election of the pope. And in order to demonstrate his worthiness, his testicles are felt by the junior cleric present as testimony of his male sex. When this is found to be so, the person who feels them shouts out in a loud voice 'He has testicles!' And all the clerics present reply 'God be praised!' Then they proceed joyfully to the consecration of the pope-elect.

He specifically confirms that this was because of Pope Joan, pointing out that it was her successor, Benedict III, who set up the pierced chair.

What are we to make of all this? Can we honestly believe that successive popes – they would have included Pope Alexander VI, who is known to have fathered any number of children – would have subjected themselves to such undignified gropings?[1] The mists begin to clear when we compare two more fifteenth-century accounts. The first is by an Englishman, William Brewin, who in 1470 compiled a guidebook to the churches of Rome. In the Chapel of St Saviour in St John Lateran, he tells us, 'are two or more chairs of red marble stone, with apertures carved in them, upon which chairs, as I heard, proof is made as to whether the pope is male or not.' The second is once again by Bishop Burchard:

> The Pope was led to the door of St Sylvester's Chapel, near which were placed two plain porphyry seats, in the first of which, from the right of the door, the pope sat, as though lying down; and when he was thus seated, the ... prior of the Lateran gave into the Pope's hand a rod, in token of ruling and correction, and the keys of the Basilica and the Lateran Palace, in token of the power of closing and opening, of binding and loosing. The Pope then moved to the other chair, from which he handed back the rod and keys.

---

[1] The Milanese historian Bernardino Coreo certainly thought so. At the close of his eyewitness account of Alexander's coronation in 1492 he writes: 'Finally, when the usual solemnities of the *sancta sanctorum* ended and the touching of testicles was done, I returned to the palace.'

'Two plain porphyry seats': these were the so-called *sedia curules*, which for some 400 years were used in papal enthronements. One was looted by Napoleon's army and taken to the Louvre';[1] the other remains in Rome, though now in the Vatican Museum, whither it was removed by Pius VI at the end of the eighteenth century. It now stands, unlabelled, in a window recess of the so-called *Gabinetto delle Maschere*. It has indeed a hole in the seat, cut in the shape of a huge keyhole; more curious, however, is the angle of the back, some forty-five degrees to the vertical. One would indeed sit on it 'as though lying down'; it could not possibly serve as a commode. One explanation that has been put forward is that it was originally intended as an obstetric or 'birthing' chair ('closing and opening, binding and loosing'?) and that it was used in the coronation ceremony to symbolise the Mother Church. It cannot be gainsaid, on the other hand, that it is admirably designed for a diaconal grope; and it is only with considerable reluctance that one turns the idea aside.

The last of the major pieces of evidence in favour of the existence of Pope Joan – or at least of the widespread belief in her legend – is the series of papal busts in the Cathedral of Siena. Their date is uncertain, but the late fourteenth century seems most likely. There are 170 of them, beginning with St Peter to the right of the crucifix in the centre of the apse and continuing anti-clockwise around the building until they end with Pope Lucius III, who died in 1185. Sure enough, Joan was included – in her proper place between Leo IV and Benedict III, her bust carrying the clear inscription *Johannes VIII, Foemina de Anglia*. Most regrettably she is no longer there, Clement VIII having had the bust removed in about 1600.

What became of it is unclear. Cardinal Baronius, Clement's librarian, claimed that it was immediately destroyed; but early in the seventeenth century Antoine Pagi, the Provincial of the Franciscans in Arles, went to stay at his Order's house in Siena, where he recorded conversations with various priests and churchmen. According to them, rather than break up the bust, it had been decided simply to relabel it. After minor remodelling, it became a portrait of Pope Zachary (741–52), who now appears in the series in his correct chronological position.

With so much conflicting evidence, can we be absolutely sure that Pope Joan never existed? Sadly, we can. Two particularly cogent

[1] Is it still there? 'When we enquired after the one in the Louvre we were told by a representative that the Museum "*ne conserve pas de trône pontifical*"' (P. Stanford, *The She-Pope*, p.50).

indications emerge, from writings respectively by a patriarch and a pope. The first comes from Photius, Patriarch of Constantinople from 858 to 865, who would therefore have been Joan's exact contemporary. Photius had no love for Rome, against which indeed he bore a considerable grudge; but he nevertheless specifically refers to 'Leo and Benedict, *successively* great priests of the Roman Church'. Two centuries later, Pope Leo IX (1049–54) wrote to Patriarch Michael Cerularius:

> God forbid that we wish to believe what public opinion does not hesitate to claim has occurred in the Church of Constantinople: namely that in promoting eunuchs indiscriminately against the First Law of the Council of Nicaea, it once raised a woman on to the seat of its pontiff. We regard this crime as so abominable and horrible that although outrage and disgust and brotherly goodwill do not allow us to believe it, nevertheless, reflecting upon your carelessness towards the judgement of Holy Law, we consider that it could have occurred, since even now you indifferently and repeatedly promote eunuchs and those who are weak in some part of their body not only to clerical office, but also to the position of pontiff.

Had Leo ever heard of the existence of Pope Joan, is it likely that he would have laid himself open to the Patriarch's obvious retort? And had the Patriarch been aware of her, would he not have so retorted? We can only conclude that in the middle of the eleventh century her legend was still unknown in Rome.

And there is solid evidence, too. Our most reliable sources record that Leo IV died on 17 July 855, and that Benedict III was consecrated on 29 September. We also know that the Emperor Lothair I died in the Ardennes within hours of Benedict's consecration. Naturally the news took some time to reach Rome, during which denarii were minted there with the words *Benedict Papa* on one side and *Hlotharius Imp Pius* on the reverse. It follows that Benedict could not have succeeded any later than the records state, and that there would simply have been no room for Joan.

But perhaps the best argument of all is the sheer improbability of a female pope, a long deception, a hidden pregnancy, a sudden birth in the street. Female popes are unlikely enough in the first place; and in real life it is rare indeed for a woman to give birth in the street. Is not all this stretching our credulity just a little too far? Of course it is; and yet there is another improbability, almost as great as these, which we are obliged to accept: that this mildly grotesque story was almost universally accepted within the Catholic Church for several centuries, and that poor incautious Joan still has her champions today.[1]

---

[1] In the eighteenth century *Pope Joan* was a popular card game; and as recently as 1972 the legend was the subject of a film starring Liv Ullmann (with Trevor Howard and Olivia de Havilland).

CHAPTER VII

Nicholas I and the Pornocracy

(855–964)

Pope Joan was a myth; Pope Benedict III – who, had Joan existed, would have succeeded her – was a nonentity. After Benedict came a joke, and after that a giant.

The joke was the bid for the papacy by Anastasius. He was born in about 815 into a distinguished Roman priestly family – his uncle was the highly influential Arsenius, Bishop of Orte. A man of outstanding abilities and culture, Anastasius mastered Greek at an early age and was created cardinal priest by Leo IV in 847 or 848; but almost immediately he quarrelled with his benefactor and fled to Aquileia. Leo, who was well aware of his ambitions and saw Anastasius as a potential rival, repeatedly summoned him back to Rome; when Anastasius refused, he was successively excommunicated, anathematised and deposed. On Leo's death in 855, his successor was duly elected as Benedict III; but Bishop Arsenius, determined that his nephew should be next on the papal throne, seized the Lateran by force, taking Benedict prisoner.

For three days confusion reigned; but it soon became clear that Anastasius lacked any degree of popular support. How, moreover, could any man under sentence of excommunication be made Pope? The Bishops of Ostia and Albano, two of the three by whom the Pope was traditionally consecrated, could not be induced – even by threats of torture – to perform the ceremony. Benedict was released from his imprisonment and finally received his consecration. Anastasius was stripped of his papal insignia and expelled from the Lateran; but Benedict treated him with more leniency than he deserved, simply confining him to the monastery of S. Maria in Trastevere.

Anastasius, however, bounced back. For the three years of Benedict's pontificate he remained in obscurity; with the accession of Nicholas I (858–67), however, his fortunes changed dramatically. He had made a fool of himself, but he remained one of the foremost scholars of his day; and Nicholas, fully aware of his abilities, first appointed Anastasius abbot of his monastery, and then Librarian of the Church – in which position (thanks, presumably, to his knowledge of Greek) he became chief adviser to the Curia on Byzantine affairs.

Nicholas I was an aristocrat and an autocrat. For him, the Pope was God's representative here on Earth – and there the matter ended. Emperors might enjoy the privilege of protecting and defending the Church; they had no right to interfere in its affairs. The Pope's authority was absolute; synods were summoned merely to carry out his orders; bishops, archbishops and even patriarchs were bound to him in loyalty and obedience. When John, Archbishop of Ravenna, got above himself, he was called to Rome, excommunicated and deposed. When Hincmar, Archbishop of Rheims, one of the most powerful churchmen in the Empire, dismissed a suffragan bishop and then tried to prevent his appeal to Rome, Nicholas immediately reinstated the bishop; and when Hincmar protested, the Pope threatened to forbid him to celebrate Mass. Nicholas also showed his mettle when a synod of Frankish bishops approved the divorce of King Lothair II of Lorraine, because he wanted to marry his mistress; the Pope simply overruled them and ordered Lothair to return to his wife. When the King deserted her for a second time, he was excommunicated. The Archbishops of Cologne and Trier came to Rome to argue the case; Nicholas excommunicated them too, as accomplices to bigamy. This time it looked as though he might have overreached himself: Lothair's brother, the Emperor Louis II, marched on Rome, ostensibly to teach him a lesson. The Pope, however, called his bluff and refused to budge; and Louis, fuming, was obliged to retreat.

Nicholas's conception of papal authority extended, it need hardly be said, over the Churches of the East. At this time the Patriarch of Constantinople was a eunuch named Ignatius – a blinkered bigot, loathed by his flock, which was determined to get rid of him. The leader of that flock was Photius, the most learned scholar of his day, capable of running rings round Ignatius, whose mind was too narrow to encompass any but the simplest theological doctrines. In one particularly successful exercise in Patriarch-baiting, Photius had even gone so far as to propound a new and deeply heretical theory that he had just thought up, according to which man possessed two separate souls, one liable to error, the other infallible. His own dazzling reputation as an intellectual ensured that he was taken seriously by many – including Ignatius – who should have known better; and after his doctrine had its desired effect, by making the Patriarch look thoroughly silly, he cheerfully withdrew it. It was perhaps the only completely satisfactory practical joke in the history of theology, and for that alone Photius deserves our gratitude.

On the Feast of the Epiphany 858 Ignatius unwisely refused the sacrament to the Emperor's uncle, who had forsaken his wife for his daughter-in-law. It took a little time to frame appropriate charges, but by the end of the year the Patriarch had been arrested and banished. Photius was his obvious successor. His lay status was unfortunate, but that difficulty was swiftly overcome: within a week he was tonsured, ordained, consecrated and enthroned. He then wrote to Pope Nicholas in Rome, giving formal notice of his elevation. Although the letter itself was a model of tactful diplomacy, containing not one word against his predecessor, it was accompanied by another, ostensibly from the Emperor himself, in which Ignatius was said to have neglected his flock and to have been properly and canonically deposed – both of which claims the Pope rightly suspected of being untrue. Nicholas received the Byzantine legates with all due ceremony in S. Maria Maggiore, but made it clear that he was not prepared to recognise Photius as Patriarch without further investigation. He therefore proposed a council of inquiry, to be held the following year in Constantinople, to which he would send two commissioners who would report back to him personally.

The two commissioners, Zachary of Anagni and Rodoald of Porto, reached Constantinople in April 861. From the moment of their arrival they found themselves under formidable pressure from Photius – swept up into a ceaseless round of ceremonies, receptions, banquets and entertainments, while the Patriarch himself remained constantly at their side, dazzling them with his erudition, captivating them with his charm. Well before the Council was to hold its opening session in the church of the Holy Apostles, Photius had satisfied himself that they would give no trouble. As for Ignatius, they were not allowed so much as to clap eyes on him until he was led into the church to give his evidence. He was then obliged to listen while seventy-two witnesses testified that his former appointment was invalid, being due to the personal favour of the Empress rather than to any canonical election. At the close of the fourth session his deposition was confirmed by a formal document – at the foot of which, prominent among the signatories, were the names of Zachary and Rodoald.

When the prelates returned to Rome, the Pope left them in no doubt of his displeasure. Their task, he reminded them, had been to discover the facts, not to appoint themselves judges. In doing so, they had betrayed the interests of the Church, succumbing to Byzantine blandishments in a manner more like that of innocent children than of senior ecclesiastics. They had allowed themselves to be made dupes of the Patriarch, and had shown themselves unworthy of their rank and position. He would consider their futures later. Meanwhile they could go.

At this point there arrived in Rome an archimandrite[1] named Theognostus who, having escaped from close surveillance in Constantinople, regaled Nicholas with tales of the iniquity of Photius and his friends, and the sufferings that the unfortunate Ignatius had been obliged to endure, ending with his enforced signature to his act of abdication. The Pope hesitated no longer. In April 863 he summoned a synod at the Lateran which divested Photius of all ecclesiastical status, restoring to their former positions Ignatius and all who had lost office in his cause. Zachary and Rodoald were dismissed from their sees. In Constantinople, however, as might have been expected, the papal ruling was ignored and the quarrel rumbled on. Up to this point, Nicholas's firmness had served only to show how powerless he was in the East; but now, quite unexpectedly, there came a stroke of good fortune – from, of all places, Bulgaria.

The Bulgars under their Khan, Boris I, were at this time a rising power in the Balkans; and in September 865 the formerly Catholic Boris had travelled to Constantinople, where he had been baptised by the Patriarch in St Sophia, the Emperor himself standing sponsor. Pope Nicholas was predictably furious; and the fact that Boris had little choice – the Byzantine fleet was lying off his Black Sea coast and his country was in the grip of the worst famine of the century – did little to assuage the papal anger. But, less than a year after his conversion, Boris was already having second thoughts. Suddenly he had found his country overrun with Greek and Armenian priests, frequently at loggerheads with each other over abstruse points of doctrine that were incomprehensible both to him and to his bewildered subjects. Moreover, wishing to keep his distance from

---

[1] In those days an archimandrite was the head of a monastery – the equivalent of an abbot in the West. Later the title would be applied to the head of a group of monasteries (Mount Athos, for example, or Meteora) and later still to a senior administrative official, ranking just below a bishop: an archdeacon, perhaps?

Constantinople, he had requested the appointment of a Bulgarian Patriarch – and had been refused.

In this refusal Photius had made a disastrous miscalculation. Now it was the Khan's turn to be furious. He was happy to be the Emperor's godson, but had no intention of being made his vassal. Fully aware of the state of affairs between Rome and Constantinople and the consequent possibility of playing one off against the other, in the summer of 866 he sent a delegation to Pope Nicholas. It carried a list of 106 points of Orthodox doctrine and social custom that conflicted with Bulgarian traditions, suggesting that much of the opposition to the new faith might be overcome if the latter were permitted to continue, and inquiring as to the Pope's views on each.

When Boris had put these points to Photius, they had either been rejected or simply ignored; for Nicholas, here was the chance he had been waiting for. He quickly set Anastasius to work, then despatched to the Bulgarian court two more bishops, bearing a remarkable document in which he gave thoughtful and meticulous answers to every one of the points on Boris's list – showing consideration for all local susceptibilities, making all possible concessions and, where these could not be granted, explaining the reasons for his refusal. Trousers, he agreed, could certainly be worn, by men and women alike; turbans too, excepting only in church. When the Byzantines maintained that it was unlawful to wash on Wednesdays and Fridays, they were talking nonsense; nor was there any reason to abstain from milk or cheese during Lent. All pagan superstitions, on the other hand, must be strictly forbidden, as must the accepted Greek practice of divination by the random opening of the Bible. Bigamy, too, was out.

The Bulgars were disappointed about the bigamy, but on the whole more than satisfied with the Pope's answers and, perhaps equally important, by the obvious trouble that he – or more accurately Anastasius – had taken over them. Boris at once swore perpetual allegiance to St Peter and, with every sign of relief, expelled all the Orthodox missionaries from his kingdom. The Roman Catholic Church was back once more in the Balkans.

Nicholas I marks a watershed: he was the last pontiff of any ability or integrity to occupy the chair of St Peter for a century and a half. His successor, an elderly cleric who took the name of Hadrian II (867–72), squandered, in only five short years, virtually all that Nicholas had gained, yielding to Archbishop Hincmar, restoring communion to King Lothair – now back with his mistress – and allowing Bulgaria to slip back into Orthodoxy. Not content with undoing virtually all the hard work of Anastasius, he even accused the Librarian of complicity in the murder of his (Hadrian's) former wife and daughter, excommunicating him for the second time in his career.[1]

But even Hadrian was a paragon in comparison with his successors. Charlemagne's Empire was gone, dissolved among the ever-bickering members of his family; without it the popes were left defenceless against the local Roman aristocracy – principally the Crescentii, the Tusculani and the Theophylacts – who established complete control over the Church and made the papacy their plaything. Hadrian's successor John VIII (872–82) was at least energetic, but also had the dubious distinction of being the first Pope to be assassinated – and, worse still, by priests from his own entourage. According to the Annals of the abbey of Fulda, they first gave him poison; then, when this failed to act quickly enough, they hammered in his skull. The enthronement of his successor Marinus (882–4) is said to have been marked by the murder of a high Roman dignitary, and that of Hadrian III(884–5) two years later by the victim's widow being whipped naked through the streets. On Hadrian's death on his way to Germany in 885 foul play was also suspected. The next two popes, Stephen V (885–91) and Formosus (891–6), died in their beds; but on the orders of his successor Stephen VI (896–7),[2] the body of Formosus was exhumed in March 896, eight months after his death, clothed in pontifical vestments, propped up on a throne and subjected to a mock trial on charges of perjury and of coveting the papacy: he was said to have accepted the see of Rome while still bishop of another diocese (no crime today). Not unpredictably, he was found guilty: all his acts, including his ordinations, were declared null and void – a judgement that caused indescribable confusion; finally his body (minus the three fingers of his right hand that he had used to give blessings) was flung into the Tiber.[3]

---

[1] The murders were in fact the work of Anastasius's cousin Eleutherius, after a failed attempt to elope with the daughter. This second excommunication was soon lifted, and we know that Anastasius attended the Eighth Ecumenical Council at Constantinople in 869–70, when he attempted unsuccessfully to arrange a marriage between Ermengard, daughter of the Western Emperor Louis II, and the son of the Byzantine Emperor, Basil I.

[2] Or, more accurately, his second successor; but the intervening Pope Boniface VI (896) – who had been twice unfrocked for immorality – died of gout after just a fortnight.

[3] It is only fair to add that it was later miraculously recovered by a hermit, rehabilitated and reinterred in its former tomb.

Almost immediately afterwards the basilica of the Lateran was largely destroyed by an earthquake – a disaster that was widely interpreted as a sign of divine displeasure at Pope Stephen's conduct. But supernatural portents were hardly necessary; to every Roman it must have been abundantly clear that the Pope had overstepped the mark. Six months later he was deposed, stripped of his papal insignia and thrown into prison, where he was shortly afterwards strangled.

After six popes in seven years, a parish priest from the unfortunately named village of Priapi was elected as Leo V in 903. How this came about is unclear, but it hardly matters: after a month there occurred a palace revolution, in the course of which a cleric called Christopher overthrew him, flung Leo into prison and had himself proclaimed and consecrated. Christopher – who has gone down in history as an antipope – fared better than Leo, lasting four months instead of one; but he in turn was toppled early in 904 by an aristocratic Roman who had taken an active part in the 'trial' of Formosus and who now assumed the name of Sergius III (904–11). Christopher was sent to join Leo in jail. Not long afterwards – moved, as he claimed, by pity – Sergius had them both strangled.

At this point there appears in papal history the ravishingly beautiful but sinister figure of Marozia, Senatrix of Rome. She was the daughter of the Roman consul Theophylact, Count of Tusculum, and of his wife Theodora, whom Bishop Liudprand of Cremona describes as 'a shameless strumpet ... who was sole monarch of Rome and wielded power like a man'. The two daughters of this unlovely couple, Marozia and another Theodora, were, he continues, 'not only her equals but could even surpass her in the exercises beloved of Venus'. He may well have been wrong about the younger sister, of whom little is known; but of Marozia he spoke no more than the truth. Lover, mother and grandmother of popes – 'a rare genealogy', sniffs Gibbon – she was born in about 890, and at the age of fifteen became the mistress of Sergius III, her father's cousin. (Their son was to be the future Pope John XI.) In 909 she married an adventurer named Alberic, who had made himself Marquess of Spoleto and by whom she had a second son, Alberic II. By this time the papal Curia, which had long been the effective government of Rome, had come completely under the control of the local aristocracy, of whom she was by far the most powerful representative; the papacy was in her hands.[1]

---

[1] Was she, one can't help wondering, the origin of Pope Joan?

Of the five popes intervening between Sergius and John XI (931–5), two were puppets of Marozia; together they reigned for less than three years. The third, John X (914–28), was of a very different calibre: it was he, together with Theophylact of Tusculum and Alberic I, who inflicted a decisive defeat on the Saracens at the Garigliano river in June 915. But Marozia hated him. Her hatred may partly have been due to the fact that he had been her mother's lover – when he had been appointed Bishop of Ravenna, the elder Theodora had actually summoned him back to Rome and thrust him into the papal chair – but can best be explained by her own ambition. John was too tough, too intelligent; and when, towards the end of 927, he began to show serious signs of opposition and even appeared, with his brother Peter, to be threatening Marozia's authority, she moved against him. Peter was struck down in the Lateran before his brother's eyes, and soon afterwards Marozia, with her second husband Guy of Tuscany[1], had the Pope himself deposed and imprisoned in the Castel Sant'Angelo, where he was soon afterwards smothered to death with pillows.

The reason for Marozia's actions was not only to eliminate a rival; it was also to leave the papal throne vacant for her son. Unfortunately the boy was still only about eighteen, so she put in two elderly puppets as stopgaps before having him installed as John XI in the early spring of 931. By this time she had disposed of Guy, in favour of a far more promising prize: Hugh of Provence, who had recently been elected King of Italy and had been duly anointed by the unfortunate John X. True, Hugh had a perfectly good wife already, but she now conveniently died, just in time to allow the marriage to take place. More of an obstacle was the fact that Guy had been Hugh's half-brother, which made the projected marriage incestuous; Hugh simply declared Guy and his other brother Lambert of Tuscany bastards – one may imagine what their mother thought about that – and, when Lambert raised his voice in protest, had him blinded and thrown into prison, where he died shortly afterwards. Few couples presenting themselves for marriage had so much blood on their hands. Unsurprisingly, their wedding ceremony in 932 was not even celebrated in church, but in the Castel Sant'Angelo. On the other hand, it was performed by the Pope himself – the first and last instance in history of a pope offici- ating at the marriage of his mother. Once the knot was tied, the couple

---

[1] Alberic I had been murdered in Orta between 924 and 926.

seemed to carry all before them; nothing, as far as could be seen, now stood between them and the imperial throne of the West.

But Marozia had miscalculated. She had forgotten another of her sons. Alberic – the Pope's half-brother – had, with each of his mother's subsequent marriages, found himself pushed further into the background. He had seen Hugh's way of dealing with unwanted relations, and had received an unmistakable warning during a feast in Sant'Angelo when his new stepfather had struck him across the face. His only hope was to act while there was still time. The Romans had no love for Hugh, whose cruelty and general boorishness were already notorious; besides, they were always ready for an uprising. In December 932 a mob stormed the castle. Hugh managed to escape through a window; Marozia and her son the Pope found themselves in prison cells. Of the formidable Senatrix of Rome nothing more was heard; John XI seems later to have been released, though he was kept under what amounted to house-arrest in the Lateran, where, according to Bishop Liudprand, Alberic treated him as his personal slave.

Alberic was now undisputed master of Rome, which he was to rule for the next twenty years, on the whole wisely and well, successfully resisting by various means – including a diplomatic marriage to Hugh's daughter – repeated attempts by Hugh to return to power. He effectively appointed the next five popes, three of whom treated him with the respect that he demanded. The first exception was Stephen VIII (939–42), who after two years of obedience seems in some way to have fallen foul of his master. What actually occurred is uncertain; but there is little doubt that the Pope was brutally mutilated and died of his injuries. The last of the five was Octavian, Alberic's bastard son, still in his teens. Stricken by a mortal fever in the summer of 954, aged barely forty, Alberic had himself carried to the altar above the tomb of St Peter, where he gathered the leading Romans around his deathbed and made them swear on the bones of the Apostle that on the death of the reigning Pope, Agapetus II (946–55), they would elect Octavian supreme pontiff. It was his last action. On 31 August he died.

It says much for Alberic's authority – if little for their wisdom – that the Romans agreed. Octavian of course immediately succeeded his father as temporal ruler of Rome; on the death of Agapetus in December 955 he changed his name to John[1] – and was duly elected

---

[1] He was only the second pope to do so. John II had been the first, in 533. As his real name had been Mercury, he had little choice. John XII in fact continued to use his former name as temporal ruler of Rome.

Pope. The choice could not have been more calamitous. Not only was the young Holy Father supremely uninterested in matters spiritual; he was to mark the nadir of the papal pornocracy. No one has put it better than Gibbon:

> ... we read, with some surprise, that the worthy grandson of Marozia lived in public adultery with the matrons of Rome; that the Lateran Palace was turned into a school for prostitution; and that his rapes of virgins and widows had deterred the female pilgrims from visiting the shrine of St Peter, lest, in the devout act, they should be violated by his successor.

Not for nothing was John XII (955–64) the grandson of Marozia and Hugh of Provence, two of the most shameless debauchees of their age. He allowed the city – indeed he encouraged it – to slide into chaos, using its wealth as well as that of the Papal States to gratify his own passion for gambling and for every kind of sexual licence. Rome's political position began to deteriorate fast; moreover, a dangerous new enemy was threatening, in the person of Hugh's nephew, the Marquess Berengar of Ivrea. Berengar had been the uncrowned but effective King of Italy since Hugh's return to Arles in 945 and had been making trouble ever since; in 959 he had seized the Duchy of Spoleto, and had now begun to ravage the papal territories to the north of Rome. By the autumn of 960 John had no alternative but to appeal to the German King, Otto of Saxony – offering him, in return for his help, the imperial crown.

Otto asked nothing better. All his life he had been guided by a single dream: to resurrect the empire of Charlemagne. As an earnest of this intention he had even arranged his German coronation in Charlemagne's beautiful circular church at Aachen. He had welded Germany together as a single state; outside Augsburg in 955 he had inflicted an overwhelming defeat on the Magyars after 500 years still the scourge of Europe; his name was known and respected across the continent. On receipt of the Pope's appeal, he crossed the Alps at the head of a sizeable army, reaching the Holy City in January 962; and on Candlemas Day, 2 February, he and his queen Adelaide, with their official sword-bearer standing guard immediately behind them, knelt before the young reprobate thirty years their junior and were crowned in St Peter's – the Pope swearing on his side to give no support to

Berengar. So it was that one of the most contemptible of all the pontiffs restored the Holy Roman Empire of Charlemagne, which was to last for a further nine and a half centuries.

Otto left Rome two weeks later, after treating John to several patronising homilies urging him to reform his scandalous ways. Ever since the day of his coronation he had insisted on addressing the Pope as a refractory schoolboy, and relations between the two had fast deteriorated; even so, he cannot have expected John to enter into negotiations with Berengar's son Adalbert as soon as his back was turned. Why John did so passes comprehension; and at the outset Otto himself seems to have been incredulous. When the report was brought to him he was busy besieging Berengar in the Apennines; his first reaction was to send a mission of enquiry to Rome. The mission returned with juicy details about the Pope's innumerable mistresses, fat and thin, rich and poor: of one whom he had made governor of cities and loaded with church treasure; of another, who had been his father's paramour before him, whom he had made pregnant and who had died of a haemorrhage; of the Pope's indiscriminate seizure of female pilgrims. 'The palace of the Lateran,' they reported, 'which had once sheltered saints, was now a harlot's brothel.'

Even now the Emperor tended towards an indulgent view. 'He is only a boy,' he is reported as saying, 'and will soon alter if good men set him an example.' Deciding to give John one more chance, he despatched another envoy, more high-powered than his predecessors: Liudprand, Bishop of Cremona.

Liudprand, as he himself reported,[1] was received by the Pope with all honour; but he soon saw clearly enough with what scorn and indifference John was prepared to treat the Emperor. Since he had given absolutely no satisfaction on any of the contested issues, there was clearly no point in remaining in Rome, and the bishop set off back to his master. Even before his arrival, however, Otto had learned that Adalbert had arrived in Rome and was preparing in his turn to receive the imperial crown. It was by now July, and the German soldiers were expiring in the heat. Otto waited until September; then he marched on Rome.

It was all over quite quickly. John made a brief show of resistance, which fooled nobody; then, as Otto approached, he scooped up what-

---

[1] His immensely entertaining *Chronicle of Otto's Reign* includes a full account of his mission – though, like all of his writings, it should be taken with more than a pinch of salt.

ever portable treasure remained and fled with Adalbert to Tivoli. The Emperor entered Rome unopposed. Three days later he summoned a synod – Liudprand lists almost a hundred of those churchmen present – and addressed it in person. He began with an expression of regret that the Holy Father had not seen fit to be present, and then called for evidence against him:

> Thereupon the cardinal priest Peter got up and testified that he had seen the Pope celebrate mass without himself communicating. John, Bishop of Narni, and John cardinal deacon then declared that they had seen the Pope ordain a deacon in a stable and at an improper season. Benedict cardinal deacon with his fellow deacons and priests said that they knew the Pope had been paid for ordaining bishops and that in the city of Todi he had appointed a bishop for ten years. On the question of his sacrilege, they said, no inquiries were necessary; knowledge of it was a matter of eyesight, not of hearsay. As regards his adultery, though they had no visual information, they knew for certain that he had carnal acquaintance with Rainer's widow, with Stephana his father's concubine, with the widow Anna, and with his own niece; and that he had turned the holy palace into a brothel and resort for harlots. He had gone hunting publicly; he had blinded his spiritual father Benedict, who had died of his injuries; he had caused the death of cardinal subdeacon John by castrating him; he had set houses on fire and appeared in public equipped with sword, helmet and cuirass. To all this they testified; while everyone, clergy and laity alike, loudly accused him of drinking wine for the love of the devil. At dice, they said, he asked the aid of Jupiter, Venus, and the other demons; he did not celebrate matins nor observe the canonical hours, nor fortify himself with the sign of the cross.[1]

Otto then addressed a letter to the Pope, rehearsing the charges and 'earnestly begging' him to return and clear himself. 'If,' he added, 'you perchance fear the violence of a rash multitude, we declare under oath that no action is contemplated contrary to the sanction of the holy canons.' But John's reply was all too typical of him. In what was clearly a studied insult, it completely ignored the Emperor's presence in Rome, while its grammar alone was enough to indicate that he had drafted it himself: 'Bishop John to all the Bishops. We hear that you wish to make another Pope. If you do, I excommunicate you by almighty God, and you have no power to ordain no one, or celebrate mass.'

---

[1] Liudprand, *Chronicle of Otto's Reign*, ch. xi.

The Emperor and synod's reply was heavy with irony, but it made its point clearly enough:

> ... We always thought, or rather believed, that two negatives made an affirmative, if your authority did not weaken that of the ancient authors ... If – which Heaven forbid – under any pretence you refrain from coming and defending yourself ... then we shall disregard your excommunication, and rather turn it upon yourself, as we have justly the power to do.

The imperial envoys arrived at Tivoli only to find that the Pope had gone hunting and was nowhere to be found. Not bothering to wait, they returned at once to Rome, where on 1 December 963 the synod assembled for the third time and the Emperor asked the bishops to consider their verdict. It did not take them long:

> 'We request your imperial majesty that this monster – whom no virtue redeems from vice – be driven from the holy Roman Church; and that another be appointed in his place, who by the example of his goodly conversation may prove himself both ruler and benefactor, living rightly himself and setting us an example of like conduct ...'
> At that all cried with one voice: 'We elect as our shepherd Leo, the venerable chief notary of the holy Roman Church ... He shall be the supreme and universal Pope, and we hereby condemn the apostate John because of his vicious life.' The whole assembly repeated these words three times, and then with the Emperor's consent escorted the aforesaid Leo to the Lateran Palace ... and later at due season elevated him to the supreme priesthood.

But the Romans refused to accept him. The problem was that Leo (963–5) was, as everyone knew, not the free choice of the bishops, but the Emperor's nominee. John may have been a monster, but he was Rome's monster; for better or for worse, the Romans had elected him, and they were not prepared to see him overthrown by a German barbarian. Their first revolt was little more than a disturbance, and was easily put down by the imperial troops. But Otto could not stay in Rome for ever. His feudal levies were committed to serve him only for a strictly limited period, and he still had to deal with Berengar and Adalbert. And so, in January 964, he left – and John returned.

His revenge was terrible. Tongues were torn out; hands, fingers and noses hacked off. All the synod's decrees were declared null and void;

a new one called on 26 February excommunicated the luckless Leo, who fled in terror to the Emperor's side. But the Emperor's mind was elsewhere. By this time he had successfully dealt with Berengar, but Adalbert was still at large and this was no time to abandon the struggle against him. Not until early May was Otto able to lead his army back to Rome, and he was still on the way when news was brought to him that John was dead – though whether of a stroke brought on by his exertions on behalf of a lady with whom he was at that time in bed, or of injuries received from her furious husband, opinion was divided. He was twenty-seven years old.

CHAPTER VIII

Schism

(964–1054)

The mutual hostility that had been steadily increasing between the German Emperor and the people of Rome was in no way diminished by the death of John XII. In the Emperor's eyes, Leo VIII continued as rightful Pope, but the Romans would have none of him. Instead of recalling Leo to Rome, they sent envoys to the Emperor in Rieti, informing him that after the libertine John, they felt the need of a devout reformer; they therefore requested leave to elect a learned and morally irreproachable deacon named Benedict. Otto of course angrily refused: having been personally responsible for Leo's elevation he could hardly have done otherwise, and he was determined to uphold his principle: no Pope could be elected or consecrated without his consent. But in refusing he must have known that he was throwing down a deliberate challenge, and the Romans had no hesitation in taking it up. Benedict V (964) was duly elected and enthroned, and it was only when Otto marched back to Rome with Leo in 964 and laid siege to the city that they surrendered him. A synod, presided over jointly by Otto and Leo, condemned Benedict, who humbly refused to defend himself, quietly submitting while he was formally stripped of his robes and insignia – Liudprand claims that he removed them himself – and his pastoral staff (or possibly his sceptre) was broken over his head. The Emperor, who seems to have been impressed despite himself, allowed him to keep his rank of deacon and exiled him to Hamburg, where two years later he died.[1]

By this time Leo VIII was already in his grave. His successor John XIII (965–72), who had been elected with the consent of just two bishops whom Otto had sent to represent him, and who made no secret of the fact that he was content to do the Emperor's bidding, was predictably detested in Rome and after only two months was

---

[1] His remains were brought back to Rome by Otto III in 988.

overthrown in a palace revolution and imprisoned in a castle in Campania. He soon escaped; and the Romans, hearing that an incandescent Otto was once more on his way, hastily welcomed him back; if they hoped, however, by so doing to avert the Emperor's wrath they were disappointed. Of those responsible for John's overthrow, the most fortunate were banished to Germany; the remainder were executed or blinded. Peter, the City Prefect, was hanged by the hair from the equestrian statue of Marcus Aurelius, now on the Capitol but then in front of the Lateran Palace; he was then subjected to the age-old humiliation of being mounted backwards on a donkey and paraded naked through the streets.

After this the Romans had no more fight left in them. Otto spent the next six years in Italy – he was to return to Germany only a few months before his death – consolidating his position and leaving the Romans in no doubt that he considered the Pope little more than his chaplain. At Christmas 967 he ordered Pope John to crown his twelve-year-old son Otto II as co-Emperor, and five years later to officiate at the marriage of young Otto to the Byzantine princess Theophano.[1] Just before Otto died in May 973 he arranged for the election of John's successor, a virtually unknown priest who became Benedict VI (973–4); but with Otto's iron hand no longer at the helm and young Otto II fully occupied with his own problems in Germany, Benedict could not hope to survive. Another coup, led this time by the increasingly powerful Roman family of the Crescentii, overthrew him and imprisoned him in the Castel Sant'Angelo, replacing him with an obscure deacon named Franco who took the title of Boniface VII (974, 984–5). Boniface gave immediate proof of his piety and holiness by having Benedict strangled; but a swift counter-revolution obliged him to flee for his life to Byzantine territory in southern Italy, with as much of the papal treasury as he could lay his hands on.

Once again the papal throne was vacant; and this time the choice fell on the high-minded Bishop of Sutri, who deliberately took the name of Benedict VII (974–83) as a mark of respect to his

---

[1] Theophano was understood to be the daughter of the Emperor Romanus II; only on her arrival was she discovered to be merely a relation of the Emperor's brother-in-law, John Tzimisces, and by no means 'born in the purple', as had been understood. Otto at first considered sending the poor girl straight back to Constantinople; fortunately, wiser counsels prevailed and two years later Tzimisces became Emperor anyway, so all was well.

unfortunate predecessor. He not only refused to recognise Boniface;[1] he excommunicated him. But Boniface was far from finished: somehow, during the summer of 980, he even managed to return to Rome and re-establish himself in the Vatican. Only in the following March were Benedict and Otto II together able to expel him for the second time. It seems, however, to have been a more definitive expulsion, since this second flight took him not to Byzantine southern Italy, but to Constantinople itself.

An additional reason for this choice of refuge may well have been that by now there was heavy fighting in the south, where, after long periods of anarchy and confusion – Bari and Taranto, to take just two examples, had spent thirty and forty years respectively under Arab domination – the Byzantines had regained their hold towards the end of the ninth century. Otto I had unfortunately seen his son's marriage to Theophano as grounds for claiming the 'restitution', as part of her dowry, of all Byzantine lands in Italy, and war had been the inevitable result. In 981 Otto II marched into Apulia, determined to settle the situation once and for all. This time the result was disaster. The Byzantines quickly arranged a temporary alliance with the Saracens, who soon afterwards cut the imperial army to pieces near Stilo in Calabria. Luckily for Otto, he was a strong swimmer. He swam to a passing ship, managed somehow to conceal his identity and later, as the vessel passed Rossano, jumped overboard again and struck out for the shore. He survived, but never recovered from the humiliation and died of malaria in Rome in September 983, aged twenty-eight. One of his last acts was to replace Pope Benedict – who had predeceased him by two months – with his Chancellor for Italy, Peter, Bishop of Pavia. As John XIV (983–4) – he modestly declined to use his own name – the first task of the new Pope was to bury the Emperor in St Peter's, the only one ever to be interred there.

Perhaps because Otto seems to have acted unilaterally and without any consultation (there is no evidence of a regular papal election), Pope John was left friendless on his death, deprived even of the support of the Empress Theophano, who had to hurry back to Germany to defend the interests of her three-year-old son Otto III. In consequence he had little hope of survival when the odious antipope Boniface returned unexpectedly to Rome from Constantinople, liberally financed by the

---

[1] Since 1904 Boniface has been officially classified as an antipope, although he appears on the ancient official lists of popes, and the next pope who took the name is known as Boniface VIII.

Emperor Basil II (the Bulgar-Slayer). John was seized, badly beaten and, as usual, consigned to the Castel Sant'Angelo, where he died four months later either of starvation or of poisoning. But Boniface had gone too far. Even for the Romans, to have murdered two popes was too much. He survived on the throne for eleven months – having blinded a cardinal deacon whom he suspected of acting against him – and then, on 20 July 985, suddenly died. Was he assassinated? There is no firm evidence, but his subsequent fate certainly suggests it. Stripped of its vestments, his body was dragged naked through the streets and exposed beneath the statue of Marcus Aurelius. There, left to the mercy of the mob, the remains of the antipope Boniface were trampled on and subjected to nameless indignities – and serve him right.

The new Pope, John XV, had been the preferred candidate both of the Curia and of his kinsman John Crescentius (head of the Crescentii Family), by now the virtual ruler of Rome. (Theophano being away in Germany with her infant son, the Empire had had no say in the matter.) He was, it must be said, a considerable improvement on Boniface; he was nevertheless greedy, rapacious and shamelessly nepotistic, and before long had made himself deeply unpopular with Church and people alike. Though quite forceful in his relations with foreign rulers and bishops (he was, incidentally, the first Pope to perform a ritual canonisation), in Rome he was content to be a puppet of John Crescentius, who in return could offer him a measure of protection; but Crescentius died in 988, and his brother John Crescentius II, on succeeding him, seized power in the Papal State and kept the Pope a virtual prisoner – so that when, in 991, a synod of French bishops complained that he had refused their envoys access to the Holy Father, Leo the Papal Chancellor was obliged to admit that his master was being held 'in such tribulation and oppression' that he could give them no satisfactory answer. Four years later in March 995, persecuted by Crescentius and detested by his clergy, John escaped from Rome and took refuge in Sutri; and that summer he sent envoys to young Otto III (now fifteen) with an appeal for help. Otto responded immediately, and the prospect of an imperial army once again on the march was enough to compel the Romans to make their peace. The Pope was invited back to Rome and reinstalled with full honours in the Lateran; but long before the army reached the city he succumbed to a violent attack of fever. A few days later he was dead.

Otto meanwhile continued to Rome. He was an extraordinary child.

Succeeding to the imperial throne at the age of three, he grew up combining the traditional ambitions of his line with a romantic mysticism clearly inherited from his mother, forever dreaming of a great Byzantinesque theocracy that would embrace Germans and Greeks, Italians and Slavs alike, with God at its head and himself and the Pope – in that order – as his twin viceroys. The pursuit of this dream made him even more preoccupied with affairs in Italy than his father had been before him. Once in Rome and crowned on Ascension Day 996 by his twenty-five-year-old cousin Gregory V (996–9) – the first German pope whom he had prudently nominated en route – he built himself a magnificent new palace on the Aventine, where he lived in a curious combination of splendour and asceticism, surrounded by a court rigid with Byzantine ceremonial, eating in majestic solitude off gold plate, occasionally shedding his purple dalmatic for a pilgrim's cloak and trudging barefoot to some distant shrine.

Ascetic or not, Otto soon found the Roman summer too much for him. In June he left in search of a cooler climate; and three months later when he was safely back in Germany the Romans, led by Crescentius, deposed Pope Gregory and threw him out of the city. The Pope sought refuge in Spoleto, from where he made two armed attempts to return; both failed. He then moved on to Pavia, where at a synod in February 997 he excommunicated Crescentius – who responded by declaring the papal throne vacant and setting upon it a Calabrian Greek named John Philagathos, who took the title of John XVI (997–8).

Despite his origins, Philagathos had already achieved remarkable success in the Roman Church. Ten years before, Theophano had appointed him first as tutor to Otto III and then Archbishop of Piacenza: the see had been raised from a simple bishopric especially for him. In 994 he had been sent as a special envoy to Constantinople to find a Byzantine bride for young Otto, but had returned empty-handed. He was visiting Rome, ostensibly as a pilgrim, when he was approached by Crescentius and allowed himself to be installed as Pope. His acceptance of Crescentius's offer remains hard to understand. He was fully aware that a canonically crowned pope was very much alive, together with an emperor who had chosen him, was related to him and could be trusted to support him. Philagathos could be looked on as nothing but an antipope, and a creature of Crescentius; how could he possibly have expected to maintain himself on the throne?

And indeed he failed to do so. In March – only a month after his so-called accession – he was dismissed; soon afterwards he was formally excommunicated. In December Otto, with his chosen Pope Gregory at his side and an army behind him, was once again heading towards Rome, which on his arrival in February 998 instantly opened its gates. Antipope John had fled just in time to the Campagna, but was soon captured. Blinded and hideously mutilated, he suffered much the same fate as the Prefect Peter half a century before, being paraded naked through the streets, sitting backwards on a donkey. He was then formally deposed and defrocked, before being incarcerated in some Roman monastery, where he lingered for another three years before a merciful death took him.

The papal history of the ninth and tenth centuries had been scarcely inspiring; but on Gregory's death in 999 the papacy suffered a sea change – with the appointment by Otto III of his old friend (and another of his tutors) Gerbert of Aurillac, then Archbishop of Ravenna. The first Frenchman to become Supreme Pontiff,[1] Gerbert took the title of Sylvester II (999–1003) as a deliberate tribute to his namesake Sylvester I, the contemporary of Constantine the Great, who had traditionally exemplified the ideal relationship between Emperor and Pope.

Gerbert had been born around 945 of humble parentage in the Auvergne, but had received a first-class education, first at Aurillac and then at Vich in Catalonia. He had been drawn across the Pyrenees by a thirst for knowledge that could be obtained nowhere else in Europe. Mathematics and medicine, geography, astronomy and the physical sciences were still deeply mistrusted in the Christian world; in that of Islam, they had been brought to a point unequalled since the days of ancient Greece. Gerbert himself is generally credited with having first popularised Arabic numerals and the use of the astrolabe, together with that of the celestial and terrestrial globes, in the Christian West. He was also a passionate lover of music, who did much to develop the organ as an instrument. Brought to Rome in 970, he impressed everyone by his extraordinary intelligence and erudition, and by his brilliance as a teacher. Soon afterwards he was summoned to the court of the fifteen-year-old Otto III, with orders 'to rid him of his Saxon rusticity and to stimulate his Greek subtlety'.

As Pope, Sylvester fulfilled every sensible expectation. He showed himself a determined reformer, denouncing the Church's two besetting

---

[1] It is mildly remarkable that, if we ignore the antipope (which we must), the first Frenchman on the papal throne should have directly succeeded the first German.

sins of nepotism and simony, forcing King Robert of France to get rid of his wife, and at the same time working – as he had always intended to work – closely with the Emperor to forge the sort of Christian Roman Empire of which they both dreamed. For a short time they were successful: together they reorganised the Church in Hungary and Poland, and it was Sylvester who sent the original Holy Crown of Hungary[1] to King Vajk, subsequently canonised as St Stephen. In recognition of what the two had achieved, Otto even returned Ravenna to the Pope, as well as the five cities of the so-called Pentapolis – Rimini, Faro, Pesaro, Senigallia and Ancona, which Pepin the Great had granted to the papacy in the eighth century – while making it clear that the transfer had nothing at all to do with the 'Donation of Constantine', which he strongly suspected of being a forgery.

For a pope of such calibre, the Romans should have been grateful; it need hardly be said that they were nothing of the kind. By some sad irony, Rome remained as unsuitable as any city could ever be, both as the centre of the universal Church and as the capital of a revived Western Empire. It was devoid alike of order and discipline, lying at the mercy of irresponsible magnates like the Crescentii or the Counts of Tusculum, or indeed its own highly volatile populace. Thus, when in 1001 a minor outbreak of trouble in Tivoli got out of hand and spread to Rome, both Pope and Emperor were forced to flee for their lives. Otto died of malaria early in 1002, aged twenty-one; Sylvester was allowed to return, but in May 1003 followed him to the grave. His pontificate had lasted just four years, barely half of which he had spent in Rome; but he had demonstrated to the world at large that there was, after all, a future for the Church; and that the papacy was not beyond hope of recovery.

The next three pontiffs were all creatures of John Crescentius II. All three were keen to establish relations with the new German king, Henry II the Holy; but Crescentius, whose Byzantine sympathies were growing stronger with age, continued to oppose any attempts to bring Henry to Rome for his imperial coronation. This state of affairs continued until May 1012 when, during another of those regular bouts of political upheaval inseparable from early medieval Rome, the Counts of Tusculum overthrew the Crescentii and seized power for themselves. The deaths of Crescentius and the last of his three puppets,

---

[1] The crown, thought to be originally Georgian work of the fourth century, is the oldest surviving in the world today. No fewer than fifty-five Kings of Hungary have been crowned with it.

Sergius IV (1009–12), within a week of each other at exactly this time cannot but suggest foul play; but there is no proof. It was scarcely surprising, in any case, that the next Pope should have been a Tusculan – the son of Count Gregory of Tusculum, and at the time of his election still a layman – who took the name of Benedict VIII. Now that there was no longer any obstacle to improving relations with the German king Henry duly visited Rome, where he was crowned by Benedict on St Valentine's Day 1014.

Unusually, the new Pope was a soldier. No sooner had he been ordained and enthroned than he was off at the head of an army to crush the remaining Crescentii in their mountain refuges, and much of the next six years was spent on campaign. In 1020 he appeared in person at the Emperor's court in Bamberg to consecrate Henry's new cathedral and to appeal for help against the Byzantium in the south. Henry agreed, and in 1022 marched down into the *mezzogiorno* with no fewer than three separate armies. They achieved one or two minor victories, but there was no significant breakthrough. The principal result was the renewed rupture of relations between Rome and Constantinople, which had somehow been patched up after the Photian schism of 861, but which were now further exacerbated by the Emperor's insistence on (and the Pope's craven acceptance of) the inclusion of the hated *filioque* in the Creed.

Dying in 1024, Benedict was followed by two more close relations – first his brother, then his nephew. All three having been laymen, each was tonsured, ordained and enthroned in a single day. The first, John XIX (1024–32), is principally remembered for having crowned Henry's successor Conrad II, in the somewhat unexpected presence of England's King Canute, who happened to be in Rome on a pilgrimage. Canute seems to have been deeply impressed; in fact John was venal, corrupt and without a ray of spirituality. The best that can be said of him was that his nephew was worse. Benedict IX (1032–45, 1047–8), elected only as a result of wholesale bribery on the part of his father, is traditionally believed to have mounted the throne at the age of ten or twelve, though later research suggests that he was more likely in his early twenties. What is beyond doubt is that he was a shameless debauchee, who recalled to the older generation the worst days of the pornocracy. The Romans, hardened as they were to corruption in high places, bore him as best they could for nearly twelve years; but in January 1045 they rose up against him and forced him to abandon the city, replacing him with the Crescentian Bishop John of Sabina, who took the title of Sylvester III (1045). Sylvester, however, lasted just two months. Benedict promptly excommunicated him and regained his throne by March; but somehow he seems to have lost his enthusiasm, and in May resigned his papal rights in favour of his godfather, the archpriest John Gratian – without, however, specifically renouncing the papacy itself.

Why he took so extraordinary a step is far from clear – but the result was chaos. There were now no fewer than three pretenders, all claiming to be the legitimate Pope. Two of the three were practically worthless; Gratian (who now called himself Gregory VI, 1045–6) was at least a serious churchman and a pious reformer, even though he was unable to shake off rumours of simony. The situation was finally resolved by the German king, Henry III. Henry had succeeded his father, Conrad II, in 1039 at the age of twenty-two. He was a conscientious ruler who took his religious responsibilities with the utmost seriousness, and was a powerful champion of reform. His original purpose in coming to Italy was to receive his imperial coronation, but he immediately saw that his first task would be to put some order in the papal affairs. On his way to Rome he saw Gregory at Piacenza, but was left unpersuaded; his conclusion – surely the right one – was to depose all three contestants. Only Benedict refused to lie down, forever making trouble from his family properties near Frascati and still breathing defiance at his successors. Sylvester (who had never wanted the job anyway) returned to his old bishopric. Gregory, by far the worthiest of the three, fared worst of all. At a synod held at Sutri he was found guilty of simony in obtaining the papal throne and was banished, accompanied by his Chancellor, Cardinal Hildebrand, to Germany. He died the following year, in Cologne.

We can hardly blame Henry III for taking the choice of pope into his own hands and, after the anarchy of previous years, for appointing a German to perform his coronation. In fact, he was to appoint four popes, one after the other. There was only one serious drawback to the choice of Germans: they were fatally susceptible to the old Roman scourge of malaria. The first, Clement II (1046–7), lasted just ten months,[1] and the odious Benedict, who was widely rumoured to have poisoned him, re-established himself for the next eight months at St

---

[1] The rumour that he was poisoned by Benedict IX is almost certainly without foundation. When his tomb was opened on 3 June 1942 there was evidence to suggest that he died of lead poisoning; but malaria remains the most likely cause.

Peter's. In July 1048 Henry's next appointee, Damasus II (1048), ruled for exactly twenty-three days before expiring at Palestrina. Whether, as some said, the heat had proved too much for him or whether Benedict was simply becoming more expert has never been properly established; but to most of the leading churchmen of his time his death made the papacy seem a less desirable prize than ever; and Henry, called upon to fill the vacancy for the third time in less than two years, was finding the task increasingly difficult. Finally, at a great council held at Worms in December 1048, German and Italian bishops called unanimously for the Emperor's second cousin, a man of tried ability and undoubted saintliness, Bruno, Bishop of Toul.

Bruno's reluctance to accept the invitation was unfeigned, and indeed hardly surprising. He agreed only on condition that his appointment would be spontaneously ratified on his arrival by the clergy and people of Rome, and accordingly set out for the Eternal City in January 1049, dressed as a simple pilgrim. Once there, however, he was immediately acclaimed and consecrated under the name of Leo IX (1049–54), and for the next six years until his death at fifty-one this tall, red-haired, military-looking Alsatian – he had in fact commanded an army in the field during one of Conrad II's expeditions into Italy – provided the Church with a quality of leadership that had long been wanting.

Hitherto the papacy had been very much a Roman institution; Leo made it genuinely international. He travelled all the time, to northern Italy, to France and to Germany; presiding at synods, fulminating against simony and against married priests, officiating at magnificent ceremonies, preaching to immense crowds. He put the papacy on the map of Europe as no pope had ever done before. He also built up an international Curia. No longer was the Pope to be surrounded by self-seeking, ever-intriguing ecclesiastics, mostly from the Roman nobility. Leo called together men as different as the fiery ascetic St Peter Damian – Doctor of the Church and forerunner of St Francis as an apostle of voluntary poverty; the brilliant Abbot Hugh of Cluny, under whose direction medieval monasticism reached its apogee; Frederick of Lorraine, Abbot of Monte Cassino, and later Pope Stephen IX (1057–8); and Cardinal Hildebrand, who as Gregory VII (1073–85) was to prove himself the greatest churchman of the Middle Ages.

The Church hardly knew what had hit it. King Henry I of France, who had no wish for the Pope to start interfering with his own ecclesiastical appointments, had forbiddden his bishops to attend the synod of Rheims, held in the very first year of Leo's pontificate. Some twenty had disobeyed him – but all too soon they regretted having done so. Leo opened the synod by demanding that each ecclesiastic stand up in turn and declare whether he had paid any money for his office. No fewer than five confessed; they were pardoned and restored to their sees. One, the Archbishop of Rheims himself, was summoned to Rome to make his defence. Another, the Bishop of Nantes, who had succeeded his own father in the diocese, was reduced to the priesthood. Yet another, the Bishop of Langres, fled and was excommunicated. The Archbishop of Besançon, who had attempted to defend him, was actually struck dumb halfway through his speech – those present being quick to draw the appropriate moral.

Yet Leo died a bitter and disappointed man, for two reasons. First, the Normans. Their story begins around 1015, with a party of some forty young Norman pilgrims at the shrine of the Archangel Michael on Monte Gargano, that curious rocky excrescence that juts out from what might be called the calf of Italy into the Adriatic. Seeing in this underpopulated, unruly land both an opportunity and a challenge, they were easily persuaded by the local Lombards to remain in Italy as mercenaries, with the object of expelling the Byzantine army of occupation from the peninsula. Word soon got back to Normandy, and the initial trickle of adventurous, footloose younger sons swelled into a steady immigration. Fighting indiscriminately for the highest bidder, they soon began to extract payment in land for their services. In 1030 Duke Sergius of Naples, grateful for their support, invested their leader, Rainulf, with the county of Aversa. Thenceforth their progress was fast. By 1050 they had effectively mopped up most of Apulia and Calabria, and Pope Leo, seeing an ever-growing threat along his southern border, proclaimed a holy war and raised an army against them.

It proved a grave mistake. The Normans may have been difficult neighbours, but they were by no means heretics and had always protested their loyalty to the Holy See. In the event, on 17 June 1053 the papal army was soundly beaten on the field of Civitate. The Byzantine army never turned up – to the fury of the papalists, who inevitably felt betrayed – and the Pope himself was taken prisoner. His captors treated him with slightly overdone respect, and nine months later, after they had got what they wanted (confirmation of their conquests and the lifting of their sentence of excommunication), they bore him back in state to Rome; but Leo never recovered from his humiliation and died only a month later.

*   *   *

The Pope's second misfortune, greater by far than the first, was that he was called upon to preside – although posthumously – over the Great Schism between the Eastern and the Western Churches. The two had been growing apart for centuries. Their slow but steady estrangement was in essence a reflection of the old rivalry between Latin and Greek, Rome and Byzantium. The Roman pontificate was rapidly extending its effective authority across Europe, and as its power grew, so too did its ambition and arrogance – tendencies that were viewed in Constantinople with resentment and not a little anxiety. There was also a fundamental difference in the approach of the two Churches to Christianity itself. The Byzantines, for whom their Emperor was Equal of the Apostles, believed that matters of doctrine could be settled only by the Holy Ghost speaking through an Ecumenical Council. They were accordingly scandalised by the presumption of the Pope – who was, in their view, merely *primus inter pares* among the Patriarchs – in formulating dogma and claiming both spiritual and temporal supremacy; while to the legalistic and disciplined minds of Rome, the old Greek love of discussion and theological speculation was always repugnant and occasionally shocking. Already two centuries before, matters had very nearly come to a head over Photius and the *filioque*. Fortunately, after the death of Pope Nicholas I and thanks to the goodwill of his successors and of Photius himself, friendly relations had been outwardly restored; but the basic problems remained unsolved, the *filioque* continued to gain adherents in the West, and the Emperor maintained his claim to rule as God's Vicegerent on Earth. It was only a matter of time before the quarrel broke out again.

That it did so at this moment might be blamed partially on Pope Leo, but was very largely the fault of the Patriarch of Constantinople, Michael Cerularius. He was as unlike his distant predecessor Photius as can possibly be imagined. Whereas the latter had been a man of intelligence and charm – as well as the greatest scholar of his day – Cerularius was a narrow-minded bigot. Already before Civitate he had fired his first salvo: learning that the Normans, with papal approval, were enforcing Latin customs (in particular the use of unleavened bread for the sacrament) on the Greek churches of southern Italy, he had immediately ordered the Latin communities of Constantinople to adopt Greek usages, and when they objected he had closed them down. There had followed a bitter correspondence, in which the Patriarch condemned certain Roman practices as 'sinful and Judaistic', while the Pope suggested – without a shred of justification – that the Patriarch's election had been uncanonical. To carry the papal letters to Constantinople, Leo (who was probably already dying) unwisely selected the three most rabidly anti-Greek churchmen in his Curia: his principal secretary Cardinal Humbert of Moyenmoutier – who in the events that followed was to prove not a jot less bigoted and waspish than the Patriarch himself – Cardinal Frederick of Lorraine and Archbishop Peter of Amalfi, both of whom had fought with him at Civitate and bore a bitter grudge against the Byzantines for having let them down.

From the moment of their arrival at Constantinople, everything went wrong. The Emperor Constantine IX received them graciously enough, but Cerularius categorically refused to recognise their authority. Then came the news that Pope Leo had died in Rome. Humbert and his colleagues had been Leo's personal representatives; his death consequently deprived them of all official standing. Their proper course in the circumstances would have been to return at once to Rome; instead, they remained in Constantinople apparently unconcerned, growing more arrogant and high-handed with every day that passed. When a certain monk of the monastery of the Studium answered the papal criticisms in polite and respectful language, Humbert replied with a stream of hysterical invective, describing the writer as a 'pestiferous pimp' and 'a disciple of the malignant Mahomet', suggesting that he must have emerged from a theatre or brothel rather than a monastery – surely confirming the average Byzantine in his opinion that the Church of Rome now consisted of little more than a bunch of crude barbarians with whom no argument, let alone agreement, could ever be possible.

At last – as Cerularius knew he would – Humbert lost the last shreds of his patience. At three o'clock on the afternoon of Saturday, 16 July 1054, in the presence of all the clergy assembled for the eucharist, the three ex-legates of Rome, two cardinals and an archbishop, all in their full canonicals, strode into the Great Church of St Sophia, the Holy Wisdom, and up to the high altar, on which they formally laid their solemn Bull of Excommunication. This done, they turned on their heels and marched from the building, pausing only to shake the dust symbolically from their feet. Two days later they left for Rome. It was only when the Bull had been publicly burned and the legates themselves formally anathematised that peace returned.

Even if we ignore the fact that the legates were without any papal authority, and that the Bull itself was consequently invalid by every standard of canon law, it remains an astonishing production: few important documents, in the words of Sir Steven Runciman, have been so full of demonstrable errors.[1] Yet such was the sequence of events, at Constantinople in the summer of 1054, that resulted in the lasting separation of the Eastern and Western Churches. It is an unedifying story because, however inevitable the breach may have been, the events themselves should never – and need never – have occurred. More strength of will on the part of the dying Pope, less bigotry on the part of the narrow-minded Patriarch or the pig-headed cardinal, and the situation could have been saved. The initial crisis arose in southern Italy, the one crucial area in which a political understanding between Rome and Constantinople was most vitally necessary. The fatal blow was struck by the disempowered legates of a dead pope, representing a headless Church – since the new pontiff had not yet been elected – and using an instrument at once uncanonical and inaccurate. Both the Latin and the Greek excommunications were directed personally at the offending dignitaries rather than at the Churches for which they stood; both could later have been rescinded, and neither was at the time recognised as introducing a permanent schism. Technically indeed they did not do so, since twice in succeeding centuries (in the thirteenth at Lyons and in the fifteenth at Florence) was the Eastern Church to be compelled, for political reasons, to acknowledge the supremacy of Rome. But though a temporary bandage may cover an open wound, it cannot heal it; and despite the balm applied in 1965 by the Second Vatican Council[2], the wound that was jointly inflicted on the Christian Church nine centuries ago by Cardinal Humbert and Patriarch Michael Cerularius still bleeds today.

[1] S. Runciman, *The Eastern Schism*. The relevant paragraph is also quoted in my own *Byzantium: The Apogee*, p.321.
[2] See Chapter XXVIII.

CHAPTER IX

Gregory VII and the Normans

(1055–85)

For almost exactly a year after the death of Leo IX on 19 April 1054 there was no pope in Rome. Henry III had already appointed three pontiffs, all Germans, and was determined to nominate a fourth; but before doing so he had long discussions at Mainz with a delegation from Rome headed by Cardinal Hildebrand. His choice finally fell on a young Swabian named Gebhard, who had been made Bishop of Eichstätt in 1042 while still in his twenties; but even then Gebhard hesitated for several months, accepting only in March 1055. The last pope to be nominated by a German king, he was enthroned on 13 April under the name of Victor II (1055–7), keeping his old bishopric throughout his pontificate. The Italian party had feared that he might prove too much a creature of the Emperor; in fact he proved a staunch defender of the rights of the Church, and a champion of reform no less determined than his predecessor. But he could not escape his countrymen's vulnerability to the miasmas of Rome, and was already a sick man when he presided at a synod at Arezzo in July 1057. When he died a few days later his German entourage wanted to take his body back to Eichstätt for burial; but the cortege was ambushed and robbed at Ravenna, where the body now rests – curiously enough, in the Mausoleum of Theodoric, at that time doing service as a church.

This time there were no consultations with the Emperor; Henry III had died suddenly at thirty-nine; his son Henry IV was a boy of six. It was the perfect opportunity for Hildebrand and his friends to recover the Italian reformist hold on the papacy, and they acted fast. Their choice fell on Frederick of Lorraine, once Pope Leo's chief lieutenant, by then Abbot of Monte Cassino. As Pope Stephen IX (1057–8) he would hardly have been popular at the imperial court, his brother – Duke Godfrey the Bearded of Lorraine – having recently married the widowed Marchioness Beatrice of Tuscany and thus assumed control of the strongest and best-organised power in northern Italy. Already there were sinister rumours of how the Pope was planning to take advantage of Henry IV's minority by transferring the imperial crown from the House of Franconia to that of Lorraine.

It is unlikely that Stephen ever entertained such an idea for a moment; but we shall never know, for in just seven months he too was dead. Feeling his end approaching, he had exacted from the Roman clergy a solemn oath that they would not elect his successor before the return of Hildebrand, who was on a mission to Germany; but the reactionaries saw their chance. Experience over the past few years had taught them that on occasions of this kind everything depended on speed. A *coup d'état* was hurriedly planned by a Tusculan-Crescentian alliance, and within a few days John Mincio, Bishop of Velletri, was enthroned as Pope under the inauspicious title of Benedict X (1058–9). From the point of view of the reformers, the choice could have been a lot worse; the new Pope may have been weak-willed, but Leo IX had made him a cardinal and Stephen had considered him a possible alternative candidate to himself. They could not, however, accept the manner of his election, which they viewed as uncanonical and corrupt. Leaving Rome in a body, they met Hildebrand in Tuscany and settled down to decide on a pope for themselves.

Their choice fell on Gérard, Bishop of Florence, an irreproachably sound Burgundian who in December 1058, once he was assured of the support of the Empress-Regent Agnes and – equally important – of Duke Godfrey of Lorraine, allowed himself to be consecrated as Pope Nicholas II (1058–61). He and his cardinals, supported by Duke Godfrey with a small military contingent, then advanced upon Rome, where the gates of Trastevere were opened to them. Quickly they occupied the Tiber Island, which they made their headquarters. Several days of street-fighting followed, but at last the Lateran was stormed, with Antipope Benedict barely managing to escape to Galeria.[1]

The reform party had won again, but the cost had been considerable. Benedict X was still at large, and he had retained a loyal following; many Romans who had been forced to swear allegiance to Nicholas raised their left hand to do so, pointing out that with their right they had already taken an oath of fidelity to his rival. More disturbing still was the knowledge that the reformists' victory could not even now

---

[1] The city of Galeria was abandoned in 1809, but its ruins may still be seen just off the Viterbo road, about twenty miles from Rome.

have been achieved without the military support provided by Duke Godfrey. In short, after all the efforts of the past decade, the papacy was once again where it had been when Pope Leo had found it: caught fast between the Roman aristocracy and the Empire, able sometimes to play one off against the other, but never sufficiently strong to assert its independence of either. The great task of reform could not possibly be accomplished in such conditions. Somehow the Church must stand on its own feet.

First came the problem of Benedict. Only thirteen years before, his odious namesake had demonstrated just how much harm could be done by a renegade antipope; Benedict X was a far more popular figure than Benedict IX, and this time there was no emperor ready to sweep down into Italy and restore order, as Henry III had done. Duke Godfrey had returned to Tuscany, though this was perhaps just as well, since he had recently displayed a curious half-heartedness that had led to suspicions of a secret intrigue with the Roman right. And so the Church took a surprising, fateful step. It called upon the Normans for aid.

The final decision to do so can only have been Hildebrand's. No other member of the Curia, not even Pope Nicholas himself, would have possessed the necessary combination of courage and prestige. Throughout Italy, and above all among the churchmen of Rome, the Normans were still considered – not unreasonably – a bunch of barbarian bandits, no better than the Saracens who had terrorised the south before them. For many of the cardinals the idea of an alliance with such men, whose record of sacrilege and desecration was notorious and who had dared, only five years before, to take arms against the Holy Father himself and hold him a captive for nine months, must have seemed more appalling by far than any accommodation with the Roman nobility, or even with Benedict himself. But Hildebrand knew that he was right. Pope and cardinals bowed, as nearly always, before his will; and in February 1059 he set off in person for discussions with one of the Norman leaders, Prince Richard of Capua.

Richard did not hesitate. Instantly he put 300 men at Hildebrand's disposal, and the cardinal hastened back to Rome with his new escort. By mid-March he and Nicholas were encamped together before Galeria, watching their army lay siege to the town. The Normans, employing their usual tactics, inflicted appalling devastation on the entire region, burning and pillaging in all directions. The Galerians resisted with courage, beating back repeated attempts to storm the walls; but in the autumn they were forced to surrender. Benedict was captured, tried, publicly unfrocked and imprisoned in the hospice of Sant'Agnese on the Via Nomentana; and the era of papal-Norman friendship had begun.

The fate of Benedict X came as a profound shock to the reactionary group in Rome. They had expected neither the degree of resolution and unity of purpose with which the cardinals had opposed his election, nor the vigour with which he had subsequently been swept aside. And now, before they were able to recover, Hildebrand dealt them a second blow, still more paralysing in its long-term effects. The procedure governing papal elections had always been vague; it was theoretically based on a settlement, originated by the Emperor Lothair in 824 and renewed by Otto the Great in the following century, according to which the election was to be carried out by the entire clergy and nobility of Rome; the new pontiff, however, was to be consecrated only after he had taken an oath to the Emperor. Such a decree, loose enough in its original conception and looser still in its interpretation through well over 200 years, was bound to lead to abuses. Apart from the power that it gave to the Roman aristocracy, it also implied a measure of dependence on the Empire, which, though counterbalanced by the need for every emperor to submit to a papal coronation in Rome, by no means accorded with Hildebrand's ideas of papal supremacy. Now, with the Romans in disarray, a child on the German throne and the assurance of armed Norman support should the need arise, it could at last be scrapped.

On 13 April 1059 Pope Nicholas held a synod at the Lateran; and there, in the presence of 113 bishops and with Hildebrand as always at his side, he promulgated the decree which, with one or two later amendments, continues to regulate papal elections to the present day. For the first time the responsibility for electing a new pope was placed squarely on the cardinals, effectively the senior clergy in Rome[1]. Only after a pontiff had been elected was the assent of the rest of the clergy and people to be sought. Lip-service was still paid to the imperial

---

[1] The word 'cardinal' comes from the Latin *cardo*, a hinge. The name was first given to the parish priests of the twenty-eight titular churches of Rome, who also served the papal basilicas (St John Lateran, St Peter's, S. Paolo fuori le Mura and S. Maria Maggiore). They were thus the 'hinges' between the Pope and his parishes. Gradually they formed a College, ranked as Roman princes, second in order of precedence only to the Pope himself. There are three ranks: cardinal-priests, cardinal-deacons and – since the eighth century – cardinal-bishops. All are nominated personally by the Pope.

connection by a deliberately vague stipulation that the electors should have regard for 'the honour and respect due to Henry, at present king and, it is hoped, future emperor', and to such of his successors as should personally have obtained similar rights from the Apostolic See, but the meaning was plain: in future the Church would run its own affairs and take orders from neither the Empire nor the aristocracy of Rome.

It was a brave decision; and not even Hildebrand would have dared to take it but for the Normans. To both the Empire and the nobility of Rome it amounted to a slap in the face, however diplomatically administered; and either side might be expected now or later to seek the restitution of its former privileges by force of arms. But Hildebrand's conversations with the Prince of Capua, to say nothing of recent events at Galeria, had given him – and, through him, the Church as a whole – new confidence. With the aid of a mere 300 Normans from Capua he had thrown the foremost of his enemies back in confusion; how much more might not be accomplished if the entire Norman strength from Apulia and Calabria could also be mobilised behind the papal banners? Such support would enable the Church to shake off once and for all the last shreds of its political dependence, and would allow the most far-reaching measures of reform to be enacted without fear of the consequences. Besides, the events of 1054 had produced a climate between Rome and Constantinople in which there was clearly no hope of an early reconciliation in the theological field; the sooner, therefore, that the perverted doctrines of the Greeks could be swept altogether from southern Italy, the better. The Normans, having at last established tolerable relations with their Lombard subjects, were at this moment forcing the Byzantines back into a few isolated positions in Apulia – notably Bari – and into the toe of Calabria. Left to themselves, they would soon finish the job; then, in all likelihood, they would start on the infidels of Sicily. They were by far the most efficient race on the peninsula, and for all their faults they were at least Latins. Should they not therefore be encouraged rather than opposed?

The Norman leaders, for their part, asked nothing better than an alliance with the Church of Rome – which would inevitably entail its alienation from the imperial court. However much they and their countrymen might have acted against individual religious foundations in the past, they had always (even at Civitate) shown respect for the Pope, and had taken arms against him in self-defence only after all

attempts at a peaceful settlement had failed. They were not so strong
that they did not welcome a guarantee against the threat of a combined
onslaught by Empire and papacy, or indeed an ally against any other
enemy – Byzantine, Tuscan or Saracen – with whom they might on
occasion be faced. On the other hand, they were quite powerful enough
to negotiate with the Pope on an equal political footing. Their hopes
were therefore high when Nicholas II left Rome in June 1059 with
an impressive retinue of cardinals, bishops and clergy and headed
south-east towards the little town of Melfi, the first Norman stronghold in southern Italy.

Slowly and magnificently the papal train passed through Campania.
It stopped at Monte Cassino where it was joined by Abbot Desiderius,
now the Pope's official representative in the south and thus in effect
his ambassador to the Normans; it wound its way through the mountains to Benevento, where the Pope held a synod; to Venosa, where
he ostentatiously consecrated the new church of the Santissima Trinità,
the foremost Norman shrine in Italy; and finally to Melfi, where he
arrived towards the end of August and found, waiting to receive him
at the gates of the town, a huge assemblage of Norman barons headed
by Richard of Capua and that other, still greater Norman leader:
Robert de Hauteville, known as the Guiscard.[1]

The Synod of Melfi, which was ostensibly the reason for the Pope's
visit, has largely been forgotten. Its purported object was to try to
reimpose chastity, or at least celibacy, on the southern Italian clergy
– an undertaking in which, despite the unfrocking of the Bishop of
Trani in the presence of more than 100 of his peers, later records
show it to have been remarkably unsuccessful. Nicholas's presence
proved to be, however, the occasion of an event of immense importance to Normans and papacy alike: their formal reconciliation. It
began with the Pope's confirmation of Richard as Prince of Capua,
and continued with his ceremonial investiture of Robert Guiscard,
first with the Duchy of Apulia, next with Calabria and finally – though
none of those Normans present had ever set foot on the island – with
Sicily.

By just what title the Pope so munificently bestowed on the Normans
territories which had never before been claimed by him or his predecessors is a matter open to doubt. But few of those present at Melfi
on that August day were likely to raise embarrassing issues of that

[1] Literally, 'the Crafty'. Compare with the English 'wiseacre'.

sort. In any event, Pope Nicholas could afford to be expansive; he was getting so much in return. He was admittedly lending papal support to the most dangerous and potentially disruptive of all the political elements in southern Italy; but by investing both its leaders – whose relations were known to be strained – he was carefully keeping this element divided. Furthermore, the two leaders now swore him an oath which effectively gave him feudal suzerainty over most of southern Italy and Sicily and changed, radically and completely, the entire position of the papacy in the region. By a lucky chance the complete text of Robert's oath – though not, unfortunately, of Richard's – has come down to us in the Vatican archives, one of the earliest of such texts still extant. The first part is of little importance, but the second is vital:

> I, Robert, by the Grace of God and of St Peter Duke of Apulia and of Calabria and, if either aid me, future Duke of Sicily, shall be from this time forward faithful to the Roman Church and to you, Pope Nicholas, my lord. Never shall I be party to a conspiracy or undertaking by which your life might be taken, your body injured or your liberty removed. Nor shall I reveal to any man any secret which you may confide to me, pledging me to keep it, lest this should cause you harm. Everywhere and against all adversaries I shall remain, insofar as it is in my power to be so, the ally of the holy Roman Church, that she may preserve and acquire the revenues and domains of St Peter. I shall afford you all necessary assistance that you may occupy, in all honour and security, the papal throne in Rome. As for the territories of St Peter ... I shall not attempt to invade them nor even [sic] to ravage them without the express permission of yourself or your successors, clothed with the honours of the blessed Peter ...
>
> Should you or any of your successors depart this life before me I shall, having consulted the foremost cardinals as also the clergy and laity of Rome, work to ensure that the Pope shall be elected and installed according to the honour due to St Peter ... So help me God and his Holy Gospels.

All those present at the ceremony could be well satisfied with what they had done; not everyone, however, shared their satisfaction. The Roman aristocracy retreated into its musty palaces, furious and frightened. The Byzantines saw that they had lost their last chance of preserving what was left of their Italian possessions. And in the Western Empire – shorn of its privileges at papal elections, faced with a new alliance as formidable militarily as it was politically and now, as a crowning insult, forced to watch in impotent silence while immense tracts of imperial territory were calmly conferred on a band of brigands – the reaction to Nicholas's behaviour can well be imagined. It was lucky for Italy that Henry IV was still a child; had he been a few years older, he would never have taken such treatment lying down. As it was, the Pope's name was thenceforth ostentatiously omitted from the intercessions in all the imperial chapels and churches, while a synod of German bishops went so far as to declare all Nicholas's acts null and void and to break off communion with him. We cannot tell how he would have reacted; before the news could reach him, the Pope had died in Florence.

The death of Nicholas II created a situation even more hopelessly confused than usual, his electoral reforms having produced the very effect that they had been specifically designed to avoid. They made a disputed succession inevitable, for how could the Empress-Regent Agnes accept any candidate canonically elected in Rome without giving implicit approval to the new dispensations? Once again, two popes struggled for the possession of St Peter's. The stronger claim was certainly that of Anselm, Bishop of Lucca, whose election as Pope Alexander II (1061–73) by the cardinal-bishops – guided, as always, by Hildebrand – had been canonically impeccable. On the other hand, his rival, the antipope Honorius II (1061–4), chosen by Agnes and supported by the Lombard bishops – who, as St Peter Damian uncharitably remarked, were better fitted to pronounce on the beauty of a woman than on the suitability of a pope – had influential partisans in Rome and plenty of money with which to nourish their enthusiasm; it was only with the military assistance of Richard of Capua (provided now for the second time, at Hildebrand's request) that Alexander was enabled to take possession of his see. Even then Honorius did not give up. As late as May 1063, after Agnes had been removed and an imperial council had declared for his rival, he even managed to recapture the Castel Sant'Angelo for several months; and though he was formally deposed the following year, he was to uphold his claims until the day of his death.

With Hildebrand continuing in his role of *éminence grise*, it was hardly surprising that the papal-Norman alliance should flourish. In 1063 Pope Alexander sent a banner to Robert Guiscard and his brother Roger, fighting the Saracens in Sicily; and three years later he sent another to William Duke of Normandy, who flew it at Hastings. He did his best, too, to heal the breach with Byzantium, sending a mission under Peter of Anagni to Constantinople; but feelings on the Bosphorus were running too high, and after the Normans under Robert Guiscard had captured Bari in 1071 – eliminating the last bastion of Byzantine power in southern Italy – the chances of a settlement were even slimmer. Even there, however, relations were a good deal easier than those with the Empire of the West.

Henry IV had come to the throne of Germany in 1056, shortly before his sixth birthday. He had not made a particularly auspicious start to his reign. His mother, the Empress Agnes, who had taken over the regency, had been totally unable to control him, and after a wild boyhood and a deeply disreputable adolescence he had acquired, by the time he assumed power at sixteen, a reputation for viciousness and profligacy that augured ill for the future. This reputation he was at last beginning to live down, but throughout his unhappy life he remained hot-tempered, passionate and intensely autocratic. Thus as he grew to manhood he became ever more resentful of what he saw as the increasing arrogance of the Roman Church and, in particular, of those reformist measures by which it was seeking to cast off the last vestiges of imperial control. It was plain that a showdown between Church and Empire was inevitable. It was not long in coming.

The setting was Milan. Nowhere in Italy did the spirit of ecclesiastical independence from the dictates of Rome burn more brightly than in this old capital of the north, where an individual liturgical tradition had been jealously preserved since the days of St Ambrose seven centuries before; nowhere were the new Roman reforms, especially those relating to simony and clerical celibacy, more bitterly resented by the diehards. On the other hand, the government of the city was now dominated by a radical left-wing party known as the Patarines who, partly through genuine religious fervour and partly through hatred of the wealth and privilege that the Church had so long enjoyed, had become fanatical champions of reform. Such a situation would have been explosive enough without imperial intervention; but late in 1072, during a dispute over the city's vacant archbishopric, Henry had aggravated matters by giving formal investiture to his own choice of aristocratic anti-reform candidate, while being fully aware that Pope Alexander had already approved the canonical election of a Patarine.

Tension between the two parties had led to the burning of Milan

Cathedral, and tempers were still running high on each side when, in April 1073, Alexander died, leaving his successor to carry on the struggle. There could be no question as to who that successor would be. Archdeacon Hildebrand had already wielded effective power in the Curia for some twenty years, during many of which he had been supreme in all but name. When, according to a carefully prearranged plan, the crowd seized him during Alexander's funeral service, carried him to the church of St Peter in Vinculis and there exultantly acclaimed him Pope, they were doing little more than regularising the existing state of affairs; and the canonical election that followed was the purest formality. Hastily he was ordained priest – a desirable qualification for the papacy, which seems to have been overlooked during the earlier stages of his career – and was immediately afterwards enthroned as Supreme Pontiff in the name of Gregory VII (1073–85).

Of the three great popes of the eleventh century – Leo IX, Gregory VII and Urban II (whom we have not yet met) – Gregory was at once the least attractive and the most remarkable. Whereas the other two were aristocrats, secure in the possession of all that noble birth and a first-class education could bestow, he was the ugly, unprepossessing son of a Tuscan peasant, Lombard by race, whose standards of learning and culture fell well below those of most leading churchmen and whose every word and gesture betrayed his humble origins.[1] They assumed the papacy almost as of right; he achieved it only after a long and arduous – though increasingly influential – apprenticeship in the Curia, and for no other reason than his immense ability and the sheer power of his will. They were both tall and of outstandingly distinguished appearance; he was short and swarthy, with a pronounced paunch and a voice so weak that, even making allowance for his heavy regional accent, his Roman colleagues often found it difficult to understand what he said. He had none of Leo's obvious saintliness, nor any of Urban's political instinct or diplomatic flair. He was neither a scholar nor a theologian. And yet there was in his character something so compelling that he almost invariably dominated, automatically and effortlessly, any group of which he found himself a member. Peter Damian had not called him a 'holy Satan' for nothing.

His strength lay, above all, in the singleness of his purpose. Throughout his life he was guided by one overmastering ideal: the

[1] Hildebrand, or Hildeprand, was a common Lombard name. His father's name, Bonizo, is an abbreviation of Bonipart, which seven centuries later we find again in the form of Buonaparte. Napoleon was also of Lombard stock. He and Hildebrand had much in common.

subjection of all Christendom, from the two emperors down, to the authority of the Church of Rome. The Church could make them and unmake them; it could also absolve their subjects from their allegiance. But just as the Church must be supreme upon Earth so too must the Pope be supreme in the Church. He was the judge of all men, himself responsible only to God; his word was not only law, it was the Divine Law. Disobedience to him was therefore something very close to mortal sin. All this and much more was spelt out in his twenty-seven propositions, known as the *Dictatus Papae*, published in 1075. These included the assertion that all popes are by definition saints, inheriting their sanctity from St Peter – a theory that must have raised a few eyebrows among Gregory's older contemporaries. Never before had the concept of ecclesiastical autocracy been carried to such an extreme; never before had it been pursued with such unflinching determination. And yet this very extremism was to prove ultimately self-destructive. Confronted by adversaries of the calibre of Henry IV and Robert Guiscard, as determined as himself but infinitely more flexible, Gregory was to learn to his cost that his persistent refusal to compromise, even when his principles were not directly involved, could only bring about his downfall.

But all that was in the future. The problem of Henry IV remained to be settled. At his Lenten Synod of 1075 the Pope categorically condemned all ecclesiastical investitures by laymen, on pain of anathema. Henry, furious, immediately invested two more German bishops with Italian sees and added, for good measure, a further Archbishop of Milan, although his former nominee was still alive. Refusing a papal summons to Rome to answer for his actions, he then called a General Council of all the German bishops and, at Worms on 24 January 1076, denounced Gregory as 'a false monk' and formally deposed him from the papacy. It was a decision he was bitterly to regret. His father Henry III had deposed three popes, and he had assumed that he could do the same. What he had failed to understand was that the papacy was no longer what it had been half a century before – and that those three miserable pontiffs were not a bit like Hildebrand.

Henry had long been eager to come to Rome for his imperial coronation, but his quarrel with successive popes over investitures had prevented him. After the Council of Worms, however, he saw that his journey could no longer be postponed. Gregory had not reacted to his deposition with the savagery that was already being rumoured in Germany, but he was clearly not going to accept it lying down. If, therefore, the Council was not to be held up to ridicule, he would have to be removed by force and a successor called. The need was for a swift, smooth military operation; and, while it was being prepared, steps must be taken to deprive the Pope as far as possible of local Italian support. North of Rome this would be difficult: the formidable Countess Matilda of Tuscany was a devout champion of the Church, her loyalty to Gregory unswerving. To the south, however, the prospects looked more hopeful. The Norman Duke of Apulia in particular seemed to have no great love for the Pope. He might well overlook his feudal responsibilities if it were made worth his while to do so. Once he and his men could be persuaded to participate in a combined attack on Rome, Gregory would not stand a chance.

Henry's ambassadors reached Robert Guiscard, probably at Melfi, early in 1076 and formally offered him an imperial investiture of all his possessions; they may even have mentioned the possibility of a royal crown. But Robert was unimpressed. He already enjoyed complete freedom of action throughout his domains, and he saw no reason to jeopardise this by giving Henry further excuses to meddle in southern Italian politics. His reply was firm, if a trifle sanctimonious. God had given him his conquests; they had been won from the Greeks and Saracens, and dearly paid for in Norman blood. For what little land he possessed that had ever been imperial, he would consent to be the Emperor's vassal, 'saving always his duty to the Church' – a proviso which, as he well knew, would make his allegiance valueless from Henry's point of view. The rest he would continue to hold, as he had always held it, from the Almighty.

Meanwhile Pope Gregory had acted with his usual vigour. At his Lenten Synod of 1076 he had deposed all the rebellious bishops and thundered out a sentence of excommunication on King Henry himself. The effect in Germany was cataclysmic. No reigning monarch had incurred the ban of the Church since Theodosius the Great seven centuries before. It had brought that Emperor to his knees, and it now threatened to do the same for Henry. The purely spiritual aspect did not worry him unduly – that problem could always be solved by a well-timed repentance – but the political consequences were serious indeed. In theory the ban not only absolved all the King's subjects from their allegiance to him; it also rendered them in their turn excommunicate if they had any dealings with him or showed him obedience. Were it to be strictly observed, therefore, Henry's government would disintegrate and he would be unable to continue on the throne any longer. Suddenly he found himself isolated.

The Pope's grim satisfaction can well be imagined as he watched his adversary struggling to retain the loyalties of those around him; his ban had been more successful than even he had dared to hope. The German princes, meeting at Tribur, had agreed to give their king a year and a day from the date of his sentence in which to obtain papal absolution. They had already called a Diet at Augsburg for February 1077. If by the 22nd of that month the ban had not been lifted, they would formally renounce their allegiance and elect another king in his place. Henry could only bow to their decision. From his point of view, it might have been worse. The princes' ultimatum called, quite simply, for his own abject self-abasement before the Pope. If this was to be the price of his kingdom, he was ready to pay it. Fortunately there was still one alpine pass – the Mont Cenis – unblocked by snow. Crossing it in the depths of winter with his wife and baby son, he hastened through Lombardy and at last found the Pope at the fortress of Canossa, where he was staying as a guest of his friend, the Countess Matilda, pending the arrival of an escort to conduct him to Augsburg. For three days Gregory kept Henry waiting for an audience; finally he saw that he had no alternative but to relent and give him the absolution he needed.

The story of Canossa, usually enlivened by an oleaginous illustration of the King, barefoot and in sackcloth, shivering in the snow before the locked doors of a brilliantly lit castle, has always been a favourite with the writers of children's storybooks, who present it as an improving object lesson in the vanity of temporal ambition. In fact Gregory's triumph was empty and ephemeral, and Henry knew it. His own humiliation had nothing to do with repentance. It was a cold-blooded political manoeuvre which was necessary to secure his crown, and he had no intention of keeping his promises once they had served their purpose. The Pope, too, can have had few delusions about the King's sincerity. Had his Christian conscience permitted him to withhold absolution he would doubtless have been only too happy to do so. He had won an unquestionable moral victory; but what was the use of a victory after which the vanquished returned unabashed to his kingdom while the victor remained cooped up in a Tuscan castle, blocked from Germany by the savage hostility of the Lombard cities and powerless to intervene?

And of course Henry showed no sign of mending his ways. He

antagonised the German princes to the point where they did indeed elect a rival king, Rudolf of Swabia. Gregory did his best to mediate between them, but eventually in 1080 he excommunicated Henry once again, sentenced him to deposition and declared Rudolf king. Alas, he had backed the wrong horse. That same year Rudolf was killed in battle; Henry, on the other hand, had never been stronger. For the second time he declared Gregory deposed; he then called a synod of German and Italian bishops at Brixen (now Bressanone) in the Tyrol, which in June 1080 dutifully elected Guibert, Archbishop of Ravenna, as Pope Clement III.

It was easy to elect an antipope, but a good deal harder to install him. Henry made three attempts to take over Rome, but only with the third was he successful. Finally, early in 1084, a mixed party of Milanese and Saxons managed to scale the walls of the Leonine City; and within an hour or two Henry's soldiers were fighting a furious battle in and around St Peter's. Pope Gregory, however, had been too quick for them. He had no intention of surrendering. Hurrying to the Castel Sant'Angelo, he barricaded himself in and watched, powerless, while on Palm Sunday Clement was enthroned in the Lateran. Just a week later, on Easter Day, Henry was crowned Emperor.

Gregory was to be saved by the Normans. Four years before, Robert Guiscard had sworn fealty to him, binding himself to give the Pope any assistance that he might need; in any event his own position would be seriously threatened if Henry, now crowned Emperor and supported by an obedient Clement III, were allowed to have his own way in southern Italy. And so it was that on 24 May 1084 Robert rode up the Via Latina with a force estimated at some 6,000 horse and 30,000 foot and, roughly on the site of the present Piazza di Porta Capena, pitched his camp beneath the walls of Rome.

Henry had not waited for him. News of the size and strength of the Norman army had been enough to make up his mind. Summoning a council of the leading citizens of Rome, he explained to them that his presence was urgently required in Lombardy. He would be back as soon as circumstances permitted; meanwhile he trusted them to fight valiantly against all attackers. Then, three days before the Duke of Apulia appeared at the gates of the city, he fled with his wife and the greater part of his army, the terrified Antipope scurrying behind.

For three days Robert waited in his camp, uncertain perhaps whether Henry's flight was genuine. Then, on the night of 27 May, under cover of darkness, he silently moved his army round to the north of the city. At dawn he attacked, and within minutes the first of his shock-troops had burst through the Flaminian Gate. They met with stiff resistance; the whole area of the Campus Martius – the quarter lying immediately across the river from the Castel Sant'Angelo – became a blazing holocaust. But it was not long before the Normans had beaten the defenders back over the bridge, released the Pope from his fortress and borne him back in triumph through the smoking ruins to the Lateran.

Alas, that triumph was short-lived. The whole capital was now given over to rapine and pillage, in which Robert's several brigades of Sicilian Saracens were not conspicuous for their restraint. On the third day, with bestiality and bloodshed still continuing unabated, the people of Rome could bear it no longer: the whole city rose against its oppressors. Robert Guiscard himself was taken by surprise and surrounded. He was saved in the nick of time by his son, who smashed his way through the hostile crowds to his father's rescue – but not before the Normans, fighting now for their lives, had set fire to the city.

Here, for Rome, was disaster, unparalleled in its history since the barbarian invasions six centuries before. Churches, palaces, ancient temples came crashing down before the advancing flames. The Capitol and the Palatine were gutted; in the whole area between the Colosseum and the Lateran hardly a single building escaped the inferno. When at last the smoke cleared away and such Roman leaders as remained alive had prostrated themselves before the Duke, a naked sword roped round their necks in token of surrender, their city lay empty, a picture of desolation and despair.

Gregory had won his battle after a fashion – but at what a price? The heroic popes of the past had saved their city from the invaders: Leo I from Attila's Huns, his own namesake, Gregory the Great, from the conquering Lombards; he, though in many ways greater than either, had delivered it up to destruction. And yet his letters show no remorse or regret. His conscience was clear. He had been fighting for a principle and, thanks to his own tenacity and courage, that principle had been upheld. God's will had been done.

So – with that sublime arrogance which was one of his chief and most unattractive characteristics – must Gregory have reasoned. But for him, too, there was to be retribution. The Roman populace, who had acclaimed him with such enthusiasm eleven years before, now saw him (and not without good reason) as the cause of all their misery and loss; and they were hungry for revenge. Only the presence of Robert Guiscard and his army prevented them from tearing their once-adored Pope limb from limb. But Robert had no desire to stay in Rome a moment longer than was necessary, and so Gregory suffered his last humiliation: the realisation that when the Normans left Rome, he would have to leave with them. At the beginning of July 1084, escorted by the mighty host of Normans and Saracens that had been at once his salvation and his undoing, he turned his back on Rome for the last time: the proudest of pontiffs, now little better than a fugitive from the city that hated him. Southward they rode to Salerno. There the Pope was settled in a palace befitting his dignity; and there, on 25 May 1085, he died. He was buried in the south-eastern apse of the cathedral 'built by Robert Guiscard at his own expense', as the façade inscription runs – where his tomb may still be seen.

In spite of the discredit that Gregory had unwittingly brought upon the papacy in his last years, the body of his achievement was greater than he knew. He had gone a long way towards establishing papal supremacy over the hierarchy of the Church, and even though he had not won a similar victory over the Empire, he had asserted his claims in such a way that they could never again be ignored. The Church had shown her teeth; future emperors would defy her at their peril. And yet Gregory died, if not a broken, then at least a disappointed, disillusioned man; and his last words – 'I have loved righteousness and hated iniquity, therefore I die in exile' – were a bitter valediction.

CHAPTER X

Innocent and Anacletus

(1086–1183)

The chaos that had driven Gregory VII from Rome was made if anything worse by his death. Antipope Clement III had his champions, but he could not hope to win over the reformist cardinals and so was never quite able to install himself permanently in the Vatican. The cardinals' problem was to find a suitable successor, for recent history had not been such as to make the pontificate a particularly attractive proposition. There was one outstanding candidate: Abbot Desiderius of Monte Cassino, who had directed the affairs of his great monastery for the past twenty-seven years, making of them its golden age. He had vastly extended its lands and its library, developing it into a centre of learning, literature and the arts; and his influence had extended far beyond its confines. He it was who in 1059 had negotiated the alliance between the papacy and the Normans, and who in 1080 had reconciled Gregory VII with Robert Guiscard. He had actually sheltered the fugitive pope at Monte Cassino on his way to exile, and had been with him when he died.

But, not surprisingly, he had absolutely no wish to be Pope himself. Why should he exchange the peace and comfort of the monastery he loved for the nightmare that was papal Rome? It took the cardinals nearly a year to persuade him – few pontiffs have ever accepted the office with greater reluctance. And it was not long before he was proved right. Just four days after his election as Victor III (1086–7) in May 1086, before he had even been consecrated, serious rioting broke out in the city and he was forced to leave. He laid aside his papal insignia, rode off at once to Monte Cassino and – with every sign of relief – took up his former duties. But he was not to be left in peace for long. Ten months later, in his earlier capacity of papal vicar in southern Italy, he convened a synod at Capua; and there he was once more persuaded to accept the office to which he had been elected. Norman troops smashed their way yet again into Rome, from which it was now the antipope's turn to flee; and on 9 May 1087

Victor was finally consecrated in St Peter's. This time he was almost a week in Rome before retiring again to his monastery, and in mid-June he was to endure the Holy City for an entire month. But that was enough. The end of July saw him back at Monte Cassino, and by mid-September he was dead.

His successor, Urban II (1088–99), was a man of a very different stamp. Odo of Lagery was a stately, scholarly aristocrat from Champagne, a zealous reformer who had been Prior of Cluny before coming south to accept the hugely important see of Ostia. He was a staunch upholder of papal supremacy on the Gregorian model – except that he possessed all the polish and diplomatic finesse that Gregory had so disastrously lacked. Since Rome was now once again in the hands of Antipope Clement and the imperialists, he had been elected and consecrated at Terracina, and he was well aware that Norman help would be necessary if he were ever to install himself in the Vatican. It was only after he had paid a personal visit to Count Roger – Robert Guiscard's younger brother, now entrusted with Sicily – that Roger was able to organise an armed expedition to Rome by means of which, in November 1088, the Pope entered the city – though even then he was confined to the tiny Tiber Island. By the following autumn he was back in exile. Not until Easter 1094, and then only through heavy bribery, was he able to penetrate to the Lateran Palace and, six years after his consecration, assume his rightful throne.

A few months later Urban sent an embassy to Constantinople. Ever since his accession he had worked hard to improve relations with Byzantium – Church union being of course the ultimate objective – and the Emperor Alexius Comnenus had been gratifyingly quick to respond; when, therefore, the papal legates delivered to Alexius an invitation to send representatives to a great Council of the Roman Church to be held at Piacenza the following March, the Emperor accepted at once. Most of the proceedings, he knew, would be concerned with domestic matters (simony, clerical marriage, the adultery of King Philip of France and the like), but the Council might also provide him with the opportunity he had long sought, to appeal for Western aid against the Turks. They had invaded his Empire a quarter of a century before, defeated a Byzantine army led by his predecessor Romanus IV and overrun practically all of Anatolia except for a few areas around the coast. They could, he believed, be driven out, but only by a military expedition on a considerable scale. Piacenza might be just the place to say so.

The Byzantine spokesmen did their work well. Sensibly, they laid their emphasis less on the prizes to be won – though we may be sure that these did not go unmentioned – than on the religious aspect of their appeal: the sufferings of the Christian communities in the East, the submergence of Asia Minor beneath an Islamic tide, the presence of the infidel armies at the very gates of Constantinople and the appalling danger they represented, not only to the Empire of the East, but to all Christendom. The listening delegates were impressed – none more so, perhaps, than Urban himself. From Piacenza he travelled on to his native France, and as his journey progressed a scheme gradually took shape in his mind, far more ambitious than any that Alexius had ever dreamed of: nothing less than a Holy War, in which the combined forces of Christian Europe would march against the Saracen.

When he arrived in France he called another Council, to gather at Clermont (now Clermont-Ferrand) on 18 November 1094. It would last for ten days, most of which would be taken up with routine Church business; on Tuesday the 27th, however, there would be a public session open to all at which, it was announced, the Pope would make a statement of immense significance to all Christendom. This promise had precisely the effect that Urban had intended. So great were the crowds that poured into the little town to hear the Pope speak that the cathedral was abandoned, and the papal throne was erected instead on a high platform set in an open field outside the eastern gate. The text of his speech has not come down to us, but he seems to have begun by repeating the points made by the Byzantine delegates at Piacenza; unlike them, however, he then turned to the plight of Jerusalem,[1] where Christian pilgrims were being regularly robbed and persecuted by the city's Turkish overlords. It was now, he emphasised, the duty of Western Christendom to march to the rescue of the Christian East. All those who agreed to do so 'from devotion only, not from advantage of honour or gain', would die absolved, their sins remitted. There must be the minimum of delay: the great army of the Crusade must be ready to march by the Feast of the Assumption, 5 August 1095.

The response to his impassioned appeal was more enthusiastic than Urban could have dared to hope. Led by Bishop Adhemar of Le Puy, several hundred people – priests and monks, noblemen and peasants

---

[1] Jerusalem had been in Muslim hands since its capture by the Caliph Omar in 638, but for most of the intervening period Christian pilgrims had been freely admitted and allowed to worship as and where they wished. The city had been taken by the Seljuk Turks in 1077.

together – knelt before his throne and pledged themselves to take the Cross. The First Crusade was under way.

Contrary to the expectations of many, the Crusade turned out to be a resounding, if undeserved, success. On 1 July 1097 the Seljuk Turks were smashed at Dorylaeum in Anatolia; on 3 June 1098 Antioch fell to Crusader arms; and finally on 15 July 1099, amid scenes of hideous carnage, the soldiers of Christ battered their way into Jerusalem, where they slaughtered every Muslim in the city and burned all the Jews alive in the main synagogue. Pope Urban, however, never knew of their victory. He died two weeks later, shortly before the reports reached Rome.

He was succeeded by a good-natured Tuscan monk, Paschal II (1099–1118). It is said that when William II (William Rufus) of England was told that the character of the new Pope was not unlike that of his own Archbishop Anselm, the King exclaimed: 'God's face! Then he isn't much good' – a remark that, though quietly memorable in its way, is hardly fair to either ecclesiastic. Paschal may have been of a gentle disposition; he may have lacked that last ounce of moral fibre. But he was no weakling: after the death of Antipope Clement he successfully disposed of three more antipopes one after another, and for the first twelve years of his pontificate staunchly upheld the principle that had by now become the central issue in the papal–imperial struggle: the right to invest bishops and abbots with ring and crozier. He was, on the other hand, prepared to negotiate; and at Sutri, where he met the Emperor Henry on his way to Rome for his coronation, he made Henry a startlingly generous offer: if the Emperor would renounce his claims to the right of investiture, he in return would surrender all the properties and rights of all churches – they were mostly German – that had come to the papacy from the Empire, retaining only those revenues, such as tithes, that were strictly ecclesiastical.

Henry was of course delighted at the prospect of acquiring the vast wealth of the German bishoprics and abbeys. He accepted with alacrity and hurried on to Rome. Strangely enough, however, neither he nor the Pope had thought to consult the German bishops of whose property they so cheerfully planned to dispose; and when, on 12 February 1111, the terms of the agreement were read out at the coronation service, there was a storm of protest so vociferous that the service had to be abandoned. This was the signal for the arrest of Pope and cardinals, which in turn proved too much for the Roman populace. They rose up against the Germans, and during the consequent street fighting Henry himself was wounded. At last he and his army retired from the Leonine City, taking Pope and cardinals with them. The churchmen were confined in various neighbouring castles while tempers cooled.

When Paschal emerged two months later there was little fight left in him. On 12 April Henry forced him to concede the right of investitures of bishops and abbots between election and consecration, and the following day the Pope – who had also been obliged to swear that he would never excommunicate him – crowned him Emperor. Once again there was an outcry in the Curia. This was craven capitulation, the abject surrender of everything for which the reformers had so long struggled. All that Paschal had given away was declared to have been extracted by force, and therefore invalid. Away in France, Archbishop Guido of Vienne pronounced a sentence of excommunication on the Emperor, a sentence that was subsequently repeated by Jordan, Archbishop of Milan. The Pope himself, deeply contrite, considered abdication; in 1112 he personally withdrew his earlier concessions, referring back to Gregory and Urban with the words 'whatever they have condemned I condemn; whatever they have rejected I reject' – which do not even suggest a firm grasp of the matters at issue, far less an assertive personality. He withdrew them again during a Lateran synod in 1116, once more forbidding all imperial investitures. But his reputation was gone; he never recovered his former authority. More rioting in Rome drove him from the city later that same year, and he left it again when Henry arrived in 1117. He returned the following January for the last time, and was dead by the end of the month.

His successor, Gelasius II (1118–19), was to reign for a year and five days; his pontificate is worth recording only because it partook of the quality of a nightmare. Papal authority was now recognised across most of Europe; within Rome, by contrast, the Pope daily took his life in his hands. By the standards of the time, Gelasius must have been already an oldish man: he had been appointed Cardinal in 1088 – thirty years before – and Papal Chancellor the following year. He had held the fort in Rome during the frequent absences of both Urban and Paschal, had accompanied the latter into captivity and had vigorously defended him at the 1116 synod. He certainly deserved a quiet ending to his days. Instead, scarcely had the tiara been set on his head than he was seized by Cencius Frangipani – head of that awesome family, which was now one of the most powerful in Rome – and locked up in one of the family castles, where he was brutally beaten. An eyewitness reported that Cencius, 'hissing like a huge snake ... grabbed the Pope by the throat ... struck him with his fists, kicked him and drew blood with his spurs ... dragging him away by the hair'. Had it not been for the swift intervention of the City Prefect, he might never have been seen again.

Even after his release, Gelasius was to remain in Rome for only a little over a month. On hearing of his election, an angry Henry V had hurried south from Lombardy; and the Pope fled with his cardinals to his home town of Gaeta. Henry summoned him back to Rome in the hope of reaching an amicable settlement; the Pope refused. Henry, now more exasperated than ever, countered by appointing an antipope, Gregory VIII (1118–21); whereat Gelasius immediately excommunicated them both. But the Emperor had the upper hand only for as long as he remained in Rome; when at last he and his army marched away, Gregory was not strong enough to maintain himself in the whole city and withdrew to within the Leonine Walls.

Unable to install himself in the Vatican, on 21 July Gelasius was saying Mass in the basilica of S. Prassede when he was once again seized by the Frangipani. This time he managed to escape, on horseback. He was eventually found by his followers sitting quietly in a field, still wearing his papal vestments. He had had enough. He returned to Rome only for as long as it took him to prepare for his departure from the city for good. Then, escorted by six of his cardinals, he rode by easy stages via Pisa and Genoa, Avignon and Vienne, to Cluny – where, on 29 January 1119, he died.

One thing was clear: there could be no peace in Rome until the vexed question of investitures could be settled. And it was fortunate indeed that Gelasius's successor both recognised its importance and possessed the strength of will to deal with it once and for all.

The son of Count William of Burgundy, Archbishop Guido of Vienne was related to the French, English and German royal houses. He had been named by Pope Gelasius on his deathbed as his ideal successor, and the small minority of cardinals who had accompanied the Pope to Cluny took it upon themselves to elect him there and then, crowning him at Vienne on 9 February 1119 as Calixtus (or Callistus) II (1119–24). Astonishingly, their decision was retrospectively ratified by the unanimous vote of the cardinals in Rome; but by that time Calixtus was already at work, having sent envoys to negotiate with Henry V at Strasbourg. Meanwhile he summoned a huge Council in Rheims for the end of October – it was to be attended by more than 400 bishops – to obtain general approval for the policy he proposed to pursue.

Despite the fact that Henry also seemed anxious for a settlement, the first attempt at reconciliation failed, largely through mutual mistrust, and Calixtus took advantage of the Rheims Council to confirm the sentence of excommunication that he had first pronounced as Archbishop of Vienne eight years before. Then, with the coming of spring, he rode south across the Alps, making a triumphal progress through Lombardy and Tuscany and entering Rome – where he was given an ecstatic reception – at the beginning of June 1120. One small preliminary problem had to be dealt with before he could settle down to the question of investitures: the Antipope Gregory was still at large. Henry had by now withdrawn his support from Gregory, who had retired to Sutri; but in April 1121 the town fell after a week's siege and Calixtus brought the wretched Antipope back to Rome. There Gregory was paraded through the streets, mounted backwards – on a camel this time – before being confined in various abbeys for the rest of his life.

Now at last the way was clear for the major challenge of Calixtus's pontificate; and early in 1122 an embassy arrived from the Emperor. Henry, they informed him, was ready for another round of talks – indeed, he had appointed a committee of twelve German princes to represent him. Calixtus despatched three of his senior cardinals (including the future Pope Honorius II 1124–30), to meet the princes at Worms; and it was there, after three weeks' hard bargaining, that the famous concordat was agreed on 23 September. Based on a model first developed in Norman England, it required the Emperor to abandon his claim to invest newly elected bishops with ring and crozier, these being symbols of spiritual authority. He would, however, confer their lands upon them with a tap of his sceptre, which represented temporal power. He would also guarantee to the higher clergy their freedom of election and consecration. In return, Calixtus promised that canonical elections to German bishoprics and abbacies would always be held in the Emperor's presence, while in disputed elections the Emperor would have the power of arbitration.

The Concordat of Worms marked the end of an important chapter in the long struggle between Church and Empire. The Pope had made concessions, which he recognised would be unpopular among the more inflexible of his flock; he was, however, at pains to emphasise that these concessions were not necessarily to be accepted in principle. All he asked was that they should be tolerated for the time being, in the interests of peace. He himself had no regrets – indeed, he felt nothing but pride in his achievement, which he celebrated in a series of frescoes that he commissioned for the Lateran.

But peace between papacy and Empire did not, alas, mean peace within Rome itself. The days of the Crescentii and the Counts of Tusculum were past; the two powerful families now confronting each other were the noble Frangipani and the far richer but relatively parvenu Pierleoni, who despite their Jewish origins had maintained a close working relationship with a number of popes since Leo IX and Gregory VII. The constant feuding between these two was to bedevil papal elections for years to come. On the death of Calixtus in 1124 the Frangipani easily won the day. The candidate favoured by the Pierleoni had already been proclaimed as Celestine II (1124), but during the service of consecration Roberto Frangipani and his followers burst into the assembly with drawn swords and insisted on the immediate acclamation of Cardinal Lamberto of Ostia. There followed a violent struggle, in the course of which Celestine was quite severely wounded and immediately resigned. The way was now clear for Lamberto, who was duly enthroned as Honorius II (1124–30).

The Pierleoni–Frangipani rivalry was reflected in a similar breach among the Curia. On the one side, and forming the majority, were the old-school Gregorians, backed by the Pierleoni; on the other was a younger group led by the Papal Chancellor Cardinal Aimeric, who had almost certainly been involved in Roberto Frangipani's coup. Honorius belonged of course to the latter faction. He had been one of the cardinals who had accompanied Gelasius to France, and one of the chief negotiators at Worms. A dedicated and determined reformer, he also worked hard to strengthen the position of the Church abroad, notably in Germany. In January 1130, however, he fell seriously ill; and Aimeric acted swiftly. The Chancellor was well aware that the obvious successor to Honorius was Cardinal Pietro Pierleoni who, after studying in Paris with the great Peter Abelard, had spent several years as a monk at Cluny before being appointed Papal Legate, first in France and then in England. His genuine piety and irreproachable Cluniac background had made him a staunch upholder of reform;[1] he was also capable, strong-willed and intensely ambitious. But he was a Pierleoni, and, for Aimeric and his party, that was enough. They seized the dying pontiff and carried him off to the monastery of S. Andrea, safe in the bosom of the Frangipani quarter, where they would be able to conceal his death until suitable dispositions could be made for the future. Then, on 11 February, Aimeric summoned to the monastery such cardinals as he felt he could trust and began preparations for a new election.

Such a proceeding, flagrantly dishonest as it was, provoked an immediate reaction from the rest of the Curia. Hurling anathemas against 'all those who would proceed to the election before the funeral of Honorius', they nominated a commission of eight electors, to meet in the church of S. Adriano. The choice of this somewhat obscure church was clearly due to their natural reluctance to put themselves at the mercy of the Frangipani; but when they arrived at S. Adriano they found that Aimeric's men had already taken possession of the church and had fortified it against them. Furious, they turned away and gathered instead at the old church of S. Marco, where they settled down to await developments.

On 13 February the rumour swept through Rome that the Pope was dead at last, and that the news was being deliberately suppressed. An angry crowd gathered around S. Andrea, and was dispersed only after the luckless Honorius had shown himself, haggard and trembling, on the balcony. It was his last public appearance; by nightfall he was dead. In theory his body should have been allowed to lie for three days in state; but since the election of a new pope could not take place before the burial of the old, Aimeric had no time for such niceties. Almost before the body was cold it was flung into a temporary grave in the monastery courtyard, and early the following morning the Chancellor and those who shared his views elected Gregory Papareschi, Cardinal-Deacon of S. Angelo, to the papacy. He was rushed to the Lateran and formally, if somewhat hastily, installed under the title of Innocent II (1130–43); he then retreated to S. Maria in Palladio (now S. Sebastiano in Pallaria), where the Frangipani could keep him out of harm's way.

Meanwhile at S. Marco the crowd had been steadily growing. It

---

[1] Accusations were from time to time made against him by such robust prelates as Manfred of Mantua and Arnulf of Lisieux (who actually wrote a book called *Invectives*) to the effect that he seduced nuns, slept with his sister, and so on; but these can be discounted as being simply the normal, healthy Church polemic to be expected at times of schism.

now included some two dozen cardinals, together with most of the nobility and as many of the populace as could squeeze through the doors. When, on the morning of St Valentine's Day, the news of Innocent's election was brought to them, there was immediate uproar. With one accord the cardinals declared the proceedings at S. Andrea and the Lateran uncanonical, and acclaimed Cardinal Pierleoni as their rightful Pope. He accepted at once, taking the name of Anacletus II. At dawn that morning there had been no Pope in Rome. By midday there were two.

Innocent or Anacletus – it is hard to say which candidate possessed the stronger claim to the papacy. Anacletus, there was no doubt, could boast more overall support, both among the cardinals and within the Church as a whole. On the other hand, those who had voted for Innocent (though fewer in number) had included the majority of the electoral commission of eight that had been set up by the Sacred College. The manner in which they had performed their duties was, to say the least, questionable, but then Anacletus's own election could scarcely have been described as orthodox. It had, moreover, taken place after another pope had already been elected and installed.

One thing was certain. In Rome itself, sweetened after years of bribery by the Pierleoni, the popularity of Anacletus was overwhelming. By 15 February 1130 he and his party were in control of the Lateran, and on the 16th they took St Peter's. Here, a week later, Anacletus received his formal consecration – while Innocent had to be content with a more modest ceremony at S. Maria Novella. Day by day Anacletus entrenched himself more firmly, while his agents dispensed subsidies with an ever more generous hand, until at last his gold – supplemented, according to his enemies, by the wholesale pillage of the principal churches of Rome – found its way into the Frangipani fortress itself. Deserted by his last remaining champions, Innocent had no choice but to flee. Already by the beginning of April we find him dating his letters from Trastevere; a month later he secretly chartered two galleys on which, accompanied by all his loyal cardinals except one, he escaped down the Tiber.

His flight proved his salvation. Anacletus had bought Rome with bribes, but elsewhere in Italy popular feeling was firmly behind Innocent. In Pisa he was cheered to the echo, in Genoa the same. From there he took ship for France, and by the time he sailed into the little harbour of Saint Gilles in Provence much of his old confidence had returned. It was well justified. When he found, awaiting him at Saint Gilles, a deputation from Cluny with sixty horses and mules in its train, ready to escort him the 200-odd miles to the monastery, he must have felt that, at least so far as France was concerned, his battle was as good as won. If the most influential of all French abbeys was prepared to give him its support in preference to one of its own sons, he had little to fear from other quarters; and when the Council of Étampes, summoned in the late summer to give a final ruling, formally declared in his favour, it merely confirmed a foregone conclusion.

France, then, was sound; but what of the Empire? Here lay the key to Innocent's ultimate success; but Lothair the Saxon, King of Germany, showed no particular eagerness to make up his mind. He was still engaged in a desperate struggle for power with Conrad of Hohenstaufen and had to weigh his actions with care. Besides, he had not yet been crowned Emperor in Rome. To antagonise the Pope who actually held the city was a step that might have dangerous implications. Innocent, however, was not unduly worried; for his case was now safely in the hands of the most powerful of all advocates and the outstanding spiritual force of the twelfth century: St Bernard of Clairvaux.

To an objective observer in the twenty-first century, safely out of range of that astonishing personal magnetism with which he effortlessly dominated all those with whom he came into contact, St Bernard is not an attractive figure. Tall and haggard, his features clouded by the constant pain resulting from a lifetime of exaggerated physical austerities, he was consumed by a blazing religious zeal that left no room for tolerance or moderation. His public life had begun in 1115 when the Abbot of Cîteaux, the Englishman Stephen Harding, had effectively released this charismatic twenty-five-year-old monk from monastic discipline by sending him off to found a daughter-house at Clairvaux in Champagne; from that moment on, almost despite himself, Bernard's influence spread; and for the last twenty-five years of his life he was constantly on the move, preaching, persuading, arguing, debating, writing innumerable letters and compulsively plunging into the thick of every controversy in which he believed the basic principles of Christianity to be involved.

The papal schism was just such an issue. Bernard declared himself unhesitatingly for Innocent. His reasons, as always, were emotional. Cardinal Aimeric was a close personal friend; Anacletus, on the other hand, was a product of Cluny, a monastery that Bernard detested, believing it to have betrayed its reformist ideals and to have succumbed to those very temptations of wealth and worldliness that it had been founded to eradicate. Worse still, Anacletus was of Jewish antecedents; as Bernard was later to write to Lothair, 'it is to the injury of Christ that the offspring of a Jew should have seized for himself the throne of St Peter'. The question of Christ's and St Peter's own racial origins does not seem to have occurred to him.

Away in Rome, Anacletus was fully aware of the need for international recognition; but whereas his rival was able to whip up support in person, he had to rely on correspondence, in which he had as yet been singularly unsuccessful. In an effort to reassure King Lothair, he had even gone so far as to excommunicate Conrad, but the King had been unimpressed and had not even had the courtesy to answer his subsequent letters. In France, too, his legates were snubbed; and now, as reports reached him of more and more declarations for Innocent, Anacletus grew seriously alarmed. The weight of the opposition was far greater than he had expected; more disturbing still, it was not only the ruling princes who favoured his antagonist, but the Church itself. During the previous half-century, thanks largely to Cluniac reforms and the influence of Hildebrand, it had developed into a strong and cohesive international authority. Simultaneously the mushroom growth of the religious orders had given it a new impetus and efficiency. Cluny under its Abbot Peter the Venerable, Prémontré under Norbert of Magdeburg – he who had persuaded Lothair to leave Anacletus's letters unanswered – and Cîteaux under St Bernard, all were vital, positive forces. All three were united in favour of Innocent, and they carried the body of the Church with them.

And so Anacletus took the only possible course: like other desperate popes in the past, he turned to the Normans. In September 1130, just about the time when the Council of Étampes was deciding in Innocent's favour, he left Rome for Avellino, where Roger II de Hauteville, Great Count of Sicily, was awaiting him. Roger had succeeded his father and namesake in 1101. First landing in Sicily just forty years before, Roger I had in that time transformed an island at once demoralised and despairing, torn asunder by internecine wars and decaying after two centuries of misrule, into a political entity, peaceful and prosperous, in which three peoples (Norman, Greek and Arab) and three religions (Catholicism, Orthodoxy and Islam) were happily coexisting in mutual respect and concord. His son had inherited the two Norman duchies of Apulia and Calabria in 1127, and had received a formal investiture from Pope Honorius the following year. His task now, as he explained to Anacletus, was to weld his three dominions into a single nation. That nation could be nothing less than a kingdom, and Roger now desperately needed a crown.

Anacletus was sympathetic. If, as now seemed likely, Roger was to be his only ally, it was plainly desirable that his position should be strengthened to the utmost. On 27 September, in the papal city of Benevento, he issued a Bull granting to Roger and his heirs the crown of Sicily, Apulia and Calabria, together with the principality of Capua, the 'honour' of Naples – a deliberately ambiguous expression since Naples, still technically independent and with vague Byzantine affiliations, was not the Pope's to endow – and the assistance of Benevento in time of war. In return Roger pledged his homage and fealty to Anacletus as Pope, together with an annual tribute of 600 schifati – a sum equivalent to about 160 ounces of gold. And so, on Christmas Day 1130, King Roger II of Sicily rode to his coronation in Palermo. In the cathedral there awaited him the Archbishop and all the Latin hierarchy of his realm, together with senior representatives of the Greek Church. Anacletus's special envoy, the Cardinal of S. Sabina, first anointed him with the holy oil; then Prince Robert of Capua, his vassal-in-chief, laid the crown upon his head.

And now at last King Lothair made up his mind. He declared for Innocent. Among all the European princes there remained to Anacletus only three adherents: King David I of Scotland, Duke William X of Aquitaine and King Roger of Sicily. This last alone would have been enough to lose him any imperial support he might have enjoyed, for by what right could any pope – legitimate or otherwise – crown some Norman upstart King over territories that properly belonged to the Empire? After Roger's coronation there could be no more sitting on the fence; Innocent it would have to be. And yet – perhaps as much to save face as for any other reason – Lothair still tried to impose a condition: that the right of investiture with ring and crozier, lost to the Empire nine years before, should now be restored to him and his successors.

He had reckoned without the Abbot of Clairvaux. When Innocent arrived with full retinue at Liège in March 1131 to receive the King's homage, Bernard was with him. This was just the sort of crisis at which he excelled. Leaping from his seat, he subjected Lothair to a merciless castigation before the entire assembly, calling upon him then and there to renounce his pretensions and pay unconditional homage

St Peter and St Paul.
Twelfth-century mosaics in the Cathedral of Monreale, Sicily.

The Crypt of the Popes, Catacomb of San Callisto, Rome, third century. Now empty, it once contained the remains of nine popes and eight bishops of the third century.

The Mausoleum of Theoderic, Ravenna. Raising that single monolith that forms the roof was an astonishing achievement for the sixth century. The mausoleum also contains the sarcophagus of Pope Victor II (1055-7).

Justinian and his entourage, including Archbishop Maximian. The shield-carrier on the far left is thought to be Belisarius. Contemporary mosaic, sixth century, San Vitale, Ravenna.

The Empress Theodora and her court.
Contemporary mosaic, sixth century, Church of San Vitale, Ravenna.

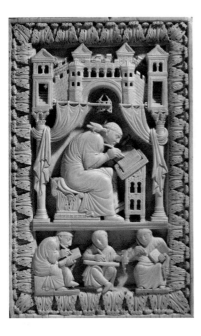

St Gregory the Great (590–604) in his study. The Holy Ghost whispers in his ear. Below, scribes are busy copying his work. Tenth-century ivory, Kunsthistorisches Museum, Vienna.

Constantine the Great (708–15) presents Pope Sylvester with the Tiara. Behind him is the Pope's horse; when Sylvester mounts it, the Emperor will hold his stirrup as the traditional mark of respect. Thirteenth-century fresco, Church of the Quattro Santi Coronati, Rome.

Pope Joan (?855–7) gives birth. Engraving, F. Spanheim, *Histoire de la Papesse Jeanne*, The Hague, 1721.

The Coronation of Charles the Bald by Pope John VIII (872–82) in 875. Musée Condé, Chantilly.

The Emperor Otto III, enthroned between representatives of the Church and Laity. *The Munich Gospels*, Staatsbibliothek, Munich.

Equestrian statue of the Emperor
Marcus Aurelius. It stood outside the
Lateran Palace in the Middle Ages,
when it was believed to represent
Constantine the Great. Piazza del
Campidoglio, Rome.

The greatest Pope of the
Middle Ages, Innocent III
(1198–1216). Thirteenth-
century fresco, Monastery
of Sacro Speco, Subiaco.

Pope Boniface VIII (1294–1303)
inaugurates, from the
benediction balcony of
the Lateran Palace,
the first Jubilee in 1300.
Biblioteca Ambrosiana, Milan.

Christ presents the Keys to St Peter. Fresco by Pietro Perugino, Sistine Chapel, Rome.

Pope Alexander VI (1492–1503) at prayer. Detail from Resurrection fresco by Pinturicchio, Borgia Apartments, Vatican Palace, Rome.

Pope Julius II (1503–1513), towards the end of his life. Raphael, National Gallery, London.

to the rightful Pope. As always, his words – or, more probably, the force of his personality behind them – had their effect. This was Lothair's first encounter with Bernard; it is unlikely that he had ever before been spoken to in such a way. He was not lacking in moral fibre, but this time he seems instinctively to have realised that his position was no longer tenable. He gave in, making his formal submission to Innocent and reinforcing it with an undertaking that the Pope probably found even more valuable: to lead him, at the head of a German army, to Rome.

It was a year and a half before Lothair kept his promise. Unrest in Germany delayed his departure; but by the summer of 1132 it was plain to him that the key to his domestic problems lay in the earliest possible acquisition of the imperial crown and the prestige it conferred; and so in August, with his queen Richenza of Nordheim and a force that amounted to little more than an armed escort, he set off over the mountains and into Italy.

He found Innocent waiting for him near Piacenza. The Pope had managed to drum up a degree of local support; the imperial army on the last stage of the journey promised to be about 2,000 strong. It was still a disappointing figure, but it was at least not shameful. What was principally lacking now was sea support. Pisa and Genoa in particular – the two great maritime republics on whose assistance Innocent had relied – could at that moment see no further than Corsica and Sardinia, over which they had long been squabbling; without their help the imperial force would stand little chance in the face of a concerted Sicilian attack. Meanwhile the autumn rains were beginning, the roads rapidly turning to mud; and Lothair decided to postpone his coronation till the spring. By then, perhaps, the warring republics might be persuaded to settle their differences.

The fact that they did so was largely due to the Abbot of Clairvaux, who appeared in Italy soon after Christmas; by March 1133, Bernard and Innocent together had alternately hectored and flattered the Pisans and Genoese into a truce, and a month later they were back at Lothair's camp, ready for the advance on Rome. The army was still sadly unimpressive, but imperial agents reported that King Roger was fully occupied with a rebellion on the part of his mainland vassals; he would be offering no serious opposition.

On the last day of April the Emperor-to-be drew up his troops before the church of S. Agnese fuori le Mura. For some days already

Rome had been in turmoil. Pisan and Genoese ships had sailed up the Tiber and were now lying threateningly under the walls; and their presence, aided by exaggerated rumours of the size of the oncoming German host, had induced many Romans to make a hurried change of allegiance. Much of the city thus lay open to Innocent and Lothair. They were received at the gates by the Frangipani nobles and their minions – who had never wavered in their opposition to Anacletus – and led in triumph to their respective palaces: the King and Queen to Otto III's old imperial residence on the Aventine, the Pope to the Lateran.

But the right bank of the Tiber, with the Castel Sant'Angelo and St Peter's, still remained firmly in the hands of Anacletus; and Anacletus was not prepared to give in. Lothair, conscious of his own weakness, proposed negotiations, but the Antipope's reply remained the same as it had always been: let the whole question of the disputed election be reopened before an international ecclesiastical tribunal. If such a tribunal, properly constituted, were to declare against him, he would accept its decision. Until then, he would stay in Rome where he belonged. Left to himself, Lothair would probably have been ready to accept this suggestion. Anything, in his view, would have been better than this continued schism; rival popes might lead to rival emperors, and in such an event his own position might be far from secure. But by now he had been joined in Rome by Bernard; and with Bernard there could be no question of compromise. If Anacletus could not be brought to his knees, he must be ignored. And so it was not at St Peter's, but at the Lateran that Innocent was reinstalled on the papal throne; and it was there – on 4 June 1133, with as much ceremony and circumstance as he could command – that he crowned Lothair Emperor of the West, and Richenza his Empress.

For the second time in half a century one putative pope had performed an imperial coronation while another had sat a mile or two away, impotent and fuming. After the previous occasion Gregory VII had been saved only by the arrival, not a moment too soon, of Robert Guiscard at the head of some 30,000 troops. Anacletus knew that he could expect nothing from that quarter; the King of Sicily, though remaining his loyal champion, was otherwise engaged. Fortunately, rescue was unnecessary. Powerless the Antipope may have been, but he was not in any physical danger. No imperial attack on the right bank would be possible without control of the two bridges spanning the river at the Tiber Island; and all approaches to these were effectively dominated by the old Theatre of Marcellus, now the principal fortress of the Pierleoni. In the circumstances, the Emperor had neither the strength nor the inclination to take the offensive. Now that his immediate aims were achieved he thought only of returning to Germany as soon as possible. Within a few days of his coronation he and his army were gone; and the Pisan and Genoese ships had returned down the river to the open sea.

For Pope Innocent, Lothair's departure was nothing short of calamitous. At once his remaining supporters in the city began to fall away. Only the Frangipani remained loyal; but they could not hold Rome unaided. By July the agents of Anacletus had everywhere resumed their activity, and the gold was beginning to flow freely once again from the inexhaustible Pierleoni coffers. In August Innocent found himself forced once again into exile. He slipped unobtrusively from his diocese – just as he had three years before – and made his way, by slow stages, to Pisa and to safety.

Meanwhile the schism rumbled on. It had now become clear to Lothair that the Antipope could never be dislodged from Rome while the King of Sicily protected him. In the autumn of 1135 an embassy from the Byzantine Emperor, John II Comnenus, arrived at the imperial court. John had his own reasons for wishing to eliminate King Roger: his Empire had never given up its claim to southern Italy, and the rich Byzantine cities of Dalmatia constituted a temptation to raiding and freebooting that Sicilian sea captains had not always been able to resist. He now offered Lothair generous financial backing for a campaign to crush their common enemy once and for all.

The Emperor needed little persuading. Thanks largely to the new prestige conferred upon him by the imperial crown, the situation in Germany had improved over the past two years, and his Hohenstaufen rivals had been forced into submission. This time he would have no difficulty in raising a respectable army. He foresaw little trouble from Anacletus. The Antipope's last remaining north Italian stronghold, Milan, had gone over to Innocent in June, and the schism was now confined to the Sicilian Kingdom and Rome itself. Once Roger was out of the way, Anacletus would be left without a single ally and would be obliged to yield. Lothair replied to John accepting his offer.

By the high summer of 1136 Lothair's army was finally gathered at Würzburg. It was on a very different scale from the sad little company that had marched with him to Rome in 1132. In the forefront were the Emperor's son-in-law, Duke Henry the Proud of Bavaria, and his old enemy and rival Conrad of Hohenstaufen, whom Lothair had confirmed in possession of his lands in return for a promise to participate in the coming campaign. It also boasted an ecclesiastical contingent that included no fewer than five archbishops, fourteen bishops and an abbot. When it reached Bologna, Lothair split the army into two. He himself proposed to continue through Ravenna to Ancona, and thence to follow the coast southwards into Apulia; meanwhile the Duke of Bavaria, with 3,000 knights and perhaps 12,000 infantry, was to press down through Tuscany and the Papal States, if possible re-establishing Innocent in Rome and assuring himself of the monastery of Monte Cassino, before meeting his father-in-law at Bari for Whitsun.

The plan succeeded well enough, and it was a joyful and triumphant German congregation that assembled on Whit Sunday, 30 May 1137, at the church of St Nicholas in Bari, to hear a High Mass of Thanksgiving celebrated by the Pope himself – even though a Sicilian garrison was still holding out in the citadel. There was, perhaps, a measure of surprise that King Roger had made no effort to oppose the invaders; but the King knew that however far Lothair might advance, sooner or later he would be driven back, as so many invading armies had been driven back before, by sickness, the relentless summer heat or the need to reach the Alps before the first snowfalls rendered them impassable. Past experience had shown that although such expeditions could be highly effective in the short term, the results they achieved seldom lasted very long after their departure. The only sensible course, Roger believed, was to encourage the Emperor to extend and exhaust himself to the limit.

And events soon proved him right. After the capitulation of the Bari garrison – whose tenacity he punished by hanging a number of them from gibbets all round the city and flinging the rest into the sea – the Emperor decided against any further advance down the coast. There were several reasons for his decision. He was seventy-one years old, and tired; besides, the whole situation had suddenly gone sour. Relations between the Germans and the papal retinue were deteriorating fast: the army, too, had been away ten months and was impatient to be home. Where Sicily was concerned, Lothair could at least feel that he had saved his honour. He had not perhaps crushed King Roger as completely as he had hoped, but he had surely dealt him a blow from which he would take long to recover. It was a pity about Pope Innocent. Although one of the purposes of the expedition had been to reinstall him in Rome, the city had been studiously bypassed and he was as far from the throne of St Peter as ever. But there: henceforth the Pope would have to fight his own battles.

Meanwhile the old Emperor could feel his life ebbing away. Though he marched with all the speed of which his dispirited army was capable, it was mid-November before he reached the foothills of the Alps. His companions implored him to winter there. The sickness was daily increasing its hold on him; it would be folly, they pointed out, to go any further so late in the year. But Lothair knew that he could not afford to wait. With all the determination of the dying, he pressed on; but at the little village of Breitenwang in the Tyrol his strength deserted him. He was carried to a poor peasant's hut; and there, on 3 December 1137, he died.

Just seven and a half weeks later, Anacletus followed him to the grave. St Bernard had already made contact with Roger of Sicily in an attempt to detach him from the Antipope; but it was Anacletus's death that effectively brought the schism to an end. A short-lived successor, the so-called Victor IV (1138), resigned after a few months, and Roger, freed now of the commitments that had cast such a blight on the first seven years of his reign, saw no point in continuing hostilities with the Holy See. He made public recognition of Innocent, and ordered all his subjects to do likewise. It is hard to see what more he could have done; but Innocent unaccountably refused a reconciliation, and at a Lateran Council on 8 April 1139 he pronounced a renewed sentence of excommunication on the King of Sicily, his sons and all those of his bishops whom Anacletus had consecrated. Then, still more unaccountably, he marched southwards from Rome with his old ally Prince Robert of Capua and perhaps a thousand knights. Half-hearted negotiations failed and gave way to open hostilities; and at the little town of Galluccio a Sicilian army suddenly attacked. Robert managed to escape, but Innocent was not so lucky. That evening, 22 July 1139, the Pope, his cardinals, his archives and his treasure were all in the hands of the King: the greatest humiliation suffered by the papacy since Robert Guiscard had annihilated the army of Leo IX at Civitate, eighty-six years before.

It was always a mistake for popes to meet Normans on the battlefield. Just as Leo had had to come to terms with his captors after Civitate, so now Innocent was forced to bow to the inevitable. On 25 July, at Mignano, he formally confirmed Roger in his Kingdom of Sicily, with the overlordship of all Italy south of the Garigliano river. He then said Mass, and left the church a free man. In the ensuing charter he managed to save a few shreds of the papal honour; but nothing could disguise the fact that, for him and his party, the treaty of Mignano spelt unconditional – or almost unconditional – surrender.

On 24 September 1143 Pope Innocent died in Rome. His long struggle with Anacletus had cost him dear. Even his allies had proved a mixed blessing. Lothair, once safely crowned, had showed him scant consideration, Henry the Proud still less. Bernard of Clairvaux had been loyal, but, deliberately or not, had seemed bent on stealing his thunder at every opportunity. Innocent's final triumph had been made possible only by the death of Anacletus; and almost at once it had been turned to dust by the rout at Galluccio. He had accepted this humiliation as gracefully as he could, and had made terms with the Sicilian King; but he had been ill repaid. Within a year Roger – emboldened by the years of schism when he had done what he liked and Anacletus had never dared take issue with him – was acting more arrogantly than ever, creating new dioceses, appointing new bishops, barring the Pope's envoys from entering his kingdom without his consent and even refusing to allow Latin churchmen in his dominions to obey papal summonses to Rome.

And even this was not all. For more than a century a movement towards republican self-government had been gathering momentum among the cities and towns of Italy. In Rome itself successive popes and the old aristocracy had done their best to save their city from the general contagion, but the recent schism had weakened their hold. Innocent in particular had never enjoyed general popularity. Coming from Trastevere, he had always been considered one degree less Roman than Anacletus, and he was known to be a good deal less generous. When, therefore, they learned that he had made a separate peace with their enemy to the south, the Romans seized the opportunity to denounce the temporal power of the Pope, revive the Senate on the Capitol and declare a republic. Innocent resisted as best he could, but he was an old man – probably well over seventy – and the effort was too much for him. A few weeks later he was dead.

He was buried in a huge porphyry sarcophagus from the Castel Sant'Angelo, which was believed to have formerly contained the bones of the Emperor Hadrian; but after a disastrous fire in the early fourteenth century his remains were transferred to the church of S. Maria in Trastevere, which he himself had rebuilt just before his death. There, immortalised in the great apse mosaic, he stares down at us from the conch, his church clutched in his hands, a strangely wistful expression in his sad, tired eyes.

CHAPTER XI

The English Pope

(1154–9)

The next ten years saw no fewer than four popes in Rome. The first, Celestine II (1143–4), detested King Roger and all he stood for and refused to ratify the Treaty of Mignano; it was a foolish policy, which he survived – just – long enough to regret. His representatives had been obliged to go cap in hand to Palermo before he died. Nor was his successor, Lucius II (1144–5), any more fortunate. During his brief pontificate the Roman commune restored the Senate as a working body, with powers to elect magistrats and even to strike its own coinage. Serious fighting broke out once again in Rome. This time Lucius unwisely decided to take the offensive, and while leading an armed attack on the Capitol was hit by a heavy stone. Mortally wounded, he was carried by the Frangipani to Gregory the Great's old monastery of S. Andrea on the Caelian; and there he died on 15 February 1145, after less than a year on the throne.

Eugenius III (1145–53) was elected on the same day to succeed him. His actual election, held on safe Frangipani territory, was smooth enough; but when he tried to proceed from the Lateran to St Peter's for his consecration he found that the commune had barred his way, and three days later he had fled the city. The speed of his flight surprised no one; indeed, the only surprising thing about Eugenius was that he should have been elected in the first place. A former monk of Clairvaux and disciple of St Bernard, he was a simple character, gentle and retiring – not at all, men thought, the material of which popes were made. Even Bernard himself, when he heard the news, made no secret of his disapproval, writing collectively to the entire Curia:

> May God forgive you what you have done! . . . What reason or counsel, when the Supreme Pontiff was dead, made you rush upon a mere rustic, lay hands on him in his refuge, wrest from his hands the axe, pick or hoe, and lift him to a throne?

To Eugenius himself he was equally outspoken: 'Thus does the finger of God raise up the poor out of the dust and lift up the beggar from the dunghill, that he may sit with princes and inherit the throne of glory.' It seems an unfortunate choice of metaphor, and it says much for the new Pope's gentleness and patience that he showed no resentment; but Bernard was after all his spiritual father, and in the months to come Eugenius was to need his old master as badly as he had ever needed him in his life – for he was now called upon to summon the Second Crusade.

It was made necessary by the fall of the Christian county of Edessa. Edessa (now the modern Turkish city of Urfa) was the first to be established of all the Crusader states of the Levant, dating from the year 1098 when Baldwin of Boulogne had left the main army of the First Crusade and struck off to the east to found a principality of his own on the banks of the Euphrates. He had not stayed there long – two years later he had succeeded his brother as King of Jerusalem – but Edessa had continued as a semi-independent Christian state until, on Christmas Eve 1144, it was conquered by an Arab army under Imad ed-Din Zengi, Atabeg of Mosul. The news of its fall horrified all Christendom. How, after less than half a century, had Cross once again given way to Crescent? Was this disaster not a clear manifestation of the wrath of God?

Although Edessa had fallen nearly eight weeks before the death of Pope Lucius, Eugenius had been more than six months on the throne before he was officially notified and began to consider the implications of a Crusade. The first question to be decided was that of the leadership. Among the princes of the West, he could see only one suitable candidate. Conrad, King of the Romans – he had not received his imperial coronation – was beset with his own troubles in Germany; King Stephen of England had had a civil war on his hands for six years already; Roger of Sicily was, for any number of reasons, out of the question. The only possible choice was Louis VII of France.

Louis asked for nothing better. He was one of Nature's pilgrims. Though still only twenty-four, he had about him an aura of joyless piety, which made him look and seem far older than his years – and which irritated to distraction his beautiful and high-spirited young wife Eleanor of Aquitaine. At Christmas 1145 he announced to his assembled vassals his determination to take the Cross. Their reaction was disappointing, but Louis had made up his mind. If he could not fill the hearts and minds of his vassals with crusading fire, he knew precisely who could. He sent for the Abbot of Clairvaux.

To Bernard, here was a cause after his own heart. Exhausted as he was, he responded to the call with that extraordinary fervour that had made him the dominant spiritual voice in all Christendom. Willingly he agreed to address the assembly that the King had summoned for the following Easter at Vézelay. At once the magic of his name began to do its work, and men and women from every corner of France poured into the little town. Since there were far too many to be packed into the cathedral, a great wooden platform was hastily erected on the hillside; there, on Palm Sunday morning, with the King at his side – displaying on his breast the cross that Pope Eugenius had sent him in token of his decision – Bernard made the speech of his life.

The text of his exhortation has not come down to us; we are told, however, that his voice rang out across the meadow 'like a celestial organ', and that as he spoke the crowd, silent at first, began to cry out for crosses of their own. Bundles of these, cut in rough cloth, had already been prepared for distribution; when the supply was exhausted, the Abbot flung off his own robe and began tearing it into strips to make more. Others followed his example, and he and his helpers were still stitching as night fell.

It was an astonishing achievement. No one else in Europe could have done it. And yet, as events were soon to tell, it were better had it not been done. The Second Crusade was to turn out an ignominious fiasco. First, the Crusaders decided to attack Damascus – the only Arab state in the whole Levant hostile to Zengi. As such, it could and should have been an invaluable ally to the Franks; by attacking it, they drove it straight into the arms of their enemy. Second, they pitched their camp along the eastern section of the walls, devoid alike of shade and water. Third, they all lost their nerve. On 28 July 1148, just five days after the opening of the campaign, King Louis gave the order for retreat.

There is no part of the Syrian Desert more shattering to the spirit than that dark-grey, featureless expanse of sand and basalt that lies between Damascus and Tiberias. Withdrawing across it in the height of the Arabian summer, the remorseless sun and scorching desert wind full in their faces, harried incessantly by mounted Arab archers and leaving in their wake a stinking trail of dead men and horses, the Crusaders must have felt despair heavy upon them. Their losses, in both men and material, had been immense. Worst of all was the shame. Having travelled for the best part of a year, often in conditions of mortal danger, and having suffered agonies of thirst, hunger and sickness and the bitterest extremes of heat and cold, this once-glorious army that had purported to enshrine all the ideals of the Christian West had given up the whole thing after just four days, having regained not one inch of Muslim territory. It was the ultimate humiliation – which neither they nor their enemies would forget.

Pope Eugenius, meanwhile, had his own problems to contend with. The most troubling of these was the political situation in Rome, where the republican movement – which had already claimed the life of his predecessor – was now gaining yet further strength, thanks to the teachings of an Augustinian monk from Lombardy whose influence in the city was growing almost daily.

His name was Arnold of Brescia. In his youth he had studied in the schools of Paris – probably under Abelard at Notre-Dame – where he had been thoroughly imbued with the new scholasticism, essentially a movement away from the old mystical approach to spiritual matters towards a spirit of logical, rational enquiry. To the medieval papacy, radical ideas of this sort would have seemed quite subversive enough; but Arnold combined with them a still more unwelcome feature: a passionate hatred for the temporal power of the Church. For him the State was, and must always be, supreme; the civil law, based on the laws of ancient Rome, must prevail over the canon; the Pope should divest himself of all worldly pomp, renounce his powers and privileges and revert to the poverty and simplicity of the early Fathers. Only thus could the Church re-establish contact with the humble masses among its flock. As John of Salisbury wrote:

> Arnold himself was frequently to be heard on the Capitol and in various assemblies of the people. He had already publicly denounced the Cardinals, maintaining that their College, beset as it was with pride, avarice, hypocrisy and shame, was not the Church of God but a house of commerce and a den of thieves ... Even the Pope himself was other than what he professed: rather than an apostolic shepherd of souls, he was a man of blood who maintained his authority by fire and sword, a tormentor of churches and oppressor of the innocent whose only actions were for the gratification of his lust and for the emptying of other men's coffers in order that his own might be filled.

Naturally, the papacy had fought back. Naturally, too, it had used the Abbot of Clairvaux as its champion. In consequence, as early as 1140 Arnold had been condemned, together with his old master Abelard, at the Council of Sens and had been expelled from France. By 1146, however, he was back in Rome; and the Roman Senate, fired by his blazing piety and recognising in his ideas the spiritual counterpart of its own republican aspirations, had welcomed him with open arms. Presumably as a sop to republican feeling, Eugenius had then released Arnold from his excommunication and ordered him to lead a life of penitence; but the action had done little to improve the Pope's popularity. In the spring of 1147, with his cardinals and Curia, he had travelled to France to give his blessing to the preparations for the coming Crusade. There and in Germany he had been received with every possible honour; only in Rome, it seemed, was he reviled. Back in Italy the following year and finding Arnold of Brescia as obstreperous as ever, he renewed the sentence of excommunication, but did not for the moment attempt a return to the city.

Queen Eleanor had accompanied her husband Louis VII on the Crusade. It had not improved their marriage. Eleanor had made no secret of the fact that her lugubrious husband bored her to distraction, and had indeed developed a relationship with her uncle, Prince Raymond of Antioch, which was generally suspected of going considerably beyond the avuncular. When she and Louis landed in Italy on their return from the Levant they were barely on speaking terms. They called on Pope Eugenius in Tusculum, the nearest town to Rome in which he could safely install himself. Eugenius was a gentle, kind-hearted man who hated to see people unhappy; and the sight of the royal pair, oppressed by the double failure of the Crusade and of their marriage, caused him deep personal distress. John of Salisbury, who was employed in the papal Curia at the time, has left us a curiously touching account of the Pope's attempts at a reconciliation:

He commanded, under pain of anathema, that no word should be spoken against their marriage and that it should not be dissolved under any pretext whatever. This ruling plainly delighted the King, for he loved the Queen passionately, in an almost childish way. The Pope made them sleep in the same bed, which he had decked with priceless hangings of his own; and daily during their brief visit he strove by friendly converse to restore the love between them. He heaped gifts upon them; and when the time came for their departure he could not hold back his tears.

Those tears were perhaps made all the more copious by the knowledge that his efforts had been in vain. Had Eugenius known Eleanor better, he would have seen from the start that her mind was made up; for the time being, however, she was prepared to keep up appearances, accompanying her husband to Rome, where they were cordially received by the Senate and where Louis prostrated himself as usual at all the principal shrines; and so back across the Alps to Paris. It was to be another two and a half years before her marriage was finally dissolved – St Bernard having persuaded Eugenius to modify his earlier attitude – on grounds of consanguinity; but she was still young and only on the threshold of that astonishing career in which, as wife of one of England's greatest kings and mother of two of its worst, she was to influence the course of European history for more than half a century.

In December 1149, with the aid of an escort of Sicilian troops, Pope Eugenius at last returned to Rome, but it was no use: the prevailing atmosphere of open hostility soon persuaded him to leave again. He then entered into correspondence with King Conrad. He knew that the commune had suggested that Conrad should come to Rome and take it over as the capital of a new-style Roman Empire, so it could hardly refuse if the King were to come to the city for his coronation. Conrad, however, never did. He died in February 1152, before he could take up the Pope's invitation. Eugenius had no choice but to transfer his attentions to Conrad's nephew and heir, Frederick of Hohenstaufen, known as Barbarossa.

Now about thirty-two, Frederick seemed to his German contemporaries the very nonpareil of Teutonic chivalry. Tall and broad-shouldered, attractive rather than handsome, he had eyes that twinkled so brightly under his thick mop of reddish-brown hair that, according to one chronicler, he always seemed on the point of laughter. But beneath that easy-going exterior lurked a will of steel, an utter dedication to a single objective. He never forgot that he was the successor of Charlemagne and of Otto the Great, and made no secret of his determination to restore the Empire to its former glory.

Frederick responded at once to the Pope, proposing a treaty by which to regularise their future relations; and the resulting agreement was duly signed at Constance. By its terms Frederick promised to subject the Romans to papal control, while Eugenius undertook to crown him in Rome at his convenience – but once again the ceremony never took place as planned. This time it was Eugenius who died, in July 1153 at Tivoli. Though never a great Pope, he had revealed a firmness of character that few had suspected at the time of his election. Like so many of his predecessors, he had been forced to spend money freely to buy support among the Romans, yet he had always remained personally incorruptible; his gentleness and unassuming ways had earned him love and respect of a kind that cannot be bought for gold. Until the day of his death he continued to wear, under his pontifical robes, the coarse white habit of a Cistercian monk. His successor, the immensely aged Anastasius IV (1153–4), survived his election by only eighteen months, and was followed by a man who was to prove to Frederick a far more formidable antagonist: the Englishman Nicholas Breakspear, who took the title of Hadrian IV (1154–9).

When he was consecrated on 4 December 1154, Hadrian was about fifty-five. He had grown up in St Albans, but, having for some reason been refused admission into the local monastery, while still little more than a boy had taken himself off to France. There he had joined the canons regular of St Rufus in Avignon, of whose house he eventually became abbot, gaining a reputation as a formidably strict disciplinarian. Back in Rome, thanks to his eloquence and his ability – and, perhaps, to his outstanding good looks – he had been spotted by Pope Eugenius. Fortunately for him, the Pope was a convinced Anglophile; he once told John of Salisbury that he found the English admirably fitted to perform any task they turned their hand to, and thus to be preferred to all other races – except, he added, when frivolity got the better of them. Frivolity, however, does not seem to have been one of Nicholas's failings. In 1152 he had been sent as Papal Legate to Norway, there to reorganise and reform the Church throughout Scandinavia. Two years later he had returned, his mission accomplished with such distinction that, on Anastasius's death the following December, the energetic, forceful Englishman was unanimously elected to succeed him.

There could have been no wiser choice, for energy and force were desperately needed. At the time of Hadrian's accession, Frederick Barbarossa had already crossed the Alps on his first Italian campaign. On his arrival in Rome he would be sure to demand his imperial coronation; but even if he were to receive it, there was little possibility that the Pope would ever be able to trust him as an ally. Indeed, with his known absolutist views, Frederick was unlikely to prove anything but a constant anxiety to the Holy See. Still more alarming was the situation in Rome itself, where Arnold of Brescia was now, to all intents and purposes, master of the city. Pope Eugenius, an ascetic who may perhaps have harboured some secret sympathy for Arnold, had allowed him to return; Pope Anastasius had turned a deaf ear to his thunderings. But Pope Hadrian was a man of a very different stamp. When, on his accession, he found himself confined by Arnold's supporters to St Peter's and the Leonine City, he had at first merely ordered the agitator to leave Rome; but when, predictably, Arnold took no notice and indeed allowed his followers to attack the venerable Cardinal Guido of S. Pudenziana as he was walking down the Via Sacra on his way to the Vatican, the Pope played his trump card. Early in 1155, for the first time in the history of Christendom, the entire city of Rome was laid under an interdict.

It was an act of breathtaking courage. A foreigner, who had been Pope only a few weeks and was able to rely on little or no popular support, had dared by a single decree to close all the churches of Rome. Exceptions were made for the baptism of infants and the absolution of the dying; otherwise all sacraments and ceremonies alike were forbidden. No Masses could be said, no marriages solemnised; dead bodies might not even be buried in consecrated ground. In the days when religion still constituted an integral part of every man's life, the effect of such a moral blockade was immeasurable. Besides, Easter was approaching. The prospect of the greatest feast of the Christian year passing uncelebrated was bleak enough; but without the annual influx of pilgrims, one of the principal sources of the city's revenue, it was bleaker still. For a little while the people held out; but by the Wednesday of Holy Week they could bear it no longer and marched on the Capitol. The Senators saw that they were beaten. Arnold and his followers were expelled; the interdict was lifted; the church bells once again pealed out their message; and on Sunday, as he had always intended to do, Pope Hadrian IV celebrated Easter at the Lateran.

Frederick Barbarossa, meanwhile, kept the feast at Pavia, where on the same day he was crowned with the traditional Iron Crown of Lombardy. His subsequent descent through Tuscany was so fast that it seemed to the Roman Curia positively threatening. Henry IV's treatment of Gregory VII seventy years before had not been forgotten, and several of the older cardinals could still remember how in 1111 Henry V had laid hands on Pope Paschal in St Peter's itself. In all the recent reports now circulating about the new King of the Romans, there was nothing to suggest that he would not be fully capable of similar conduct. No wonder the Curia began to feel alarm.

Hurriedly Hadrian sent two of his cardinals north to the imperial camp. They found it at S. Quirico near Siena, and were cordially received. Then, as an earnest of his goodwill, they asked Frederick for help in laying hands on Arnold of Brescia, who had taken refuge with some local barons. Frederick readily obliged; he detested Arnold's radical views almost as much as the Pope himself and welcomed this new opportunity to show his power. Sending a body of troops to the castle, he had one of the barons seized and held as a hostage until Arnold himself should be delivered. The fugitive was immediately given up to the papal authorities; and the cardinals, reassured, applied themselves to their next task: making arrangements for the first, critical interview between Pope and King.

The meeting was fixed for 9 June 1155 at Campo Grosso, near Sutri. It began auspiciously enough with Hadrian, escorted by a great company of German barons sent forward by Frederick to greet him, riding in solemn procession to the imperial camp. But now trouble began. At this point, according to custom, the King should have advanced to lead in the Pope's horse by the bridle and to hold the stirrup while its rider dismounted; he did not do so. For a moment Hadrian seemed to hesitate. Then, dismounting by himself, he walked slowly across to the throne that had been prepared for him and sat down. Now at last Frederick stepped forward, kissed the Pope's feet and rose to receive the traditional kiss of peace in return; but this time it was Hadrian who held back. The King, he pointed out, had denied him a service that his predecessors had always rendered to the Supreme Pontiff. Until this omission was rectified, there could be no kiss of peace.

Frederick objected that it was no part of his duty to act as a papal groom; but Hadrian would not be shaken. He knew that what appeared on the surface to be a minor point of protocol concealed in reality something infinitely more important – a public act of defiance that struck at the very root of the relationship between Empire and papacy. Suddenly and surprisingly, Frederick gave in. He ordered his camp to be moved a little further south; and there, on the morning of 11 June, the events of two days before were restaged. The King advanced to meet the Pope, led in his horse by the bridle and then, firmly holding the stirrup, helped him to dismount. Once again Hadrian settled himself on his throne; the kiss of peace was duly bestowed; and conversations began.

Hadrian and Frederick would never entirely trust one another; but the ensuing discussions seem to have been amicable enough. The terms agreed at Constance were confirmed. Neither party would enter into separate negotiations with Byzantium, Sicily or the Roman Senate. Frederick would defend all papal interests, while in return Hadrian would excommunicate all enemies of the Empire who after three warnings persisted in their opposition. The two then rode on together towards Rome.

From the side of the papacy there was no longer any objection to the imperial coronation. This ceremony, however, had not been performed since the establishment of the Roman commune; how would Rome itself now greet its Emperor-to-be? It was an open question, and Frederick's recent move against Arnold of Brescia had made it more problematical still. But he and Hadrian were not long kept in suspense. While they were still some distance from the city they were met by a deputation sent out by the Senate to greet them and to spell out the conditions on which they would be received. Their spokesman began with a bombastic and patronising speech, suggesting that Rome alone had made the Empire what it was, and that the Emperor would therefore do well to consider his moral obligations to the city – obligations that apparently included a sworn guarantee of its future liberty and the *ex gratia* payment of 5,000 pounds of gold.

The spokesman was still in full spate when Frederick interrupted him to point out that all Rome's ancient glory and traditions had now passed, with the Empire itself, to Germany. He had come only to claim what was rightfully his. He would naturally defend Rome as necessary, but he saw no need for any formal guarantees. As for gifts of money, he would bestow them when and where he pleased. His quiet assurance took the delegates off-guard. Stammering that they must return to the capital for instructions, they took their leave. As soon as they were gone, Pope and King held an urgent consultation. Hadrian, with his experience of the Senate, had no doubt that trouble was to be expected. He advised the immediate despatch of a body of troops to occupy the Leonine City by night. Even with this precaution, he pointed out, the danger would not be entirely averted. If they wanted to avoid bloodshed, he and Frederick would have to move quickly.

The date was Friday, 17 June 1155. Such was the urgency of the situation that Hadrian decided not even to wait for the following Sunday, as he would normally have done. Instead, at dawn on Saturday, Frederick rode down from Monte Mario and entered the Leonine City, already occupied by his troops. The Pope, who had arrived an hour or two previously, was awaiting him on the steps of St Peter's. They entered the basilica together, a throng of German knights following behind. Hadrian himself celebrated Mass; and there, over the tomb of the Apostle, he hurriedly girded the sword of St Peter to Frederick's side and laid the imperial crown on his head. As soon as the ceremony was done, the Emperor – still wearing the crown – rode back to his camp outside the walls, his huge retinue following on foot. The Pope meanwhile took refuge in the Vatican to await developments.

It was still only nine o'clock in the morning; and the Senate was assembling on the Capitol to decide how best to prevent the coronation when the news arrived that it had already taken place. Furious to find themselves outwitted and outmanoeuvred, they sprang to arms; soon one mob was pressing across the Ponte Sant'Angelo into the Leonine City, while another – having crossed the river further downstream at the Tiber Island – advanced northwards through Trastevere. The day was growing hotter. The Germans, tired by their march through the night and the excitement of the past few hours, wanted to sleep and to celebrate. Instead, they were ordered to prepare at once for battle. For the second time that day Frederick entered Rome, but he wore his coronation robes no longer. This time he had his armour on.

All afternoon and evening the fighting continued; night had fallen before the imperial troops had driven the last of the insurgents back across the bridges. Losses had been heavy on both sides. Bishop Otto of Freising, who was probably an eyewitness, reports that among the Romans almost 1,000 were slain or drowned in the Tiber, and another 600 taken captive. The Senate had paid a high price for its arrogance. But the Emperor, too, had bought his crown dearly. His victory had not even gained him entrance into the ancient city, for the sun rose the next morning to show the Tiber bridges blocked and the gates barricaded. Neither he nor his army was prepared for a siege; the heat of the Roman summer, which for a century and a half had consistently undermined the morale of successive invading armies, was once again beginning to take its toll, with outbreaks of malaria and dysentery among his men. The only sensible course was to withdraw and

– since the Vatican was clearly no longer safe for the papacy – to take Pope and Curia with him. On 19 June he struck camp again and led his army up into the Sabine Hills. A month later he was heading back to Germany, leaving Hadrian powerless at Tivoli.

The story of the coronation of Frederick Barbarossa is almost told, but not quite. Apart from the Emperor who was crowned and the Pope who crowned him, there is a third character who, although he was not in Rome on that fateful day, influenced the course of events as much as either of them. No record exists to tell us exactly when or where Arnold of Brescia suffered his execution. We know only the manner in which he met his death. Condemned by a Church tribunal on charges of heresy and rebellion, he remained firm to the end and walked calmly to the scaffold without a trace of fear; and as he knelt to make his last confession, we read that the executioners themselves could not restrain their tears. They hanged him nonetheless; then they cut him down and burned the body. Finally, in order to ensure that no relics should be left for veneration by the people, they threw his ashes into the Tiber. For a martyr, misguided or not, there could be no greater honour.

Pope Hadrian, on the other hand, felt betrayed. His southern frontier was under attack from King William of Sicily[1], and he had hoped that in accordance with the terms agreed at Constance the newly crowned Emperor would march against him. Frederick himself would have been perfectly ready to do so, if only he could have carried his knights with him; but they were determined to leave the south and return at once to Germany, and he knew that he could not press them too far.

Friendless and alone, unable to return to Rome since Frederick's coronation, Hadrian spent the winter with his Curia at Benevento. As far as he was concerned the Emperor, his one hope, had shown himself to have feet of clay. Meanwhile the situation in the south was fast deteriorating. King William, having overcome opposition from the Byzantines and his own rebel subjects, was on the march towards the papal frontier. As he approached, Hadrian sent most of his cardinals away to Campania – mainly for their greater safety, but also, perhaps, for another reason. He knew that he would now have to come to terms with William. Diehard cardinals had scuppered too many potential

---

[1] William I (the Bad), King of Sicily, had succeeded his father, Roger II, in 1154.

agreements in the past; if he were to save anything from a coming disaster, he would need the utmost freedom to negotiate.

As soon as the vanguard of the Sicilian army appeared over the hills, the Pope sent his Chancellor, Roland of Siena, and two other cardinals who had remained with him to greet the King and to bid him, in the name of St Peter, to cease from further hostilities. They were received with due courtesy, and formal talks began at Benevento. The going was not easy. The Sicilians were in a position of strength and drove a hard bargain, but the papal side fought every inch of the way. It was not until 18 June 1156 that agreement was finally reached. William gained papal recognition over a far larger body of territory than had ever been granted before, on payment of an annual tribute. In return he acknowledged the Pope's feudal suzerainty; but there could be no doubt as to which party profited the most. We have only to look at the language in which the papal document of acceptance was drafted:

> William, glorious King of Sicily and dearest son in Christ, most brilliant in wealth and achievement among all the kings and eminent men of the age, the glory of whose name is borne to the uttermost limits of the earth by the firmness of your justice, the peace which you have restored to your subjects, and the fear which your great deeds have instilled into the hearts of all the enemies of Christ's name.

Even when allowance is made for the traditional literary hyperbole of the time, it is hard to imagine Hadrian putting his signature to such a document without a wince of humiliation. He had been Pope just eighteen months, but already he had learned the bitterness of desertion, betrayal and exile; and even his broad shoulders were beginning to bow. He appears now in a very different light from that in which we saw him when he placed Rome under an interdict or pitted his will against that of Frederick Barbarossa just twelve short months before. Perhaps it was John of Salisbury who best summed up his mood:

> I call on the Lord Hadrian to witness that no one is more miserable than the Roman Pontiff, nor is any condition more wretched than his ... He maintains that the papal throne is studded with thorns, that his mantle bristles with needles so sharp that it oppresses and weighs down the broadest shoulders ... and that had he not feared to go against the will of God he would never have left his native England.

* * *

The fury of Frederick Barbarossa when he heard of the Benevento agreement can well be imagined. Had not Hadrian given him a personal undertaking not to enter into any private communications with the King of Sicily? Had he not now actually signed a treaty of peace and friendship – a treaty, moreover, by which he not only recognised William's claim to a spurious crown but, in ecclesiastical affairs, granted him privileges more far-reaching even than those enjoyed by the Emperor himself? By what right did Hadrian so graciously confer imperial territories on others? Was there no limit to papal arrogance?

It was not long before his worst suspicions were confirmed. In October 1157 he held an imperial Diet at Besançon. Ambassadors converged on the town from all sides: from France and Italy, from Spain and England – and, of course, from the Pope. The effect of all Frederick's arrangements was, however, slightly spoilt when, in the presence of the assembled company, the Papal Legates read out the letter they had brought with them from their master. Instead of the customary greetings and congratulations, the Pope had chosen this of all moments to deliver himself of a strongly worded complaint. The aged Archbishop of Lund, while travelling through imperial territory, had been set upon by bandits, robbed of all he possessed and held to ransom. Such an outrage was serious enough in itself; but it was aggravated by the fact that although the Emperor had been furnished with full details of the case, he appeared as yet to have taken no steps to bring to justice those responsible. Turning to more general topics, Hadrian recalled his past favours to the Emperor – reminding him in particular of his coronation at papal hands and adding, perhaps a trifle patronisingly, that he hoped at some future date to bestow still further benefices upon him.

Whether the Pope was deliberately intending to assert his feudal overlordship we shall never know. Unfortunately the two words he used, *conferre* and *beneficia*, were both technical terms used in describing the grant of a fief by a suzerain to his vassal. This was more than Frederick could bear. If the letter implied, as it appeared to, that he held the Holy Roman Empire by courtesy of the Pope, in the same way as any petty baron might hold a couple of fields in the Campagna, there could be no further dealings between them. The assembled German princes shared his indignation; and when Cardinal Roland, the Papal Chancellor, blandly replied by enquiring from whom Frederick held the Empire if not from the Pope, there was general uproar. Otto of Wittelsbach, Count Palatine of Bavaria, rushed forward, his hand on his sword; only the rapid intervention of the Emperor himself prevented an incident compared with which the misfortunes of the Archbishop of Lund would have seemed trivial indeed.

When Hadrian heard what had happened he wrote Frederick another letter, couched this time in rather more soothing terms, protesting that his words had been misinterpreted; and the Emperor accepted his explanation. It is unlikely that he really believed it, but he had no wish for an open breach with the papacy. Nonetheless, the *bagarre* at Besançon, as anyone could have seen, was merely a symptom of a far deeper rift between Pope and Emperor, one that no amount of diplomatic drafting could ever hope to bridge. The days when it had been realistic to speak of the two swords of Christendom were gone – gone since Gregory VII and Henry IV had hurled depositions and anathemas at each other nearly a hundred years before. Never since then had their respective successors been able to look upon themselves as two different sides of the same coin. Each must now claim the supremacy, and defend it as necessary against the other. When this involved the confrontation of characters as strong as those of Hadrian and Frederick, flashpoint could never be far off. Yet the root of the trouble lay less in their personalities than in the institutions they represented. While the two of them lived, relations between them – exacerbated by a host of petty slights, both real and imagined – became even more strained; though it was only after their deaths that the conflict was to emerge into open war.

The Treaty of Benevento proved to be of immeasurably greater significance than either of its signatories could have known at the time. For the papacy it inaugurated a new political approach to European problems – one that it was to follow, to its own considerable advantage, for the next twenty years. Hadrian himself was gradually brought to accept what he must always have suspected: that the Emperor was not so much a friend with whom he might occasionally quarrel as an enemy with whom, somehow, he must live. His concordat with King William gave him a powerful new ally and enabled him to adopt a firmer attitude in his dealings with Frederick than could ever otherwise have been possible – as the Besançon letter bears witness.

In papal circles, so radical a change in policy was bound to meet with opposition at first. Many leading members of the Curia still clung to their imperialist, anti-Sicilian opinions; and the news of the terms agreed had caused almost as much consternation in the Sacred College as in the imperial court. Gradually, however, opinion swung round in

William's favour. One reason was Barbarossa's arrogance, as shown at Besançon and confirmed by several other incidents before and since. Besides, the Sicilian alliance was now a fait accompli; it was useless to oppose it any longer. William, for his part, seemed sincere enough. On the Pope's recommendation, he had made his peace with Constantinople. He was rich, he was powerful; and, as several of Their Eminences could – if they wished – have testified, he was also generous.

And now Frederick Barbarossa set out to sack and ravage the Lombard cities, and a great wave of revulsion against the Empire swept down through Italy. With it, too, was an element of terror: when the Emperor had finished with Lombardy, what was to prevent him from continuing to Tuscany, Umbria, and even Rome itself? Only an alliance forged between an English pope and a Norman king. In the spring of 1159 came the first great counter-thrust against Frederick that can be directly ascribed to papal–Sicilian instigation. Milan suddenly threw off the imperial authority, and for the next three years the Milanese stoutly defied all the Emperor's efforts to bring them to heel. The following August representatives of Milan, Crema, Piacenza and Brescia met the Pope at Anagni; and there, in the presence of envoys from King William, was sworn the initial pact that was to become the nucleus of the great Lombard League. The towns promised that they would have no dealings with the common enemy without papal consent, while the Pope undertook to excommunicate the Emperor after the usual period of forty days. Finally it was agreed by the assembled cardinals that on Hadrian's death his successor should be elected only from those present at the conference.

It was perhaps already obvious that the Pope had not long to live. While still at Anagni he was stricken by a sudden angina, from which he never recovered. He died on the evening of 1 September 1159. His body was carried to Rome, and was laid in the undistinguished third-century sarcophagus in which it still rests and which can still be seen in the crypt of St Peter's. During the course of the demolition of the old basilica in 1607 it was opened; and the body of the only English pope was found entire, dressed in a chasuble of dark-coloured silk. It was described as being 'that of an undersized man, wearing Turkish slippers on his feet and, on his hand, a large emerald'.

Hadrian's pontificate is hard to assess. He certainly towers over the string of mediocrities who occupied the throne of St Peter during the first half of the century, just as he himself is overshadowed by his magnificent successor. He left the papacy stronger and more generally respected than he found it, although much of this success was due to its identification with the Lombard League; but he failed utterly to subdue the Roman Senate. He was Pope for fewer than five years; but those years were hard and of vital importance to the papacy, and the strain told on him. Before long his health had begun to fail, and with it his morale. He died embittered and disappointed – as all too many of his predecessors had died before him.

CHAPTER XII

Alexander III and Frederick Barbarossa

(1159–98)

On 5 September 1159, the day after the body of Pope Hadrian had been laid to rest in St Peter's, about thirty cardinals assembled in conclave behind the high altar of the basilica.[1] Two days later all but three of them had cast their votes for the former Chancellor, Cardinal Roland of Siena, who was therefore declared to have been elected. One of the three, however, was the violently pro-imperialist Cardinal Octavian of S. Cecilia; and just as the scarlet mantle of the papacy was brought forward and Roland, after the customary display of reluctance, bent his head to receive it, Octavian dived at him, snatched the mantle and tried to don it himself. A scuffle followed, during which he lost it again; but his chaplain instantly produced another – presumably brought along for just such an eventuality – which Octavian this time managed to put on, unfortunately back to front, before anyone could stop him.

There followed a scene of scarcely believable confusion. Wrenching himself free from the furious supporters of Roland, who were trying to tear the mantle forcibly from his back, Octavian – whose frantic efforts to turn it the right way round had only resulted in getting the fringes tangled round his neck – made a dash for the papal throne, sat on it and proclaimed himself Pope Victor IV.[2] He then charged off through St Peter's until he found a group of minor clergy, whom he ordered to give him their acclamation – which, seeing the doors suddenly burst open and a band of armed cut-throats swarming into the basilica, they hastily did. For the time being at least, the opposition was silenced; Roland and his adherents slipped out while they could and took refuge in St Peter's tower, a fortified corner of the

---

[1] By the end of the conclave there may have been only twenty-nine; according to Arnulf of Lisieux, Bishop Imarus of Tusculum – a renowned epicure – left early because he refused to miss his dinner.

[2] Oddly enough, it was the second time that this title had been chosen by an antipope. See Chapter X, p.129.

Vatican. Meanwhile, with the cut-throats looking on, Octavian was enthroned a little more formally than on the previous occasion and escorted in triumph to the Lateran – having been at some pains, we are told, to adjust his dress before leaving.

However undignified in its execution, the coup could now be seen to have been thoroughly and efficiently planned in advance – and on a scale which left no doubt that the Empire must have been actively implicated. Octavian himself had long been notorious as an imperial sympathiser and his election was immediately recognised by Frederick's two ambassadors in Rome, who at the same time declared a vigorous war on Roland. Once again they opened their coffers, and German gold flowed freely into the purses and pockets of all those Romans (nobles, senators, bourgeoisie or rabble) who would openly proclaim their allegiance to Victor IV. Meanwhile Roland and his faithful cardinals remained blockaded in St Peter's tower.

But almost at once Octavian – or Victor, as we must now call him – saw his support begin to dwindle. The story of his behaviour at the election was by now common knowledge in the city and, we may be sure, had lost nothing in the telling. Everywhere the Romans were turning towards Roland as their lawfully elected Pope; a mob had formed around St Peter's tower and was now angrily clamouring for his release. In the street, Victor was hooted at and reviled; lines of doggerel were chanted mockingly at him as he passed. On the night of 16 September he could bear it no longer and fled from Rome; and the following day the rightful pontiff was led back into the capital amid general rejoicing.

But Roland knew that he could not stay. The imperial ambassadors were still in Rome, and still had limitless money to spend. Victor's family, too, the Crescentii, remained among the richest in the city. Pausing only to assemble an appropriate retinue, on 20 September the Pope travelled south to Ninfa, which was then under the sway of his friends the Frangipani; and there, in the church of S. Maria Maggiore, he at last received formal consecration as Alexander III (1159–81). One of his first acts, predictably, was to excommunicate the Antipope, who soon afterwards (and equally predictably) excommunicated him in return. For the second time in thirty years the Church of Rome was in schism.

Had Frederick Barbarossa bowed to the inevitable and accepted Alexander as the rightful Pope that he indubitably was, there is no reason why the two should not have reached some accommodation. Instead, at the Council of Pavia in February 1160, the Emperor formally recognised the ridiculous Victor, thereby forcing Alexander – whose claim was soon accepted by all the other rulers of Europe – into even closer alliance with William of Sicily and saddling himself with a new series of vain and useless obligations which were to cripple him politically for the best part of twenty years. The Pope excommunicated Frederick in March (after Pavia he had little choice) and absolved all imperial subjects from their allegiance, but he was still unable to return to Rome. For nearly two years he divided his time between Terracina and Anagni, two papal cities conveniently close to the Sicilian kingdom, to which he looked both for his physical protection and for the financial subsidies he so desperately needed. Then, in the last days of 1161, he boarded a Sicilian ship for France.

For the next three and a half years he was to live in exile, mostly at Sens, working to form a great European League comprising England, France, Sicily, Hungary, Venice, the Lombard towns and Byzantium, against Frederick Barbarossa. He failed, as he was bound to fail. Henry II of England in particular he found impossible to trust. In the early days of the schism Henry had been a firm friend; as early as 1160 Bishop Arnulf of Lisieux had reported that while the King 'received all Alexander's communications with respect, he would not so much as touch Octavian's letters with his hands, but would take hold of them with a piece of stick and throw them behind his back as far as he could'. But in 1163 Henry's difficulties with Thomas Becket had begun, and the following year his promulgation of the Constitutions of Clarendon – deliberately designed to strengthen his hold over the English Church at the expense of the Pope – had caused a distinct chill in Anglo-papal relations.

But Alexander's disappointment at his diplomatic failure must have been forgotten when, early in 1165, he received an invitation from the Roman Senate to return to the city. The Antipope Victor, who had also been forced to spend his last years in exile, had died the year before in pain and poverty at Lucca, where he had been keeping himself alive on the proceeds of not very successful brigandage and where the local hierarchy would not even allow him burial within the walls. Frederick, stubborn as ever, had immediately given his blessing to the 'election', by his two tame schismatic cardinals, of a successor under the name of Paschal III (1164–8); but the action had earned him and his new antipope nothing but scorn, and it may well have been the ensuing wave of resentment and disgust at the absurdity of the schism and the pig-headedness of the Emperor that had at last brought the Romans to their senses. Besides, the pilgrim trade had dried up. Without a pope, medieval Rome lost its *raison d'être*.

For all that, the homecoming was not an easy one. Frederick did everything he could to prevent it, even hiring pirates to waylay the papal convoy on the high seas. But Alexander took a roundabout route and landed, in September 1165, at Messina. Two months later he reached Rome, where, escorted by senators, nobles, clergy and people bearing olive branches in their hands, he rode in state to the Lateran.

Early in 1167 Frederick Barbarossa led his army over the Alps and across the plain of Lombardy; he then split it into two parts. The smaller, under the Archbishop of Cologne, Rainald of Dassel – who was also imperial Chancellor and the Emperor's right hand – and another warlike ecclesiastic, Archbishop Christian of Mainz, was to march on Rome, enforcing the imperial authority as they went, and open up a safe road for the Antipope Paschal, still sitting nervously in Tuscany. Frederick himself, with the bulk of his army, pressed on across the peninsula towards Ancona, the nucleus of Byzantine influence in Italy, to which he laid siege. The inhabitants put up a spirited resistance. Their defences were strong and in good order, and they were determined not to be deprived of their association with the Empire of the East, which brought them considerable profit. Luck, too, was on their side. First, the Emperor was diverted by the appearance down the coast of a Sicilian force; soon after his return he received news which caused him to raise the siege altogether and leave at once for Rome. The Anconitans were saved.

The Romans, on the other hand, were as good as lost. On Whit Monday, 29 May, just outside Tusculum, their large but undisciplined army had attacked the Germans and Tusculans under Christian of Mainz and, though outnumbering them many times over, had been utterly shattered. Imperial messengers had sped to Frederick with the news. Rome, they reported, was still holding out, but – failing massive reinforcements – it could not last long; still less could it hope to resist a new German attack at full strength. The Emperor was jubilant. With Rome ripe for the plucking, Ancona could wait. His arrival in Rome sealed the fate of the Leonine City. A single savage onslaught smashed the gates; the Germans poured in, only to find an unsuspected inner fortress: St Peter's itself, ringed with strongpoints and hastily dug trenches. For eight more days it held out; it was only when the besiegers set fire to the forecourt, destroying the great portico so lovingly restored by Innocent II and finally hacking down the huge portals of the basilica itself, that the defending garrison surrendered. Never had there been such desecration of the holiest shrine in Europe. Even in the ninth century the Saracen pirates had contented themselves with tearing the silver panels from the doors; they had never penetrated the building. This time, according to a contemporary – Otto of St Blaise – they left the marble pavements of the nave strewn with dead and dying, the high altar itself stained with blood. And this time the outrage was the work not of infidel barbarians, but of the Emperor of western Christendom.

St Peter's fell on 29 July 1167. The following day, at that same high altar, the Antipope Paschal celebrated Mass and then invested Frederick – whom Pope Hadrian had crowned twelve years before – with the golden circlet of the Roman *Patricius*: a deliberate gesture of defiance to the Senate and people of Rome. Two days later still he officiated at the imperial coronation of the Empress Beatrice, her husband standing at her side. Pope Alexander had no alternative; disguised as a simple pilgrim, he slipped out of the city and made his way to the coast, where he was discovered – fortunately by friends – three days later, sitting on the beach and waiting for a ship. He was rescued and taken to safety in Benevento.

Frederick's triumph in Rome marked the summit of his career. He had brought the Romans to their knees, imposing on them terms which, though moderate enough, were calculated to ensure their docility in the future. He had placed his own pope on the throne of St Peter. Northern Italy he had already subdued; and now, with his strength still undiminished, he was ready to mop up the Kingdom of Sicily. Poor Frederick – how could he possibly have foreseen the catastrophe that was so soon to overtake him, one that in less than a single week was to destroy his proud army in a way that no earthly foe could ever have matched? On that memorable 1 August the skies had been clear and the sun had blazed down on his triumph. Then, on the 2nd, a huge black cloud suddenly obscured the valley beneath Monte Mario. Heavy rain began to fall, followed by a still and oppressive heat. On the 3rd came pestilence. It struck the imperial camp with an unparalleled swiftness and force; and where it struck, more often than not it killed. Within a matter of days it was no longer possible to bury all the dead; and the rising piles of corpses, swollen and putrefying in the merciless heat of a Roman August, made their own grim contribution to the sickness and the pervading horror. Frederick, seeing the flower of his army dead or dying around him, had no choice but to strike camp; and by the second week of August he and his silent, spectral procession were dragging themselves homeward through Tuscany.

And even now the nightmare was not over. Reports of the plague had already spread through Lombardy, and the Germans arrived to find town after town closed against them. At last, and with considerable difficulty, they reached the imperial headquarters at Pavia; and there – with the alpine passes already impassable – Frederick was forced to halt, watching in impotent rage when, on 1 December, no fewer than fifteen of the leading cities formed themselves into the greater Lombard League, the foundations of which had been laid at Anagni eight years before. It was his crowning humiliation; such was his Italian subjects' contempt for him that they had not even waited until he was back over the Alps before making their ultimate gesture of defiance. And indeed, when the spring finally came and the snows began to melt, he saw that even this last lap of his homeward journey was to be a problem; the passes were all controlled by his enemies and closed to him and his shattered army. It was secretly, shamefully and in the guise of a servant that the Emperor of the West finally regained his native land.

While Frederick Barbarossa was tasting his triumph and disaster, what had happened to his old enemy the Pope? Alexander had first taken refuge with his Frangipani friends. Serious as the situation was, he seems to have thought that he might still be able somehow to maintain himself in the capital; and when two Sicilian galleys sailed up the Tiber, he had actually refused their captains' offer to carry him away to safety. It was a courageous decision, but, as he soon saw, an unwise one. The Romans, fickle as ever, turned against him. Disguised as a pilgrim, he had finally embarked in a small boat and slipped down the river to freedom. Landing at Gaeta, he then made his way to Benevento, where he was joined by his loyal cardinals. He had escaped not a moment too soon. Had he fallen into the Emperor's hands, that surely would have been the end of his active pontificate; even if he had somehow avoided capture, he would probably have perished in the epidemic – which, it need hardly be said, did not confine itself to the imperial army, but raged through Rome until the Tiber was thick with corpses. The Almighty, perhaps, had been on his side after all.

Such was certainly the view of the papal supporters. God-fearing men everywhere, and in Germany perhaps most of all, saw in that dreadful visitation on Barbarossa the hand of the exterminating angel – not only a just retribution for his crimes, but also proof of the rightness of Alexander's cause. The Pope's popularity soared, and with it his prestige. The Lombard cities made him patron of their new League, and even invited him (though he did not accept) to take up residence among them. Meanwhile they founded a new city between Pavia and Asti and named it Alessandria in his honour.

In Rome, the Antipope Paschal had meanwhile lost what derisory support he had ever enjoyed. His health too was failing fast, and everyone knew that he had not long to live. In such circumstances it would have been a simple matter for Alexander to return to the Lateran; but Alexander refused. He had come to hate Rome, and he despised the Romans for their faithlessness and venality. Three times in eight years they had welcomed him to their city; three times they had turned against him and driven him into exile. He had no wish to go through it all again. Benevento, Terracina, Anagni – there were plenty of other places from which the business of the papacy could be transacted with efficiency and despatch, free from the intrigues and the ceaseless violence of the Eternal City. He preferred to remain where he was.

It was eleven years before he saw Rome again.

On Saturday, 29 May 1176, at Legnano just outside Milan, Frederick Barbarossa suffered at the hands of the Lombard League the most crushing defeat of his career. He had lost much of his army, and had narrowly escaped with his own life; but the disaster had brought him to his senses. After four long Italian campaigns he saw that the Lombard cities were as determined as ever to resist him and, since the formation of their League, were well able to do so. Pope Alexander was now recognised almost everywhere – even in much of the Empire itself – as the rightful pontiff. For Frederick to persist any longer in the policy on which he had already wasted the best years of his life would earn him the derision of Europe.

His ambassadors met the Pope at Anagni to negotiate the terms of the reconciliation. In essence, they were simple enough: on the imperial side, recognition of Alexander, restitution of Church possessions and the conclusion of peace with Byzantium, Sicily and the Lombard League; on the papal, confirmation of Frederick's wife as Empress, of his son Henry as King of the Romans and of several distinguished prelates in sees which they originally owed to schismatic antipopes. The next question was where the great meeting was to take place. After prolonged argument it was agreed that Pope and Emperor should meet in Venice, on condition that Frederick should not be admitted into the city until Alexander had given his consent.

On 10 May 1177 the Pope arrived with his Curia. He was received by the Doge and the Patriarchs of Grado and Aquileia and, after High Mass in St Mark's, was carried in the state barge to the Patriarchal Palace at S. Silvestro, which was put at his disposal for as long as he cared to remain. Before his meeting with the Emperor there was much work to be done; during the discussions at Anagni he had had no brief to speak for either Sicily or the League, both of which would have to reach agreement with the imperial plenipotentiaries if the promised Kiss of Peace were to have the significance he intended for it. So now, in the Patriarchal Chapel, a second round of negotiations began. Meanwhile the Emperor, to whom by the terms of the reconciliation Venetian territory was still forbidden, held himself in readiness – first at Ravenna, and later (with Alexander's permission) at Chioggia.

The League representatives in particular proved hard bargainers, and the talks dragged on for over two months; but on 23 July agreement was complete. At the Pope's request, a Venetian flotilla left for Chioggia and brought Frederick to the Lido, whither a delegation of four cardinals sailed out to greet him. In their presence he solemnly abjured his antipope and made formal acknowledgement of Alexander; the cardinals in their turn lifted his seventeen-year excommunication. Now at last he could be admitted into Venice. Early next morning the Doge himself arrived at the Lido, where Frederick had spent the night, with an impressive retinue of nobles and clergy. He personally escorted the Emperor to a barge specially decorated for the occasion, and together they were rowed in state to the Piazzetta.

In Venice itself the last preparations had been completed. Flags were flying, windows dressed. For much of that summer the city was crowded as never before, with her normal floating foreign population of travellers and merchants now swollen to many times its normal size by the greatest princes and prelates of Europe, each bent on outshining his rivals in the splendour of his retinue. One, the Archbishop of Cologne, brought with him a suite of 400 secretaries, chaplains and attendants; the Patriarch of Aquileia boasted 300, as did the Archbishops of Mainz and Magdeburg. Count Roger of Andria, the second envoy of the King of Sicily, had 330; Duke Leopold of Austria, with a train of just 160, must have cut a sorry figure indeed.

Of the several eyewitness accounts that have survived, perhaps the most vivid is the so-called *De pace veneta relatio*, whose author seems to have been a German churchman:

> At daybreak, the attendants of the Lord Pope hastened to the church of St Mark the Evangelist and closed the central doors ... and thither they brought much timber and deal planks and ladders, and so raised up a lofty and splendid throne ... Thither the Pope arrived before the first hour of the day [6 a.m.] and having heard mass soon afterwards ascended to the higher part of his throne to await the arrival of the Emperor. There he sat, with his patriarchs, cardinals, archbishops and bishops innumerable; on his right was the Patriarch of Venice, and on his left that of Aquileia.
>
> And now there came a quarrel between the Archbishop of Milan and the Archbishop of Ravenna as to which should be seen to take precedence; and each strove to sit himself in the third place from that of the Pope, on his right side. But the Pope determined to put an end to their contention, and leaving his own exalted seat descended the steps and placed himself below them. Thus was there no third place to sit in, and neither could sit on his right. Then about the third hour there arrived the Doge's barge, in which was the Emperor, with the Doge and cardinals that had been sent to him on the previous day; and he was led by seven archbishops and canons of the Church in solemn procession to the papal throne. And when he reached it, he threw off the red cloak he was wearing, and prostrated himself before the Pope, and kissed first his feet and then his knees. But the Pope rose, and taking the head of the Emperor in both his hands he embraced him and kissed him, and made him sit at his right hand, and at last spoke the words 'Son of the Church, be welcome.' Then he took him by the hand and led him into the Basilica. And the bells rang, and the *Te Deum laudamus* was sung. When the ceremony was done, they both left the church together. The Pope mounted his horse, and the Emperor held his stirrup and then retired to the Doge's Palace ...
>
> And on the same day the Pope sent the Emperor many gold and silver jars filled with food of various kinds. And he sent also a fatted calf, with the words 'It is meet that we should make merry and be glad, for my son was dead, and is alive again; and was lost, and is found.'

The Treaty of Venice marked the climax and the culmination of Alexander's pontificate. After all the sufferings and humiliations he had had to endure, through eighteen years of schism and ten of exile, and in the face of the unremitting hostility of one of the most redoubtable figures ever to wear the imperial crown, here at last was his reward. He had lived to see the Emperor's recognition not only of himself as legitimate Pope, but of all the temporal rights of the papacy over the city of Rome – those same rights that Frederick had so arrogantly claimed for the Empire at his coronation. It was a triumph, greater by far than that which Pope Gregory had scored over Henry IV exactly a century before; but to the faithful who rejoiced with the old Pope at Venice during those sweltering summer days, it was also a tribute to the patience and tenacity with which he had steered the Church through one of the most troubled periods in her history.

And now that that period was over, those qualities remained with him. Neither on the day of his triumph nor at any other time during the Emperor's stay in Venice did Alexander show the slightest inclination to crow over his former enemy. One or two subsequent historians have perpetuated the legend of the Pope placing his foot on Frederick's neck, of the Emperor muttering under his breath, 'Not to you, but to St Peter' and Alexander replying sharply: 'To me *and* to St Peter'. But this story is told by no contemporary writer and is inconsistent with all the first-hand evidence that has come down to us. The Emperor, too, seems to have behaved impeccably. On the day following the great reconciliation he tried to carry courtesy even further: having again held the papal stirrup on leaving the basilica, he would have led Alexander's horse all the way to the point of embarkation if the Pope had not gently restrained him. Did Frederick, one cannot help wondering, remember then the two days spent at Sutri when he had refused to perform the same service for Pope Hadrian, on the way to Rome for his coronation twenty-two years before?

If, as is generally believed, Pope Alexander was born in about 1100, he would now have been approaching his eightieth year. He had, however, one more task to perform. Early in 1179 he convoked the Third Lateran Council, the most important result of which was the decree governing papal elections. Until the mid-eleventh century popes were usually appointed, sometimes by the people of Rome, sometimes by the Emperor; but in 1059, as we have seen, it was agreed that they should be the responsibility of the Church alone. Even then the elections tended to be hit-and-miss affairs, their rules never formally laid down; but now at last Alexander ordained that the right to elect a new pope was to be restricted to the College of Cardinals, with a two-thirds majority required before any candidate could be elected. Apart from the fact that since the pontificate of John Paul II the right to vote has been restricted to those cardinals aged under eighty, virtually the same rules apply today.

Alexander had achieved peace with the Empire; he had not, alas, achieved peace in Rome. The Roman Senate remained so hostile that in the summer of 1179 he left the city for the last time. He had never liked it, never trusted its people; to him, all through his life, it had been enemy country. And when, after his death at Cività Castellana on the last day of August 1181, his body was brought back to the Lateran, the Romans proved him right. Not four years before, they had welcomed him back from exile to the sound of trumpets; now, as his funeral cortege entered the city, the populace threw filth at the bier, scarcely suffering his body to be buried in the basilica.

Alexander III was one of the greatest of the medieval popes. Innocent III, who was elected to the Papacy in 1198, was another. In the seventeen years that separated them, no fewer than five men occupied the throne of St Peter; all were Italians, all had to contend, as Alexander had contended, with the two continuing nightmares of the twelfth-century papacy: the Hohenstaufen emperors and the Senate and people of Rome. Lucius III (1181–5), a Cistercian monk who had been singled out for promotion by St Bernard, soon found the city too hot for him and retired to Segni. He had one rather inconsequential meeting with the Emperor at Verona in 1184, during which he learned to his deep consternation that Frederick had betrothed his son Henry to Constance, daughter of Roger II and (her nephew William II being childless) heir to the throne of Sicily. This meant that Sicily would effectively become part of the Empire: the papacy would be virtually surrounded.

Lucius died while still at Verona, and was buried in the Duomo. On the same day the cardinals unanimously elected Umberto Crivelli, Archbishop of Milan, to succeed him under the name of Urban III (1185–7). Urban made no effort to live in Rome, but continued in Verona, whence he reluctantly sent legates to represent him at the wedding of Henry and Constance in Milan Cathedral; he refused, however – as Lucius had done before him – to crown Henry co-Emperor, and was furious when Frederick characteristically had the ceremony performed by the Patriarch of Aquileia instead. Relations between Pope and Emperor rapidly deteriorated, to the point where Frederick ordered Henry to invade and occupy the Papal States; Urban was forced to capitulate, but the quarrel continued, and Frederick was spared a further sentence of excommunication only by the Pope's sudden death in October 1187 at Ferrara.

Urban had died of shock, on hearing the news of Saladin's capture of Jerusalem following the disastrous Christian defeat at Hattin in Galilee. His successor Gregory VIII (1187), not far short of eighty at the time of his election, lost no time in calling upon Christendom to take up arms for its recovery. Gregory could not, in the nature of things, have expected a long pontificate; in fact it lasted just eight weeks. He was busy trying to negotiate a truce between Genoa and Pisa – both of whose fleets would be vitally necessary to the success of the coming Crusade – when he died at Pisa just a week before Christmas, leaving the planning of the expedition to his successor Clement III (1187–91). It was agreed that the Crusade would be led by Frederick Barbarossa; he would be joined by Richard Coeur-de-Lion of England, Philip Augustus of France and William II (the Good) of Sicily.[1] William in fact died (aged just thirty-six) in November 1189 before he could embark, but the other two kings met in Sicily to make the rest of the journey together.

Frederick, on the other hand, elected to take the land route. He made the long and arduous journey across eastern Europe, over the Dardanelles into Asia and across Anatolia, until at last, on 10 June 1190, he led his army out of the last of the Taurus valleys and on to the flat coastal plain. The heat was sweltering and the little river Calycadnus that ran past the town of Seleucia[2] to the sea must have been a welcome sight. Frederick spurred his horse towards it, leaving his men to follow. He was never seen alive again. Whether he dismounted to drink and was swept off his feet by the current, whether his horse slipped in the mud and threw him, whether the shock of falling into the icy mountain water was too much for his tired old body – he was nearing seventy – remains unknown. He was rescued, but too late. The bulk of his army reached the river to find their Emperor lying dead on the bank.

---

[1] William the Good had succeeded his father, William the Bad, in 1166.
[2] In modern Turkish Seleucia has become Silifke, while the Calycadnus is now less euphoniously known as the Göksu.

Frederick's death resulted in an immediate improvement in papal-imperial relations. Clement III had virtually no diplomatic experience; in the three years of his papacy he was nevertheless able to come to a mutually acceptable agreement with Henry (now the new German king, Henry VI), promising him his imperial coronation. Henry for his part restored the Papal States that he had occupied in 1186. Equally remarkable, the Pope also entered into successful negotiations with the Senators of Rome. As a result he was able to settle back in the Lateran, in which neither of his two immediate predecessors had once set foot. In return for regular payments and control of most of the city administration, the Senators recognised his sovereignty, agreed to swear allegiance and restored the papal revenues. With these two over-riding problems out of the way, Clement devoted all his energies to preaching the coming Crusade.

He need not have bothered. The Third Crusade, though not a complete fiasco like the Second, failed utterly in its main object of recovering Jerusalem. Immediately on Frederick's death his army began to disintegrate. Many of the German princelings returned at once to Europe; others took ship for Tyre, then the only major port in the Levant still in Christian hands; the rump, carrying the Emperor's body, preserved – not very successfully – in vinegar, marched grimly on, though it lost many more of its men to an ambush as it entered Syria. The survivors who finally limped into Antioch had no more fight left in them. By this time, too, what was left of Frederick had gone the same way as his army; his rapidly decomposing remains were hastily buried in the cathedral, where they were to rest for another seventy-eight years – until a Mameluke army under the Sultan Baibars burned the whole building, together with most of the city, to the ground.

Fortunately for the Crusading East, Richard and Philip Augustus arrived with their armies essentially intact; thanks to them, all was not lost. Acre became the capital of the kingdom; but that kingdom, now reduced to the short coastal strip between Tyre and Jaffa, was but a pale shadow of what Crusader Palestine had once been. It would struggle on for another century, and when it finally fell to Baibars in 1291 the only surprise was that it had lasted so long.

After the death of William the Good, Frederick's son Henry had become – by virtue of his marriage to Constance – King of Sicily. He was due to set out for his coronation in Palermo in November 1190; but just before his departure news arrived of his father's fate. Henry now had two crowns to claim instead of one. Inevitably his departure was delayed by several weeks; fortunately the winter was mild, the alpine passes still open. By January 1191 he and his army were safely across. Then, after a month spent strengthening his position in Lombardy and securing the assistance of a fleet from Pisa, he headed towards Rome, where Pope Clement was expecting him.

But before he could reach the city Pope Clement was dead. Hurriedly – for the imperial army was fast approaching – the Sacred College met in conclave and selected as his successor the cardinal-deacon Giacinto Bobo. It seemed, in the circumstances, a curious choice. The new Pope was of illustrious birth (his brother Ursus was the founder of the family of Orsini) and could boast a long and distinguished ecclesiastical record, having stoutly defended Peter Abelard against St Bernard at Sens more than fifty years before. But he was now eighty-five: hardly, one might have thought, the man to handle the overbearing young Henry during a crisis that threatened the position of the Church almost as much as it did that of the Kingdom of Sicily. There is every indication that he shared this view himself; only the proximity of the German army, together with widespread fears of another schism if there were any delay in the election, at length persuaded him to accept the tiara. A cardinal since 1144, it was only on Holy Saturday, 13 April 1191, that he was ordained priest; the following day, Easter Sunday, he was enthroned in St Peter's as Pope Celestine III (1191–8); and on the 15th, as the first formal action of his pontificate, he crowned Henry and Constance Emperor and Empress of the West.

So far, everything had gone Henry's way; but before he continued his journey, the old Pope had a warning for him. Some time during the first weeks of 1190, in a desperate effort to avoid absorption into the Empire, the Sicilians had crowned a rival king of their own: Count Tancred of Lecce, the bastard son of King Roger's eldest son (also called Roger), who had died before his father. Tancred had his problems, but he was energetic, able and determined; Henry could expect serious opposition; indeed, he would have been better advised to return at once to Germany.

Henry of course took no notice, and headed south. To begin with, he continued to carry all before him. One town after another opened its gates; only at Naples was he brought to a halt. The city's defences were in good order – Tancred had them repaired the year before, at his own expense – and its granaries and storehouses full. When the

Emperor appeared with his army beneath their walls, the citizens were ready. The ensuing siege was not even, from their point of view, particularly arduous. Thanks to the incessant harrying of the Pisan ships by the Sicilian fleet, Henry never managed properly to control the harbour approaches, and the defenders continued to receive regular reinforcements and supplies. Despite heavy battering, the defences held firm; and it became clear, as the sweltering summer dragged on, that it was the besiegers rather than the besieged who were feeling the strain. Finally, on 24 August, Henry gave the order to raise the siege, and within a day or two the imperial host had trailed off northwards over the hills.

Back in Germany, the insufferable young Emperor continued to make trouble: nominating bishops as he liked, even condoning the murder of a certain Albert of Brabant, whom Celestine had confirmed as Bishop of Liège. Then, shortly before Christmas 1192, King Richard I – although under papal protection while returning from the Crusade – was captured by Leopold V of Austria, who shortly afterwards handed him over to Henry. The ransom demanded (150,000 marks, more than double the annual income of the English Crown) was eventually raised, and was used by the Emperor to buy off his German opponents. Thus, when Tancred of Lecce died in February 1194, just two weeks after Richard's release, Henry was free to travel to Palermo without fear of opposition and to claim his crown. He received it on Christmas Day of that same year.

Constance was not present at her husband's coronation. Pregnant for the first time at the age of forty, she had determined on two things: first, that her child should be born safely; second, that it should be seen to be unquestionably hers. She did not put off her journey to Sicily, but travelled more slowly and in her own time; and she had progressed no further than the little town of Jesi, some twenty miles west of Ancona, when she felt the pains of childbirth upon her. There, the day after her husband's coronation, in a tent erected in the main square to which free entry was allowed to any matron of the town who cared to witness the birth, she brought forth her only son Frederick – whom, a day or two later, she presented in that same square to the assembled populace, proudly suckling him at her breast.

Three years later, in November 1197, after putting down a rebellion in Sicily with his customary brutality, Henry VI died of malaria at Messina. He was thirty-two. Pope Celestine, just sixty years older, survived him by three months.

CHAPTER XIII

Innocent III

(1198–1216)

In August 1202 Pope Innocent III and his Curia were travelling through Latium and stopped at Subiaco, some thirty miles east of Rome. The town possessed a monastery, where the Pope could easily have lodged; but – presumably because it could not accommodate his large retinue and he did not wish to leave them – the entire party, Pope included, pitched camp on a hill above the lake. Innocent's health was poor; he loathed the heat and always tried to avoid the Roman summer when he could. But that year there was no escape. All he had was a small tent; the sun was murderous, the flies an additional torture. Work was out of the question; everyone sat around in whatever shade they could find and tried to forget their discomfort in conversation. Many of them could not bring themselves to make the precipitous descent to the cool lake and the hard climb back to the camp. The Pope, on the other hand, did – dipping his hands gratefully into the water and throwing it on his face.

This little vignette (taken from a letter written at the time by a member of the papal staff to an absent colleague) sheds a warm and somewhat unexpected light on the man under whom the medieval papacy reached its zenith. No pope ever had a more elevated conception of his position than Innocent III; he was indeed the Vicar of Christ on Earth (a designation that first became current in his day), standing, as it were, halfway between God and man. But his complete confidence in himself – together with a sense of humour rare in the Middle Ages – made him patient, simple and always approachable, genuinely loved by those around him.

Lotario di Segni was born around 1160. His father was Trasimondo, Count of Segni; his mother Claricia was a Roman, of the patrician Scotti family. There were strong papal connections: Clement III (1187–91) was his uncle; his nephew was to be Gregory IX (1227–41). Blessed with a first-class intellect, Lotario had studied theology in Paris and law at Bologna; in his youth he had made the pilgrimage to Canterbury, only a year or two after Thomas Becket's murder. Clement had made him a cardinal in 1190, but Celestine III (1191–8) – since his family and the Scotti were longtime enemies – had kept him firmly in the background. This gave the young cardinal time to compose several religious tracts – one of which, *De Contemptu Mundi, sive De Miseria Conditionis Humanae*, must (despite the gloom of its title[1]) have enjoyed extraordinary popularity, since it survives in no fewer than 700 separate manuscripts. At any rate this small, handsome, humorous man must have impressed himself mightily upon the Curia, because on the very day of the death of Pope Celestine on 8 January 1198 he was unanimously elected, at the age of thirty-seven, as his successor.

Within less than two years Innocent found himself without a secular rival in Europe. The death of Henry VI and the traditional enmity of the House of Guelf towards the Hohenstaufen had left the Western Empire rudderless and Germany in a state of civil war. Byzantium under its ridiculous Emperor, Alexius III Angelus, was also in near-chaos; the independent Norman Sicily was gone; and both England and France were occupied with inheritance problems after the death of Richard I in 1199. The Pope was consequently in a stronger position than any of his recent predecessors; and without a hostile Emperor to intrigue against him, he was soon able to reassert his authority both in the Papal States – which had been reduced to near-anarchy by Hohenstaufen policies – and in Rome itself, reconciling the various aristocratic factions, to several of which he was related through his mother. He even managed to acquire the Duchy of Spoleto and the March of Ancona, a territory that stretched from Rome to the Adriatic and provided an invaluable cordon sanitaire between northern Italy and the Sicilian Kingdom – where he pulled off another diplomatic masterstroke by persuading the Empress Constance to make Sicily a papal fief and to appoint the Pope as Regent during her son Frederick's minority.

He was less fortunate in giving his blessing to the Fourth Crusade. Like his predecessors, Innocent had determined on the liberation of the Holy Places from Muslim occupation, and as early as 1198 had called for a Crusade for the recovery of Jerusalem, imposing a tax of 2½ per cent on clerical incomes to pay for it. When, however, the Crusaders finally gathered in Venice in the summer of 1202, they were

---

[1] *Concerning the Contempt of the World, or the Wretchedness of Man's Lot.*

unable to pay the agreed 84,000 silver marks for the transport of their army across the Mediterranean; the Venetians therefore refused to sail unless the Crusaders helped in the recapture of Zara (now Zadar) on the Dalmatian coast. Zara was duly taken and sacked, but fighting broke out almost at once between the Crusaders and the Venetians over the division of the spoils, and when order was finally restored the two groups settled down in separate quarters of the city for the winter. Before long news of what had happened reached the Pope; outraged, he excommunicated the entire expedition. (Later he was to reconsider, and to restrict the sentence – most unfairly – to the Venetians only.)

And worse was to follow. While the Crusade was still in Zara, Duke Philip of Swabia – Barbarossa's fifth and youngest son, who had married the daughter of the dethroned Byzantine Emperor, Isaac II – arrived with a proposal: if the Crusade would escort his brother-in-law, Isaac's son Alexius, to Constantinople and enthrone him there in the place of the present usurper, Alexius would finance its future advance and supply an additional army of 10,000. He would also heal the 150-year schism by submitting the Byzantine Church to the authority of Rome. The invitation sounded tempting indeed, and was accepted by both the Crusaders and the Venetians, who quickly forgot their differences; but it led, in April 1204, to the most unspeakable of the many outrages in the whole hideous history of the Crusades: the brutal sacking and near-destruction, by men wearing the Cross of Christ on their shoulders, of Constantinople – capital of the Roman Empire and Christendom's most vital outpost in the East. As a result, a succession of Frankish thugs (most of them hardly able to write their names, and none of them speaking a word of Greek) occupied the throne of the emperors for the next fifty-seven years. Byzantium was to endure for almost two centuries more, but only as the palest shadow of what it once had been.

Pope Innocent, who had tried unsuccessfully to deflect the Crusaders from Constantinople altogether, was as horrified as anyone when he heard of the atrocities for which they had been responsible; but he could hardly ignore the fact that the Latin occupation brought with it a Roman Catholic Patriarch, and so deluded himself into thinking that the schism was effectively at an end. 'By the just judgement of God,' he wrote, 'the kingdom of the Greeks is translated from the proud to the humble, from the disobedient to the faithful, from schismatics to Catholics.' How wrong he was: the rape of Constantinople, far from putting an end to the schism, set it in stone.

Meanwhile Innocent's belief in the Crusading ideal remained unshaken – as the Albigenses were to learn to their cost.

The Albigenses were a heretical Christian sect that had first appeared in the Languedoc towards the beginning of the eleventh century. Their particular heresy – Catharism – did not exist only in western Europe. In former times Cathars had existed in Armenia (where for centuries, under the name of Paulicians, they had been a thorn in the flesh of successive Byzantine rulers) as well as in Bulgaria and Bosnia, where they were known as Bogomils. Essentially, they espoused the Manichaean doctrine that good and evil constituted two distinct spheres – that of the good, spiritual god and that of the devil, creator of the material world – and that the Earth was a constant battleground between them. Their leaders, the *perfecti*, abstained from meat and from sex; they also rejected saints, holy images and relics, together with all the sacraments of the Church, particularly baptism and marriage. To Pope Innocent, such departures from strict orthodoxy could not be tolerated. At first he attempted peaceable conversion, sending a Cistercian mission headed by a Legate, Peter of Castelnau, and by the Abbot of Cîteaux, and subsequently joined by the Spaniard Domingo de Guzman, better known as St Dominic; but in 1208 Peter was murdered by a henchman of Count Raymond VI of Toulouse, and Innocent proclaimed a Crusade.

That Crusade was to continue for the next twenty years, pitting the northern barons, led by Simon de Montfort, against those of the south. It led to several hideous massacres – the worst of them all in the town of Montségur – and it utterly destroyed the dazzling Provençal civilisation of the early Middle Ages. Even when the war ended in 1229 with the Treaty of Paris (after the wholesale massacres of countless adherents) the heresy refused to die. It was another hundred years before the Inquisition, unleashed on the region with all its terrifying efficiency, succeeded in crushing it at last.

By a curious irony the year 1209, which marked the beginning of the Albigensian Crusade, also saw the establishment of the first of the two great Mendicant Orders, those of St Francis of Assisi and St Dominic respectively. Both men were well known to Pope Innocent, who – according to the old Franciscan tradition – orally approved St Francis's Order of Friars Minor in Rome on 16 April. Those first friars were, quite simply, wandering preachers who accepted whatever employment (normally agricultural) or hospitality was offered to them and, if absolutely necessary, begged for their bread.[1] They preached the simplest of sermons to townsfolk and peasants alike and took particular pains over the care of the sick. The Order proved hugely popular and grew with astonishing speed; ten years after its foundation it boasted more than 3,000 members. The second Order, that of St Dominic, was to be sanctioned in 1216, five months after the Pope's death.

During the early years of Innocent's pontificate, one of his most abiding concerns was the future of the German crown which, it must be remembered, was elective rather than hereditary. Frederick of Sicily, as the only son of Henry VI, had an obvious claim; but Frederick was far away in Palermo and still a child. Of the two rival claimants in Germany, one was his uncle Philip, Duke of Swabia; the other was Otto, Duke of Brunswick, son of the Guelf leader Henry the Lion and his wife Matilda, daughter of Henry II of England. Otto was consequently the nephew of Richard Coeur-de-Lion and of Richard's younger brother, King John. Since Philip refused to give any undertakings with regard to Sicily, while Otto readily agreed to respect papal rights both there and in the enlarged Papal States, Pope Innocent had no hesitation in supporting the Duke of Brunswick; Frederick's future authority could, he felt, with any luck be restricted to Sicily. Hostilities between the two factions delayed any final solution to the problem for several years; gradually, however, the Duke of Swabia grew dangerously strong, to the point where Innocent might well have had to revise his position; the Pope cannot have mourned unduly when Duke Philip was murdered in 1208 by the Palatine Count of Bavaria, to whom he had refused one of his daughters in marriage. The way was now clear for Otto's coronation, which Innocent performed in Rome on Sunday, 4 October 1209.

But the Duke of Brunswick proved a sad disappointment. Within weeks he was showing himself every bit as arrogant and bullying as Barbarossa or Henry VI had ever been, and in the summer of 1210 he invaded the Sicilian Kingdom and took possession of all southern Italy. Unfortunately for him, however, he went too far: his invasion of the papal province of Tuscany led to his instant excommunication, and in September 1211 a council of the leading German princes met

---

[1] The term 'Mendicant Orders' is in fact not strictly accurate where the Franciscans are concerned, St Francis having recommended that they should live as far as possible by manual labour, begging only as a last resort.

in Nuremberg and declared him deposed. They then despatched ambassadors to Palermo, with an invitation to Frederick (now just seventeen) to assume the vacant throne.

The invitation came as a complete surprise. Frederick's principal councillors strongly advised against acceptance. He had no ties of his own with Germany; indeed, he had never set foot on German soil. His hold on his own Sicilian kingdom was still far from secure; it was scarcely a year since the Duke of Brunswick had been threatening him from across the Straits of Messina. Was this really the moment to absent himself from Sicily for several months at least, for the sake of an honour that, however impressive, might yet prove illusory? On the other hand a refusal would, he knew, be seen by the German princes as a deliberate snub, and could not fail to strengthen the position of his chief rival. Both in Italy and in Germany, the Duke of Brunswick still had plenty of support. Having renounced none of his long-term ambitions, Otto was fully capable of launching a new campaign – and he would not make the same mistake next time. Here was an opportunity to deal him a knockout blow. It was not to be missed.

Pope Innocent, after some hesitation, gave his approval. Frederick's election would admittedly tighten the imperial grip to the north and south of the Papal States, and it was in order to emphasise the independence – at least theoretical – of the Kingdom of Sicily from the Empire that the Pope insisted on Frederick's renunciation of the Sicilian throne in favour of his newborn son, with Queen Constance acting as Regent. Once these formalities had been settled, Frederick could set off. At the end of February 1212 he sailed from Messina. His immediate destination, however, was not Germany, but Rome; and there, on Easter Sunday, 25 March, he knelt before the Pope and performed the act of feudal homage to him – technically on behalf of his son the King – for the Sicilian Kingdom.

His way north, however, was by no means clear. On 28 July he was given a warm welcome in Pavia; but the Lombard plain was constantly patrolled by bands of anti-imperialist Milanese, and it was one of these bands that surprised the imperial party as they were leaving the town the next morning. Frederick was lucky indeed to be able to leap on to one of the horses and, having forded the River Lambro bareback, make his way to friendly Cremona. By the beginning of autumn he was safely in Germany where, in December, he was crowned King. It was his first step towards the Empire of the West.

From Innocent's point of view, Frederick began promisingly enough.

In the summer of 1213 he guaranteed, in what was known as 'the Golden Bull of Eger', free elections of all bishops and abbots in his realms, and allowed, in cases of religious litigation, the right of appeal to the Holy See, which had previously been denied in Sicily. It was inevitable that imperial–papal relations should sooner or later turn sour – they always did – but for the remaining three years of Innocent's life he had good reason to congratulate himself on the success of his policy towards the Empire.

Otto of Brunswick had done enough to blacken himself in the Pope's eyes; and his image was not improved by the fact that he was the nephew of King John of England. Already in 1208, before Otto had fallen from grace and when John had refused to recognise the Pope's nominee (and old personal friend) Stephen Langton as Archbishop of Canterbury, Innocent had laid the whole kingdom under an interdict. John had retaliated by the seizure of all clerical property, and by ordering the arrests of all the mistresses of priests and clerks – though he soon allowed them to buy back their freedom. Negotiations had begun between King and Pope, but John continued to be as refractory as ever and in 1209 Innocent excommunicated him – at which nearly all the English bishops and abbots went into voluntary exile. Now the ban of the Church had in the past been known to bring kings and even emperors to their knees (we have only to think of Henry IV at Canossa); the difficulty was that when sees and abbacies became vacant their revenue reverted to the Crown. By 1211 the King's profits from seven of one and seventeen of the other were such that he seemed to be actually enjoying his excommunication and in no hurry to have it lifted.

A year later, however, by now some £100,000 the richer, John determined to win back extensive territories in France – Normandy, Anjou, Maine and parts of Poitou – that he had lost to Philip Augustus early in his reign. This would clearly involve a massive continental campaign; and such a campaign, he knew, would be impossible while he was an excommunicate. And so, in November 1212, he agreed to accept Langton. He need not have bothered: the ensuing campaign was a disaster. His chief ally was his nephew, the Duke of Brunswick, whom he had long supported and largely financed; there were also units from the Low Countries commanded by the Count of Flanders, making a total of perhaps 15,000 men in all. Undaunted, the 10,000-strong army of Philip Augustus, supported only by Frederick of Sicily, rode out to meet the invaders on 27 July 1214 at Bouvines, between

Lille and Tournai – and won a decisive victory. The Count of Flanders was taken prisoner, while Otto fled back to Brunswick. As for John himself, Bouvines marked the end of his coalition, and of all his continental ambitions. At home, his position was now so weak that he was obliged to sign the Magna Carta the following year.

Such is the reputation of this most celebrated of all historic documents that it comes as something of a surprise to learn that the more intransigent barons almost immediately rendered it unworkable. Far from ensuring a healthier relationship between themselves and the monarchy, it led to a civil war that soon became an international one when Prince Louis of France (later Louis VIII) invaded England at the barons' invitation. Pope Innocent – who saw it not as an assertion of the law against tyranny, but as an attempt at feudal insurrection against royal authority – was predictably furious, and at John's request declared it null and void on the grounds that it had been imposed upon the King against his will.

By this time, however, the Pope was immersed in preparations for the climax of his pontificate, and indeed of all medieval papal legislation: the Fourth Lateran Council, which opened in November 1215. Present were more than 400 bishops and archbishops, including the Latin Patriarchs of Constantinople and Jerusalem and representatives of those in Alexandria and Antioch. Among the rest were more than 800 abbots and priors, together with the envoys of Frederick of Sicily (now King of the Germans), the Latin Emperor of Constantinople and the Kings of England, France, Aragon, Sicily, Hungary, Cyprus and Jerusalem. Conspicuous by their absence were representatives of the Greek Church in the East; the horrors of the Fourth Crusade were still too fresh in their minds.

The Council concerned itself with two problems in particular: the occupation by the Infidel of the Holy Places and the recrudescence of heresy. The starting date for the proposed new Crusade was fixed for 1 June 1217, and a tax of one-fortieth of their income was imposed on all the clergy, with the Pope and cardinals paying one-tenth; but Innocent's death on 16 July 1216 deprived the preparations of their momentum and the project was of necessity postponed. Where heresy was concerned, it is noteworthy that the first speaker after the Pope himself was the Bishop of Agde, who discussed the Albigensian problem at considerable length. Later the Catharist doctrine was formally condemned, and crusading privileges were extended to all those who took part in campaigns against it.

Some time during the early sessions of the Council, St Dominic arrived in Rome to request from Pope Innocent the official confirmation of his Order; but there were various problems to be solved, and it was Innocent's successor Honorius III who finally gave the Dominicans his blessing. They were to prove as successful as the Franciscans; by the time of Dominic's death in 1221, six priories had been founded in Lombardy, four in Provence, four in France, three in Tuscany and Rome and two in Spain.

Altogether, the Council promulgated seventy-one canons, or decrees, covering a remarkably wide field. The very first defined the doctrine of transubstantiation; the thirteenth forbade the foundation of any new religious orders – St Dominic got over this one by adopting the Rule of St Augustine; the eighteenth abolished the use of boiling water and red-hot iron in trials by ordeal; the twenty-first insisted on confession and communion for all Catholics at least once a year at Easter; the thirty-first prohibited illegitimate sons of the clergy from inheriting their fathers' churches. The closing canons were directed against the Jews. No Christian was to have commerce with Jewish usurers; both Jews and Muslims were to wear distinctive dress; no Jew might appear in public during Holy Week, nor might he exercise any public function involving power over Christians.

These last provisions seem shocking to us today; they would not have done so in the early thirteenth century. Innocent and his colleagues were children of their time; they discriminated against the Jews, but it was their fellow-Christians whom they persecuted. Before condemning them too harshly we should perhaps consider the position of the Jews in medieval England, remembering how before the end of the century, after innumerable arrests and executions, King Edward I was to banish the entire Jewish community from English soil.

Quite apart from the decrees of the Council, Innocent was responsible for a huge corpus of legislation; he left more than 6,000 letters, many of which were decretals of canon law, issuing his first collection of them as early as 1210 and entrusting it to the University of Bologna. His reign marks the apex of the temporal power of the medieval papacy; but none could have foreseen the suddenness with which it came to an end. In July 1216 the Pope left Rome for the north, hoping to settle the age-old quarrel between Genoa and Pisa so that the two great maritime republics could collaborate in the projected Crusade. Some years before, he had suffered a severe attack of malaria, which had brought him to the edge of the grave; he had got no further than Perugia when the same disease struck again. A day or two later he was dead. He was fifty-five.

The following night, the house in which he had died was broken into and his body stolen. It was found the next day stripped naked, rapidly decomposing in the summer heat, and was hastily buried in the church of S. Lorenzo.[1] At some later date, we are told, the bones of one of the greatest – if not *the* greatest – of medieval popes were heedlessly thrown, together with those of Urban IV and Martin IV, into a box that was stored in a cupboard in the sacristy of the new cathedral. At the end of the nineteenth century Leo XIII ordered that they should be brought back to the Lateran; and so they were finally returned to Rome, in the suitcase of a priest, by rail.

---

[1] According, at least, to his biographer Helene Tillman, in *Pope Innocent III*, to whom I am indebted for this entire paragraph. She quotes L. Bonazzi, *Storia di Perugia dalle origini al 1860*, vol. I, 1865. I have not traced this book; nor, more surprisingly, have I traced the church, which appears in none of the guidebooks to the city.

CHAPTER XIV

The End of the Hohenstaufen

(1216–1303)

Two days after Pope Innocent's death in Perugia in July 1216, the cardinals met in that same city and elected the elderly and already frail Cardinal Cencio Savelli, who took the name of Honorius III (1216–27). He came from an aristocratic Roman family and had already given many years' service in the Curia; in 1197 he had even served briefly as tutor to Frederick of Sicily – though as Frederick was not yet three years old, he is unlikely to have made much impression.

From the day of his installation, Honorius saw as his first duty the continuation of his predecessor's plans for a Crusade. To achieve the political unity necessary for its success he worked hard on the diplomatic front, arbitrating between the kings of France and Aragon, persuading Philip Augustus to abandon his invasion of England, helping John's son Henry to succeed to the throne after his father's death in 1216. Alas, the Fifth Crusade proved as ill-starred as the Second, Third and Fourth. It had as its object the capture of the Egyptian city of Damietta, which it was hoped to exchange later for Jerusalem. A fleet set out in 1218, initially under the leadership of John of Brienne, titular King of Jerusalem, but on the arrival (four months late) of the papal contingent under the Spanish Cardinal Pelagius of St Lucia, the cardinal insisted on assuming overall command.

After Damietta had endured a seventeen-month siege, the Egyptian Sultan al-Kamil in desperation offered the whole Kingdom of Jerusalem west of the Jordan in return for the Crusaders' departure; idiotically, the offer was refused by Pelagius, who was determined to shed as much blood as possible, conquering Cairo and indeed the whole of Egypt. Damietta duly fell on 5 November 1219, but the war dragged on for nearly two more years and would have continued even longer, had not the Crusading army been trapped by the Nile floods – from which it extricated itself only by surrender. The Crusade, so nearly a success, had been yet another disaster, thanks entirely to the pig-head-edness of its leader.[1]

Pope Honorius, on the other hand, was inclined to lay the blame elsewhere: on the massive shoulders of the man who was now the Emperor Frederick II. As early as 1214 Frederick had announced his intention of taking the Cross. Why he did so remains a mystery. He had never been particularly pious; moreover he had been brought up by Muslim scientists and scholars, whose language he spoke perfectly and whose religion he deeply respected. Nor at this time was he under pressure from the Pope or anyone else. Indeed, there is plenty of reason to believe that he later regretted his promise; he certainly showed no eagerness to fulfil it, remaining in Germany until 1220 and allowing the Fifth Crusade to depart without him. Had he accompanied it as its leader, the Pope believed – probably rightly – that there would have been a very different outcome; and it was at least to some extent to hasten him on his way that Honorius had crowned him Emperor when he passed through Rome on his journey back to Sicily.

For the failure of the Fifth Crusade had served only to increase the Pope's determination to launch a Sixth, to be led by the Emperor himself. Frederick remained markedly unenthusiastic, but there was now a further complication to be considered. The Empress Constance had died in 1221, and it had recently been proposed that Frederick should marry the twelve-year-old Yolande de Brienne, the hereditary Queen of Jerusalem. Her title came from her mother, the grand-daughter of King Amalric I; she, at the age of seventeen, had married the sexagenarian John of Brienne, who had promptly assumed the title of King. After his wife's early death a year or two later his claim to it was clearly questionable, but he had continued to govern the country now based on Acre as Regent for his little daughter Yolande. Moreover, as we have seen, he had initially led the recent Crusade.

Frederick had not at first been greatly attracted by the proposal. Yolande was penniless, and little more than a child; he was more than twice her age. As for her title, few were emptier; Jerusalem had now been in Saracen hands for half a century. On the other hand, the king-ship – purely titular though it might be – would greatly strengthen his claim to the city when he eventually left on his long-postponed Crusade. And so, after some deliberation, he agreed to the match. He

---

[1] The siege was further complicated by the unexpected arrival of St Francis of Assisi, who gained an audience with the Sultan and tried to convert him to Christianity. That was a failure too.

agreed, too, in the course of further discussions with Honorius, that the Crusade (to which the marriage was indissolubly linked) would set out on Ascension Day, 20 May 1227. Any further delay, Honorius made clear, would result in Frederick's excommunication.

It was in August 1225 that fourteen galleys of the imperial fleet arrived at Acre – the last surviving outpost of Crusader Outremer[1] – to conduct Yolande to Sicily. Even before her departure she had been wedded to the Emperor by proxy; on her arrival at Tyre, being now deemed to have come of age, she received her coronation as Queen of Jerusalem. Only then did she embark on the journey that was to take her to a new life, accompanied by a suite that included a female cousin several years her senior. Frederick, together with her father, was awaiting her at Brindisi, where a second marriage took place in the cathedral on 9 November. It was, alas, ill-fated. The following day the Emperor left the city with his bride, and without previously warning his father-in-law; by the time John caught up with them he was informed by his tearful daughter that her husband had already seduced her cousin. When Frederick and Yolande reached Palermo the poor girl was immediately packed off to the palace harem. Her father, meanwhile, had been coldly informed that he was no longer Regent. Still less did he have any further right to the title of King.

Whether John's fury was principally due to the Emperor's treatment of his daughter or to the loss of his titular kingdom is unclear; at any rate he went at once to Rome, where Honorius predictably took his side and refused to recognise Frederick's assumption of the royal title. This could hardly have failed to exacerbate the strain in imperial–papal relations, already at an abysmal level owing to Frederick's continued dilatoriness and his refusal to acknowledge the Pope's authority over northern and central Italy. The quarrel took a further downward plunge when Honorius died in 1227 and was succeeded by Cardinal Ugolino of Ostia, who took the name of Gregory IX (1227–41). Already in his seventies, he started as he meant to go on. 'Take heed', he wrote to Frederick soon after his accession, 'that you do not place your intellect, which you have in common with the angels, below your senses, which you have in common with brutes and plants.' To the Emperor, whose debauches were rapidly becoming legendary, it was an effective shot across the bows.

---

[1] Outremer – literally, 'beyond the sea' – was the name given to the Crusading states in the Levant, established after the First Crusade.

By this time the Crusade was gathering its forces. A constant stream of young German knights was crossing the Alps and pouring down the pilgrim roads of Italy to join the Emperor in Apulia, where the army was to take ship for the Holy Land. But then, in the savage heat of an Apulian August, an epidemic broke out. It may have been typhoid, or it may have been cholera; it swept relentlessly through the Crusader camps. And now Frederick himself succumbed; so too did the Landgrave of Thuringia, who had brought with him several hundred cavalry. The two sick men embarked nonetheless and sailed from Brindisi in September, but a day or two later the Landgrave was dead, and Frederick realised that he himself was too ill to continue. He sent the surviving Crusaders ahead, with instructions to make what preparations they could; he himself would join them when sufficiently recovered – by May 1228 at the latest. Ambassadors were simultaneously despatched to Rome, to explain the situation to the Pope.

Gregory, however, refused to receive them. Instead, in a blistering encyclical, he accused the Emperor of having blatantly disregarded his crusading vows. Had he not, after repeated postponements, himself set a new date for his departure? Had he not agreed to his own excommunication if he did not fulfil his pledge? Had he not foreseen that, with thousands of soldiers and pilgrims crowded together in the summer heat, an epidemic was inevitable? Had he not therefore been responsible for that epidemic, and for all the deaths that it had caused, including that of the Landgrave? And who was to say that he had really contracted the disease anyway? Was this not just a further attempt to wriggle out of his obligations?[1] On 29 September Gregory declared Frederick excommunicated.

In doing so, however, he created for himself a new problem. It was self-evident that excommunicates could not lead Crusades, and as the weeks passed it became increasingly clear that this was precisely what Frederick intended to do. Another awkward fact was also beginning to emerge: the Pope had badly overplayed his hand. Frederick had replied with an open letter addressed to all those who had taken the Cross, explaining his position quietly and reasonably, appealing for understanding and conciliation – setting, in short, an example to the Holy Father of the tone that he would have been well advised to adopt

[1] The article on Gregory IX in *The New Catholic Encyclopedia* – in spite of conclusive evidence to the contrary – endorses this view with the words 'on September 8, a large fleet made its appearance, but, feigning illness, Frederick ordered it to turn back to Otranto'. The illness was not feigned, and the fleet was not ordered to turn back.

himself. The letter had its effect. When, on Easter Sunday 1228, Pope Gregory launched into yet another furious diatribe against the Emperor, his Roman congregation rioted; hounded from the city, the Pope was obliged to seek refuge in Viterbo. From there he continued his campaign, but whereas only a few months before he had been urgently calling upon Frederick to leave on the Crusade, he was now in the ludicrous position of preaching equally urgently against it, knowing as he did that were the Emperor to return victorious, papal prestige would sustain a blow from which it would take long indeed to recover.

At last, On Wednesday, 28 June 1228, Frederick II sailed from Brindisi with a fleet of about sixty ships, bound for Palestine. He was now fully restored to health, but his relations with Pope Gregory had not sustained a similar improvement; indeed, on discovering that he really was preparing for departure, the Pope had fired off another excommunication on 23 March. (Yet another was to follow on 30 August.) Frederick, meanwhile, had once again become a father. Two months earlier the sixteen-year-old Yolande had given birth to a boy, Conrad, only to die of puerperal fever shortly afterwards.

After spending some months in Cyprus, the Emperor landed in Tyre towards the end of 1228. Impressive detachments of Templars and Hospitallers were there to greet him, still further swelling the ranks of what was already a considerable army; but Frederick had no intention of fighting if his purposes could be achieved by peaceful diplomacy – as he had reason to think they might be. Some months before, the Sultan al-Kamil in Cairo, at loggerheads with his brother al-Mu'azzam, Governor of Damascus, had secretly appealed to Frederick with a proposal: if he would drive al-Mu'azzam from Damascus, then he – al-Kamil – would be in a position to restore to Frederick the Kingdom of Jerusalem.

In the interim al-Mu'azzam had died (rather surprisingly, of natural causes) and it looked as though al-Kamil, who had come to claim what he conceived was his birthright, might now be rather less enthusiastic about the proposed alliance; but Frederick still had high hopes. An embassy was despatched, pointing out that the Emperor had only come on the Sultan's invitation, but that the world now knew that he was here; how then could he leave empty-handed? The resulting loss of prestige might well prove fatal, and al-Kamil would never be able to find himself another Christian ally. As for Jerusalem, it was nowadays a relatively insignificant city, defenceless and largely depopulated, and, even from the religious point of view, far less important to Islam than it was to Christendom. Would its surrender not be a small price to pay for peaceful relations between Muslim and Christian – and, incidentally, for Frederick's own immediate departure?

There were no threats – none, at least, outwardly expressed. But the imperial army was on the spot, and its strength was considerable. The Sultan was in an impossible position. The Emperor was there on his very doorstep, waiting to collect what had been promised, and unlikely to leave until he had got it. Meanwhile the situation in Syria, where al-Kamil's attempts to capture Damascus were having no effect, was once again causing him increasing alarm. Perhaps an alliance might be no bad thing after all. And so the Sultan capitulated, agreeing to a ten-year treaty – on certain conditions. First, Jerusalem must remain undefended. The Temple Mount, with the Dome of the Rock and the al-Aqsa Mosque opposite it, might be visited by Christians, but must remain in Muslim hands, together with Hebron. The Christians could have their other principal shrines in Bethlehem and Nazareth, on the understanding that they would be linked to the Christian cities of the coast only by a narrow corridor running through what would continue to be Muslim territory.

On Saturday, 17 March 1229, Frederick – still under sentence of excommunication – entered Jerusalem and formally took possession of the city. The following day, in open defiance of the papal ban, he attended Mass in the Church of the Holy Sepulchre, deliberately wearing his imperial crown. He had effectively achieved everything he had set out to achieve, and had done so without the shedding of a drop of Christian or Muslim blood. Among the Christian community a degree of rejoicing might have been expected; instead, the reaction was one of fury. Frederick, while still under the ban of the Church, had dared to set foot in the most sacred shrine of Christendom, which he had won with the collusion of the Sultan of Egypt. The Patriarch of Jerusalem,[1] who had studiously ignored the Emperor ever since his arrival, now showed his displeasure – somewhat illogically, it must be said – by putting the entire city under an interdict. Church services were forbidden; pilgrims visiting the Holy Places could no longer count on the remission of their sins. The local barons, meanwhile, were outraged that they had not been consulted. How anyway, they asked

---

[1] All the Eastern patriarchates were allowed to continue under Muslim occupation – as, indeed, they still do.

themselves, were they expected to retain all these territories that Frederick had so dubiously acquired, once the imperial army had returned to the West?

The last straw, to priests and laymen alike, was the Emperor's obvious interest in – and admiration for – both the Muslim faith and Islamic civilisation as a whole. He insisted, for example, on visiting the Dome of the Rock (of whose architecture he made a detailed study[1]) and the al-Aqsa Mosque, where he is said to have expressed his disappointment at not having heard the call to prayer. (The Sultan had ordered the muezzins to be silent as a gesture of respect.) As always, he questioned every Muslim he met: about his faith, his calling, his way of life or anything else that occurred to him. To the Christians of Outremer, such an attitude was profoundly shocking; even the Emperor's fluent Arabic was held against him. With every day that he remained in Jerusalem his unpopularity grew, and when he moved on to Acre – narrowly escaping an ambush by the Templars on the way – he found the city on the verge of open rebellion.

By this time he too was in a dangerous mood, shocked by the apparent ingratitude of his fellow-Christians and ready to give as good as he got. He ordered his troops to surround Acre, allowing no one to enter or leave. Churchmen who preached sermons against him were bastinadoed. Meanwhile he had the fleet made ready to sail on 1 May. Soon after dawn on that day, as he passed through the butchers' quarter to the waiting ships, he was pelted with offal. It was his last experience of the Holy Land.

Stopping only very briefly in Cyprus, the Emperor reached Brindisi on 10 June. He found his kingdom in a state of helpless confusion. Pope Gregory had taken advantage of his absence to launch what almost amounted to a Crusade against him, calling on the princes and churches of western Europe for men and money to launch an all-out attack on Frederick's position both in Germany and in Italy. In Germany the Pope's attempts to establish a rival Emperor in the person of Otto of Brunswick had had little effect; in Italy, on the other hand, he had organised an armed invasion, with the object of driving Frederick out of the south once and for all, so that the whole territory could be ruled directly from Rome. Furious fighting was at that moment in progress in the Abruzzi and around Capua, while several cities in

---

[1] Its octagonal shape may well have been the inspiration for his magnificent hunting lodge, Castel del Monte in Apulia.

Apulia, believing the rumours (assiduously circulated by papal agents) of Frederick's death, were in open revolt. To encourage others to follow their example, Gregory had recently published an edict releasing all the Emperor's subjects from their oaths of allegiance.

The situation could hardly have been worse; yet from the moment of Frederick's arrival the tide began to turn. Here was the Emperor, once again among his own people, not dead but triumphant, having recovered without bloodshed the Holy Places for Christendom. His achievement may not have impressed the Christian communities of Outremer, but to the people of southern Italy and Sicily it appeared in a very different light. Moreover, with his return to his kingdom, Frederick himself instantly became a changed man. Gone were the anger, the bluster, the insecurity, the lack of understanding; he was back now in the land he knew and loved; once again, he was in control. All that summer he spent tirelessly on campaign, and by the end of October the papal army was broken.

Gregory IX, however, was not; and the final reconciliation between the two was a long and painful process. In the following months the Emperor made concession after concession, knowing as he did that the obstinate old Pope still retained his most damaging weapon. Frederick was still excommunicate: a serious embarrassment, a permanent reproach and a potentially dangerous diplomatic liability. As a Christian, too – insofar as he was one – Frederick would have had no wish to die under the ban of the Church. But still Gregory prevaricated; it was not until July 1230 that, very reluctantly, he agreed to a peace treaty (signed at Ceprano at the end of August) and lifted his sentence. Some weeks later, the two men dined together in the papal palace at Anagni. The dinner, one feels, must have been far from convivial, at least in its early stages; but Frederick was capable of enormous charm when he wanted to use it, and the Pope seems to have been genuinely gratified that the Holy Roman Emperor should have taken the trouble to pay him an informal visit. So ended – for the time being – yet another of those Herculean struggles between Pope and Emperor on which the history of medieval Europe seems so frequently to turn.

The truce proved, inevitably, uneasy; but it lasted for nine years, during which time each party rendered the other useful service. When, in 1234, the Romans staged one of their periodic revolts, demanding the abolition of clerical immunities as well as the right to raise taxes and to strike coinage, Frederick instantly answered Gregory's appeal for aid and forced their submission. In return the Emperor sought papal assistance in his difficulties with the Lombard cities; Gregory did his best to mediate and obligingly excommunicated Frederick's refractory son, Henry, King of the Germans, who was plotting with the Lombards against his father. All too soon, however, the rifts began to appear. His attempts at mediation having failed, the Pope was seriously concerned when Frederick summoned the help of German princes in subduing the Lombard cities by force; he clearly could not allow the Emperor to ride roughshod over northern Italy and impose on it the same degree of autocracy as he enjoyed in the south. Were he to do so, what was to prevent an imperial invasion of the Papal States and the consequent absorption of the whole of Italy into the Empire?

Then, in November 1237, Frederick smashed the Lombards at Cortenuova. They fled by night, leaving behind the splendid Milanese *carroccio*, the ceremonial war chariot that carried the standards and served as a rallying point for the army. To heighten the impact of his victory, the Emperor then entered Cremona, where he awarded himself a triumph on the ancient Roman pattern. Behind him and his victorious soldiers marched the captured Lombard commanders in fetters; the *carroccio* itself was drawn through the streets by an elephant from the menagerie that accompanied Frederick on all his travels, with Pietro Tiepolo – son of the Doge of Venice and sometime *podestà* (or governor) of Milan – bound to its central flagpole. For Gregory, this was additional proof that the papacy was in mortal danger; and when the following year Frederick sent his bastard son Enzio to Sardinia (a papal fief), arranging for him to marry a noble Sardinian girl and designating him King, his worst suspicions were confirmed.

By 1239 relations between the two were once again as bad as they had ever been. Papal agents were sowing dissension in Germany; others were working on the Lombards, stiffening their resolve after Cortenuova. Meanwhile the Emperor was secretly intriguing with the cardinals to get rid of Gregory once and for all. The inevitable result was yet another sentence of excommunication. Frederick was quite accustomed to this by now, but it served as a useful excuse for war. Insults flew back and forth: the Pope was 'a Pharisee seated on the chair of pestilence, anointed with the oil of wickedness', who should be deposed forthwith; the Emperor was the forerunner of Antichrist, the monster of the Apocalypse, 'the furious beast from the sea'.[1] Then Frederick marched. In 1240 his troops surrounded Rome, though they did not enter the city. The Pope retaliated by summoning a General Council of the Church, to convene at Easter 1241. It was, in a sense, a challenge: would or would not those attending be allowed unrestricted passage? But the Emperor called his bluff. The German churchmen were forbidden to attend. With all land routes closed, the French cardinals and bishops were obliged to travel by sea; their ships were intercepted by the imperial fleet and more than 100 distinguished churchmen were taken prisoner.

For Pope Gregory, now in his late eighties, this last blow was too much. His spirit was unbroken, but his old body was ravaged by kidney disease. He struggled on as best he could, but the Roman summer proved too much for him, and on 22 August 1241 he died. Frederick, who was probably well aware that his old enemy's end was near, had remained outside Rome. He had always maintained that he had no quarrel with the Church, only with the Pope personally; on Gregory's death, therefore, he quietly returned to Sicily.

The pontificate of Gregory IX was completely overshadowed by his battle with the Emperor. He did, however, make one significant contribution to canon law, publishing in 1234 what was known as the *Liber extra*, the first complete collection of papal decretals, which was to remain the fundamental authority until the early twentieth century. Like his predecessor, he looked benevolently on the Mendicant Orders, canonising Francis in 1228 and Dominic six years later. It was unfortunate that he should have entrusted to these Orders – and particularly to the Dominicans – the administration of the papal Inquisition, which, among the Albigenses in the Languedoc, was becoming increasingly brutal.

If Gregory's successor (the hopeless old Celestine IV, 1241) had lived, Frederick's worries might have been almost at an end; but after just seventeen days Celestine followed Gregory to the grave. For the next year and a half the Emperor, while simultaneously preparing a huge fleet to sail against Genoa and Venice, did everything he could to influence the next election, but in vain; the Genoese cardinal Sinibaldo dei Fieschi who in June 1243 became Pope Innocent IV (1243–54), though he lacked his predecessor's vehement intemperance, was to prove if anything an even more determined adversary than Gregory

[1] Revelation XIII, 1.

had been. Only two years after his accession, at a General Council in Lyons, he declared the already excommunicated Frederick deposed, stripping him of all his dignities and titles.

But emperors could not be thrown out so easily. The Hohenstaufen name retained immense prestige in Germany, while in Frederick's own kingdom his endless peregrinations had ensured him a consistently high profile, to the point where he seemed omnipresent: part of life itself. Loftily ignoring the papal pronouncement, he continued the struggle; Innocent fought back, supporting two successive anti-kings whom he had had elected by the German princes, using the Mendicant Orders to preach a Crusade against the Emperor, and even at one point conniving in a plot to assassinate him. He spent considerable sums of money on bribes, and would have spent more if the papal treasury had not been virtually empty: on his accession he had been besieged by a mob of creditors demanding the repayment of debts incurred by Pope Gregory.

King Louis IX of France did his best to mediate, but the quarrel was too deep; and the two were still at daggers drawn when, in December 1250 during a hunting trip in Apulia, Frederick suffered a violent attack of dysentery. He died a few days later at Castel Fiorentino, just thirteen days short of his fifty-sixth birthday. His body was taken to Palermo Cathedral where, at his request, it was consigned to the magnificent porphyry sarcophagus that had been prepared for his grandfather, Roger II, and can still be seen there today.

As his heir in Germany and in the *Regno* – as his southern Italian and Sicilian kingdom was now called – Frederick had named Conrad, his son by Yolande of Jerusalem; and during Conrad's absence in Germany he had entrusted the government of Italy and Sicily to Manfred, the favourite of his eleven illegitimate children. Manfred proved a worthy scion of his father. He re-created Frederick's brilliant court, founded the Apulian port of Manfredonia and – by marrying his daughter to the Despot of Epirus – acquired for the Empire the island of Corfu and a considerable stretch of the Albanian coast. Before long he had absorbed much of the Papal State, the March of Ancona, Spoleto and the Romagna. He did not (to the Pope's inexpressible relief) claim authority over northern Italy; nevertheless, his increasing power in the south could not but reawaken anxieties in Rome, and these became greater still when, in August 1258, the Sicilian baronage proclaimed him King.

Ever since Frederick's theoretical deposition, Innocent IV – and, after his death in 1254, his successor (and Gregory IX's nephew), the gentle, easy-going and ultimately ineffectual Alexander IV (1254–61) – had been seeking an 'athlete of Christ', who would rid southern Italy once and for all of the House of Hohenstaufen and lead the army of the Church to victory in the peninsula. Richard, Earl of Cornwall, brother of the English king Henry III, had seemed at one moment a possibility, but had finally refused to take up the challenge; so too – after the Pope had actually invested him with the southern kingdom – had King Henry's son Edmund. In 1261, however, Alexander died at Viterbo where, to avoid the factional strife in Rome, he had spent most of his pontificate; and after three months of inconclusive deliberations the cardinals elected a rank outsider, the Patriarch of Jerusalem, who happened to be visiting the Curia at Viterbo in his official capacity. Jacques Pantaléon was a Frenchman, the son of a poor cobbler in Troyes. He took the name of Urban IV (1261–4); and his eye soon fell on a compatriot, Charles of Anjou.

The brother of Louis IX, Charles was now thirty-five. In 1246 he had acquired through his wife the county of Provence, which had brought him untold wealth; he was also lord, inter alia, of the thriving port of Marseilles. To this cold, cruel and vastly ambitious opportunist the Pope was now offering a chance not to be missed. In return for a lump sum of 50,000 marks and the promise of an annual tribute of 10,000 ounces of gold, together with military aid as required, Charles would be enfeoffed with the kingdom of southern Italy and Sicily. The army that he was to lead against Manfred, and which began to assemble in northern Italy in the autumn of 1265, would be officially designated a Crusade – which meant that it would be as always something of a ragbag, with the usual admixture of adventurers hoping to secure fiefs in southern Italy, pilgrims seeking the remission of their sins and ruffians simply out for what they could get. With them, however, was an impressive number of knights from all over western Europe – French, German, Spanish, Italian and Provençal, with even a few English thrown in for good measure – who, Charles firmly believed, would be more than a match for anything Manfred could fling against them.

On 6 January 1266 – Epiphany – a group of cardinals in Rome invested Charles of Anjou with the crown of Sicily. (Neither Pope Urban nor his successor, Clement IV [1265–8], ever went near the Holy City, preferring to remain at Anagni or Viterbo.) Less than a month later, on 3 February, Charles's troops crossed the frontier into the *Regno* and met Manfred's on the 26th outside Benevento. It was all over quite quickly. Manfred, courageous as always, stood his ground and went down fighting, but his troops, hopelessly outnumbered, soon fled from the field. The battle had been decisive: the Crusade was over.

And so – or very nearly – was the House of Hohenstaufen. Two years later Conrad's son Conrad (better known as Conradin) made a last desperate attempt to save the situation, leading an army of Germans, Italians and Spaniards into the *Regno*. Charles hurried up and met them on 23 August 1268 at the border village of Tagliacozzo. This time the battle proved a good deal harder, resulting in hideous slaughter on both sides; but the Angevins again won the day. Conradin escaped, but was captured soon afterwards. There followed a show trial in Naples after which, on 29 October, the young prince – he was just sixteen – and several of his companions were taken down to the market place and publicly beheaded.

Manfred and Conradin were both, in their different ways, heroes. It was hardly their fault that they were overshadowed by their father and grandfather; so, after all, was much of the known world. The fact remains that, politically, Frederick had been a failure. Like virtually all the Hohenstaufen, he had a dream of making Italy and Sicily a united kingdom within the Empire, with its capital at Rome; the overriding purpose of the papacy, aided by the cities and towns of Lombardy, was to ensure that that dream should never be realised. It was unfortunate for the Emperor that he should have had to contend with two such able and determined men as Gregory and Innocent, but in the long run the struggle could have had no other outcome. The Empire, even in Germany, had lost its strength and cohesion; no longer could the loyalty of the German princes be relied upon, or even their deep concern. As for northern and central Italy, the Lombard cities would never again submit to imperial bluster. Had Frederick only accepted this simple truth, the threat to the papacy would have been removed and his beloved *Regno* might well have been preserved. Alas, he rejected it, and in doing so he not only lost Italy; he signed the death-warrant of his dynasty.

The Hohenstaufen were defeated; but it would be a mistake to see the papacy as victorious. Urban and Clement were both Frenchmen; they had done everything they could to support their compatriot, Charles of Anjou. Clement had not even protested at the cruel and vindictive execution of Conradin. It had been the intention of both popes, however, that Charles's authority should be confined to his new Sicilian kingdom; instead, his early victories had awoken in him far greater ambitions. These now encompassed the domination of all Italy, the reduction of the Pope to the status of a submissive puppet, the reconquest yet again of Constantinople – now once more in Greek hands – with its return to the Latin faith and, ultimately, the establishment of a Christian Empire that would extend the length and breadth of the Mediterranean. With every day that passed it was becoming clearer that his threat to the independence of the Holy See was potentially as great as Frederick's had ever been.

In November 1268 Pope Clement died at Viterbo; and it says much for Charles's influence in the Curia that he was able to keep the papal throne unoccupied for the next three years – conveniently covering the period that he was away crusading in Tunisia with his brother, Louis IX. The vacancy ended only when the authorities at Viterbo (where the conclave was being held) actually removed the roof of the palace in which the cardinals were deliberating. Their hasty choice had then fallen on Tedaldo Visconti, Archdeacon of Liège, who as Gregory X (1271–6) proved from Charles's point of view distinctly unhelpful, thwarting his attempts to have his nephew, Philip III of France, elected Holy Roman Emperor and allying himself with Byzantium to the extent of actually effecting, at the Council of Lyons in 1274, a temporary union of the Eastern and Western Churches. Only in 1281, after four more popes had come and gone,[1] did Charles get his way at last with the election of another Frenchman, Simon de Brie, who was crowned at Orvieto as Pope Martin IV (1281–5). Already master of Provence and the greater part of Italy, titular King of Jerusalem[2] and by a long way the most powerful – and dangerous – prince in Europe, Charles was now free to realise his greatest ambition by marching against Constantinople, whose Emperor, Michael VIII Palaeologus, Pope Martin obligingly redeclared schismatic. It was only twenty years since the Greeks had recovered their capital from

---

[1] Innocent V (1276) lasted for five months, Hadrian V (1276) for five weeks. John XXI (1276–7), a formidably intellectual Portuguese, had been Pope for eight months when the ceiling of his study in his new palace at Viterbo collapsed on his head. Because of his avariciousness and nepotism, Nicholas III (1277–80) had the distinction of being consigned by Dante to an eternity upside down in hell; after thirty-three months of dedicated opposition to Charles, he was carried off by a stroke.
[2] He had bought the title in 1277 from Princess Maria of Antioch, granddaughter of King Amalric II of Jerusalem.

the Franks; as 1282 opened, their chances of keeping it looked slim indeed.

They were saved by the people of Palermo. The French were already hated throughout the *Regno*, both for the severity of their taxation and the arrogance of their conduct; and when, on the evening of 30 March, a drunken French sergeant began importuning a Sicilian woman outside the church of Santo Spirito just as Vespers were about to begin, her countrymen's anger boiled over. The sergeant was set upon by her husband and killed; the murder led to a riot, the riot to a massacre. By morning 2,000 Frenchmen were dead. Palermo, and soon afterwards Messina, was in rebel hands. And now Peter III of Aragon, husband of Manfred's daughter Constance, saw his chance to make good his somewhat shadowy claim to the Sicilian crown. He reached Palermo in September, and by the end of October had captured Messina, where the French had made their last stand.

For Charles of Anjou, who had established his court in Naples, the War of the Sicilian Vespers and the consequent loss of Sicily spelt disaster. His kingdom was split down the middle, his reputation gone. His vaunted Mediterranean empire was seen to have been built on sand; he had ceased to be a world power. There could no longer be any question of an expedition against Byzantium. Little more than two years later Charles died at Foggia. But it was not only the reputation of the House of Anjou that had suffered. There was also the fact that Sicily and the *Regno* had been granted to Charles by the Pope; the papacy too had to look to its prestige. Martin had promptly proclaimed a Crusade against the Aragonese, but nobody took it very seriously; and it was a sad and disappointed Pope who – having in March 1285 dined too well on milk-fed eels from Lake Bolsena – followed his friend Charles to the grave.

The principal task of the next two popes was to expel the House of Aragon from southern Italy and restore that of Anjou. The first of the two, Honorius IV (1285–7),[1] being of a distinguished Roman family, was at least allowed to take up residence in the palace he had recently built on the Aventine; but he was already seventy-five on his accession, and almost paralysed by gout. He could hardly stand, let alone walk; he said Mass sitting on a stool, while his hands needed a mechanical contrivance to raise them from the altar. He reigned for

---

[1] Honorius was, incidentally, the last pope to have been married before his ordination.

only two years, and nearly a year was to pass before his successor was elected. The summer of 1287 was stiflingly hot, and killed off no fewer than six cardinals. The rest fled to the hills, returning in the autumn for their conclave. Even now they took their time: it was not until February 1288 that they elected – as a compromise – the first Franciscan pope and former General of the Order, Girolamo Masci (1288–92). As Nicholas IV, he was no more successful at restoring the Angevins than Honorius had been; nor, in 1291, could he do anything to prevent the Mameluke Sultan Qalawun from capturing Acre, thus putting an end, after 192 years, to Crusader Outremer. From its beginnings it had been a monument to intolerance and territorial ambition, its story one of steady physical and moral decline accompanied by monumental incompetence. Few people in western Europe were sorry to see it go.

After Nicholas died in April 1292 the twelve living cardinals met in Perugia – Rome at that time suffering one of its all-too-frequent visitations of the plague. They took their time, deliberating for twenty-seven months before picking on one of the most unsuitable men ever to occupy (however briefly) the papal throne. He was Pietro del Morrone, an eighty-five-year-old peasant who had lived for more than six decades as a hermit in the Abruzzi, and his only qualification was that once, appearing briefly at the court of Gregory X, he had hung up his outer habit on a sunbeam. There is a fascinating account by one of its members of the journey of a five-man papal embassy to Pietro's mountain hermitage – only to find that Charles II of Naples[1] had already got there. They found the new Pope in a state verging on panic; but he recovered at last and, after a prolonged period of prayer, reluctantly accepted the papal throne.

True, there had long been a prophecy of an 'angel pope', who would usher in the Age of the Spirit; but it is hard to see how anyone, viewing the agonised old man astride a donkey being led to his consecration at L'Aquila, could have believed that the Papacy was in safe hands – or, indeed, any hands at all. Indeed, Celestine V (1294) quickly proved himself to be nothing more than a puppet of Charles II, even taking up residence in the Castello Nuovo that still dominates the harbour of Naples. Within it he ordered the building of a small wooden cell, the only place where he could feel at home. He normally refused to

---

[1] Charles II was the son of Charles of Anjou. After the Sicilian Vespers, the Aragonese held Sicily; the House of Anjou retained Naples alone.

see his cardinals, whose worldliness and sophistication terrified him; when he did so, they were obliged to abandon their elegant Latin and adopt the crude vernacular that was the only language he could understand. The duties of the papacy, political, diplomatic and administrative, he ignored; favours were bestowed on anyone who asked for them. No wonder he lasted for just five months, then wisely announced his abdication: the only one in papal history.

The architect of this abdication was Cardinal Benedetto Caetani, who is said to have introduced a secret speaking-tube into Celestine's cell through which, in the small hours of the night, he would simulate the voice of God, warning him of the flames of hell if he were to continue in office. It was certainly Caetani who drafted the deed of renunciation that, on 13 December 1294, the Pope read out to the assembled cardinals, before solemnly stripping off the papal robes and revealing himself once again in his hermit's rags.

Poor Celestine: he is usually identified with the unnamed figure whom Dante meets in the Third Canto of the *Inferno* and accuses of 'having made through cowardice the great refusal' – *il gran rifiuto*. In fact he was no coward; he simply asked to return to the hermitage that he should never have left.

It was somehow inevitable that the successor to the luckless Pope Celestine, elected on Christmas Eve 1294 only twenty-four hours after the opening of the conclave in Naples, should have been that same Cardinal Benedetto Caetani, who now took the name of Boniface VIII (1294–1303). Of all his fellow-cardinals he was by far the most able, the most strong-willed and the most ambitious; he it was who had engineered Celestine's removal, and we may be sure that in doing so he had taken care to smooth his own path to the papal throne. Born around 1235 at Anagni of a modestly aristocratic family with papal connections (his mother was a niece of Alexander IV), he was now in his early sixties, with forty years of experience behind him. In his youth he had been member of a legation to England, where, during the civil war caused by the efforts of Simon de Montfort to curb the misgovernment of King Henry III, he had at one moment found himself besieged in the Tower of London, from where he was rescued in the nick of time by the future Edward I. On his return to Rome he had settled down to work for his own advancement, acquiring a steadily increasing number of benefices to help him on his way.

Having been appointed Cardinal by the Frenchman Martin IV,

Boniface had always been a steadfast supporter of the Angevin cause in Naples and Sicily; at his first coronation ceremony in Naples, his white horse had been led by Charles II. No sooner was he crowned, however, than he made it known that he was returning at once to Rome – and that his predecessor Celestine would be coming with him. The old man was predictably horrified: the whole object of his abdication had been to enable him to return to his mountain hermitage. With his vast following of the faithful, however, he might easily have become unwittingly the focus of opposition; and Boniface was taking no chances. On reaching Rome, the Pope was furious to learn that Celestine had somehow slipped away and taken once again to the hills; he gave immediate orders for his pursuit and arrest, by force if necessary. It took some time – despite his age, Celestine was still remarkably quick on his feet – but at last he was found and brought before his formidable successor. It was then that Celestine is said to have uttered his famous prophecy. 'You have entered like a fox,' he declared to Boniface, 'you will reign like a lion – and you will die like a dog.'

His words probably had little effect on his own fate; he was, whether he liked it or not, too dangerous to be allowed his liberty. Boniface imprisoned him in a remote castle at Fumone – it was in fact just the sort of place where Celestine felt at home – and there, ten months later at the age of ninety, he died.

Pope Boniface was recrowned in Rome on 23 January 1295. He was the epitome of the worldly cleric – indeed, he was as unlike his predecessor as it is possible to be. A first-class legist and a scholar, he founded Rome University, codified canon law and re-established the Vatican Library and Archive. But there was little of the spiritual in his nature. For him the great sanctions of the Church existed only to further his own temporal ends and to enrich his family. Foreign rulers he treated less as his subjects than as his menials. As for his office, he saw it in exclusively political terms, determined as he was to reassert the supremacy of the Apostolic See over the emerging nations of Europe. For this task he possessed abundant energy, self-confidence and strength of will; what he lacked was the slightest sense of diplomacy or finesse. Concepts such as conciliation, or compromise, simply did not interest him; he charged forward regardless – and ultimately he paid the price.

It was in a way typical of him that he should have declared 1300 a Holy Year, the first in Christian history. Attracted by the promise of 'full and copious pardon' to all who visited St Peter's and the Lateran after making their confession, some 200,000 pilgrims are said to have converged on Rome from all over the continent, vastly enriching the city – in certain of the basilicas, the sacristans were said to have had to gather in the offerings with rakes – and adding immeasurably to the papacy's prestige. Among the pilgrims was the poet Dante, who set the *Divine Comedy* in the Holy Week of that year; in Canto XVIII of the *Inferno* he actually compares the regimentation of the crowds in hell to the one-way system that he had seen controlling the traffic on the Ponte Sant'Angelo.

Among those thousands, however, there was not a single crowned head. King Charles was soon antagonised, as was Edward I of England when the Pope tried to claim Scotland as a papal fief. That operation failed, as did Boniface's attempts to dictate the succession in Hungary and Poland. Ironically enough, however, the Pope's most implacable enemy was the French king, Philip the Fair. Their mutual hostility had begun in 1296, when Philip imposed a heavy tax on the French clergy to help finance his campaign against England in Gascony – the curtain-raiser, as it were, to the Hundred Years War. Since the days of Innocent III such taxes had been customary for Crusades; but Philip's campaign could hardly be so described. Furious, the Pope replied with a Bull, *Clericis laicos*, which formally prohibited the taxation of clergy or Church property without express authorisation from Rome. Had he given the matter any serious consideration, he would have seen in an instant just how short-sighted his action was; Philip simply forbade the export of currency and valuables, simultaneously barring the entry of papal tax collectors into the country. Since the papal exchequer relied heavily on income from France, Boniface had no alternative but to climb down – attempting to recover some of his lost prestige by formally canonising Philip's grandfather, Louis IX.

Simultaneously, and quite unnecessarily, he made enemies of the immensely powerful family of Colonna. Although the family was a traditional rival of the Caetani, the two Colonna cardinals had originally supported his election; but they had quickly become disenchanted with his arrogance and autocratic style. Matters came to a head when in 1297 a party of Colonna supporters hijacked a consignment of bullion on its way to the papal treasury, claiming that it had been extracted 'from the tears of the poor'. Boniface as usual overreacted, threatening to send papal garrisons to their home city of Palestrina and other Colonna strongholds and expelling the two cardinals – who had no connection with the hijacking – from the Sacred College. Finally he excommunicated the family en masse, seizing and devastating its lands in the name of a Crusade. When the Colonna all fled to France, his principal enemies in Italy became the *Fraticelli*, a spiritual branch of the Franciscans, who had rebelled against the increasing worldliness of their Order to return to their founder's principles of asceticism and poverty. Boniface they loathed, not only for his wealth and arrogance, but because they held him responsible for Celestine's abdication, imprisonment and death.

Now the gloves were off. The Pope was made the victim of a campaign of scurrilous abuse, probably unequalled even in papal history. Its authors did not confine themselves to charges of nepotism, simony or avarice, which could all too easily be justified; they accused him of idolatry – because he had erected so many statues of himself – of atheism and even of sodomy. (Sex with boys, he was accused of saying, was no worse than rubbing one hand against the other.) All these accusations, and many others still more outlandish, were enthusiastically echoed in France – if indeed France was not their original source. Within three or four years of his accession Boniface VIII was probably the most widely detested pope there had ever been.

Then, in the autumn of 1301, King Philip summarily imprisoned the obscure but contumacious Bishop of Pamiers, charging him with treason and insulting behaviour. The Pope, without having troubled even to look into the case, angrily demanded the Bishop's release; Philip refused; and the battle between the two entered its final phase. Boniface, in yet another Bull, *Ausculta fili* ('listen, son'), loftily summoned the King himself, together with his senior clergy, to a synod in Rome in November 1302. Philip, it need hardly be said, once again refused; but thirty-nine French bishops, somewhat surprisingly, found the courage to attend. It was after this that Boniface fired his last broadside, *Unam sanctam*, in which – after liberal quotations from St Bernard of Clairvaux and St Thomas Aquinas – he claimed in so many words that 'it is altogether necessary for salvation for every human creature to be subject to the Roman Pontiff'. There was nothing particularly new in this; similar claims had been made by Innocent III and several other popes. Nonetheless, papal absolutism could hardly go further, and there was no question that it was King Philip whom Boniface had principally in mind.

Probably on the advice of his new minister, Guillaume de Nogaret (whose Albigensian grandfather had been burned at the stake, and who consequently had no love for the papacy), Philip now returned to his former tactic of all-out personal attack. All the old charges – together with several new ones, such as illegitimacy and heresy, which included disbelief in the immortality of the soul – were repeated, and an insistent demand made for a General Council at which the Supreme Pontiff should be arraigned. An army of 1,600 under de Nogaret in person was despatched to Italy with orders to seize the Pope and bring him, by force if necessary, to France. Boniface was meanwhile in his palace at Anagni, putting the finishing touches to a Bull excommunicating Philip and releasing his subjects from their allegiance. He was due to publish it on 8 September; but on the 7th de Nogaret and his troops arrived, together with Sciarra Colonna and a band of Italian mercenaries. The Pope donned his full papal regalia and faced them with courage, challenging them to kill him. They briefly took him prisoner; but he was rescued by the people of Anagni – he was, after all, one of their number – and spirited away. De Nogaret, seeing that there was no way of laying hands on him short of a massacre, wisely decided to retire.

His mission, however, had not been in vain. The old Pope's pride had suffered a mortal blow. After a few days' rest, his Orsini friends escorted him back to Rome; but he never recovered from the shock. He died less than a month later, on 12 October 1303. Dante, by anticipation – since Boniface died just three years after the poet's visit to hell – places him in the eighth circle, upside down in a furnace. His judgement may be thought a little harsh; but one sees, perhaps, what he meant.

CHAPTER XV

Avignon

(1309–67 and 1370–6)

The next Pope, Benedict XI (1303–4), was a humble Dominican who, we are told, felt at ease only with other Dominicans. He was one of his predecessor's few supporters. Despite his gentle demeanour, he had stood shoulder to shoulder with Pope Boniface at Anagni; now he applied himself to the delicate task of pacifying King Philip, and persuading him to drop his plans for a General Council as a means of bringing Boniface posthumously to justice. In this he was temporarily successful, though only after he had revoked all Boniface's existing papal decrees and pronouncements against Philip and his subjects, including every Frenchman who had been involved in the affair at Anagni – with the sole exception of de Nogaret himself. De Nogaret, Sciarra Colonna and the Italians, on the other hand, he denounced as being guilty of sacrilege in laying hands on the Supreme Pontiff, ordering them to present themselves before 29 June 1304. They never did so, because – apart from anything else – by that date the Pope was already mortally ill of dysentery in Perugia; ten days later he was dead.

The physical attack on Pope Boniface at Anagni had not been forgotten; hated as he had been, many right-thinking churchmen remained deeply shocked by King Philip's action, which they saw as an insult to the papacy and all it stood for. There were others, however, who had been equally disgusted by the Pope's treatment of the two Colonna cardinals and who wanted in any case to see an end to the long dispute with France – for which, with Boniface gone, there was no longer any real justification. The conclave that opened in Perugia in July 1304 was split down the middle, and the deadlock continued for eleven months; it was finally agreed that if a new pope were ever to be elected, he would have to come from outside the College of Cardinals. And so he did: Bertrand de Got, Archbishop of Bordeaux, who took the name of Clement V (1305–14). Not being a cardinal, he had not been present at the conclave; he had, however, attended Boniface's synod in 1302, despite which he had managed to maintain a friendly working relationship with Philip.

Although a shameless nepotist, the new Pope was a distinguished canon lawyer and an efficient administrator. He concentrated on the missionary role of the Church, going so far as to establish chairs in Arabic and other oriental languages at the universities of Paris, Oxford, Bologna and Salamanca. In his dealings with countries other than his own he was to show an impressive independence of spirit, releasing Edward I of England from his vows to his barons, suspending the Archbishop of Canterbury, excommunicating King Robert the Bruce of Scotland for the murder in church of his old enemy John Comyn, and settling a fifteen-year dispute over the Hungarian succession. Had he been an Italian, elected and crowned in Rome, he might well have proved himself, if not a great pope, at least a strong one. Being a subject of King Philip, however, from the moment of his election he found himself under almost intolerable pressure from his master. Philip began as he meant to go on, insisting first of all that, since the new Pope was already in France, he should be crowned there. The beginning of Clement's pontificate was far from auspicious: when he was riding to his coronation ceremony at Lyons, a wall onto which spectators had climbed to watch the procession suddenly collapsed. The Pope was knocked off his horse, but escaped with only bruises; others taking part in the procession were not so lucky. Several were seriously injured, and the Duke of Brittany was killed.

At that time there is no reason to believe that Clement did not fully intend to move to Rome in due course; his justification for remaining temporarily in France was his hope of bringing about an end to the hostilities between France and England, so that the two could combine their forces for another Crusade to the Holy Land. For four years he had no fixed abode; he moved constantly between Lyons, Poitiers and Bordeaux, his cardinals following as best they could. (By now they were mostly Frenchmen: of the ten he created in December 1305, nine were French – four of them his nephews – and the French element was to be increased still further in 1310 and again in 1312.) Philip meanwhile maintained the pressure to keep him in France; but in 1309 Clement decided to settle in Avignon – which, lying as it did on the east bank of the Rhône,[1] was at that time the property of Philip's

---

[1] The two banks were linked by the twelfth-century Pont Saint-Bénézet, the last bridge across the Rhône before it reached the Mediterranean. Originally it had twenty-two arches; unfortunately all but four were swept away by a great flood in 1680. This is the bridge that still lives in the old song, though there is a theory that the dancing actually took place under it, rather than upon it, on the little island of la Barthelasse.

vassal, Charles of Anjou, King of Sicily and Count of Provence. The little town (with around 5,000 inhabitants, it was at that time scarcely more than a village) was to be the home of six more popes after him, and the seat of the papacy for the next sixty-eight years.

Those years are often referred to as the 'Babylonian captivity'. It was nothing of the kind. The popes were in no sense captive; they were in Avignon because they wanted to be. Nonetheless, it was not a comfortable place. The poet Petrarch described it as 'a disgusting city', battered by the mistral, 'a sewer where all the filth of the universe is collected'. The Aragonese ambassador was so nauseated by the stench of the streets that he fell ill and had to return home. As papal territory, it was also a place of refuge for criminals of every kind, and its taverns and brothels were notorious. Nor was it designed to accommodate a papal court. The Pope and his immediate entourage moved into the local Dominican priory; a few fortunate cardinals managed to requisition the larger houses; the rest found a roof wherever they could.

The move to Avignon should at least have allowed Clement a degree of independence; but Philip was too strong for him. The Pope was a sick man (he suffered from stomach cancer throughout his pontificate) and he soon showed himself little more than a puppet of the French king. Unshaken in his determination to bring Pope Boniface to justice, Philip obliged Clement to open a full inquiry in 1309. Delays and various complications ensued, and in April 1311 the proceedings were suspended; the Pope, however, had to pay a heavy price: the complete rehabilitation of the Colonna cardinals, full compensation for their family, the annulment of all Boniface's actions that were prejudicial to French interests and the absolution of Guillaume de Nogaret. And a still greater humiliation was in store: the part that Clement was forced to play in Philip's plan for the elimination of the Knights Templar.

It is difficult for us nowadays to understand the influence of the Templars in the later Middle Ages. Founded in the early twelfth century to protect the pilgrims flocking to the Holy Places after the First Crusade and owing much to the patronage of St Bernard, these warrior-monks were within fifty years firmly established in almost every country of Christendom, from Denmark to Spain, from Ireland to Armenia; within a century 'the poor fellow-soldiers of Jesus Christ' were – despite their Benedictine vows of poverty, chastity and obedience – financing half of Europe, the most powerful bankers of the civilised world. By 1250 they were thought to possess some 9,000 landed properties; both in Paris and in London their houses were used as strongholds in which to preserve the royal treasure. From the English Templars, Henry III borrowed the purchase money for the island of Oléron in 1235; from the French, Philip the Fair extracted the dowry of his daughter Isabella on her ill-starred marriage to Edward II of England. For Louis IX – taken prisoner in Egypt at the end of the Sixth Crusade – the Templars provided the greater part of his ransom, and to Edward I they advanced no fewer than 25,000 *livres tournois*, four-fifths of which they were later to remit.

Of all the countries in which the Templars operated they were most powerful in France, where they effectively constituted a state within a state; and as their influence increased, it was not surprising that King Philip should have become seriously concerned. But Philip also had another, less honourable reason for acting against them: he was in desperate need of money. He had already dispossessed and expelled the Jews and the Lombard bankers; similar treatment of the Templars – which promised to secure him all the Templar wealth and property in his kingdom – would solve his financial problems once and for all. The Order would, he knew, prove a formidable adversary; fortunately, he had a weapon ready to hand. For many years there had been rumours circulating about the secret rites practised by the Knights at their midnight meetings. All he now needed to do was institute an official inquiry; it would not be hard to find witnesses who – in return for a small consideration – would be prepared to give the evidence required.

And so King Philip set to work; and the results of his inquiry proved even more satisfactory than he had dared to hope. The Templars, it now appeared, were Satanists. They worshipped an idol of their own, whom they had named *Baphomet* (possibly a corruption of Mahomet). They underwent a secret ceremony of initiation, in which they formally denied Christ and trampled on the crucifix. Their vow of poverty, as the whole world knew, had long gone out of the window; it was now revealed that their vow of chastity had suffered a similar fate. Sodomy in particular was not only permitted: it was actively encouraged. Such illegitimate children as were, nevertheless, happened to be engendered were disposed of – frequently by being roasted alive.

On Friday, 13 October 1307,[1] the Grand Master of the Temple,

---

[1] This is believed to be the origin of Friday the 13th's grim reputation.

Jacques de Molay, was arrested in Paris with sixty of his leading brethren. To force them to confess, they were put to the torture – first by the palace authorities and then by the Inquisition. Over the next six weeks no fewer than 138 Knights were subjected to examination, of whom (not surprisingly) 123, including de Molay himself, finally confessed to at least some of the charges levelled against them. Philip, meanwhile, wrote to his fellow-monarchs urging them to follow his example. Edward II of England – who probably felt on somewhat shaky ground himself – was initially inclined to cavil with his father-in-law, but when firm instructions arrived from Pope Clement he hesitated no longer. The English Master of the Order was taken into custody on 9 January 1308. All his Knights followed him soon afterwards.

The Templars had their champions. When de Molay was interrogated by three cardinals sent expressly to Paris by the Pope, he formally revoked his confession and bared his breast to show the unmistakable signs of torture. In consequence, at Clement's first consistory, no fewer than ten members of the Sacred College threatened to resign in protest against his policy; and early in February the Inquisition was instructed to suspend its activities against the Order. But it was impossible to reverse the tide. In August the Grand Master, examined and tortured yet again, pleaded guilty for the second time.

The public trial of the Templars opened on 11 April 1310, when it was announced that any of the accused who attempted to retract an earlier confession would be burned at the stake; on 12 May fifty-four Knights suffered this fate, and during the next fortnight nine others followed them. The whole contemptible affair dragged on for another four years, during which Pope and King continued to confer – a sure sign of the doubts that refused to go away – and to discuss the disposition of the Order's prodigious wealth. Meanwhile Jacques de Molay languished in prison until his fate could be decided. Only on 14 March 1314 did the authorities finally bring him out onto a scaffold before the Cathedral of Notre-Dame, to repeat his confession publicly for the last time.

They had reason to regret their decision. As Grand Master, Jacques de Molay had hardly distinguished himself over the previous seven years. He had confessed, retracted and confessed again; he had shown no heroism, few qualities even of leadership. But now he was an old man, in his middle seventies and about to die; he had nothing more to lose. And so, supported by his friend Geoffroy de Charnay, he spoke out loud and clear: as God was his witness, he and his Order were totally innocent of all the charges of which they had been accused. At once he and de Charnay were hurried away by the royal marshals, while messengers hastened to the King. Philip delayed his decision no longer. That same evening the two old Knights were rowed out to a small island in the Seine, where the stake had been prepared.

It was later rumoured that, just before he died, de Molay had summoned both Pope Clement and King Philip to appear at the judgement seat of God before the year was out; and it did not pass unnoticed that the Pope was dead in little more than a month, while the King was killed in a hunting accident towards the end of November. De Molay and de Charnay faced the flames with courage and died nobly. After night had fallen, the friars of the Augustinian monastery on the further shore came to collect their remains, to be revered as those of saints and martyrs.

A great pope – Gregory VII, for example, or Innocent III – could and would have saved the Templars; Clement, alas, fell a long way short of greatness. His craven subservience to Philip in the most shameful chapter of the King's reign constitutes an indelible stain on his memory. In one instance only did he show any inclination to go his own way: Philip – who had instituted the campaign solely to get his hands on the Templars' money – cannot have welcomed the Bull by which, on 2 May 1312, the Pope decreed that all their property (outside the kingdoms of Castile, Aragon, Portugal and Majorca, on which he deferred his decision) should devolve upon their brethren the Hospitallers, who suddenly found themselves richer than they had ever dreamed. But the King was dead long before the decree could be put into effect.

Throughout this period of Templar persecution the Pope's health was steadily deteriorating; the end came at the castle of Roquemaure on the Rhône on 20 April 1314. Clement V is remembered today principally for being the first of the Avignon popes; the important thing to remember, however, is that there was at no time any official transference of the papal capital. Clement himself never altogether abandoned the idea of a return to Rome; it was just that he constantly postponed it – and no wonder. North and central Italy were in greater turmoil than ever. Across Lombardy and Tuscany the Guelfs and Ghibellines were at each other's throats, as were the Colonna and the Orsini factions in Rome; when Prince Henry of Luxembourg arrived in Rome in 1312 for his coronation as the Emperor Henry VII, he had to fight his way into the city. (The ceremony was performed by three cardinals amid the ruins of the Lateran, which had been largely destroyed by fire four years before.) There was, in short, little temptation to cross the Alps; the Pope, already mortally ill, preferred to die in his homeland.

For two years and four months after the death of Clement V the papacy lay vacant. The conclave met first at Carpentras, but broke up when some of the Gascon cardinals incited an armed attack on the Italian faction. The disorder spread to the town, much of which was set on fire. One of Clement's nephews looted the papal treasury and disappeared. There followed a long cooling-off period, with the cardinals not reassembling until March 1316; even then, it was five more months before they could agree, which they did only after Philip V (who had succeeded his father in May) had imprisoned them in the Dominican convent, daily reducing their rations of food and drink until they reached a decision. Their choice fell on Jacques Duèse, who took the title of John XXII (1316–34). He was already sixty-seven but, unlike his predecessor, was a superb administrator; he was also possessed of boundless energy and was always ready to plunge into the fray. It was not long before he did so, in a long engagement with the Franciscan 'Spirituals', an extremist group akin to the *Fraticelli*, which called for a return to the original precepts of St Francis and the literal observance of his rule and testament, especially in relation to the principle of poverty. John, when appealed to, had no hesitation in pronouncing that there was nothing in the Scriptures to suggest that Christ and his Apostles were 'paupers', possessing no property of their own. Obedience, he declared, was a greater virtue than either poverty or chastity. He then went even further, by repudiating that convenient arrangement whereby Franciscan property was theoretically vested in the Holy See, which simply allowed the Order the 'use' of it. Henceforth the Franciscans were property owners – in many cases rather rich ones – whether they liked it or not.

All this had the effect of splitting the Order more than ever; and many Franciscans went into open schism. Among them were the General of the Order, Michael of Cesena, and the English theologian William of Ockham, both of whom fled from Avignon to the court of the Pope's arch-enemy, the German king Louis IV the Bavarian. Louis's hostility stemmed from 1322, when he had defeated and captured Frederick of Austria in battle, a victory that he believed entitled him to the crown of the Holy Roman Empire. John, however, had forbidden him to exercise imperial authority until he, as Pope, had settled the dispute. Louis had replied with what was known as the Sachsenhausen Appellation, in which he first denied papal authority over imperial elections and then went on to attack the Pope's condemnation of the Spirituals. To this John had replied with a sentence of excommunication; but in January 1328 Louis arrived in Rome – where he was crowned by the aged Sciarra Colonna, 'captain of the people' – and three months later solemnly deposed 'Jacques of Cahors' (that being the Pope's birthplace) from the pontificate, replacing him with an antipope in the person of a Franciscan Spiritual who called himself Nicholas V, and on whose head the Emperor himself laid the papal crown.

But Louis had gone too far. He was not an Otto the Great or a Frederick Barbarossa, a maker of popes and antipopes, and the Romans knew it. Moreover he had only a token army with him, and when King Robert of Naples sent an army northwards he fled, taking his antipope with him. In January 1329 the two of them were present at Pisa, with Michael of Cesena and William of Ockham, at a ceremony in the cathedral in which a straw effigy of Pope John, sumptuously attired in full canonicals, was formally condemned on a charge of heresy. This bizarre performance did little to enhance the reputation of either Emperor or Antipope, and Nicholas accompanied his protector and patron no further. With such little authority as he had ever possessed waning rapidly, he left Louis to return alone to Germany, and after a few months of wandering gave himself up. Pope John treated him with surprising leniency, with an official pardon and even a small pension – though he took the precaution of confining Nicholas, for the remaining three years of his life, to the papal residence.

The charge of heresy was obviously nonsense; but towards the end of his life, indeed when he was in his middle eighties, John XXII sailed a good deal closer to the wind. It was generally agreed by orthodox theologians that the saints in heaven were immediately admitted to a full vision of God; in a series of sermons delivered in the winter of 1331–2, John claimed this to be untrue, maintaining that the full Divine Vision would be withheld until after the Last Judgement; until then they could contemplate only the humanity of Christ. The ensuing storm of protest led to his condemnation by a committee of doctors of the University of Paris and to insistent demands for an Ecumenical Council. Finally the Pope made a modified retraction, confessing that the souls of the blessed would have their vision 'as clearly as their condition allowed' – a mildly ridiculous formula that nevertheless seemed to satisfy his critics. Like his predecessor, he was an unrepentant nepotist: of the twenty-eight cardinals he created, twenty were from southern France and three were his nephews. Unlike Clement, however, he never seriously considered a move to Rome[1]; at his death the Papacy was more thoroughly French – and under the influence of the French king – than it had ever been.

Avignon was by now a great deal larger (and richer) than it had been on the arrival of Clement V. After a quarter of a century as the home of the papacy, it was no longer a stinking village. It had now become a city, to which the fiscal system created by Popes Clement and John together had brought untold wealth. Whole districts had been swept away, fine palaces and mansions built for the cardinals and ambassadors, the bankers and merchants, the architects, painters and craftsmen who came from all over Europe to make their fortunes[2]. Papal Avignon was rapidly becoming the first great financial power of Europe. Petrarch, writing in 1340, was profoundly shocked:

> Here reign the successors of the poor fishermen of Galilee; they have strangely forgotten their origin. I am astounded, as I recall their ancestors, to see these men loaded with gold and clad in purple, boasting of the spoils of princes and nations; to see luxurious palaces and heights crowned with fortifications, instead of a boat turned downward for shelter . . .
>
> Instead of holy solitude we find a criminal host with crowds of infamous cronies; instead of soberness, licentious banquets; instead of pious pilgrimages, foul and preternatural sloth; instead of the bare feet of the Apostles, the snowy coursers of brigands fly past us, the horses decked with gold and fed on gold, soon to be shod with gold, if the Lord does not check this slavish luxury.

In all this vapid display, John was happy to give the lead. He it was who founded the vineyards of Châteauneuf-du-Pape; and a record has survived of the provisions laid in for the banquet he gave in

---

[1] There was at one moment a half-hearted proposal to move to Bologna; but it was almost immediately dropped.

[2] One of these palaces, the *Petit Palais*, still stands a hundred yards north-west of the cathedral. Its Renaissance façade was added in the late fifteenth-century by the Papal Legate Giuliano della Rovere, the future Pope Julius II.

November 1324 on the occasion of the marriage of his great-niece. They included nine oxen, fifty-five sheep, eight pigs, four wild boars, 200 capons, 690 chickens, 3,000 eggs, 580 partridges, 270 rabbits, forty plovers, thirty-seven ducks, fifty-nine pigeons, four cranes, two pheasants, two peacocks, 292 small birds, three hundredweight of cheese, 2,000 apples and other fruit, and eleven barrels of wine.

Perhaps the Spirituals had a point, after all.

Pope John XXII died on 4 December 1334. This time, for once, the cardinals acted reasonably quickly. The new Pope was inducted on the 20th: the Bishop of Pamiers, a baker's son and former Cistercian monk named Jacques Fournier, who took the name of Benedict XII (1334–42). He was not an attractive figure. Tall and heavily built, with an exceptionally loud voice, he had made his name as an Inquisitor, and had taken it upon himself to eliminate the last vestiges of Catharism from the south-west of France. In this he had been entirely successful: in the presence of five bishops and the King of Navarre, 183 men and women were burned at the stake – a spectacle described by a contemporary as 'a holocaust, very great and pleasing to God'.[1] Pope John had then made him a cardinal, as a reward for a job well done.

And yet, dour and unbending through he may have been, Benedict had his qualities. He possessed none of John's arrogance; despising all luxury, he continued to dress in the Cistercian habit. Nepotism he detested – none of his relatives achieved advancement – and he declared war on all the countless abuses that had grown up during the pontificates of his two predecessors. All the clerical hangers-on and vagabond monks who had no good reason for staying at Avignon were dismissed; fees payable for documents issued were fixed for the first time; strict new constitutions were drawn up for the Cistercians, Franciscans and Benedictines. In the diplomatic field, however, his touch was less sure. He failed miserably in his attempts to prevent the outbreak of the Hundred Years War between France and England – putting an end to any prospect of a joint Crusade – and his efforts to mend fences with the Emperor Louis were easily frustrated by the French king Philip VI and the King of Naples.

There is evidence to suggest that at the very beginning of his pontificate Benedict may have seriously contemplated a return to Italy, though

---

[1] E. Mullins, *Avignon of the Popes*. The appalling story is told in detail by Emmanuel Le Roy Ladurie in *Montaillou*.

probably – since the situation in Rome showed no improvement – only as far as Bologna in the first instance. Almost immediately on his accession he had ordered the restoration and reroofing of St Peter's, and for some years he continued to spend large sums on both it and the Lateran. Before long, however, he seems to have been dissuaded from the idea by the cardinals (nearly all of whom were French) and by King Philip; and by the end of 1335 his subjects were no longer in any doubt that the papacy was to remain, for the foreseeable future – perhaps even in perpetuity – on the banks of the Rhône. Work had begun on the *Palais des Papes*.

The chosen site was immediately to the south of the cathedral. The first building to rise was a 150-foot tower, the lower part designed to house the papal treasury, the upper to contain the Pope's personal apartments. To this Benedict added a two-storey chapel and what is now the whole of the northern section of the palace; he left his successor to contribute the rather more elaborate west and south wings, thus forming a spacious cloister – later to become the *cour d'honneur* – to the south of which is the huge vaulted audience chamber. A somewhat awkward combination of palace, monastery and fortress, the *Palais des Papes* can hardly be counted an architectural success; nowadays, too, it suffers from an almost embarrassing lack of furniture. But it remains an undeniably impressive monument to the exiled papacy.

Pope Benedict died on 25 April 1342. Petrarch claimed that he was 'weighed down by age and wine'; in fact he was only in his early sixties, but there may be something in the accusation: despite his otherwise rigorous austerity, he was known for his prodigious appetite. His successor could hardly have provided more of a contrast. Pierre Roger, though not of illustrious birth – he was the son of a landed squire in the Corrèze – had already had an astonishing career. Possessor of a double doctorate in theology and canon law, Archbishop of Sens at twenty-eight and of Rouen at twenty-nine, he had shortly afterwards been appointed Chancellor and Chief Minister of France by Philip VI. The King had actually been so anxious for him to succeed Benedict that he had sent his son to Avignon in the hope that he could sway the election, but the Prince arrived to find that there was no need: the cardinals had already elected Roger as Pope Clement VI (1342–52).

'My predecessors,' announced Clement, 'did not know how to be Pope.' He set out to show them, though in fact he lived less like a pope than an oriental potentate. Sumptuously dressed, surrounded by a vast entourage of attendants, showering wealth and favours on all who approached him ('a pope,' he also declared, 'should make his subjects happy'), in his extravagance and outward display he easily outclassed all the crowned heads of Europe; the cost of his court is said to have been ten times that of King Philip's in Paris. Three thousand guests sat down to his coronation banquet, at which 1,023 sheep, 118 head of cattle, 101 calves, 914 kids, sixty pigs, 10,471 hens, 1,440 geese, 300 pike, 46,856 cheeses, 50,000 tarts and 200 casks of wine were consumed. Yet it was not just his surroundings that dazzled; it was the man himself. He was formidably intelligent, the finest orator and preacher of his day; his charm was irresistible. But all the old abuses returned. Back, with a vengeance, came the bad old days of nepotism. Of the twenty-five cardinals whom Clement appointed during his ten-year pontificate, twenty-one were French and at least ten his close relations; one of them, who was later to become Gregory XI – the last of the seven Avignon popes – was widely believed to be his son. There were other rumours, too, where women were concerned: many of them tending to centre on the lovely Cécile, Countess of Turenne, sister-in-law of the Pope's nephew, who regularly acted as hostess at the palace. Petrarch, as usual, became almost hysterical with indignation:

> I will not speak of adultery, seduction, rape, incest; these are only the prelude to their orgies. I will not count the number of wives stolen or young girls deflowered. I will not tell of the means employed to force into silence the outraged husbands and fathers, nor of the dastardliness of those who sell their womenfolk for gold.

Prostitutes, he maintained, 'swarmed on the papal beds'. Poets, perhaps, never make the best witnesses; but Petrarch – one of the great writers of the Middle Ages – could, had he wished, have given us a brilliant and accurate description of papal Avignon. It is a pity that instead he has left us a travesty that borders on the grotesque.

Did Pope Clement ever for a moment consider a papal return to Rome? Certainly not. Not only did he complete the Papal Palace begun by Benedict; in 1348 he bought Avignon and the surrounding County of Venaissin from Joanna, Queen of Naples and Countess of Provence. Joanna was twenty-two, and famed for her beauty; but she had come to Avignon as a fugitive. Three years before, her young husband Prince

Andrew of Hungary, who was living with her in Naples, had been assassinated, on the orders of her great-aunt Catherine of Valois, but not without suspicion of Joanna's own complicity. Andrew's brother, King Lewis of Hungary, on the pretext of avenging the murder, then invaded Naples, claiming the kingdom for himself. Joanna had fled to Avignon with her second husband, Louis of Taranto, to seek protection from her brother-in-law and to beg Pope Clement to clear her name.

Clement, who made no secret of his taste for beautiful women, was only too happy to agree. The result of the inquiry that followed was almost certainly a foregone conclusion, but it was obviously important to go through the motions. The Pope's throne was set on a dais, with his cardinals ranged on each side of him to form a semicircle. The prosecution was conducted by two ambassadors of King Lewis; Joanna, we are told, defended herself – and did so quite brilliantly. Clement then rose to his feet and pronounced her innocent. Her first objective attained, Joanna now had a further appeal to make. Her odious brother-in-law had seized the treasury and she was penniless. He had now gone back to Hungary, and she had been recalled to Naples by the local barons; but she and her husband did not even have the money to make the journey. The Pope was once again delighted to oblige. He immediately made available 80,000 gold florins, in return for which he took possession of the city and county.

What makes this story more remarkable still is that it took place in the year of the Black Death. The plague had reached Avignon in January 1348; by September it had claimed no fewer than 62,000 – perhaps three-quarters of the population of the city and its surroundings – including Petrarch's lover Laura and every single one of the English community of Austin Friars.[1] Pope Clement, who could easily have taken refuge in the countryside, showed considerable courage by remaining in Avignon, where he arranged for carters to take away the dead and gravediggers to bury them – though all too soon both groups were obliged to give up the struggle. He also bought a huge field to be converted into a cemetery. By the end of April 11,000 had been buried there and another layer of corpses had to be laid on top. According to a Flemish canon who happened to be there at the moment of the outbreak:

---

[1] 'Nor,' wrote Canon Henry Knighton of Leicester towards the end of the century, 'did men care.' 'At Marseilles,' he added still more uncharitably, 'of one hundred and fifty Franciscans not one survived to tell the tale – and a good job too!'

about the middle of March the Pope, after mature deliberation, gave absolution till Easter to all those who, having confessed and being contrite, should happen to die of the sickness. He likewise ordered devout processions, singing the litanies, to be made on certain days each week. To these events, it is said, people sometimes gather from all the neighbouring districts to the number of up to two thousand; among them many of both sexes are barefoot, some are in sackcloth, some with ashes, walking with tears and tearing their hair, and beating themselves with scourges even to the drawing of blood.

In the early days of the epidemic the Pope himself would join these processions, but realising that they could only spread the infection, he soon put a stop to them. He himself then wisely retired to his private apartments, where he received no one and spent the entire day and night roasting himself between two blazing fires. When at the height of the Avignon summer this became impossible, he retired briefly to his castle near Valence, but with the coming of autumn he returned to the roasting. The treatment proved successful – he survived – but it was not until Advent that the scourge was finally seen to be on the wane; and by then there were few people in Avignon left to celebrate.

As Europe emerged from the nightmare, it began to look for scapegoats; and – perhaps inevitably – it settled on the Jews. Was the Jew not Antichrist? Did he not kidnap and torture Christian children? Did he not regularly desecrate the Host? Had he not poisoned the wells of the Christian communities, infecting all their members with the plague? In vain did the Jews point out that they had suffered every bit as much as the Christians – arguably even more, thanks to the swarming ghettos in which they were obliged to live; their accusers refused to listen. As early as May, there was a massacre of Jews in Provence, and in Narbonne and Carcassone the entire Jewish communities were liquidated. In Germany and Switzerland the persecutions fell not far short of a holocaust. Pope Clement acted swiftly. Twice, on 4 July and 26 September, he published Bulls that condemned the massacres, wherever they might occur, and called on all Christians to conduct themselves with tolerance and restraint. Those who continued to victimise any Jew would be instantly excommunicated.

Alas, for many Jews he was too late. Communications were slow in the fourteenth century; despite his efforts some 350 separate massacres took place and more than 200 Jewish communities suffered complete annihilation. But for this Clement cannot be blamed. On the contrary, he should be remembered as the first pope in history to undertake an active defence of the Jewish people, wherever they might be found. It was the noblest and most courageous act of his life – an example that all too many of his successors might usefully have followed.

In an attempt to revive the spiralling Roman economy, Pope Clement had declared 1350 a Holy Year, but it had not been a success. Pilgrims arriving in Rome had been shocked by the general dilapidation and decay. The city, now without a pope for nearly half a century, was as sad as it had ever been. There had been a brief moment when it seemed as though the Romans might recover their self-respect; this was in 1344, when Cola di Rienzo, the son of a Roman washerwoman who happened to be a demagogue of genius, had launched a blistering campaign against the local aristocracy, inflaming the popular imagination with his evocations of the city's past greatness and his prophecies of a glorious rebirth. Such was his success that three years later, on the Capitol, he was invested with the title of Tribune and given limitless dictatorial powers; then, summoning a 'national' assembly, he solemnly conferred Roman citizenship on all the cities of Italy and announced plans for the election of an Italian emperor, presumably himself.

But appeals for Italian unity, whether pronounced by German princes or Roman agitators, were always doomed to failure. The dictatorial powers that Cola had so effortlessly acquired went to his head. He took up residence in what was left of the Lateran Palace; he adopted the title of 'White-robed Knight of the Holy Spirit'; he took a ritual bath in the porphyry basin in which it was believed that Pope Sylvester had baptised Constantine the Great;[1] finally, we are told, he was crowned with six separate crowns. No wonder that by 1347 the Roman mob had turned against him and forced him into exile. Excommunicated by the Papal Legate, he first found refuge with the *Fraticelli*; then in 1350 he moved on to Prague, to seek the aid of the King of Germany, Charles IV. This, however, proved a serious mistake: Charles recognised a madman when he saw one, locked him up for two years and then handed him over to the Pope. Clement, who could never quite resist Cola, had him put on trial for heresy, but secretly arranged for his acquittal.

---

[1] In fact, Constantine was baptised in Nicomedia, on his deathbed. See Chapter II.

When, in December 1352, Pope Clement died at the age of sixty-one, Cola di Rienzo was still languishing in captivity at Avignon. The following year he stood trial, and was duly found not guilty. Then in 1354 Clement's successor Innocent VI (1352–62), who had set his heart on a return of the papacy to Rome, conceived the idea of sending Cola back there with the rank of Senator, trusting that he would help his Vicar-General, the Spanish cardinal Gil Alvarez Carrillo de Albornoz, to prepare the way – reasserting papal authority in the city, leading the opposition to the ever-hostile aristocracy and winning over the masses to the papal cause. Cola accordingly made his way back to the scene of his former triumphs, where he was given a guarded welcome; but the old magic was gone. The mob, fickle as always, rose against him. In vain he showed himself on the balcony of the Capitol, clad in shining armour and bearing aloft the banner of Rome; they only jeered the louder. Disguising himself as a beggar, he tried to flee, but the gold bracelets glinting under his rags betrayed him. Minutes later his body was hanging by the feet in a public square, a fate eerily similar to that which befell, six centuries later, his most successful imitator – Benito Mussolini.

Innocent VI was already seventy years old; but he had lost none of his energy. Many of the cardinals, accustomed as they were to the splendour of life under Clement, must, one feels, have bitterly regretted their choice. Under the new regime Avignon suffered a sea change. Away went the colour, the luxury and extravagance, the parades and processions; back came austerity, parsimony, impartiality and discipline. As in the reign of Benedict XII, reform was the order of the day. The new Pope himself offered his mansion at Villeneuve – on the far side of the Rhône – to the Carthusians, adapting it to monastic life largely at his own expense.[1] But Rome remained constantly in his mind; and he could have had no better representative there than Albornoz. More a general than a churchman, the Cardinal rapidly subdued the various despots and feudal lords who had taken effective control of the Papal States. One after another, the rebellious cities fell: Viterbo, Orvieto, Spoleto, Rimini, Ancona. Most important of all, he recovered Bologna from the Visconti of Milan. Not all his conquests were achieved by force of arms – bribery too played its part, not least at Bologna – but by 1364 the Papal States once again all acknowledged papal authority.

---

[1] Now known as the Chartreuse du Val de Bénédiction, it was badly damaged in the Revolution. But the double nave can still be seen, with Pope Innocent's tomb.

The Pope had worked hard (and on the whole successfully) to put his house in order. Under him Avignon was certainly a gloomier, greyer place than it had been in the days of his glittering predecessor; but the worst abuses were eliminated and the books were balanced. In the diplomatic field he maintained friendly relations with Charles IV – who in 1355 paid a whirlwind visit to Rome, there to be crowned by the Cardinal-Bishop of Ostia – even after Charles published his so-called Golden Bull, which regulated the election of the German kings, making no mention of the Pope's right to approve the candidates. But his plans for a new Crusade failed (as by now such plans always did) and his attempt to heal the schism with Byzantium was equally unsuccessful. (Since he followed the usual papal policy of making this conditional on the Byzantines' total subjection to Rome, the failure was hardly surprising.)

Perhaps Innocent's greatest diplomatic achievement was to negotiate in 1360 the Treaty of Brétigny, which brought nine years of comparative peace in the middle of the Hundred Years War. All too soon, however, he had reason to regret his action. During hostilities the mercenary armies, which accounted for much of the fighting strength of both sides, were generously paid and did, on the whole, pretty well for themselves; now, with the peace, they suddenly found themselves unemployed. What could they do but form themselves into 'free companies' and take to brigandage? And where could they expect richer pickings than in the papal capital? In December 1360 – only seven months after the signature of the treaty – they seized the little town of Pont-Saint-Esprit, some twenty-five miles up the Rhône, and cut off Avignon's communications with the outside world. Before long the city itself was under siege; and that siege was still in progress when, early in 1361, the plague returned. By the beginning of summer there were another 17,000 dead, including nine cardinals.

And Pope Innocent, now approaching eighty, gave in. He bought off the brigands, offering them a large sum of money (which he had to borrow) in return for their departure. The precise terms of the agreement have not come down to us. It may well be that it involved their undertaking to move down into Italy, there to assist Cardinal Albornoz in his campaign of pacification. The Cardinal is known to have had several free companies in his pay, but did they include the besiegers of Avignon? We shall never know.

*   *   *

Pope Innocent died, a sad and disappointed man, in September 1362. The cardinals' first choice as his successor was the brother of Clement VI – they clearly longed for a return of the good old days – but he refused; failing to agree on one of themselves, they then picked a Benedictine monk, Guillaume de Grimoard, who became Pope Urban V (1362–70). Thanks to various missions to Italy as Papal Legate, he was not completely inexperienced in public affairs; but he remained unworldly, austere and deeply pious. Throughout the eight years of his pontificate he insisted on wearing the black habit of his Order, and at night slept on bare boards in a specially contrived monk's cell. Several hours of each day he spent in study and prayer. A serious scholar himself and patron of the arts and sciences, he distributed bursaries to poor students with a generous hand – at one moment he is said to have personally supported 1,400 of them – endowed a college at Montpellier and founded universities not only at nearby Orange, but as far afield as Vienna and Cracow.

Urban cherished two overriding ambitions: first, a Crusade against the Turks, which, he hoped, might also bring the Eastern Church back into the Catholic fold; second, the return of the papacy to Rome. Once again, the Crusade failed to get off the ground. It was to have been led by the French king John II, who had been captured by the English at the battle of Poitiers and had only recently been released – in exchange for several hostages (including his son), pending the raising of the ransom money. He had come to Avignon, where he had sworn to lead an army of 150,000 men to deliver the Holy Land. But before he could do so his hostage son escaped, and John – as a point of honour – voluntarily returned to his English captivity. He was still in England when he died.

As for the long-discussed return to Rome, conditions were now more favourable than they had been for half a century. Albornoz had done his work well; Bernabò Visconti had continued to make trouble over Bologna but had finally been bought off, and the Papal States were – more or less – at peace. And so, in June 1366, Pope Urban publicly announced, not only to his cardinals but to all the princes of Europe, that the papacy was leaving Avignon for Rome. Whatever the princes may have thought, the papal court was horrified. By now virtually all its members, from the cardinals down to the humblest of scribes, were Frenchmen. Their homes, on many of which they had spent small fortunes, were in Avignon or Villeneuve. Their language was French or Provençal. The last thing they wanted was to leave it all for a malarial, malodorous city known to be in the last stages of dilapidation and decay, perpetually torn apart by a corrupt aristocracy and a famously unpredictable rabble. But the Holy Father had spoken. There was nothing they could do but start packing.

For a glorious moment it looked as if the dreaded journey might be indefinitely postponed: the French freebooter-general Bertrand du Guesclin, ordered by his king Charles V to lead an army of some 30,000 – mostly free companies – against Pedro the Cruel of Spain, took it upon himself to make a detour to Avignon, where he cheerfully demanded 200,000 gold florins to pay (he said) for his coming campaign. The Pope replied by excommunicating the lot of them, but they only became more threatening, laying waste the surrounding countryside, terrorising the entire neighbourhood, raping prodigious numbers of nuns and generally behaving like occupying armies at their worst. Urban, in despair, instituted a special tax on everyone in the city and paid the sum demanded; but du Guesclin, on learning that the money had been extracted from the populace, immediately returned it, insisting that he had no wish to impoverish the people. The funds that he had demanded would be accepted only if they came exclusively from the papal coffers. The result was a new levy, still more unpopular, which fell on churchmen alone; only then did the General lead his men away across the Pyrenees to Spain.

The court returned to its melancholy preparations. A rump was to be left at Avignon, so that day-to-day papal business could continue until such time as Rome was ready to take over; for the rest, the date of the great departure was fixed for 30 April 1367. It is difficult to imagine the sheer scale of the operation: the transfer of hundreds (perhaps thousands) of people, their families and all their worldly goods, together with the entire papal archives, furniture and equipment, all to be loaded on to barges and floated downstream to Marseilles. From there, on 19 May, the Pope and his cardinals embarked on a flotilla of vessels supplied by Venice, Genoa, Pisa and – from their base in Rhodes – the Knights of St John. The Knights also agreed to escort the bulk of the party, which took the land route, first to Genoa and then south-eastwards down the west coast of Italy.

After seventeen days on heavy seas the papal fleet arrived on 5 June at the port of Corneto, where Albornoz was waiting. Urban naturally wished to press on to Rome at once, but the Cardinal dissuaded him. The Lateran Palace, Albornoz pointed out, was utterly uninhabitable. The Vatican was in the course of preparation, but was by no means ready: how much better it would be if the Holy Father were to remain in Viterbo as his guest until the autumn. It was thus not until 16 October, escorted by an armed force of 2,000, that Urban entered Rome – the first pope for sixty-three years to set foot in the city.

He was to remain for only three; but during that time he began a complete rebuilding of the Lateran and instituted an ambitious programme of repair to the churches of Rome, nearly all of which were by now crumbling. Meanwhile the presence of a pope acted on the Romans like a tonic; at last, it seemed, there was a chance of stability, even of prosperity. Their morale was raised still further by the lavish celebrations that were organised to greet the various princes of Europe who beat a congratulatory path to the papal door: Peter I of Cyprus, Queen Joanna of Naples, the Holy Roman Emperor Charles IV and – most remarkable of all – the Emperor John V Palae-ologus of Byzantium, who on Thursday, 18 October 1369 formally signed a document declaring his personal acceptance of the Roman Catholic faith, sealing it with his imperial golden seal. There was no question of any union of the two Churches, which remained as far apart as they had ever been – not a single Orthodox churchman had accompanied the Emperor to Rome. John signed with one purpose only in his mind: to persuade western Europe to send military help against the Ottoman Turks, whose threat to Constantinople was growing day by day. His signature was binding on himself, but on no one else. Urban was the first and the last pontiff to receive visits from both Eastern and Western Emperors; and John's arrival should have marked the triumphant vindication of his decision to bring the papacy back to Rome – achieved in the face of considerable phys-ical danger and appalling administrative upheaval, to say nothing of the determined opposition of the King of France and virtually the entire College of Cardinals. But the truth was that the Pope had had enough. He was now approaching sixty, his heart was still in France – of the eight new cardinals he had created in September 1368, six had been Frenchmen and only one a Roman – and since arriving in Rome the College had, if anything, increased its pressure. Moreover Albornoz was now dead, and without his firm grip on Italian affairs the political situation in Italy was again deteriorating fast. Perugia had actually gone so far as to revolt against Roman authority and to hire a free company of mercenaries to threaten papal Viterbo. This was under the command of the notorious English soldier of fortune Sir John Hawkwood, who had fought at both Crécy and Poitiers and had now settled in Italy, where he was cheerfully selling his sword to the highest bidder.

Probably after he had been made an offer that he could not refuse, Hawkwood was persuaded to come to terms; but now the Pope received even more alarming news. In 1369 Charles V of France had summarily annexed the province of Aquitaine, which had been part of the dowry of Queen Eleanor when she had married the future Henry II of England in 1152. Henry's great-great-great-grandson King Edward III, had outraged, launched not one but two separate expeditions to recover it. The Treaty of Brétigny was forgotten; the Hundred Years War raged again, as fiercely as ever it had. To Pope Urban this was a catastrophe. He had given his word to John Palaeologus that he would do his utmost to organise a major Crusade against the Ottoman Turks, but he was well aware that this would only be possible if the French and the English could forget their differences and agree to act together in the cause of Christendom. Somehow he must restore peace between them. Clearly, there was no way that he could do so from distant Rome; from Avignon, however, there might just be a chance. And so, with outward reluctance but, one suspects, a good deal of inner relief, he gave the order to return.

The papal flotilla of thirty-four ships sailed from Corneto on 4 September 1370; before the end of the month the Pope was back in Avignon, where on the 27th he was given a hero's welcome. Few among those present, whether lay or ecclesiastic, can have believed that, after this disastrous experiment, the papacy would ever leave Avignon again. Rome was quite simply too remote, too dangerous, too unhealthy, too impractical. No one in his right mind, surely, would dream of returning there. Did Pope Urban himself share this view? Possibly; and yet however glad he may have been to be back in civilisation, he must have felt a profound sense of disappointment, even of failure. There is no record of his having opened negotiations with the kings of France or England; but he had little opportunity. Within six weeks of his return he fell seriously ill, and on 19 December he died. He was buried in Avignon Cathedral; but in 1372 his body was transferred by his brother to the Abbey of St Victor in Marseilles. There it became the object of a cult – which is presumably why, five centuries later in 1870, Pope Pius IX saw fit to beatify him.

Technically, as we know, papal Avignon did not form part of France. Culturally and emotionally, on the other hand, its people saw themselves as Frenchmen – or as Provençaux, which at that time was much the same thing. With its population now risen to some 30,000, their city might be only a quarter the size of Paris; but as an intellectual and religious centre and a focus of banking and international trade, it could invite comparison with the capital itself. The University Law School attracted students from all over Europe, as did the School of Theology, which was accommodated in the Papal Palace. Here too was the magnificent Library with its renowned collections of Arabic and Hebrew manuscripts, to say nothing of its volumes of Greek and Latin literature and philosophy, which were to make the city an early centre for humanist studies. The dirty, smelly old Avignon castigated by Petrarch had long since passed away; visitors in 1370 saw a fine and prosperous city, dominated by the great palace itself, its streets lined with smaller palaces and mansions fit for cardinals and bishops to live in. Churches and monasteries had sprung up in profusion, both inside and outside the walls. The commercial district was thronged; few were the luxuries from East or West that the merchants of Avignon were unable to supply.

It was therefore, perhaps, with a feeling of slightly smug told-you-so satisfaction that the overwhelmingly French College of Cardinals met in conclave to choose, after just two days, one of their own number: Pierre-Roger de Beaufort, to be known as Gregory XI (1370–8). He had been a churchman since childhood. Canon of Rodez at eleven, cardinal – appointed by his uncle, Clement VI – at nineteen, he was deeply religious, ascetic and inclined towards mysticism, but he also possessed a quality of steely self-will that frequently astonished those who knew him. His one weakness was his health, which constantly gave his doctors cause for anxiety, and occasionally even for alarm.

It was probably the mystical element in his character which convinced him that, despite the obvious advantages of Avignon and the unfortunate experience of his predecessor, the papacy belonged in Rome. True, Avignon was more favourably situated if there were to be any brokering of peace between England and France; but the situation in the Papal States was every bit as important for Christendom, and it was plain that the troublemaking rebel warlords of that region could be kept in check only from Italy. Besides, Gregory was one of the very few Avignon churchmen who genuinely liked the peninsula. In his youth he had studied law in Perugia, where he had known many of the foremost humanist scholars of the day and learned excellent Italian. Later, during Urban's years in Rome, he had been one of the Pope's principal deputies.

And so he made up his mind; and on 9 May 1372 he announced to his cardinals that they would all be leaving 'very shortly' for Rome.

Of course, as he should have known, it was not as easy as that. There was the opposition to be faced down not only from the cardinals, but from the kings of France and England. Second, there was no money in the treasury to pay the costs of transportation. Campaigns in Italy, to say nothing of the removal two years before of most of the papal court and Curia to Rome and back, had emptied the papal coffers. Gregory was obliged to borrow – 60,000 gold florins from the Duke of Anjou and another 3,000 from the King of Navarre – simply to keep the papacy on its feet. Moreover, as always, Italy was in turmoil; once again it was the Visconti of Milan on the warpath, threatening Piedmont (which did not worry the Pope too much) and Romagna (which worried him a great deal). The strong measures that he took against Milan – a military league, an interdict, even the preaching of a Crusade – all came to nothing and he eventually had to conclude a humiliating peace. Meanwhile Bologna had declared its independence, and the Pope had to summon Albornoz's successor as his Legate in Italy, Cardinal Robert of Geneva, to recruit a troop of free companies to assert his authority.

Cardinal Robert possessed none of the diplomatic subtlety of his predecessor. He immediately blockaded Bologna in an attempt to starve its citizens into surrender, laying waste all the surrounding countryside and allowing his mercenaries to rape and murder to their hearts' content. His final atrocity was to turn them loose on the neighbouring town of Cesena; the result was a massacre of more than 4,000 men, women and children. Bologna, however, continued to hold out; it was not until after the Pope was back in Rome that a truce was finally concluded.

All this could only delay matters further, as did a last-minute appeal for arbitration from the kings of England, France and Aragon. For all these reasons it was not until some four and a half years after his first announcement that Pope Gregory eventually left Avignon. He might have delayed still longer, had it not been for a formidable young Dominican nun, Caterina Benincasa, better known today as St Catherine of Siena, who appeared in Avignon to demand a new anti-Muslim Crusade, simultaneously calling on Gregory to return the papacy to its historical and spiritual home.[1] He eventually left, with

---

[1] She is not to be confused with another female saint, St Bridget of Sweden, who had put similar pressure on Urban V and is now (since 1999) patron saint of Europe.

his cardinals and court, on 12 September 1376, bound in the first instance for Marseilles, where the ships provided by Queen Joanna and other rulers were waiting. Almost at once the little fleet was caught up in a violent storm, in which several of the vessels were lost. The survivors took two months to reach Corneto, whence they slowly made their way down the coast to Ostia and thence up the Tiber to Rome. Gregory finally disembarked on Tuesday, 13 January 1377.

The papacy was back in Rome. This time it stayed. It was never to leave the city again. But the Italy to which it had returned, though in some respects unchanged, in others differed radically from the Italy it had left seventy years before. Unity was as remote a possibility as ever: Guelf and Ghibelline, their original quarrels long forgotten, still hammered away at each other, and the blood continued to flow as it always had, copious and unavailing. But seven decades without either a pope or an effective emperor had removed the old polarities, and the Black Death had drawn yet another curtain across the past, while exposing the present still more mercilessly to the winds of change. The secular, enquiring spirit that now spread across the land was not in itself new. Its roots went back to Roger of Sicily and his Greek and Arab sages, to Frederick II and his falcons, to Manfred and his troubadours, to Arnold of Brescia and the scholastics, to the doctors and lawyers of Bologna and Salerno. But the fourteenth century had given it a new momentum – in the political sphere with Cola di Rienzo and the despots of the north; in the cultural sphere with Dante, Petrarch, Boccaccio and the humanists – and at the same time the papal barriers that had so long blocked its progress had suddenly disappeared. The Renaissance was under way.

CHAPTER XVI

Laetentur Coeli!

(1378–1447)

Avignon, however, was far from finished. The immense machine of the papacy could not be dismantled and transported in a matter of weeks. The popes might be back on the Tiber, but many of the papal departments remained by the Rhône, together with the magnificent library and the bulk of the archives, which by now filled a whole wing of the palace. Among those departments was that which dealt with finance; for the fourteen months that remained of Pope Gregory XI's pontificate, his entire expenses were met by regular shipments of gold from Avignon. In fact, of the innumerable papal staff, it was only a comparatively small proportion, consisting mainly of the senior hierarchy, that had travelled with Gregory to Rome; the vast majority of the many hundred clerks, accountants, secretaries and scribes had remained behind. Among them were even half a dozen cardinals, charged to continue the attempts to mediate between England and France. Avignon, in short, after the Pope's departure, was by no means the sad, abandoned city that might have been imagined – though no one could possibly have foreseen the whole new, if slightly dubious, lease of life that awaited it.

Away in Rome Pope Gregory, though still only forty-eight, was aware that he was dying and was giving much thought to the question of his successor. Acutely conscious that the Church was still split down the middle, he was fully aware that if the papacy were now to remain in Rome for good, it must become Italian again – and that meant, in the first instance, an Italian pontiff. He in turn would appoint Italian cardinals, and so the French influence in the Sacred College would gradually be reduced. When Gregory died on 27 March 1378, it was clear that the Romans agreed with him. They had by no means always treated their popes with particular affection or respect, but they were determined not to let them go again. '*Romano lo volemo, o almeno italiano,*'[1] they

---

[1] 'We demand a Roman, or at least an Italian!'

shouted throughout the ensuing conclave; and – up to a point – they got what they wanted.

Bartolomeo Prignano, who took the name of Urban VI (1378–89), was in many ways a surprising choice. He was not a Roman aristocrat, but a member of the working class of Naples, who had never lost his heavy Neapolitan accent. Though now titular (and absentee) Archbishop of Bari, he had spent virtually his whole adult life in the papal chancery and was a bureaucrat through and through: austere, efficient, conscientious. In other circumstances he might have made a perfectly satisfactory pope. But the years of being patron- ised and generally ordered about by the French cardinals had had their effect. No sooner had he assumed supreme power than his character underwent a sea change; the quiet, competent civil servant turned overnight into a raging tyrant, hurling insults at the cardi- nals during the consistories and sometimes even physically attacking them.

Although several distinguished laymen were also the objects of the Pope's abuse – they included the Duke of Fondi and even the ambas- sadors of Queen Joanna of Naples – it was perhaps inevitable that the thirteen French cardinals suffered the most. One by one they slipped away to Anagni, where on 2 August they made a public state- ment to the effect that Pope Urban's election had taken place under the threat of mob violence and was therefore invalid; they called upon him to abdicate at once. A week later, there still being no reaction from Rome, they moved to Fondi – within the Kingdom of Naples, where Joanna could give them protection – and declared Urban deposed. Then, on 20 September, they elected Robert of Geneva as Clement VII. Each pope excommunicated the other, placing his supporters under an interdict. The Great Schism of the West had begun. It was to continue for nearly forty years.

If Urban had been a surprising choice for the papacy, Clement was an astonishing one. True, the fact that he was neither French nor Italian may have counted in his favour; but his record in Italy had been one of barbaric brutality, and Urban had no difficulty in raising troops to oppose him. Clement first fled to Joanna in Naples; but though she personally supported him, her subjects made no secret of their preference for Urban – who was, after all, one of their own – and Clement soon returned with his cardinals to Avignon. Urban meanwhile created a new College by appointing no fewer than twenty- nine new cardinals from all over Europe.

Western Christendom now faced a dilemma unique in its history. Antipopes as such were nothing new; but the present rivals had both been elected by the same cardinals, and while Urban's election had been unquestionably canonical – no one took the plea of intimidation too seriously – the manner of his deposition had been unprecedented: could popes be unmade by those who made them? On the other hand, Urban was clearly becoming ever more unbalanced. And so the continent was split down the middle: England, Germany, northern and central Italy and central Europe remained loyal to Urban, while Scotland, France, Savoy, Burgundy and Naples accepted the authority of Clement. So, after long hesitation, did Aragon and Castile.[1]

The Church had been able to tolerate a papacy exiled to Avignon; but the existence of two rival popes, one in Avignon and one in Rome, was too much for it to cope with. Two popes meant two Colleges of Cardinals, two papal chanceries, two appointments to a single see or abbey – and double the expenditure. In this last field Clement at Avignon had the advantage, since the departments in charge of finance had never properly moved back to Rome. He was able to create a court rivalling that of his namesake Clement VI for luxury and extravagance – from which he continued his struggle against his rival. But Urban too was busy. His most immediate enemy was Joanna of Naples, who courageously remained loyal to Clement. She was soon to pay the price. Urban deposed her in 1380 and in her place crowned her cousin, the young Charles of Durazzo. Entering Naples the following year, Charles imprisoned her in the castle of Muro; and there shortly afterwards he had her suffocated.

All too soon, however, Urban found the new king just as intractable as Joanna had been. The Pope had now become obsessed with obtaining valuable Neapolitan fiefs for his utterly worthless nephew, and when Charles refused to grant them he began interfering in the internal affairs of the kingdom. Now seriously paranoid, he moved with his cardinals to Nocera, where he heard that six of these cardinals were conspiring with Charles to create a council of regency that would effectively act for him. Flying into a fury, he excommunicated the King and had the cardinals brutally tortured. Charles now hastened to Nocera and put the city under siege; Urban and his entourage escaped

---

[1] 'Even saints were confused about the rights and wrongs of the situation. St Catherine of Siena supported Urban, St Vincent Ferrar supported Clement' (Eamon Duffy, *Saints and Sinners*).

to Genoa. There five of the six cardinals were put to death; the sixth, an Englishman named Adam Easton, was released only at the personal request of his sovereign, Richard II. Not until 1386 – a few weeks after Charles had been assassinated in Hungary – did the Pope return to Rome, where he died three years later.

Pope Clement – technically he is now seen by the Church as an antipope, though he himself would have been horrified by the description – outlived his rival by five years. Never for a second did he doubt the validity of his own election; and it was a bitter disappointment to him when, on Urban's death, the ensuing conclave did not recognise him as the legitimate pope and so put an end to the schism once and for all. Instead, they insanely elected another Neapolitan, Pietro Tomacelli, as Boniface IX (1389–1404); and there was an alarming moment in 1391 when King Charles VI of France announced his intention of personally conducting Boniface to Rome, though fortunately nothing came of it. In his last years Clement, while still at Avignon, came under heavy pressure (largely from France and, in particular, the University of Paris) to agree to a solution whereby both popes should resign and open the way for a new conclave; but he, like Boniface, firmly rejected all such suggestions, and he was still stubbornly resisting when he died, of a sudden apoplexy, on 16 September 1394.

It would have been so easy to end the schism; all that was required was that when one of the popes died, his conclave should refuse to elect a successor, so leaving the survivor in undisputed authority. But Rome had passed up the chance in 1387, and Avignon in 1394 did no better. Pope Boniface, apart from an unfortunate tendency to simony, was young and energetic, and Charles VI wrote letters to each of the twenty-one Avignon cardinals, begging them to accept him. But it was no use: on the grounds that they must on no account be swayed by outside influences, they left his letters unopened. Each of them, however, swore to work for the resolution of the schism; and each undertook, if elected, to abdicate if ever there were a majority decision that he should do so. They then proceeded to elect – unanimously – the Aragonese cardinal Pedro de Luna, who now took the name of Benedict XIII (1394–1417).

Benedict had an impressive record. He had been among the last of the original cardinals to abandon Pope Urban, but once he had finally become convinced of the legitimacy of Urban's deposition he had given unwavering support to Clement, who had appointed him to the Iberian peninsula as his Legate. It was thanks to him that Aragon and Castile, Portugal and Navarre had all eventually given their support to the Avignon papacy. In 1393 he had been transferred to Paris, where he had publicly championed the scheme of ending the schism by the abdication of both popes, declaring that he would certainly follow such a course in the event of his own election. Whether or not this attitude told in his favour at the conclave, we shall never know; but on finding himself Pope he instantly changed his mind. A proud and unbending Spaniard, he now made it plain that he – and he alone – was the rightful pontiff, and that no power on Earth could persuade him to relinquish his responsibilities.

And he proved it. In May 1395 there arrived in Avignon an embassy consisting of three royal dukes sent by Charles VI; in June 1397 an Anglo-French mission; in May 1398 ambassadors from Germany. All of them implored the Pope to remember his sworn oath and make his formal abdication. He remained immovable. Then, in June of that year, a French national synod decided to withdraw from his obedience. This came as a serious blow, since it deprived him of the all-important revenues from the Church in France; it also induced Navarre and Castile to follow the French example. Several panic-stricken cardinals also deserted him. But Benedict kept his nerve, allowing himself to be blockaded in his palace, confident that sooner or later the pendulum would swing back in his favour.

As indeed it did. The French Church had not gone over to Boniface; it had opted for independence, and in so doing had made many of the hierarchy profoundly uneasy. The people, too, who had complained bitterly at paying taxes to the papacy, were still more resentful at seeing them go straight into the royal coffers. One March night in 1403, with the aid of his most influential ally, the Duke of Orleans, Pope Benedict slipped out of his palace into Provence – where he was immediately and enthusiastically acclaimed. There was nothing to be done. France, Navarre and even the errant cardinals all returned to the fold. Benedict had won that round; but he was still committed to work for the end of the schism, and in September 1404 he at last felt strong enough to send an embassy to Rome, proposing a meeting of both pontiffs, or at least their plenipotentiaries.

But Boniface in Rome proved every bit as intractable as Benedict in Avignon; and anyway he died (of gallstones) on 1 October. All in all he had been a competent pope, repairing much of the damage done by his predecessor, regaining the allegiance of Naples and – perhaps most important of all – imposing his authority on Rome, putting an end to its republican independence and creating a new senate (nominated by himself) to be responsible for the city's administration. He had also undertaken a major reconstruction of the Castel Sant'Angelo. His principal fault was his unscrupulousness in financial affairs: indulgences, simonies, annates (the practice by which a year's income from a benefice or see was paid directly to Rome) – it seemed that there was no abuse that he would not happily tolerate, so long as it kept the gold flowing into his coffers. But with the main treasury and the financial departments still at Avignon, it is not easy to see how he and his Curia would otherwise have survived.

Boniface's successor, Innocent VII (1404–6), similarly rejected proposals for a meeting; but he was nowhere near as adroit as his predecessor in his dealings with the Romans, and matters came to a head when eleven of the leading citizens, arriving at the Vatican for negotiations, were murdered by his idiotic nephew who commanded the papal militia. At this, the mob stormed the palace; Innocent and his cardinals were lucky to get out alive and make their way to Viterbo. Not until the spring of 1406 was it safe to return, and six months later the Pope was dead – though not before he had established a chair of Greek at the Sapienza University of Rome, founded by Boniface VIII just a century before.

Why the Roman cardinals should now have chosen the Venetian Angelo Correr – Gregory XII (1406–15) – to succeed him is not immediately easy to understand. Gregory was certainly a distinguished churchman (for fifteen years he had been the Latin Patriarch of Constantinople) and had long protested that his dearest wish was to see the end of the schism; but he was already eighty years old, and it seemed on the face of it unlikely that his wish would be granted. Since, as it happened, he was to live for another nine years, it very nearly was – though by no means thanks to him.

Before Gregory's election, each of the fourteen cardinals had sworn a personal oath that, if elected, he would immediately stand down in the event of the death or abdication of Pope Benedict in Avignon. Each had also promised that within three months of his election he would open negotiations with Benedict to decide on a place where the two popes might meet. Gregory kept his word and sent an embassy to his rival; and after long and occasionally acrimonious discussions it was finally agreed that the meeting should take place at Savona on

29 September 1407. Only after this decision was made did the old man begin to waver. The pressure came principally from King Ladislas of Naples, Doge Michele Steno of Venice and the future Emperor Sigismund of Luxembourg, all of whom dreaded seeing the papacy fall once more into French hands. Benedict went as far as Portovenere, near La Spezia; but Gregory stopped at Lucca, where he firmly announced that he was no longer willing to meet his rival. Nor in any circumstances would he abdicate.

It was an astonishing volte-face, which lost Gregory much support. Now at last the Sacred Colleges of the two rival popes forgot their separate allegiances and gathered in June 1408 at Livorno, where they issued an appeal to both hierarchies – including the popes themselves – together with the princes of Europe or their representatives, to meet at a General Council, to be held at Pisa on 25 March 1409. The popes refused; but the invitation to Pisa received a most gratifying response, being accepted by no fewer than four patriarchs, twenty-four cardinals, eighty bishops (102 others sent delegates to represent them), the heads of four religious orders and an impressive number of distinguished theologians from universities and religious houses. The Council's fifteen sessions lasted for more than ten weeks. Both Gregory and Benedict were condemned as 'notorious schismatics and heretics' – though there were many who enquired of what heresies they had been guilty – and were formally deposed. The cardinals then formed a conclave and elected the Cardinal Archbishop of Milan, Pietro Philarghi, who had started life as an orphaned beggar boy in Crete and was to end it as Pope Alexander V.

But the Council had made one disastrous mistake. By calling the two rival popes to appear before it – and declaring them contumacious when they refused – it had implied its superiority over the papacy itself, a principle that neither of the rival pontiffs could have been expected to endorse. Before long it became clear that its only real effect had been to saddle Christendom with three popes instead of two. But it was unrepentant, and when Pope Alexander died suddenly in May 1410 it lost no time in electing his successor.

Baldassare Cossa, who now joined the papal throng under the name of John XXIII (1410–15),[1] was widely believed at the time to have

---

[1] The circumstances of his election and subsequent deposition have denied him a place on the canonical list of popes. It was nonetheless mildly surprising that Cardinal Angelo Roncalli should have adopted the same name on his election to the papacy in 1958 (see Chapter XXVIII).

poisoned his predecessor. Whether he actually did so is open to doubt. He had, however, unquestionably begun life as a pirate; and a pirate, essentially, he remained. Morally and spiritually he reduced the papacy to a level of depravity unknown since the days of the pornocracy in the tenth century. A contemporary chronicler records in shocked amazement the rumour current in Bologna – where Cossa had been Papal Legate – that during his time there he had seduced 200 matrons, widows and virgins, to say nothing of an alarming number of nuns. His score over the three following years is regrettably not recorded; he seems, however, to have maintained a respectable average, for on 29 May 1415 he was arraigned on similar charges before another General Council, meeting this time at Constance – the only such council ever to be held north of the Alps.

There was a certain irony here, since the Council of Constance had originally been Pope John's idea. He had plenty of energy and intelligence, but in the circumstances found it difficult indeed to put himself forward as a spiritual leader of men. His first synod had been a disaster – constantly interrupted, we are told, by an owl that flew into the Pope's face and screeched at him. (True or not, the very existence of the story is an indication of the contempt in which he was generally held.) To preside at a General Council would, he felt, give him the prestige he lacked, and there was plenty of work for it to do. First of all there were his two rivals to be dealt with: Gregory and Benedict, who had refused to accept the authority of those gathered at Pisa to depose them. There was also an urgent need to investigate the teachings of John Wycliffe in England and John Hus in Bohemia. What he needed now was a powerful patron; and so towards the end of 1412 he approached one of the leading figures on the European stage, Sigismund of Luxembourg.

Sigismund was now forty-four. Son of the Emperor Charles IV, King of Germany and (through his wife) of Hungary, he was the halfbrother of King Wenceslas of Bohemia (whose crown he was also to inherit seven years later) and was therefore much concerned by the influence of Hus, which was spreading rapidly across Europe. He conferred with Pope John personally at Lodi just before Christmas 1413, and it was jointly announced that the Council would meet at Constance on 1 November of the following year. In the ensuing discussions the two quickly reached agreement on all points except one: Sigismund made it clear that he expected to preside over the Council himself. To John, this was a serious blow. Had he been in sole charge of the proceedings, he could have steered them more or less as he wished. With Sigismund in control, however, things might well turn against him. It was thus with serious misgivings that, in early October 1414, he set out for Constance.

The attendance at Pisa had been impressive enough, but most of those present had been Italian or French. The Council of Constance, with the most powerful prince of central Europe behind it, was on an altogether different scale. Altogether there were nearly 700 delegates, including twenty-nine cardinals and some 180 bishops. John Hus was there in person, his security guaranteed – as he thought – by a letter of safe conduct from Sigismund; but he was arrested on the Pope's orders after only a preliminary hearing, handed over to the King when he arrived just before Christmas and – still at Constance – was burned at the stake on 6 July 1415.

Pope John, meanwhile, had fled from his own Council. During the first weeks of the new year the mood had turned against him, and there were insistent demands that he should be put on trial for his countless crimes. He had one firm ally, Frederick of Habsburg, Duke of Austria; and on the night of 20 March 1416, when the Duke had obligingly arranged a tournament in Sigismund's honour, John disguised himself with some difficulty as a stable-boy and slipped out of the city, heading first to Frederick's castle at Schaffhausen and then, as he hoped, to the protection of the Duke of Burgundy across the Rhine. But it was to no avail. The Council having called without success for his immediate and unconditional abdication, Sigismund sent his soldiers to find and arrest him. Meanwhile John was tried in his absence, and duly condemned. As Edward Gibbon delightedly noted, 'the most scandalous charges were suppressed: the Vicar of Christ was only accused of piracy, murder, rape, sodomy and incest'. John spent the next four years in the custody of the Elector Ludwig III of Bavaria, from whom he eventually purchased his liberty for a vast sum. Returning to Italy, he was, somewhat surprisingly, forgiven; and his long career of debauch and depravity was rewarded by the bishopric of Tusculum and one of the grandest of early Renaissance tombs, the joint work of Donatello and Michelozzo, in the baptistery of Florence Cathedral.

It was at Constance that matters were finally settled. John XXIII and Benedict XIII – now eighty-seven – were alike deposed; Gregory XII was prevailed upon to abdicate with honour, with the promise that he would rank second in the hierarchy, immediately after the future pope – a privilege that was the more readily accorded in view of the fact that, since he was now approaching ninety and looked a good deal older, it was not thought likely that he would enjoy it for long. Indeed, two years later he was dead, and with the election of Cardinal Oddone Colonna as Pope Martin V (1417–31), the schism was effectively at an end.

As the schism ended, the Renaissance papacy began – with Martin as its first representative. Although a member of one of the oldest and most distinguished Roman families, he could not immediately establish himself in Rome. The city was, as so often in the past, a battle-ground – this time being fought over by two warring soldiers of fortune – and it was not until three years after his election that he was finally able to enter it for the first time as Pope. And he was shocked by what he saw. Rome was in ruins, its total population having shrunk to some 25,000, hopelessly demoralised and in many cases half-starving. Foxes, even wolves, roamed the streets. The once magnificent buildings stood roofless and untenanted. The restoration of the Vatican, set in train half a century before, had long since been suspended, and the Pope even had difficulty in finding somewhere decent to live. Fortunately one of his own family's palaces was still up to a point habitable; here he was obliged to stay while the work was resumed, and until it was eventually completed.

Meanwhile he got down to business. He took in hand the chaotic papal finances, and initiated a hugely ambitious programme of restoration and reconstruction of the whole city: the walls and fortifications, the bridges, the ruined basilicas and churches. He summoned three great painters from the north – Pisanello, Masaccio and Gentile da Fabriano – for the redecoration of the Lateran alone. In the diplomatic field he succeeded (at least to a considerable degree) in bringing under his control the Church in France, which during the Avignon years had become quite impossibly arrogant and overbearing. He took the first significant steps in internationalising the College of Cardinals – weakening the Italian and French elements and introducing numbers of Englishmen, Germans and Spaniards. He got rid of the countless bands of brigands that were terrorising the city and the surrounding countryside. Finally he re-established order in the Papal States.

His purpose behind all these achievements was to reassert the power and prestige of the papacy after the chaos into which it had fallen during the schism. The two recent assemblies, at Pisa and at Constance, had asserted several worrying new principles. The Pope, it appeared, was no longer supreme: he was now at the mercy of a General Council, which stood above him and could depose him at will. Now – according to the conciliarists – it was the Council, rather than the Pope, that constituted the ultimate authority in the Church; the Pope was its servant, bound to give it his obedience and to respect its decisions. Councils, it had been agreed, were to be held regularly. In short, the papacy was now undergoing the process already familiar to most nations of western Europe: the process of slow democratisation, the gradual substitution of absolute monarchy by parliamentary government.

To these ideas Martin V was not entirely unsympathetic. The Council of Constance had, after all, rescued the Church from forty years of schism and, quite possibly, from ultimate disintegration; to it, indeed, he very largely owed his own crown. On the other hand, Councils were unwieldy things that met infrequently, spoke with many different voices and took an eternity to reach any major decision. They were no substitute for a single strong hand at the helm; and that Pope Martin was determined – and well able – to supply. He took his own decisions, keeping both cardinals and Curia under his own strict personal control. When, for example, in September 1423 the time came for the next Council, to be held at Pavia, he announced that he would not be attending. In consequence of this, and of a sudden outbreak of plague that necessitated the Council's last-minute transfer to Siena, there were relatively few delegates present; and when their discussions turned to the question of further restrictions on papal power, he made the poor attendance a pretext for closing down the whole assembly. The Church would have to wait until the next Council, which was to meet in July 1431 in Basel.

As 1430 drew to its close, the sixty-two-year-old Pope showed himself if anything still less enthusiastic about the Basel meeting than he had been about its predecessor. Once again, he made it clear that there would be no question of his being there himself; in his stead he appointed Cardinal Giuliano Cesarini as its president, giving him authority to dissolve it at any moment if it threatened to tread on dangerous ground. In the event, he could not have attended even had he wished to do so; on 20 February 1431 he died of an apoplectic stroke. He had been, if not a great pope, at least an outstandingly good one; and he had restored peace and good government to his city. Once again Michelozzo and Donatello worked together on a papal tomb; but this time it stood in Rome rather than Florence, and its inscription, TEMPORUM SUORUM FELICITAS ('the joy of his times'), was a testimonial of which, surely, any pope would have been proud.

That epitaph, however, is unlikely to have been suggested by the College of Cardinals. They had never liked Martin. They had resented his arrogance, his unwillingness to listen, his reluctance even to consult them, let alone to take their advice. The conciliar spirit was in the air, and to a greater or lesser extent had infected all of them. He had paid it lip-service, up to a point; but as time went on he had become increasingly impatient with the whole idea. Now that the Basel Council was about to open, it was essential that the next pope, whoever he might be, should show himself to be in sympathy with the reforms that were to be proposed. Thus it was that the cardinals all undertook that whoever should be elected would give the Council his wholehearted support, working with the Sacred College, rather than in opposition to it, in the government of the Church.

Unfortunately, things did not turn out quite as they had planned. Their choice fell on Gabriele Condulmer, a Venetian – though not, like his uncle Gregory XII, an aristocrat – who had spent much of his early life as an Augustinian hermit on an island in the lagoon. His rise to power, first as Bishop of Siena and from 1408 as Cardinal, had been unashamedly nepotistic; and whatever promises he may have made before the conclave, once reigning as Pope Eugenius IV (1431– 47) he showed little more goodwill towards the coming Council than Pope Martin had before him. Indeed, when the Council eventually opened on 23 July 1431 the attendance was so sparse – among the absentees were Cardinal Cesarini, appointed by Martin to preside – that after six months Eugenius attempted to dissolve it. This, however, proved a serious mistake. The delegates may have been comparatively few; but they were conciliarists to a man, and they absolutely refused to be dissolved. The Pope, they claimed, had no authority to dismiss them. It was they, and not he, who were supreme in the Church; and unless he presented himself before them and withdrew his Bull of dissolution it was he, and not they, who would be dismissed.

But Eugenius refused to budge, and the ensuing deadlock was broken only by King Sigismund. As King of Germany and Emperor-to-be, he needed the support of the Pope to strengthen his position in northern Italy and that of the Council in his struggle against the Hussites. In May 1433 he made his way to Rome, where he was duly crowned by Eugenius; and for the next six months he worked hard on both parties, persuading them to moderate their respective attitudes until, at the end of the year, the two reached an uneasy agreement. It was in fact rather more like a papal surrender. Eugenius was obliged to withdraw his Bull of dissolution and to recognise – with all too few reservations – the primacy of the Council.

Seeing his humiliation, other enemies took full advantage. First were the Colonna. In the spring of 1434, furious at being ordered to return the Church treasures that they had acquired under their kinsman Martin V, they engineered a rising in the streets of Rome; and at much the same time the pro-conciliar Filippo Maria Visconti of Milan sent two *condottieri* (mercenary generals) to invade the Papal States. Then, when Eugenius found himself blockaded in the city, the Romans rose again and proclaimed a republic. For the luckless Pope, it was all too much. Disguised as a monk but soon identified, and defending himself as best he could under a hail of missiles, he made his escape in a small boat down the Tiber to Ostia and thence transferred to a galley that took him to Pisa. June found him in Florence, where he was soon to be joined by the Sacred College and the Curia.

In Florence, as guest of Cosimo de' Medici, he remained for the next nine years, fighting a constant battle against the conciliarists in Basel, who – their numbers now greatly increased by legists and theologians from the universities – were becoming daily more radical and anti-papal. For the moment there was little that he could do to resist them, though in the summer of 1436 he circulated a formal denunciation of their pretensions to all the princes of Christendom. On the other hand, he had considerable success in re-establishing his political position. Among the Curia was an ex-soldier of long experience named Giovanni Vitelleschi; Eugenius singled him out, promoted him to Bishop and sent him off with a small force to Rome. Energetic and utterly ruthless, Vitelleschi showed no mercy on the rebels and quickly restored order both in Rome and in the Papal State.

Basel, however, remained to be dealt with; and the deadlock might have dragged on indefinitely but for a single, immensely significant development: the arrival in the West of John VIII Palaeologus, Emperor of Byzantium.

Faced with the remorseless advance of the Ottoman Turks, the Byzantine Empire was at its last gasp. Massive military assistance from western Europe represented its only chance of survival, but all attempts to obtain it foundered on the same rock: the Eastern and Western Churches were in schism. Only if that schism were ended could a united Christendom take up arms in the longed-for Crusade.

To John Palaeologus the Council of Basel seemed to offer a ray of hope. Once again, representatives of all the Christian nations of the West were present; and although the ambassadors of his predecessor, Manuel II, had returned from Constance disappointed, much had happened in the past fifteen years – including a reluctant acceptance by the Pope of what the Byzantines had never ceased to maintain: that true union could be achieved only by means of a Council of the whole Church, to be attended by representatives of both East and West. This time, perhaps, a Byzantine appeal might fall on more receptive ears.

But all this would mean a fresh start; and it was obvious that Basel was not the place. The past years had seen too much ill-feeling and bitterness; if the new Council were to have any chance of success, a change of *venue* was essential. The more hidebound of the conciliarists naturally objected – in 1439 going so far as to declare the Pope deposed and to elect an antipope in his stead – but this arbitrary renewal of the papal schism cost them what little prestige they had left, and one by one the Christian nations submitted to the authority of Pope Eugenius.

Ideally the Emperor would have wished the new Council to be held in Constantinople; but he was obliged to admit that in present conditions this was no longer practicable. He therefore willingly accepted the Pope's choice of Ferrara, confirming that he personally, together with his Patriarch, would head the imperial delegation. Eugenius, hearing this welcome news, lost no time. By September 1437 his legates were already in Constantinople to work out the details, while others were negotiating with the Venetians for the hiring of a fleet to bring the Byzantine delegation in proper state to Ferrara. Thus it was that John Palaeologus left his brother Constantine as Regent and on Wednesday, 27 November embarked on his historic journey, taking with him a party some 700 strong, among them the most distinguished group of Eastern churchmen ever to visit the West. There was the Patriarch himself, Joseph II – nearly eighty years old, crippled by heart disease, but beloved of all who met him; eighteen Metropolitans, some of them representing his fellow-Patriarchs of Alexandria, Antioch and Jerusalem, and including the brilliant young Metropolitan Bessarion of Nicaea; and a dozen other bishops, including Isidore, Abbot of St

Demetrius in Constantinople, who had been promoted the previous year to Bishop of Kiev and All Russia.

On 8 February 1438 the party reached Venice, where the Emperor was greeted by Doge Francesco Foscari and conducted with immense pomp and ceremony up the Grand Canal to the great palace of the Marquis of Ferrara.[1] There he remained for the next three weeks, writing letters to all the European princes, urging them to attend the Council or at least to send representatives. Only at the end of the month did he leave on the last stage of his journey. Compared to his Venetian reception, his arrival in Ferrara was a lacklustre affair, not improved by pouring rain. Pope Eugenius gave him a warm welcome, but even this was somewhat clouded when the Emperor was informed that his Patriarch, on his arrival a few days later, would be expected to prostrate himself and kiss the pontiff's foot. Of this, he politely pointed out, there could be no question; and at last the Pope was obliged to yield. Had he not done so, it is doubtful whether the Council of Ferrara would ever have taken place.

The Council got off to a bad start. John had stipulated that four months should pass before the formal discussions on doctrine were begun; one of his principal reasons for attending was to seek help from the other European princes, and he was determined that no important decisions should be taken before their arrival. But spring turned to summer, and no princes appeared. The Latins grew more and more impatient, the Pope – who was responsible for the board and lodging of the entire Greek delegation – more and more concerned as his financial reserves fell ever lower.

With August came the plague. Strangely enough, the Greeks appeared immune – the Emperor was in any case away from Ferrara for most of the time, indulging in his favourite sport of hunting – but there was heavy mortality both among the Latin delegates and in the city as a whole. Meanwhile the Latins grew even more irritated with their guests. The Greeks too were losing patience. They had been away from home for the best part of a year, and had so far achieved nothing. Many of them were short of money, for the papal subsidies were becoming increasingly irregular. Finally it was by now plain that none of the European princes had any intention at all of showing up, so there was no point in waiting for them any longer. It was to everyone's

---

[1] This thirteenth-century palace, restored with majestic insensitivity in the 1860s and – in consequence of its later history – known today as the Fondaco dei Turchi, still stands on the upper reaches of the Canal, opposite the S. Marcuola *vaporetto* station.

relief when deliberations began in earnest on 8 October. For the first three months they were concerned almost exclusively with the *filioque* clause – a tricky enough point anyway, having played a major part in the schism four centuries before,[1] but now further complicated by linguistic problems. Few of the delegates spoke any language other than their own, and there were no qualified interpreters. The sessions ended on 13 December with agreement as far away as ever.

At this point the Pope managed to persuade the delegates to move to Florence. He gave as his reason the continued presence of the plague in Ferrara, but his true motives were almost certainly financial: the Council had been sitting for eight months, showed every sign of going on indefinitely and had already made alarming inroads on the papal treasury. In Florence, on the other hand, the Medici could be trusted to help out. But the move also proved beneficial in other ways. When the sessions were resumed towards the end of February 1439 the Greeks – tired, anxious, homesick and quite possibly hungry – seemed distinctly readier to compromise than they had been the previous year. By the end of March they had agreed that the Latin formula according to which the Holy Spirit proceeded from the Father *and* the Son meant the same as a recently accepted Greek formula whereby it proceeded from the Father *through* the Son. It was soon after this breakthrough that Patriarch Joseph finally expired; but then, as one observer rather unkindly remarked, after muddling his prepositions, what else could he decently do?

With the *filioque* at last out of the way, the other outstanding questions were quickly settled. The Greeks disapproved of the Roman dogma on purgatory and on the use of unleavened bread at the sacrament. They also deplored the Latin practice of giving communion in both kinds to the laity, and of forbidding the marriage of non-monastic priests. But on all these issues they put up only token opposition. The question of papal supremacy might at other times have caused difficulties, but since the Council of Basel this had been a delicate subject and was consequently glossed over as far as possible. Thanks largely to the Emperor himself – who employed persuasion and threats in equal measure to ensure the amenability of his subjects – agreement had been reached by midsummer on every major issue, and on Sunday 5 July 1439 the official Decree of Union (little more than a statement of the Latin position, apart from one or two concessions permitting

---

[1] See Chapter VIII.

Greek usages) was signed by all the Orthodox bishops and abbots except the Metropolitan of Ephesus, who had given in on absolutely nothing, but was forbidden by John to exercise a veto. The Latins then added their own signatures; and the following day the decree was publicly proclaimed in Florence Cathedral, being recited first in Latin by Cardinal Cesarini and then in Greek by the Metropolitan Bessarion of Nicaea. The Latin version began with the words *Laetentur Coeli* – 'let the heavens rejoice'; but the heavens, as soon became clear, had precious little reason to do so.

Pope Eugenius had won a major victory. On paper at least he had brought the Orthodox Church back into the Roman fold.[1] In doing so he had established his personal supremacy. The radical conciliarists at Basel were speechless with rage. First they suspended him, then they deposed him and finally, on 5 November 1439, they elected an antipope – in the surprising shape of Duke Amadeus VIII of Savoy. Amadeus was a deeply pious layman, founder (and himself a member) of an order of knightly hermits on the Lake of Geneva. He accepted with great reluctance, calling himself Felix V (1439–49); but he soon had reason to regret his decision, for no one took him very seriously. The Council, too, had succeeded only in making itself look ridiculous. From that moment on it gradually dissolved, though it was to limp on until 1449.

After a nine-year absence, in September 1443 Pope Eugenius returned to Rome and set about countering the effects of the schism with the invaluable help of his friend Aeneas Silvius Piccolomini. The future Pope Pius II, Piccolomini – although at this time still a layman – had been one of Antipope Felix's most trusted advisers; but he had now transferred his allegiance, and it was thanks to his diplomatic skill that in 1447 the German princes declared as one man for Eugenius – and just in time, for within a week or two he was dead. His sixteen-year reign had not been easy: more than half of it had been spent in his Florentine exile. But his long struggle with the Council of Basel had ended in victory; never again would papal supremacy be challenged from within the Church itself.

---

[1] No one in the West could have foreseen that by the time the Emperor returned to Constantinople in February 1440 *Laetentur Coeli* would already be dead in the water, repudiated by the three surviving Patriarchs, its signatories condemned as traitors to the faith, castigated throughout the capital and in some cases physically attacked.

CHAPTER XVII

The Renaissance

(1447–92)

If, as has been suggested, Martin V was the first Renaissance pope, Eugenius was the second. He was not temperamentally a Renaissance figure – on his deathbed he expressed bitter regrets that he had ever left his hermitage – but his nine years with the Medici in Florence could not have failed to have their effect; and when he returned to Rome (accompanied, incidentally, by Fra Angelico) he devoted himself, in the four years remaining to him, to the continuation of Martin's work on the city. To bring Rome up to the standards now set by Milan, Genoa, Venice and the other great cities of the north would have taxed the powers of Hercules; but Eugenius worked hard, and when his apostolic secretary Flavio Biondo dedicated to him his three books on the restoration work, *Roma Instaurata*, the compliment was not undeserved.

Artistically and culturally, however, Rome was still something of a backwater when Tommaso Parentucelli (1447–55), the son of a modest physician in Liguria, was elected pontiff in March 1447, taking the name of Nicholas V. Of the previous 140 years the popes had been absent for well over half, and thanks to the consequent chaos the flowering of classical and humanistic learning that had swept away the last vestiges of the Middle Ages from Tuscany and Umbria had left the city almost untouched. A Dante, a Petrarch, a Boccaccio – all of them Florentines – would have been unthinkable in Rome. Although both Boniface VIII in 1303 and Innocent VII a hundred years later had worked hard to give the city the university it deserved, they had had only moderate success.

With the beginning of the fifteenth century, however, there was a change in the air. First of all, Greek influence had begun to make itself felt. When in 1360 Boccaccio had wished to learn the language, he had had the utmost difficulty in finding anyone in Italy capable of teaching him; he had eventually unearthed an aged Calabrian monk of revolting habits, whom he had lodged in his house for three years, preparing one of the first – and worst – translations of Homer into Latin. But around the turn of the century there had appeared in Florence a first-rate Greek scholar named Manuel Chrysoloras. He taught there for the next fifteen years until his death, leaving behind him a book, the *Erotemata*, which – though not quite as exciting as it sounds – was essentially a Greek grammar, set out in the form of questions and answers. Among his pupils were two of the most distinguished early Italian humanists, Leonardo Bruni and Poggio Braccolini, who both became members of the Curia and were thus able to inject some of the new learning into the papal court. Soon, too, Chrysoloras was joined by the impressive company of Greek intellectuals who accompanied John Palaeologus to the Councils of Ferrara and Florence.

These Greeks brought with them a new awareness of antiquity. For a thousand years the pagan splendours of ancient Rome had been ignored or forgotten, being of no interest to either pope or pilgrim. Then there had been the seventy years of absence in Avignon, followed by the forty years of schism; and disastrous as these years had been in many ways, they did make it possible for subsequent popes to look upon the city with completely fresh eyes – eyes that were shocked by the sight of cattle grazing in the Forum or antique statuary being ground to powder to provide local jerry-builders with cement. That is why, from the middle of the fifteenth century, the entire institution of the papacy underwent a radical change. Imbued as they were with humanist ideas, the Renaissance popes were ambitious and energetic men of the world, determined not just to revive Rome's former greatness, but to create a new city that would combine the best of both classical and Christian civilisations, bearing witness to their own greatness and that of their families and arousing the admiration and envy of all who saw it.

Like his predecessor, Nicholas V had spent some years in Florence, where he had been tutor to the Strozzi family and had made friends with all the scholars who clustered around the Medici. In consequence he had become far more deeply imbued with Renaissance culture than Eugenius ever was. He was also a good deal less confrontational and far more politically astute, restoring order to Rome and self-government to the Papal States, granting virtual independence to Bologna and persuading history's last antipope, Felix V, to abdicate. One of his greatest successes was his declaration of 1450 as Jubilee Year, which brought perhaps 100,000 pilgrims, tempted by the offer of plenary indulgence for their sins, flocking to Rome. This completely restored the papal finances. The high point of the celebrations was the canonisation of S. Bernardino of Siena, a Franciscan friar who had died only six years before and whose extraordinary charisma had earned him a place in the hearts of Italians comparable, perhaps, to that of Padre Pio in our own day.

Admittedly, not everything in that Jubilee Year went according to plan. An outbreak of the plague in the early summer caused hundreds of deaths: 'all the hospitals and churches,' wrote an eyewitness, 'were full of the sick and dying, and they were to be seen in the infected streets falling down like dogs.' On 19 December a pack of horses and mules was frightened by the crowds on the Ponte Sant'Angelo and stampeded; some 200 pilgrims were trampled to death or drowned in the Tiber. Yet even these disasters made little difference in the long term. The Jubilee Year showed conclusively that, after a century and a half, the papacy was back on track. Avignon was now past history, and the schism, and all the anti-papal excesses of the conciliar movement. The popes were fully and firmly restored to Rome, where they belonged, and had every intention of staying there.

In 1452 Frederick III of Habsburg[1] crossed the Alps, with a suite of more than 2,000, to receive from the Pope the crown of the Holy Roman Empire; it was to be combined with the new Emperor's marriage to Donna Leonora, daughter of the King of Portugal. In every Italian city through which Frederick passed he was cheered to the echo and deluged with presents. In Ferrara he was greeted not only by the Marquis Borso d'Este, but also by Galeazzo Maria Sforza, eldest son of the usurping Duke of Milan, and was obliged to listen to a speech of welcome 'as long as two chapters of St John's Gospel', pronounced by Galeazzo Maria's eight-year-old brother. In Bologna and Florence the receptions were more elaborate still, and in Siena he met his bride for the first time. The two then rode to Rome together, entering the city on 9 March. On the 16th Pope Nicholas performed the marriage ceremony in St Peter's, after which he crowned Frederick with the Iron Crown of Lombardy. The imperial coronation took place three days later, and was followed by the coronation of the young Empress, with a crown that had been specially made for her. When the service was over the Emperor made a point of bringing the Pope's horse to

---

[1] Frederick was the nephew of his namesake, Frederick, Duke of Austria, the protector of the Antipope John XXIII (see Chapter XVI).

the door of the Basilica and holding his stirrup while he mounted. The festivities ended with a ceremonial banquet at the Lateran.

That ceremony – it was the last imperial coronation ever to take place in Rome – marked the apogee of Nicholas's pontificate. All too soon, however, came disaster: on Tuesday, 29 May 1453, after a fifty-five-day siege, the army of the Ottoman sultan, Mehmet II, smashed down the walls of Constantinople and put an end to the Christian Empire of the East. The news was received with horror throughout western Europe. The Byzantine Empire had lasted 1,123 years; although it had never recovered from the Fourth Crusade two and a half centuries before, it had remained the eastern bastion of Christendom. As the refugees spread westwards from the conquered city they carried with them the epic story of its heroic defence, which doubtless lost nothing in the telling. But western Europe, for all its deep and genuine dismay, was not profoundly changed; indeed, the two states most immediately affected, Venice and Genoa, lost no time in congratulating the Sultan and making the best terms they could with the new regime.

In Rome, Pope Nicholas showed none of the cynicism and self-interest of the merchant republics. He did his utmost to galvanise the West for a Crusade, a cause that was enthusiastically supported by the two Greek cardinals, Bessarion and Isidore – who had remained in Italy after the Council of Florence and embraced Catholicism – as also by the Papal Legate in Germany, Aeneas Silvius Piccolomini, the future Pope Pius II. But it was no use. Two or three hundred years before, Christian zeal had been enough to launch military expeditions for the recovery of the holy places of pilgrimage; with the advent of Renaissance humanism, the old religious fire had been extinguished. Europe had dithered, and Byzantium had died. With the Ottoman army stronger now than it had ever been, the old Empire was beyond all hope of resurrection.

It was Nicholas's only important failure. He had no choice but to accept it, and returned to the two chief interests of his life, books and buildings – the only things, he said, that it was worth spending money on. His two predecessors had both been enthusiastic builders, but neither had shown much interest in literature; Pope Martin, indeed, had generally disapproved of classical (and consequently pagan) authors, and had maintained that nothing of antiquity was worth preserving beyond what was contained in the works of St Augustine. Nicholas, by contrast, was scarcely ever seen without a book in his hand. He read everything that came his way, annotating copiously in the margins in his exquisite handwriting. His legate Piccolomini wrote admiringly:

> From his youth he has been initiated into all liberal arts, he is acquainted with all philosophers, historians, poets, cosmographers, and theologians; and is no stranger to civil and canon law, or even to medicine.

Thus, on his accession, Nicholas deliberately set out to create, 'for the common convenience of the learned, a library of all books, both in Latin and in Greek, worthy of the dignity of the Pope and the Apostolic See'. He had to start virtually from scratch: the old papal library had been left at Avignon, where most of the volumes had by now been lost or stolen; of the remainder, the old Antipope Benedict XIII had carried off a good many after his deposition and had taken them to the castle of Peniscola near Valencia. Now papal agents travelled all over Europe in search of rare manuscripts, and scholars were set to work to make properly accurate Latin translations of the Greek texts, both Christian and pagan. Forty-five copyists were kept permanently employed. By Nicholas's death he had spent 30,000 gold florins and had collected some 1,200 volumes – the nucleus of today's Vatican Library.[1]

Meanwhile he continued the work of his predecessors in the rebuilding of Rome. He strengthened the old Leonine Walls and other more recent defences, supervised the restoration of forty early Christian churches, repaired aqueducts, paved streets and initiated a major restoration of the Castel Sant'Angelo. His most important work, however, was on the Vatican – which, he now decided, should replace the Lateran as the principal papal residence – and on St Peter's. Of the late thirteenth-century palace, essentially the work of Nicholas III, he restored and enlarged the north and west sides, using Leon Battista Alberti and Bernardo Rossellino as his architects. He also commissioned Fra Angelico (with his assistant Benozzo Gozzoli) to paint the stories of St Stephen and St Lawrence in his chapel and study, and a further cycle of scenes from the life of Christ in the Chapel of the Sacrament.[2]

His plans for St Peter's were still more ambitious. Like all the other

---

[1] There were as yet no printed books. The invention of printing cannot be ascribed to a single year, but 1450 is as good a date as any.
[2] Giorgio Vasari tells us that the latter was destroyed when Paul III put in a new staircase. The only survivor of Nicholas's work is his chapel. In the fresco depicting the ordination of St Lawrence, the representation of the third-century Pope Sixtus II is said to be a portrait of Nicholas himself.

great buildings of Rome, it had been allowed to fall into decay; Alberti maintained that its complete collapse was only a matter of time. Nicholas, however, had in mind something more than just a programme of repair; he envisaged lengthening the building by about a third, adding transepts and a new apse around the shrine of the Apostle. There was also a plan for a magnificent new space outside, where three great new avenues through the Borgo would converge and where the crowds could congregate for mass blessings. These plans all lapsed at the Pope's death, but it is interesting to speculate on what would have happened if they had been put into effect. Julius II, half a century later, would probably not have ordered the complete rebuilding; on the other hand, we should almost certainly have been deprived of the great Bernini piazza, which to this day remains one of the most magnificent open spaces of Europe.

Pope Nicholas V died in March 1455 at the age of fifty-seven. His pontificate had lasted only eight years, but his influence had been enormous. Martin and Eugenius had both been affected by Renaissance ideas, but neither had wholeheartedly embraced the humanist ethos. Nicholas was the first pope who saw absolutely no contradiction or conflict between humanism and the Christian faith. To him, the arts were neither vain nor frivolous; they too bore witness to the glory of God. It was only right, therefore, that the Church should give a lead in the artistic field, just as it did in the spiritual. Other popes who thought as he did were to follow him; but Nicholas, and Nicholas alone, combined his views with a genuine piety, humility and integrity. It was entirely typical of him that in 1449 he should have ordered a retrial of Joan of Arc, who had been burned at the stake in Rouen on 30 May 1431 on charges that included heresy and witchcraft. This was to continue for the next seven years, during which 115 witnesses were heard; it ended only in the reign of his successor – who is normally, and most unfairly, given the credit – with her complete rehabilitation.

Unlike so many of those who preceded or followed him, Nicholas V was untouched by greed or nepotism. Greatness – which he unquestionably possessed – never went to his head. In earlier years he had described himself, to his friend Vespasiano da Bisticci, as 'a mere bell-ringing priest'; and so, in a very real sense, he remained.

On 4 April 1455 the fifteen cardinals in Rome assembled for the conclave – and badly missed their chance. They might have elected

Cardinal Bessarion, by far the most intelligent and cultivated churchman in Rome. As a former Metropolitan of the Orthodox Church he was better qualified than any of his colleagues to end the 400-year schism, and he would have steered the papacy in a new and healthier direction. Alas, his Greek origins (which should have counted in his favour) militated against him; the cardinals instead chose a seventy-seven-year-old Catalan jurist, Alfonso de Borja – subsequently Italianised to Borgia – who took the name of Calixtus III (1455–8).

Deeply pious, dry as dust and crippled by gout, Calixtus devoted his pontificate to two consuming ambitions. The first was to organise a European Crusade that would deliver Constantinople from the Turks; the second was to advance the fortunes of his family and compatriots. Art and literature interested him not a jot. 'See how the treasure of the Church has been wasted!' he is said to have exclaimed on walking into the Vatican Library for the first time. During his three-year pontificate, the Renaissance in Rome was suspended. Painters and sculptors, metal-workers and cabinet-makers were all dismissed. To raise money for his Crusade, Calixtus had no hesitation in selling off many of the most valuable gold and silver works of art in the Vatican Treasury, together with a number of the Papal Library's most precious books. He built galleys in the boatyards of the Tiber, despatched preachers across the continent to sell indulgences and imposed swingeing taxes throughout western Christendom. The response, however, was lukewarm. The courts of Europe grieved for Constantinople, but they were far too deeply preoccupied with their own concerns to go into battle on its behalf. A combined land and sea force was nevertheless despatched, and was not altogether abortive: the Hungarians under Janos Hunyadi routed the Turks at Belgrade in July 1456, and a year later a squadron of the Ottoman fleet was destroyed off Lesbos. But neither victory produced further results, or was of any long-term importance.

Calixtus pursued his second ambition with similar energy and rather more success. Two of his great-nephews were given red hats; being the grandsons of his sisters, they were first required to change their name to Borgia. One of them, Rodrigo, was additionally appointed Vice-Chancellor of the Holy See, a post that placed him in the forefront of Vatican affairs for the next thirty-five years, until his own succession as Pope Alexander VI. On a more humble level, the Pope filled his court and Curia with Spanish and Catalan nominees – though few of them survived in their posts for very long after his death. This came on 6 August 1458 and was generally welcomed.

Nobody had much liked Pope Calixtus; everybody liked Aeneas Silvius Piccolomini. Born one of eighteen children, of an old Sienese family that had gone down in the world, he had pulled himself up by his own efforts and spent eight years in humanistic studies in Siena and Florence; he had then become secretary to various cardinals attending the Council of Basel, one of whom, Cardinal Nicholas Albergati, sent him in 1435 on the greatest adventure of his young life, a secret mission to Scotland.

The purpose of this mission was to try to persuade King James I to launch an attack on England, in yet another attempt to end the Hundred Years War. Aeneas had hoped to travel via London, but the English – doubtless suspecting that he was up to no good – refused him permission to land; he was obliged to return to the continent and take a ship from Sluys direct to Scotland. The journey almost ended in disaster. Violent westerly gales drove the vessel towards the coast of Norway, and the terrified Aeneas vowed, if he survived, to walk barefoot to the nearest shrine of the Virgin Mary. At last, on the twelfth day, the ship – which was now taking on terrifying quantities of water – limped into port near Dunbar, and he duly trudged over the frozen earth to the holy well at Whitekirk. Fortunately for him, the distance was only about five miles and he made it; but after resting there for a time he found that he had lost all sensation in his feet. At first he feared that he might never walk again; in fact he recovered, but suffered from arthritis for the rest of his life, and for much of his pontificate had to be carried about in a sedan chair.

His *Commentaries* – an account of his life written in the third person – cast an interesting light on early fifteenth-century Britain:

> The cities have no walls. The houses are usually constructed without mortar; their roofs are covered with turf; and in the country doors are closed with oxhides. The common people, who are poor and rude, stuff themselves with meat and fish, but eat bread as a luxury. The men are short and brave; the women fair, charming and easily won. Women there think less of a kiss than in Italy of a touch of the hand ... There is nothing the Scotch like better to hear than abuse of the English ...
>
> Then Aeneas ... disguised himself as a merchant and left Scotland for England. A river, which rises in a high mountain, separates the two countries. When he had crossed this in a small boat and had reached

a large town about sunset, he knocked at a farmhouse and had dinner there with his host and the parish priest. Many relishes and chickens and geese were served, but there was no bread or wine. All the men and women of the village came running as if to see a strange sight and as our people marvel at Ethiopians or Indians, so they gazed in amazement at Aeneas, asking the priest where he came from, what his business was, and whether he was a Christian ...

When the meal had lasted till the second hour of the night, the priest and the host together with all the men and children took leave of Aeneas and hastened away, saying that they were taking refuge in a tower a long way off for fear of the Scots, who were accustomed, when the river was low at ebb tide, to cross by night and make raids upon them. They could not by any means be induced to take him with them, although he earnestly besought them, nor yet any of the women, although there were a number of beautiful girls and matrons. For they think the enemy will do them no wrong – not counting outrage a wrong. So Aeneas remained behind with two servants and his one guide among a hundred women ...

But after a good part of the night had passed, two young women showed Aeneas, who was by this time very sleepy, to a chamber strewn with straw, planning to sleep with him, as was the custom of the country, if they were asked. But Aeneas, thinking less about women than about robbers, who he feared might appear at any minute, repulsed the protesting girls ... So he remained alone among the heifers and nanny-goats, which prevented him from sleeping a wink by stealthily pulling the straw out of his pallet.

Though still a layman, he returned to work in the Council Secretariat in Basel, and soon afterwards found himself secretary to the Antipope Felix V. In 1442 Felix sent him to the Diet of Frankfurt where, almost immediately on his arrival, Aeneas caught the attention of the German king Frederick III – whose history he was later to write. The King fully recognised his literary gifts, as well as his outstanding intelligence and efficiency, and appointed him Poet Laureate. For the next three years the young man worked in the royal chancery in Vienna, turning out in his spare time not only a quantity of mildly pornographic poetry,[1] but also a novel in much the same vein, *Lucretia and Euryalus*, celebrating the amorous adventures of

[1] Much of his verse was inspired by the poet Francesco Filelfo, who had been commissioned by Nicholas V to write a book of stories – later described as 'the most nauseous compositions that coarseness and filthy fancy ever spanned'. Nicholas, we are told, had much enjoyed them.

his friend, the Chancellor Caspar Schlick. He himself seems to have been no slouch where amorous adventures were concerned, as several acknowledged bastards could testify.

But such an existence could not continue indefinitely, and in 1445 Aeneas's life underwent a dramatic change. First he broke with the Antipope and was formally reconciled with Eugenius IV; then, in March 1446, he was ordained priest. Thereafter he was a genuinely reformed character and his progress was fast: Bishop of Trieste in 1447, of Siena in 1450, Cardinal in 1456. Two years later he was elected pope and characteristically, remembering Virgil's *pius Aeneas*, took the name of Pius II (1458–64) and settled down to organise a Crusade.

He should have known better. With all his long diplomatic experience, it should have been clear to him that the princes of Europe were simply not prepared to shelve all their other preoccupations in order to march against the Turk; this, however (like so many of his predecessors), he refused to accept. Within two months of his accession he issued a Bull summoning Christendom to a Holy War, and called a Congress of all Christian rulers to meet at Mantua on 1 June 1459. Nearly all of them declined the invitation; those who did not were evasive or non-committal. Pius arrived at Mantua to find virtually no one there. The sad decline in papal influence could, he decided, be due only to the conciliar movement, of which he himself had previously been a staunch upholder; in January 1460 he promulgated another Bull, condemning as heretical all appeals to a General Council. There could hardly have been a more radical about-turn.

He refused, however, to be discouraged. If he could not defeat Sultan Mehmet in battle, perhaps he could persuade him by force of reason to see the error of his ways. In 1461 he drafted an extraordinary letter to the Sultan, in which he included a detailed refutation of the teachings of the Koran, an equally thorough exposition of the Christian faith and a final appeal to renounce Islam and accept baptism. It now seems that the letter may never have been sent; if it was, it unsurprisingly received no reply. But then good news arrived from Venice and Hungary: these states had at least agreed to join forces in a Crusade. Now all Pius's hopes revived. The troops, he announced, would rendezvous with the fleet the following summer in Ancona; he himself would march at their head.

The Piccolomini Library in Siena Cathedral contains a superb cycle of frescoes by Pinturicchio depicting scenes from Pius's life, the last of which shows his arrival at Ancona. The truth, however, was very far from what the picture suggests. The Pope who took the Cross in St Peter's and set off on his litter from Rome on 18 June 1464 was already a sick man – so sick, indeed, that it was a whole month before he reached his destination. And when at last he arrived at Ancona it was to find only a handful of Crusaders awaiting him. There were no obvious leaders, and hardly any equipment. The Venetian fleet, he was told, had been delayed. It eventually sailed into harbour on 12 August with the current Doge, Cristoforo Moro, at its head; but instead of the great armada the Pope had expected, it consisted of just twelve small galleys. For Pius, the disappointment was too great. He turned his face to the wall, and two days later he was dead. His broken heart was interred at Ancona, but his body was brought back to Rome. It was a sad end to one of the most talented popes of his century. Pius was not above nepotism and filled his court with Sienese compatriots; but his literary and intellectual gifts, his skill as an administrator, his discriminating patronage of the arts and his long diplomatic experience gave him a distinction matched by few of his contemporaries. He also remains the only pope to have created a city. In just five years between 1459 and 1464 he transformed his birthplace, the little village of Corsignano, redesigning it on classical lines according to all the latest theories of urban planning, giving it a cathedral and a magnificent palazzo for the use of his family, and renaming it after himself: Pienza.

Pius was a hard act to follow, and his successor Paul II (1464–71) was a distinct comedown. Born Pietro Barbo, scion of a rich family of Venetian merchants, he is said to have thought himself outstandingly good-looking – a view difficult indeed to reconcile with the existing portraits – and had at first tried to call himself Formosus (the Handsome); fortunately his cardinals had been able to dissuade him. Such physical beauty as he may or may not have possessed was in any case not reflected in his intellectual attainments. Shamelessly uncultured, he lost no time in getting rid of the humanists whom Pius had loved; when their leader, Bartolomeo Sacchi – known as Platina, who was subsequently Papal Librarian and author of *The Lives of the Popes* – protested and talked threateningly of a Council, he spent the next four months in the dungeons of the Castel Sant'Angelo. Several members of the Roman Academy, who professed what the Pope regarded as an exaggerated interest in antiquity and insufficient respect for the Church, suffered a similar fate and were released only after the personal intervention of Cardinal Bessarion.

What Paul liked was wealth and display. As a young cardinal (being the nephew of Eugenius IV, he had become a cardinal-deacon at twenty-three) he had rather surprisingly amassed a superb collection of antiques and works of art. He encouraged carnivals, horse-racing and public entertainments of every kind. The celebrations on the occasion of the visit of the Emperor Frederick III on his second visit to Rome in 1468 were long remembered in the city. Meanwhile, equally surprisingly, he set about the restoration of Rome's ancient monuments. The Pantheon, the Arches of Titus and Septimius Severus and the equestrian statue of Marcus Aurelius were all taken in hand. He also built, and inhabited for the last five years of his pontificate, the magnificent Palazzo Venezia (from the first-floor balcony of which Mussolini would later harangue the crowds). Finally, it was thanks to him that two enterprising Germans were allowed to set up the first Roman printing press.

The Pope's sexual proclivities aroused a good deal of speculation. He seems to have had two weaknesses – for good-looking young men and for melons – though the contemporary rumour that he enjoyed watching the former being tortured while he guzzled himself on the latter is surely unlikely. The stroke that killed him on 26 July 1471, at the age of only fifty-four, was said to have been brought on by a surfeit of both.

There was general surprise when his successor, Francesco della Rovere, took the name of Sixtus IV (1471–84); Sixtus III had died in 440, more than a thousand years before. The new pope had been a Franciscan – indeed, General of the Order – and as a distinguished theologian was deeply respected by Cardinal Bessarion and other senior churchmen. Much in demand as a preacher, he had to all appearances been zealous for reform. Franciscans are noted for their love of poverty; it can only be said that Sixtus, on becoming Pope, proved an exception to the rule. From one day to the next, his whole character changed. He spent money like water; his coronation tiara alone cost 100,000 ducats, more than one-third of the papacy's annual income. To raise additional funds he sold plenary indulgencies on a scale previously unparalleled, together with high-sounding papal titles and sinecures. He bestowed the see of Milan on an eleven-year-old and the archbishopric of Lisbon on a boy of eight. His nepotism was on a similar scale. Among his first actions was the bestowal of red hats on two of his eleven nephews, Giuliano della Rovere and Pietro Riario (who was widely rumoured to be the Pope's son, by his own sister). A third nephew, Girolamo Basso, had to wait a year or two until after his cousin, Cardinal Pietro, had died of dissipation at twenty-eight. Four more nephews and two nieces were married into the ruling houses of Milan, Naples and Urbino and to the Orsini and Farnese families in Rome.

Meanwhile the rebuilding of the city went on. Sixtus continued where Nicholas V had stopped. He gave Rome its first new bridge – the Ponte Sisto – across the Tiber since the days of antiquity, to ensure that there was no repetition of the disaster of 1450; he was also responsible for the churches of Santa Maria della Pace and Santa Maria del Popolo, which was to become effectively the mausoleum of the della Rovere family. He revived the Roman Academy. He restored the Ospedale di S. Spirito (still a hospital today) and the equestrian statue of Marcus Aurelius on the Capitol. He carved out new piazzas, replacing the medieval labyrinths of narrow alleys with broad new thoroughfares. He left Rome a Renaissance city. Within the Vatican, he carried on Nicholas's work in the Library, trebling it in size and appointing the formerly disgraced Platina as its librarian.

But above all the name of Sixtus lives on in the Sistine Chapel, greatest of all his benefactions, intended primarily for the holding of conclaves, but also for the regular services attended by the *cappella papalis*, that exalted group of cardinals and other dignitaries who accompanied the Pope at his devotions. When the basic construction was completed in 1481, a whole troop of painters was brought in to provide the frescoes. Chief among them were Botticelli, Ghirlandaio and Perugino, though several others – including Pinturicchio and Signorelli – also contributed. (Michelangelo was at this time only six; it was to be another twenty-seven years before he was reluctantly persuaded by Julius II to take over the east wall and the ceiling.)

It is ironical indeed that the originator of one of the most beautiful buildings in the world should also have been the inspiration for one of its most odious institutions. In Spain the *Reconquista* – the recovery of those parts of the country that had been conquered by the Moors – was almost complete; but there was grave concern over the many thousands of forcibly baptised Jews, the Marranos. In the previous reign (that of King Henry IV) they had enjoyed considerable power, reaching high positions in government, business and finance, and even in the Church. Now the suspicion was growing that a large number of them were tenaciously clinging to their old beliefs. Accordingly, in 1478, Sixtus issued a Bull ordering a major inquiry. This was the beginning of the notorious Spanish Inquisition, which enabled the Dominican friar Tomás de Torquemada to introduce – with the full approval of the monarchs, Ferdinand and Isabella – a regime of brutality and terror unparalleled in Spain until the twentieth century and the Civil War.[1]

Where Italy was concerned, Sixtus could perfectly well have elected to stand aside from the power struggle that continued to lacerate the peninsula – as Venice, Milan, Florence, Naples and other, lesser powers endlessly jockeyed for supremacy; alas, he did not. He plunged in, and by doing so did untold damage to the moral prestige of the Holy See, which became just another party to the eternal squabble. Historians are still debating how far he was implicated in the so-called Pazzi conspiracy of 1478, the purpose of which was to replace the Medici as de facto rulers of Florence with the Pope's nephew, Girolamo Riario.

Already in 1473 the Pazzi bank (a lesser rival to that of the Medici) had lent Sixtus most of the purchase price of 40,000 ducats for the town of Imola, which the Pope wanted for two of his nephews. The Medici – who had already, for their own reasons, refused the loan – were predictably furious, and more furious still the following year when Sixtus dismissed them as his principal bankers, adding insult to injury by appointing to the archbishopric of Pisa (which was under Florentine authority) one of the closest associates of the Pazzi, Francesco Salviati. Lorenzo de' Medici (the Magnificent) refused to recognise the appointment, forbidding the new Archbishop entry into Pisa or even into Florence itself; Sixtus replied by threatening excommunication and an interdict over the whole Florentine state.

And so, as relations between the two factions grew steadily worse, the plot was hatched; and on Sunday, 26 April 1478, principally on the orders of Francesco de' Pazzi and Archbishop Salviati, it went into operation. At a pre-arranged moment – it was, typically, the ringing of the bell marking the elevation of the Host – in the course of High Mass in Florence Cathedral, a whole team of assassins (which included Francesco) fell upon Lorenzo's younger brother Giuliano, stabbing him in the chest

---

[1] There had been earlier inquisitions, like the so-called Papal Inquisition that ultimately eradicated the Cathars in the thirteenth century. The Spanish Inquisition was on an altogether different scale.

and back at least a dozen times (some witnesses say nineteen). A moment later they turned on Lorenzo. He, however, seized his short sword and fought back, before leaping over a low rail into the choir and taking refuge in the sacristy. He was quite badly hurt, but his wounds were not life-threatening; Giuliano, on the other hand, was dead.

Immediately, all Florence was up in arms. The conspirators were quickly rounded up, and were shown no mercy. The official place of execution outside the eastern walls was ignored; the punishments, Lorenzo decided, must be exemplary. Jacopo Bracciolini, son of the great humanist Poggio, was hanged from a high window overlooking the Piazza della Signoria; Francesco de' Pazzi met a similar fate from a top window of the Loggia de' Lanzi, as did the Archbishop and his brother, Jacopo Salviati. Angelo Poliziano, the humanist and classical scholar who was a protégé of Lorenzo de' Medici, reports that – presumably through some involuntary spasm – the dying Archbishop, hanging as he was next to Francesco, bit so savagely into him that long after his death his teeth remained locked in the other's chest.

Was Pope Sixtus indeed embroiled in the conspiracy? Certainly he must have known about it, and quite probably gave it his active encouragement, for no one was more anxious than he to dislodge the Medici once and for all. He is said to have insisted that there should be no bloodshed; but since the object of the conspiracy was assassination, it is difficult to see how he could have had it both ways. And now at last he decreed the excommunication of the Medici that he had long threatened, and the interdict over Florence; and all Italy flared up in war. The attempted coup had failed – just. But if Lorenzo had been a little less lucky and had suffered the fate of his brother, the successful conspirators could easily have brought about a change of government in Florence; and no one would have applauded this change more heartily than Pope Sixtus IV.

It is somehow characteristic of Sixtus that his death – on 12 August 1484 – should have been generally attributed to frustration at having peace forced upon him by the princes of Italy. He certainly died unlamented; indeed, the news of his death caused two weeks of celebration in Rome, inspired by his greatest Roman enemies, the Colonna. Characteristic too is his superb free-standing bronze tomb by Pollaiuolo in the Vatican – probably the most magnificent of any pope, if we except that by Michelangelo which was planned by Sixtus's nephew Giuliano (the future Julius II) for himself, but never properly completed.

It need hardly be said that Giuliano had his eye on the papacy; so too did Cardinal Rodrigo Borgia. Neither, however – despite offers of huge bribes and lucrative promotions – was able to raise the necessary degree of support in the Sacred College. And so, rivals as they were, they worked together to ensure that at the ensuing conclave the cardinals' choice should fall on some second-rate puppet whom they could dominate. It can only be said that they succeeded. The Genoese Giambattista Cibo, Pope Innocent VIII (1484–92), was a hopeless nonentity. He too was much given to nepotism, with the difference that the beneficiaries were not his nephews, but his own children by a Neapolitan mistress – one of whom, his hopelessly dissolute son Franceschetto, he was to marry off to the daughter of Lorenzo the Magnificent in return for the grant of a red hat to Lorenzo's thirteen-year-old son Giovanni.[1] When, three years later in 1479, Giovanni took his place in the College, his father wrote to him warning him of the evils of Rome – 'that sink of all iniquity' – and urging him 'to act so that you convince all who see you that the wellbeing and honour of the Church and the Holy See are more to you than anything else in the world'. Above all, Giovanni must beware of the temptations to evil-doing of the College of Cardinals, which is 'at this moment poor in men of worth ... If the Cardinals were such as they ought to be, the whole world would be better for it, for they would always elect a good pope and thus secure the peace of Christendom.'

Sixtus had left the papacy with enormous debts, and when it came to spending, Innocent himself was no slouch; despite, therefore, the continued sale of indulgences, offices and titles, his financial situation would certainly have become desperate but for a sudden windfall from a most unexpected source: the Ottoman Empire. On the death of an Ottoman sultan the usual practice – to avoid any dispute over the succession – was for his eldest son instantly to have all his brothers garrotted; but when Mehmet II, the conqueror of Constantinople, died in 1481, his son and successor Bayezit had unaccountably failed to despatch his younger brother Cem,[2] who also made a bid for the throne. He failed, and fled for his life, taking refuge on Rhodes with the Knights of St John, whose Grand Master Pierre d'Aubusson had become famous all over Europe for his successful

---

[1] Giovanni was not new to Church preferment. An abbot at the age of eight, he had been nominated to the great Benedictine abbey of Monte Cassino at eleven. Later he was to become Pope Leo X.
[2] This is the modern Turkish spelling. The name is pronounced *Gem*.

defence of the island against Cem's father, Mehmet, in 1480. D'Aubusson welcomed him, but secretly came to an agreement with the Sultan to keep him under guard in return for an annual subsidy of 40,000 ducats. Soon, realising that Rhodes was too close to Ottoman lands for comfort, d'Aubusson sent Cem on to one of the Knights' commanderies in France. There he remained until 1489, when Pope Innocent took him over (he was, after all, an invaluable diplomatic and political asset) in return for red hats for d'Aubusson and a nominee of the French king. On his arrival in Rome Cem was given a splendid reception and escorted by Franceschetto to the Vatican, where he and his suite were lodged in magnificent apartments and lavishly entertained.

The subsidy, however, continued to be payable, and the following year the Pope received a Turkish embassy that presented him with 120,000 ducats – almost the total annual income of the Papal State – for the prince's maintenance over the next three years. He also brought as a present the Holy Lance that had pierced Christ's side at the time of the Crucifixion; a special chapel was built for it in St Peter's. Cem had by this time settled contentedly down with his court in the Vatican, where the appearance of groups of Muslims in their kaftans and turbans must have caused even more raised eyebrows than the sight of the papal grandchildren playing in the gardens.

By this time, however, the pope was sinking fast. To quote a recent authority:

> He slept almost continuously, waking to gorge himself on gargantuan meals . . . He grew grossly fat and increasingly inert, being able, toward the end of his life, to take for nourishment no more than a few drops of milk from the breast of a young woman. When he seemed to be dying, an attempt to save his life was made by sacrificing the lives of three healthy young men to provide a blood transfusion. (Ironically, this attempt was made by a Jewish doctor.) The young men supplying the blood were paid one ducat each. They perished in the process and, with the onset of rigor mortis, the coins had to be prised from their clenched fists.[1]

Innocent himself died on 25 July 1492, having lived just long enough to learn of the final expulsion of the Moors from Spain. His had been a deeply undistinguished pontificate. Under his governance, Rome –

---

[1] G. Noel, *The Renaissance Popes*.

which always needed a firm hand at the helm – had subsided into hopeless disorder, and the Papal States were not far off anarchy. On his deathbed he begged the assembled cardinals for their forgiveness for his shortcomings, and enjoined them to choose a worthier successor.

Unfortunately, they did not do so.

CHAPTER XVIII

The Monsters

(1492–1513)

Few years in all history have proved more fateful than the year 1492. It began dramatically enough, with the completion on 2 January of the Spanish conquest of Granada, ending the Moorish Kingdom and consolidating the rule of Ferdinand and Isabella; in March, the Jews in Spain were given three months to accept Christianity or leave the country; April saw the death, in his family villa at Careggi, of Lorenzo the Magnificent; in late July, Pope Innocent VIII died in Rome; and in early August Christopher Columbus sailed, all unwittingly, for the New World.

Innocent's successor Rodrigo Borgia, now sixty-one years old, took the name of Alexander VI (1492–1503). His great-uncle Calixtus III had given him a good start: a cardinal at twenty-five and already in possession of a whole clutch of bishoprics and abbeys, at twenty-six he had become Vice-Chancellor of the Holy See, an office that guaranteed him the vast income which he was to hold over the next four pontificates. There can be little doubt that he owed his election principally to the huge bribes that he shamelessly distributed: it is said that four mule-loads of bullion were carried from the Borgia palace to that of Cardinal Ascanio Sforza. His principal rival, Cardinal Giuliano della Rovere, could not match his wealth and was obliged to contain his fury as best he could.

Alexander was, however, known to be highly intelligent and an experienced administrator, almost certainly better able than any of his rivals to restore order to Rome, which under Innocent had been allowed to fall dangerously out of control. He was said never to have missed a consistory (the cardinals' regular meeting), except when he was ill or absent from Rome; no one had a deeper understanding of the workings of the Curia. He was also witty, charming and excellent company: 'women,' wrote an envious contemporary, 'were attracted to him like iron to a magnet'. What he lacked was the slightest glimmering of religious feeling. He made no secret of the fact that he was in the Church for what he could get out of it – and he got a very great deal. By the time of his election, which was celebrated with a bullfight in the piazza in front of St Peter's, he had fathered no fewer than eight children by at least three different women, earning him a severe rebuke from Pius II, which had had no effect whatsoever. Those of his offspring who remained closest to him were his four children by the aristocratic Roman, Vannozza Catanei: Giovanni, Cesare, Lucrezia and Goffredo (or Gioffrè; in Catalan Jofré). No fewer than five of his family were to receive the red hat: Cesare at the age of only eighteen, by which time he was already an archbishop.

Alexander had occupied the papal throne for only two years when King Charles VIII of France – described by the historian H.A.L. Fisher as 'a young and licentious hunchback of doubtful sanity' – led an army of some 30,000 into Italy, inaugurating a whole series of invasions, which over the next seventy years were to put much of the peninsula under foreign domination. The *casus belli* was Naples. The old Angevin royal line had died out in 1435 with Queen Joanna II, and the Neapolitan throne had been seized by the King of Sicily, Alfonso of Aragon, who had been succeeded by his illegitimate son Ferdinand[1] and then by Ferdinand's son, another Alfonso. But, the bastard grandson of a usurper, it was generally agreed, had only a tenuous claim to the throne; and Charles, as a descendant of his namesake Charles of Anjou, believed that he had a very much better one. All this was bad news indeed for Pope Alexander. In 1493 he had married his son Goffredo to Ferdinand's granddaughter, and on Ferdinand's death had immediately recognised and crowned the young Alfonso. He was not encouraged by Charles's repeated threats to depose him, or by the news that his bitterest enemy, Cardinal Giuliano della Rovere, had declared for the French king and had headed north to join him.

For Charles, the invasion began promisingly enough. With his cousin, the Duke of Orleans, he crossed the Alps without incident, his heavy cannon having been shipped separately to Genoa. Milan, now under the brilliant Ludovico Sforza (Ludovico 'il Moro'), received him with enthusiasm, as did Lucca and Pisa. In Florence, welcomed as a liberator by the Dominican firebrand Savonarola, the King took the opportunity to expel Piero de' Medici – who displayed none of

---

[1] Not to be confused with Ferdinand of Spain, husband of Isabella.

the statesmanship of his father Lorenzo, dead two years before. On 31 December 1494 Rome opened her gates and Charles installed himself in what is now Palazzo Venezia, while Alexander (who had unsuccessfully appealed to the Sultan Bayezit for assistance) briefly took refuge in the Castel Sant'Angelo; but a fortnight later King and Pope met for the first time – and Alexander's famous charm did the rest. On 17 January 1495 he said Mass before 20,000 soldiers of the French army in the great piazza in front of St Peter's, with Charles himself acting as server.

The French remained in Rome for another ten days. Already, like all armies of occupation, they were becoming increasingly unpopular. They showed little respect for the local people; every day brought new stories of violence, robbery and rape. Even the palace of Vannozza Catanei was ransacked. It was with unconcealed joy and relief that on 27 January the Romans watched them march away to Naples, accompanied by Cesare Borgia – ostensibly as Papal Legate, but in fact as a hostage for his father's good behaviour. With them too went Prince Cem, the only man in the whole immense company whom they were sorry to see depart.

On 22 February Charles entered Naples. King Alfonso immediately abdicated and entered a monastery; his son Ferrante fled for his life. The Neapolitans, on the other hand, who had never looked on the House of Aragon as anything other than usurping foreigners, gave the French king a hero's welcome. On 12 May he was crowned for the second time. But, as he was soon to discover, there is all the difference in the world between a lightning offensive and a sustained programme of occupation. The Neapolitans, delighted as they had been to get rid of the Aragonese, soon discovered in their turn that one foreign oppressor was very much like another. Unrest also grew among the inhabitants of many of the smaller towns, who found themselves having to support, for no good reason that they could understand, discontented and frequently licentious French garrisons.

Beyond the Kingdom of Naples, too, men were beginning to feel alarm. Even those states, Italian and foreign, who had previously looked benignly upon Charles's advance were asking themselves just how much further the young conqueror might be intending to go. Ferdinand and Isabella, who wanted Naples for themselves, made an alliance with the Emperor Maximilian, cementing it by offering the hand of their daughter Joanna – later to be known, with good reason, as 'the Mad' – to Maximilian's son Philip, and preparing an invasion fleet; and even the King's former ally Ludovico Sforza 'il Moro' of Milan, by now as alarmed as anyone, was further disconcerted by the presence at nearby Asti of the Duke of Orleans, whose claims to Milan through his grandmother, the Duchess Valentina Visconti, he knew to be no less strong than his own, or than those of Charles to Naples. Pope Alexander, who had by this time recovered his sangfroid, found plenty of support for his anti-French alliance, the so-called Holy League, which was ostensibly pacific, but in fact had a single objective: to send the new King packing.

When news of the League was brought to Charles in Naples, he flew into a fury, but did not underestimate the danger with which he was now faced. To make matters worse, he had lost both his distinguished hostages. Cesare had simply slipped away; Cem had contracted a high fever at Capua and died a few days later. Thus it was that only a week after his Neapolitan coronation Charles left his new kingdom for ever and headed – together with 20,000 mules loaded with loot from Naples – back to the north. Rome was panic-stricken at the thought of his return. Alexander and most of his Curia slipped away to Orvieto, leaving just one unfortunate cardinal to greet the King.

Fortunately, on this occasion the French army proved surprisingly well behaved – probably because Charles was reluctant to waste any more time before getting safely across the Alps. He would have liked an audience with the Pope, to discuss the possible dissolution of the Holy League and obtain full papal recognition of his Neapolitan coronation; but in the face of Alexander's determination to avoid him, there was nothing he could do. The march, which involved dragging his heavy artillery across the Apennines in midsummer, proved a nightmare; and on 5 July he reached the little town of Fornovo near Parma to find himself facing some 30,000 soldiers of the League under the command of Francesco Gonzaga, Marquis of Mantua. The only battle of the whole campaign, fought on the following day, was over in a flash; but it was the bloodiest that Italy had seen for 200 years. Gone were the days of the old mercenary *condottieri*, whose object was always to prolong a war as far as possible and to live to fight again; they often tended to see a battle as little more than a stately pavane, with fighting – such as it was – hand-to-hand and artillery-fire too weak and inaccurate to do much serious harm. The French had introduced a warfare of a very different kind: they, together with their Swiss and German mercenaries, fought to kill – and the heavy iron balls that burst from the mouths of their cannon inflicted hideous wounds.

Gonzaga managed to present the battle of Fornovo as a victory; few dispassionate observers would have agreed with him. The French admittedly forfeited their baggage train – which included Charles's sword, helmet, gold seal and a 'black book' containing portraits of his female conquests – but their losses were negligible compared with those of the Italians, who had utterly failed to stop them. They continued their march that same night and reached Asti unmolested a few days later. There, however, bad news awaited them. Alfonso's son, Ferrantino, had landed in Calabria where, supported by Spanish troops from Sicily, he was rapidly advancing on Naples. On 7 July he reoccupied the city. Suddenly, all the French successes of the past year evaporated. A week or two later Charles led his army back across the Alps, leaving the Duke of Orleans behind to maintain a French presence as best he could.

But the soldiers whom he disbanded at Lyons that November carried something far deadlier than any dream of conquest. Columbus's three ships, returning to Spain from the Caribbean in 1493, had brought with them the first cases of syphilis known to the Old World; through the agency of the Spanish mercenaries sent by Ferdinand and Isabella to support King Alfonso the disease had quickly spread to Naples, where it was rife by the time Charles arrived. After three months of *dolce far niente*, his men must in turn have been thoroughly infected, and it was almost certainly they who were responsible for introducing the disease north of the Alps.

With Charles safely out of the way, Alexander was free to settle down to his principal task, the aggrandisement of his family. His eldest son Giovanni, already Duke of Gandia, he had destined for the throne of Naples; this ambition, however, came to nothing when in June 1497 Giovanni disappeared. Two days later his body was recovered from the Tiber. His throat had been cut, and there were no fewer than nine stab wounds. Who was the murderer? Giovanni was only twenty, but his violent, unstable character and his penchant for other men's wives had already made him countless enemies.

Of all the possibilities, the likeliest seems to have been his brother Cesare; there were ugly rumours that the two had been rivals for the love of their sister-in-law, Goffredo's wife Sancia, or even of their sister Lucrezia. Cesare was well capable of fratricide – three years later he almost certainly murdered his brother-in-law Alfonso of Aragon, second husband of Lucrezia – and his jealousy of his elder brother was well known. There is also the curious fact that although Pope Alexander was genuinely shattered by the assassination of his favourite son (he is said to have touched neither food nor water for three days) he seems to have been content that no one was ever formally accused, far less convicted, of the crime. Cesare too, had he been innocent, would surely have moved heaven and earth to find his brother's murderer.

For a time, it seemed that Alexander was a reformed character. Indeed, he said as much. 'The blow that has fallen upon us,' he declared:

> is the heaviest that we could possibly have sustained. We loved the Duke of Gandia more than anyone else in the world. We would have given seven tiaras to be able to recall him to life. God has done this as a punishment for our sins. We for our part are resolved to mend our own life and to reform the Church.

It certainly needed reforming. The cost of the wars required to maintain the Papal States and the ambitious building programmes of successive popes meant that there was a constant search for new sources of income. The discovery in 1462 of an alum mine near Tolfa had come as a godsend to the papal treasury. Alum was indispensable for both the cloth and leather trades. Heretofore it had to be imported at considerable expense from Asia Minor; henceforth the popes could declare a ban on supplies from the Muslim world and establish their own monopoly. But alum alone was nowhere near enough. Indulgences were another invaluable source of income, as was the sale of offices. More and more sinecures were invented; these were bought for large sums and guaranteed an income for life. The result was a vast increase in the membership of the Curia, many of whose members had absolutely nothing to do.

As part of his proposed reforms, Alexander now nominated a commission of six of the most pious cardinals; and less than two months later a draft Bull of Reformation had been prepared. The Pope was banned from selling benefices and from transferring Church property to lay persons. As for the cardinals – who were to be drawn from all the nations – none should possess more than one bishopric; their households were limited to eighty people and thirty horses; they were banned from hunting, theatres, carnivals or tournaments; and their funeral expenses were not to exceed 1,500 ducats. The lesser clergy were similarly reined in: they must refuse all bribes and put away their concubines.

Who, however, was expected to enforce these new rules? Only those who stood to lose by them. And so the draft Bull remained precisely that, and Pope Alexander soon slipped back into his old ways. Cesare – who had never renounced his – gradually replaced Giovanni in his father's affections, and in 1498 persuaded Alexander to release him from the cardinalate and his religious vows and allow him to return to the outside world. As a layman once again (he was the first man in history to lay down the red hat) he soon became the Pope's *éminence grise*. It was largely thanks to his influence that by the end of that same year Alexander had abandoned his anti-French policies and had willingly given his consent to the annulment of the marriage of the new French king Louis XII, assuring him at the same time that he would not oppose Louis's claims to Milan and Naples. In doing so, he opened the way to new French adventures in Italy; but such considerations were of minimal interest to Cesare, who travelled in magnificent state as papal envoy to France, where he was made Duke of Valentinois and given as a bride Charlotte d'Albret, sister of the King of Navarre. On his return to Italy he directed his energies to the Papal States, eliminating one by one – by expulsion or poisoning – the feudal lords of Umbria and Lazio, Romagna and the Marches until the whole area had become a personal fief of the Borgia family.

The year 1498 also saw the solution of a problem that had plagued Pope Alexander since the beginning of his pontificate. It was personified by the Dominican friar Girolamo Savonarola. Originally from Ferrara, since 1490 Savonarola had lived in Florence, preaching fierce and fiery sermons, delivering apocalyptic prophecies and claiming direct communication with God. The chief objects of his wrath were the Medici, the Duke of Milan and – particularly after Alexander's accession – the papacy; and he did not mince his words:

> Popes and prelates speak against worldly pride and ambition, and are plunged in it up to their ears. They preach chastity and keep mistresses ... They think only of the world and worldly things; for souls they care nothing ... They have made of the Church a house of ill fame ... a prostitute who sits upon the throne of Solomon and signals to the passers-by ... O prostituted Church, you have unveiled your abuse before the eyes of the whole world, and your poisoned breath rises to the heavens.

The overthrow of the Medici and their expulsion from Florence in 1494 was, as we know, the simple result of the French invasion; but to the Florentines it was Savonarola's doing, and he emerged as the new leader of the city, setting up a 'Christian and religious republic' and ordering regular 'bonfires of the vanities' – mirrors, cosmetics, fine clothes, secular books and pictures (including paintings by Michelangelo and Botticelli), musical instruments, gaming tables, even chessmen. While it lasted, the general atmosphere must have been more like that of Puritan England in the seventeenth century than of Renaissance Florence in the fifteenth.

Already by 1497 the Pope had had enough. He excommunicated the turbulent friar and, when Savonarola took no notice, called for his arrest and execution. By this time the Florentines were sick of him too. On 8 April 1498 a mob attacked the convent of S. Marco, of which he was prior; in the ensuing struggle several of his supporters were killed and, along with his two closest associates, he finally surrendered. All three were tortured to exact their confessions; and on 23 May they were led out into the Piazza della Signoria, where they were stripped of their friars' robes and hanged in chains from a single cross. A huge fire was lit beneath them, so that Savonarola should burn just as the vanities had burned before him. The ashes of all three were then flung into the Arno, to ensure that no relics would be rescued for future veneration.

Outside Italy, Pope Alexander's most fateful decision was taken in 1493, when he made the all-important adjudication between Spain and Portugal over their recent territorial discoveries in Africa and America. For most of the century the Portuguese, inspired and encouraged by their Infante, Dom Henrique – better known as Prince Henry the Navigator – had been steadily exploring the west coast of Africa; and during the last decade Vasco da Gama and Bartholomew Diaz had rounded the Cape of Good Hope and opened up the Cape Route to the Indies. In these achievements the Spanish monarchs had shown markedly little interest; their time came only when Columbus returned from his first voyage in 1493 and announced that he had planted the flag of Castile in the New World. At their request, therefore, Pope Alexander drew a line of demarcation from north to south 100 leagues west of the Azores, decreeing that all zones of exploration to the east of that line should be allotted to Portugal, all those to the west to Spain. In 1494, after protests by the Portuguese, the line was moved further westwards by the Treaty of Tordesillas; this made it possible in 1500 for Portugal to claim Brazil, and explains why Brazil remains Portuguese-speaking today.

The last four years of Alexander's pontificate were largely taken up with his own and Cesare's ambition to appropriate the entire Papal State and turn it into a Borgia family fief. The programme was mapped out and put into execution by Cesare, who by now utterly dominated his father. It involved the crushing of many of the great Roman families – above all, the Orsini; it necessitated several assassinations, which were normally followed by seizures of property, and was further financed by the open sale of the highest offices of the Church, including that of cardinal. Cesare Borgia was hated and feared for his violence and cruelty. 'Every night,' the Venetian Ambassador reported to his government, 'four or five men are discovered assassinated, bishops, prelates and others, so that all Rome trembles for fear of being murdered by the Duke.'

And yet, although he was hideously disfigured by syphilis – towards the end of his life he never showed himself in public without a mask – few who came into contact with Cesare failed to be impressed. His energy was boundless, his courage absolute. He appeared to need no sleep, and his speed of movement was astonishing: he was said to arrive at a city before he had left the last. At the same time he shared to the full his father's love of women. In his short life he left at least eleven bastards; and the diary of the Papal Master of Ceremonies, Johannes Burckhardt, leaves us in no doubt of how Cesare spent his leisure:

> On Sunday evening, 30 October [1501], Don Cesare Borgia gave a supper in his apartments in the apostolic palace, with fifty decent prostitutes or courtesans in attendance, who, after the meal, danced with the servants and others there, first fully dressed and then naked. Following the supper, too, lampstands holding lighted candles were placed on the floor and chestnuts strewn about, which the prostitutes, naked and on their hands and knees, had to pick up as they crawled in and out amongst the lampstands. The Pope, Don Cesare and Donna Lucrezia were all present to watch. Finally, prizes were offered – silken doublets, pairs of shoes, hats and other garments – for those men who could perform the act most frequently with the prostitutes.

At this point it might be useful to say a word about Donna Lucrezia. She has been cast as the femme fatale of the Borgia dynasty; but to what extent she deserved the role remains uncertain. She was certainly not just a pretty face: on two occasions her father handed over to her complete control of the Vatican Palace, with authority to deal with his correspondence. As for her reputation, there is absolutely no evidence for the rumours of incest with one or more of her brothers – or, indeed, with her father – apart from that given by her first husband, Giovanni Sforza, during the divorce proceedings, during which several other baseless accusations were levelled in both directions. She seems to have been very largely the hapless instrument of her father's and brother's political ambitions. Her marriage to Sforza in 1493 at the age of thirteen (after two earlier betrothals) was due to Alexander's eagerness to establish an alliance with Milan; before long, however, the Sforza were no longer necessary and the Pope's son-in-law became an inconvenience. In 1497 there seems to have been a plot to assassinate him – though which of the three Borgias was implicated we shall never know – but he escaped from Rome just in time, and it was then decided that a divorce would be sufficient. Giovanni (who stood to lose not only his wife, but also her dowry and the city of Pesaro, which he held in fief from the Pope) fought hard, but was eventually forced to agree on the humiliating grounds of impotence, despite his testimony that the marriage had been consummated more than a thousand times. There was the additional embarrassment that at the time of the divorce Lucrezia was actually pregnant; but the paternity of the child Giovanni, who was born in secret, has never been established.

Lucrezia's next marriage was even more ill-starred; her second husband, Alfonso of Aragon, whom she genuinely loved, was murdered by Cesare – quite possibly out of jealousy, though there were also political overtones. She was, we are told, broken-hearted; but Alexander soon had a third marriage lined up: to another Alfonso, the Este Prince of Ferrara. The attendant festivities, on the usual sumptuous scale, were paid for by the sale of eighty new offices in the Curia and the appointment of nine new cardinals (five of them Spaniards) at 130,000 ducats per red hat. (At about the same time the Pope also appropriated the entire fortune of the Venetian cardinal Giovanni Michiel, who had recently died in agony, almost certainly poisoned by Cesare.) This marriage was also ostensibly successful, in that Lucrezia bore her husband a number of children; but it did not prevent her from having passionate affairs with the poet Pietro Bembo and her bisexual brother-in-law, Francesco Gonzaga, Marquis of

Mantua. Despite these profligacies, she achieved comparative respectability and outlived the rest of her family, dying in Ferrara in 1519 after giving birth to her eighth child.

The month of August 1503 saw Rome at its hottest and most unhealthy. The nearby Pontine marshes had not yet been drained; malaria was rife and several cases of plague had also been reported. It was a time of year when all those who could afford to do so left the city; but these were critical times – a French army was on the march to Naples – and the Pope had remained in the Vatican. On the 12th, both Alexander and Cesare were stricken with fever. Cesare recovered, but the seventy-two-year-old Pope could not fight the infection, and six days later he was dead.

The fact that father and son had collapsed on the same day inevitably aroused suspicions of foul play. It was pointed out that on 3 August the two of them had dined with the recently appointed Cardinal Castellesi in his nearby villa; the rumour rapidly spread round Rome that they had intended to poison their host, but had inadvertently drunk the poisoned wine themselves. For some reason this mildly ridiculous story has survived and found its way into a number of serious histories; it ignores the fact that although by this time the Borgia father and son had a good many murders to their credit, they had no ascertainable motive to kill Castellesi. Nor are there any known poisons that take over a week to have their effect. The likelihood is that Alexander and Cesare were simple victims of the epidemic, and that the Pope – improbable as it may have seemed – died a perfectly natural death.

Thanks to the two of them (and in lesser measure to Lucrezia), the Borgias have become a legend for villainy and cruelty. Much of this was clearly justified; but all legends contain an element of exaggeration and often tend to obscure the truth. Moreover, because the Borgia legend concentrates on their crimes, the credit side tends to be forgotten. At the time of his election Alexander had been Vice-Chancellor to five successive popes; he understood the ways of the Vatican as well as anyone alive. For the past fifty years it had done its best to build up the reputation of the Holy See as one of the European superpowers, able to negotiate with France and Spain as a political equal. Unfortunately, as Alexander well knew, it was nothing of the kind. It lacked the money, it lacked the manpower, it lacked even the basic security of its own home ground, constantly threatened as it was by the Orsini and the Colonna, as well as by the notoriously inflammable Roman populace. The 'papal vicars' – mostly *condottieri* who were, by definition, out for what they could get – were not to be trusted for a moment; equally faithless were the major Italian states, Venice and Florence, Naples and Milan, and other cities less important but equally independent. Then there were the French, forever threatening a new invasion, and in the background Spain and (now apparently on the crest of the wave) the Ottoman Turks.

In short, the papacy had real or potential enemies on every side, and no firm friends. To survive with its independence intact, it desperately needed adequate finance, firm administration and astute diplomacy; and these Alexander was able to provide in full measure, however questionable his means of doing so. He proved it in only the second year of his pontificate, when he persuaded Charles VIII to leave Rome, thus saving himself and his successors from being nothing more than satraps of the French. For this alone, he deserves the gratitude of posterity. The fact that he has not received it is largely due to his private life and to the incessant vilification that he received both during his lifetime and after his death, and which he tolerated with quite extraordinary equanimity. On more than one occasion he chided Cesare for not showing the same tolerance; it could be argued, however, that he might have done better to follow his son's example. Many of the accusations levelled against him he could easily have disproved, had he bothered to do so; by leaving them unanswered, he contributed to his own unspeakable reputation.

Despite his eventual recovery, the sickness that struck Cesare Borgia on that fateful 12 August was to destroy his life. The disappearance of Alexander from the scene created a vacuum that brought chaos in its train; several cities rose in open revolt. A French army under Francesco Gonzaga had already reached Viterbo, only forty miles from Rome; meanwhile a Spanish army under its brilliant young general Gonsalvo de Córdoba was hurrying northwards from Naples. In normal times Cesare might have been able to deal with the situation; but now, desperately ill in the Vatican, he was powerless to take the swift military measures necessary to save his career. Political action was his only hope; and that meant ensuring the support he needed from his father's successor. He managed to secure some 100,000 ducats from his family's private treasury; and with this considerable sum, from his sickbed, he hoped to bribe the coming conclave. At all costs he was determined to prevent the election of his most dangerous enemy, Cardinal Giuliano della Rovere – nephew of Pope Sixtus IV – who had been living in exile in France during the greater part of Alexander's pontificate. The surest way of achieving this was, he knew, to block the Cardinal's return to Rome.

He failed. Della Rovere arrived unscathed, together with Cardinal Georges d'Amboise, Louis XII's chief counsellor, who was as ambitious for the tiara as he was. A third determined candidate was Cardinal Ascanio Sforza, who had broken with Alexander over his pro-French policies; now released from prison by d'Amboise in order to cast his vote for the Frenchman, Sforza found himself unexpectedly popular and began lobbying on his own account. In fact d'Amboise was soon effectively eliminated: a French pope at such a moment seemed almost as bad an idea as another Spanish one, particularly after della Rovere had spread the word that it would mean the second removal of the papacy to France. The struggle seemed to be between della Rovere and Sforza; neither, however, could accumulate the votes necessary to carry the day, and the choice of the cardinals finally fell on a compromise candidate, Francesco Todeschini-Piccolomini, Bishop of Siena, who took the name of Pius III (1503) as a tribute to his uncle, Pius II. He was already sixty-four, but looked and acted a good deal older and was crippled by gout. There was a general feeling that he would not last long.

In fact, he lasted just twenty-six days – one of the shortest pontificates in history. He had been a fine, upstanding churchman of unquestioned integrity, and had been the only cardinal brave enough to protest when Alexander transferred papal territories to his son, the Duke of Gandia. There were strong indications that, had he lived, he would have summoned a General Council and driven through the reforms that were so desperately needed. With his death on 18 October 1503 the opportunity was lost – and it was the Church that paid the price.

One of the shortest pontificates was followed by the shortest conclave. It lasted for only a few hours on 1 November. Giuliano della Rovere had done his work well, and had spread his money astutely; he had even managed to secure the vote of Ascanio Sforza, the only other serious potential contender. And it was plain to all that he was born to command. In the words of the Venetian envoy:

> No one has any influence over him and he consults few or none. It is almost impossible to describe how strong and violent and difficult he is to manage. In body and soul, he has the nature of a giant. Every-

thing about him is on a magnified scale, both his undertakings and his passions. He inspires fear rather than hatred, for there is nothing in him that is small or meanly selfish.

It might have been thought that the election of this terrifying figure as Pope Julius II (1503–13) – he had scarcely bothered to change his name – would spell the end for Cesare Borgia. It did not. Just two weeks before the Orsini had stormed Cesare's palace in the Borgo, and he (by now fully restored to health) had taken refuge in the Castel Sant'Angelo. He was still there when messengers arrived from della Rovere assuring him of his protection in the event of his being elected. Accordingly, the moment he heard of the election, Cesare had returned to his old quarters in the Vatican. But, as he well knew, he was only there on sufferance. It was in Julius's interest to string him along, simply because his power base was the Romagna, where Venice was helping herself to more and more cities; Julius for the moment had no army, and consequently needed Cesare's. When he had no further use for the Duke of Valentinois, he would unquestionably ditch him.

As of course he did. Cesare Borgia still retained much of his old fire, but without his father's protection and support, the days of power and glory were gone and he fades out of our story. Exiled to Spain in 1504, he died in 1507, fighting for his brother-in-law, King John of Navarre, at the siege of Viana. He was thirty-one years old.

There is a story that when Michelangelo was working on his fourteen-foot bronze statue of Pope Julius II and suggested putting a book in the Pope's left hand, Julius replied, 'Nay, give me a sword, for I am no scholar!'[1] He spoke no more than the truth; he was indeed a soldier, through and through. Not since Leo IX (at Civitate in 1053) had a pope led his army personally in battle; Julius did so, on several occasions – notably when, in January 1511, in full armour and aged sixty-eight, he personally trudged with his army through deep snowdrifts to capture Mirandola from the French. His world, like that of his enemy Alexander VI, was exclusively temporal; for the spiritual he had no time or inclination, and to establish the papacy firmly as a temporal power was the primary task to which he devoted his pontificate. This involved, inevitably, a good deal of fighting. Already by the autumn of 1504 he had succeeded in bringing both France and the

---

[1] Shortly afterwards the statue was toppled by the Bolognesi. They sold it for scrap to the Duke of Ferrara, who recast it into a huge cannon, which he affectionately christened Julius.

Empire into an alliance against Venice – another instance of foreign armies being invited into Italy to settle what are essentially domestic differences; and in April 1506, immediately after laying the corner-stone of the new St Peter's, he led his entire Curia on an expedition to regain Perugia and Bologna from the local families who saw them-selves as independent despots and ruled accordingly. The Baglioni in Perugia surrendered – one suspects rather to the Pope's disappoint-ment – without a fight; the Bentivoglio in Bologna put up rather more resistance, but eventually the paterfamilias Giovanni (who had ruled there for more than forty years) fled to France and the Pope made his triumphal entry into the city.[1]

Venice, however, remained the Pope's arch-enemy. Five years before he had been her most trusted friend in the whole of the Sacred College; but she had recently seized several cities in the Romagna that had previously fallen to Cesare Borgia. These cities, which had tradition-ally belonged to the Holy See, Venice had refused to surrender; so now Julius was determined on her destruction. Italy, as he saw it, was divided into three. In the north was French Milan, in the south Spanish Naples. Between the two there was room for one – but only one – powerful and prosperous state; and that state, Julius was determined, must be the papacy. A new stream of emissaries was despatched from Rome: to France and Spain, to the Emperor Maximilian, to Milan, Hungary and the Netherlands. All bore the same proposal, for a joint expedition by western Christendom against the Venetian Republic, and the consequent dismemberment of its empire.

The states of Europe could not be expected to feel much sympathy for such a policy. Their motive for joining the proposed league was neither to support the papacy not to destroy Venice, but to help them-selves. However much they might try to present their action as a blow struck for righteousness against iniquity, they knew perfectly well that their own conduct was more reprehensible than ever Venice's had been. But the temptation was too great, the territories promised them irresistible. They accepted. So it was that the death-warrant of the Venetian Empire was signed, at Cambrai on 10 December 1508, by Margaret of Austria on behalf of her father Maximilian and by Cardinal d'Amboise for the King of France. Julius himself, though his legate was present at Cambrai, did not formally join the League until the

---

[1] It was on 21 January of that same year that the Swiss Guard was founded – a perma-nent corps of mercenary soldiers to protect the person of the Pope. During Julius's pontifi-cate they certainly earned their keep.

following spring; he seems to have been uncertain whether the other signatories were in earnest. But when in March 1509 King Ferdinand II of Aragon announced his formal adherence, he hesitated no longer. On 5 April Julius openly associated himself with the rest and placed Venice under an interdict, and on the 15th the first French soldiers marched into Venetian territory. A month later, on 14 May, the French met the Venetians just outside the village of Agnadello. For Venice, it was a catastrophe. Her casualties were about 4,000, and her entire mainland empire was as good as lost. Before the end of the month the Pope's official legate received back those fateful lands in the Romagna with which the whole tragedy had begun.

In early July the Pope agreed to accept a six-man Venetian embassy in Rome, and it was soon clear that he had done so only in order to inflict still more humiliation on the Republic. On their arrival in early July the envoys had been forbidden, as excommunicates, to enter the city until after dark, to lodge in the same house or even to go out together on official business. Only one was granted an audience, which rapidly deteriorated into a furious diatribe by Julius himself. Not, he vowed, until the provisions of the League of Cambrai had been carried out to the letter and the Venetians had knelt before him with halters around their necks would he consider giving them absolution. Then, very soon, the pendulum began to swing. Less than two months after Agnadello came the first reports of spontaneous uprisings on the mainland in favour of Venice; and on 17 July, after just forty-two days as an imperial city, Padua returned beneath the sheltering wing of the Lion of St Mark. There had as yet been no sign of Maximilian in Italy, but the news of Padua's defection quickly brought him down with an army. His siege began on 15 September; for a fortnight the German and French heavy artillery pounded away at the walls, reducing them to rubble. And yet, somehow, every assault was beaten back. On the 30th the Emperor gave up.

When Pope Julius was told the news from Padua he flew into a towering rage; and when, after Maximilian's failure to recover it, he heard that Verona too was likely to declare for Venice, he is said to have hurled his cap to the ground and blasphemed against St Peter. His hatred of Venice was as vindictive as ever, and the war continued. At first Venice had rejected the Pope's terms outright; she had even appealed to the Turkish sultan for support, requesting as many troops as he could spare and a loan of not less than 100,000 ducats. But the Sultan remained silent, and by the end of the year the Venetians saw that they must capitulate. And so, on 24 February 1510, Pope Julius II took his seat on a specially constructed throne outside the central doors of St Peter's, with twelve of his cardinals around him. Five Venetian envoys, dressed in scarlet (the sixth had died a few days before), advanced towards him and kissed his foot, then knelt on the steps while their spokesman made a formal request on behalf of the Republic for absolution, and the Bishop of Ancona read out the full text of the agreement. This must have made painful listening for the envoys – not least because it lasted for a full hour, during which time they were forced to remain on their knees. Rising with difficulty, they received twelve scourging rods from the twelve cardinals (the actual scourging was mercifully omitted), swore to observe the terms of the agreement, kissed the Pope's feet again and were at last granted absolution. Only then were the doors of the basilica opened, and the assembled company proceeded in state for prayers at the high altar before going on to Mass in the Sistine Chapel – all except the Pope, who, as one of the Venetians explained in his report, 'never attended these long services'.

The pendulum, it seemed, was swinging again. The news of the Pope's reconciliation with Venice had not been well received by his fellow-members of the League; at the absolution ceremony the French, imperial and Spanish ambassadors to the Holy See, all of whom were in Rome at the time, were conspicuous by their absence. Although Julius made no effort to dissociate himself formally from the alliance, he was soon afterwards heard to boast that by granting Venice absolution he had plunged a dagger into the heart of the King of France – proof enough that he now saw the French, rather than the Venetians, as the principal obstacle to his Italian policy and that he had effectively changed sides. By the high summer of 1510 his volte-face was complete, his new dispositions made. His scores with Venice had been settled; now it was the turn of France.

By all objective standards, Pope Julius's action was contemptible. Having encouraged the French to take up arms against Venice, he now refused to allow them the rewards that he himself had promised, turning against them with all the violence and venom that he had previously displayed towards the Venetians. He also opened new negotiations with the Emperor in an attempt to turn him, too, against his former ally. His claim, regularly resurrected in his defence by later apologists, that his ultimate objective was to free Italy from foreign invaders would have been more convincing if he had not invited in these particular invaders in the first place.

There was, in any case, another motive for the Pope's sudden change of policy. Having for the first time properly consolidated the Papal States, he was now bent on increasing them by the annexation of the Duchy of Ferrara. Duke Alfonso, during the past year, had become little more than an agent of the French king; his salt-works at Comaccio were in direct competition with the papal ones at Cervia; finally, as husband of Lucrezia Borgia, he was the son-in-law of Alexander VI – a fact that, in the Pope's eyes, was alone more than enough to condemn him. In a Bull circulated throughout Christendom, couched in language that St Peter Martyr said made his hair stand on end, the luckless Duke was anathematised and excommunicated.

In the early autumn of 1510 Pope Julius had high hopes for the future. A joint papal and Venetian force had effortlessly taken Modena in mid-August, and although Ferrara was strongly fortified, there was good reason to believe that it would not be able to withstand a well-conducted siege. The Pope, determined to be in at the kill, travelled north by easy stages and reached Bologna in late September. The Bolognesi gave him a frosty welcome. Since the expulsion of the Bentivoglio in 1506 they had been shamefully misgoverned and exploited by papal representatives and were on the verge of open revolt. The Governor, Cardinal Francesco Alidosi, had already once been summoned to Rome to answer charges of peculation, and had been acquitted only after the intervention of the Pope himself – whose continued fondness for a man so patently corrupt could be explained, it was darkly whispered in Rome, only in homosexual terms. But the tension inside the city was soon overshadowed by a still graver anxiety. Early in October a French army under the French Viceroy of Milan, the Seigneur de Chaumont, marched south from Lombardy and advanced at full speed on Bologna. By the 18th it was just three miles from the gates.

Pope Julius, confined to bed with a high fever in a fundamentally hostile city and knowing that he had fewer than a thousand of his own men on whom he could rely, gave himself up for lost. 'O, chè ruina è la nostra!'[1] he is reported to have groaned. His promises to the Bolognesi that they would be exempted from taxation in return for firm support were received without enthusiasm; and he had already opened peace negotiations with the French when, at the eleventh hour,

---

[1] 'Oh, what a ruin is ours!'

reinforcements arrived from two quarters simultaneously: a Venetian force of light cavalry and a contingent from Naples, sent by King Ferdinand as a tribute after his recent papal recognition. The Pope's courage flooded back at once. There was no more talk of a negotiated peace. Chaumont – who seems to have felt some last-minute qualms about laying hands on the papal person – was persuaded to withdraw: a decision that did not prevent Julius from hurling excommunications after him as he rode away.

It is hard not to feel a little sorry for the Seigneur de Chaumont. He was dogged by ill-luck. Again and again we find him on the point of a major victory, only to have it plucked from his grasp. Often, too, there is about him more than a touch of the ridiculous. When Julius was besieging Mirandola, Chaumont's relief expedition was twice delayed: the first time when he was hit on the nose by an accurately aimed snowball which happened to have a stone lodged in it; and then again on the following day when he fell off his horse into a river and was nearly drowned by the weight of his armour. He was three days recovering, only sixteen miles from the beleaguered castle; as a result, Mirandola fell. A month later his attempt to regain Modena failed hopelessly; and on 11 March 1511, aged thirty-eight, he died of a sudden sickness, which he – though no one else – ascribed to poison, just seven hours before the arrival of a papal letter lifting his sentence of excommunication.

But by this time the Duke of Ferrara, on whom the ban of the Church weighed rather less heavily, had scored a brilliant victory over a papal army that was advancing towards his city along the lower reaches of the Po, and Julius was once again on the defensive. In mid-May Chaumont's successor, Gian Giacomo Trivulzio, led a second march on Bologna; and on his approach the inhabitants, seeing their chance of ridding themselves once and for all of the detested Cardinal Alidosi, rose in rebellion. The Cardinal panicked and fled for his life, without even troubling to warn the Duke of Urbino, who was encamped with the papal troops in the western approaches, or the Venetians, a mile or two away to the south; and on 23 May Trivulzio entered Bologna at the head of his army and restored the Bentivoglio to their former authority.

Cardinal Alidosi, who in default of other virtues seems at least to have possessed a decent sense of shame, barricaded himself in the castle of Rivo to escape the papal wrath; but he need not have bothered. Julius, who had prudently retired a few days earlier to Ravenna, showed not a trace of anger. Even now, in his eyes, his beloved friend could do no wrong: he unhesitatingly laid the entire blame for the disaster on the Duke of Urbino, whom he summoned at once to his presence. The interview that followed is unlikely to have diminished the Duke's long-standing contempt for Alidosi, for whose cowardice he was now being made the scapegoat. When, therefore, on emerging into the street he found himself face-to-face with his old enemy – who had left his castle and had just reached Ravenna to give the Pope his own version of recent events – his pent-up rage became too much for him. Dragging the Cardinal from his mule, the Duke attacked him with his sword; Alidosi's retinue, believing that he might be acting under papal orders, hesitated to intervene, and moved forward only when the Duke remounted his horse and rode off to Urbino, leaving their master dead in the dust.

The grief of Pope Julius at the murder of his favourite was, we read, terrible to behold. Weeping uncontrollably, waving aside all sustenance, he refused to stay any longer in Ravenna and had himself carried off at once to Rimini in a closed litter, through whose drawn curtains his sobs could plainly be heard. But there were further blows in store. Mirandola, for whose capture he had always felt himself personally responsible, was within a week or two to be lost to Trivulzio. The papal army, confused, demoralised and now without a general, had disintegrated. With the recapture of Bologna, the way was open to the French to seize all the Church lands in the Romagna for which he had fought so hard and so long. All the work of the last eight years had gone for nothing. And now, at Rimini, the Pope found a proclamation nailed to the door of the church of S. Francesco, signed by no fewer than nine of his own cardinals with the support of Maximilian and Louis of France, announcing that a General Council of the Church would be held at Pisa on 1 September to investigate and reform the abuses of his pontificate.

Both as a pope and a man, Julius had many faults. He was impetuous – 'so impetuous,' wrote the contemporary historian Francesco Guicciardini, 'that he would have been brought to ruin had he not been helped by the reverence felt for the Church, the discord of the Princes and the condition of the times' – mercurial, vindictive, a poor organiser and a deplorable judge of character. Though an adept diplomatic tactician, he had little sense of long-term strategy. Eaten up by worldly ambition, he was utterly unscrupulous in the pursuit of his ends.

Certain qualities, however, he possessed in full measure. One was courage, and another was indomitability of spirit. On his journey back to Rome, at the age of nearly seventy, he was already contemplating a new league, headed by himself and comprising Venice, Spain, England and if possible the Empire, whose combined forces would drive the French once and for all from the Italian peninsula; and by the beginning of July 1511 negotiations had begun.

They presented no serious problems. Ferdinand of Spain had already gained all he could have hoped for from the League of Cambrai and had no desire to see any further strengthening of the French position in Italy. In England, Ferdinand's son-in-law Henry VIII willingly agreed to keep his rival occupied in the north while his allies did the same in the south – although he was obliged to point out to the Pope, while accepting his proposals, that it would have been better if they had not been carried by an obvious double-agent (recommended, it appears, by the late Cardinal Alidosi) who was regularly reporting all developments to King Louis. Venice, which throughout the negotiations was fighting hard – and on the whole successfully – to resist French offensives in the Veneto and Friuli, asked nothing better. Maximilian, as usual, dithered; but even without him, the new league promised to prove a force to be reckoned with.

One reason, apart from his natural temperament, for the Emperor's ambivalent attitude was the proposed Church Council at Pisa, which he and King Louis had jointly sponsored. Already Louis was beginning to regret the idea, and support for it was rapidly falling away. After two short sessions, local hostility was to force its removal to Milan; and there, although under French protection, it was openly ridiculed to the point where a local chronicler forbore to record its proceedings because, he claimed, they could not be taken seriously, and anyway he was short of ink.

Meanwhile the Pope, having almost miraculously recovered from an illness during which his life had been despaired of, was able to proclaim the 'Holy League' on 4 October and begin preparations for war. He soon found, however, that King Louis also held an important new card in his hand: his nephew, Gaston de Foix, Duc de Nemours, who at the age of twenty-two had already proved himself one of the outstanding military commanders of the day. Courageous, imaginative and resourceful, this astonishing young man could take a decision in an instant; and, having taken it, could move an army like lightning. A dash from Milan in early February 1512 was enough to thwart an attempt to recover Bologna by a papal army; unfortunately it also suggested to the citizens of Bergamo and Brescia that, with the French forces away on campaign, this was an opportune moment to rise in revolt and return to their former Venetian allegiance. They were quickly proved wrong. Marching night and day in bitter weather – and incidentally smashing a Venetian division that tried to intercept him, in a battle fought by moonlight at four o'clock in the morning – Nemours was at the walls of Brescia before the defences could be properly manned, and he and his friend Bayard led the assault, fighting barefoot to give themselves a better grip on the sloping, slippery ground. Brescia was taken by storm, the leader of the revolt was publicly beheaded in the main square and the whole city was given over to five days' sack, during which the French and German troops fell on the local inhabitants, killing and raping with appalling savagery. It was another three days before the 15,000 corpses could be cleared from the streets. Bergamo hastily paid 60,000 ducats to escape a similar fate, and the revolt was at an end.

The campaign, however, was not. Nemours, determined to give his enemies no rest, returned to Milan to gather fresh troops and then immediately took to the field again. With an army that now amounted to some 25,000, he marched on Ravenna and laid siege to the town. As a means of drawing out the papal army, the move was bound to succeed. Its commander, the Spanish Viceroy in Naples, Ramón de Cardona, could not allow a city of such importance to be captured under his nose without lifting a finger to save it. And so on Easter Sunday, 11 April 1512, on the flat, marshy plain below the city, the battle was joined.

Of all the encounters recorded in Italy since Charles VIII had taken his first, fateful decision to establish a French presence in the peninsula nearly twenty years before, the battle of Ravenna was the bloodiest. When at last the papalists fled from the field they left behind them nearly 10,000 Spanish and Italian dead. Several of the leading Spanish captains, some of them seriously wounded, were in French hands, as was the Papal Legate, Cardinal de' Medici. Ramón de Cardona himself, who had taken flight rather earlier in the day – he is said not to have drawn rein until he reached Ancona – was one of the few to survive unharmed. But it had been a pyrrhic victory. The French losses had also been considerable, and – worst of all – Nemours himself had fallen at the moment of triumph, in a characteristically impetuous attempt to head off the Spanish retreat. His place was taken by the elderly Seigneur de la Palice, who was possessed of none of his speed and panache. Had the young man lived, he would probably have rallied what was left of the army and marched on Rome and Naples, forcing Julius to come to terms and restoring King Louis to the Neapolitan throne; but la Palice was cast in a more cautious mould. He contented himself with occupying Ravenna, where he was unable to prevent an orgy of butchery and rape which surpassed even that suffered by the Brescians a few weeks before.

And now there suddenly occurred one of those extraordinary changes of political fortune that render Italian history as confusing to the reader as it is infuriating to the writer. When the news of Ravenna reached him, Julius, foreseeing an immediate French advance on Rome, prepared for flight. Just before he was due to leave, however, he received a letter from his captive legate, whom la Palice had unwisely permitted to correspond with his master. The French, wrote Cardinal de' Medici, had suffered losses almost as great as those of the League; they were tired and deeply demoralised by the death of their young leader; their general was refusing to move without receiving instructions and confirmation of his authority from France. At about the same time the Venetian Ambassador in Rome sought an audience with the Pope to assure him that, contrary to widespread rumours, the Republic had not accepted any French proposals for a separate peace, and had no intention of doing so.

At once Julius took new courage. Overpowered, at least temporarily, in the military field, he flung all his energies into the Church Council that he had summoned for May 1512. This had now become more necessary than ever, since King Louis's renegade Council of Milan had taken advantage of the victory of Ravenna to declare the Pope contumacious and suspend him from office. It was true that even in Milan itself few people took the findings of so transparently political a body very seriously; nonetheless, this open split in the Church could not be allowed to go unchecked or unanswered. On 2 May, with all the state ceremonial of which the papal court was capable, the Supreme Pontiff was borne in his litter to the Lateran, followed by fifteen cardinals, ten archbishops, fifty-seven bishops and three heads of monastic Orders: a hierarchical show of strength that made the handful of rebels in Milan seem almost beneath notice – precisely as it was intended to do. At its second session this Lateran Council formally declared the proceedings of the Council of Pisa/Milan null and void, and all those who had taken part in it schismatics.

On that very same day Pope Julius also proclaimed the adhesion of the Emperor Maximilian to the Holy League; and Maximilian now gave orders that all subjects of the Empire fighting with the French army should immediately return to their homes on pain of death. To la Palice, this was disastrous news. He had already suffered a serious depletion of his French troops, most of whom had been recalled to deal with the impending invasion of Henry VIII in the north; the precipitate departure of his German mercenaries now left him in the ridiculous position of a general without an army – or at least without any force capable of holding the Swiss and Venetians whom he suddenly found ranged against him. Meanwhile the Spanish and papal forces were also back in the field and, although only a shadow of what they had been before their recent defeat, were able to advance virtually unopposed on all fronts. By the beginning of July the Pope had not only regained all his territories, but had even extended them to include Reggio Emilia, Parma and Piacenza. La Palice, with what was left of his army, had no choice but to return to France, where Louis XII, who only three months before might have had the entire peninsula within his power, now saw all his hopes annihilated.

Pope Julius II died on 21 February 1513 of a fever, probably brought on by the syphilis from which he had suffered for many years. There had been little of the priest about him, apart from his dress and his name. His pontificate was dominated by politics and by war; his strictly ecclesiastical activities were largely confined to routine matters – though it was he who issued the fateful dispensation that authorised Henry VIII to marry Catherine of Aragon, the widow of his elder brother Arthur.

Julius's most important legacy by far was as a patron of the arts. He had a passion for classical statuary, enriching the Vatican collections with masterpieces such as the *Apollo Belvedere* and the *Laocoön*. (The latter had been accidentally unearthed in 1506 by a man digging in his vineyard.) But he is nowadays chiefly remembered for his decision to replace the old basilica of St Peter with a new building, infinitely more magnificent than its predecessor. The plans for this he eventually entrusted to Bramante[1] – who, abandoning his original design for a Greek cross-in-square church with the tomb of St Peter directly beneath a vast dome, eventually decided on a more traditional Latin basilica with nave and aisles, together with a portico derived

---

[1] His real name was Donato d'Angelo Lazzari. He was nicknamed *Bramante* – the word means 'soliciting' in Italian – since he was constantly seeking jobs for himself.

from the Pantheon. Away went the ancient mosaics, the icons, the huge medieval candelabra; it was not long before the architect had acquired a new nickname, *Il Ruinante*. The work on St Peter's alone would have kept Bramante fully employed for the rest of his life, but Julius made him additionally responsible for a radical redesign of the Vatican gardens.

The Pope also gave encouragement and employment to the twenty-six-year-old Raphael, whom he commissioned to fresco his own apartments, the so-called *Stanze* (he refused absolutely to inhabit those of the hated Alexander), and to Michelangelo – whom, as we know, he had to bully mercilessly ('I'm a sculptor, not a painter,' the artist protested) into painting the Sistine Chapel ceiling. It has been suggested that, despite the bullying, the two men were lovers. Both, certainly, were homosexual, and Julius – although he had engendered three daughters while still a cardinal – was widely accused of sodomy. On the whole the idea seems improbable; but we shall never know.

Excessive modesty was never one of the failings of Pope Julius II; and as early as 1505 he also commissioned Michelangelo to design his tomb. This was originally intended to stand thirty-six feet high and to contain forty statues, all of them more than life-size; according to Vasari, the principal reason for his decision to rebuild St Peter's was in order to provide suitable accommodation for it. Unfortunately the money ran out and the project had to be radically revised. A far more modest version can now be seen in S. Pietro in Vincoli in Rome; but Julius was actually buried in what there was of his new St Peter's – as, doubtless, he would have wished.

CHAPTER XIX

The Medici Pair

(1513–34)

Pope Leo X (1513–21), who followed Julius after a short and trouble-free conclave untinged for once by simony, was born Giovanni de' Medici, the second son of Lorenzo the Magnificent. 'God has given us the Papacy,' the thirty-seven-year old Pope is said to have written to his brother Giuliano soon after his accession, 'let us now enjoy it.' The words themselves may or may not be apocryphal; but they are an accurate enough summing-up of the new Pope's attitude to his office, and indeed of his whole outlook on life. At the same time, they are open to misconstruction. It was not in Leo's nature to enjoy his pontificate as Alexander VI had done. There were to be no orgies, no unseemly roistering. The sale of indulgencies and Church appointments went on as it always had – money had to be raised somehow – but, for all that, Leo remained genuinely pious: he took his religious duties seriously and fasted twice a week.

The fact remains that he was less a pope than a Renaissance prince. Homosexual like his predecessor, he was a cultivated and polished patron of the arts, far more magnificent than his father Lorenzo had ever dared to be. A passionate huntsman, he would ride out with an entourage of 300; an insatiable gourmet, he gave lavish banquets and willingly attended those given by his friends. In 1494, when his family was exiled from Florence, he had travelled to France, Germany and the Netherlands, where he had met Erasmus; but six years later he was back in Rome, rapidly acquiring political influence in the Curia, and by 1512 he had successfully re-established Medici control in Florence, of which he was to be the effective ruler throughout his pontificate.

He began as he meant to continue: with a procession from the still-unfinished St Peter's to the Lateran, a procession that for sheer sumptuous extravagance surpassed anything Rome had ever seen. Though suffering agonies from fistula and piles, he rode on a snow-white horse escorted by 112 equerries – to say nothing of countless cardinals, prelates and ambassadors, and detachments of both cavalry and infantry, while papal chamberlains flung gold coins into the crowd. But even that was only the beginning. He ordered tapestries of gold and silken thread from Brussels – based on Raphael's cartoons, now in the Victoria and Albert Museum – at a cost of 75,000 ducats, then willingly paid out double that sum for the festivities attendant on the wedding of Giuliano to Filiberta of Savoy, aunt of Francis I of France. He commissioned from Michelangelo a new façade for the church of S. Lorenzo in Florence, where three generations of his family were already buried, building a road running for 120 miles to a Tuscan quarry; and when this project had to be abandoned – the money ran out, and Leo complained, understandably, that the artist was impossible to work with – he instituted another: the Medici Chapel in the same building, which was finally to be completed during the pontificate of his cousin, Pope Clement VII.

And there was intellectual and scientific work also to be done. Leo revived Rome's university, the Sapienza, which had not functioned for the past thirty years, appointing nearly a hundred professors and substantially increasing the number of subjects offered – which now included medicine, mathematics, botany and astronomy. He founded chairs of Greek and Hebrew, each with its own printing press. He even encouraged the theatre (until now non-existent in Rome), staging, among much else, a refreshingly sexy comedy by his close friend Cardinal Bibbiena.

Leo's biographer, Paolo Giovio, saw his reign as a Golden Age. The city's most powerful banker, Agostino Chigi, had erected a huge triumphal arch beneath which the procession passed, inscribed with the words 'The time of Venus has passed, and the time of Mars. Now is the rule of Minerva.' The Romans had no difficulty in identifying the reigns of Alexander VI and Julius II; the reference to Minerva, goddess of wisdom, was perhaps rather more problematical. Leo, highly educated and sophisticated as he was, could hardly have been described as wise. However many indulgences he sold, however many new offices he created, he remained permanently in hock to the bankers of Rome and Florence, and the papacy fell further and further into debt.

Politically, Leo was an incorrigible waverer. When in 1515 Francis marched on Milan the Pope joined the Holy League to resist him; but in the ensuing battle of Marignano – in which the French army destroyed that of the League – the papal troops, though entrenched only fifty miles away, took no part, and Leo subsequently hurried off to meet the victorious king at Bologna. The result, which he hardly deserved, was a concordat in which the Papacy surrendered Parma and Piacenza, but the continuation of Medici rule in Florence was assured.

Florence, however, was no longer enough. Leo had benefited from unbridled nepotism in his own youth, and did all he could to continue the tradition to the next generation. Two of his cousins and three of his nephews he had made cardinals; but for his favourite nephew, Lorenzo – the son of his deceased elder brother Piero – he intended something more: the Duchy of Urbino. The present Duke (he was Francesco della Rovere, nephew of Julius II) had rebelled in 1508 against his papal suzerain; now, in 1516, Leo simply excommunicated him, seizing and torturing the envoy whom the Duke sent to Rome to protest. The war that followed lasted for two years and cost 800,000 ducats; by the time it was finished Lorenzo – its intended beneficiary – was dead. (His daughter Catherine, however, was to win a far greater prize than Urbino; she married Henry, son and successor of Francis I, and became Queen of France.)

In the summer of 1517 Rome was rocked by the most scandalous, but at the same time the most mysterious, chapter in Leo's pontificate. The Pope suddenly announced – and the announcement itself must have been embarrassing enough – that he had discovered a conspiracy by several cardinals, led by Cardinal Alfonso Petrucci (who was widely believed to be the Pope's lover), to assassinate him. They had, it seemed, bribed a Florentine doctor named Vercelli to inject him with poison while operating on his fistula. Interrogated under torture, Vercelli not surprisingly confessed and was immediately hanged, drawn and quartered. Petrucci suffered similar treatment, and implicated a number of other cardinals. He too was sentenced to death. Because it was unlawful for a Christian to lay hands upon a Prince of the Church, he was strangled by a Moor, with a cord made of crimson silk. The lives of the other cardinals were spared – on payment of huge fines.

The accusations seem improbable in the extreme. All the accused cardinals had small grievances against Leo, but none had any that could be generally accepted as a motive for assassination. And even had they wished to murder the Pope, would they really have selected that particular method of doing so? Of them all, only Petrucci had made any attempt to flee; and yet, curiously enough, they all confessed. We shall never know the truth; popular opinion in Rome, however, persisted in believing that there had in fact been no conspiracy, and that Leo had fabricated the whole thing for the sake of the fines he was able to exact. At all events the papacy was still further discredited, and Leo's subsequent creation of no fewer than thirty-one new cardinals, who together paid him half a million ducats for their red hats, did little to restore its prestige.

Nor, apparently, did the Pope have the faintest comprehension of how much that prestige needed restoring. Like many of his predecessors he paid lip-service to the idea of reform; reading of his pontificate, one tends to forget that for the first four years of it the Fifth Lateran Council was in progress. But the Council achieved virtually nothing. There was no sense of urgency in its deliberations, or any sign that it received any firm direction from the Pope. Meanwhile the shameless extravagance, the blatant marketing of indulgences and offices, the sexual shenanigans – for Leo had long since given up any attempt to conceal his preferences and was now positively flaunting his latest catamite, the singer Solimando, son of Prince Cem – all these abuses, and many others besides, had given still greater strength to the reform movement, and it was by now plain to any unprejudiced observer that, unless the Church were quickly to buckle down and clean out its own stables, a serious rebellion could not be long in coming.

It was on 31 October 1517 – just at the time when, in the aftermath of the Petrucci conspiracy, Pope Leo was appointing his thirty-one new cardinals – that Martin Luther nailed his notice to the church door at Wittenberg, announcing that he was prepared to defend, in open debate, ninety-five theses that claimed to establish the invalidity and illegality of indulgences.[1] It would not have been a difficult task. The idea that spiritual grace could be sold commercially for hard cash was obviously nonsense; and in recent times new and improved indulgences had come onto the market. It was now possible, for example, to acquire them in respect of sins not yet committed: to lay up, as it were, a credit balance of advance absolution; alternatively, indulgences could be bought on behalf of deceased relatives; the more money paid, the shorter their time in purgatory.

---

[1] Scholars now tell us that Luther never nailed it to the door, but distributed it in the usual way. They would.

By now the Church was teetering on the edge of an abyss; yet still Leo failed to see that Luther's crusade was more than a 'monkish squabble'. The man was clearly an irritation; but Savonarola had been a good deal worse, and was now almost forgotten. This tiresome German would doubtless go the same way. Meanwhile, in November 1518 the Pope published a Bull: all who denied his right to grant and issue indulgences would be excommunicated. But no one in Germany took any notice. Reverence for the papacy, as Guicciardini lamented, 'had been utterly lost in the hearts of men'. Half-heartedly Leo tried to enlist the help first of the General of the Augustinian Order and then of Luther's protector, the Elector Frederick of Saxony, to bring the monk to order; but neither attempt was successful. Then in 1520 he published another Bull, *Exsurge Domine*, condemning Luther on forty-one separate counts. This Luther publicly burned – and was consequently excommunicated. On 11 October 1521 the Pope bestowed the title *Fidei Defensor*[1] – Defender of the Faith – on King Henry VIII of England, in recognition of his book *The Defence of the Seven Sacraments against Martin Luther*.

On New Year's Day 1515 King Louis XII of France died in Paris. Just over a year later, on 23 January 1516, King Ferdinand of Aragon followed him to the grave. These two deaths brought two young men, still relatively unknown, to the forefront of European affairs. They could hardly have been more unlike. King Francis I was twenty years old at the time of his succession, and in the first flush of his energy and virility. He was already an accomplished ladies' man – not particularly handsome, perhaps, but elegant and dashing, with a quick mind, a ready wit, a boundless intellectual curiosity and an unfailing memory which astonished all who knew him. He loved spectacle and ceremonial, pomp and parade; and his subjects, bored out of their minds by a long succession of dreary, colourless sovereigns, took him to their hearts.

Charles of Habsburg, born in 1500 to the Emperor Maximilian's son Philip the Handsome and Ferdinand and Isabella's daughter Joanna the Mad, had inherited neither of his parents' primary attributes. His appearance was ungainly, with the characteristically huge Habsburg chin and protruding lower lip; he suffered also from an appalling stammer, and showered his interlocutors with spittle. He had little imagination, and no ideas of his own; few rulers have ever been so

---

[1] The abbreviation *Fid. Def.* (or the initials *F.D.*) appears to this day on British coins.

utterly devoid of charm. What saved him was an innate goodness of heart and, as he grew older, a tough sagacity and shrewdness. Though far the most powerful man in the civilised world, he never enjoyed his empire in the way that Francis I and Henry VIII enjoyed their kingdoms – or Leo X his pontificate.

At the age of sixteen, Charles (already ruler of the Netherlands) had assumed the regency of Aragon and the Two Sicilies on behalf of his mother, now hopelessly insane. Three years later came the death of his grandfather, the Emperor Maximilian. The Empire remained elective, and the succession of Charles was by no means a foregone conclusion. There were still many who preferred his younger brother, the Archduke Ferdinand. A still more formidable rival was Francis I – who, in the early stages of his candidature, had the enthusiastic support of Pope Leo. (Henry VIII of England also at one moment threw his cap into the ring, but no one took him very seriously.) Fortunately for Charles, the German electors hated the idea of a French emperor; the Fuggers – that hugely rich banking family from Augsburg – lined as many pockets as was necessary; and at the last moment Leo withdrew his opposition. On 28 June 1519 Charles was elected, and on 23 October of the following year he was crowned – not in Rome, but in the old Carolingian capital of Aachen – as the Emperor Charles V. In addition to the Netherlands and Spain, Naples and Sicily and the New World, there now devolved on him all the old Empire, comprising most of modern Austria, Germany and Switzerland. Milan, Bohemia and western Hungary were to follow a little later. For a man of modest talents and mediocre abilities, here was an inheritance indeed.

It is uncertain whether Pope Leo, when he withdrew his opposition to Charles's coronation, entirely understood that by doing so he was giving his approval to the last stage of the polarisation of continental Europe. The King of France was now trapped in a vice, virtually encircled by the Empire; conversely, the Emperor now found himself sovereign of a divided dominion, its two parts cut off from each other by a hostile state. The result was inevitable: a long and deadly struggle between the two men for dominance in Europe and mastery of the western Mediterranean. The part that the papacy was to play in this struggle was to be largely concerned with maintaining the balance of power; but Leo's own sympathies, despite his earlier support for Francis, were now firmly with Charles.

It was plain from the start that the young Emperor was not going to accept the presence of the French in Italy. He himself had no Italian ambitions except to maintain his hold on Sicily, Naples and Sardinia, all of which he had inherited from his grandfather Ferdinand; these he was determined to pass on to his successors. For the rest, he was only too pleased that the native rulers should remain in possession of their states, provided only that they recognised his position and showed it due respect. French influence, on the other hand, could not be tolerated. King Francis, for as long as he remained in Italy, constituted a challenge to the imperial hold on Naples and seriously endangered communications between the Empire and Spain. In 1521 the Emperor signed a secret treaty with Leo, as a result of which a combined papal and imperial force expelled the French once again from Lombardy, restoring the house of Sforza in Milan. This victory enabled the papacy to recover Parma and Piacenza, lost six years before.

For Pope Leo, here was a reason for celebration; but in the course of the ensuing banquet, which seems to have been more than usually riotous and lasted all night, he caught a chill that rapidly became a fever; and on 1 December he died. As a Renaissance prince he would have been superb; as Pope he was a disaster. In seven years he is estimated to have spent some five million ducats, and at his death was well over 800,000 in debt. At that time it was calculated that there were more than 2,150 saleable offices in the Vatican, worth some 3,000,000 ducats. Leo X had left Italy in its usual state of turmoil, northern Europe on the verge of religious revolution, and the papacy in the lowest depths of degradation.

Such was the state of the papal treasury after Leo's death that the candles used at his funeral were the leftovers from that of Cardinal Gianantonio di Sangiorgio, held the day before; and such was the state of popular feeling against the Church that the thirty-nine cardinals who assembled for the conclave on 28 December needed a bodyguard to protect them.

Conclaves were well known to be uncomfortable things, but this was one of the worst. In the depths of a bitter winter, the Vatican was entirely unheated; several windows had lost their glass and had to be roughly boarded up. Most of those present had spent the greater part of their lives in conditions of extreme luxury; now they found themselves herded together, shivering in a dim half-light, with little to eat – their food was passed to them 'at a round turning wheel made in the wall' – and only the most rudimentary sanitation. On the sixth day, by which time one elderly cardinal had been carried out half-dead, the meagre rations were still further reduced. Few better ways, one might have thought, could be devised to encourage a quick decision; but almost at once there was deadlock. Cardinal Giulio de' Medici, with fifteen avowed supporters, at first seemed the favourite, but the sinister Cardinal Francesco Soderini turned the remainder firmly against him; Giulio then declared himself in favour of Cardinal Alessandro Farnese – upon whom, however, a similar hatchet job was now performed by Cardinal Egidio di Viterbo. As Egidio happened to be Alessandro's confessor, the propriety of his diatribe was questioned; but the damage was done.

At this moment a letter was produced from the Emperor Charles V, warmly recommending his erstwhile tutor, a sixty-two-year-old Dutchman from Utrecht named Adrian Florensz Dedal. Hardly anyone in Rome had ever heard of him, but there: he had no enemies in the city and, given his age, was unlikely to last too long. After Pope Leo, perhaps a compromise candidate with (as far as anyone knew) a spotless reputation would be no bad thing. And did not a vote for him represent the best chance of escaping from a freezing Vatican back to their own warm palaces? And so, after fourteen nightmare days, he was elected on 9 January 1522.

Having deliberately delayed his departure owing to an outbreak of plague and then having travelled to Rome by sea, Pope Adrian (or Hadrian) VI (1522–3) – he made no attempt to change his name in the traditional manner – arrived only in August. He spoke no Italian, his Latin was incomprehensible and before the end of the year he had antagonised everyone: the populace, who considered him a northern barbarian; the Curia, who were furious at his refusal to distribute the usual benefices; Charles V, who had expected him to join his league against Francis I; and Francis himself, who actually stopped the transfer of Church money from France to Rome when the Pope arrested and imprisoned Cardinal Soderini for secretly plotting to hand over Naples to the French. Meanwhile he lived like a monk. Gone were Alexander's courtesans, Julius's armies, Leo's catamites and banquets. Hadrian spent precisely one crown a day on catering and employed as domestic staff only his old Flemish housekeeper, who did all his cooking, washing and cleaning. For the art and architecture of the Renaissance he cared not a jot: he threatened to have the Sistine Chapel whitewashed, and the *Laocoön* – 'an effigy of heathen idols' – thrown into the Tiber.

It need hardly be said that his promised reforms all came to nothing. He failed to control the cardinals, who continued to live like fighting cocks; nor could he do anything to check the sale of indulgences, without which the Church would have faced bankruptcy. All his initiatives ended in disaster: his attempts to form a European coalition against the Sultan; his handling of the Reformation (whose importance he consistently failed to recognise, just as Pope Leo had before him); even his proposal – after the Turkish capture of Rhodes and the eviction of the Knights of St John – for a three-year truce over the whole of Christendom. When he fell sick and died in September 1523, little more than a year after his arrival in Rome, there was nothing but relief. It was to be another four and a half centuries before the election of the next non-Italian pope.

The cardinals' relief was tempered, however, by the realisation that they would have to face another conclave. Fortunately, this opened in the autumn (1 October) rather than the depths of winter, but as usual the conditions worsened as time went on. From the beginning there was no heating, fresh air or natural light; then, towards the end of the month, the midday and evening meals were reduced to a single course; shortly afterwards the cardinals received only bread, wine and water. Once again, the argument for a quick election could hardly have been more persuasive; but feelings ran high, much was at stake, and it was fifty remorseless days before the choice was made.

The obvious candidate was Giulio de' Medici, who was supported by the Emperor and consequently by the Spanish contingent; but there were many Italian cardinals – including Soderini (who had been instantly released on Hadrian's death) and the powerful Pompeio Colonna – who were determined to do him down. The English were stubbornly and somewhat ridiculously backing Cardinal Wolsey; the French were divided. Back and forth went the arguments; devious conspiracies were hatched, and dark intrigues; intricate deals were planned, compromise candidates proposed and rejected. As it turned out, the cardinals could have saved themselves a lot of trouble, to say nothing of physical misery, because on 19 November the majority choice finally fell on the favourite, Cardinal Giulio, who somewhat surprisingly took the name of the brutal Antipope of the Schism, Clement VII (1523–34).[1]

Giulio de' Medici was the bastard son of Giuliano, Lorenzo the Magnificent's brother, who had been assassinated by the Pazzi in Florence

---

[1] See Chapter XVI.

Cathedral forty-five years before. Lorenzo had tracked down the mother and had persuaded her to allow him to bring up the boy as his own. Then, when Lorenzo himself died in 1492, Giulio was placed under the guardianship of Lorenzo's second son, Giovanni. Since the guardian was only three years older than the ward, the two became close friends; and when Giovanni became Pope Leo X one of his first acts was to legitimise his cousin, making him a cardinal and effectively ruler of Florence.

Despite their mutual affection, the two could hardly have been more different. Leo was unusually ugly, with a huge head and a fat, red face; but he possessed a charm that many found irresistible. Clement, now forty-eight, was tall and slim; he might have been good-looking but for his thin, tightly compressed lips, haughty expression and almost perpetual frown. He was pious, conscientious, industrious; but nobody – with the single exception of his friend Benvenuto Cellini – liked him much. Guicciardini went so far as to describe him as 'somewhat morose and disagreeable, reputed to be avaricious, far from trustworthy and naturally disinclined to do a kindness'. Anyone who thought that the election of another Medici signalled a return to the extravagant and easy-going days of Pope Leo was in for a disappointment.

It might reasonably be supposed that such a man would prove at least a competent pope. Alas, Clement was nothing of the kind. He was vacillating and irresolute, apparently terrified when called upon to make a decision. He might have made a moderately good major; as a general he was a disaster. Leopold von Ranke, the great German historian, dubbed him the most disastrous of all the popes, which – if one remembers the papacy in the tenth and eleventh centuries – seems a little unfair; the fact remains that the eleven years of his pontificate saw the worst sack of Rome since the barbarian invasions, the establishment in Germany of Protestantism as a separate religion and the definitive breakaway of the English Church over Henry VIII's divorce.

Finding himself – as Hadrian had before him – caught in the whirlpool caused by the rivalry between Charles V and the King of France, Clement dealt with the situation even more clumsily than his predecessor. His first loyalty should clearly have been to the Emperor, to whom he largely owed his election; but in 1524 he joined with Venice and Florence in a secret alliance with France, and Francis, with an army of some 20,000, marched back over the Mont-Cenis pass into Italy. In late October he recaptured Milan, then turned south to

Pavia, where he spent the winter, trying unsuccessfully to divert the River Ticino as a means of taking the city. He was still there four months later when there arrived an imperial army. The two armies met just outside Pavia, and on Tuesday, 21 February 1525, battle was joined.

The battle of Pavia proved to be one of the most decisive engagements in European history. It was also the first to prove conclusively the superiority of firearms over pikes. When the fighting was over the French army had been virtually annihilated; Francis himself had shown, as always, exemplary courage; after his horse had been killed under him he had continued to fight on foot until at last, overcome by exhaustion, he had been obliged to give himself up. He was captured and sent to Spain, where he remained for a year in not uncomfortable confinement; then Charles released him in return for his signature to what was known as the Treaty of Madrid, by which he renounced all claims to Burgundy, Naples and Milan. When he returned to Paris, however, and the terms of the treaty were made public, there was a general outcry. Pope Clement in particular was aghast: without a French presence in Italy, how could he hope to defend himself against the Emperor? Hastily he recruited Milan, Venice and Florence to form an anti-imperialist league for the defence of a free and independent Italy – and invited France to join. Though the ink was scarcely dry on the Treaty of Madrid, and though he and the Pope held widely differing views on Milan (the Pope favouring the Sforzas, while Francis wanted the city for himself), on 15 May 1526 the King, with his usual flourish, signed his name.

The League of Cognac, as it was called, introduced an exciting new concept into Italian affairs. Here, for perhaps the first time, was an agreement dedicated to the proposition that Milan, and by extension all other Italian states, should be free of foreign domination. Liberty was the watchword. It need hardly be said, however, that Charles V did not view the League in quite this light. To him it was a direct and deliberate challenge, and over the next few months relations between himself and the Pope steadily deteriorated. Finally, in September, two letters from the Emperor were despatched to Rome. They could hardly have been more outspoken if they had been written by Martin Luther himself. The first, addressed personally to the Pope, accused him of failing in his duties towards Christendom, and Italy, and even the Holy See. The second, to the cardinals of the Sacred College, went further still. If, it suggested, the Pope refused to summon a General

Council for the reform of the Church, it was the responsibility of the College to do so without his consent. Here was a clear threat to papal authority. To Pope Clement, indeed, it was tantamount to a declaration of war.

In and around Milan the fighting had hardly ever stopped; there must have been many Milanese who, on waking in the morning, found it difficult to remember whether they owed their allegiance to the Sforzas, the Emperor or the King of France. An imperial army had marched into the city in November 1525, and had spent the winter besieging the unfortunate Francesco Maria Sforza in the citadel, and Sforza had finally capitulated on 15 July 1526. The news of his surrender had plunged the Pope into black despair. His treasury was empty, he was detested in Rome, and his theoretical ally Francis was not lifting a finger to help him. Meanwhile the Reformation was gaining ground and the Ottoman threat still loomed. And now, as autumn approached, there were rumours that the Emperor was preparing a huge fleet, which would land some 10,000 troops in the Kingdom of Naples – effectively on the Pope's own doorstep. More serious still, Clement was aware that there were imperial agents in the city, doing everything they could to stir up trouble against him with the enthusiastic help of a member of his own Sacred College, Cardinal Pompeio Colonna.

For well over two centuries Rome had been split by the rivalry of two of its oldest families, the Colonna and the Orsini. Both were enormously rich, and both ruled over their immense domains as if they were themselves sovereign states, each with its own cultivated court. Their wealth in turn enabled them to contract advantageous marriages; people still talked of the wedding festivities of Clarice Orsini with Clement's uncle, Lorenzo the Magnificent, as the most sumptuous celebrations of the fifteenth century. But the Orsini had long enjoyed what might be called a special relationship with the papacy, by reason of the fact that all the principal roads leading north out of Rome passed through their territory. Successive popes, therefore, had taken care not to offend them.

This alone was more than enough to antagonise their rivals, whose outstanding representative in the 1520s was Pompeio Colonna. The Cardinal had begun life as a soldier and should probably have remained one. He had entered the Church only because of family pressures; never could he have been described as a man of God. Julius II, indeed – who was even less of one – had refused to promote him; it was Leo

X who had eventually admitted him to the Sacred College, but any gratitude that Pompeio may have felt was certainly not extended to Leo's cousin. For Clement he cherished a bitter hatred, powerfully fuelled by jealousy, and a consequent determination to eliminate him – either by deposition or, if necessary, by death.

In August 1526 Pompeio's kinsman Vespasiano Colonna came to Rome to negotiate a truce between his own family on the one hand and the Pope and the Orsini on the other. Clement, much relieved, disbanded his own troops – whereupon the army of the Colonna instantly attacked the city of Anagni, effectively blocking communications between Rome and Naples. The Pope had still not recovered from his surprise or had a chance to remobilise when, at dawn on 20 September, that same army smashed through the Gate of St John Lateran and poured into Rome. At about five o'clock that same afternoon, after hours of heavy fighting, Clement fled along the covered passage that Alexander VI had built for just such eventualities, leading from the Vatican to the Castel Sant'Angelo. Meanwhile the looting and plundering had begun. As one of the secretaries of the Curia reported:

> The papal palace was almost completely stripped, even to the bedroom and wardrobe of the Pope. The great and private sacristy of St Peter's, that of the palace, the apartments of prelates and members of the household, even the horse-stalls were emptied, their doors and windows shattered; chalices, crosses, pastoral staffs, ornaments of great value, all that fell into their hands was carried off as plunder by this rabble.

The mob even broke into the Sistine Chapel, where the Raphael tapestries were torn from the walls. Golden and jewelled chalices, patens and all manner of ecclesiastical treasures were seized, to a value estimated at 300,000 ducats.

With proper preparations made, a pope could hold out in the Castel Sant'Angelo for months; on this occasion, however, the fortress was completely unprovisioned. Clement had no choice but to make what terms he could. The ensuing negotiations were delicate, but their results were less than satisfactory to Pompeio Colonna, who now realised that his attempted coup had been a failure. Public opinion had swung dramatically against his own family. Rome had been plundered and the Colonna had – rightly – been blamed. In November the cardinal was deprived of all his dignities and benefices, and the leading members of his family suffered similar fates. Apart from three small fortresses, the Colonna had lost all their property in the Papal States.

Clement had survived, but only just. According to another member of the Curia, writing towards the end of November 1526:

> The Pope sees nothing ahead but ruin: not just his own, for which he cares little, but that of the Apostolic See, of Rome, of his own country and of the whole of Italy. Moreover, he sees no way of preventing it. He has expended all his own money, all that of his friends, all that of his servants. Our reputation, too, is gone.

He had good reason to be depressed. Strategically he was vulnerable on every side, and the Emperor was exploiting his vulnerability to the full. The previous August Süleyman the Magnificent had won one of his greatest victories at Mohacs in Hungary. And now there came news of the defection of Ferrara, whose Duke, Alfonso d'Este, had joined the imperialists. 'The Pope,' wrote the Milanese envoy, 'seems struck dead. All the attempts of the ambassadors of France, England and Venice to restore him have been in vain ... He looks like a sick man whom the doctors have given up.' And still Clement's tribulations were not over. On 12 December a Spanish envoy delivered a personal letter from the Emperor repeating his demand for a General Council. Early the following year it was learned that an imperial army under the Duke of Bourbon was advancing on the Papal States.

Charles, second Duke of Bourbon, was one of the exalted members of the French nobility and the hereditary Constable of the Kingdom. He should have been fighting for his king, to whom he was distantly related; but Francis's mother, Louise of Savoy, had contested his inheritance and in a fit of pique he had sold his sword to the Emperor. Despite his treachery he was a charismatic figure, admired by all his men for his courage. He never shirked an engagement and could always be found where the fighting was thickest, easily distinguishable by the silver and white surcoat that he always wore and by his black, white and yellow standard on which was emblazoned the single word 'Espérance'. Now, as he advanced southwards from Milan at the head of an army of some 20,000 German and Spanish troops, the citizens of all the towns along his route – Piacenza and Parma, Reggio, Modena and Bologna – worked frantically on their defences. They could have saved themselves the trouble: the Duke had no intention of wasting time on them. He led his army directly to Rome, drawing it up on the Janiculum Hill immediately outside the city wall; and at four o'clock in the morning of 6 May 1527 the attack began.

In the absence of heavy artillery, Bourbon had decided that the walls would have to be scaled – a technique far more difficult and dangerous than that of simply pounding them until they crumbled. He himself was one of the first casualties. He had just led a troop of Germans to the foot of the wall and was actually positioning a scaling ladder when he was shot through the chest by an arquebus. (Benvenuto Cellini, who was present, goes a long way towards claiming personal responsibility.) The fall of the unmistakable white-clad figure was seen by besiegers and besieged alike, and for an hour or so the fate of the siege hung in the balance; then the thought of revenge spurred the Germans and Spaniards on to ever greater efforts, and between six and seven in the morning the imperial army burst into the city. From that moment on there was little resistance. The Romans rushed from the wall to defend their homes, and many of the papal troops joined the enemy to save their own skins. Only the Swiss Guard and some of the papal militia fought heroically on until they were annihilated.

As the invaders approached the Vatican, the Pope was hustled out of St Peter's and led for the second time along the covered way to the Castel Sant'Angelo, already thronged with panic-stricken families seeking refuge. Such were the crowds that it was only with the greatest difficulty that the portcullis could be lowered. One cardinal had to be pushed in by his servants through a window; another was pulled up in a basket. Outside in the Borgo and Trastevere the soldiers embarked on an orgy of killing. Cardinal Giovanni Maria Ciocchi del Monte, the future Pope Julius III, was hung up by his hair. Almost all the patients in the Hospital of Santo Spirito were massacred; of the orphans of the Pietà, not one was left alive.

The imperial army crossed the Tiber just before midnight, the Germans settling in the Campo dei Fiori, the Spaniards in Piazza Navona. The sack that followed has been described as 'one of the most horrible in recorded history'. The bloodbath that had begun across the river continued unabated: to venture out into the street was to invite almost certain death, and to remain indoors was little safer; scarcely a single church, palace or house of any size escaped pillage and devastation. Monasteries were plundered and convents violated, the more attractive nuns being sold in the streets for a *giulio* apiece.

At least two cardinals were dragged through the streets and tortured; one of them, who was well over eighty, subsequently died of his injuries. 'Hell,' reported a Venetian eyewitness, 'has nothing to compare with the present state of Rome.'

It was four days and four nights before the city had any respite. Only with the arrival on 10 May of Pompeio Colonna and his two brothers, with 8,000 of their men, was a semblance of order restored. By this time virtually every street in the city had been gutted and was strewn with corpses. One captured Spanish sapper later reported that on the north bank of the Tiber alone he and his companions had buried nearly 10,000, and had thrown another 2,000 into the river. Six months later, thanks to widespread starvation and a long epidemic of plague, the population of Rome was less than half what it had been before the siege; much of the city had been left a smouldering shell, littered with bodies lying unburied during the hottest season of the year. Culturally, too, the loss was incalculable. Paintings, sculptures, whole libraries – including that of the Vatican itself – were ravaged and destroyed, the pontifical archives ransacked. The painter Parmigianino was imprisoned, saving his life only by making drawings of his jailers.

The imperial army, meanwhile, had suffered almost as much as the Romans. It too was virtually without food; its soldiers – unpaid for months – were totally demoralised, interested only in loot and pillage. Discipline had broken down: Germans and Spaniards were at each other's throats. Pope Clement, however, had no course open to him but once again to capitulate. The official price he paid was the cities of Ostia, Civitavecchia, Piacenza and Modena, together with 400,000 ducats – a sum that could be raised only by melting down all the papal tiaras and selling the gold and jewels with which they were encrusted; the actual price was higher still, since the Venetians (in spite of their alliance) seized Cervia and Ravenna. The Papal States, in which an efficient government had been developing for the first time in history, had crumbled away. Early in December the Pope escaped from Rome and travelled in disguise to Orvieto; it was there that he received ambassadors from Henry VIII of England, seeking their master's release from his marriage to Catherine of Aragon. One of them reported:

> The Pope lieth in an old palace of the bishops of the city, ruinous and decayed; as we came to his privy chamber we passed three chambers, all naked and unhanged, the roofs fallen down, and, as one can guess,

30 persons – riffraff and others – standing in the chambers for a garnishment. And as for the Pope's bedchamber, all the apparel in it was not worth 20 nobles . . . it were better to be in captivity in Rome than here at liberty.

Where the annulment was concerned, the Pope – who had other things to think about – dithered as usual; the ambassadors returned disappointed.

Peace, when it came, was the result of negotiations begun during the winter of 1528–9 between Charles's aunt, Margaret of Savoy, and her sister-in-law, Louise, mother of King Francis. The two met at Cambrai on 5 July 1529, and the resulting treaty was signed in the first week of August. The Ladies' Peace, as it came to be called, confirmed Spanish rule in Italy. Francis again renounced all his claims there, receiving in return a promise from Charles not to press the imperial claims to Burgundy; but France's allies in the League of Cognac were left completely out of the reckoning and were thus obliged to accept the terms that Charles was to impose at the end of the year – terms that included, for Venice, the surrender of all her possessions in southern Italy to the Spanish Kingdom of Naples. Francesco Maria Sforza was restored to Milan (though Charles reserved the right to garrison its citadel); the Medici, who had been expelled from Florence in 1527, were also restored (though it took a ten-month siege to effect the restoration); and the island of Malta was given in 1530 to the Knights of St John.

To those who felt that the King of France had betrayed them, it was a shameful settlement. But at least it restored peace to Italy and put an end to the long and unedifying chapter in her history, a chapter that had begun with Charles VIII's invasion of 1494 and had brought the Italians nothing but devastation and destruction. To seal it all, the Emperor now crossed the Alps, for the first time, for his imperial coronation. This was no longer an indispensable ceremony; his grandfather Maximilian had done without it altogether, and Charles himself had been nearly ten years on the throne without this final confirmation of his authority. The fact remained, nonetheless, that until the Pope had laid the crown on his head, the title of Holy Roman Emperor was technically unjustified; to one possessing so strong a sense of divine mission, both title and sacrament were important.

Imperial coronations were traditionally performed in Rome. On landing at Genoa, however, in mid-August 1529, Charles received reports of Sultan Süleyman's steady advance on Vienna; at once he decided that a journey so far down the peninsula at such a time would be folly. It would take too long, besides leaving him dangerously cut off in the event of a crisis. Messengers sped to Pope Clement, and it was agreed that in the circumstances the ceremony might be held in Bologna, a considerably more accessible city, which still remained firmly under papal control. Even then the uncertainty was not over: while on his way to Bologna in September Charles received an urgent appeal from his brother Ferdinand in Vienna, and almost cancelled his coronation plans there and then. Only after careful consideration did he decide not to do so. By the time he had reached Vienna, either the city would have fallen or the Sultan would have retired for the winter; in either event, the small force that he had with him in Italy would have been insufficient to tip the scales.

And so, on 5 November 1529, Charles V made his formal entry into Bologna where, in front of the Basilica of S. Petronio, Pope Clement was waiting to receive him. After a brief ceremony of welcome, the two retired to the Palazzo del Podestà across the square, where neighbouring apartments had been prepared for them. There was much to be done, many outstanding problems to be discussed and resolved, before the coronation could take place. It was, after all, only two years since papal Rome had been sacked by imperial troops, with Clement himself a virtual prisoner of Charles in the Castel Sant'Angelo; somehow, friendly relations had to be re-established. Next, there were the individual peace treaties to be drawn up with all the Italian ex-enemies of the Empire. Only then, when peace had been finally consolidated throughout the peninsula, would Charles feel justified in kneeling before Clement to receive the imperial crown. Coronation Day was fixed for 24 February 1530, and invitations were despatched to all the rulers of Christendom. Charles and Clement had given themselves a little under four months to settle the future of Italy.

Surprisingly, it proved enough. And so the peace was signed, and on the appointed day, in S. Petronio, Charles received from the papal hands the sword, orb, sceptre and finally the crown of the Holy Roman Empire. It was the last time in history that a pope was to crown an emperor; on that day the 700-year-old tradition, which had begun when Pope Leo III had laid the imperial crown on the head of Charlemagne, was brought to an end. The Empire was by no means finished, but never again would it be received, even symbolically, from the hands of the Vicar of Christ on Earth.

There remained the problem of Henry VIII's annulment. The King was determined to get it: he desperately needed a son, which Catherine was increasingly unlikely to produce. Fortunately for him, there seemed to be a way out. Catherine was the widow of his elder brother Arthur, and canon law forbade marriage to a dead brother's wife. Julius II had stretched a point and had given him a special dispensation to marry her; Henry now pleaded that the prohibition was the law of God rather than simply that of the Church. The dispensation was thus itself uncanonical and his marriage consequently invalid. His and Catherine's inability to have a son was clearly a sign of divine displeasure.

For the Pope, one would have thought, the granting of the annulment was a small price to pay to keep England in the Catholic fold. There was, however, one insuperable problem: the King's unwanted wife was the aunt of the Emperor whom he had so recently crowned. It was safer to declare Henry excommunicate; which, on 11 July 1533 – when Henry had forced Archbishop Cranmer to declare his marriage to Catherine null and void and had already married Anne Boleyn – Clement finally did. And Henry fought back. Defender of the Faith he may have been; but he now unhesitatingly broke with Rome and established the Church of England, placing himself at its head.

And yet, despite all his misfortunes – for many of which he had himself been responsible – the Pope never forgot that he was a Medici and a Renaissance prince. He was a patron of Cellini and Raphael, and he commissioned Michelangelo to paint the Last Judgement on the east wall of the Sistine Chapel, as well as completing his work on the Medici tombs in S. Lorenzo. His family had fought its way back into Florence in 1530, and the city was now ruled by Alessandro, generally believed to have been the bastard son of Lorenzo the Magnificent's grandson, Lorenzo II.[1] Now Clement, within a year of his death, achieved the only real diplomatic success of his career: a double marriage, linking the Medici with the two most powerful (yet always bitterly opposed) royal houses of Europe, the Valois and the Habsburg. The first of these was between Lorenzo II's daughter Catherine

---

[1] Several historians, however, have suggested that he was the son of Clement himself.

and Henry, Duke of Orleans, son of Francis I and future King Henry II of France; the second was between Alessandro and Margaret of Austria, the natural daughter of Charles V. It was to officiate at the first of these that the Pope travelled to Marseilles in October 1533;[1] when he returned to Rome at the end of the year he was already a sick man. He never recovered his health, and on 25 September 1534 he died.

[1] Fourteen years later, his kinswoman was Queen of France. The second marriage was less successful, Alessandro being assassinated in 1537 by his distant cousin Lorenzino.

CHAPTER XX

The Counter-Reformation

(1534–1605)

Alessandro Farnese, who on 13 October 1534 was elected as Pope Paul III (1534–49), was the senior member of the Sacred College. He was only sixty-seven, but had not worn well. Bent almost double, with a long white beard and hobbling on a stick, he gave the impression of being at least a decade older; it comes as something of a surprise to learn that he was elected unanimously after just two days and was to reign for the next fifteen years. Already in 1522, at the conclave that elected Hadrian VI, he had been an early favourite; but his character assassination by Cardinal Egidio had utterly destroyed his chances. By now, however, he had distanced himself from his former life and Egidio's objections had been forgotten; moreover, Farnese had made meticulous plans in advance to pave the way to the papacy.

Paul had been known in former days as the 'petticoat cardinal', since – according to popular belief – he owed his red hat entirely to the fact that his sister Giulia had been a favourite mistress of Alexander VI. From the start, however, he made it clear that he was to be no petticoat pope. Like Giulia, he was a child of the Renaissance, reared in the court of Lorenzo the Magnificent; as Egidio had been at pains to point out, although a cardinal at twenty-five he had since cheerfully fathered four children. He was equally shameless in his nepotism, raising two of his grandsons to the Sacred College at the ages of sixteen and fourteen respectively. He revived the Carnival in 1536; Rome resounded to the cheers of bullfights, horse-races and firework displays, the Vatican to the music of balls and banquets. And yet – and this is what makes Paul III one of the most interesting popes of the sixteenth century – he turned out to be a man of strong moral conscience and a reformer.

Let us look at his worldly side first. Architecturally, his supreme achievement is the Palazzo Farnese, on the Via Giulia in Rome.[1] He

---

[1] It provides the setting for Act II of Puccini's *Tosca*, and is today the French Embassy.

had begun it in 1517; but such was its size and splendour that it was not completed until 1589, forty years after his death. One of its four architects was Michelangelo, whom Paul also commissioned to redesign the Campidoglio – into which the equestrian statue of Marcus Aurelius was now moved to provide a centrepiece – and to succeed Antonio da Sangallo as architect of St Peter's. Michelangelo worked on the new basilica for seventeen years (during which he designed the great dome) until his death at the age of eighty-nine. Throughout that time he refused all fees; it was, he said, an offering to God.

Dynastically, like all Renaissance popes, Paul III was determined to further his family fortunes. The Farnese were an old and distinguished family of *condottieri* with estates around Viterbo and Lake Bolsena, but they were not aristocrats like the Orsini or the Colonna. Clearly, there was room for improvement: Paul first appointed his notoriously dissolute son Pierluigi as Captain-General of the Church.[1] Next he made Pierluigi's son, Ottavio, Duke of Camerino; then in 1538 he married Ottavio to Margaret of Austria – the fifteen-year-old widow of the assassinated Alessandro de' Medici.[2] Finally in 1545 he made Pierluigi Duke of Parma and Piacenza, a dynasty that was to continue for almost two centuries.

But these artistic and dynastic considerations, important as they were, occupied relatively little of his time. Most of this was taken up by the Church and the perils that beset it. The first of these was posed by the Turks. Under their brilliant Sultan Süleyman the Magnificent they were not only steadily advancing through central Europe; they were threatening the coasts of Italy as well as the remaining Christian outposts in the eastern Mediterranean. If they could be defeated at all, it could only be by a concerted effort of all the Catholic nations. Somehow, therefore, those two arch-rivals, Francis of France and the Emperor Charles, must be reconciled.

The other peril was Protestantism. It was by now far too late to eradicate it: most of northern Europe had already been engulfed in the tide. He could concentrate only on damage limitation. The more he considered how best to contain the surge, the more convinced he became that the prime necessity was for a General Council – and one that would include a strong contingent of Lutherans. Objections, inevitably, were raised on all sides. The cardinals saw any reform as

---

[1] In 1535 Paul sent Pierluigi to the court of the Emperor Charles V. Pierluigi was particularly enjoined to refrain from sodomy during his stay.
[2] See Chapter XIX p.298.

a threat to their own comfortable lifestyles; the Emperor, terrified that the proposed Council might take so rigid a stand on doctrine as to make a compromise with his Protestant subjects impossible, preferred that it should leave aside all theological questions and confine itself to measures of reform; the Lutherans demanded a totally uncommitted meeting of all Christians, and steadfastly refused to attend any assembly that was held on Italian soil, or presided over by the Pope. As for the King of France, he was only too pleased to see Charles enmeshed in religious problems, and had no wish to see them resolved. But Paul persisted, and meanwhile summoned a special commission, which he ordered to report on all the ills of the Church and to recommend on the measures that should be taken to remedy them. It was composed of a number of cardinals, specially admitted to the Sacred College for the task; they included the devout English humanist Reginald Pole, a cousin of Henry VIII, and Giampietro Carafa (the future Paul IV), an elderly Neapolitan who had served as Papal Nuncio in England and had subsequently founded the Theatine Order.[1] The commissioners submitted their report in March 1537. One of our leading church historians[2] describes it in a single word: dynamite. It listed the current abuses and laid the blame for all of them – the sale of indulgences and Church benefices, the sinecures, stockpiling of bishoprics and countless others – squarely on the papacy. The result of all this had been the Protestant Reformation, and no wonder: had the Church kept its house in order, the Reformation would never have occurred. The horrified Curia (deliberately unrepresented on the commission) did all it could to sweep the report under the carpet; but a copy was leaked, and before long a German translation was going the rounds of the Lutheran churches.

Now at last reform – serious reform – was in the air, and Pope Paul did everything he could to encourage it. He gave an enthusiastic reception to the young Filippo Neri, whose mission was concentrated in the seedy inns and whorehouses of the Roman underworld; and a few years later he accorded a similar welcome to the rather older Ignatius Loyola, a Basque who had arrived with half a dozen like-minded colleagues from Spain, grouped together in what they called

---

[1] The Theatines were a reformist Order, forbidden to own property or to beg. They were to play an important part in the Counter-Reformation. 'They observed the strictest austerity of life, and their habit was distinguished from that of the secular clergy only by their white socks' (*Oxford Dictionary of the Christian Church*).

[2] E. Duffy, *Saints and Sinners*.

the Society of Jesus. In 1540 the Pope issued a Bull giving the Society his official approval. The Jesuits, with no distinctive dress for their Order, no fixed headquarters and no choral prayer, were bound together by two things only: strict discipline and unconditional obedience. They were to have a chequered history; but they were the spearhead of the Counter-Reformation.

Finally the Pope had his reward: on 13 December 1545 the long-delayed Council opened at Trent, a city recommended by the Emperor because it lay safely in imperial territory. It got off to a shaky start, its first sessions being attended by only a single cardinal, four arch-bishops and thirty-one bishops; but it was gradually to gather momentum and to continue on and off for the next eighteen years. It was overwhelmingly weighted in favour of the Italians; even when best attended, with more than 270 bishops, the Germans never numbered more than thirteen. But the important thing about the Council was that – in the teeth of all the opposition to it – it had actually happened; moreover, it showed itself ready to defy the Emperor and fearlessly debate the hoary old questions of doctrine: justification by faith, transubstantiation, purgatory and many more.

It was never to be more than a partial success. When it was at last dissolved the Protestants, who understandably saw it as little more than a Roman puppet-show, naturally remained unsatisfied – how could they have been anything else? Even for the Catholics its reforms were less radical and comprehensive than many had hoped for. Not a word was said, for example, about the reform of the papacy, which was far more necessary than anything else. Owing largely to the undiminished mutual hostility of the Emperor and the King of France (Francis I was succeeded by Henry II in 1547), it sat only intermittently, often without the French contingent. It never came near to being the ecumenical council of union for the whole of Western Christianity that had been so long hoped and prayed for; it was simply the confessional council of the Counter-Reformation, with the purpose of recatholicising Europe, if necessary by force. The results were all too evident: in France, no fewer than eight civil wars against the Huguenots (more than 3,000 of whom perished in the Massacre of St Bartholomew in Paris in 1572); a war between Spain and the Netherlands that lasted for more than eighty years; and the night-mare Thirty Years War (1618–48), which caused untold devastation through northern Europe.

But the Council nonetheless established a solid basis for the renewal of discipline and spiritual life in the Church, which emerged a good deal stronger and more focused than before. It is thanks only to the Council of Trent that the Protestant tide was eventually halted; and thanks only to the vision and determination of Pope Paul III that it was held at all.

Had Pope Paul died at the end of 1545, he would probably have closed his eyes a happy man; sadly for him, he was to live another four years, during which personal tragedy struck. In September 1547 the people of Piacenza rose up against his son Pierluigi and assassinated him; then, to escape papal vengeance, they sought the Emperor's protection. Charles granted it; once Piacenza was under his guardianship it was virtually his, and if he played his cards right he might soon acquire Parma as well. For Paul, this was a betrayal of trust. His initial reaction was angrily to reclaim Parma as papal territory, only to find that Pierluigi's son Ottavio refused to give it up and that his other grandson – one of his own cardinals – had taken Ottavio's side. Ottavio was beyond his jurisdiction; the Cardinal was not so lucky. Summoned to the papal presence, he felt his biretta snatched from his head and hurled to the ground. But the Pope was by now in his eighty-second year, and the emotion was too much for him. A few hours later he was dead.

Paul III having died in mid-November, the conclave to elect his successor was held the following winter. Despite the hardships involved, it lasted nearly three months. In the fifteenth century conclaves had been attended only by those members of the Sacred College who formed part of the Curia and were consequently in Rome; by the sixteenth, cardinals were summoned from all over Europe – although this did not mean that their colleagues necessarily waited for them. During the early stages in 1548 the dominant figure was the Englishman Reginald Pole: on the first round he secured twenty-five votes out of the twenty-eight required. Had he been prepared to lobby in his own interest he would probably have swept the board; but that was not his way. He made no effort to convince the xenophobe Italians who were determined on one of their own number, and the conclave was still undecided when the French cardinals arrived. Horrified at the thought of an English pope, they accused Pole of heresy and managed to alienate several of his supporters. Pole's principal champion, the Pope's grandson, Cardinal Alessandro Farnese, proposed the magnificently Machiavellian ploy of a late-night scrutiny during which the majority would be too sleepy (or drunk) to take much interest; but that was not Pole's way, either. If, he said, he was to enter the Vatican, he would do so through the open door, not like a thief in the night.

This conclave was probably the only one in papal history that incorporated a deliberate tease. The victim was Cardinal Ippolito d'Este, whose brother had already made a fool of himself by being caught scrambling over the roof of the Sistine Chapel in a vain attempt to eavesdrop on what was going on. The Cardinal was at that moment suffering from an unfortunate condition in which his hair and beard were falling out in handfuls. The cause – as everyone knew perfectly well – was almost certainly alopecia; but he was arraigned before his fellows, who strongly hinted that the problem was due to syphilis. Indignantly poor d'Este fell into the trap and protested that he had led a life of exemplary chastity for more than a year. After that he was no longer considered a serious contender.

Finally, after the usual intrigues, the French and Italian factions agreed – despite the Emperor's opposition – on a relative nonentity. Giovanni Maria Ciocchi del Monte (henceforth to be known as Julius III, 1550–5) was a competent canon lawyer who had suffered grievously during the sack of Rome a quarter of a century before[1] and had later been co-president at the opening of the Council of Trent. He was, however, better known for his infatuation with a seventeen-year-old boy, somewhat inappropriately named Innocenzo, whom he had picked up in the streets of Parma two years before, and whom on his accession he instantly made a cardinal.

He began as he meant to go on. Here once again was a typical Renaissance pope, shamelessly self-indulgent and nepotistic, whose banquets – it was widely whispered in Rome – tended to deteriorate into homosexual orgies after the principal guests had taken their leave. He lavished vast sums on his exquisite country villa, the Villa Giulia;[2] he took an active interest in Michelangelo's work on St Peter's; he appointed Palestrina as choirmaster and *magister puerorum* of his personal chapel. He was, perhaps surprisingly, a staunch believer in the need for Church reform – he encouraged the Jesuits and certainly did everything he could to keep the Council of Trent firmly on the rails – and he genuinely rejoiced when, with the succession of Mary

---

[1] See Chapter XIX, pp.293–4.
[2] The city has now grown to the point where this is a country villa no more. It now houses the National Etruscan Museum.

I to the English throne, her country returned to the Catholic fold. But there can be no doubt that his principal object was the pursuit of pleasure. For a man notorious, inter alia, for his gluttony, there was a certain poetic justice in his end: his digestive system ceased to function and on 23 March 1555 he died – effectively, of starvation.

Marcello Cervini was a humanist and a scholar. He had translated Greek works into Latin, and Latin works into Italian; he had been appointed Bishop of three successive sees, where (despite long absences) he had assiduously promoted reforms; he had been one of the three co-presidents of the Council of Trent; and he had reorganised the Vatican Library. When, after a short conclave in which, thanks to a stalemate between the French and imperialists, he was elected as a compromise candidate, he chose to keep his own name and became Pope Marcellus II (1555). He was a reformer through and through. He cut his coronation expenses to a minimum and pared his court to the bone. Such was his horror of nepotism that he forbade all members of his family to show their faces in Rome. Aged only fifty-three at the time of his coronation, he might have achieved great things; unfortunately, after just twenty-two days in office he suffered a massive stroke, which killed him. Palestrina's *Missa Papae Marcelli* is his only lasting memorial.

On his election on 23 May as Pope Paul IV (1555–9), Giampietro Carafa was seventy-nine years old – the oldest pope of the sixteenth century and by far the most terrifying. In his intolerance, his bigotry, his refusal to compromise or even to listen to any opinions other than his own, he was a throwback to the Middle Ages. He suspended the Council of Trent, replacing it with a commission of cardinals and theologians; he introduced the *Index of Forbidden Books,* including on it the complete works of Erasmus;[1] he took a special delight in the Inquisition, never missing its weekly meeting; finally, he opened the most savage campaign in papal history against the Jews – to the point where, in the five short years of his pontificate, the Jewish population of Rome was halved.

Anti-Semitism had first manifested itself in Rome soon after Constan-

---

[1] By a curious irony, another of the first books to appear on the Index was a work of which Paul IV himself had been the principal author. It was the report of the committee called by Paul III to investigate the principal abuses of the Church, and the areas most in need of reform (see above, p.301). The intention was to keep it secret, for the Pope's eyes only; after it was leaked to the Protestants it was immediately placed on the Index – in an unsuccessful attempt to keep it out of Catholic hands.

tine the Great adopted Christianity in the fourth century, and with succeeding centuries it had grown steadily worse. But it was under Paul IV that the Jews were first rounded up into a ghetto, forbidden to trade in any commodity except food and second-hand clothing, permitted only a single synagogue in each city (in Rome seven were demolished), compelled to speak only Italian or Latin and obliged to wear yellow hats in the street. The Bull *Cum nimis absurdum* of 17 July 1555, which laid down these and innumerable other similar regulations, was to remain in force for the next three centuries.

Next to the Jews, Paul IV hated the Spaniards. Coming as he did from an old Neapolitan family, this was hardly surprising; but his immoderation led him, as always, to go too far. He never forgave the Emperor Charles for concluding the Peace of Augsburg, which in 1555 pacified Germany by conceding to the Lutherans all those areas that had Lutheran rulers. Two years later, abandoning the neutrality of his immediate predecessors and ignoring the fact that Charles was now the principal champion of the Catholic Reformation, he allied himself with Henry II of France and declared war on Spain. The result was disaster. The Spanish Viceroy of Naples, the Duke of Alba, led an army north and the Romans prepared for yet another siege; fortunately for the Pope, Alba proved merciful, taking Ostia, but sparing Rome itself. The Duke was generous, too, in the terms of the Treaty of Cave that followed. But Paul refused to be mollified. His hatred of the Habsburgs even led him to quarrel with Charles's daughter-in-law, Queen Mary I of England, who had restored her country to Catholicism. He deprived the estimable Cardinal Pole of his legateship, summoning him back to Rome to answer charges of heresy, and generally made himself so unpleasant as greatly to facilitate the efforts of Queen Elizabeth – Mary's half-sister and successor – in returning her realm to the Protestant religion.

The blame for some of the Pope's actions (especially where Spain was concerned) can perhaps be laid at the door of his two worthless nephews, Charles – on whom he also bestowed a red hat – and Giovanni, whom he made Duke of Paliano. Both were deeply venal, but he trusted them implicitly – until, some six months before his death, the scales at last fell from his eyes. He immediately stripped them of all their offices and honours and expelled them from Rome, but it was too late: the damage was done. And he himself never recovered from the shock. He died on 18 August 1559 a broken man, and the most generally detested pope of the sixteenth century. As the news was carried through Rome, the populace exploded with joy. They first attacked the headquarters of the Inquisition, smashing the building to pieces and releasing all its prisoners; then they marched to the Pope's statue on the Capitol, tore it down, knocked its head off and threw it into the Tiber.

There followed a long conclave. For four months the French and Spanish cardinals were deadlocked, and it was not until Christmas Day that the new pope was finally elected. Giovanni Angelo Medici – he was a humble notary's son from Milan, no relation to his grand Florentine namesakes – took the name of Pius IV (1559–65) and proved as different from his alarming predecessor as any pope could possibly be. Paul, for all his faults, had been a figure of irreproachable integrity; Pius took little trouble to conceal his three natural children. Paul's austerity had been such that when he strode through the Vatican sparks were said to fly from his feet; Pius was convivial and relaxed. He restarted the Council of Trent; he mended fences with the Habsburgs, opening up friendly relations with Charles's son, Philip II of Spain, and his brother, the Emperor Ferdinand I;[1] he restricted the powers of the Inquisition; he cut the papal Index, which had already proved itself unworkable, down to size; Paul's two dreadful nephews – one of whom, the Duke of Paliano, had his wife strangled on suspicion of adultery, personally stabbing her presumed lover – he arrested; after the wife had been proved innocent, both were executed.

Not that Pius scorned a little nepotism himself; but he was a good deal luckier in his nephew. Charles Borromeo (later to be canonised), whom he created Cardinal and Archbishop of Milan, was to prove one of the greatest reformers and administrators of his day, dominating the final sessions of the Council of Trent. In Milan his firm discipline aroused a good deal of hostility, but he worked tirelessly among the poor and the sick, notably during the terrible plague year of 1576. Nowadays the nephew's reputation tends to overshadow that of the uncle, but Pius's own achievements were impressive enough. It was he who – through the Archbishop – guided the Council to its conclusion, who confirmed its decrees in the Bull *Benedictus Deus* and who was largely responsible for its acceptance throughout the Catholic world. He also began a compilation of the catechism and a reform of the missal and breviary, though these were still unfinished at his death. Last but not least, he revived the Renaissance tradition, encouraging artists and scholars, founding universities and printing presses and

---

[1] Charles V had abdicated in 1556 and retired to the monastery of Yuste in Extremadura.

enriching Rome with more fine buildings, including the Porta Pia and (in the Baths of Diocletian) the church of S. Maria degli Angeli.

Pius's principal failure was in his attempts to check the spread of Protestantism in England and France. In England he refused to excommunicate Queen Elizabeth, in the vain hope that he could persuade her to maintain the fanatical Catholicism of Mary. Meanwhile he sent large subsidies to the King of France for use in his struggle against the Huguenots. He was naturally disappointed when Elizabeth continued staunchly to uphold her father's Church of England and when the strength of the Huguenots continued to grow; but before he died in December 1565 he could nevertheless look back on six remarkably successful years – and congratulate himself on having left the Church in a considerably better state than he had found it.

But then, alas, the pendulum swung again. Archbishop Charles Borromeo, having made it clear that he was not interested in the papacy for himself, eventually recommended the formidable Cardinal Michele Ghislieri. Ghislieri had begun life as a shepherd – which was, metaphorically at least, a suitable qualification for the papacy. Later, however, Paul IV had appointed him Inquisitor-General, which was not. Pius V (1556–62) – one is somehow surprised that he did not take the name of Paul – was cast very much in the Carafa mould. Deeply ascetic himself (he continued as Pope to wear a hair shirt and the rough habit of a Dominican friar under his papal robes, regularly walking barefoot and bareheaded in penitential processions), he expected a similar asceticism from all those around him. In a whole series of decrees he sought to stamp out blasphemy – rich blasphemers were heavily fined, poor ones flogged – and ensure the proper observance of holy days and fasts. Doctors were forbidden to treat patients who had not confessed or lately received the sacraments.

Sex was, as always, a particular bugbear. Finding that he could not abolish prostitution altogether, the Pope decreed that all unmarried prostitutes must be whipped, and all men found guilty of sodomy burned at the stake. He was only with difficulty persuaded not to make adultery a capital offence. As it was, no bachelor might employ a female servant; no nun might keep a male dog. Women were barred from the classical sculpture in the Vatican collections. The figures of Michelangelo's *Last Judgement* in the Sistine Chapel were chastely overpainted. After a few months of this the Romans were complaining that Pius wanted to turn their city into one enormous monastery.

Pius had spent long years as an Inquisitor; and an Inquisitor, essentially, he remained. He continued his predecessor's tradition of personally attending all sessions of the Roman Inquisition and frequently extended his visits to include the torture-chamber, from which he would emerge utterly unmoved. Those found guilty of heresy he had no hesitation in sentencing to death. The general commanding the small papal army that he sent to France to help the King in his religious war had special instructions to kill all Huguenot prisoners. With the Jews, too, he kept up Paul's policy of persecution; outside the Roman ghetto (and another small one in Ancona) they were banned from all papal territories.

Throughout his pontificate the Pope had one overriding objective: to keep the dread infection of Lutheranism out of Italy. And in this, whatever may be said of his methods, he was remarkably successful. Across the Alps in Germany, it was true that the fighting was more or less over since the Peace of Augsburg; but more than half of Germany was now Lutheran. France was being torn in two, as were the Spanish Netherlands, where the Dutch Calvinists were steadily increasing their hold. England and Scotland were lost; Pius's excommunication and 'deposition' of Queen Elizabeth in 1570 succeeded only in making life more difficult for her Catholic subjects. Outside Italy, only the Spain of Philip II stood firmly for the Faith. Besides, Protestantism was not the only enemy. Elsewhere in the Mediterranean, Venice was forced in 1570 to cede Cyprus to the Turks; and even when in October of the following year the combined fleets of Spain, Venice and the papacy destroyed the Ottoman navy at Lepanto – the last great naval engagement in history to be fought by oared galleys – the victory was to have no lasting effect: only seventeen years later came the defeat of the Spanish Armada, and in the following century Crete was to go the way of Cyprus.

Pope Pius V lived for just seven months after Lepanto. He had been a dedicated reformer, and he did much to impose upon Christendom the findings and decisions of the Council of Trent; but he was too extreme, too narrow-minded, too bigoted for the good of his flock. Not, on the other hand, for his own: he is the only pope between the mildly ridiculous Celestine V (1294) and the wholly admirable Pius X (1903–14) to have been made – quite unaccountably – a saint.

Ugo Boncompagni, who after an unusually short conclave now mounted the papal throne under the name of Gregory XIII (1572–85), was a seventy-year-old Bolognese of still-undiminished energy. Starting his career as a lecturer in canon law, he had soon found himself a leading figure at the Council of Trent; in recognition of his services there he had received his red hat and had been sent as legate to Philip II in Spain. There he had once again distinguished himself – winning the confidence and trust of the pathologically suspicious Philip II – and on his return to Rome was generally agreed to be the obvious choice for Pope.

Gregory's name is chiefly remembered today in the Gregorian Calendar, which he introduced in a Bull of 1582. The old Julian Calendar, which dated from 46 BC, was now ten days behind; the Gregorian therefore cut ten days out of the year 1582, so that 4 October was followed immediately by 15 October. Fine-tuning was provided by making only the fourth of the final years of successive centuries a leap year. (Thus 1600 had 366 days; 1700 did not.) Desirable as it was, the reform could hardly have been more ill-timed. With Catholic, Protestant and Orthodox at each other's throats, it was at first adopted only by those states in the Roman obedience. Broadly speaking, the Protestants accepted the reform at various times during the eighteenth century (Great Britain and her American colonies in 1752) while Russia, Greece and the Balkan States delayed until the twentieth.

To Gregory, however, the calendar would have seemed of relatively minor importance. From the outset he made it clear that the principal objective of his pontificate would be the fight against Protestantism, together with the steadfast promotion of the decrees of the Council of Trent; he would, in other words, continue the policy of his predecessor. Since he was a far more amenable and easy-going character than Pius, he was considerably more successful. It had been proved again and again at Trent that far-reaching reform was impossible without a clergy properly trained in theology and the art of disputation, so he set about building colleges and seminaries. First he enlarged the Jesuit College in Rome – originally founded by Julius III; it now became known as the Gregorian University. The Jesuits were also entrusted with the running of the German College, which proved so effective that more colleges were built in other cities of the Empire, including Vienna, Prague and Fulda in Germany. Rome also saw the establishment of an English seminary, from which a steady stream of missionaries made their perilous way to Elizabethan and Jacobean England, where several found martyrdom. Other colleges were established for Greeks, Maronites, Armenians and Hungarians.

Had he contented himself with the intellectual and doctrinal training of the new generation of priests and missionaries, Gregory's record as Pope would have been a good deal more distinguished than it was. One could wish, for example, that he had not reacted to the news of the St Bartholomew's Day massacre of the Huguenots by ordering a special *Te Deum* to be sung and personally attending a mass of thanksgiving at the French church of St Louis; or that he had not tried to persuade King Philip of Spain to launch an invasion of England from Ireland or the Netherlands; or, when these dreams collapsed, that he had not given active encouragement to a plot to assassinate Queen Elizabeth of England – 'the Jezebel of the North'. Such an act, he had declared, would be seen as the work of God.

In other enterprises, however, Gregory was more enlightened, and more successful. He replaced the old legates, previously the Pope's official representatives abroad, with a new order whom he called nuncios, normally of archiepiscopal rank, trained diplomats who were henceforth to be the chosen instruments of papal policy in every Catholic country, where they were expected to work long and hard to ensure that their master's will was done. He won over Poland for the Church, though in Russia his unfortunate nuncio to Ivan the Terrible was lucky to escape with his life; he sent Jesuit missionaries across the world: westwards to Brazil, eastwards to India, China and even Japan. He spent vast sums on the restoration and further improvement of Rome, adorning the city with several new churches, including the tremendous Gesù, one of the most spectacular examples in Europe of the high baroque. In 1578 his scholarly mind was fascinated by the discovery of the Roman catacombs, and he insisted that the early Christian remains that had now suddenly come to light should be subjected to proper scientific study.

By this time, however, Gregory's extensive building programmes and his subsidies to Catholic rulers in their struggle to hold the Protestants at bay – to say nothing of the cost of running all his colleges and foundations – were rapidly emptying the papal coffers. In an effort to remedy the situation, he had taken to claiming the reversion to himself of any property on papal territory whose occupier could not produce cast-iron evidence of his title; this practice, however, resulted only in a furious body of dispossessed landowners, who took their revenge by resorting to open brigandage. When Gregory died aged eighty-three, after a thirteen-year pontificate, he left the papacy almost penniless, and the Papal State faced with near-anarchy.

Morale, on the other hand, was probably higher than it had been for half a century. The Roman Church was now fighting back. Given new spirit by the Council of Trent, it had launched its own Counter-Reformation, symbolised above all by the city itself: by the new St Peter's, not yet altogether finished, but already hugely impressive; by the quantity of other great churches springing up on every side; by the vast numbers of seminarists of every race and nation, living proof of the sheer vitality of the revived Catholicism. The tens of thousands of pilgrims who flocked to Rome to celebrate the Jubilee Year of 1575, making their solemn visits to the seven great basilicas of the holy city,[1] could not have failed to be impressed, encouraged and strengthened in their faith.

Pope Sixtus V (1585–90), who was elected on 24 April 1585, exactly a fortnight after Gregory's death, continued where his predecessor had left off, with still greater energy and determination. As Felice Peretti, a farmworker's son from near Ancona, he had joined the Franciscans at the age of twelve and, thanks to his high intelligence and brilliant gifts as a preacher, had rapidly risen through the Church ranks. In 1557 Paul IV had recognised him as a kindred spirit and sent him to Venice, first to reform the Franciscan monastery of the Frari and then, later, as Inquisitor. It was in this last capacity that he had seriously overstepped the mark. The Venetians were devout and conscientious Catholics, but they had always resisted papal attempts to limit their freedom of action. They were merchants; their life was trade, and their commercial prosperity depended on good relations with Protestants and Muslims alike. They refused to allow the Pope to tell them what to do. They could not keep out the Inquisitors altogether, but insisted that their own representatives should sit alongside them and, when necessary, exercise a moderating influence.

This arrangement had worked successfully enough until the appearance of Peretti. He, however, had tried to bully and browbeat them, and their indignation at his severity and arrogance had led to his recall; but Pius IV had characteristically reappointed him three years later, and Pius V had promoted him to Vicar-General of his Order, Grand Inquisitor and Cardinal. Out of favour under Pope Gregory, he had languished in his villa on the Esquiline preparing what is described by

---

[1] St Peter's, St John Lateran, S. Maria Maggiore, S. Croce in Gerusalemme, S. Paolo fuori le Mura, S. Lorenzo fuori le Mura, and S. Sebastiano fuori le Mura.

the *Oxford Dictionary of Popes* as 'a distinctly uneven edition of St Ambrose'; but with Gregory's demise, his sheer force of personality made him the obvious choice as successor. He was elected unanimously.

Of all the popes of the Counter-Reformation, Sixtus V was the most alarming. Stern and inflexible, utterly ruthless, brooking no opposition to his will, he ruled Rome as the autocrat he was. The power of the Sacred College was drastically reduced. He fixed the maximum number of cardinals at seventy, at which it remained for the next 400 years. He then instituted fifteen separate Congregations – or strictly speaking fourteen, since one of them, the Holy Office, was already in existence – to be concerned with every aspect of government, religious and secular alike. These too were to endure well into the twentieth century. One of them was responsible for the university, another for the Vatican printing press, which in 1587 produced a copy of the Septuagint, the Greek translation of the Hebrew Testament. This was to be followed by a revised text of the whole Latin Bible, the Vulgate. Sixtus entrusted the task to a special committee of learned cardinals, but their progress was so slow that he eventually took it over himself. Alas, as he had already shown with St Ambrose, textual analysis was never his strong suit. When the work finally appeared, all serious scholars were horrified; on his death it was immediately withdrawn, and was heavily revised before being republished by Clement VIII in 1592.

The Pope was a good deal more successful where Church discipline was concerned. One of the principal issues that had dogged the final sessions of the Council of Trent had been the question of the divine right of bishops: did they derive their authority through the Pope, or directly from God Himself? This was not a question that many people dared to put to Sixtus V: he now laid down that every new bishop must submit himself to the Pope in Rome before taking up his appointment, and must make regular return visits to report on the state of his diocese.

Within two years, thanks to a reign of terror, Sixtus had restored law and order throughout the papal lands. No fewer than 7,000 brigands were publicly executed; there were, we are told, more heads impaled on spikes along the Ponte Sant'Angelo than melons in the market. Meanwhile, to restore the Vatican finances, expenditure was pared to the bone (Sixtus was not a Franciscan for nothing), while food prices were rigidly controlled. New taxes were raised, new loans floated, agriculture encouraged, marshes drained, the wool and silk industries subsidised. His sale of offices – but only bureaucratic and administrative, never ecclesiastical – earned the Pope some 300,000 scudi a year. Long before his death he had become one of the richest princes in Europe.

His foreign policy, like that of his predecessors, was based on his hatred of Protestantism, as the chief obstacle to the realisation of his dream of a universal Catholic Church. He promised vast subsidies to Philip II for his projected invasion of England – but after the expedition ended in catastrophe with the defeat of the Spanish Armada in 1588, refused to pay them. The following year he let Philip down for the second time, when he relaxed his opposition to the Huguenot Henry IV (whom he had excommunicated in 1585) on Henry's agreeing to convert to Catholicism in return for the French crown.

But we remember Pope Sixtus V above all for his building. He enabled Giacomo della Porta to complete the dome on St Peter's. Meanwhile his favourite architect, Domenico Fontana, designed a new Lateran Palace, a new papal residence within the Vatican and a major reconstruction of the Vatican Library. The huge Egyptian obelisk that had once stood in Nero's Circus was erected, in a scene of considerable drama, in Bernini's great piazza; on the left bank of the Tiber, three lesser obelisks lent additional majesty to the squares in front of the Lateran, Santa Maria Maggiore and Santa Maria del Popolo. Broad new avenues connected the main pilgrimage churches. A superb aqueduct, the *Acqua Felice*, brought water to the city from Palestrina, a good twenty miles away. Two other aqueducts made possible the hundreds of ornamental fountains that soon sprang up all over the city. Sixtus reigned for just five years, but it is to him more than to any other pope that we owe the full baroque splendour of Counter-Reformation Rome.

He deserved well of his city; alas, his arrogance and choleric temper made him generally detested. Few popes since the Middle Ages had been more unpopular. When he died, on 27 August 1590, after successive bouts of malaria, there was general rejoicing throughout the city; and his statue on the Capitol was gleefully torn down by the mob, just as Paul IV's had been thirty-one years before.

The next sixteen months saw no fewer than three popes in Rome. In any history of the papacy, the names of Urban VII (1590), Gregory XIV (1590–1) and Innocent IX (1591) may very largely be ignored. Urban was a wholly admirable churchman and would probably have made an excellent pope; it was not his fault that on the very night after his election he was struck down by malaria; he died less than a fortnight later. He rather charmingly left his considerable personal fortune to provide dowries for impecunious Roman girls; by them, at least, he was not forgotten. Gregory – a friend of both Charles Borromeo and Filippo Neri, pious, well-meaning but as weak as water – is chiefly remembered as a killjoy, who prohibited one of the most popular amusements of the citizens of Rome: the betting on papal elections, the duration of pontificates and the creation of cardinals. Innocent, despite only two months as Pope, was arguably the most effective of the three. He forcibly opposed the still-Protestant Henry IV in France, took strong measures against banditry, regulated the course of the Tiber and did what he could to improve sanitation. A week before Christmas 1591 he fell ill, but insisted on making the traditional pilgrimage to the seven basilicas; an act of devotion that unfortunately proved fatal.

Stability returned with Ippolito Aldobrandini, the son of a distinguished Florentine barrister driven from his native city by the Medici. He took the name of Clement VIII (1592–1605). In many ways Clement personified the ideals of the Counter-Reformation. He led a deeply pious life, spending hours daily in prayer and meditation, making a daily confession and visiting the seven pilgrimage churches on foot fifteen times a year. Unfortunately his austerities proved too much for his health – he was a martyr to gout – and as the years went by he tended to rely more and more on his two nephews, Cinzio and Pietro, on both of whom (together with a fourteen-year-old greatnephew) he bestowed red hats. With these two taking much of the weight of the administration off his shoulders, he was free to devote much of his time to scholarship. In 1592 he published a corrected version of the Vulgate – hopelessly mangled by Sixtus V – together with revisions of the pontifical, the missal and the breviary. Four years later there appeared a greatly enlarged Index, including for the first time a ban on Jewish books. This reflected Clement's besetting sin, his intolerance. Throughout his pontificate he gave every encouragement to the Inquisition, which during his reign sent more than thirty heretics to the stake; they included the former Dominican Giordano Bruno, who met his death on 17 February 1600 in the Campo dei Fiori, where his statue still stands.

Politically, Clement's most important decision – taken after long hesitation and with deep reluctance – was to recognise Henry IV as

King of France. Henry, a former Huguenot, had been received into the Catholic Church in 1593, famously remarking, '*Paris vaut bien une messe*'.[1] Clement still remained unconvinced; it was only after the King had been crowned at Chartres the following year that he finally accepted his nuncio's advice, lifted Sixtus V's sentence of excommunication and granted Henry his recognition. He may well have regretted doing so when, on 13 April 1598, Henry published his Edict of Nantes, granting extensive rights to the Huguenots, allowing them free exercise of their religion (except in certain towns, which included Paris) and civil equality with Catholics. This caused, it need hardly be said, a furious outburst from Spain, which he felt strong enough to ignore.

Clement VIII died on 5 March 1605. If he left the papacy stronger than he had found it, this was largely due to the elaborate Jubilee celebrations of 1600, which brought perhaps half a million pilgrims to Rome. The city was now at last – thanks to the sixteenth-century popes – worthy of its position as the capital of Christendom. In the past century the Catholic Church had sustained fearful blows: England and Scotland were now Protestant beyond redemption; in the Spanish Netherlands the Dutch Calvinists had defied all attempts by King Philip to crush them; in Germany the Emperor Maximilian himself was showing alarming signs of Lutheran sympathies; in France the effects of Henry IV's conversion had been largely nullified by the Edict of Nantes. But Rome was now more magnificent than it had ever been; and the 80,000 faithful who watched when, at midnight on 31 December 1599, the Pope ceremonially opened the *Porta Santa* – the Holy Door – bore witness to the extraordinary success of the Counter-Reformation.

---

[1] 'Paris is well worth a Mass.'

CHAPTER XXI

Baroque Rome

(1605–1700)

On Pope Clement's death the Sacred College awarded the papacy to Cardinal Alessandro de' Medici. The cardinal – who took the name of Leo XI (1605) – had been largely responsible for persuading Clement to lift the sentence of excommunication on Henry IV, and had afterwards served for two years as Papal Nuncio in France. Deeply devout and highly intelligent, he would probably have made an excellent pope; but he was already seventy years old, and reigned for just twenty-six days before succumbing to a sudden chill. King Henry, who had spent 300,000 scudi in securing his election, cannot have been best pleased. Leo was succeeded by a Sienese, Cardinal Camillo Borghese, who at only fifty-two could confidently expect a reasonably long pontificate. He was to reign for the next sixteen years.

Pope Paul V (1605–21), as he chose to be called, was every bit as devout as his predecessor, but not nearly as intelligent. He failed absolutely to understand that the papacy was now one of a number of European powers; it was no longer possible to uphold the ideal of absolute papal supremacy as it had existed in the Middle Ages. Paul attempted to do so, and immediately met his match – in the Republic of Venice. The Venetians would not have dreamed of questioning their duty of doctrinal obedience; their political independence, on the other hand, they held to be sacrosanct. Besides, the very existence of their city depended on international commerce; how could they be expected to discriminate against heretics, any more than in the past they had discriminated against the infidel?

Already under Clement VIII, they had scored a few victories. In the face of considerable papal pressure, they had maintained their rights over the little town of Ceneda; then in 1596 Venetian printers and booksellers had somehow managed to obtain a special concordat allowing them to handle – under certain conditions – works included on the Index. The Republic had also staunchly defended the religious freedom of foreign diplomats. When Clement reproached it in 1604 for allowing Sir Henry Wotton to import Protestant prayer books and hold Anglican services in his private chapel, Venice had sent him a firm reply: 'The Republic can in no wise search the baggage of the English Ambassador, of whom it is known that he is living a quiet and blameless life, causing no scandal whatever.' The Pope did not insist, and Sir Henry continued to perform his devotions undisturbed throughout the fourteen years of his Venetian embassy.

Paul V, on the other hand, was made of sterner stuff. Papal Legates now sought ever more frequent audiences with the Doge, to remonstrate and protest. Why had the Senate recently prohibited the erection of any more religious buildings in the city without special licence? Venice argued in vain that it was becoming impossible to maintain even the existing churches and monasteries, which already occupied half the area of the city; but such arguments were simply not accepted, and the papal communications began to acquire a new, menacing edge. The two parties were thus, from the very beginning of Paul's reign, set on a collision course. Venice did her best to maintain friendly relations, even going so far as to enrol the Borghese family among the ranks of her nobility; but the polite veil could not be maintained for long.

The storm broke in the late summer of 1605, when two professed clerics – one of whom was subsequently found never to have taken holy orders – were denounced to the Venetian authorities, the first for persistent attempts on the honour of his niece, the second for 'murders, frauds, rapes and every kind of violence against his dependants'. In each case the Council of Ten ordered an immediate inquiry and arrogated to itself the responsibility for the trial and punishment of the two offenders. Instantly the Pope went on the attack. These two prisoners, he objected, were members of the clergy and consequently outside the Republic's jurisdiction. They must be handed over at once to the ecclesiastical authorities.

All through the autumn the argument went on; then, in December, the Pope sent two briefs to the Doge. One dealt with the question of Church property, the other with the two clerics. If Venice did not forthwith annul her decrees in the first instance and surrender her two prisoners in the second, the ban of the Church would be laid upon her. Venice, it need hardly be said, had no intention of doing either. But the time for diplomacy was past. What the Republic now needed, to present her case before the world, was an expert on canon law who was also a theologian, a dialectician, a political philosopher and a polemicist, who could argue with clarity and logic. The Senate did not hesitate. It sent for Paolo Sarpi.

Sarpi was fifty-three, and had been a Servite friar since the age of fourteen. He was renowned for his learning, which extended far beyond the field of the spirit; indeed, the whole cast of his mind seems to have been scientific rather than theological. As an anatomist, he has been credited with the discovery of the circulation of the blood, a quarter of a century or more before Harvey; as an optician, he earned the gratitude of Galileo himself. Now, as official counsellor to the Senate, he drafted the Republic's reply. 'Princes,' it ran, 'by divine law which no human power can abrogate, have authority to legislate on matters temporal within their jurisdictions; there is no occasion for the admonitions of Your Holiness, for the matters under discussion are not spiritual but temporal.'

The Pope had no patience with such arguments, which, he claimed, 'reeked of heresy'. On 16 April 1606 he announced at a consistory that unless Venice made full submission within twenty-four days, the sentence of excommunication and interdict would come into force. Venice, however, was not prepared to wait. On 6 May, Doge Leonardo Donà set his seal on an edict addressed to all patriarchs, archbishops, bishops, vicars, abbots and priors throughout the territory of the Republic. In it he made a solemn protest before Almighty God that he had striven by every means possible to bring the Pope to an understanding of the Republic's legitimate rights. Since, however, His Holiness had closed his ears and had instead issued a public monitory 'against all reason and against the teachings of the Holy Scriptures, the Fathers of the Church and the Sacred Canons', that monitory was formally declared to be worthless. The clergy were therefore adjured to continue as before with the care of the souls of the faithful and the celebration of the Mass. The protest ended with the prayer that God would lead the Pope to the knowledge of the vanity of his action, the wrong he had done to the Republic and the justice of the Venetian cause.

Next, the Doge on Sarpi's advice banished all Jesuits – who had taken a strongly papalist line from the outset – from the territory of the Republic, dismissing the Papal Nuncio with the words:

Monsignor! You must know that we are, every one of us, resolute and ardent to the last degree, not merely the Government but the whole nobility and people of our State. We ignore your excommunication: it is nothing to us. Think now where this resolution would lead, if our example were to be followed by others.

For Pope Paul and his Curia, there was now a terrible truth to be faced. The interdict had failed. The most dreaded weapon in the papal armoury – that same weapon the very threat of which, in the Middle Ages, had been enough to bring kings and emperors to their knees – had lost its power. Worse, its failure had been revealed to the world. The effect on papal prestige, already incalculable, was growing with every day that this farcical sentence continued in operation. It must be lifted, and quickly. To do so would not be easy, but somehow a formula would have to be found.

For some time Paul was unable even to contemplate so crushing a blow to his pride, but at last even he was obliged to agree. The French offer of mediation was accepted and negotiations began. Venice, advised as always by Sarpi, drove a hard bargain. She refused outright to petition for any removal of the ban; any such request must come from the King of France. As for the two prisoners, once the ban was lifted she would consign them to the French Ambassador as a token of her regard for the King, but without prejudice to her right to judge and punish them. On no account would she readmit the Jesuits (who were to remain banned for the next half-century). Finally, thanks largely to the mediation of the irresistibly named French cardinal François la Joyeuse, a carefully drafted decree was prepared stating that in view of the Pope's change of heart and the lifting of the sentence, Venice would rescind her solemn protest; it contained, however, no word to suggest that she had at any time been in the wrong or regretted her actions.

And so, in April 1607, after almost exactly a year, the interdict was lifted. It was the last in the history of the Church. No Pope would ever dare risk another, and papal authority over Catholic Europe was never quite the same again. But the end of the interdict did not mean reconciliation in any but the most formal sense. Paul V had been publicly humiliated; there were, moreover, several issues that remained unsettled and which he had no intention of allowing to be forgotten. Foremost in his mind was a determination to be revenged on those clergy who had defied his edict – and above all on the architect of his defeat, Paolo Sarpi.

Sarpi did not immediately give up his office on the resumption of relations with Rome. There was still work for him to do, and he continued to make the daily journey on foot from the Servite monastery to the Doges' Palace, waving aside all suggestions that his life might be in danger. Returning to the monastery in the late afternoon of 25 October 1607, he was descending the steps of the S. Fosca bridge when he was set upon by assassins, who stabbed him three times before making their escape, leaving the knife deeply embedded in his cheek-bone. Miraculously, he recovered; later, on being shown the weapon, he tested its point and was able to pun that he recognised the 'style' of the Roman Curia. There is no proof that he was right; but the fact that the would-be assassins – who had by this time been identified – fled at once to Rome, where they flaunted themselves, fully armed, in the streets and where no charges were ever preferred against them, suggests that the attack, if it were not actually instigated by the papal authorities, at least had not incurred their disapproval.

There were to be two more attempts on Sarpi's life, one from within his own cloister. These too he survived, finally dying in his bed on 15 January 1623. But papal rancour followed him beyond the grave. When the Senate proposed a monument in his honour, the Papal Nuncio raised violent objections, threatening that if anything of the sort occurred, the Holy Office would declare him an impenitent heretic. This time Venice gave in; and it was only in 1892 that the present distinctly undersized bronze statue was erected in the middle of the Campo S. Fosca, a few yards from the spot where he so narrowly escaped martyrdom.

Paul V never recovered from the Venice affair, nor from the botched attempts on the life of Paolo Sarpi. In England, memories of the Gunpowder Plot[1] – which took place only five months before the interdict was pronounced – were reawakened; in France, blame for the assassination of Henry IV in 1610 was laid at the papal door; all over Europe, the Pope's ultimate weakness had been revealed. He continued, however, to act according to his convictions, forever tightening Church discipline and otherwise pursuing the narrow (and by now distinctly old-fashioned) conservatism that seemed to belong more to the sixteenth century than to the seventeenth. He it was, for example, who in 1616 first took issue with Galileo for his championship of the Copernican theory that the sun, rather then the earth, was the centre of the universe.

---

[1] A Catholic conspiracy to assassinate the King and blow up Parliament on 5 November 1605. The conspirators were discovered and the plot failed.

For the rest, Paul continued the Counter-Reformation tradition of the renovation of Rome – above all of St Peter's itself. When the work on the new basilica had begun in 1506, Bramante's original plan had been that of a Greek cross; later, Raphael had favoured that of a Latin, with an extended nave to the west,[1] but Michelangelo had reverted to the original Greek idea. It was Paul V and his architect Carlo Maderno who, for liturgical reasons and to cover the space occupied by the Constantinian basilica, finally decided on the Latin alternative, adding the extension to the nave and the western façade. The Pope also gave every encouragement to his nephew, Cardinal Scipione Caffarelli – who had in gratitude changed his name to Borghese – in his building of the magnificent Villa Borghese, the first of the great Roman park villas, surely inspired by that of the Emperor Hadrian at Tivoli.

Cardinal Scipione was, in a way, a throwback to Renaissance times. By the seventeenth century the concept of the 'cardinal nephew' had long since ceased to arouse comment; for a pope to appoint such a figure from his immediate family as his chief confidential adviser was by now normal practice. Where Scipione differed from the norm was in the immense wealth that he acquired through a veritable flood of benefices, and in the conspicuousness of his spending. Few popes – and not a single cardinal – had ever before shown themselves such lavish patrons of the arts.[2] But he was equally generous in his restoration of the many churches for which, as Cardinal, he was responsible – in particular that of S. Sebastiano fuori le Mura, one of the seven pilgrimage basilicas, on which he worked for seven years.

While apparently giving them his wholehearted approval, Pope Paul shared none of his nephew's tastes. His own lifestyle, while in no way exaggeratedly austere, was simple and unassuming. He possessed, however, like nearly all his Counter-Reformation predecessors, that same unshakeable self-confidence that has done so much to hold the Catholic Church together through the greatest crises in its history. With virtually all Europe except Italy and the Iberian peninsula in continuing religious turmoil and with the ultimate outcome of the long confessional struggle still undecided, firm leadership from Rome

---

[1] When referring to St Peter's, which is built in defiance of the normal liturgical rules whereby the high altar is placed at the east end, the points of the compass have to be reversed: east is west and west is east (see Chapter I, p.5).
[2] His collection was transferred to the Villa Borghese only in 1891; before that it was housed in the Palazzo Borghese, which Pope Paul had bought in 1605, the year of his accession.

had been essential; fortunately, even the faults of the Counter-Reformation – the Inquisition, the Index, the overinsistence on papal supremacy, the enthusiasm of the Jesuits and one or two other recently founded religious Orders – were all manifestations of confidence rather than of cowardice. When in November 1620 (just over a century after Martin Luther had posted his ninety-five theses on the church door at Wittenberg) Paul V suffered a sudden stroke during the victory celebrations after the battle of the White Mountain, it must have seemed to many that the worst was over, and that the Church had survived.

The battle of the White Mountain is today largely forgotten among the English-speaking peoples; but it had a huge impact in the history of central Europe. It was a triumph for the Catholic cause, and in particular for the Emperor Ferdinand II, who had succeeded to the imperial throne the previous year. Educated and heavily influenced by the Jesuits, Ferdinand was a staunch Catholic, determined to impose religious conformity across his Empire. This had not improved his popularity in Bohemia, which had been fiercely Protestant since the days of John Hus; and when on 23 May 1618 two of his representatives were thrown out of a window of Hradcany Castle in Prague – they fell a good fifty feet, but fortunately into a pile of horse manure – he found that he had a full-scale national revolt on his hands. The following year he was officially deposed from the Bohemian throne and replaced by the Protestant Elector Palatine, Frederick V; and the national revolt had developed into what was to become the Thirty Years War, the bloodiest European cataclysm until the twentieth century.

Ferdinand's Catholic army – which included in its ranks the philosopher René Descartes – met Frederick's Protestants under the White Mountain, a few miles west of Prague, on 8 November 1620. The early-morning attack took the defenders by surprise; they broke and fled. Of their army of about 15,000, more than one-third were killed or captured. Among those who took flight was Frederick himself, the shortness of his reign earning him the title of the Winter King.[1] He and his queen – Elizabeth, daughter of King James I of England – were to live the rest of their lives in exile. As for his kingdom, Bohemia, it was delivered into Habsburg (and therefore Catholic) hands, in which it was to remain for nearly 300 years.

* * *

---

[1] He had actually reigned for a year and four days.

Pope Paul partially recovered from his first stroke; a second, however, occurring some ten weeks later, finished him off. By the time of his death at the end of January 1621 he had contributed well over half a million florins to the Emperor and the leader of the Catholic League, Maximilian I, Elector of Bavaria. His successor, Gregory XV (1621–3), assisted by his cardinal nephew Ludovico Ludovisi, was to bring this figure up to very nearly two million. Such vast subsidies enabled the Catholics to follow up their success at the White Mountain and drive back the Protestants on all fronts, to the point where Maximilian in gratitude presented the Pope with the entire Palatine Library of recently captured Heidelberg – fifty wagon-loads of priceless volumes – to be incorporated into that of the Vatican.

Gregory's pontificate lasted little over two years. The sequence of Catholic victories continued well into the twenty-one-year reign of his successor Urban VIII (1623–44), but the subsidies soon dried up. It was not that Maffeo Barberini, member of a rich merchant family long established in Florence, was any less committed to the Catholic cause; merely that the course of the hostilities took a different turn with the appearance on the scene of a new Protestant protagonist, King Gustav II Adolf – better known to us as Gustavus Adolphus – of Sweden. Just why Gustav decided to enter the war remains uncertain; he was presumably concerned at the growing power of the Holy Roman Empire, and may well have cherished ambitions to increase his own economic and commercial influence around the Baltic. At all events, he invaded the Empire in 1630 – and immediately the pendulum swung. He consistently drove back the Catholic forces until the Protestants had regained much of the land they had lost since 1618.

The successes of Gustavus Adolphus, like those of the Catholics in the previous decade, would have been impossible without heavy financial backing, and this came from what might have been thought a most unlikely source: Cardinal Richelieu, since 1624 the chief minister of King Louis XIII of France. For some time Richelieu had been worried by the growing power of the Habsburgs, who held a number of territories along the eastern border of France, including the Spanish Netherlands; and to keep this power in check – even though he himself was a member of the Sacred College – he had no hesitation in backing the Protestant cause. In return, therefore, for a Swedish promise to maintain an army in Germany to resist the Habsburgs (and for an additional undertaking that Sweden would not conclude a peace with the Emperor without French approval), he was happy to pay King Gustav an annual subsidy of one million livres.

All would have been well for Richelieu had Gustav not been killed at the battle of Lützen in November 1632. For two more years the Swedes, though deprived of their leader, continued to hold their own; but on 6 September 1634 an imperial army under the Emperor's son, the Archduke Ferdinand (the future Ferdinand III), destroyed their army at Nördlingen in the Danube valley, leaving 17,000 dead and taking another 4,000 prisoner. After Nördlingen the whole complexion of the war changed again. The Swedes were relegated to a minor role and Richelieu took over the leadership, allying France with Sweden and declaring war on Spain in May 1635. Henceforth the protagonists on both sides were Catholics, and a war that had been begun on purely religious issues became political – no longer a contest between Catholic and Protestant, but now one between the Habsburg and Bourbon houses.

Pope Urban did his best to reverse this trend. His task, as he saw it, was to reconcile the three great Catholic powers – France, Spain and the Habsburgs – in order to create a united front against Protestantism. On the other hand, having served as Papal Nuncio in France, he was a Francophile through and through, and he was deeply suspicious of Spanish ambitions in Italy. However hard he tried (and perhaps he never tried very hard), he never managed to conceal the direction in which his natural sympathies lay. When the Gonzaga line in Mantua failed in 1624, he unhesitatingly supported the French candidate for the succession. He doubtless deplored in his heart the Franco-Swedish alliance, but despite continued pressure from Philip IV of Spain never took any action.

In fact the situation was hopeless, and Urban knew it. Not surprisingly, he turned his attention to two areas in which he could make his presence felt: Church administration and the fine arts. He worked hard on a revision of the breviary, providing several new hymns of his own. He codified the proper procedures for beatification and canonisation and sanctioned several new religious Orders. Missionary work was another special interest: he founded the Collegio Urbano for the training of missionaries (a number of which he sent off to the Far East) and established a polyglot printing press. Where the arts were concerned, his best-known contribution – perhaps the summation of all that is most vulgarly ostentatious in baroque Rome – was the vast *baldacchino* that he commissioned from Gianlorenzo Bernini for St Peter's (which he consecrated in 1626), to mark the

tomb of St Peter and the high altar above it. It is wholly characteristic of the time (and of Urban himself) that the four barley-sugar
columns should have enormous bees – emblem of the Barberini –
crawling up them; for not since the Renaissance had any pope so
shamelessly promoted and enriched his own family. He made a brother
and two nephews cardinals, and presented another brother and his
son with enormous benefices; altogether the Barberini family is said
to have left the papacy the poorer by some 105 million scudi.
Conscience-stricken at the end of his life, he sought advice from canon
lawyers and theologians on whether such expenditure had been sinful.
There was still time for repentance; not, however, for compensation.

Urban has also been bitterly criticised for his treatment of his friend
Galileo. Perhaps surprisingly, the popes of the Counter-Reformation
had encouraged astronomy – Gregory XIII is said to have founded
the Vatican Observatory – and Nicholas Copernicus had actually dedicated to Paul III his book maintaining that the Earth revolved round
the sun, rather than vice versa. Although this idea was clearly incompatible with the story of creation as told in the Book of Genesis, it
was some seventy years before the Church raised any objection; and
when the heliocentric theory was finally condemned by Paul V in
1616, Galileo – who had been its most powerful champion – was
given a personal admonition not to advocate or teach it, though he
was still allowed to discuss it hypothetically. For the next few years
he occupied himself principally with other matters and stayed well
away from the controversy.

As Cardinal Barberini, Pope Urban had done everything he could
to protect his friend. He had great personal admiration for Galileo,
and had even written a Latin poem to celebrate his discovery of spots
on the sun. When, in 1632, Galileo sought his personal permission
to publish his *Dialogue Concerning the Two Chief World Systems*,
Urban willingly granted it, asking only that his own views on the
matter should be included in the book. And it was now that Galileo
made the greatest mistake of his life. The character in the *Dialogue*
who defends the old Aristotelian earth-centred theory is named Simplicius, and is often made to look a fool. To put the Pope's words in
the mouth of Simplicius, as Galileo did, was understandable, even
logical; but it was hardly diplomatic. Urban – who had an extremely
well-developed sense of his own dignity – was furious; moreover the
whole tone of the book made it clear that it was a work of advocacy,
which the Inquisition had expressly forbidden.

Galileo had unnecessarily antagonised his most powerful supporter; now he had to pay the price. In 1633 he stood trial in Rome. The result was a foregone conclusion. He was sentenced to perpetual imprisonment (later, because of his age and eminence, commuted to house-arrest) and was required formally to abjure the heliocentric theory. The *Dialogue* was banned, together with all his other works and any that he might write in the future. The Pope even pursued him after his death. When the great man died aged seventy-seven on 8 January 1642, the Grand Duke of Tuscany proposed to bury him in the basilica of S. Croce in Florence, next to his father and other members of his family, and to erect a marble mausoleum in his honour; but Urban and his nephew, Cardinal Francesco Barberini, objected, and the body was eventually laid to rest in a small room at the end of a corridor. There it was to remain for almost a century, until it could be moved to the main body of the church and a worthier sepulchre.

Pope Urban VIII died just two and a half years after Galileo, on 29 July 1644. At the end of his life – encouraged by his nephews, who sniffed the possibilities of further financial gain – he had allowed himself to be dragged into a minor war with one Odoardo Farnese, lord of Castro (a papal fief), on the grounds that Odoardo had defaulted on his debts. Odoardo fought back, having somehow found support in France and in an Italian league that included Venice, Tuscany and Modena, and the papal army was completely crushed. For the Romans, remembering the vast sums that Urban and his family had already appropriated for themselves, this extremely expensive defeat proved the last straw. The news of the Pope's death provoked open jubilation in the streets.

His successor, the seventy-year-old Giambattista Pamfili, who took the name of Innocent X (1644–55), represented a violent reaction against everything Urban had stood for. He hated France, which he considered had shamelessly enriched itself at the papacy's expense, and favoured Spain – the only nation, he claimed, on which the Holy See could safely rely. Indeed, he owed his election entirely to the Spanish veto of a rival candidate. (Cardinal Mazarin, who had succeeded Richelieu as Louis XIII's chief minister in 1642, had tried to veto Pamfili in his turn, but his letter had arrived too late.)[1] One of the Pope's first acts after his enthronement was to set up a commission of inquiry to

---

[1] By this time the Emperor, together with the kings of France and Spain, had gradually established the right of veto on any candidate for the papacy of whom they disapproved.

investigate the fortunes that the Barberini had amassed and to put their possessions under sequestration – an act that caused a degree of panic among the Barberini cardinals, one of whom took flight. The remainder, however, appealed to Mazarin, who managed to persuade Innocent to pursue the matter no further.

Although a model of propriety in comparison with his predecessor, when it came to nepotism Innocent was by no means guiltless. Although there was no cardinal nephew, there were plenty of Pamfili purses to be filled, and the Pope was happy to fill them. The most dangerously powerful of his beneficiaries was his sinister sister-in-law, Donna Olimpia Maidalchini – a woman, in the words of a contemporary, 'of nauseating greed' – who amassed a vast fortune and at the same time exerted the most extraordinary power over him. There was inevitably much speculation in Rome on the precise nature of their relationship; all that was known was that the Pope consulted her on every issue and took no decisions without her approval.

The state of the papal exchequer made it impossible for Innocent to attempt a building programme on the scale adopted by his predecessors. We owe him, nonetheless, the Piazza Navona with its glorious Bernini fountain, and Borromini's baroque transformation of the interior of St John Lateran. Not altogether surprisingly, there also appeared a Villa Pamfili – the work of Innocent's nephew Camillo – on the Via Aurelia to the west of the city. Innocent is best remembered, however, not by the architecture he commissioned, but by his superb portrait by Velázquez, which now hangs in the Galleria Doria Pamphilj in Rome.[1] ('All too true,' he is said to have commented on seeing it for the first time.)

When Innocent died on New Year's Day 1655, the ensuing conclave took three months to elect his successor. The delay was due largely to the French, Cardinal Mazarin lodging strong objection to the most popular candidate, Fabio Chigi, Bishop of Imola. At last, however, he grudgingly withdrew his opposition, and Chigi was elected as Pope Alexander VII (1655–67). But his difficulties with Mazarin were by no means over; the Cardinal could not forgive Rome for having offered a home to his arch-rival Cardinal de Retz who, having intrigued bitterly against him, had escaped from France the previous year. In consequence Mazarin gave active support to the Farnese family – who were

---

[1] Now better known as the Villa Doria Pamphilj. It is not to be confused with the Palazzo Doria Pamphilj – with its art gallery – at the beginning of the Corso, just north of Piazza Venezia.

attempting to reclaim land in the Papal State – and, as a deliberate snub, refused to allow the papacy to mediate when France concluded the Peace of the Pyrenees with Spain in 1659. Mazarin died in 1661, but the young Louis XIV refused to make up the quarrel; indeed, he exacerbated it by breaking off diplomatic relations altogether, invading the papal territories of Avignon and the Venaissin in 1662 and threatening a further invasion of the Papal State itself. Had Alexander possessed more strength and determination, he might have been able to resist the relentless pressure; unfortunately, he did not. Quiet, scholarly and deeply spiritual, he was designed for a gentle and contemplative life; tough and aggressive statesmanship in the unforgiving seventeenth century was not for him. And so it was that he unprotestingly submitted to Louis, accepting without a murmur the humiliating conditions that the King forced on him with the Treaty of Pisa in 1664.

The single event of his reign that probably gave him more pleasure than any other was the baptism of Queen Christina of Sweden. Christina, having abdicated the Swedish throne, had taken a long ceremonial route through Italy, arriving in Rome – travelling in a sedan chair specially designed by Bernini and sent out by the Pope – on 20 December. On Christmas morning 1655, in a magnificent ceremony in St Peter's, Alexander personally confirmed her in the Catholic faith, with Christina taking the additional name of Alexandra in his honour.[1] That night she formally took up residence in the Palazzo Farnese.[1] She was to live in Rome for the next thirty-five years until her death, causing a good deal of trouble to Alexander and his three successors, but – by her eccentricities of dress and behaviour and the sheer force of her extraordinary personality – leaving a far more indelible mark upon the city than they ever did.

The first two of those three successors, Giulio Rospigliosi and Emilio Altieri, both took the name of Clement. Clement IX (1667–9), who was enthroned in June 1667, reigned only two and a half years, during which his principal achievement was to repair relations with France and, at least temporarily, settle the continuing agitation over Jansenism. This depressing doctrine – first proposed by Cornelius Jansen, a former

[1] She subsequently moved to the Palazzo Riario (built by the nephew of Sixtus IV), now the Palazzo Corsini. This was to be the home of her astonishing art collection, and also of the Arcadian Academy, intended for the study of art, literature and philosophy, which still exists in Rome.

Bishop of Ypres – emphasised original sin, human depravity, predestination and the necessity of divine grace; it had split the Church in France for most of the century. Louis XIV was determined to wipe it out, and it was at his stern request that in 1653 Innocent X had condemned five key propositions contained in Jansen's principal treatise, the *Augustinus*.

Clement mended his fences, too, with the Venetians. Venice was at the time engaged in a desperate war with the Turks, who for the past twenty years had been laying siege to her last surviving colony in the Mediterranean, the island of Crete. Innocent X had sent out a papal squadron as early as 1645, but its admiral – Nicolò Ludovisi, Prince of Piombino – had shown extreme distaste for the whole expedition and had almost immediately returned home. After that the Pope had made all further help conditional on his being given control of Venetian bishoprics – a suggestion that the Republic had refused even to contemplate. Alexander VII had also imposed a condition, the readmission of the Jesuits, banned from Venetian territory since the 1606 interdict; this too had been rejected. Now, however, the situation was desperate; and when Pope Clement (who was determined to give the Venetians all the help he could) repeated the offer, it was accepted. The Jesuits returned, and the Pope succeeded in organising – with the cooperation of France, Spain and the Empire – two relief expeditions to the beleaguered island.

Alas, it was too late. The first expedition sailed in 1668 and consisted largely of aristocratic young Frenchmen, who fought only for their own glory; in their opening battle they showed considerable courage, but when it was over the survivors could not get out fast enough. (Many of them, even then, never saw France again; they had carried the plague bacillus with them.) The second, which left the following year, was also predominantly French, but sailed under the papal banner. Its story was much the same, but without the courage. Within two months of their arrival the French ships had weighed anchor, and in the general despair that ensued the few auxiliaries from the papacy, the Empire and the Knights of Malta likewise set their sails for the west. The Venetians, left alone, could fight no longer and on 6 September 1669 their Captain-General, Francesco Morosini, surrendered.

By this time Pope Clement's health was already giving cause for concern; soon after hearing the news from Crete he suffered a serious stroke, and on 9 December he died. His successor Emilio Altieri, or

Clement X (1670–6) – elected after a five-month conclave because France and Spain determinedly vetoed each other's candidates – was already in his eightieth year and was hopelessly ineffectual. In the absence of a true cardinal nephew he bestowed the role on Cardinal Paluzzi degli Albertoni (whose nephew had married the Pope's niece), requiring him to adopt the name of Altieri. This proved a grave mistake: the Cardinal immediately took over the entire administration, accumulating vast wealth on behalf of himself and his family, and Clement's reputation in Rome suffered accordingly.

Such personal influence as the Pope was able to exert was largely confined to the diplomatic field. Since the fall of Crete, the Turkish threat loomed larger than ever. The Sultan had now turned his attention to Poland, the largest state in Europe, and both Clement and Cardinal Benedetto Odescalchi – soon to succeed him as Innocent XI – sent heavy financial subsidies to the Polish general John Sobieski, who was able to inflict a crushing defeat on an Ottoman army at Chocim on the Dniester river in November 1673 and was elected King of Poland six months later. In his dealings with Louis XIV of France, however, Clement was less successful. As he grew older and more powerful, Louis adopted an increasingly bullying attitude, claiming royal control over French episcopal appointments and the revenues of bishoprics that had been allowed to fall vacant (the *régale*). During an audience in 1675, the French Ambassador (himself a cardinal) actually laid hands on the eighty-five-year-old Pope, pushing him back into his chair when he tried to rise.

It was only with the succession of Innocent XI (1676–89) the following year that the papacy began to assert itself. A man of total integrity and by far the greatest pope of the seventeenth century, Innocent publicly warned Louis to press no longer for further extension of his royal privileges. Such conduct, he pointed out, was an offence to God, who might well punish him by depriving him of heirs to the throne.[1] The result was an open breach between Paris and Rome. In March 1682 an assembly of the French clergy formally adopted what were known as the four Gallican Articles, which denied the Pope any temporal authority, asserted the superiority of General Councils and reaffirmed the ancient rights and liberties of the Gallican Church. A month later Innocent predictably rejected these articles, and refused to ratify the appointments of any French bishops until the matter was

---

[1] God very nearly did: Louis was to be succeeded by his great-grandson.

settled. By January 1685, no fewer than thirty-five French bishoprics were vacant.

Nine months later the King, whose treatment of his Huguenot subjects had been growing steadily more repressive, revoked the Edict of Nantes by which Henry IV had granted them extensive privileges almost a hundred years before. But if he thought thereby to regain the Pope's favour, he was disappointed; Innocent publicly condemned the violence of what now amounted to an out-and-out religious persecution. King and Pope were also at loggerheads over the all-important issue of resistance to the Turks, who never relaxed their pressure on Christian Europe. Innocent had worked hard to unite the Emperor Leopold I and John Sobieski, now King of Poland, in a 'Holy League' against them, and it was thanks only to this that an Ottoman army had been driven back from Vienna in 1683. King Louis, however, would have none of it. The Emperor, he well knew, suffered from Turkish pressure far more than he did, and he was only too happy that it should continue. Thus it was that throughout Innocent's pontificate Franco-papal relations steadily deteriorated. In 1687 the Pope refused to receive the new French Ambassador; in January 1688 he excommunicated Louis and all his ministers, and the same year he rejected the King's nominee for the archbishopric (and electorship) of Cologne, adopting instead the candidate proposed by Leopold. In September the French once again occupied the papal enclave of Avignon and the Venaissin. But if Innocent failed to bring King Louis to heel, he at least showed him (as his predecessors never had) that the papacy was still a force to be reckoned with. And, even without Louis's support, he continued his campaign against the Turks, recruiting to his Holy League both Venice and Russia, thus enabling the League to turn the Ottoman tide, liberating Hungary in 1686 and Belgrade the following year.

There has long existed a somewhat surprising theory according to which Pope Innocent secretly encouraged and supported the plans of the Protestant William of Orange to supplant the Catholic James II on the English throne. Despite James's attempts to bring England back into the Catholic fold, Innocent deeply distrusted him: he was too close to Louis, for one thing, and far too aggressive and confrontational, for another. Certainly the Pope never gave him any support, and he was probably neither surprised nor especially concerned when William ousted him. Still, no serious evidence for this theory has ever been adduced, and the idea can almost certainly be discounted.

Innocent died on 12 August 1689. In his lifetime he had not been particularly popular among his flock; utterly incorruptible, stern and uncompromising, he had lived austerely and parsimoniously – having inherited a debt of 500,000 scudi, he had little choice – and, avoiding the faintest breath of nepotism himself, had done all he could to persuade his cardinals to follow his example. After his death, however, his many outstanding qualities gradually came to be recognised, and it was only a quarter of a century before Pope Clement XI began the process of canonisation. But French memories were long, and French influence in Rome had lost none of its power: in 1744, at the insistence of Louis XV, the process was suspended. Only in the mid-twentieth century, under Pius XII, did the wheels begin to turn again. Innocent is now at last beatified; but sainthood is not yet his.

Innocent XI was seventy-eight when he died; Alexander VIII (1689–91) was seventy-nine when he succeeded him. The conclave by which Cardinal Pietro Ottoboni was chosen was the first to be attended by official ambassadors of both the Emperor and the King of France, but even before these had arrived the cardinals were virtually agreed on their choice. Needless to say, the French representative had initially protested: Ottoboni had after all been the right-hand man of Pope Innocent, who had appointed him Grand Inquisitor of Rome and Secretary of the Holy Office. But in the preliminary discussions the Cardinal gave his assurances that Franco-papal relations would be his first priority, and the objections were withdrawn.

The new pope had already been a cardinal for thirty-seven years. He was a Venetian, the first Venetian pope for two centuries. Blameless in his personal life, he was a fine scholar, possessed of one of the largest private libraries in Italy. In marked contrast to his predecessor, he was warm, generous and endlessly charming to young and old alike. Alexander carried his years well; his mind remained as alert as ever it had been. And he cheered Rome up. He made frequent public appearances, driving informally through the city. He used to say that his twenty-third hour had already struck, so he had to work fast. Back came the lavish spending and extravagance; the manifestations that marked his enthronement were, according to an eyewitness, 'the most beautiful seen in our lifetime'. Back, too, came the Carnival, and public performances of operas – one of which, *Colombo*, had come from the pen of Cardinal Pietro Ottoboni himself.

Back, finally, came the old nepotism. On his accession Alexander had appointed to the post of cardinal nephew his twenty-year-old grand-nephew Pietro, making his nephew Giambattista Secretary of State; both were loaded with rich benefices. As more members of his family hastened down from Venice, they too were appointed to highly lucrative posts. Nor was the Republic itself forgotten. Venice was at that time engaged in an ambitious campaign to drive the Turks from the Peloponnese, led by that same Francesco Morosini who had been Captain-General in Crete and was now himself Doge; Alexander threw himself behind it with enthusiasm, sending a large subsidy together with a number of galleys and a force of 1,500 fighting men. In April 1690 he even went so far as to send Morosini a hat and a sword blessed by himself.

From the beginning of his pontificate, however, he never forgot that his primary concern must be to improve relations with France. Fortunately Louis XIV – whose position had been much weakened by the Glorious Revolution in England and the deposition of James II – was in a receptive mood. He willingly restored Avignon and the Venaissin to papal hands, and raised no objection when the Pope put an end to the rights of asylum and immunity from taxes claimed by foreign embassies in Rome. In return, and despite vociferous protests from the Emperor, Alexander raised to the cardinalate Toussaint de Forbin Janson, Bishop of Beauvais, for whose elevation Louis had been pressing for years. Forbin had been a signatory to the Assembly of 1682, in consequence of which Innocent XI had repeatedly refused to consider him; but to Alexander, in the improved atmosphere of conciliation, his red hat was a small price to pay.

Despite these minor concessions, the fundamental issue remained unresolved: the Pope absolutely refused to ratify the appointment of any French bishops unless they formally renounced and repudiated the Gallican Articles – which Louis, on his side, was determined to uphold. In vain did Alexander write personally and privately to the King, and even to Madame de Maintenon – to whom Louis was now secretly married and who was said to exercise considerable influence over him. The replies he received dashed his hopes – such as they were – to the ground. Ruefully he had to accept that all his efforts at a reconciliation with the French king had come to nothing, and had succeeded only in seriously damaging the good relations he had previously enjoyed with the Emperor. With Leopold the elevation of Cardinal Forbin still rankled – the more so since none of his own nominees had been similarly promoted. He resented, too, the impressive sums that the Pope had sent to Venice for her Peloponnesian campaign, which had resulted in much-reduced subsidies for his own struggle against the Turks. But Pope Alexander probably cared little for the Emperor's feelings. As late as mid-November 1690 he appointed two more cardinals. Neither was an imperial nominee; both were related to his nephews.

At this time Alexander was still in excellent health; but in January 1691 he developed a severe inflammation of the leg, which rapidly became gangrenous. On the 29th he summoned to his bedside the twelve cardinals who had been involved in the dispute with France and delivered to them a Brief, declaring that the Declaration of 1682 – upholding the Gallican Articles – was legally null and void. It was his parting shot; three days later he was dead.

The ensuing conclave continued for more than five months, the longest since 1305. It would probably have lasted even longer had it not been for the summer heat – exceptional even by Roman standards – which raised the temperature in the Sistine Chapel to intolerable levels. The delay was largely due to King Louis, who strongly supported the Venetian Cardinal Gregorio Barbarigo; but the French finally gave way and the vote was cast for the seventy-six-year-old Archbishop of Naples, Antonio Pignatelli, henceforth to be known as Innocent XII (1691–1700). A Neapolitan aristocrat born in the Basilicata, he was the last pope from southern Italy – and, incidentally, the last to grow a beard.

Having assumed the name of his indirect predecessor, he also took him as his model – with the difference that whereas Innocent XI had been stern and unapproachable, Innocent XII held regular public and private audiences, talking easily and freely with all classes. Nepotism he hated; he refused to confirm the nephews of Alexander VIII in their posts, and by means of a Bull, *Romanum decet ponteficem* of 22 June 1692, decreed that all relatives of the reigning pontiff should be forbidden to accept estates, offices or revenues. If a member of a pope's family was admitted to the Sacred College it must be on grounds of merit alone, and his annual revenues were not to exceed 12,000 scudi. This Bull was to be sworn to at every future conclave, by all the cardinals and by the Pope himself. It made a widespread impression throughout the Catholic world and effectively marks the end of nepotism in the Holy See.[1]

Innocent maintained that *his* nephews were the poor; after the welfare of the Church, they were always his principal concern. In 1692 he converted the old Lateran Palace into a hostel for no fewer than 5,000 homeless unemployed, and in 1693 took over the Ospizio (hospice) di S. Michele on the Ripa Grande, a boys' orphanage founded by the family of Innocent XI, commissioning the architect Carlo Fontana[2] to remodel it so that it should accommodate 300 orphans instead of the original thirty. These two buildings, combined with Sixtus V's hospice and with another asylum for foundlings, now formed a united Apostolic Hospice, which the Pope placed under the care of three cardinals, and which was henceforth so near his heart as to arouse complaints that he often forgot everything else.

As Innocent's favourite architect, Fontana was given many other commissions during his pontificate. The most ambitious was to complete and enlarge the Palazzo di Montecitorio – which Bernini had begun forty-five years before on the orders of Innocent X – and to use it as a vast *Palais de Justice*, finally bringing all Rome's various tribunals and courts of law under one roof. The work was never carried out as originally planned (the expense would have been astronomical), but the building as we see it today remains one of the city's most magnificent examples of the high baroque[3]. In St Peter's, Fontana also designed the baptistry[4] and the monument to Queen Christina in the right-hand aisle.

Another long-standing abuse against which Innocent took firm action was the sale of Church offices. Here he had to face a good deal of opposition, since the practice was highly profitable; but he offset the loss by cutting his own expenses to the bone. He then turned his attention to the harbours of Civitavecchia and Nettuno, both of which were greatly enlarged in order to increase the corn trade. Civi-

---

[1] Careful investigation has revealed that the nephews of Paul V had received 260,000 scudi, those of Urban VIII 1,700,000, those of Innocent X 1,400,000, those of Alexander VII 900,000, those of Clement X 1,200,000 and those of Alexander VIII 700,000 from the Apostolic Camera alone. On top of this there was the considerable income derived from various vacant offices.

[2] Not, of course, to be confused with the sixteenth-century Domenico Fontana. The two were, so far as is known, unrelated.

[3] Since 1871 it has been the seat of the Italian Chamber of Deputies.

[4] The huge porphyry font is said originally to have come from the Mausoleum of Hadrian, and later to have adorned the tomb of the Holy Roman Emperor Otto II.

tavecchia he also made a free port, endowing it with a magnificent new aqueduct and in May 1696 even paying the city a personal visit, being the first pope for more than a century to do so.

The Pope's greatest diplomatic achievement was to end the fifty-year deadlock between Louis XIV and the Holy See. First, he ratified the appointments of all the bishops nominated by the King who had not taken part in the 1682 Assembly – that which had adopted the four Gallican Articles. In return, Louis revoked the declaration of the French clergy by which the bishops had been obliged to subscribe to the Articles, and the bishops formally retracted their signatures. It was, on the whole, a satisfactory accommodation, of which the only serious drawback was that the Articles themselves were left intact: the French Church was largely to ignore Vatican authority until the Revolution and beyond. Inevitably, too, this burying of the hatchet aroused imperial suspicions. Innocent had done his best to improve relations with the Emperor Leopold, just as he had with King Louis, and had sent him 80,000 scudi for his struggle against the Turks. But the unconcealed hostility and arrogance of successive imperial ambassadors in Rome seemed expressly designed to provoke conflict; moreover the bitter war that was raging between the French and the Empire made it impossible to be friends with both. The Holy See was not represented at the peace talks that led to the Treaty of Ryswick[1] in September 1697, but somehow managed to arrange for the inclusion of a clause that the Roman Catholic faith should be preserved intact in all countries that were subjected to Protestant rule by the terms of the Treaty.

At the beginning of November 1699 the eighty-four-year-old Pope fell dangerously ill. He never properly recovered, but somehow found the strength to celebrate the Holy Year of 1700 with public appearances, blessing the thousands of pilgrims from the balcony of the Quirinal Palace[2] and even visiting the principal churches. Then on 1 August he suffered a serious relapse. He lingered for another eight weeks, dying in the early hours of 27 September. In the nine years of his pontificate he had achieved much: the end of nepotism, reconciliation with France. He may even have decided the whole future of Spain; despite his differences with Louis XIV, he certainly advised the childless Spanish king Charles II to nominate as his heir Louis XIV's

---

[1] The treaty settled the Nine Years War, which had pitted France against the Grand Alliance of the Empire, England, Spain and the United Provinces (Netherlands).
[2] The Quirinal was the principal residence of the popes from Clement VIII until 1870 (Pius IX).

grandson Philip, Duke of Anjou, rather than the Emperor Leopold's younger son Charles. On 3 October 1700 – just a week after Innocent's death – Charles II changed his will accordingly, dying himself a month later.

Although he never knew it, Innocent XII was to have one further claim to fame. After some 170 years in his grave, he was to enter the canons of English literature. Readers – if such there be – of Robert Browning's *The Ring and the Book* will recognise him as one of the twelve narrators in whose words the interminable story is told. It does not improve his reputation; fortunately, his reputation does not need improving.

CHAPTER XXII

The Age of Reason

(1700–48)

The seventeenth century had closed with two very old men occupying the throne of St Peter; the eighteenth began with a very young one. Gian Francesco Albani was only fifty-one when, after long hesitation, he accepted his election as Pope Clement XI (1700–21). A cardinal since 1690, he had enjoyed considerable influence under his two predecessors, and had actually drafted Innocent's Bull prohibiting nepotism. Thanks to his intelligence, scholarship and gifts as an orator he had long been considered *papabile*, yet curiously enough he had been ordained a priest only two months before his election.

The deathbed decision of Charles II of Spain to name Philip of Anjou as his successor had had, not surprisingly, an explosive effect: for Charles had been the last male descendant of the Emperor Charles V, and the Spanish crown was now coveted – and indeed claimed – by the two mightiest dynasties of Europe. Philip III of Spain (who reigned from 1598 to 1621) had two daughters: the elder, Anne, had been married off to Louis XIII of France; the younger, Maria, to the Emperor Ferdinand III of Austria. Anne had in due course given birth to the future Louis XIV; Maria to the Emperor Leopold I. In the fullness of time Leopold had married Charles II's younger sister, Margaret; and their small grandson Joseph Ferdinand was consequently the Habsburg claimant. Already the scene seemed set for a struggle. When in 1698 King Charles made a will confirming Joseph Ferdinand as his heir, the matter might have been thought to be settled; but in February 1699 the young prince unexpectedly died. His sudden death was attributed, rather unconvincingly, to smallpox: there were many, among them the boy's own father, who suspected poison and did not hesitate to say so. In any event it was Leopold's younger son, the Archduke Charles, who now claimed the Spanish throne on behalf of the Empire.

Like Innocent before him, Clement favoured Philip of Anjou as the next King of Spain. Philip's grandfather, Louis XIV, might have his faults, but he was unquestionably the most powerful existing champion of Roman Catholicism. Moreover, where papal territory in Italy was concerned, the Spanish record was abysmal; it was clear to Clement that the papal lands would be far safer if a Frenchman, rather than a Spaniard, were in control of Spanish-held Naples, Milan and Sicily. But he could hardly expect the Emperor Leopold to agree with him, and nor indeed could King Louis, who lost no time in packing off the young claimant to Madrid to assume his throne without delay, in the company of a bevy of French officials prepared to take over all the key posts of government. What Louis could not have known was how long and how desperate the ensuing war would be, or what a price he would have to pay for his grandson's crown.

And so it was that in February 1701 – less than three months after Pope Clement's enthronement – Philip of Anjou was welcomed in Madrid as King Philip V of Spain while, almost simultaneously, French troops occupied the Spanish Netherlands. Almost before anyone knew it, Europe had been swept up in the War of the Spanish Succession.

The Emperor Leopold, too, was moving fast. If Spain were to pass from the hands of the weakest monarch in Europe into those of the strongest, what chance was there that trade would be allowed to continue? Just as the Pope had feared, Leopold was determined to seize all Spanish territories in Italy, beginning with Milan, to prevent their falling into French hands. He found his allies in England and Holland. These two maritime countries were both carrying on an immensely profitable trade with Spain; there were several English and Dutch merchants permanently resident in Cadiz and other Spanish ports. Through much of the seventeenth century the two had been at loggerheads; now, however, they shared with the Emperor a common concern: to keep out the French. And so the Grand Alliance was born.

As for Pope Clement, everyone knew of his pro-French sympathies – he had actually sent a letter of congratulation to King Philip in Madrid – so it came as no surprise when his offer to mediate was ignored. On the outbreak of war he did his best to take a neutral stand, though this was by no means easy when both Leopold and Philip demanded to be invested with Naples and Sicily (in which Philip had already been proclaimed without opposition). If we are to believe the Venetian Ambassador, the Pope feared the power, the boldness and the pride of the Habsburgs and the frivolity, presumption and violence of the Bourbons – to say nothing of their Gallican ideas. His greatest weakness had always been indecision; now he vacillated, desperately trying to gain time and thus successfully antagonising both parties.

And, inevitably, the peninsula became once again a battleground. First the French swept in and captured Milan; but then in 1706 the Empire's brilliant general Prince Eugene of Savoy drove them out of northern Italy. A year later the Austrian troops of Leopold's successor Joseph I invaded papal territory and took possession of Naples, threatening Rome itself. The Pope, who had no army worthy of the name, was forced to accept Joseph's terms, recognising both his capture of Naples and the claim of his younger brother the Archduke Charles to the throne of Spain – which led, of course, to a serious worsening of papal-Spanish relations.

Then, on 17 April 1711, Joseph died in Vienna at the age of only thirty-three – this time it was definitely smallpox – and the whole European political scene was once again transformed overnight. In his six-year reign Joseph had enthusiastically espoused Charles's claims to Spain; but Charles was now not just a Spanish claimant; he was his brother's obvious successor on the imperial throne. The Grand Alliance had been formed to prevent a single family, the Bourbons, from becoming too powerful; if Charles were to succeed to the Empire (as indeed he did, being elected the following year), the Habsburgs threatened to become more powerful still, with all their dominions once more united as in the days of Charles's great-great-great-great-uncle, Charles V. Inevitably, many months were to pass before the European powers were able to come to terms with the new situation; it was not until New Year's Day 1712 that negotiations began between the Allies and France in the Dutch city of Utrecht.

What is generally known as the Treaty of Utrecht was in fact a whole series of treaties in which, after a European upheaval that had lasted eleven years, France and Spain attempted once again to regulate their relations with their neighbours. Pope Clement, as usual, found himself disregarded. Charles surrendered his Spanish claims to Philip, and was granted Milan and Naples. France and Spain both formally recognised Duke Victor Amadeus II of Savoy – who happened to be King Philip's father-in-law – as King of Sicily.[1] On none of these

---

[1] In 1720 he was obliged to surrender Sicily to the Emperor, receiving in exchange the comparatively unimportant island of Sardinia. From then until 1861, when his distant cousin Victor Emmanuel II became the first King of a united Italy, he and his successors were also known as Kings of Sardinia, though they continued to reign from their ancestral capital of Turin.

occasions was the Pope consulted. Even the old papal fiefs of Parma and Piacenza were disposed of without his consent.

The political and diplomatic prestige of the Holy See was indeed in sorrowful decline; only in doctrinal matters was the Pope still listened to – up, at least, to a point. Here his principal headache was caused by Jansenism[1] in France. By this time it had been causing trouble for well over half a century, defying all Louis XIV's efforts to stamp it out. It had recently flared up again when forty doctors at the Sorbonne had ruled that it was permissible for Catholics to listen to a condemnation of Jansenism 'in respectful silence'. This roused the King to a new fury. He now demanded that Pope Clement, who had already rebuked the doctors, publish a Bull declaring that passive acquiescence was not enough; the abominable doctrine must be actively and positively denounced, whenever and wherever it should raise its head. Clement did so – but with consequences very different from those he had expected. There was an immediate outcry in France, spreading far beyond Jansenist circles and spearheaded by that most aristocratic of churchmen, Cardinal Louis-Antoine de Noailles, Archbishop of Paris. Louis, angrier than ever, insisted on yet another Bull, which would be nothing less than an out-and-out condemnation of Jansenism. Once again the Pope did as he was bid, with the celebrated Bull *Unigenitus*, which condemned 101 propositions taken from a recent and hugely popular publication by a leading Jansenist named Pasquier Quesnel, *Moral Reflections on the Gospels*; but Noailles, together with fifteen bishops, categorically refused to accept it – Gallicanism, it will be seen, was far from dead – and the stalemate continued until the King's death in 1715.

As Louis XV, his great-grandson and heir, was only five years old, the regency was entrusted to Philip, Duke of Orleans. The Duke took no interest in religion; he wished only to be rid of the whole problem once and for all. He forbade any further discussion of the controversial Bull and left it to the Pope to find a solution. Clement responded with a third Bull, upholding *Unigenitus* and excommunicating all those who disobeyed it. This too was widely condemned, not only by de Noailles, but by several bishops, the French *parlements* and the Sorbonne. It was naturally upheld by the Regent, but still the dispute went on, doing more and more to destroy the rapidly waning prestige of the papacy in France, and it was still raging when

---

[1] See Chapter XXI, pp.329–30.

the Pope died, after a long illness, on 19 March 1721. He was seventy-one, and had been in office for twenty years – during which Rome had suffered two catastrophic floods and, in early 1703, a hurricane so furious that the church bells rang of their own accord. This had been followed by a whole series of earthquakes, one of which accounted for three arches on the second tier of the Colosseum.

Clement XI was a man of many virtues. He was deeply devout, hard-working, incorruptible and a generous patron of the arts. His besetting fault was indecision. He lacked the instinctive political sense that guides a natural leader, and was consequently unable to impose his prestige – let alone his will – upon his foreign flock. He had been genuinely reluctant to accept his elevation to the papacy, and he never deluded himself that he had been a success. Some months before his death he dictated his epitaph to his nephew, Cardinal Annibale Albani. It read: 'Clement XI, Pope, once a chaplain then a canon of this basilica, died on . . . after a pontificate of . . . years. Pray for him.'

As the eighteenth century continued it gradually became clear that the papacy had a new enemy with which to contend: an enemy a good deal more insidious than the doctrinal differences that had plagued Christendom for well over a millennium. For this was the Age of Reason. For many churchmen, even heretics were preferable to sceptics, agnostics (there were still relatively few who dared call themselves atheists) or anticlericals.

In the face of this new intellectual climate it is not easy to see what measures the Holy See could have taken; what is clear, however, is that it did not take them. The first two successors of Clement XI were pious enough – they had both renounced dukedoms for the sake of the Church – but neither reigned for long (Innocent XIII, already a sick man and enormously fat, lasted less than three years, 1721–4; Benedict XIII less than six, 1724–30) and neither made much impact in Rome. Innocent, it is true, had some success in resolving tensions abroad. In 1721 he endeared himself to Louis XV by raising his dissolute and debauched chief minister, the Abbé Guillaume Dubois, to the cardinalate, and the following year he invested the Emperor Charles VI with Naples and Sicily – something that Clement IX had always refused to do.

When Innocent's successor Benedict XIII was elected, much against his will, on 29 May 1724 he was already seventy-six and in his dotage.

Apart from forbidding the clergy to wear wigs, he refused to act as Pope and dealt with Charles, Louis and Philip of Spain simply by ignoring them; meanwhile he lived the life of a simple parish priest, sleeping in a small whitewashed room on the top floor of the Quirinal (he subsequently moved to the Vatican), hearing confessions, visiting the sick and giving religious instruction. Several times a week he waited on thirteen paupers at table. Most of the papal business he entrusted to a certain Niccolò Coscia, whom he had known when Archbishop of Benevento and whom in 1725 he promoted – in the face of heavy opposition – to the Sacred College. He could hardly have made a more disastrous choice. Coscia was a scoundrel, deeply corrupt, who thought only of his own self-enrichment, selling off church offices, accepting bribes, filling the Curia with his own Beneventan cronies and leaving the papal treasury bare. Meanwhile Benedict accepted all his recommendations without question and would not have a word said against him. Nepotism had been formally abolished by Clement XI; but now the Church, in the words of a recent historian,[1] 'had all the evils of nepotism without the nephews'.

It was somehow typical of Benedict that when he did show firmness he usually did so on the wrong occasion, and at the wrong time. A good example of this tendency was provided when John V of Portugal claimed the right – enjoyed by several other courts – of proposing candidates for the Sacred College. When the Pope refused, John broke off diplomatic relations, recalled all Portuguese residents in papal territory, forbade all communication with the Curia and even tried to prevent the sending of alms from Portugal to Rome.

Thanks to the greed of Niccolò Coscia and the childish gullibility of his master, the Holy See suffered grievously – not only in terms of its finances, but also in its political prestige. The Pope was too old to learn the arts of statesmanship and good government, and too innocent to see the corruption and duplicity of those in whom he put his trust. He died, more of old age than anything else, on 21 February 1730 – not a moment too soon.

But the moment Benedict had been lowered safely into his grave the Roman populace exploded in rage. Despite everything, they had loved the old man – just as they had detested Coscia and his Beneventans. Coscia himself, who had been living in the Vatican in far greater comfort and grandeur than the Pope himself, escaped without being

---

[1] E. Duffy, *Saints and Sinners*.

recognised (he was carried out on a stretcher) and took refuge with his friend, the Marchese Abbati, in his house on the Corso; but he was tracked down soon enough. The house was surrounded and narrowly escaped complete devastation. Soon afterwards the unspeakable cardinal was arrested and put on trial. He managed to draw out the proceedings for a considerable time, but in April 1733 was sentenced to excommunication, ten years' imprisonment in the Castel Sant'Angelo and a fine of 100,000 scudi. It was one of the harshest judgements ever given against a member of the Sacred College, but not a word was raised in objection.

The doddering old Benedict XIII was succeeded by a man only three years younger. Pope Clement XII (1730–40) was a wealthy Florentine, already seventy-nine and – like so many of his predecessors[1] – in constant pain from gout. He was an intellectual and a scholar who in former days, as Cardinal Lorenzo Corsini, had maintained a distinguished *salon* in the Palazzo Pamfili on Piazza Navona; but within two years of his accession he had become so blind that he could sign papers only if his hand were placed on the spot where his signature was required; and by August 1736 the imperial ambassador Count Harrach was writing: 'he has almost completely lost the wonderful memory he once possessed and his colour is so pale that there is reason to fear his demise at the turn of the season'.

On the other hand, Pope Clement had lost none of his youthful energy, and he was by no means ineffectual. He acted with firmness and promptitude against Coscia; in a determined attempt to rescue the papal finances he revived the state lotteries, which Benedict XIII had forbidden, and approved the issue of paper money. He also created a free port at Ancona, and cancelled some of the more excessive examples of Benedict's generosity. But although all these measures proved moderately beneficial, they failed to diminish appreciably the burden of debt.

Moreover, as the economy of the papacy continued to decline, so too did its international prestige. When Duke Antonio Francesco Farnese of Parma and Piacenza died in 1731 without male issue and Charles VI once again asserted his suzerainty over the duchy, Clement's protests were simply ignored. He was similarly powerless a year later

---

[1] So many, indeed, that one finds oneself wondering whether 'gout' in those days was not a portmanteau word, covering rheumatism, arthritis and probably a good many other diseases as well.

when it was transferred to Don Carlos of Spain, son of Philip V and his formidable Italian queen, Elizabeth Farnese.[1] In 1732 Don Carlos – who, thanks to his mother, was far more of an Italian than a Spaniard – was formally installed as Duke of Parma and Grand Prince of Tuscany. Later the same year the Papal Nuncio was expelled from Venice. In 1733 the French blockaded Avignon, which was still under papal control. In the spring of 1734 the Pope watched with impotent anxiety while Don Carlos, backed by Louis XV, marched south through the Papal States and made his triumphal entry into Naples; and by the late autumn, despite some resistance from the citadels of Messina, Trapani and Syracuse, he had effectively taken over Sicily as well. In 1735 the prince resigned Parma to the Empire in exchange for recognition as King of Naples; and in 1736 Spain and Naples both broke off diplomatic relations with the Holy See. To restore them Clement was obliged to invest Don Carlos unconditionally with the Kingdom of Naples.

Meanwhile the Pope's health was giving increasing cause for concern, his misery now increased by a painful hernia and bladder trouble. On 28 January 1740 he asked to be given the last rites, and on 6 February he died in his eighty-eighth year. Considering his sufferings, his energy almost to the end had been astonishing, and if so many of his diplomatic initiatives failed he can hardly be held responsible; the times were against him. Thanks to his family's wealth and the profits from his lotteries, he left Rome richer and more beautiful than he found it, building a museum of antique sculptures on the Capitol (the first public museum of antiquities in Europe), providing St John Lateran with a new façade and the superb Corsini Chapel (both by Alessandro Galilei), laying out the Piazza di Trevi and commissioning from Nicola Salvi the glorious Trevi Fountain.[2] He also enlarged and greatly enriched the Vatican Library, presenting it with some 200 Etruscan vases and more than 300 antique medals. It was, for an octogenarian, an impressive record.

The conclave that followed the death of Clement XII lasted more than six months – the longest since the Great Schism. The final choice was a totally unexpected compromise candidate, the Bolognese Prospero

[1] Elizabeth claimed it as of right, the duchy having been in Farnese hands since its creation in 1545 as a fief for Paul III's illegitimate son, Pierluigi (see Chapter XX, p.300).
[2] Begun in 1732, the fountain was completed after 1751 by Giuseppe Pannini and inaugurated in 1762 by Clement XIII.

Lorenzo Lambertini. 'If you want a saint, take Gotti; if you want a statesman, take Aldovrandi; if you want a good fellow, take me,' he is said to have joked during the conclave's last days. The cardinals, it appeared, wanted a good fellow; Lambertini was duly elected, taking the name of Benedict XIV (1740–58) in honour of the pope who had raised him to the Sacred College. He proved worth waiting for. A deeply learned theologian and Church lawyer who had written what is still the standard work on canonisation, he was also genial and approachable, with a ready wit and an excellent sense of humour. He enjoyed nothing more than wandering informally around Rome, chatting to passers-by; it was typical of him that when the King of Naples visited Rome in 1744 the Pope received him not in his palace on the Quirinal, but in a neighbouring coffee-house.[1]

But Benedict's easy-going charm concealed an underlying serious-ness and unremitting industry. His task, as he saw it, was to restore the dignity and influence of the Holy See, and somehow drag it into the eighteenth century. Only two months after his accession, however, came the first and greatest crisis of his pontificate: the death, in October 1740, of the Emperor Charles VI. Charles had taken care to obtain solemn guarantees from all the principal European powers that they would respect the right of his twenty-three-year-old daughter Maria Theresa to succeed him in the monarchy, if not in the elected Empire. The papacy and the Republic of Venice, England and Holland had all willingly agreed; Louis XV, though unwilling to commit himself, had been friendly and reassuring, while the new King of Prussia, Frederick II (later to be known as 'the Great') not only confirmed his recognition, but even offered military assistance should it ever be needed. He spoke, as was soon apparent, with a forked tongue; but Maria Theresa was not to know it until, just two months later on 16 December 1740, a Prussian army of 30,000 invaded the imperial province of Silesia. The War of the Austrian Succession had begun.

Charles's body was scarcely cold before Elizabeth Farnese forced her ever-compliant husband Philip V to lay claim to all the Habsburg hereditary possessions. Their grounds were shaky, and she knew it. What she was really after, as always, was the Italian provinces, and she had a valuable ally on the spot: her son Don Carlos, now King Charles of Naples. Within weeks a Spanish army had crossed the Pyre-nees and was advancing – with King Louis's blessing – through the

---

[1] There is a delightful painting of this event by Pannini in the Capodimonte Museum, Naples.

Languedoc and Provence; meanwhile the Spanish Duke of Montemar sailed a further division to Orbetello (near the modern Porto Ercole), where it was joined by Neapolitan troops. At this point King Charles Emmanuel of Sardinia[1] threw in his lot with Maria Theresa, so henceforth Austria and Sardinia were pitted against the two Bourbon kingdoms of France and Spain. They had other allies too: in August 1742 a British naval squadron commanded by the sixty-six-year-old admiral Thomas Matthews appeared off Naples and threatened to bombard the city unless King Charles withdrew at once from the Bourbon coalition. The threat was gratifyingly effective; Matthews then turned against a squadron of French and Spanish ships, driving it back into Toulon and thus cutting off all naval communications between Naples and Spain.

Throughout this period the attitude of the Holy See was uncertain. Despite previous papal assurances, the Pope delayed his formal recognition of Maria Theresa's hereditary right of succession until the very end of 1740. The Empire, on the other hand, remained elective. There were two obvious candidates: Maria Theresa's husband, Francis of Lorraine, and the Elector Charles Albert of Bavaria. Benedict secretly favoured Charles Albert; since Francis was already Grand Duke of Tuscany,[2] his election would bring the Empire to the Pope's very doorstep. Benedict gave careful instructions, however, to his legate at Frankfurt (where the election was to be held) on no account to commit himself, but simply to encourage the choice of a candidate who would be able and willing to protect the interests of the Church.

When, on 24 January 1742, Charles Albert was unanimously elected as the Emperor Charles VII, being crowned three weeks later, Benedict lost no time in according him his recognition. Maria Theresa, on the other hand, showing all the spirit for which she would soon be celebrated, immediately declared the election null and void and sent an army to Bavaria. On 13 February it marched into Munich, and in August the furious Queen announced the sequestration of all Church benefices in Austria. By this time, too, the Papal States had been overrun by Spanish, French and Neapolitan troops. The pontificate of Benedict XIV had not begun well.

It was a relief for almost everyone – not least the Pope, to whom

---

[1] See p. 341.
[2] At the request of the Emperor – who wished to compensate the ex-King of Poland Stanislas Leszczinski (father-in-law of Louis XV) for the loss of his kingdom – he had received Tuscany in 1736 in exchange for his former Duchy of Lorraine.

the new Emperor had been a considerable disappointment – when Charles VII died after a short illness on 20 January 1745, less than three years after his coronation. This time there was little question as to his successor, and the Grand Duke of Tuscany was duly crowned in October as Francis I. Despite heavy pressure from France and Spain and his own lively suspicions, the Pope recognised him. There were still outstanding questions to be settled, and it was almost a year before Francis made his formal act of obedience; but the way was then clear for a resumption of relations, and diplomatic representatives were duly exchanged.

When at last, after eight years, the war came to an end with the Treaty of Aix-la-Chapelle in 1748, the only true victor was Frederick of Prussia, who had started it in the first place. Charles Emmanuel kept Savoy and Nice; the Duchy of Parma and Piacenza, after twelve years as part of the Empire, was entrusted to Philip of Bourbon, the younger brother of Charles III, who thus founded the House of Bourbon-Parme, which still exists today. Maria Theresa's husband was duly recognised as the Emperor Francis I. To many people, the War of the Austrian Succession must have seemed hardly worth the fighting.

CHAPTER XXIII

The Jesuits and the Revolution

(1750–99)

Both during the war and after it, Pope Benedict spent much of his time in diplomatic negotiations with the European powers. Conciliatory by nature, he was not afraid to make substantial concessions in return for good relations and the smooth running of the Church machine. With Spain, he even went so far as to negotiate the transfer of some 12,000 ecclesiastical appointments to the King, retaining just fifty-two. The Curia was horrified; Benedict merely pointed out that King Ferdinand would almost certainly have appropriated them anyway, and that by negotiating he had secured 1,300,000 scudi in compensation.

Turning his attention to Portugal – which had broken off diplomatic relations in the time of Benedict XIII[1] – the Pope willingly granted all King John's demands and even awarded him the title of *Fidelissimus*, 'Most Faithful'. But the country began to cause him serious anxiety after John's death in 1750, with the rise to power in that same year of Sebastian de Carvalho e Mello, better known as the Marquis of Pombal. Since the new King, Joseph I, was a pleasure-loving nonentity, Pombal soon became the most powerful man in the kingdom – and the most feared, to the point where in 1759 the Papal Nuncio in Lisbon wrote that he was the most despotic minister there had ever been, not only in Portugal, but in the whole of Europe. Pombal believed – as it happened, nearly always mistakenly – that he knew what was best for his country, and he brooked no opposition: those who expressed contrary opinions or stood in his way were imprisoned or executed. Not surprisingly he hated the Church, which he made every effort to bring under his control, and had a particular detestation for the most active group within it, the Society of Jesus.

For some years already the Jesuits had been growing increasingly unpopular. Founded in 1534 as a humble Order of missionaries, they

---

[1] See Chapter XXII, p.344

were now seen as a vast, intellectually arrogant, power-hungry and hugely ambitious organisation, enmeshed in international intrigue and totally unscrupulous in their operations. For years they had been pilloried by Jansenist pamphleteers; Blaise Pascal in his *Lettres provinciales* had attacked them as shameless hypocrites. They were blamed for every atrocity, every outrage. Who else, people asked, had been responsible for the assassinations of Henry III and Henry IV of France, or for the attempts on the lives of Queen Elizabeth and James I of England? Had not the English Civil War been the fruit of a Jesuit conspiracy?

In Portugal the Society had five confessors at court, and a near-monopoly of colleges and schools. Its power had to be broken, and Pombal was determined to break it. In 1755 (the year of the great Lisbon earthquake) a Jesuit was expelled for having preached a disloyal sermon, despite the fact that none of those who heard it had noticed anything to which the King might have objected. Two years later the Jesuit confessor to the royal family was forcibly evicted, and the next day all Jesuits were banned from the court and struck off the list of preachers in the cathedral. Pombal told the nuncio that the principal reason was the conduct of the Society in its missionary colonies in Spanish Paraguay and Portuguese Brazil, where Jesuit missionaries were alleged to have incited the Indians to rebellion. At much the same time the Portuguese envoy in Rome strongly hinted to Pope Benedict that if he did not take firm measures against the Society, King Joseph would expel it altogether from his realm.

It was always the Pope's instinct to temporise. He had no wish to offend the King, but he resented Pombal's attitude, which demanded his unquestioning acceptance of the truth of his accusations. He politely replied that he would appoint one of his cardinals to investigate the charges, and on consideration of his report would take whatever measures seemed appropriate. On 1 April 1758 – just a month before his death – he duly named the Portuguese cardinal Francesco Saldanha as Reformer and Visitor of the Jesuits of Portugal.

In his dealings with Prussia, Benedict smoothed his path by recognising the Protestant Frederick II – whose conquest of Silesia had greatly increased the number of his Catholic subjects – as King, a title previously denied him by the Holy See; on the other hand, he refused absolutely to allow him to transfer to Berlin the seat of the Cardinal-Bishop of Breslau, Vicar-General of all the Catholics in his realm, even when the King promised to upgrade the Catholic chapel there to the status of a cathedral. The result, the Pope realised, would have been tantamount to the establishment of a Prussian state church, effectively independent of Rome – and he would have none of it.

Another serious problem was the heavy burden of debt that he had inherited. He instituted drastic economies in every department of the administration, but they did little more than counterbalance the depredations of the foreign armies; the burden remained crushing. In his canonical and liturgical reforms he had rather more success. Mixed marriages were regularised; Christians of the Eastern rite in communion with Rome – the Maronites of Lebanon, for example, and other uniate Churches of the Middle East – were formally assured that they might continue in all their traditional forms of worship. The Congregation of the Index (effectively the papal Board of Censorship) was instructed to avoid excessive zeal, interpreting its instructions as liberally as possible. (Freemasonry, however, and the works of the Pope's openly confessed admirer Voltaire[1] remained proscribed.)

As might have been expected, Benedict XIV was an enthusiastic patron of the arts and sciences. Unlike his predecessor, he had never been a rich man; no magnificent buildings stand to his memory. He managed nonetheless to found chairs of mathematics, chemistry and physics at the University of Rome, and a chair of surgery (with an institute of anatomy) at that of Bologna; and he greatly enriched both the Vatican Library and the Capitoline Museum. It was thanks largely to him that, during the mercifully peaceful last ten years of his pontificate, Rome became not only the religious but also the intellectual capital of Catholic Europe: the Rome in which Johann Joachim Winckelmann invented art history; the Rome that was also a few years later to inspire Edward Gibbon. Gibbon's contemporary Horace Walpole summed up Benedict accurately enough: 'A priest without insolence or interest, a prince without favourites, a pope without nephews'. His Roman flock adored him, and when he died on 3 May 1758 the whole city went into mourning.

'Who would have thought it?' wrote Cardinal Carlo della Torre Rezzonico to his brother on hearing that he had been elected pope. 'I am completely bewildered before God and man ... You know my failings; if others had known them they would never have acted as they have.' When his mother was informed, she died of shock.

---

[1] Voltaire had gone so far as to dedicate his tragedy *Mahomet* to Pope Benedict.

Rezzonico, who took the name of Clement XIII (1758–69) after the Pope who had raised him to the purple, came from a rich Venetian family that had bought itself into the nobility some seventy years before. The Jesuit historian Giulio Cesare Cordara, who knew him well, wrote:

> He had all the virtues which could grace a prince and a pope. He was naturally kind-hearted, generous, candid and truthful, abhorring any kind of dissembling or exaggeration. He had a lively mind, great powers of endurance and an indefatigable capacity for work. It was easy to gain admittance to him; his conversation was kind but not unmeasured; pride and contempt for others were utterly foreign to his nature. Although destiny allotted him the highest dignity, he succeeded in preserving a notable humility and meekness.

The one thing Clement lacked was self-confidence. Shy and timid to a fault, he was incapable of taking his own decisions. In consequence he became increasingly dependent on his Secretary of State, Cardinal Luigi Torrigiani, whose deep admiration for the Society of Jesus did much to shape the Pope's own attitude in the crisis that was to come.

The problem of the Jesuits was to overshadow Clement's entire pontificate. At the time of his accession the principal battlefield remained Portugal, where the Marquis of Pombal was stepping up his persecutions. Benedict XIV's choice of Cardinal Saldanha as investigator had been a disastrous mistake. Saldanha was a distant relation of Pombal, to whom he owed his successful career and whom he obeyed in every particular. On 5 June 1758, barely a month after his appointment, he issued an edict announcing that he had certain knowledge that scandalous commercial transactions had been in operation in every Jesuit college, residence, noviciate and in all houses of other kinds owned by the Order and under the protection of Portugal, in Europe, Asia, Africa and America. All further trade was now forbidden under penalty of excommunication, all account books were to be surrendered. Two days later the Jesuits were formally suspended from preaching and the hearing of confessions.

The reaction in Portugal, among both the nobility and the people, was one of horror. In Rome, where the conclave was still in progress, it was much the same. The Apostolic Nuncio in Lisbon was instructed to inform Saldanha that his edict was excellent, but for one slight omission: evidence. Without that, it was simple calumny. It was further remarked that although the cardinal's inquiry was officially opened on 31 May, the decree had been printed four days earlier, on the 27th. Regarding the Jesuits' suspension, the nuncio was to point out that this was entirely uncanonical: individual members of an Order might be suspended, but not the Order as a whole. The Patriarch of Lisbon was subsequently found to have signed the edict under duress. On its publication he retired to his country retreat; a month later he was dead.

And all this was only the beginning. On the night of 3 September, shots were fired at King Joseph. Responsibility can almost certainly be laid at the door of a group of dissatisfied noblemen, twelve of whom were publicly executed; but soon the rumour was spreading that the attempted assassination had been instigated by the Jesuits – and Pombal had the perfect pretext for which he had been waiting. The seven Jesuit establishments in Lisbon were surrounded and searched, and on 5 February 1759 everything within them was sequestrated. This included all foodstuffs; had not pious benefactors taken pity on them, the fathers would have been reduced to beggary. On 20 April the King – by now quite recovered – wrote to Pope Clement reiterating the familiar charges against the Society and informing him that he had consequently expelled it from Portugal. The Pope protested in vain. Soon afterwards his nuncio suffered a similar expulsion and, for the second time in thirty years, diplomatic relations were broken off.

And now the anti-Jesuit fever spread to France. For the past half-century the France of Voltaire and Rousseau, of Diderot and his *Encyclopédie*, had been the European focus of anti-religious thought. 'So long as there are rogues and fools in the world,' wrote Voltaire to Frederick the Great, 'there will always be religion. There can be no question but that ours is the most ridiculous, absurd and bloodthirsty that ever infected the earth.' The papacy was detested, and the Jesuits were its most vocal champions. They also had a virtual monopoly of education, and stood, in the minds of the *philosophes* (or French free-thinkers), as the principal bastion of reaction and obscurantism. No wonder, then, that Pombal's activities against them had been viewed by many Frenchmen with approval. In short, France was a tinderbox; and its fuse was lit, ironically enough, by a Jesuit: Father Antoine Lavalette.

Father Lavalette was the procurator of a mission run by his Order on the island of Martinique, who in 1753 became Apostolic Prefect of all the Jesuit settlements in the West Indies. He was, however, a man of business as well as a priest, and he also ran a large plantation on the neighbouring island of Dominica where he employed some 500 slaves, sending the produce of their labours back to France. All might have been well had it not been for the Seven Years War (1756–63), on which Britain and France fought on opposite sides. Two of Lavalette's valuable shiploads were seized by the British outside Bordeaux, and the business was left a total of 1,500,000 livres in debt. The Paris *parlement* pronounced the Society of Jesus responsible, further declaring its assets subject to confiscation and forbidding it to give instruction or to accept novices pending a thorough review of its constitution. A suggestion by the French government that the Order should be administered by a special Vicar-General independent of Rome was instantly vetoed by the Pope: 'Let them be as they are or let them cease to be,' he said – a command rendered somewhat more pithily in Latin by the words *Sint ut sunt aut non sint.* The government chose the latter alternative, and on 1 December 1764 a royal decree declared the Society abolished and expelled from France.

Now it was the turn of Spain, to which King Charles had returned from Naples in 1759 on the death of his mentally unhinged half-brother, King Ferdinand. Though far more Catholic than its French neighbour, the country had been by no means unaffected by the Age of Enlightenment, and there were many who attributed its general backwardness to the influence of the Church. The Jesuits in particular were blamed – as they had been in Portugal – for the disturbances in Paraguay, for which they continued to disclaim all responsibility. They were equally innocent of the charge that led to their third expulsion.

On 10 March 1766 a decree was published in Madrid forbidding the wearing of the traditional flowing cloak and broad-brimmed *sombrero* in all royal residential towns, university towns and provincial capitals in Spain. Instead, men were enjoined to wear the short French wig and *tricorne*. The forbidden costume, it was claimed, was un-Spanish, and served only to enable criminals to conceal their faces and so to pass unrecognised. A fortnight later, on Palm Sunday, serious riots – they were known as the 'hat and cloak riots' – broke out, directed primarily against the finance minister, Squillace; the Jesuits played no part, but were once again held responsible. On 27 February 1767 Charles III banished them from Spain and all its

overseas territories. In November of the same year they were similarly expelled from Naples and Sicily, and in 1768 from the island
of Malta (still in the hands of the Knights of St John), as also from
the Duchy of Parma and Piacenza, whose Duke Ferdinand was the
nephew of Charles III.

Although the duchy had been created as a fief for a bastard son of
Pope Paul III, it had long since ceased to acknowledge the historic
suzerainty of the Holy See. Successive popes, on the other hand, had
continued to assert their claims. Most recently, Clement XIII had reaffirmed the papal claims when in 1765 Philip was succeeded by his
fifteen-year-old son Ferdinand. But Parma – or more accurately the
duchy's chief minister Guillaume du Tillot, Marquis of Felino – was
spoiling for a fight. Within months of Ferdinand's accession he had
issued a law imposing swingeing dues on ecclesiastical property, and
in January 1768 he promulgated another – forbidding the reference
of disputes to Rome and the publication of any ecclesiastical decree
without ducal permission. This was too much for Pope Clement, who
immediately convened a Congregation of cardinals and bishops to
consider a suitable response. The result was a Brief that reiterated the
feudal rights of the Holy See over the Duchy and declared all Parma's
anticlerical laws null and void. For good measure Clement included
all those responsible for the two laws in the Bull *In coena Domini*,
which contained a list of those excommunicated for reasons of faith
or morals and, according to an age-old tradition, was read out on
Maundy Thursday every year.

Here was just the pretext du Tillot needed. Not only Parma, but
the three great Bourbon monarchies of France, Spain and Naples
reacted in fury. The Pope's ban, they maintained, applied as much to
themselves as it did to the duchy; Clement had effectively released all
their subjects from their duty to their sovereigns. Bernardo Tanucci,
the chief minister in Naples, went so far as to suggest depriving him
of all his worldly possessions. The French foreign minister, the Duc
de Choiseul, abandoned diplomatic language altogether:

> The Pope is a complete ninny, and his minister is a first-class fool. The
> insult is aimed not only at the Duke of Parma: it applies to the whole
> House of Bourbon. It is an act of revenge, a reprisal against those
> monarchs who have driven out the Jesuits. If this first detestable step
> is tolerated, the Roman Court, led by a man that knows no bounds,
> will stop at nothing. The dignity of the monarchs and the Family

Compact demand that we allow no prince of this House to be insulted with impunity.

The best way to resolve the crisis, he believed, was for the House of Bourbon – France, Spain and Naples – to send a joint memorandum to the Pope, expressing its astonishment that he should have addressed such a missive, as insulting as it was unjust, to the Duke of Parma. The Holy See must now formally countermand its Brief. If the Pope were to refuse, diplomatic relations with Rome would be broken off for the remainder of his pontificate. Predictably Clement did refuse, and in June 1768 a French army reoccupied Avignon and the Venaissin, together with Neapolitan Benevento, which had been a papal fief since the eleventh century.

Meanwhile there was another problem that refused to go away: what was to be done with the luckless exiles? It had been vaguely assumed that they would all be accommodated in Rome, but a special Congregation of cardinals decided, by a majority of six to two, to deny them admission. These exiles numbered in their thousands; the Society's houses had no spare capacity, or any spare funds to pay for their lodging elsewhere. An attempt was made to land some 3,000 Spanish Jesuits on the island of Corsica, but this proved disastrous. For nearly forty years the island had been in revolt against its Genoese overlords; there was fighting all over; the inhabitants had barely enough food for themselves. The new arrivals were not permitted even to disembark for well over a month, and then they were obliged to forage for themselves amid a resentful and often openly hostile peasantry. Within five months sixteen members of the Castilian Province were dead.

Then, on 15 May 1768, Corsica was purchased by France. Having expelled all Jesuits from his territory four years earlier, King Louis was certainly not going to allow them to overrun his new island. They were collected up again, embarked on French ships and dropped off at Sestri Levante, between Genoa and La Spezia, from which it was hoped that they would gradually and secretly make their way, in small parties, into the Papal States. But from the moment of their arrival on Italian soil, the attitude towards them changed. The more compassionate Italians were horrified to see these hundreds of homeless and penniless men of God, tattered and emaciated, physically and emotionally exhausted, wandering without even a definite destination in view. Clement could no longer close his doors against them. At long last they were allowed admission into papal territory, though they were forbidden to enter Rome without special permission from the Society's General.

No similar degree of pity, however, was shown by the Bourbon powers. Nothing would now satisfy them but the universal suppression of the Jesuit Order; and on Monday, 16 January 1769 the Spanish envoy in Rome handed the Pope a communication from his government. Clement took it, and dismissed the envoy with his blessing; only then did he open it – and cancelled all his audiences for the next two days. The shock and humiliation were too much for him, and he never properly recovered. He summoned a special consistory for 3 February, but the night before suffered a massive heart attack. He was dead by morning.

His had been a sad pontificate, poisoned by the implacable hatred of the House of Bourbon for the Society of Jesus, for which Clement could hardly be blamed. He was, however, unimaginative and – for a Venetian – surprisingly narrow-minded.[1] Perhaps, had he been a greater pope than he was, more self-confident and more decisive, he might have been able to defend the Society rather more effectively, but even then he would have been unlikely to make much difference. The fault was in the age; the Enlightenment approved of the Pope as little as the Pope approved of the Enlightenment. The papacy had lost its prestige, and with it much of its power. Christian Europe might pay it lip-service, but very little more.

Clement XIII died fighting to save the Jesuit Order; Clement XIV (1769–74) killed it. Lorenzo Ganganelli was a Franciscan of humble origins who in 1743 had, ironically enough, dedicated a book to the founder of the Jesuits, St Ignatius Loyola. The conclave that, after three and a half months, elected him Pope was from the very beginning dominated by the Jesuit question. It also had the distinction of being visited by Joseph II of Austria. Joseph had been Emperor since the death of his father Francis I, but exerted little real power, his mother Maria Theresa being still alive and very much in control. In answer to polite questioning, he gave it as his opinion that she was too pious to do anything to bring about the suppression of the Order; nor, however, would she do anything to oppose that suppression, and

---

[1] He continued the work of Paul V, ordering the covering or painting over of the papacy's more provocative works of art, including more of the frescoes in the Sistine Chapel.

she would on the whole be happy if it occurred. He himself felt much the same way.

It was plain from the start of the conclave that any candidate who openly favoured the Jesuits would be vetoed by one or all of the Catholic powers; on the other hand, to win the election on the strength of a previous promise to abolish them would smack of simony. Ganganelli was therefore careful to tread a middle path. He let it be known that he considered the complete suppression of the Order to be a possibility, no more. He probably had no very strong views one way or the other; but he was an ambitious man and he was determined to play the Jesuit card quietly – but only very quietly – to his advantage. On 19 May 1769, at the age of sixty-four, he was elected Pope.

Clement XIV possessed many admirable qualities. He was highly intelligent, friendly and unassuming, totally incorruptible, with a fine sense of humour. When, on 26 November 1769, he was taking part in the *possesso* – the immense procession preceding the ceremonial taking possession of the Lateran – his horse, terrified by the cheering of the vast crowd, reared up and threw him. He remarked later that he hoped that when he was on his way up to the Capitol he looked like St Peter, but hoped even more that when he fell he looked like St Paul. He was handicapped by a sad lack of political experience: he had never been out of Italy, and had never held a diplomatic post abroad. It was perhaps his consciousness of this disadvantage that sapped his confidence. In the words of an anonymous contemporary who knew him well:

> ... he lacks courage and stability; he is unbelievably slow in taking any decision. He deceives people with fine words and promises, weaves his web around them and enchants them. He begins by promising them the world, but then makes difficulties and in true Roman fashion withholds a decision ... Anyone who seeks a favour should endeavour to obtain it at his first audience.

Cardinal de Bernis, the French Ambassador to Rome, wrote:

> Clement XIV is intelligent, but his knowledge is confined to theology, church history and a few anecdotes of court life. He is a stranger to politics, and his love of secrecy is more than his mastery of it; he takes a delight in friendly intercourse and in the process he lays bare his inmost thoughts. He has a pleasant manner. He wants to please and is

in mortal fear of displeasing. In vain he arms himself with courage; timidity is the fundamental feature of his character. In his government he will show more kindness than firmness; to the church finances he will bring order and thrift. He is frugal and active, though not a quick worker. He is cheerful and he wants to be at peace with everyone and to live long.

That love of secrecy was to cause him serious difficulties with the Sacred College. His cardinals were never confided in, or even asked for their opinions. They began to complain, and when their complaints went unheeded took matters into their own hands, boycotting the great ceremonies of the Church and leaving the Pope to officiate virtually unattended. Moreover, Clement's habit of surrounding himself with men of low degree put a severe strain on his relations with the Roman nobility – to the point where, only four months after his accession, they refused to give the ceremonial attendance that was their traditional duty. A particular irritation to them was the Pope's private secretary and favourite, his fellow-Franciscan Bontempi, son of a cook in Pesaro. It was to Bontempi, far more than to the papal Secretary of State Cardinal Opizio Pallavicini, that he confided his innermost thoughts and secrets.

The Pope's instinctive wish to conciliate led him, immediately on his accession, to open up discussions with Portugal and the Bourbon powers. Portugal was easily dealt with. After ten years of severed relations, virtually every Portuguese from the King down wished heartily to end the quarrel. The only exception was Pombal; but after Clement had confirmed all his nominees in various bishoprics and offered a red hat to his brother, even the dreaded Marquis was persuaded to relent. Then, in 1770, the Pope took another major step. He discontinued the annual reading of the Bull *In coena Domini*, in which the inclusion of Parma two years before had precipitated the Bourbon ultimatum – thereby ending for ever a tradition that had continued since at least the early thirteenth century.

These gestures and others like them did something to improve relations between the two sides; but Clement was still under constant pressure, and was well aware that the breach could never be healed until the Society of Jesus was dissolved once and for all. He delayed action for as long as he could; but then in 1773 came the news that the Bourbon states were preparing for a showdown, which would almost certainly result in a complete rupture – nothing less than the secession of the most powerful Catholic states of Europe from the authority of the Holy See. Some doubts remained over Habsburg Austria, since Maria Theresa had formerly favoured the Jesuits, entrusting them with the education of her children; but in April the Empress – who had high hopes of marrying off her daughter Marie Antoinette to the French Dauphin, the future Louis XVI – wrote to Charles III of Spain confirming that, despite the high esteem in which she held the Society, she would put no obstacle in the way of its suppression if the Pope considered it expedient in the interests of Catholic unity. We have the evidence of several of those closest to her that she regretted this letter for the rest of her life; her remorse would have been greater still had she known the ultimate fate of her daughter, for whose sake she had sacrificed the Jesuit Order.

With the publication of Maria Theresa's letter, the Pope had no other cards left to play. The Bull authorising the suppression, *Dominus ac redemptor noster*, was accordingly prepared in the offices of the Curia, and was published on 16 August 1773. The following day the General of the Order, Lorenzo Ricci, was taken to the English College in Rome, from which, a month later, he was transferred to Castel Sant'Angelo. Meanwhile the contents of his wine-cellar were shared out among the cardinals. The same was true of much of the Jesuits' art collection, though the most important items found their way to the Vatican Museums.

Ricci was joined in the castle by his secretary, his five assistants (Italian, Polish, Spanish, Portuguese and German) and seven others. On the orders of their jailer, the odious Monsignor Alfani, and of the Spanish Ambassador to Rome, José Monino, they were prevented from speaking to each other and their windows were boarded up to ensure they made no effort to communicate with the outside world. In October they were forbidden to say Mass, and the sum set aside for their food was reduced by half. A prolonged and exhaustive investigation failed to prove anything against them, but their confinement continued. Despite repeated appeals to Clement and his successor, the seventy-four-year-old Ricci died in November 1775, still in the Castel Sant'Angelo – though he was to be buried in the Jesuit church of the Gesù. After his death, however, the proceedings against his colleagues were suspended. Two had predeceased him; the last were released in February 1776.

The inhuman treatment of these men, all priests, against whom no evidence of any wrongdoing was ever found, leaves a further permanent stain on the record of Clement XIV – which, it must be said, was stained enough already. He himself had nothing against the Jesuits; why, otherwise, would he have delayed his action against them for three years? He had always been aware, however, that their suppression was the price he would have to pay for the papacy, and he was fully prepared to sacrifice them. He might have argued that by then he had no choice, that the Holy See could never hope to regain the respect of Catholic Europe while the Order survived; alas, after it had gone the papacy was, if anything, even less respected than before, its international prestige lower than at any time since the Middle Ages.

The last year of the Pope's life was miserable. The painful skin disease from which he had suffered for years suddenly grew much worse; at the same time he became deeply depressed and paranoid, being in constant fear of attempts on his life – to the point where he stopped kissing the feet of his favourite crucifix because he was afraid that the Jesuits had put poison on them. In a matter of months he deteriorated dramatically, until by August, according to Centomani, the Neapolitan agent in Rome, 'he was emaciated and utterly bereft of all colour, his eye distracted, his mouth open and slobbering'. It was a relief to everyone around him, and surely to himself, when Clement died on the morning of 22 September 1774. Even then, his body decomposed so quickly there were many who thought that the Jesuits had succeeded after all.

Giovanni Angelo Braschi, who was elected in February 1775 after a four-month conclave and took the name of Pius VI (1775–99), was a genial aristocrat who had been engaged to be married before making a last-minute decision to enter the priesthood instead. His pontificate was to last very nearly twenty-five years – at the time the longest in papal history;[1] it was unfortunate indeed that for so fateful a quarter-century the Church should have fallen into such feckless hands.

Pius was neither particularly intelligent nor deeply spiritual. He was, however, tall and handsome – and he was in love with being Pope. The Grand Tour was now at its height, and he took enormous pleasure in appearing, superbly robed, at all the great ceremonies in St Peter's, giving audiences to the young *milords* who were flocking to Rome and dispensing his blessings with a graceful hand. In other ways, too, he seemed a throwback to the Renaissance. Nepotism

---

[1] But his record has been beaten three times since – by Pius IX, Leo XIII and John Paul II.

returned with a vengeance: he built Palazzo Braschi on Piazza S. Pantaleo for his nephew Luigi (the last palace to be commissioned by a pope for his own family) and hugely enriched several other relatives at the Church's expense. He spent lavishly on the arts, raised three more Egyptian obelisks in Rome and vastly extended the Museo Pio-Clementino in the Vatican. He even tried, unsuccessfully, to drain the Pontine Marshes – characteristically passing the freehold of much of the reclaimed land to his nephews.

Whereas his two predecessors had to cope primarily with the Bourbon princes, Pius found his chief enemy in the Emperor Joseph II. While his mother Maria Theresa was alive Joseph had given little trouble, but from the moment of her death in 1780 he was a changed man. The Church in Austria was, he decided, in urgent need of reform, and in matters pertaining to it he was no longer prepared to be dictated to, by either popes or their nuncios. There were, for a start, too many monasteries – more than 2,000 of them; 1,300 were promptly dissolved. As for the priesthood, it was far too blinkered in its outlook; in future all seminaries would be put under state supervision and required to give their students a proper liberal education as well as a religious one. In October 1781 the Emperor struck yet another series of blows to the papacy: a so-called Edict of Toleration effectively subjected the Church to the State, allowed freedom of worship and equal opportunities to his Protestant and Orthodox subjects, suppressed the contemplative religious Orders altogether and transferred the surviving monasteries from the jurisdiction of the Pope to that of the local bishops.

For Pius, there was only one thing to be done: he must travel personally to Vienna. He left in the early spring of 1782, arriving shortly before Easter. It was a courageous step – no pope had left Italy since the Reformation – but there seemed just a chance that with his strong personality and undoubted charm he might be able to win the Emperor round. He was disappointed. Joseph gave him an enthusiastic welcome, provided him with a palatial lodging in the Hofburg and staged several magnificent ceremonies at which the Pope's good looks and proud bearing impressed all those present; but in their long discussions he conceded nothing. (The Austrian Chancellor, Prince Kaunitz, later remarked that he had given the Pope a black eye.) Pius returned to Rome via Bavaria, at the invitation of its ruler, the Elector Charles-Theodore. There too he enjoyed a rousing reception, cheered to the echo wherever he went; no one present could have guessed that only four years later a congress held at Ems would very nearly succeed in creating a German Catholic Church virtually independent of Rome. That same year – 1786 – in Italy itself, something very similar was being planned at Pistoia with the support of the Emperor's brother, the Grand Duke Leopold of Tuscany; this time, however, Pius was able to exert his authority. He forced the resignation of the synod's moving spirit, Bishop Scipione Ricci (nephew, as it happened, of the unfortunate General of the Jesuits), and condemned all the resolutions passed at Pistoia in a Bull, *Auctorem fidei*.

The correct balance between the spiritual and the temporal power in the nations of Catholic Europe might long have continued as a major issue, to be discussed – and quite possibly fought over – for many years to come. But already in France the storm-clouds were gathering, and such questions were to be altogether forgotten in the cataclysm that was on its way. On 5 May 1789 the States-General of France were summoned to a meeting at Versailles.

France was bankrupt: bankrupt because of the exorbitant tax demands of her monarchy and the unbridled power of her aristocracy. In the early days of the Revolution, the Church was not blamed; neither Louis XIV nor Louis XV had been easy friends of the papacy, but France had remained fundamentally Roman Catholic. The last Protestant pastor to be martyred had died in prison in 1771, the last Protestant galley-slaves freed as recently as 1775. The chief minister was the Cardinal Archbishop of Toulouse, Etienne Loménie de Brienne.[1] But the yawning gulf that existed between aristocracy and Third Estate – the people – was reflected in that between the noble bishops and the poverty-stricken majority of the parish clergy, who struggled to keep body and soul together; and as the great wave of the Revolution gathered force, the Church was inevitably engulfed. It was another agnostic prelate, Charles-Maurice de Talleyrand-Périgord, Bishop of Autun, who proposed, on 2 November 1789, that Church property should be put 'at the disposal of the nation'. Three months later all religious Orders were suppressed.

At this stage the pastoral structure of the Church remained

---

[1] 'He was not in fact a Christian. Like many other fashionable clergy, he shared Voltaire's sardonic rejection of revealed religion, and when it had been proposed to promote him to Paris, Louis XVI had refused, on the ground that the Archbishop of Paris "must at least believe in God"'. For this quotation and much of the paragraph I am indebted to E. Duffy, *Saints and Sinners*, pp.199–200.

Pope Pius II (1458–64) at Ancona, awaiting the arrival of the Princes of Europe for a crusade.
Pinturicchio, Piccolomini Library, Siena Cathedral.

Pope Leo X (de' Medici, 1513–21) and his nephews. Painted by Raphael in 1518, soon after Leo had appointed him architect of the new St Peter's. Galleria degli Uffizi, Florence.

Pope Clement VII (de' Medici, 1523–34). It was he who refused to allow the annulment of Henry VIII's first marriage, and endured the Sack of Rome, 1527. Sebastiano del Piombo, Museo di Capodimonte, Naples.

Pope Paul III (Farnese, 1534–49). Father of four illegitimate children before his election. One of two portraits by Titian, Museo di Capodimonte, Naples.

Pope Paul V (Borghese, 1605–21).
An arch-reactionary, he first took issue with
Galileo for his espousal of Copernicus's
theory that the sun, rather than the earth, was
the centre of the universe. Gianlorenzo Bernini,
Statens Museum for Kunst, Copenhagen.

Pope Innocent X (Pamphilj,
1644–55). Dominated through
most of his reign by his reputed
mistress, the sinister and corrupt
Olimpia Maidalchini. Velázquez,
Galleria Doria Pamphilj, Rome.

Pope Pius VII (Chiaramonti,
1800–23). Obliged to deal as
best he could with Napoleon,
who treated him abominably.
Jacques-Louis David,
Musée du Louvre, Paris.

2 December 1804. The Emperor Napoleon crowns himself and the Empress Josephine in Notre-Dame, watched by Pope Pius VII on right, seated. Jacques-Louis David, Musée du Louvre, Paris.

Pope Pius IX (1846–78) and
King Victor Emmanuel II.
Popular print.

Pope Leo XIII (1878–1903).
Mass-produced popular print,
Museo del Risorgimento, Milan.

Pope Pius XII (1939–58) at his coronation in 1939, seated on the Sedia Gestatoria.

Pope John Paul I (1978): his first blessing from the balcony overlooking St Peter's Square.

Pope John Paul II (1978–2005), obliged to use his 'Popemobile'
after an attempt on his life in 1981.

untouched; but the following July saw the passing by the Assembly of the Civil Constitution of the Clergy, which was revolutionary indeed. Fifty-two episcopal sees were abolished; henceforth each *département* would have its own bishop, designated a 'public official' and subject to the authority of an elected diocesan council. The clergy were henceforth to be elected by the laity, Catholic or not, and known as citizen-priests, *curés-citoyens*. All of this was proposed, it need hardly be said, without any reference to the Pope – who, it was plain, would be expected to accept the Constitution in its entirety. If he did not, there was a strong possibility that France would once again annex Avignon (where the revolutionary party had already declared the annexation as a fait accompli) and the Comtat Venaissin.

When in 1789 the Assembly had unilaterally abolished the annual payment of St Peter's Pence for the maintenance of the Holy See, Pope Pius had made no objection. In the absence, therefore, of any word from Rome, on 22 July Louis XVI gave his preliminary sanction – though with many misgivings – to the Civil Constitution. It was unfortunate that on the very next day he received a private letter from the Pope, written on the 10th, to the effect that the Constitution 'would lead the entire nation into error, the kingdom into schism, and perhaps be the cause of a cruel civil war'. The King suppressed the letter, and entered into rather desperate negotiations with Pius in the hope that some compromise might be reached – although, given the present mood of the Assembly, there was no indication that they would be prepared to take any papal demands, or even opinions, into account.

The French clergy, who knew nothing of the Pope's letter and most of whom hated the Constitution, longed for guidance in the shape of a public pronouncement from Rome; but they were disappointed. Pius was prepared to write privately to King Louis, but he could never give the new legislation his blessing, and if he were to speak openly against it he risked driving the whole country into schism, as had happened in England two centuries before. So he remained silent, and the clergy were still without instructions when, on 27 November, the Assembly directed that all men of the Church should swear an oath of obedience to the Constitution. About half the parish priests did so, but only seven bishops (including, of course, Talleyrand). Those who refused were removed from their posts, but remained theoretically free to worship as they liked. As time went on, however, and the Revolution grew in force and intensity, they came to be considered traitors; many were deported.

It was the imposition of the oath that finally induced Pius to break his silence. In March 1791 and again in April he denounced the Constitution as schismatical, declared the ordinations of the new state bishops to be sacrilegious and suspended all prelates and priests who had taken the oath. The Church in France was now split down the middle. Diplomatic relations were broken off, Avignon and the Venaissin annexed yet again. Finally, on 10 August 1792, the monarchy was abolished – and the bloodletting began. In Lyons a campaign of mass executions accounted for well over a hundred priests and nuns; further massacres took place in Paris, Orleans and several other cities. No fewer than eight bishops were to die on the scaffold. Loménie de Brienne would almost certainly have been among them, had he not cheated the guillotine by poisoning himself in prison. On 21 January 1793 the King of France followed hundreds of his subjects to the scaffold. Nine months later his Queen suffered the same fate.

By now the persecutions were no longer confined to refractory priests; they were directed against Christianity itself. Some 20,000 left holy orders altogether. Churches were locked, or converted into 'temples of reason', or rededicated to any one of a number of bogus religions, such as 'Fertility' or Robespierre's 'Supreme Being'. The public practice of the Christian religion almost ceased; by the spring of 1794, only about 150 of the pre-revolutionary parishes were still celebrating Mass. The situation improved to some extent after the fall of Robespierre in July of that year, but three years later the violence was renewed and the persecutions became worse than ever.

From Rome, Pope Pius followed these events with horror. The old Europe that he had known on his accession in 1775 had been transformed. The Bourbons were gone from France. They still ruled in Spain, but Charles IV – who had succeeded his father Charles III in 1788 – was a virtual cipher who thought only of hunting. In Austria, Joseph II had died in 1790 and his brother, Leopold II, two years later; the imperial throne was now occupied by Leopold's son Francis II, and Joseph's ideas of Church reform were long forgotten. Meanwhile Austria was heading the great European coalition against France. Pius was reluctant to join it, firstly because of the old tradition of neutrality in wars between Catholic nations, and secondly because he had no wish to give France an excuse to invade the Papal States; but it was only natural that, from the sidelines, the Holy See should give it all possible support.

What neither the Pope or anyone else could have foreseen was that

Europe was about to undergo yet another transformation, more radical and more dramatic than any since the days of the Roman Empire. Napoleon Bonaparte was on his way.

When the French Directory was established in October 1795, Bonaparte had been appointed second-in-command of the Army of the Interior; and five months later, when it resolved to launch a new campaign against Austria through Italy, the still slim, solemn young Corsican, bilingual in Italian, seemed the obvious choice to lead it. No one – except possibly himself – could have foreseen the measure and speed of his success. Towards the end of April 1796 Piedmont was annexed to France, King Charles Emmanuel IV abdicating and retiring to his other kingdom of Sardinia. On 8 May the French crossed the Po, and on the 15th Bonaparte made his formal entry into Milan, where he established a republic. His orders were to annihilate the papacy, 'the centre of fanaticism', but there was still an Austrian army in Lombardy and he was reluctant to press too far to the south. Instead he took over the Legations (so called because they were ruled by a Papal Legate) of Ravenna, Bologna and Ferrara, and concluded an armistice with the Pope on terms hugely favourable to himself. By these terms he would retain the Legations, place a garrison in Ancona and enjoy free access to all papal ports. He also demanded an indemnity of 21 million scudi, and the choice of 500 ancient manuscripts and 100 works of art from the papal collections. On his side the Pope undertook to urge all French Catholics to accept and observe their country's religious laws. In February 1797 these terms were confirmed by the Treaty of Tolentino, which also provided for the permanent surrender to France of Avignon and the Venaissin, an additional vast indemnity and many more works of art. Three months later, the French army moved against Venice.

Meanwhile Napoleon's elder brother Joseph was sent to Rome as Ambassador, together with his prospective brother-in-law, General Léonard Duphot. The two had instructions to make all the trouble they could and so prepare the way for the overthrow of the papacy and its replacement by a Roman Republic. On 22 December 1797 they engineered an armed demonstration against the Pope – in the course of which, however, Duphot was shot by a papal corporal. Joseph, deaf to the Curia's explanations, reported to the Directory that one of his country's most brilliant young generals had been murdered by the priests. As a result, General Louis Berthier was ordered to march on Rome. He met with no opposition and on 10 February 1798 occupied the city. Five days later the new republic was proclaimed in the Forum. Pius, who was now eighty, was treated abominably – the Fisherman's Ring was forcibly torn from his finger – and was carried off to Siena, the crowds kneeling in the rain to watch him pass.

In May Siena was shaken by a series of earthquakes, and the miserable Pope was transferred to a Carthusian monastery outside Florence. By this time he was so weak that the doctors feared for his life, and positively refused when the Directory ordered that he should be sent to Sardinia. But still he was not allowed to rest. The following March, when French troops occupied Florence and abolished the Grand Duchy, he was moved again, this time to France. Now virtually paralysed, he was carried in a litter over the freezing Alpine passes to Briançon and finally to Valence where, on 29 August 1799, his long martyrdom came to an end.

For Pius VI was indeed a martyr. Few popes in history had been made to suffer so much, and so unnecessarily. And the courage and fortitude with which he bore his tribulations did much to redeem his reputation – because he had, after all, much to answer for. It is unlikely that he could have saved the Catholic Church in France from the insensate fury of the Revolution. The fact remains, however, that when called upon to give a lead he failed to do so; instead he dithered – and French Christianity very nearly died.

CHAPTER XXIV

Progress and Reaction

(1799–1846)

The French did not stay long in Italy. Napoleon had set off on his expedition to Egypt, from which he had slipped stealthily away in August 1799 – just a week before the death of Pius VI – back to Paris; Joseph Bonaparte had proved incapable of holding Rome, anti-French and pro-papal risings by the *Sanfedisti* – 'those of the Holy Faith' – had broken out all over the peninsula, and the French army had beaten a hasty retreat. It had, however, immediately been replaced by another army of occupation, Neapolitan this time, and there was a general feeling among the cardinals that the forthcoming conclave should be held in some city other than Rome, one that promised to be safer and generally more tranquil. They chose Venice.

The Most Serene Republic was dead. Napoleon had put an end to it in May 1797. A 'Tree of Liberty' had been erected in St Mark's Square, surmounted by the symbolic scarlet Phrygian cap that bore more than a passing resemblance to the Doge's *corno*. The *corno* itself, together with other symbols of the ducal dignity and a copy of the Golden Book in which the names of all the noble families of the Republic were inscribed, had been publicly burned beneath it. But Napoleon had held Venice for just five months; in October, by the Treaty of Campo Formio, he had handed it over to Austria. It was therefore under Austrian auspices that the conclave was held, with the Emperor Francis even offering to pay its expenses.

The selected meeting place was the island monastery of S. Giorgio Maggiore; and it was there, in November 1799, that the conclave assembled. From the outset it was clear that its task was not going to be easy. Austria wanted above all a pope who would uphold the monarchist counter-revolution, and who would not interfere with her increasingly ambitious plans for northern Italy; she was anxious in particular to assert her permanent possession of the Legations – Ravenna, Bologna and Ferrara – which Pius VI had been obliged to cede to Napoleon at Tolentino. The Sacred College held no brief for the Revolution, but most of the cardinals felt a good deal more strongly about the Legations, which they held to be an integral part of the territory of the Papal State. Only after fourteen weeks of argument was the stalemate eventually broken, with the election of Barnaba Chiaramonti, Bishop of Imola, as Pope Pius VII (1800–23).

The Emperor Francis was, to say the least, displeased. The new Pope, though gentle, mild-mannered and deeply pious, was known to have preached in 1797 a Christmas sermon that welcomed democracy (in the revolutionary sense) as a Christian virtue; moreover, being himself a native of the Papal State, he could hardly be expected to look kindly on an Austrian annexation of the Legations. With reluctance the Emperor invited him to Vienna for talks; the Pope declined, and Francis somewhat pettishly refused him the use of St Mark's for his coronation. This consequently had to be held in S. Giorgio, a small island site where conditions were cramped and no ceremonial procession was possible. And now there came a still more ominous sign of imperial displeasure: fearful of pro-papal demonstrations in the Legations, Francis ordered that Pius must return to Rome by sea. The vessel put at his disposal proved to be barely seaworthy and totally without cooking facilities; the journey took twelve nightmare days.

When the Pope finally reached Rome in July 1800 he found the political situation once again transformed. Napoleon Bonaparte, now First Consul and de facto ruler of France, had smashed the Austrians at Marengo and was once again master of northern Italy. Would Pius follow the same path as his predecessor, to deposition and exile? It seemed more than likely. But Napoleon was a lot more intelligent than the members of the Directory had been – intelligent enough to see that the French people were sick and tired of the excesses and extremes of the Revolution: that the reaction had set in, and that they wished to return to their old faith. One of his first actions on achieving supreme power had been to order full funeral honours for Pius VI, whose body was lying, still unburied, at Valence.[1] On 5 June 1800 he had addressed the clergy of Milan:

> I am convinced that the Catholic religion is the only one capable of making a stable community happy, and of establishing the foundations of good government. I undertake always to defend it ... I intend that [it] should be practised publicly and in all its fullness ... France has

---

[1] It was brought back to Rome in 1802, and was buried at St Peter's.

had her eyes opened through suffering, and has seen that the Catholic religion is her single anchor amid the storm.

The first communication from Napoleon to be received by Pius VII, therefore, was a good deal friendlier than the Pope had expected. It informed him that the First Consul would welcome proposals for a new concordat, even going so far as to suggest that if agreement could be reached, the papacy might recover at least some of its lost possessions. But the ensuing negotiations were long and hard. One of the thorniest problems was that of the appointment of bishops. At this moment in her history France had two competing hierarchies, the old pre-revolutionary one and that which had been established by the Civil Constitution. Each had its own bishops, among whom no reconciliation was possible. Napoleon's solution was to abolish the lot, and to nominate a new set himself without consultation with the Pope – a proposal that left the Sacred College horrified. Another headache was caused by the question of clerical celibacy. During the Revolution priests had been permitted (indeed, encouraged) to marry, and many of them had done so. An additional complication here was Talleyrand, who was now Foreign Minister of France; a former Bishop of Autun, he had married a lady who was not only English, but a Protestant to boot. He was understandably determined that no action should be taken against married priests.

But it was not only the French who made the difficulties. For many of the cardinals, Napoleon continued to represent the Revolution, that same Revolution that had persecuted the Church, stolen its property, massacred its priests, abducted its Pope and deprived it of its secular power – which included its schools, hospitals and care for the poor. Let Napoleon throw his tantrums; let him threaten schism on the English pattern or even turn Calvinist and take Europe with him; were not even these things preferable to an accommodation with Antichrist? In May 1801 the talks were on the point of breaking down altogether, and the French troops in Florence were preparing to march on Rome. Only a frantic rush from Paris to Rome by the papal Secretary of State, Cardinal Consalvi, saved the day – and the long-awaited concordat was finally signed on 15 July. Even then the difficulties were not over: hardly was the ratification complete and the necessary legislation under way when Napoleon unilaterally published his seventy-seven 'Organic Articles', tightening the grip of the State and further restricting papal intervention. The Legations remained in French hands, as did Avignon and the Venaissin. There was no restoration of Church property. The two sides were still arguing when, in May 1804, Napoleon had himself proclaimed Emperor of the French. Shortly afterwards the Pope was invited to Paris for the imperial coronation.

This put Pius in a quandary. The monarchies of Europe had been shocked by the concordat, which they saw as an act of capitulation. If the Pope were now to attend – let alone perform – the coronation of this Corsican adventurer, the reputation of the papacy would sink lower still. As for the Emperor Francis, who had defended the Church throughout the Revolution, how would he react to the spectacle of a pope crowning an upstart rival, devoid alike of birth and breeding? At the same time, Pius knew that he could not refuse. Telling himself that the very act of laying the crown on Napoleon's head must at least increase his prestige, he set off, escorted by six cardinals, across the Alps.

On his arrival in Paris he found an unexpected opportunity to assert his authority: Josephine confessed to him that she and Napoleon had never gone through a wedding ceremony in church, and the Pope refused point-blank to attend the coronation until they had done so. A secret marriage service, without witnesses, had to be performed by Napoleon's uncle, Cardinal Fesch, the afternoon before the coronation, much to the bridegroom's disgust. But the Emperor had his revenge. On the day of the coronation, 2 December 1804, in Notre-Dame, he first kept the Pope waiting for a full hour and then personally performed the actual crowning – first of himself and then of Josephine. Pius was allowed to bless the two crowns, but that was all: for the rest, he was relegated to the role of a simple spectator. In Jacques-Louis David's great painting of the occasion his displeasure can clearly be seen on his face.

The Pope remained in France for the next four months. Despite repeated efforts, he failed to achieve any of his main objectives: the 'Organic Articles' remained in force. On the other hand, he enjoyed huge personal success. Whenever he appeared in public – which he did as often as possible – he was greeted by cheering crowds, all surging forward to receive his blessing. The pendulum had swung a long way since the Revolution; France was on the threshold of a dramatic Catholic reaction, and the presence of the Pope was exactly what it needed. When the time at last came for Pius to return to Rome, more crowds lined his route; it was a very different journey from that which had followed his election in Venice only five years before.

*   *   *

One year to the day after the Emperor's coronation, his army of 68,000 triumphed over a combined force of 90,000 Austrians and Russians at Austerlitz in Moravia. On the day after Christmas 1805, by the terms of a treaty signed at Pressburg (now Bratislava), Austria was obliged to return to France all the Venetian territories she had acquired in 1797 at Campo Formio – to constitute, together with the coasts of Istria and Dalmatia, the new Napoleonic Kingdom of Italy. But for Napoleon this was only the beginning: he was determined to take over the entire peninsula. He had already annexed, without warning and to the Pope's furious indignation, the papal port of Ancona; now a French army of 40,000 men under Marshal André Masséna marched through the Papal States into southern Italy, with Joseph Bonaparte as the Emperor's personal representative. When Pius registered a some-what nervous protest, Napoleon put him firmly in his place: 'Your Holiness will show the same respect for me in the temporal sphere as I bear towards him in the spiritual . . . Your Holiness is the Sovereign of Rome, but I am its Emperor.'

On 11 February 1806 King Ferdinand and Queen Maria Carolina of Naples – she was the sister of Marie Antoinette – fled to face the winter miseries of Palermo; and on the 14th, in drenching rain, a French division entered Naples. There was virtually no resistance. The Neapoli-tans looked on in silence when on the following day Joseph staged his own procession and took up residence in the royal palace. Later that year, by imperial decree, he was proclaimed King. The Holy See was now surrounded by French-controlled territory, and henceforth rela-tions between France and the papacy suffered a steady deterioration – leading in January 1808 to another French occupation of Rome itself, with the Pope a prisoner in the Quirinal and under immense pressure to abdicate all his temporal power. He continued to refuse, and on 10 June 1809 Rome was declared a 'free imperial city' while the tricolour replaced the papal flag on the Castel Sant'Angelo. Three weeks later French patience gave out altogether: a body of French soldiers climbed the walls of the Quirinal with scaling ladders and burst into the papal study, where Pius was in conference with his secretary, Cardinal Pacca. Still fully robed, the two were seized and bundled into a coach and driven north. Pacca was held in Florence, but the Pope was rushed with all possible secrecy over the Alps to Grenoble.

When Napoleon was informed of the abduction he flew into a rage. His men had acted irresponsibly and without orders; he would have infinitely preferred to leave Pius at the Quirinal where he belonged.

On the other hand, to send him straight back to Rome would make the Emperor look foolish. Finally he decided to send the unfortunate pontiff to the bishop's palace at Savona, on the Italian Riviera. Here, though treated with every consideration where his physical comfort was concerned, he remained a prisoner – totally cut off from the outside world, with paper and ink alike forbidden. Rome meanwhile had become a dead city, the entire papal establishment having been virtually liquidated: the cardinals, the heads of the religious Orders, the archives and seals of authority had all been removed to Paris.

By now, however, the Emperor had two new problems on his hands. Josephine had failed to provide him with a son and heir and was now, at forty-six, obviously too old to do so. His only hope lay in remarriage; but for that he needed a divorce – which Pius, he knew, would never grant. Fortunately his first marriage had been undertaken only under pressure and without witnesses; in the circumstances, the ecclesiastical courts in Paris saw no obstacle to annulment. In April 1810 Napoleon married Marie Louise, daughter of the Emperor Francis I of Austria[1] – though thirteen cardinals who remained loyal to the Pope refused to attend the ceremony.

The second problem was Pius's continued refusal to confirm any bishops nominated by Napoleon. By 1810 there were twenty-seven sees without prelates in France alone, and countless more in French-occupied Europe. Napoleon hoped to persuade the council of existing bishops to override the Pope, but the council – even though led by Cardinal Fesch, his own uncle – would not hear of it. Pius himself knew nothing of all this until, on 9 June 1812, he was snatched away from Savona and brought forcibly to France. The journey (most of which, for reasons of speed and secrecy, was effected in the hours of darkness) proved a further nightmare, every bit as bad as that endured by his predecessor: by this time, too, he was suffering from a serious urinary infection, which obliged him to stop the coach every ten minutes. The poor man was on the point of death when, after twelve hideous days, he arrived at Fontainebleau – only to be informed that the Emperor had just departed on his Russian campaign.

Napoleon remained in Russia only about six months. In December, learning of an attempted *coup d'état* in Paris, he abandoned his army

---

[1] Formerly Francis II of the Holy Roman Empire. This, however, had been dissolved after Austerlitz. In 1804 he had founded the new Empire of Austria, of which he was now the Emperor Francis I. He was thus named *Doppelkaiser* ('double Emperor') – the only one in history.

– just as he had in Egypt – and took a sleigh back to the west. He arrived back at Fontainebleau in mid-January 1813. By this time the Pope had made a partial recovery; but, remaining as he did in poor health and entirely alone, without a single cardinal to support him against the furious bullying by the Emperor that now began, it was hardly surprising that he finally capitulated, signing on a scrap of paper a draft basis for a formal concordat whereby he would be shorn of all his temporal power. No longer would he rule in Rome; the seat of the papacy was now to be transferred to France. New bishops would be invested by their metropolitans if the Pope failed to approve their appointments within six months.

It was still only a scribbled draft; but Napoleon instantly proclaimed the concordat a fait accompli. Now at last the cardinals Pacca and Consalvi, both horrified by the news, were allowed to join their master. They found him a broken man, his head buried in his hands, appalled by what he had done and by the way the Emperor had first tormented and then tricked him. Slowly the two cardinals managed to breathe new life and hope into him, until eventually he wrote to Napoleon in his own hand, repudiating the 'concordat' on the grounds that he had signed only a draft – and that under severe duress. Napoleon predictably suppressed the letter, but by now he had other, more important things to think about. After his defeat at Leipzig in October his empire had begun to crumble; by January 1814 he was writing to the Pope withdrawing the concordat unconditionally. His Holiness was free to return to Rome at his convenience. Pius left first for Savona, then in March travelled on to the Holy City. Arriving on the 24th, he was given a rapturous welcome; his carriage horses were unharnessed from the shafts and he was drawn in triumph to St Peter's by thirty young scions of the greatest families in Rome.

On 1 November 1814, with Napoleon exiled to Elba, the Congress of Vienna met to redraw the map of Europe. The papal representative was Cardinal Consalvi, whose superb diplomatic skills succeeded in recovering almost all the former papal territories with the exception of Avignon and the Venaissin – for which by now there was little real justification anyway. The Legations and the Marches of Ancona, however (which in 1798–9 had formed part of the Cisalpine and Roman Republics and in 1808–9 of Napoleon's Kingdom of Italy) were returned once more to the Holy See.

But it was not only Europe that needed reconstruction; it was also the Church. The Holy Roman Empire, which had begun with Charlemagne just over a thousand years before, had been abolished in 1806; the great prince-bishoprics of Germany were gone. The religious Orders had been largely suppressed. All over the continent episcopal sees were vacant, seminaries closed down, Church property taken over; and in all those lands that had been subject to the revolutionary law of France, divorce, civil marriage and freedom of religion were now deeply rooted and would be hard indeed to abolish. As a first step in what would clearly prove a Herculean task, on 7 August 1814 Pius VII revived the Society of Jesus.

The Pope was now seventy-two, and respected in Europe more than he had ever been. The cruelties and excesses of the Revolution and the megalomaniac ambitions of Napoleon had brought about a vigorous spirit of reaction of which the Church, which had endured persecution from the one and consistently harsh treatment from the other, had emerged as the leading symbol; and Pius, whose pontificate had been one of the most troubled in all history and whose own personal sufferings had been acute, was now seen as the personification of resistance, which had ultimately led to the destruction of both. No longer was the Pope looked upon – as he had been in the previous century – as a fairly insignificant anachronism; he was once again back on the map of Europe, recognised by the Catholic princes as a temporal ruler as well as the supreme spiritual authority. This consequently put him in a substantially stronger position as a negotiator; and during the nine years remaining of his pontificate he was able to conclude more than twenty different concordats with foreign states – including Orthodox Russia in 1818 and Protestant Prussia in 1821 – setting out the terms and conditions under which the work of the Church could be done in each. In most countries he lost the right to appoint bishops (one of the great points at issue between Church and State throughout history) but monasteries and seminaries reopened, and schools were once more subjected to religious authority. Not all the changes were for the best: there were cases where democracy was suppressed, or the censorship of books reimposed. In Spain the hopelessly reactionary Ferdinand VII even reintroduced the Inquisition. But Pius himself did his utmost to adapt the papacy to the modern world, and when he died on 20 July 1823 – of the aftereffects of a broken femur – the prospects for the papacy looked brighter than they had for half a century.

* * *

In fact, appearances proved deceptive. Cardinal Consalvi, the Pope's devoted Secretary of State and the guiding spirit behind many of his reforms, died six months after his master; and the way was now clear for the *Zelanti* – the more reactionary cardinals, who hated those reforms and looked for a conservative regime dictated by spirituality rather than pragmatism – to select one of their own. Their choice fell on the sixty-three-year-old Cardinal Annibale Sermattei della Genga, who had spent much of his career in the papal diplomatic service until he was dismissed by Consalvi after disastrously bungling the negotiations for the return of Avignon. He took the name of Leo XII (1823–9). Pious but narrow-minded, in constant pain from piles, he represented a throwback to the most blinkered days of the eighteenth century, condemning toleration, reinforcing censorship and the Index, restricting Jews once again to ghettos and in Rome obliging 300 of them to attend a weekly Christian sermon. In the Papal States the old aristocracy was re-established, the old ecclesiastical courts reintroduced. Education was strictly controlled, morality enforced by a thousand pettifogging regulations. The playing of games on Sundays or feast days was punishable with a prison sentence. The free sale of alcohol was forbidden. The enlightened modern state that Consalvi had been so carefully building up was replaced by a police regime of spies and informers, of the kind all too accurately depicted in Puccini's *Tosca*.

During the first months after his accession there were fears both in Rome and abroad that Leo would reverse all the conciliatory policies of Pius VII. Fortunately they were unfounded. Bigoted the Pope might be; but he well understood the advantages of good relations with the European powers. Indeed, it was thanks to his intervention with the Ottoman Sultan Mahmud II that the Armenian Catholics were at last emancipated in 1830. But by then the Pope was dead. His five-and-a-half-year pontificate had been a near-disaster. He had undoubtedly meant well, but his lack of any understanding of the modern world made him a detested figure in Rome and undid much of the splendid work of his predecessor.

Since Francesco Saverio Castiglione, who succeeded him in March 1829 as Pope Pius VIII (1829–30), was to reign for only twenty months, he might have been seen as a stopgap. He was in fact a good deal more. A brave man of high principle, he had served an eight-year prison sentence for refusing to swear allegiance to Napoleon. Pius VII (whose name he had deliberately adopted) had greatly admired him and had hoped that he might be chosen as his successor; and the new Pope's declared aim was to continue in the great man's footsteps. He could not altogether abolish Leo's police state, but he drew its teeth and made life for the average Roman infinitely more bearable that it had been; and when in July 1830 France deposed her morbidly pious and hugely unpopular Charles X, the Pope was not slow in recognising Louis-Philippe as King of the French and bestowing upon him the traditional title of 'Most Christian King'.

Four months later, however, Pius was dead. His successor – elected after sixty-four days and eighty-three ballots – was a former Camaldolese[1] monk from the monastery of S. Michele on the island of Murano in the Venetian lagoon. His name was Bartolomeo Alberto Cappellari, and he took the name of Pope Gregory XVI (1831–46). Just as Pius VIII had continued the work of Pius VII, so – alas – was Gregory XVI to follow in the footsteps of Leo XII. Like Leo, he was the creature of the *Zelanti*; he also had the backing of the Austrian Chancellor, Prince Metternich, who had set his heart on an absolutist pope who would not surrender to what he described as 'the political madness of the age'. The Prince certainly got what he wanted.

Gregory succeeded to the papacy in a moment of crisis. Since the fall of Bonaparte, a wave of radical discontent had been steadily gathering force the length and breadth of the Italian peninsula, deriving much of its strength from a vast semi-secret society known as the 'charcoal-burners', or *Carbonari*. Their principal ideals were, first, political liberty; second, the unification of Italy. And – although few of them were yet aware of the fact – there was another group still in the process of formation for whom a united Italy was to be the only goal. This group was called *La giovane Italia* ('Young Italy') and was founded in 1831 by an exile in Marseilles, a young man of twenty-six named Giuseppe Mazzini.

In 1830 rebellion broke out in the Papal States, several of the cities falling into rebel hands. Gregory had to move swiftly. Terrified that the unrest might spread, he appealed to the Austrian Emperor to send troops to defend Rome. Francis did not need to be asked twice. His firm action quickly restored order in the Papal States, but solved none of the fundamental problems that underlay the uprising; and with the immediate danger averted, the Pope settled down to a policy of grim

---

[1] The Camaldolese were a strict and austere branch of the Benedictines, who lived only part of their life in the monastery, spending the rest of it as hermits.

repression. He openly condemned the very idea of freedom of conscience or of the press, or the separation of Church and State. On those who upheld these ideals he clamped down mercilessly, by means of a police regime even more severe than that of Leo before him. Before long the papal prisons were overflowing, the papal exchequer emptied by the cost of spies and informers.

Gregory's mind was totally closed to progress, or indeed to any innovation. It was typical of him, for example, that he should have banned the new railways – which he called *chemins d'enfer* – from all papal territories. Less than four months after his accession the great powers came together to demand radical reforms in the Papal States. The Pope refused; civil disorder broke out once again; the Austrian troops were recalled and Louis-Philippe – in a remarkable display of ingratitude – seized Ancona. For the next seven years the Papal States lay under foreign military occupation.

But Gregory's worst failure was in Poland. By the terms of the Third Partition in 1795, Poland as a state had ceased to exist, its territory split between Russia, Prussia and Austria; and ever since his accession in 1825 Tsar Nicholas I had been making life as difficult as he could for the Catholics – and the Poles were virtually all Catholics – under his rule. Upon the Uniates (those who, while accepting papal supremacy, followed the Eastern rite) he put heavy pressure to join the Russian Orthodox Church, while those bishops (the vast majority) who followed the Latin rite found that communications with Rome had been made well-nigh impossible. Resentment of the Russians grew steadily, until in November 1830 the Poles rose against them. Everything that could go wrong did so; yet somehow they managed to establish a provisional government, and when in February 1831 a force of 115,000 Russian troops marched on Warsaw, the Poles fought back. A great wave of pro-Polish feeling now swept across Europe, and from all over the continent men hastened to join the Polish colours, including hundreds of officers from Napoleon's *Grande Armée*. Other contingents came from Germany, Italy, Hungary and Britain. In France, Louis-Philippe made sonorous speeches suggesting military support, and James Fenimore Cooper started a Polish-American Committee.

Alas, their efforts were in vain. On 8 September Warsaw was forced to capitulate. Tsar Nicholas took hideous vengeance. The leaders of the revolt were beheaded, 350 sentenced to hang, 10,000 officers sent off to hard labour. More than 3,000 families had their estates confiscated. In the countryside, whole villages were burned:

> The accent was on humiliating the proud, degrading the noble, removing the vertebrae. Prince Roman Sanguszko, who was of Rurik's blood and might have qualified for some respect in Russia, was sentenced to hard labour for life in Siberia and made to walk there chained to a gang of convicts. When his wife, a friend and former lady-in-waiting to the Empress, fell at the feet of Nicholas and begged for mercy, she was told she could go too. She did.[1]

At some stage it might have been expected that Gregory XVI would utter a word or two of support for his Catholic flock; he did nothing of the kind. Instead, in June 1832, he published a Brief in which he categorically condemned the insurrection and denounced 'those who, under cover of religion, have set themselves against the legitimate power of princes'. Two months later, in his encyclical *Mirari Vos*, he went still further, referring to 'that absurd and erroneous doctrine, or rather delirium, that freedom of conscience is to be claimed and defended for all men'. As for any ideas for the regeneration of the Church:

> it has been instructed by Jesus Christ and his Apostles and taught by the Holy Spirit ... It would therefore be completely absurd and supremely insulting to suggest that the Church stands in need of restoration and regeneration ... as though she could be exposed to exhaustion, degradation or other defects of this kind.

Mirari Vos was primarily directed against the priest Félicité-Robert de Lamennais, editor of the newspaper *L'Avenir* – which carried the words '*Dieu et Liberté*' as its masthead – and spokesman of the French liberal clergy. Lamennais maintained that the Church must ally itself with the people rather than their oppressors: with the Catholic Poles against Tsar Nicholas; with the Catholic Belgians against the Dutch Protestant William I; with the Catholic Irish against Protestant Westminster. But, as the encyclical made all too clear, Pope Gregory would have none of it; and by his refusal – perhaps his inability – to accept progressive ideas he cut off both himself and the papacy from modern political thought. Lamennais later denounced Rome as 'the most

---

[1] A. Zamoyski, *The Polish Way*, p.275.

hideous cloaca that has ever soiled the human eye'. He was going, arguably, a little too far; but few things in the world are more infuriating than blinkered bigotry on the scale then demonstrated by the Roman papacy, and it is hard not to feel some sympathy for him.

Gregory's record was not wholly disastrous. He reorganised all foreign missions, bringing them more firmly under papal control. He established some seventy new dioceses across the world, and nearly 200 missionary bishops. He denounced slavery and the slave trade. He founded the Christian Museum in the Lateran, and the Etruscan and Egyptian Museums in the Vatican. But he brought sad discredit on the Church; and when on 1 June 1846 he died after a short illness, there were few indeed to mourn him.

CHAPTER XXV

Pio Nono

(1846–78)

Each day the Pope shows himself more lacking in any practical sense. Born and brought up in a *liberal* family, he has been formed in a bad school; a good priest, he has never turned his mind towards matters of government. Warm of heart and weak of intellect, he has allowed himself to be taken and ensnared, since assuming the tiara, in a net from which he no longer knows how to disentangle himself, and if matters follow their natural course, he will be driven out of Rome.

Those prophetic words were written by the Austrian State Chancellor, Prince Metternich, in October 1847 to his ambassador in Paris. Their subject was Giovanni Maria Mastai-Ferretti, who in the previous year, at the age of only fifty-four and after a forty-eight-hour conclave, had been elected Pope Pius IX (1846–78). He was as unlike his predecessor as it was possible to be: indeed, he was known to have been openly critical of Gregory's rule in the Papal States, just as he was of the Austrian presence in Italy. Gregory had made him a cardinal, but had never trusted him: even Ferretti's cats, he maintained, were liberals.

The reaction of the cats to Pius's election is not known; but by the liberals of Italy, and indeed all western Europe, the news had been greeted with excitement and delight. The new pontiff, it seemed, was one of themselves. In his first month of office he amnestied more than a thousand political prisoners and exiles.[1] A few weeks later he was giving garden parties – for both sexes – at the Quirinal. Meanwhile he actively encouraged plans for the railways that his predecessor had so detested, and for gas lighting in the streets of Rome.

---

[1] 'God doesn't grant amnesties,' growled Metternich; 'God pardons.'

He established a free (or very nearly free) press. He made a start on tariff reform, introduced laymen into the papal government and abolished Leo XII's grotesque law that obliged Jews to listen to a Christian lecture once a week. Mobbed wherever he went, he was the most popular man in Italy.

But his reputation carried its own dangers. Every political demonstration, from the mildest to the most revolutionary, now claimed his support; his name appeared on a thousand banners, frequently proclaiming causes to which he was strongly opposed. With the outbreak of the revolutions of 1848 – they occurred in Sicily, Paris, Vienna, Naples, Rome, Venice, Florence, Lucca, Parma, Modena, Berlin, Milan, Cracow, Warsaw and Budapest – his position became still more untenable. '*Pio Nono! Pio Nono! Pio Nono!*': the name became a battle-cry, endlessly chanted by one mob after another as it surged through the streets of city after city. When the Pope concluded one speech with the words 'God bless Italy', his words were immediately seen as an endorsement of the popular dream of a united peninsula, freed for ever from Austrian rule. (Pius, it need hardly be said, had no desire to see Italy united; apart from anything else, what would then become of the Papal States?) In short, he now found himself on a runaway train; his only hope was to try to apply the brakes whenever he could.

Already by the end of January of that fateful year the spate of new constitutions had begun. King Ferdinand had given one to Naples on the 29th; in Florence, just a week later, the Grand Duke had offered his subjects another. On 5 March, after the Paris revolution and the flight of Louis-Philippe, King Charles Albert of Savoy had granted one to the Piedmontese in Turin. Then on 13 March it had been the turn of Vienna, and Metternich himself had taken to his heels. This was the most important event of all; new hope surged in the breast of every Italian patriot – who, as always, looked to the Pope for a lead. There was nothing for it: on 15 March Pope Pius granted a constitution to the Papal States, providing for an elected chamber. It was not exaggeratedly liberal – his chief minister, Cardinal Giacomo Antonelli,[1] had seen to that – nor, as things turned out, did it last

---

[1] Antonelli was largely responsible for enabling the papacy to cling to temporal power for as long as it did. He was a brilliant politician with immense charm and – as his countless bastards attested – an extremely *mouvementé* sex life. 'When he stops in a salon near a pretty woman, when he stands close to speak to her, stroking her shoulders and looking deeply into her corsage, you recognise the man of the woods and you tremble as you think of post-chaises overturned at the roadside' (E. About, *La question romaine*).

very long; but it served its purpose. Pius, unwilling as he was to spearhead European revolution, could hardly be seen to be lagging behind.

Metternich's resignation and flight left Austria in chaos. The government was rudderless, the army bewildered and uncertain in its loyalties. Here, unmistakably, was the signal to insurgents and revolutionaries throughout Italy. In Milan, the great insurrection known to all Italians as the *cinque giornate* – the five days of 18–22 March – drove the Austrians from the city and instituted a republican government. On the last of those days, in Turin, a stirring front-page article appeared in the newspaper *Il Risorgimento*, written by its editor, Count Camillo Cavour. 'The supreme hour has sounded,' he wrote. 'One way alone is open for the nation, for the government, for the King. War!'

Two days later King Charles Albert proclaimed the readiness of Piedmont to take up arms against the Austrian occupiers. Grand Duke Leopold II of Tuscany despatched an army composed of both regular troops and volunteers. Rather more surprisingly, there was a similar response from King Ferdinand of Naples, who sent a force of 16,000 under a huge Calabrian general called Guglielmo Pepe. Strategically these contributions probably made little difference; they showed, however, beyond all possible doubt, that the cause was a national, Italian one. As they took their places beside the Piedmontese, Charles Albert's fellow-rulers saw themselves not as allies, but as compatriots.

On 24 March General Giovanni Durando led the advance guard of a papal army out of Rome, to protect the northern frontier of the Papal States against any possible Austrian attack. This was conceived as a purely defensive measure, but the warmongers refused to accept it as such. Austria, they claimed, had declared war on Christian Italy. This was therefore a holy war, a Crusade, with the divine purpose of driving the invader from the sacred Italian soil. Pope Pius was horrified. Never for a moment would he have condoned such a policy of aggression, least of all against a Catholic nation. It was clearly essential for him to make his position clear once and for all. The result was the so-called Allocution of 29 April 1848. Far from leading the campaign for a united Italy, he declared, he actively opposed it. God-fearing Italians should forget the whole idea of unification and once again pledge their loyalty to their individual princes.

The news of the Allocution was received with horror by all true Italian patriots up and down the country. As things turned out, the cause of unification was virtually unaffected: the movement was by now so widespread as to be unstoppable. The only real damage done was to the reputation of Pius himself. Until now he had been a hero; henceforth he was a traitor. Moreover, the Allocution had shown, as perhaps nothing else could have shown, just how powerless he was to influence events. All his popularity disappeared overnight; now it was his turn to look revolution in the face. For seven months he struggled to hold the situation; but when on 15 November his chief minister, Antonelli's successor Count Pellegrino Rossi, was hacked to death as he was entering the Chancellery, Pius realised that Rome was no longer safe for him. On the 24th, aided by the French Ambassador and the Bavarian minister and disguised as a simple priest, he slipped secretly out of the Quirinal Palace by a side door and fled to Gaeta – in Neapolitan territory – where he was joined by Cardinal Antonelli and a small staff. King Ferdinand gave him a warm welcome and settled Pius in his local palace, where he established a small Curia and continued the papal business.

At first the Piedmontese army enjoyed a measure of success. All too soon, however, on 24 July 1849, Charles Albert was routed at Custozza, a few miles south-west of Verona. He fell back on Milan, with the old Austrian Marshal, Josef Radetzky,[1] in hot pursuit; and on 4 August he was obliged to ask for an armistice, by the terms of which he and his army withdrew behind their own frontiers. Two days later the Milanese also surrendered, and the indomitable old marshal led his army back into the city. The first phase of the war was over, and Austria was plainly the victor. It was not only that she was back in undisputed control of Venetia-Lombardy. Naples had made a separate peace; Rome had capitulated; France, in the person of her Foreign Secretary, the poet Alphonse de Lamartine, had published a republican *Manifesto* that had made encouraging noises, even if it had offered no material help. The forces of the counter-revolution were triumphant across mainland Italy.

Except in Venice. On 22 March 1848 a Venetian lawyer named Daniele Manin and his followers had occupied the Arsenal and commandeered all the Austrian arms and ammunition that were stored there. Manin had then led a triumphal procession to the Piazza, where he had formally proclaimed the rebirth of the Republic, abolished by

---

[1] Radetzky had taken part in the very first Austrian campaigns against Napoleon more than half a century before, and had been Chief of Staff at the battle of Leipzig in 1813. He had fought in seventeen campaigns, had been wounded seven times and had had nine horses shot from under him.

Napoleon half a century before. The Austrian governor had signed an act of capitulation, promising the immediate departure of all Austrian troops. But now Venice stood alone. Her only hope was Manin, whom in August she invited to assume dictatorial powers. He refused; it was nevertheless under his sole guidance that the Venetian Republic was to fight on throughout the following winter, courageously but with increasing desperation.

For all the states of Italy, the *quarantotto* – 'the forty-eight' – had been a momentous year. Strategically, the situation had changed remarkably little; in most places Austria remained in control. Politically, on the other hand, there had been a dramatic shift in popular opinion. When the year began, most patriotic Italians were thinking in terms of getting rid of the Austrian forces of occupation; when it ended, the overriding objective – everywhere except in Venice – was a united Italy. Change was in the air. At last, it seemed, the Italians were on the verge of realising their long-cherished dream. The Risorgimento had begun.

The hurried departure of the Pope had taken Rome by surprise. The chief minister of the papal government, Giuseppe Galletti – an old friend of Mazzini's who had returned to Rome under the amnesty and had courageously succeeded the murdered Rossi – first sent a delegation to Gaeta to persuade Pius to return; only when this was refused an audience did Galletti call for the formation of a Roman Constituent Assembly, of 200 elected members, which would meet in the city on 5 February 1849. Time was short, but the need was urgent, and 142 members duly presented themselves in the Palace of the Cancellaria on the appointed date. Just four days later, at two o'clock in the morning, the Assembly voted – by 120 votes to ten, with twelve abstentions – to put an end to the temporal power of the Pope and establish a Roman Republic. It was dominated by a forty-one-year-old adventurer named Giuseppe Garibaldi.

Born in 1807 in Nice – which would be ceded to France only in 1860 – Garibaldi was, like Mazzini, a Piedmontese. He had begun his professional life as a merchant seaman, and had become a member of Mazzini's *Giovane Italia* in 1833. Always a man of action, he was involved the following year in an unsuccessful mutiny (one of the many failed conspiracies of those early years) and a warrant was issued for his arrest. Just in time, he managed to escape to France; meanwhile, in Turin, he was sentenced *in absentia* to death for high treason.

After a brief spell in the French merchant navy he joined that of the Bey of Tunis, who offered him the post of Commander-in-Chief. This, however, he declined; and finally, in December 1835, he sailed as second mate on a French brig bound for South America. There he was to stay for the next twelve years, the first four of them fighting for a small and now-forgotten state that was trying – unsuccessfully – to break away from Brazilian domination. In 1841 he and his Brazilian mistress, Anita Ribeiro da Silva, trekked to Montevideo, where he was put in charge of the Uruguayan navy, also taking command of a legion of Italian exiles – the first of the Redshirts, with whom his name was ever afterwards associated. After his victory at the minor but heroic battle of San Antonio del Santo in 1846 his fame quickly spread to Europe. By now he had become a professional rebel, whose experience of guerrilla warfare was to stand him in good stead in the years to come.

The moment Garibaldi heard of the revolutions of 1848 he gathered sixty of his Redshirts and took the next ship back to Italy. His initial offers to fight for the Pope and then for Piedmont having both been rejected – Charles Albert, in particular, would not have forgotten that Garibaldi was still under sentence of death – he headed for Milan, where Mazzini had already arrived, and immediately plunged into the fray. The armistice following Charles Albert's defeat at Custozza he simply ignored, continuing his private war against the Austrians until at the end of August, heavily outnumbered, he was obliged to retreat to Switzerland. Three months later, however, on hearing of the Pope's flight, he hurried at once with his troop of volunteers to Rome. There he was elected a member of the new Assembly, and it was he who formally proposed that Rome should thenceforth be an independent republic.

On 18 February 1849 Pope Pius in Gaeta addressed a formal appeal for help to France, Austria, Spain and Naples. By none of these four powers was he to go unheard; to the Assembly, however, the greatest danger was France – whose response would clearly depend on the complexion of its new republic and, in particular, on Prince Louis-Napoleon, its newly elected President. Nearly twenty years before, the Prince had been implicated in an anti-papal plot and expelled from Rome; he still cherished no particular affection for the papacy. But it was all too clear to him that Austria was more powerful than ever in Italy; how could he contemplate the possibility of the Austrians now marching south and restoring the Pope on their own terms? If he himself were to take no action, that – he had no doubt at all – was exactly what they would do.

Louis-Napoleon gave his orders accordingly, and on 25 April 1849 General Nicholas Oudinot (the son of one of Napoleon's marshals) landed with a force of about 9,000 at Civitavecchia and set off on the forty-mile march to Rome. From the start he was under a misapprehension. He had been led to believe that the Roman Republic had been imposed by a small group of revolutionaries on an unwilling people and would soon be overturned; he and his men would consequently be welcomed as liberators. His orders were to grant the Assembly no formal recognition, but to occupy the city peacefully, if possible without firing a shot.

He was in for a surprise. The Romans, although they had little hope of defending their city against a trained and well-equipped army, were busy preparing themselves for the fight. Their own forces, such as they were, consisted of the regular papal troops of the line, the *carabinieri* – a special corps of the Italian army entrusted with police duties – the 1,000-strong Civic Guard, the volunteer regiments raised in the city, which amounted to some 1,400 and – by no means the least formidable – the populace itself, with every weapon it could lay its hands on. But their total numbers were still pathetically small, and great was their jubilation when, on 27 April, Garibaldi rode into the city at the head of 1,300 legionaries whom he had gathered in the Romagna. Two days later there followed a regiment of Lombard *bersaglieri*, with their distinctive broad-brimmed hats and swaying plumes of black-green cock's feathers. The defenders were gathering in strength; but the odds were still heavily against them, and they knew it.

The first battle for Rome was fought on 30 April. The day was saved by Oudinot's ignorance and misunderstanding of the situation. He had brought no siege guns with him, and no scaling ladders; it was only when his column, advancing towards the Vatican and the Janiculum Hill, was greeted by bursts of cannon-fire that he began to realise the full danger of his position. Soon afterwards Garibaldi's legion swept down upon him, swiftly followed by the *bersaglieri* lancers. For six hours he and his men fought back as best they could, but as evening fell they could only admit defeat and take the long road back to Civitavecchia. They had lost 500 killed or wounded, with 365 taken prisoner – but perhaps the humiliation had been worst of all.

That night all Rome was illuminated in celebration, but no one pretended that the invaders were not going to return. The French had learned that Rome was going to be a tougher nut to crack than they had expected; nonetheless, they intended to crack it. Little more than a month later – during which time Garibaldi, at the head of his legionaries and the *bersaglieri*, marched south to meet an invading Neapolitan army and effortlessly expelled it from republican territory – Oudinot had received the reinforcements he had requested, and it was with 20,000 men behind him and vastly improved armament that, on 3 June, he marched on Rome for the second time.

Advancing once again from the west, his primary objectives were the historic Villa Pamfili and Villa Corsini, high on the Janiculum Hill. By the end of the day both were safely in his hands, his guns drawn up into position. Rome was effectively doomed. The defenders fought back superbly for nearly a month, but on the morning of 30 June Mazzini addressed the Assembly. There were, he told them, three possibilities: they could surrender; they could continue the fight and die in the streets; or they could retire to the hills and continue the struggle. Around midday Garibaldi appeared, covered in dust, his red shirt caked with blood and sweat; his mind was made up. Surrender was obviously out of the question. Street fighting, he pointed out, was also impossible; when Trastevere – the area of Rome lying west of the Tiber – was abandoned, as it would have to be, French guns could simply destroy the city. The hills, then, it would have to be. '*Dovunque saremo*,' he told them, '*colà sarà Roma.*'[1]

Rome now awaited the Pope's return; but Pius took his time. It would be weeks or months, he knew, before the city reverted to normal; in any case, what would his own policy be? He was glad on the whole that Louis-Napoleon had agreed to leave a French garrison indefinitely in or near Rome – he might have need of it – but he was resolved not to let the Prince-President tell him what to do. On no account would he reintroduce the Constitution of 1848; he would allow nothing more than a limited amnesty, a State Council and a Legislative Assembly. Only when the French agreed to these conditions did he consent to return; it was not until 12 April 1850 that he made his formal re-entry into the city. This time, however, he avoided the Quirinal Palace: it had too many unhappy memories. Instead he went straight to the Vatican – where his successors have lived ever since.

* * *

---

[1] 'Wherever we are, there shall be Rome.'

Had the *quarantotto* been in vain? By early 1850 it certainly seemed so. Pius IX had returned to a French-occupied Rome; the Austrians were back in Venice and in Lombardy; in Naples, King Ferdinand II ('King Bomba') had torn up the constitution and once again wielded absolute power; Florence, Modena and Parma, all under Austrian protection, were in much the same state. In the whole peninsula, only Piedmont remained free – but Piedmont too had changed. The tall, handsome, idealistic Charles Albert was dead. His son and successor, Victor Emmanuel II, was short, squat and unusually ugly, principally interested (or so it seemed) in hunting and women. But he was a good deal more intelligent than he looked; despite his genuine shyness and awkwardness in public, he missed very few tricks. It is hard to imagine the Risorgimento without him.

Yet even Victor Emmanuel might have foundered had it not been for Count Camillo Cavour, who became his chief minister at the end of 1852 and remained in power, with very brief intermissions, for the next nine years – years that were crucial for Italy. Cavour's appearance, like that of his master, was deceptive. Short and pot-bellied, with a blotchy complexion, thinning hair and spectacles that looked like goggles, he was shabbily dressed and on first acquaintance distinctly unprepossessing. His mind, on the other hand, was like a rapier, and once he began to talk, few were impervious to his charm. Domestically, he pursued a programme of ecclesiastical reform – often in the teeth of opposition from a pious and conscientiously Catholic king; his foreign policy, meanwhile, was ever directed towards his dream of a united Italy, with Piedmont at its head. But how could this be achieved with Austria in control in Venetia-Lombardy and a French army protecting the Papal States? By early 1866, when he and Napoleon III[1] found themselves sitting together at the Paris peace table after the Crimean War, Cavour began to entertain a new and exciting hope that the Emperor, despite his distinctly unhelpful policies in the past, might now be prepared to assist in the long-awaited Austrian expulsion.

Surprisingly enough, what seems finally to have decided Louis-Napoleon to take up arms on Italy's behalf was a plot by Italian patriots to assassinate him. Their attempt took place on 14 January 1858, when bombs were thrown at his carriage as he and the Empress

---

[1] Louis-Napoleon had revived his uncle's Empire – and himself assumed the title of Emperor – on 2 December 1852.

were on their way to the Opera. Neither was hurt, though there were several casualties among their escort and the surrounding bystanders. The leader of the conspirators, Felice Orsini, was a well-known republican who had been implicated in a number of former plots. While in prison awaiting trial he wrote the Emperor a letter, which was later read aloud in open court and published in both the French and the Piedmontese press. It ended: 'Remember that, so long as Italy is not independent, the peace of Europe and Your Majesty is but an empty dream . . . Set my country free, and the blessings of twenty-five million people will follow you everywhere and forever.'

Although these noble words failed to save Orsini from the firing squad, they seem to have lingered in the mind of Louis-Napoleon, who by midsummer had come round to the idea of a joint operation to drive the Austrians from the Italian peninsula once and for all. His motives were not, it need hardly be said, wholly idealistic. True, he had a genuine love for Italy and would have been delighted to present himself to the world as her deliverer, but he was also aware that his prestige and popularity at home were fast declining. He desperately needed a war – and a victorious war at that – to regain them, and Austria was the only potential enemy available. The next step was to discuss the possibilities with Cavour, and in July 1858 the two met secretly at the little health resort of Plombières-les-Bains in the Vosges. Agreement was quickly reached. Piedmont would engineer a quarrel with the Duke of Modena and send in troops, ostensibly at the request of the population. Austria would be bound to support the Duke and declare war; Piedmont would then appeal to France for aid, and France would help her to expel the Austrians from Italy and annex Venetia-Lombardy. In return, she would cede to France the county of Savoy and the city of Nice. The latter, being the birthplace of Garibaldi, was a bitter pill for Cavour to swallow; but if it was the price of liberation, then swallowed it would have to be.

The Emperor landed with his army of 54,000 at Genoa on 12 May 1859; and on 4 June the first decisive battle was fought – at Magenta, a small village some fourteen miles west of Milan, where the French scored a decisive victory over some 60,000 Austrians. Casualties were high on both sides, and would have been higher if the Piedmontese, delayed by the indecision of their commander, had not arrived some time after the battle was over. This misfortune did not, however, prevent Louis-Napoleon and Victor Emmanuel from making a joint triumphal entry into Milan four days later.

After Magenta the Franco-Piedmontese army was joined by Garibaldi, who had been invited by Victor Emmanuel to assemble a brigade of *cacciatori delle Alpi* ('Alpine hunters') and had won another battle against the Austrians some ten days before at Varese. They then all advanced together and met the full Austrian army on 24 June at Solferino, just south of Lake Garda. The ensuing battle – in which well over a quarter of a million men were engaged – was fought on a grander scale than any since Leipzig in 1813. The French were able now to reveal a secret weapon: rifled artillery, which dramatically increased both the accuracy and range of their guns. Much of the fighting, however, was hand-to-hand, beginning early in the morning and continuing throughout most of the day. Only towards evening, after losing some 20,000 of his men in heavy rain, did the twenty-nine-year-old Emperor Franz Josef order a withdrawal across the Mincio. But it was a pyrrhic victory; the French and Piedmontese lost almost as many men as the Austrians, and the outbreak of fever (probably typhus) that followed the battle accounted for thousands more on both sides. The scenes of carnage made a deep impression on a young Swiss named Henri Dunant, who chanced to be present and organised emergency-aid services for the wounded. Five years later, as a direct result of his experience, he was to found the Red Cross.

Louis-Napoleon, too, had been profoundly shocked; and this was certainly one of the reasons why, a little more than a fortnight after the battle, he made a separate peace with Austria. There was another reason, too: recent events had persuaded several of the smaller states – notably Tuscany, Romagna and the Duchies of Modena and Parma – to think about overthrowing their rulers and seeking annexation to Piedmont. The result would be a formidable state, immediately across the French border, covering much of north and central Italy: a state that might well absorb some or all of the Papal States and even the Two Sicilies. Was it really for this that the gallant Frenchmen who fell at Solferino had given their lives?

And so, on 11 July 1859, the Emperors of France and Austria met at Villafranca near Verona, and the future of northern and central Italy was decided in under an hour. Austria would keep Venetia, as well as Mantua and Peschiera, the great fortress on Lake Garda; the rest of Lombardy she would surrender to France, who would pass it on to Piedmont. The former rulers of Tuscany and Modena would be restored to their thrones, and an Italian confederacy would be established under the honorary presidency of the Pope. Venetia – including Venice itself – would be a member of this confederacy, while remaining under Austrian sovereignty.

The fury of Cavour when he read the details of the Villafranca Agreement can well be imagined. Without Venice, Peschiera or Mantua, not even Venetia-Lombardy would be entirely Italian; as for central Italy, that was lost even before it had been properly gained. After a long and acrimonious interview with Victor Emmanuel, he submitted his resignation. 'We shall return,' he wrote to a friend, 'to conspiracy.' Gradually, however, he recovered himself. There had a least been no mention in the agreement of the French annexation of Savoy and Nice, which he had reluctantly agreed to at Plombières; the present situation, if not all that he had hoped, was certainly a good deal better than it had been the year before.

Over the next few months it improved still further, as several of the smaller states categorically refused to accept the fate prescribed for them; nothing, they made it clear, would induce them to take back their former rulers. In Florence, Bologna, Parma and Modena dictators had sprung up, all of them determined on fusion with Piedmont. The only obstacle was presented by Piedmont itself; the terms agreed at Villafranca were now incorporated in a formal treaty signed at Zurich, and General Alfonso La Marmora, who had succeeded Cavour as chief minister, was unwilling to take any action in defiance of it. But the dictators were quite prepared to bide their time. Florence, meanwhile, kept her independence; Romagna (which included Bologna), Parma and Modena joined together to form a new state, which – since the Roman Via Aemilia ran through all three of them – they called Emilia.

Camillo Cavour followed these developments with satisfaction, and in January 1860 returned to Turin to take over a new government. Scarcely was he back in office when he found himself swept up in negotiations with Napoleon III, and it was not long before the two reached agreement. Piedmont would annex Tuscany and Emilia; in new return, Savoy and Nice would be ceded to France. There was a predictable explosion of wrath from Garibaldi, whose immediate reaction was to start planning his personal recapture of his native city and its return to Piedmont; but before he could do so another far more promising opportunity suddenly presented itself – an opportunity not just to fight for a noble cause, but to make history.

*　　*　　*

On 4 April 1860 there was a popular insurrection in Palermo. It was not a success – the Neapolitan authorities had been secretly informed in advance – but it provided a spark for others throughout northern Sicily, and the authorities could not cope with them all. When Garibaldi heard the news he acted at once. Cavour refused his request for a Piedmontese brigade, but within less than a month he had assembled a band of volunteers, who sailed from the little port of Quarto (now part of Genoa) on the night of 5 May, landing unopposed at Marsala in western Sicily on the 11th. They represented a broad cross-section of Italian society, about half consisting of men from the professions (lawyers, doctors and university lecturers) and the other half drawn from the working class. Some were still technically republicans, but their leader made it clear to them that they were fighting not just for Italy, but also for King Victor Emmanuel – and this was no time to argue.

From Marsala the Thousand (as they came to be called, although there were actually 1,089 of them) headed inland. There was a degree of somewhat half-hearted resistance from Bourbon troops, but by the end of May Garibaldi was master of Palermo, and two months later of all Sicily. In mid-August he and his men crossed the Straits of Messina; and on 7 September he entered Naples in an open carriage, King Francis II having fled the previous day.

Naples was the largest city in Italy, the third largest in Europe. For two months Garibaldi ruled it – and Sicily – as a dictator, while planning his next step: a march on the Papal States and Rome. But this step was never taken. Cavour, knowing full well that to allow Garibaldi to continue might mean war with France, was determined to stop him in his tracks. Besides, Garibaldi was now far more popular than Victor Emmanuel himself; the Piedmontese army was deeply jealous of his recent successes; and there was always the lurking danger that Mazzini, who had arrived in Naples in mid-September, might persuade him to desert the King of Piedmont and espouse the republican cause.

Suddenly Garibaldi found two formidable armies ranged against him: the Neapolitan and the Piedmontese. King Francis had managed to raise a new army, and not long after the Redshirts left Naples on the first stage of their journey north, they found a force of some 50,000 drawn up along the bank of the Volturno river. It was here that they suffered their first defeat since landing in Sicily: outside the little town of Caiazzo, in their leader's temporary absence, one of his generals tried and failed to cross the river, losing 250 men in the attempt. But on 1 October Garibaldi had his revenge. It was an expensive victory, with some 1,400 killed or wounded in and around the little village of S. Angelo in Formis; but it may well have saved Italy.

Meanwhile the Piedmontese army was also advancing south, into the papal territories of Umbria and the Marches. Its campaign was unspectacular, but effective, its papalist opponents consisting of little more than an international brigade of volunteers, recruited from Catholic communities throughout Europe.[1] It overcame a spirited resistance at Perugia, scored a small victory over a papal army at the little village of Castelfidardo near Loreto and a rather larger one when it captured Ancona, taking 7,000 prisoners including the commander of the papal forces, the French general Christophe de Lamoricière. That was the end of the papal army; henceforth there was no further trouble.

Victor Emmanuel himself, accompanied by his long-term mistress Rosina Vercellana – she was dressed, we are told, to kill – now came to take titular command of his army. From that moment Garibaldi's star began to set. The battle of the Volturno had already persuaded him that a march on Rome was no longer a possibility; and now, with the King himself on his way, he saw that his rule in the south must come to an end. He gave in gracefully. He rode north with a large escort to meet the King, and on 7 November the two of them entered Naples side by side in the royal carriage. Victor Emmanuel offered him the rank of full general together with a splendid estate, but Garibaldi would have none of it. He remained a revolutionary, and for as long as Austria still occupied the Veneto – and the Pope continued as temporal ruler in Rome – he was determined to preserve his freedom of action. On 9 November he sailed for his farm on the little island of Caprera off the Sardinian coast. He took with him only a little money (borrowed, since he had made none during his months of power) and a bag of seeds for his garden.

On Passion Sunday, 17 March 1861, Victor Emmanuel II was proclaimed King of Italy. Old Massimo d'Azeglio, Cavour's predecessor and successor as chief minister, is reported to have said when he heard the news: '*L'Italia è fatta; restano a fare gli italiani.*'[2]

Less than three months after the royal proclamation Cavour was dead.

---

[1] 'Pio Nono had been doubtful about the Irish volunteers at first, because he feared the effects on Irishmen of the ready availability of cheap Italian wine' (Eamon Duffy, *Saints and Sinners*).
[2] 'Italy is made; now we have to make the Italians.'

He had spent his last weeks in furious debate over the future of Rome – in which, it should be recorded, he had never once set foot. All the other major Italian cities, he argued, had been independent municipalities, each fighting its own corner; only Rome, as the seat of the Church, had remained above such rivalries. But though the Pope must be asked to surrender his temporal power, papal independence must at all costs be guaranteed: 'a free Church in a free state'. He encountered a good deal of opposition: the most vitriolic from Garibaldi, who emerged from Caprera in April 1861, strode into the Assembly in his red shirt and grey South American poncho and let loose a stream of abuse at the man who, he thundered, had sold off half his country to the French and had done his best to prevent the invasion of the Two Sicilies. But he succeeded only in confirming that, however brilliant a general he might be, he was no statesman. Cavour easily won the vote of confidence that followed. It was his last political victory. He died suddenly on 6 June of a massive stroke. He was just fifty years old.

If Camillo Cavour had lived just one more decade he would have seen the last two pieces of the Italian jigsaw fitted into place. Where Rome was concerned, Pope Pius was refusing to yield an inch; he held the Papal States for the Catholic world and was obliged by his coronation oath to pass them on to his successor. Napoleon III, by contrast, was becoming steadily more amenable to negotiation, and by what was known as the September Convention, signed on 15 September 1864, he agreed to withdraw his troops from Rome before September 1866. The new Kingdom of Italy in return pledged itself to defend papal territory against any attack, and agreed to transfer its capital within six months from Turin to Florence. Rather than improving the prospects of incorporating Rome into the new Italian state, the Convention – which was to remain in force for six years – seemed to guarantee, at least temporarily, the status quo. On the other hand, by putting an end to the fifteen years of French occupation it cleared the ground for the next steps, whatever these might be; and by freezing the situation in Rome it enabled the government to turn its mind to the other overriding necessity : the recovery of the Veneto.

But now, by a stroke of good fortune, there appeared a *deus ex machina*, who was effectively to drop into Italy's lap both of the coveted territories. This took the unexpected shape of the Prussian Chancellor, Otto von Bismarck, who was now well on the way to uniting all the German states into a single Empire. The one stumbling block was Austria. Bismarck therefore proposed to Victor Emmanuel a military alliance: Austria would be attacked simultaneously on two fronts, by Prussia from the north and by Italy from the west. In the event of victory, Italy's reward would be the Veneto. The King agreed, and Napoleon III had no objection. The treaty was signed on 8 April 1866, and on 15 June the war began. Six weeks later it was over. A single battle did the trick. It was fought at Sadowa, some sixty-five miles north-east of Prague, and engaged the largest number of troops (one-third of a million) ever assembled to that date on a European battlefield. The Prussian victory was total, and the armistice that followed duly provided for the cession of the Veneto. This was confirmed by a plebiscite, the result of which was a foregone conclusion. Venice was an Italian city at last, and Italy could boast a new and invaluable port on the northern Adriatic.

Only Rome remained.

On 8 December 1864 Pope Pius published his encyclical *Quanta cura*. It was prompted by a speech by the liberal Count Charles de Montalambert at a Catholic Congress held the previous year at Malines in Belgium. The time had come, Montalambert had declared, to scrap the age-old alliance of throne and altar, which was now dead on its feet. Instead, he called for a fresh attitude on the part of the Church. Let it now embrace the new democratic principles, doing away with the Index, the Inquisition and similar repressive institutions and opening the way to free discussion. To Pius, this was dangerous talk indeed. Montalambert and the Archbishop of Malines both received letters of stern reprimand, and work began on the encyclical – to which, when it appeared, was attached what was described as a *Syllabus of Errors*. It was this, rather than the encyclical itself, that caused widespread consternation, consisting as it did of a list of no fewer than eighty condemned propositions. Some of these were uncontroversial enough; others, seemed to many of the faithful profoundly shocking. Did the Pope really believe that non-Catholics in Catholic countries should be forbidden to practise their religion? Did he genuinely condemn the idea that 'the Roman Pontiff can and should reconcile himself with progress, liberalism and recent civilisation'?

Pius IX never lost his easy-going charm, his ready smile, his ever-present sense of humour; and yet here was proof – if proof were needed – that the Pope had now identified himself with one of the most reactionary, intolerant and aggressive movements of modern

Church history. To the Ultramontanists (as they had come to be called) the Pope was absolute ruler, unquestioned leader, infallible guide. No discussion was permitted, no suggestion that there might be two sides to an argument. Roman Catholicism was in danger of becoming something akin to a police state, illiberal and bigoted. As the Anglican convert John Henry Newman wrote disgustedly: 'We are shrinking into ourselves, narrowing the lines of communication, trembling at freedom of thought, and using the language of dismay and despair at the prospect before us.' No wonder Britain's representative in Rome, Odo Russell, reporting back to his government, wrote of the Pope's 'unbounded pretensions to absolute control over the souls and bodies of mankind', and of his position 'at the head of a vast ecclesiastical conspiracy against the principles which govern modern society'. 'Liberal Catholics,' he wrote, 'can no longer speak in her [the Church's] defence without being convicted of heresy.'

The shockwave soon spread across Europe. In France, the *Syllabus* was banned; in Naples, it was publicly burned; Bishop Dupanloup of Orleans wrote that 'if we do not succeed in checking this senseless Romanism, the Church will be outlawed in Europe for half a century'. Pope Pius, however, was unrepentant. Almost in defiance of the opposition, he summoned a General Council of the Church, to be known as the First Vatican Council and to meet on 8 December 1869 in St Peter's.

It was by far the largest Council in history, attended by nearly 700 bishops from all five continents – 120 of them English-speaking. (There would have been more bishops still if Russia had allowed its Catholic priests to attend.) The proceedings, it was agreed, should take place under two heads, the Faith and the Church. The Constitution on the Faith formally deplored the pantheism, materialism and atheism of the time and caused few problems. That on the Church proved a good deal trickier. It had not originally been intended that the main issue should be that of Papal Infallibility, but as the Council continued its work this gradually assumed overriding importance. The debate was long and spirited, and the wording as finally accepted – by a majority of 533 to two, but with many abstentions – disappointed the extremists on both sides. The Roman pontiff, it declared, was indeed infallible, his definitions 'being irreformable of themselves, and not from the consent of the Church'; his infallibility was, however, restricted only to those occasions 'when he speaks *ex cathedra*, that is when, in discharge of the office of Pastor and Doctor of all Christians, by virtue of his supreme Apostolic authority he defines a doctrine regarding faith or morals to be held by the Universal Church'.

This decree was promulgated on 18 July 1870 – not a moment too soon. The very next day saw the declaration of the Franco-Prussian War; and the instant withdrawal of French troops from Rome, followed by the Italian occupation of the city, brought the Council to a somewhat abrupt finish.

By the end of 1866 Garibaldi was preparing for a march on Rome, even issuing a proclamation calling upon all freedom loving Romans to rise in rebellion against the Pope. Since the September Convention still had four more years to run, the Piedmontese government had no choice but to arrest him and send him back to Caprera; but he soon escaped – he was by now in his sixtieth year – reassembled his volunteers and resumed his promised march.

He had reckoned without the French. Napoleon III, who had withdrawn his troops in 1866 in conformity with the September Convention, now sent a fresh army, equipped with the deadly new *chassepot* rifles, which landed at Civitavecchia in late October. The volunteers, outnumbered and outclassed, stood no chance. Garibaldi himself managed to slip back across the frontier into Italy – and into the arms of the authorities. Back he was sent to Caprera, where he remained (this time heavily guarded) under house-arrest. Of his men, no fewer than 1,600 were taken prisoner.

Yet again, by his swift reaction, the Emperor Napoleon had saved the temporal power of the papacy; no one could have guessed that less than three years later he would be instrumental in bringing about its downfall. The prime mover, once again, was Bismarck, who had cunningly drawn France into a war by his threat to place a prince of the ruling Prussian House of Hohenzollern on the throne of Spain. That war was declared – by France, not Prussia – on 19 July 1870. It was to prove a bitter struggle: Napoleon was going to need every soldier he had for the fighting that lay ahead. By the end of August there was not a uniformed Frenchman left in Rome.

Pope Pius was fully aware of the danger. Only his little mercenary army remained to protect him. Napoleon's defeat at Sedan[1] on 1 September and his capitulation on the 2nd spelled the end of the

---

[1] '*La France*,' the Pope is said to have remarked to a remaining French representative, '*a perdu ses dents*' (Sedan) – 'France has lost her teeth.' Pius IX was famous for the awfulness of his puns; but even for him this must have been one of the worst.

Second Empire and the destruction of Pius's last hopes. In the minds of the Italian government, the only question still to be decided was one of timing: should their army occupy Rome immediately – the September Convention was on the point of expiry, and with the elimination of one of the signatories was a dead letter anyway – or should they wait for a popular rising?

Meanwhile Victor Emmanuel sent a special emissary, Count Gustavo Ponza di San Martino, with a last appeal to the Pope, writing (as he put it) 'with the affection of a son, the faith of a Catholic, the loyalty of a king and the soul of an Italian'. The security of Italy and of the Holy See itself, he continued, depended on the presence of Italian troops in Rome. Would His Holiness not accept this unalterable fact and show his benevolent cooperation? Alas, His Holiness would do no such thing. He would yield, he declared, only to violence, and even then he would put up at least a formal resistance. He allowed the emissary to take his leave with a final assurance: that San Martino and his friends would never enter Rome. Only when the Marquess was halfway to the door did he call him back. 'That last assurance,' he said with a smile, 'is not infallible!' Nonetheless, he was as good as his word. When Italian troops entered Rome by the Porta Pia on the morning of 20 September 1870, they found a papal detachment waiting for them. The fighting was soon over, but not before it had left nineteen papalists and forty-nine Italians dead in the street.

Over the next few hours Italian troops swarmed through Rome, leaving only the Vatican and the Castel Sant'Angelo, from which there now flew the white flag of surrender. There was no further resistance. In May 1871, by the so-called Law of Guarantees, the government assured the Pope of his personal inviolability, and of his continued exclusive occupation of the Vatican, the Lateran and his country residence at Castel Gandolfo. All three, however, would henceforth be the property of the Italian State, which would pay him three and a half million lire a year in compensation. The papal court would remain as it had always been, as would the Papal Guard; the Supreme Pontiff would continue to maintain his own diplomatic service, and a diplomatic corps would continue to be accredited to the Holy See. Papal communications with the outside world would be assured by the Vatican post and telegraph office, which would issue its own stamps. But Pius doggedly refused to recognise what was obviously a fait accompli, or to accept the compensation money. As 'Vicar of a Crucified God', he declared, he was perfectly prepared to suffer; but voluntarily to surrender the Patrimony of Peter, 'the seamless robe of Jesus Christ' – that he could never contemplate.

There was, however, one provision of the Law of Guarantees that he did accept: the right to appoint all Italian bishops. With the unification of Italy, all such appointments – 237 of them – had been in the hands of Victor Emmanuel; their transfer to the Holy See completely transformed the attitude of the Italian episcopate towards the Pope and immeasurably increased the power of the pontificate over the Church. It did not, on the other hand, do anything to change the Pope's view of the Italian government. Already, three years before, his decree *Non Expedit* – which was to remain in force until after the First World War – had forbidden Catholics to stand or vote in elections, or in any way take part in the political life of the new kingdom; now he voluntarily withdrew inside the walls of the Vatican, where he remained for the last eight years of his life. The plebiscite that was held shortly afterwards registered 133,681 votes in favour of the incorporation of Rome into the Kingdom of Italy, and 1,507 against. Rome was now part of Italy not by right of conquest, but by the will of its people. Only the Vatican City remained an independent sovereign state.

It was not until 2 July 1871 that Victor Emmanuel made his official entry into his new capital. The streets were already being decorated for the occasion when he sent a telegram to the Mayor forbidding all signs of festivity. As a pious Catholic, he had been not only saddened but terrified when sentence of excommunication had been passed upon him. Ferdinand Gregorovius, the Prussian historian of medieval Rome, wrote in his diary that the procession was 'without pomp, vivacity, grandeur or majesty; and that was as it should have been, for this day signals the end of the millenary rule of the Popes over Rome'. In the afternoon the King was urged to cross the river to Trastevere, where some small ceremony had been prepared by the largely working-class population. He flatly refused, adding – in the Piedmontese dialect of which few of those about him would have understood a word – 'The Pope is only two steps away, and would feel hurt. I have done enough already to that poor old man.'

Pope Pius made his last journey through Rome on 19 September 1870. It was to St John Lateran, where he left his carriage and slowly and painfully made the long ascent of the *scala santa* on his knees. When he reached the top, he prayed and then, rising to his feet, blessed the papal troops who had escorted him. Then he returned to the Vatican, which he never again left until his death seven and a half years later, outliving Napoleon III by five years and King Victor Emmanuel by a month. One of his last acts was to remove the excommunication by which the King would have been barred from receiving the last sacraments. In the weeks immediately before his death his most regular visitor was the Archbishop of Westminster, Cardinal Henry Manning, an Ultramontanist through and through. Just before his death Pius gave Manning a remarkably bad photograph of himself, scribbling on the bottom the words of Christ as he walked on the waters: 'Fear not, it is I'. One wonders whether Manning appreciated the joke.

Pius died on the morning of 8 February 1878. According to custom, Cardinal Pecci – soon to succeed him as Leo XIII – tapped his forehead three times with a little silver hammer, calling him by his baptismal name, Giovanni Maria. When there was no reply he turned to the other cardinals present with the traditional words: 'The Pope is truly dead.' The body lay in state in the Chapel of the Blessed Sacrament, behind a grille which the feet touched, so that they could be kissed by the faithful. A vast crowd filed by to do so, day and night, for three days.

It had been the longest pontificate – thirty-one years – in papal history. Politically it had been (from Pius's point of view) a disaster; but Pius did not spend all his life trying to maintain his temporal power. His first concern was always for the health and well-being of the Church itself; and for this no Pope had ever worked harder, or with greater effect. He founded more than 200 new dioceses, particularly in the United States and the British Empire; he re-established the Catholic hierarchies in Britain and the Netherlands; and he concluded concordats with an impressive number of states, Catholic or otherwise.

And there were other achievements, too, still more lasting, though not perhaps in every case universally acclaimed. Already in 1854 the Pope had proclaimed the doctrine of the Immaculate Conception, according to which the Blessed Virgin (not, as many people assume, Jesus Christ) was born without original sin. The manner of the proclamation was as significant, if not more so, as the doctrine itself; though Pius had consulted several bishops in advance, he dared – as no pope had ever dared before – to put forward the dogma on his own sole authority. In doing so he gave an enormous boost to the burgeoning cult of Mary, which continued to gather momentum as the century advanced. (Only four years later came the stamp of divine approval:

in Lourdes, the Virgin appeared to young Bernadette Soubirous and introduced herself with the words 'I am the Immaculate Conception'.) Another cult to which the Pope gave great encouragement was that of the Sacred Heart of Jesus. Eighteenth-century Jansenists had dismissed it as 'cardiolatry', but Pius placed its feast day firmly on the Church calendar. It is no coincidence that the church of the Sacré Coeur in Paris was built during his pontificate on the Butte Montmartre – the highest point of Paris.

All his life he had been alternately loved and hated, respected and despised; and in 1881, three years after his death, the pendulum swung again. It had been decided that his body should find its final resting place in the patriarchal basilica of S. Lorenzo fuori le Mura; but since Italy was by now in the grip of a furious wave of anticlericalism inspired by her Prime Minister Agostino Depretis, it was thought safer for it to be transported by night. Unfortunately, word of the intended operation had somehow reached the Roman mob, which almost succeeded in hurling the coffin into the river. By the time it was carried into S. Lorenzo it had been dented by stones and was heavily spattered with mud. Pio Nono, it seemed, was as controversial a figure as ever he had been. He still is.

CHAPTER XXVI

Leo XIII and the First World War

(1878–1922)

The conclave that, on its third ballot, elected Cardinal Gioacchino Vincenzo Pecci as Pope Leo XIII (1878–1903) on 20 February 1878 was the first to be held by the Holy See since its loss of temporal power. The Cardinal was ten days short of his sixty-eighth birthday, and was known to be in poor health; but those who saw him as little more than a stopgap pope soon had cause to revise their opinions. He was to run the Church with remarkable efficiency for more than a quarter of a century.

His early career had been unpromising. A nunciature to Belgium in 1843 had ended in disaster, with his ignominious departure at the request of King Leopold I. His next thirty-two years were spent as the not particularly important Bishop of Perugia. In 1853 Pius IX had made him a cardinal, but the all-powerful Antonelli had disliked and distrusted him, and it was only after Antonelli's death in 1876 that Pecci had been recalled to Rome. He was then appointed *Camerlengo*, the cardinal who administers the Church between the death of a Pope and the election of his successor; but even this was less significant than might have been supposed, since there was a long-standing tradition that *Camerlenghi* did not become popes.

The problems that Leo inherited were formidable indeed. Throughout the 1870s and 1880s, and especially under the ministries of Agostino Depretis and Francesco Crispi, the attitude of the Kingdom of Italy to the papacy was frankly hostile: the Law of Guarantees was infringed again and again. Leo was not even allowed to bless the crowd in the traditional manner after his coronation, from the loggia of St Peter's; instead, the whole ceremony had to take place in the seclusion of the Sistine Chapel. Over the next few years the situation grew steadily worse. Processions and outdoor services were banned; the bishops suffered from unremitting government interference; tithes were withheld; priests were conscripted into the army, while fewer and fewer of them were allowed to involve themselves in education.

The Catholic faithful, alarmed by what was beginning to look suspiciously like persecution, implored the Pope to form his own parliamentary party, in order to tackle the government on its own ground; but Leo remained firm. If Catholics wished to express their feelings by voting in the local or municipal elections, they might do so; anything more would mean recognition of the Italian state – and that remained out of the question.

As Supreme Pontiff, on the other hand, he could speak out for the Church – which he regularly and vigorously did. The views Leo expressed were essentially those of his predecessor, of the Vatican Council and even of the *Syllabus*; but the tone was markedly different. Gone was the shrillness that had informed so many of Pius IX's later pronouncements; Leo spoke with a voice of calm, reason and regret. Why was the Kingdom of Italy so hostile? Surely the Church should be a friend, not an enemy. Had it not led humanity out of barbarism and into enlightenment? Why, then, was its teaching rejected? As anyone could see, that rejection was causing nothing but lawlessness and strife. If Italy would only return to the Catholic fold, all her present troubles would vanish away.

With other nations, Leo adopted an even gentler approach. The Franco-Prussian War had changed the religious face of Europe. The dominant power was no longer Catholic Austria, but fiercely Protestant Prussia, and this new dispensation had left the Catholic areas of Germany (particularly Bavaria) gravely concerned. German Protestants had been outraged by Pius IX's *Syllabus* and by the definition of infallibility, while the Catholics had organised themselves into a powerful political party, which made a considerable nuisance of itself in the Berlin parliament; Bismarck had consequently come to look upon them as a potentially dangerous enemy. With the help of the odious Dr Adalbert Falk, whom in 1872 he made his Minister of Education, he had instituted what was known as the *Kulturkampf* – the Culture Struggle – and this in turn had given rise to the so-called Falk Laws, which expelled the Jesuits and several other religious Orders, subjected all Catholic educational establishments to rigid state control and made any discussion of politics from the pulpit punishable by imprisonment.

Once enthroned, Leo lost no time in seeking a reconciliation. Fortunately for him, Bismarck was already losing confidence in his anticlerical policy, which was proving singularly unsuccessful; it had aroused furious protestations, one or two serious riots and even occasional bloodshed. He was now only too pleased to find an excuse to abandon it, and the overtures made by the Pope provided a perfect face-saving opportunity to do so. The Chancellor could not, of course, be seen to give in too quickly; but by the end of 1880 the worst of the anticlerical laws had been rescinded, and by 1886 the *Kulturkampf* was a thing of the past. The only important exception was the ban on the Jesuits, which was to remain in force until 1917.

Unfortunately, just as Prussia was giving up her anticlericalism, France was reviving hers. The recent war had been followed by the horrors of the Paris Commune, in the course of which the Archbishop of Paris and several other distinguished churchmen had been executed by firing squad; the atrocity had led, not surprisingly, to a right-wing reaction, which had continued through most of the decade. By 1879, this in turn was spent, and the French political scene was dominated by Léon Gambetta, who two years before had defined his position with the words, '*Le cléricalisme, c'est l'ennemi.*' On the last day of 1882 Gambetta died at the age of only forty-four, in the company of his mistress, from the "accidental" discharge of a revolver; but his policies lived on after him. Throughout the 1880s and 1890s in France it was the *Kulturkampf* all over again. Under the famous Article VII of the educational code of the radically left-wing Jules Ferry, religious and lay schools might no longer compete on an equal footing. Just as they had been under Louis XV, the Jesuits were driven from their religious houses. They, the Marist Fathers and the Dominicans were deprived of the right to teach in either state or private schools. Primary education was completely secularised. Seminarists were no longer excused military service. The first state secondary schools for girls were established – a major (and to many a shocking) reform, since the education of young women had until now always been the preserve of the Church. Finally, divorce was permitted for the first time.

With the Third Republic and the Church at daggers drawn, Pope Leo did his best. In encyclical after encyclical he urged the French government to put an end to its hostility, damaging surely to the very soul of France: Church and State, he endlessly repeated, were not incompatible; they were complementary to each other, and should consequently be working together for the general good of the French people. But to the right-wing, monarchist, Catholic faction he was just as outspoken. There was, he declared, nothing illegal or immoral in the principle of republicanism as such; whatever their feelings, it was the duty of all good Catholics to support the established Republic.

The Church could fight hostile legislation; it must never oppose a legitimate Constitution. But the Pope's words had little effect; and France's narrow escape in 1888–9 from a dictatorship under the consumingly ambitious, but ultimately somewhat absurd General Georges Boulanger[1] did still more to polarise the Catholic right.

From 1893 to 1898 France was governed by a set of rather more moderate ministers, and it seemed at first that the worst of the Church's troubles might be over. Another of Pope Leo's encyclicals assured French Catholics that a bishop might quite reasonably support a republican candidate so long as that candidate gave him guarantees of religious freedom. This led to the establishment of a Catholic Republican party, which caused the parliamentary majority to shift towards the centre. But then in November 1894 came the conviction on a charge of treason of the Jewish Colonel Alfred Dreyfus, and his subsequent sentence to life imprisonment on Devil's Island. On the question of his guilt or innocence France was split in two, with the always anti-Semitic Catholic right predictably campaigning against Dreyfus. (Of all the publications involved, the most venomously malignant was the journal of the Assumptionist Order, *La Croix*.[2]) The *affaire* was to drag on until the summer of 1906, when Dreyfus was finally restored to his former rank, promoted and decorated.

By then, however, Catholicism in France had suffered its greatest blow of all. In June 1902 the government was taken over by Emile Combes, a provincial politician who had himself studied for the priesthood, but had later developed a bitter hatred of the Church and everything it stood for. The wholesale expulsion of all 'unauthorised' religious Orders was now set in train; on 19 April 1903 the entire monastic community of the Grande Chartreuse was forcibly ejected by two squadrons of dragoons with fixed bayonets. By the end of 1904 more than 10,000 Catholic schools had been closed. Thousands of priests, monks and nuns had fled France to escape persecution; and

---

[1] Boulanger came close to a *coup d'état*, but lost his nerve. He fled to Brussels, later shooting himself on his mistress's grave. In the words of the journalist Caroline Rémy, who wrote under the pseudonym of Séverine, 'he began like Caesar, continued like Catiline, and ended like Romeo'.

[2] *Civiltà Cattolica*, the journal of the Jesuits in Rome, continued to proclaim Dreyfus's guilt even after his pardon – the editor, Fr Raffaele Ballerini, claiming that the Jews had 'bought all the newspapers and consciences in Europe' in order to acquit him. A few years before, in 1881 and 1882, the same journal had claimed that the blood of a Christian child was required by a general law 'binding on the conscience of all Hebrews'. Every year, it went on, the Jews 'crucify a child', who 'must die in torment' (J. Cornwell, *Hitler's Pope: The Secret History of Pius XII*, p.28).

in December 1905 the Concordat of 1801 was formally abrogated, bringing about the complete separation of Church and State.

It was a sad day for the pontificate; happily for him, Leo XIII did not live to see it.

Leo's most significant work, however, was not political or diplomatic, but sociological. He was the first pope to face up to the fact that the world had moved into an industrial age. It was not that the appearance of a teeming urban proletariat in Italy had somehow escaped the notice of his predecessor; Pius IX had been bitter indeed in his repeated attacks on socialism, nihilism and what he saw as the other evils of the time. He had failed, on the other hand, to appreciate that this immense new working class was the responsibility of the Church, which was largely ignoring it. It was Leo who reopened the dialogue between them, and introduced programmes of social action. His *Opera dei Congressi e dei Comitati Cattolici* sponsored fourteen congresses during his pontificate alone; but he also supervised the formation of Catholic trade unions, which had considerable success until in 1927 Mussolini made voluntary withdrawal of labour a punishable offence.

His greatest monument is probably his encyclical *Rerum Novarum*, published in May 1891. It was in fact the papacy's shamefully belated response to *Das Kapital* and *The Socialist Manifesto*, and was later to be described by Pope John XXIII as the Magna Carta of Catholic social doctrine. Already in the preamble, Leo nailed his colours to the mast. In the present industrial society, he wrote:

> a small number of very rich men have been able to lay upon the teeming masses of the labouring poor a yoke which is very little better than slavery itself . . . The conflict now raging derives from the vast expansion of industrial pursuits and the marvellous discoveries of science; from the changed relations between masters and workmen; from the enormous fortunes of some few individuals and the utter poverty of the masses; from the increased self-reliance and closer mutual combination of the working classes; and also, finally, from the prevailing moral degeneracy.

Class and inequality, he emphasised, would always be present; at the same time he vehemently condemned the Marxist theory of class war. The fault lay in the unthinking callousness and greed of contemporary capitalism; every worker had the right to demand a fair wage and even, if absolutely necessary, to go on strike. The business of the

State was to ensure that contracts between employers and employees were properly drawn up and respected, and to regulate factory hours, safety measures and working conditions. It should not, however, concern itself with the elimination of social abuses; this could be achieved only through Christian charity. Religion was thus the once sure guide to industrial peace. Without it, the world would subside into godless anarchy; and in the spate of public assassinations that occurred during the last decade of his life – of the French President Sadi Carnot in 1894, of the Empress Elizabeth of Austria in 1898, of King Umberto I of Italy in 1900, and of President McKinley of the United States in 1901 – he seemed to see the realisation of his worst nightmare.

There was nothing particularly revolutionary about all this; much of it was wrapped up in the old papal paternalistic language, and there were plenty of passages about the natural inequality of men and the duty of the poor to accept their station in life, which, when taken out of context, could be used by right-wing apologists to argue that nothing had really changed. The true significance of *Rerum Novarum* is that it represents the thinking of the first pope of the twentieth century, of the successor to Pio Nono. From now on the door was open for future generations of Catholic socialists to develop that thinking further, and to carry it forward.

Pope Leo XIII died on 20 July 1903, in his ninety-fourth year, as lucid as he had ever been and very nearly as energetic. Few popes had had to fight harder than he for the well-being – one might almost say the survival – of the Catholic Church in two leading nations of Europe that should have known better, and during his twenty-five year struggle he had suffered many setbacks and disappointments. He could, however, look back on one tremendous achievement: he had proved that the Pope, even when shorn of his temporal power, indeed even when 'prisoner of the Vatican', could still be a potent force in the world. He had given the papacy a new image, and a prestige greater than it had enjoyed for many centuries.

Leo XIII had been respected and revered across the globe; he had not, however, been loved. No temporal monarch had ever surrounded himself with more ceremonial. Leo had insisted that all his visitors should kneel throughout the audience; members of his entourage had been obliged to remain standing in his presence; we are told that not once in twenty-five years did he address a single word to his coachman.

It was not surprising that after his death the cardinals wanted a change; and they got one. Giuseppe Sarto, who took the name of Pius X (1903–14), was a peasant – the first since Sixtus V, more than three centuries before – the son of a village postman and a seamstress from the Veneto. He had spent eight years as a parish priest, and although he had later served as Bishop of Mantua and Patriarch of Venice, a parish priest is essentially what he had remained; throughout his pontificate he personally gave classes on the catechism every Sunday afternoon. There was about him not a trace of the grandeur, the austerity or the cool detachment of his predecessor; he was warm, approachable and above all down-to-earth.

Once enthroned, he lost no time in introducing reforms within the Church itself. He streamlined the Curia, reducing its thirty-seven different departments to nineteen. He revised and recodified the canon law. He virtually rewrote the breviary and the catechism. He also made far-reaching changes in Church music. In the nineteenth century its traditionally medieval character had given way to compositions heavily influenced by Italian opera; Verdi's *Requiem* and Rossini's enchanting *Petite Messe Solonelle* are obvious examples. This the Pope firmly denounced, calling for a return of Gregorian chant and plainsong. He also launched a campaign to encourage all Catholics to take Holy Communion more often. A few times a year, he stressed, was simply not enough – good Catholics should communicate every day, or at least once a week. The First Communion was another far-reaching change: previously, a child celebrated it between the ages of twelve and fourteen; henceforth the age was to be seven. This was the beginning of the tradition still seen all over the Catholic world: the little girls in their white dresses and veils, the little boys with their sashes, the presents and family celebrations afterwards.

Pius worked hard, and achieved much; but he failed altogether to make an impact on Europe and the world in the way that Pius IX and Leo had done. He was too quiet, too humble, too holy; and his very holiness closed his mind to original thought. The Catholic intellectual theologians in Italy and France, Germany and England, doing their best to free religion from the shackles of medieval scholasticism and to reconcile their faith with the philosophical ideas and the thrilling scientific, historical and archaeological discoveries that informed the opening century, found the Pope not just unsympathetic, but an active and implacable enemy. In 1907 he published the encyclical *Pascendi*, which ran to no fewer than ninety-three pages, condemning what he called 'modernism' as 'a compendium of all the heresies'. This has been described by one recent historian[1] as 'the opening shot in what rapidly became nothing less than a reign of terror'; the Pope and his Secretary of State, Cardinal Rafael Merry del Val (an Englishman of Spanish ancestry), personally approved an organisation named 'The Society of St Pius V', which amounted effectively to a secret police, suppressing liberal Catholic newspapers, steaming open letters, even using *agents provocateurs* to trap liberals into incriminating themselves. It was run by a distinctly sinister priest, Mgr Umberto Benigni. Among its victims were the Cardinal Archbishops of Paris and Vienna, and the entire Dominican community of Fribourg.

Despite his preoccupation with Church affairs, during the second half of his pontificate Pius X saw all too clearly the relentless advance of the European powers towards war – a war that would inevitably involve Catholics fighting Catholics, and would probably wreak more destruction than any other war in history. This caused him deep distress, the more so since he knew that he was powerless to prevent it. Its outbreak at the end of July 1914 is often said to have hastened his death, which occurred just three weeks later on 20 August. Indeed, it may well have done so; but he was already seventy-nine, was plagued by gout and had suffered a heart attack the previous year. He would probably not have lasted very much longer.

Especially in the theological field, Pius had his detractors; but no one doubted his essential goodness of heart. After the appalling earthquake that struck Messina in 1908, he had filled the Vatican with homeless refugees long before the Italian government had lifted a finger. He sought no favours, either for himself or his family: his brother remained a postal clerk, his three sisters lived together in straitened circumstances in Rome; his nephew continued as a simple parish priest. In consequence he was loved as neither of his two immediate predecessors had been, and before long crowds of pilgrims were coming to pray at his tomb in the crypt of St Peter's. In 1923, twenty years after his enthronement, the long process of canonisation began. It did not go altogether smoothly: the Secretary of State, Cardinal Pietro Gasparri, gave evidence that the Pope had 'approved, blessed and encouraged a secret espionage association outside and

[1] E. Duffy, *Saints and Sinners*, p.250.

above the hierarchy . . . a sort of Freemasonry in the Church, something unheard of in ecclesiastical history'. But such peccadillos were
ignored; and in 1954, before a crowd estimated at some 800,000,
Pope Pius XII formally declared him a saint – the first pope to be
so elevated since Pius V, who had died the best part of four centuries
before.[1]

The election of a Genoese aristocrat, the appropriately named Giacomo
della Chiesa, as Benedict XV (1914–22) at the sixteenth ballot caused
an immediate problem in the Vatican: owing to a dangerously premature birth, he had never attained normal height; even the smallest of
the papal robes kept in readiness for the new pope hung on him like
a curtain. He is said to have turned to the Vatican tailor and said
with a smile, '*Caro*, had you forgotten me?' In Bologna, where he
had been Archbishop, he had been known as *il piccoletto*; but it was
less on account of his size than for the fact that Pius X and Cardinal
Merry del Val deeply distrusted him that the membership of the Sacred
College, which normally went with the see, had been deliberately withheld; he had finally received his red hat little more than three months
before his coronation. He may not even have been particularly surprised
immediately afterwards, when one of the very first documents that
appeared on his desk proved to be a denunciation of himself, recently
prepared at the request of his predecessor. One of his first actions was
to dismiss his old chief, Merry del Val, to whom he hardly gave the
time to clear his desk. He went on to eliminate Mgr Benigni and his
espionage network, and the Curia once again breathed more easily.
    Benedict's pontificate was doomed before it started, overshadowed
as it had to be by the First World War. With so many of his flock
fighting on each side, Benedict could assume only a position of the
strictest neutrality, blaming both sides equally for the bloodshed and
devoting all his energies to bringing about an end to what he described
as 'this horrible butchery', by means of a negotiated peace. Meanwhile he did everything he could to mitigate the suffering: opening
up an agency in the Vatican for exchanging wounded prisoners of war
– it eventually achieved the repatriation of some 65,000; persuading

---

[1] 'The extent to which Roman canonisations have meanwhile deteriorated in our day to
gestures in church politics is shown by the canonisation of this very pope by Pius XII in
1954 and the beatification of Pius IX in 2000. That even most recently the Vatican has
opened the archive of the Inquisition only up to 1903, to the accession of Pius X, shows
how fearful people there are of the truth' (The Revd Hans Küng, *The Catholic Church*,
2001).

Switzerland to accept tuberculosis patients from whatever army they came; and almost bankrupting the Vatican with his countless relief operations.[1]

But strive as he might to be impartial, the inevitable result was that each side accused him of favouring the other – the Allies arguably having rather more reason to do so, since the Germans had actually offered, once the Italians were defeated, to help him to recover temporal authority over Rome for the papacy[2]. Benedict was terrified, too, in the event of a victory by the Russians, of a vast westward expansion of Orthodoxy; but with the advent of the Russian Revolution this fear suddenly turned to hope – that at last it might be possible to bring about a reconciliation with Orthodoxy, bringing it back within the Catholic fold. As early as May 1917 he had established a Congregation for the Eastern Church, following it up with a Pontifical Eastern Institute in Rome; but his efforts came to nothing – indeed, Lenin declared war on religion, and on assuming power was immediately to subject both the Orthodox and the Roman Catholic Churches in Russia to murderous persecution.

It was the success of the Italian government, when it entered the war in 1915, in persuading the Allies to have nothing to do with the Pope that denied him, to his unconcealed disappointment, representation at the peace negotiations of 1919. He could only denounce the government as 'vengeful' – as indeed it was. The remaining years of his life were spent attempting to secure the position of the Church in post-war Europe. Here his success was remarkable. When his pontificate had begun in 1914 the number of foreign countries with diplomatic representation at the Holy See numbered fourteen; when it ended in 1922 there were twenty-seven. These included Britain, whose chargé d'affaires was the first British representative there since the seventeenth century. In 1921 relations were even resumed with France, much mollified after the Pope was tactful enough to canonise Joan of Arc in 1920. True, the Vatican's relations with the Italian government remained a problem, but Benedict at least took the first steps towards its solution. He gave his blessing to the Italian People's Party founded by Don Luigi Sturzo – father of Christian Democracy in Italy – in 1919, thereby effectively abrogating Pius IX's *Non*

---

[1] According to the Italian historian Nino lo Bello, the Secretary of State, Cardinal Gasparri, was obliged to raise a loan from Rothschild's to pay for the 1922 Conclave.
[2] Papal relations with Germany were also greatly eased after 1917 through the smooth diplomacy of the nuncio, Monsignor Eugenio Pacelli, the future Pius XII.

Expedit;[1] three years later it was the second largest group in the parliament. Then, in 1920, he lifted the Church's ban on official visits to the Quirinal (since 1870 the official residence of the King of Italy) by Catholic heads of state.

Benedict's death, at the age of only sixty-seven, on 22 January 1922 – an attack of influenza having suddenly turned to pneumonia – took Europe by surprise. Throughout his pontificate he had remained relatively obscure; a recent biography even bears the title *The Unknown Pope*. This was not entirely due to the war. Unlike his two predecessors he was not handsome, nor was he remotely charismatic. 'With his unimpressive figure and his expressionless face,' wrote an American journalist, 'there is neither spiritual nor temporal majesty.' The Secretary to the British Legation went even further:

> . . . the present pope is a decided mediocrity. He has the mentality of a parochial Italian who has hardly travelled at all and a tortuous method of conducting affairs . . . He is capable of rising neither to great heights nor of efficiently controlling the ordinary routine of his administration . . . he is obstinate and bad-tempered to a degree.

This is not altogether fair. Benedict had after all had twenty years' experience at the Vatican, and his control of Bologna – always a difficult see – had been exemplary. He could not help his appearance or his public persona; nor could he, like Leo and Pius, impress himself on a constant stream of pilgrims whom he would daily receive in audience; thanks to the war, this stream had almost dried up. But the fact remains that, despite his immense humanitarian support to both sides, Benedict made little impression either on Italy or on the world at large. It is somehow significant that, apart from his tomb in St Peter's, his only monument was erected by – of all people – the Turks, in the courtyard of the Saint-Esprit Cathedral in Istanbul. It bears the inscription: 'The great Pope of the world tragedy . . . the benefactor of all peoples, irrespective of nationality or religion'. At least somebody was grateful.

---

[1] The decree of 1868 forbidding Catholics to take part in Italian political life (see Chapter XXV, p.401).

CHAPTER XXVII

Pius XI and Pius XII

(1922–58)

Elected at the fourteenth ballot, and then only to break a deadlock in the conclave, Pope Pius XI (1922–39) came as a considerable surprise. Achille Ratti was a sixty-five-year-old scholar, an expert on medieval palaeography who had spent most of his working life as a librarian and much of his leisure time mountain-climbing in the Alps. In 1919 Benedict XV had sent him as nuncio to Poland, which had, after 123 years, just regained its independence as a sovereign state. It was not a happy mission: Ratti was resented and mistrusted by the Polish hierarchy, which saw him simply as the agent of a pro-German pope. Within fourteen months of his arrival, however, the situation had changed dramatically. The Bolsheviks had invaded Poland, and in the summer of 1920 had marched on Warsaw. Had they captured the city, there would have been nothing to stop them taking over the whole of eastern Europe. No foreign observer would have given the Poles a chance against them, but somehow – and many both inside and outside the country considered it nothing short of a miracle – Marshal Jozef Pilsudski managed to launch a massive counter-attack and at the last moment turned the tide.

Ratti could easily have escaped back to Rome; instead, he had categorically refused to leave Warsaw. It was many centuries since a papal envoy had stood with the army of Christendom as it defended its frontier and, with the danger finally averted, it was no wonder that his popularity soared. He himself never forgot the experience, which left him with the lifelong conviction that of all the enemies with which Christian Europe was faced, communism was by far the most terrible. In the spring of 1921 he returned to Italy, first to the cardinalate and then, in June, to the archbishopric of Milan; but his life as an archbishop was short – only seven months later he was elected Pope.

He started as he meant to go on. After informing the cardinals of his chosen name, his first act as Supreme Pontiff was to announce that he would give the traditional papal blessing, *Urbi et Orbi*, from the outside balcony of St Peter's. It would be for the first time since 1870; but there was no consultation, no seeking advice; that, as his entourage quickly discovered, was not his way. Pius knew precisely what he wanted, and was determined to get it.

His strength of character – one might almost say his ruthlessness – was soon amply demonstrated in his dealings with France. The restoration of friendly relations had begun with his predecessor Benedict; the canonisation of Joan of Arc had had a remarkable impact, and had been attended by representatives of the French government as well as by no fewer than eighty parliamentary deputies from Paris. There was, however, a problem – in the shape of a dangerously popular right-wing movement and newspaper, pseudo-Catholic, monarchist and deeply anti-Semitic, both known as *Action Française*. Their founder, a deeply unpleasant demagogue named Charles Maurras, had long since lost whatever faith he might once have possessed, but he saw the Church as a pillar of the reaction in which he fanatically believed and had no scruples in exploiting it for his own ends. Large numbers of French Catholics, including several bishops, read his newspaper and shared his views – which included a detestation of the French Republic. It thus became clear to Pope Pius that there could be no further improvement in relations with France while Maurras and *Action Française* continued to claim papal backing. In 1925 he put them both on the Index, and two years later formally excommunicated all the movement's supporters. When the eighty-one-year-old French Jesuit Cardinal Louis Billot subsequently wrote to the newspaper expressing his sympathy, the Pope summoned him to an audience and obliged him to resign his red hat.[1]

A still greater challenge to the Pope's statesmanship was the rise of Fascist Italy. At the end of October 1922, less than nine months after the papal election, Benito Mussolini staged his 'March on Rome' and was accepted by King Victor Emmanuel as his Prime Minister. In the early days, before he became 'Il Duce', Mussolini might still have been overturned in a parliamentary election. The socialists and Don Luigi Sturzo's People's Party together easily outnumbered the thirty-five

---

[1] 'Support for Maurras was strong among the French Holy Ghost Fathers, one of whom was the Rector of the French Seminary in Rome where the students had a strong *Action Française* group. Pius sent for the ancient, bearded superior of the Order, and told him to sack the Rector. The old man replied, "Yes, Holy Father, I'll see what I can do", upon which the Pope grabbed his beard and shouted, "I didn't say see what you can do, I said fire him".' (E. Duffy, *Saints and Sinners*, pp.256–7).

1929

Fascist deputies; had they formed an alliance they might have ensured the survival of freedom in Italy. But Pius would have none of it. For him any association with socialism was out of the question; moreover, he was becoming increasingly concerned by certain distinctly left-wing tendencies of the People's Party. Don Luigi was accordingly informed that His Holiness considered his political activities incompatible with his priesthood and obediently withdrew into exile, first in London and later in the United States (where, much to the Vatican's irritation, he continued his political activity). In Italy his party, powerless without papal support, quietly faded away.

The Fascists, by contrast, were growing steadily stronger. In 1923 the Italian government passed the so-called Acerbo Law, which decreed that any party gaining 25 per cent of the votes should have a two-thirds majority in the Parliament. Its purpose was transparently to ensure this majority for the Fascists, and after the election of the following year there was no further obstacle to Mussolini imposing his dictatorship. By this time he had moderated his early anti-religious attitude and was making conciliatory gestures to the Church – reintroducing religion into state schools, erecting crucifixes in the law courts, even in 1927 himself undergoing a Roman Catholic baptism; and in that same year he proposed a treaty and a concordat which, after endless argument and much hard bargaining, were eventually signed at the Lateran Palace, by himself and by Pius's Secretary of State, Cardinal Pietro Gasparri, on 11 February 1929.

Under this Lateran Treaty the Pope regained a vestige of his temporal power. Admittedly the land over which he was sovereign ruler amounted to a mere 109 acres – about a quarter of the area of the Principality of Monaco – with a population of rather fewer than 500, but the Holy See was once again to rank among the nations of the world. Moreover, in return for his renunciation of his claim to the previous papal territories, the Pope was given a payment, in cash and Italian state securities, of 1,750 million lire – which at that time amounted to some £21 million. Anticlerical laws passed by the Italian government since 1870, including the Law of Guarantees, were declared null and void. In return, the Vatican promised to remain neutral and not to involve itself in international politics or diplomacy.

The Concordat dealt with the status of the Church in Italy. It declared Roman Catholicism to be the only recognised religion of the State, recognised canon law alongside state law, provided for Catholic religious teaching in state schools and validated Catholic church

417

marriages. The Roman catacombs were entrusted to the Holy See, on the understanding that the Vatican would allow archaeological excavation and exploration by the Italian government to continue. On the face of it, the papacy had done remarkably well. It could not be denied, however, that it had given its implied approval to Fascism. The Pope had even hailed Mussolini as 'a man sent by Providence', and in the 1929 elections most Catholics were encouraged by their priests to vote Fascist.

The honeymoon could not last. The rupture began with Catholic Action, a movement founded by Pius X, which was really little more than a nationwide society dedicated, as the Pope had put it, to 'restoring Jesus Christ to his place in the family, in the school and in the community'. Mussolini – who instinctively mistrusted any national organisation that he did not personally control – claimed that it was politically inspired, serving as a front for the People's Party of the now-exiled Sturzo. The Catholic Scout movement aroused his anger even more: no one understood better than he the importance of early brainwashing. 'Youth,' he declared, 'shall be ours.' As these and similar bodies suffered increasing physical harassment from the Fascist thugs who came in force to break up their meetings or to seize and impound their records, the Pope raised his voice in protest. His encyclical *Non abbiamo bisogno* of June 1931 – drafted, significantly, in Italian – began by answering the Duce's charges *seriatim*; as it continued, however, it turned into a general attack on Fascism and all it stood for:

> What is to be thought about the formula of the oath, which even little boys and girls are obliged to take, that they will execute orders without discussion from an authority which . . . can give orders against all truth and justice? . . . Takers of this oath must swear to serve with all their strength, even to the shedding of blood, the cause of a revolution which snatched the young from the Church and from Jesus Christ, and which inculcates in its own young people hatred, violence and irreverence . . . Such an oath is unlawful . . .
>
> We have not said that we wish to condemn the [Fascist] party as such . . . It [recently] declared that 'respect for the Catholic religion and for its Supreme Head, is unchanged'. [But this] is the respect which has had its expression in vastly extended and hateful police measures, prepared in the deep silence of a conspiracy, and executed with lightning-like suddenness, on the very eve of our birthday . . .

In the same context there is an allusion to 'refuges and protections' given to the still remaining opponents of the party; 'the directors of the 9,000 groups of Fascists in Italy' are ordered to direct their attention to this situation . . . [We have received] sad information about the effect of these remarks, these insinuations and these orders, which have induced a new outbreak of hateful surveillance, of denunciations and of intimidations . . .

Interestingly enough, the encyclical had a measure of success. It was widely read in Italy and abroad, and caused Mussolini appreciably to relax his pressure on the Church. It must also have been very much in the mind of Cardinal Eugenio Pacelli, who in February 1930 had succeeded Gasparri as Pius's Secretary of State. From the outset, Pacelli was fixated on Germany. He knew the country well, having served as nuncio in Munich for three years from 1917 and in Berlin throughout the 1920s. He loved the Germans and spoke their language perfectly, often in preference to Italian. He was also aware that in pre-war days Germany had contributed more funds to the Holy See than all the other nations of the world combined. It was not of course technically a Catholic country – in 1930 the Catholics represented about one-third of the population, although by 1940, after Hitler's annexations of the Saar, the Sudetenland and Austria, the proportion had increased to about half – and neither Pacelli nor Pius had any delusions about the Nazis, whom they saw as little better than gangsters; but they nevertheless believed that National Socialism represented a firm bulwark against communism, in their eyes the far greater enemy.

And so, on 20 July 1933, the German Concordat was signed in Rome, by Pacelli on behalf of Pope Pius XI and by Franz von Papen, Vice-Chancellor of the Reich, for Adolf Hitler. Generous privileges were granted to the Catholic clergy and to Catholic schools in Germany, in return for the withdrawal by the Catholic Church, with its various associations and its newspapers, from all social and political action. This withdrawal involved, as it had in Italy, the loss of a political party. In the hope of an understanding with Mussolini, Pius had effectively sacrificed the *Partito Populare*; now, at Hitler's insistence, Pacelli intimated that the Centre Party – the second-strongest in the *Reichstag*, which was also led by a priest, Mgr Ludwig Kaas, and included the vast majority of German Catholics in its ranks – was, so far as the Vatican was concerned, dispensable. It was duly wound up, and Mgr Kaas, who had by this time fallen completely under Pacelli's spell and seldom left his side, was brought to Rome, where he was given charge of the fabric of St Peter's.[1]

As did the Italian, the German Concordat came in for heavy international criticism. The Catholic Church could have set itself up in determined opposition to National Socialism; instead, by agreeing to the abdication of all its political rights and morally obliging all German Catholics to obey their Nazi leaders, Pacelli and Pius had together cleared the way for the unobstructed advance of Nazism – and of its treatment of the Jews. In the minutes of a cabinet meeting held on 14 July 1933, Hitler is recorded as having boasted that 'the Concordat gave Germany an opportunity and created an area of trust that was particularly significant in the developing struggle against international Jewry'.[2] By the outside world the Pope was accused of giving both regimes respectability and of increasing their prestige – which indeed, in the short term, he did. But he was soon to show still greater dissatisfaction with the Nazis than he had with the Fascists: in the first three years of their regime between 1933 and 1936, during which their oppression of the Church steadily increased, he was obliged to address no fewer than thirty-four separate notes of protest to the German government. It is worth noting, however, that no protest was made against the publication of the Nuremberg race laws of 1935.[3]

The final break came on Passion Sunday 1937 – when the encyclical *Mit brennender Sorge*, having been smuggled into Germany, secretly printed there on twelve different presses and distributed by bicycle or on foot, was read from every Catholic pulpit. It should have come at least three years earlier; even now it failed to condemn Hitler and National Socialism by name. But its meaning was clear enough – particularly since it had been written in German rather than the usual Latin. The government of the Reich, it declared, had 'sown the tares of suspicion, discord, hatred, calumny, of secret and open hostility to

---

[1] It is to Mgr Kaas that we owe the discovery of the ancient shrine now claimed to be that of St Peter, revealed while he was reordering the crypt of St Peter's to accommodate Pius XI's tomb.

[2] Catholic priests in Germany were instructed – and in most cases seem willingly to have agreed – to provide the authorities, through the local registers of marriages and baptisms, with details of blood purity. The Concordat also trapped the Church into accepting Hitler's Law for the Prevention of Genetically Diseased Offspring, which was to result in the sterilisation of some 350,000 people, in most cases without their own or their familiy's consent.

[3] Nor, incidentally, would there be a word of condemnation for *Kristallnacht*, the first major German pogrom of 9–10 November 1938, in which ninety-one Jews were killed and some 30,000 arrested and sent to concentration camps. More than 200 synagogues were burned, and thousands of homes and businesses ransacked.

Christ and his Church, fed from a thousand different sources and making use of every available means'.

The eleventh paragraph of the encyclical is of particular interest because – though once again there is no specific condemnation of anti-Semitism – its target is clear. It stresses the value of the Jewish Old Testament, which it describes as being 'exclusively the word of God and a substantial part of His revelation':

> Whoever wishes to see banished from Church and school the Biblical history and the wise doctrines of the Old Testament blasphemes the name of God, blasphemes the Almighty's plan of salvation and makes limited and narrow human thought the judge of God's designs over the history of the world . . .

Non abbiamo bisogno and *Mit brennender Sorge* together left no doubt in anyone's mind about the Pope's opinions of the Fascist and National Socialist regimes; and no one was surprised that, when in March 1938 the Führer paid a state visit to Rome, Pius deliberately slipped away to Castel Gandolfo. But he was not yet finished: only five days after the second encyclical he published a third, for which he reverted to the traditional Latin. *Divini Redemptoris* was primarily directed against his greatest bugbear, communism:

> This modern revolution . . . exceeds in amplitude and violence anything yet experienced in the preceding persecutions launched against the Church. Entire peoples find themselves in danger of falling back into a barbarism worse than than that which oppressed the greater part of the world at the coming of the Redeemer.
>
> This all too imminent danger . . . is bolshevistic and atheistic communism, which aims at upsetting the social order and at undermining the very foundations of Christian civilisation . . .
>
> Communism, moreover, strips man of his liberty, robs human personality of all its dignity, and removes all the moral restraints that check the eruptions of blind impulse . . .
>
> For the first time in history we are witnessing a struggle, cold-blooded in purpose and mapped out to the last detail, between man and 'all that is called God'.

This hatred of communism was enough to ensure that when the Spanish Civil War broke out in July 1936 the Pope immediately gave his support to General Franco, though after the republican government's brutal separation of Church and State in 1931 – which had led to mob attacks on churches and monasteries, and massacres of priests, monks and nuns – he could hardly have done otherwise. It was nonetheless embarrassing for him to see Franco's victory being achieved on the backs of the two dictators – the more so when the Spanish Falangists began to emulate the worst characteristics of the Nazi and Fascist regimes that Pius had so frequently denounced.

But Pius's pontificate, overshadowed as it was by the European dictatorships, was by no means exclusively political. It saw the number of Catholic missionaries more than doubled, and at the same time a far greater degree of responsibility devolving on recently converted communities; as early as 1926 the Pope personally consecrated the first six Chinese bishops, and the total of native priests in India and the Far East increased from 3,000 to more than 7,000. It was a considerable disappointment to him that his efforts towards a reunion of the Catholic and Orthodox Churches met with so little response. (They might have had more success if he had not called the Churches back to the fold quite so patronisingly, as if they were lost sheep.)

Fortunately, he could always seek consolation in science. Pius was a genuine scholar – the first since Benedict XIV nearly two centuries before – and was not afraid to show it. He modernised and enlarged the Vatican Library, founded the Pontifical Institute of Christian Archaeology and the Pontifical Academy of Sciences, built the Pinacoteca for the Vatican's by now superb collection of pictures and transferred the old observatory from Rome to Castel Gandolfo. In 1931 he shocked many of the more old-fashioned faithful by installing a radio station and becoming the first pope to make regular broadcasts to the world. One of the most important of these transmissions was made at the time of the Munich crisis of September 1938, when the British Prime Minister Neville Chamberlain flew to Munich to meet Hitler in a vain attempt to prevent the imminent world war. Pius had little respect for Chamberlain who, as he instantly saw, was no match for his opponent; but he broadcast a moving appeal for peace, which was heard across Europe.

Unfortunately he was by now a sick man, and failing fast. Diabetes was rapidly taking hold, and both his legs were hideously ulcerated. On 25 November he suffered two heart attacks within a few hours of each other. He continued to give audiences – though now from his sickbed – and in January 1939 received Chamberlain and the Foreign Secretary Lord Halifax, in whom he did his best to instil a degree of courage and determination to resist Hitler's demands. But he was unsuccessful, as he had known he would be: 'Sono due limaccie,' he is said to have murmured as they left, 'They're a pair of slugs.'

By this time he was already working on what was to be his most vehement attack on the dictatorships, to be delivered at a meeting of all the Italian bishops on 11 February 1939. He implored his doctors to keep him alive long enough to make what he felt might be the most important speech of his life; alas, they failed to do so. Pius died the day before the speech was due to be made. Almost immediately the rumour began to spread that he had been murdered on Fascist orders by one of the doctors, Francesco Petacci.[1] What we know for a fact – on the authority of Mussolini's son-in-law and Foreign Minister, Count Gian Galeazzo Ciano – is that the Duce was later extremely anxious to find a copy of the speech and actually sent the Italian Ambassador to the Holy See to Pacelli (now Pope Pius XII) to enquire about it. Pacelli assured him that it had been consigned to the secret archives, where it would remain a dead letter.

Pius XI had his faults. He was an autocrat through and through. In his concept of Christianity he was bigoted, reactionary and inflexible: the Roman Catholic Church was right, everyone else was wrong. He had no time for the incipient ecumenical movement: so far as he was concerned, there could be no bargaining over God's revealed truth. 'The encyclical *Mortalium Annos*, of 1928 made it clear that the ecumenical message of the Vatican for the other Churches was simple and uncompromising: "Come in slowly, with your hands above your head."'[2] In the earlier period of his pontificate his detestation of communism – which, let it never be forgotten, he had seen at first hand in Poland – made him more tolerant of the Fascists, and at first perhaps even of the Nazis, than he might otherwise have been; but in his last years his open and unflinching hostility to both earned him the respect and admiration of the free world.

Pope Pius XI died on 10 February 1939; Pope Pius XII (1939–58) was elected on 2 March – his sixty-third birthday – on the third ballot, the very first day of the conclave. It was the shortest for 300 years. According to his sister, Eugenio Pacelli had been 'born a priest'; while still a child, he would dress up in cassock and surplice and act out

---

[1] Dr Petacci's daughter Claretta was, incidentally, the mistress of Mussolini and was to be summarily hanged with him six years later.
[2] E. Duffy, *Saints and Sinners*, p.262.

the celebration of the Mass in his bedroom. As soon as he was old enough he studied at the Gregorian University and the Capranica College in Rome, and he was still only twenty-three when he was ordained in 1899. Two years later he had entered the papal service, after which he never looked back, serving as nuncio first in Munich and then in Berlin, becoming a cardinal in 1929 and in the following year succeeding Gasparri as Secretary of State. In this capacity he had negotiated concordats with Austria and, in July 1933, with Nazi Germany. Although no Secretary of State had been elected Pope since Clement IX in 1667, Pacelli was by far the best-known, the most experienced and the most intelligent member of the Sacred College. His predecessor had had a huge admiration for him, and – as his own health had progressively collapsed – had entrusted to him more and more of the papal business. His election was, effectively, a foregone conclusion.

Cardinals are known as 'Princes of the Church'; few in the last three centuries have been more princely than Pacelli. When on 18 May 1917 he set off from Rome to Munich, his train included an additional sealed carriage – brought expressly from Zurich – containing sixty cases of food, in case the wartime rations of Germany should offend his notoriously delicate digestion. His private compartment, a luxury specifically forbidden during the war, had had to be specially requisitioned from the Italian State Railways, and all the stationmasters between Rome and the Swiss border were put on red alert. Six weeks later he travelled, in similar state, to Berlin, where he discussed Benedict's peace plan first with the imperial Chancellor, Theobald von Bethmann-Hollweg, and subsequently with Kaiser Wilhelm himself. Not surprisngly, the talks came to nothing: there could be no accommodation while both sides believed that they could win. Pacelli returned to Munich, and devoted himself once again to war relief.

At this, it must be said, he worked hard – visiting prison camps, distributing food parcels to the prisoners, giving spiritual assistance whenever and wherever he could. Only one incident strikes a sour note: when he dealt with a request to the Pope by the Chief Rabbi of Munich to use his influence for the release of a consignment of Italian palm fronds, which his Jewish flock needed for the forthcoming celebration of the Feast of Tabernacles. These fronds, it appeared, had already been purchased, but were held up in Como. Pacelli replied that although he had forwarded the request to Rome, he feared that thanks to wartime delays and the fact that the Holy See had no diplomatic relations with the Italian government, it was unlikely that anything could be done in time. He explained confidentially to Gasparri, however, that:

> it seemed to me that to go along with this would be to give the Jews special assistance not within the scope of practical, arm's-length, purely civil or natural rights common to all human beings, but in a positive and direct way to assist them in the exercise of their Jewish cult.

In April 1919, in the confusion following the armistice of the previous November, a trio of Bolsheviks – Max Levien, Eugen Leviné and Towia Axelrod – seized power in Bavaria. There followed a brief reign of terror, during which the foreign missions came under particular attack; the diplomatic corps consequently decided that it should send representatives to register a protest with Levien. Pacelli, then nuncio, reported to Gasparri:

> Since it would have been totally undignified for me to appear in the presence of this aforesaid gentleman, I sent the *uditore* [a certain Mgr Schioppa] . . .
> The scene that presented itself at the palace was indescribable. The confusion totally chaotic, the filth completely nauseating . . . and in the midst of all this, a gang of young women, of dubious appearance, Jews like all the rest of them, hanging around in all the offices with lecherous demeanour and suggestive smiles. The boss of this female rabble was Levien's mistress, a young Russian woman, a Jew and a divorcée, who was in charge. And it was to her that the nunciature was obliged to pay homage in order to proceed.
> This Levien is a young man, of about thirty or thirty-five, also Russian and a Jew. Pale, dirty, with drugged eyes, hoarse voice, vulgar, repulsive, with a face that is both intelligent and sly. He deigned to receive the Monsignor Uditore in the corridor, surrounded by an armed escort, one of whom was an armed hunchback, his faithful bodyguard. With a hat on his head and smoking a cigarette, he listened to what Monsignor Schioppa told him, whining repeatedly that he was in a hurry and had more important things to do.[1]

Much was to be written in later years of Pius XII's deep love and admiration for the Jewish people. These last two quotations suggest that such reports may have been somewhat exaggerated. On matters

---

[1] For fuller versions of these two quotations, see J. Cornwell, *Hitler's Pope*, pp.70 and 74–5.

of colour, on the other hand, there was no pretence. As early as 1920 Pacelli had complained to Gasparri that black soldiers in the French army were routinely raping German women and children in the Rhineland. To these accusations – which included no suggestion that white soldiers might be inclined to do the same – the army, not surprisingly, issued vehement denials; but Pacelli continued to believe the charges and to urge papal intervention. A quarter of a century later, as Pope, he was to ask the British Foreign Office for assurances that 'no Allied coloured troops would be among the small number that might be garrisoned in Rome after the occupation'.

Nazi Germany had annexed Austria in March 1938. Exactly a year later, after the fiasco of the Munich Agreement, German troops were massing on the border of Czechoslovakia. And yet, on 6 March 1939, just four days after his election, Pope Pius XII could personally draft a letter to Hitler:

> To the Illustrious Herr Adolf Hitler, Führer and Chancellor of the German Reich! Here at the beginning of Our Pontificate We desire to express the wish to remain united by the bonds of profound and benevolent friendship with the German people who are entrusted to your care ... We pray that Our great desire for the prosperity of the German people and for their progress in every domain may, with God's help, come to full realisation.

This letter was not only the first addressed by the new Pope to any head of state; we have the word of Mgr Alberto Giovanetti, one of the official historians of Pius XII, that 'in length and in the sentiments it expresses, it differs totally from the other official letters sent by the Vatican at that time'.

On 15 March 1939 the Germans occupied Czechoslovakia. A week later Diego von Bergen, German Ambassador to the Vatican, reported to his government:

> I learn from a well-informed source that urgent attempts have been made, especially on the French side, to prevail upon the Pope to associate himself with the protests of the democratic States against the annexation of Bohemia and Moravia to the Reich. The Pope has declined these requests very firmly. He has given those around him to understand that he sees no reason to interfere in historic processes in which, from the political point of view, the Church is not interested.

And even this was only the beginning. On 1 September 1939 the *Wehrmacht* marched into Catholic Poland, and two days later Britain and France declared war on Germany. Over the next five weeks the Poles lost some 70,000 men. From the Vatican, however, despite repeated intervention by the British and French Ambassadors, there came not a word of sympathy or regret, still less of denunciation. This deafening silence continued until the third week of October, when the Pope published his first encyclical, *Summi Pontificatus*. In this, at long last, Poland received a mention:

> The blood of countless human beings, noncombatants among them, has been shed and cries out to heaven, especially the blood of Poland, a nation very dear to us. Here is a people which has a right to the human and brotherly sympathy of the whole world, because of its devotion to the Church and by reason of the ardour that it has poured into the defence of Christian civilisation, so that its titles are carved indelibly on the tablets of history.

Not altogether surprisingly, the encyclical was welcomed by the Allies; the French air force dropped 88,000 copies of it over Germany. The language was clear enough for the German Foreign Office: 'Pius XII,' it informed its Ambassador to the Holy See, 'has ceased to be neutral.' It should be noted, however, that there is no mention anywhere in the text of Germany, or Nazis, or Jews.

There was a curious incident in November 1939, when the Pope was secretly approached by a group of German conspirators with a request for help. Their intention was to overthrow Hitler and return Germany to democracy; but before they could do so they needed a guarantee that the Western powers would not take advantage of any period of chaos that might result and impose on Germany terms as humiliating as those imposed after the First World War at Versailles. Would the Pope be prepared to act as go-between, seeking assurances that Britain and her Allies would agree to an honourable peace?

Pius was fully aware that he was being asked to take part in a conspiracy. This obviously represented a huge risk. Had any intervention by him become known, Hitler would almost certainly have vented his anger on the Catholic Church in Germany; Mussolini for his part might have claimed a breach of the Lateran Treaty and invaded the Papal State, or at least cut off its water and electricity supplies. Not surprisingly, Pius asked for twenty-four hours to consider. He consulted none of his Curia, not even his Secretary of State; the answer which he returned the next day – that he was prepared to do all he could for the sake of peace – represented his own decision and no one else's.

The decision, however, left him deeply uneasy. When the British Minister to the Holy See, Sir d'Arcy Osborne, had an audience shortly afterwards, he reported:

> He wished to pass the communication [from the German conspirators] on to me purely for information. He did not wish in the slightest degree to endorse or recommend it. After he had listened to my comments . . . he said that perhaps, after all, it was not worth proceeding with the matter and he would therefore ask me to regard his communication to me as not having been made. This, however, I promptly declined, as I said I refused to have the responsibilities of His Holiness's conscience unloaded on to my own.

In the final event, the whole thing came to nothing. Neville Chamberlain's government insisted on far more information than the conspirators were prepared to give, and was anyway unimpressed by the thought of making any sort of peace while the German military machine remained intact. It insisted, too, on bringing in the French, which the conspirators were extremely reluctant to do. It may be that the latter lost their nerve; for whatever reason, the plot simply ran out of steam. It has seemed worth recording here simply as an indication of Pius's basic anti-Nazi feelings, of his courage in taking a quite exceptionally dangerous decision, and of his strange insecurity once that decision was made.

And so we come to the mighty question mark that casts its shadow over the pontificate of Pope Pius XII: his attitude to the Holocaust. A strong vein of anti-Semitism had always run through Catholic thinking: had not the Jews murdered Christ? The Tridentine Mass, promulgated by the Council of Trent in the sixteenth century,[1] contained a Good Friday prayer for the conversion of 'the perfidious Jews'[2], and the right-wing Catholic parties in France, Germany and Austria made no secret of their anti-Semitic feelings. It is hardly necessary to say that such views found no place in the official teaching of

---

[1] See Chapter XVIII.
[2] The phrase was later eliminated on the orders of John XXIII (see Chapter XXVIII).

the Church; but the passages quoted earlier in this chapter make it clear that they were shared at least to some extent by the young Pacelli – and he is unlikely to have been alone.

'The Jews,' declared Hitler in a broadcast on 9 February 1942, 'will be liquidated for at least a thousand years.' Within a month, active persecution was under way not only in Germany, Austria and Poland, but in Hungary, Croatia, Slovakia and Marshal Pétain's Unoccupied France. All this was well known in the Vatican; indeed, it was common knowledge throughout Europe. On 21 April Sir d'Arcy Osborne wrote to his friend Bridget McEwen: 'Yesterday being Hitler's birthday, I wore a black tie in mourning for the millions he has massacred and tortured.' The Pope could hardly have worn a black tie, but he could have spoken out against the continuing atrocities. Despite Osborne's continued entreaties, he refused to do so. On 31 July Osborne wrote again to Mrs McEwen:

> It is very sad. The fact is that the moral authority of the Holy See, which Pius XI and his predecessors had built up into a world power, is now sadly reduced. I suspect that H.H. [His Holiness] hopes to play a great role as peacemaker and that it is partly at least for this reason that he tries to preserve a position of neutrality as between the belligerents. But, as you say, the German crimes have nothing to do with neutrality . . . and the fact is that the Pope's silence is defeating its own purpose because it is destroying his prospects of contributing to peace.

By now the mass deportations had begun; before the end of the year 42,000 French Jews had been sent to Auschwitz alone. In September President Roosevelt sent a personal envoy to the Pope to beg him to condemn the German war crimes; but still the Pope refused. The papal Secretary of State, Cardinal Maglione, would only repeat that the Holy See was doing all that it could.

It was not – if only because as 1942 drew to its close, the Vatican clearly had something else on its mind. It was terrified that the Allies were going to bomb Rome. Poor Osborne was being summoned almost daily to the Secretariat of State and entreated to extract a firm undertaking from the British government that there would be no air raids on the Holy City. In vain he pointed out that Britain was at war, and that Rome was an enemy capital; and he well knew that, even if the city was to be spared, it was highly unlikely the Italians would be given advance information of the fact. He wrote on 13 December:

The more I think of it, the more I am revolted by Hitler's massacre of the Jewish race on the one hand, and, on the other, the Vatican's apparently exclusive preoccupation with the effects of the war on Italy and the possibilities of the bombardment of Rome. The whole outfit seems to have become Italian.

The following day he had another talk with Cardinal Maglione:

I urged that the Vatican, instead of thinking of nothing but the bombing of Rome, should consider their duties in respect of the unprecedented crime against humanity of Hitler's campaign of extermination of the Jews, in which I said Italy was an accomplice as the partner and ally of Germany.

Finally, on Christmas Eve 1942, Pius XII made a broadcast to the world. It was long and, for the most part, stiflingly turgid. Only at the very end, when the majority of his listeners had probably switched off through sheer boredom, did he come, after a fashion, to the point, calling on men of good will to make a solemn vow 'to bring back society to its centre of gravity, which is the law of God'. He continued:

Mankind owes that vow to the countless dead who lie buried on the field of battle. The sacrifice of their lives in the fulfilment of their duty is a holocaust offered for a new and better social order. Mankind owes that vow to the innumerable sorrowing host of mothers, widows and orphans who have seen the light, the solace and the support of their lives wrenched from them. Mankind owes that vow to those number-less exiles whom the hurricane of war has torn from their native land and scattered in the land of the stranger, who can make their own the lament of the Prophet: 'Our inheritance is turned to aliens, our house to strangers'. Mankind owes that vow to the hundreds and thousands of persons who, without any fault on their part, sometimes only because of their nationality or race, have been consigned to death or to a slow decline.

And that was it. Once again there was no mention of Jews, or of Nazis, or even of Germany. The racial element of the Holocaust had been toned down by the addition of the two weasel words 'sometimes only'; millions of victims – even by Christmas 1942 – had been deli-cately reduced to 'hundreds and thousands'. When Mussolini heard it, he said to Ciano, 'This is a collection of platitudes which might better have been made by the parish priest of Predappio.'[1] He was not very far wrong.

Until now, in comparison with their central-European brethren, the Italian Jews had been relatively lucky. Although the 8,000-odd people who comprised the Jewish community of Rome doubtless shared in full measure the general indignation at the Pope's apparent spinelessness, while the Duce continued in power they were left for the most part undisturbed. Mussolini had enacted a number of anti-Semitic laws, but they had been largely disregarded. Then, in July 1943, everything changed. The Allies invaded Sicily, and bombed Rome. Mussolini was arrested. Nearly two years later, on 29 April 1945, he and Claretta Petacci were summarily executed, and left hanging from the roof of a garage. On 11 September Rome came under German occupation, and Marshal Albert Kesselring declared martial law. On 18 October the SS gave the order to round up the Jews.

There had been Jews in Rome before there had been Christians. The first Jewish settlers had arrived in 139 BC. After the coming of Christianity the fortunes of their community had varied; several of its tribulations have been recorded in earlier chapters of this book. Never in all its history, however, had Italian Jews faced a threat such as this. Already at the end of September the Jewish community had been compelled to collect fifty kilograms of gold within thirty-six hours; they had succeeded only through the generosity of their fellow-citizens, Christian and Jewish alike, who had rallied with donations. (After several hours' hesitation, the Vatican had offered a *loan*; it was politely rejected.) There was a general assumption that this gold had been the price of security; only when the long line of open army trucks took up its position in the ghetto in the early hours of 16 October did it become clear that it had been nothing of the sort.

As the trucks threaded their way through the pelting rain to their gathering point at the Collegio Militare – from which their human cargo was to be transported to Auschwitz – powerful voices were raised to stop the operation. Several of these voices were German: one was that of Baron Ernst von Weizsäcker, Ambassador to the Holy See, while another was that of Kesselring himself. Yet another objector was Albrecht von Kessel, the German Consul in Rome. All three were convinced that if the deportations were allowed to go ahead there

---

[1] The village of his birth.

might easily be a general rising against the occupying forces. What was needed now was for the Pope to make a vehement protest against this new outrage, which was taking place on his very doorstep. But nothing came. Weizsäcker himself wrote to his colleague Dr Karl Ritter in Berlin:

> Although pressed on all sides, the Pope did not allow himself to be drawn into any demonstration of reproof at the deportation of the Jews of Rome. The only sign of disapproval was a veiled allusion in *Osservatore Romano* on 25–28 October, in which only a restricted number of people could recognise a reference to the Jewish question.

And so the deportation went ahead.

How can we explain this contemptible silence on the part of Pius XII? It all goes back first to his innate anti-Semitism, and then to his fear of communism – always, both to his predecessor and to himself, a far greater bugbear than Nazi Germany. As he himself put it in a conversation with the American representative at the Vatican, Harold Tittman, he believed that a protest would provoke a clash with the SS; he might have added – but did not – that such a clash might well have resulted in a German occupation of the Vatican and his own capture and imprisonment. This in turn would have played directly into the hands of the Communists. He himself had come up against them in Munich, and he was fully aware of the atrocities they had committed against the Church in Russia, Mexico and Spain. With Europe in its present state of chaos, a communist takeover in Rome could not be discounted; and to avoid that, even the deportation of Roman Jewry would be a small price to pay.

This argument in itself seems hard enough to swallow; but even if we accept the papal silence to have been justified, another astonishing fact remains to be explained. After the end of the war Pius continued as Pope for another thirteen years, during which time not one word of apology or regret, not a single requiem or Mass of remembrance was held for the 1,989 Jewish deportees from Rome who had met their deaths at Auschwitz alone. There were many people too who wondered, in retrospect, why a pope who had thought nothing of excommunicating all members of the Communist Party throughout the world had never apparently considered doing the same to the Catholic Nazi war criminals – including Himmler, Goebbels, Bormann and Hitler himself.

No condemnation either was expressed for the last Nazi atrocity to take place in Rome before its liberation. It occurred on 24 March 1944, the day after a company of German soldiers was bombed as it marched down Via Rasella; thirty-three men died. The following evening, on Hitler's personal orders, 335 Italians, including some seventy Jews, were herded into the Ardeatine Caves south of the city and massacred. Once again there was no protest from the Vatican – though two days later its newspaper *L'Osservatore Romano* ran an article expressing sympathy with the German casualties and regretting 'the 320 [*sic*] persons sacrificed for the guilty parties who escaped arrest'.

On the same day as the bombing, 23 March, the Germans occupied Hungary; and Adolf Eichmann, Hitler's 'architect of the Holocaust', began to apply the 'final solution' to the country's 750,000 Jews. Now at last the Vatican took note: the nuncio in Budapest, Mgr Angelo Rotta, made official representations to the Hungarian government – the very first time that such a thing had been done by a papal diplomatic representative. Even then, the phrasing was unexpected:

> The office of the Apostolic Nuncio . . . requests the Hungarian Government once again not to continue its war against the Jews *beyond the limits prescribed by the laws of nature and God's commandments*,[1] and to avoid any action against which the Holy See and the conscience of the entire Christian world would feel obliged to protest.

It was not, however, until 25 June that the Pope cabled the Hungarian President Admiral Horthy, asking him to 'use all possible influence to stop the suffering and torments which countless people are undergoing simply because of their nationality or their race'. There was still no mention of the Jews by name – though President Roosevelt, cabling on the following day, showed less delicacy and in fact threatened dire consequences.

At this point, it is only fair to record, the Catholic Church in Hungary stepped in firmly and efficiently. Vast numbers of hunted Jews were given refuge in monasteries, convents, churches and often with private Catholic families. During the autumn and winter of 1944, we are told, 'there was practically no Catholic Church institution in Budapest where persecuted Jews did not find refuge'. Countless lives

[1] Author's italics.

were saved; nevertheless, two questions remain. Eichmann started his loathsome work in March; could not the rescue operation have begun then, instead of four or five months later? And did this operation have papal blessing?

With the coming of peace in the spring of 1945, Pope Pius XII – who since the death of Cardinal Maglione the previous August was acting as his own Secretary of State – found himself once again confronted by his old arch-enemy, communism. The Italian Communist Party under its brilliant leader Palmiro Togliatti saw itself as the true conqueror of Fascism, and thus as the legitimate inheritor of power. It was fortunately counterbalanced by the glamour of America, whose forces had flooded the country with all the accoutrements of a capitalist-consumerist society. Against both these extremes Pius urged a programme of Catholic renewal that, unlike communism or capitalism, would be Italian through and through; if he had to choose, however, there was no doubt in his mind that American materialism was by far the lesser of the two evils. On 2 July 1949 he went so far as to publish a decree declaring that no Catholic could be a member of the Communist Party or advocate communism in any way; anyone found guilty of doing so would have the sacraments withheld. The previous year he had violently opposed – as had the entire Curia – the foundation of the state of Israel. This surprised no one; for Pius, as for the Church down the ages, the Jews were the people who had murdered God.

By this time the Pope was seventy-three. Physically, he was still strong, while his autocratic spirit and self-confidence were growing with every year that passed. The old anti-Semitism was still in evidence: to his dying day he was to refuse recognition to the state of Israel. And his vision was narrowing; he was tending more and more to entrench himself in the tried old orthodoxies and to close his mind to new theological ideas. On 2 September 1950 he issued an encyclical, *Humani generis*, which paralysed contemporary scholarship and categorically condemned any new or original Christian thinking. And it went further still. Papal encyclicals had never been considered infallible; henceforth, they made it clear that they were settling a disputed matter once and for all: 'It is obvious that that matter . . . cannot be any longer considered a question open to discussion among theologians.'

There followed something not unlike the reign of terror that had existed under Pius X. The American Jesuit Daniel Berrigan reported:

'I saw at close hand intellectual excellence crushed in a wave of orthodoxy, like a big Stalinist purge.'[1] One of the principal victims was the
celebrated Jesuit palaeontologist Pierre Teilhard de Chardin, whose
work was denied publication and who was eventually exiled to the
United States. Another casualty was the French worker-priest experiment, the most exciting and probably the most successful of all the
attempts to bring Christianity to the world of heavy industry. Its
members exchanged their clerical clothes for overalls and signed on
as bargees, miners or factory hands; missionary work had never been
like this before, and its success was dramatic. But for Pius it was too
dangerous, an open invitation to communism. He showed more and
more hostility towards it, and finally in November 1953 dissolved it
altogether.

For forward-looking Christian thinkers, this was a miserable time;
it was in a way a reflection of Senator Joseph McCarthy's America,
when reds were found under every bed. Nor was it improved by the
Pope's *ex cathedra* proclamation, on 1 November 1950, of the doctrine
of the Assumption of the Virgin Mary – in other words, that the
Virgin's body, instead of corrupting after her death, was immediately
assumed into heaven. There was nothing new in this theory; the
Assumption had long been one of the most popular subjects in Italian
religious painting – one has only to think of Titian's tremendous altar-
piece in the church of the Frari in Venice – and its feast day on 15
August one of the most important dates in the Christian calendar. On
the other hand, it was unknown to the early Church and had no
confirmation in the Scriptures; and the non-Catholic Churches resented
what they saw as the arrogance of the Pope in claiming infallibility –
for the first time since its definition at the First Vatican Council in
1870 – when prescribing an article of faith in which they did not for
a moment believe.

By the mid-1950s, Pope Pius's health was giving cause for concern.
Much of the deterioration seems to have been due to the ministra-
tions of his oculist, Professor Riccardo Galeazzi-Lisi, who took over
complete responsibility for his physical well-being and was generally
considered (by everyone but Pius himself) to be a charlatan and a
quack. Galeazzi-Lisi was bad enough, but he also introduced two more
of the same kind: first the then-fashionable Swiss doctor Paul Niehans,
who claimed to have discovered the secret of eternal youth in the cells

---

[1] Quoted in J. Cornwell, *Hitler's Pope*.

drawn from the foetuses of sheep and monkeys, and then a mad dentist who prescribed industrial quantities of chromic acid, a substance principally used in those days for the cleaning of brass musical instruments. It is thought to have been this which was responsible for the chronic hiccups that plagued the Pope in the last years of his life.

He died in the early hours of the morning of Thursday, 9 October 1958. The funeral ceremony was long and impressive; the body was driven slowly through Rome in an open coffin to its lying-in-state in St Peter's. It was unfortunate indeed that the embalming had been left to Galeazzi-Lisi, who announced that he would be employing a new technique, similar to that used on Jesus Christ himself, 'which would leave the body in its natural state'. This it singularly failed to do. From time to time appalling eructations were heard coming from the coffin, and during the lying-in-state the smell was such that one of the attendant Swiss Guards fainted. Meanwhile the nose fell off. It was to the considerable relief of all those present when the lid was finally screwed down and Pope Pius XII was lowered into the grottoes beneath the Basilica, to take up his final resting place only a few feet from the tomb of St Peter.

It is painful to have to record that, on the orders of his successor, the process of his canonisation has already begun. Suffice it to say here that the current fashion for canonising all popes on principle, if continued, will make a mockery of sainthood.

CHAPTER XXVIII

Vatican II and After

(1958–present)

When Angelo Giuseppe Roncalli was elected Supreme Pontiff at the twelfth ballot on 28 October 1958, he was less than a month short of his seventy-seventh birthday. Fat, kindly and convivial, with an easy charm and a ready wit, he endeared himself to all those with whom he came in contact; while no one had really loved Pope Pius XII, it was impossible not to love Pope John XXIII (1958–63). Nonetheless, he was generally expected to be little more than a *papa di passaggio* – a caretaker pope. His pontificate did indeed last for less than five years, but there was little of the caretaker about it. On the contrary, it shook the world.

The first surprise was the name he chose: John. There had been twenty-two legitimate popes of that name, the most recent of whom had reigned at Avignon in the early fourteenth century; few were men of much distinction, while John XII was one of the most depraved pontiffs in all history.[1] There had also been a previous John XXIII, an antipope deposed by the Council of Constance in 1415.[2] Later, the Pope was to maintain that one of the reasons for his choice was to retrieve this evangelical name from dishonour; at the time of his election, however, he claimed to have chosen it because it was the name of his father, of the humble parish church near Bergamo where his family of thirteen were all baptised, and of innumerable cathedrals throughout the world, including his own Lateran. Later, he characteristically produced yet another reason: that there had been more popes called John than any other name, and that most of them had remarkably short reigns.

The new pope was a scholar, author of a five-volume study of his hero, St Charles Borromeo, the great sixteenth-century Archbishop of Milan and towering figure of the Counter-Reformation;[3] and this

---

[1] See Chapter VII.
[2] See Chapter XVI, and Gibbon's comment: 'The most scandalous charges were suppressed: the Vicar of Christ was only accused of piracy, murder, rape, sodomy and incest.'
[3] See Chapter XX, p.307.

work had naturally brought him into contact with Mgr Ratti, the Vatican Librarian who later became Pope Pius XI. It was he who in 1925 launched Roncalli on a diplomatic career, during which he served first in Bulgaria, then in Turkey and Greece – where, during the German occupation, he worked tirelessly on behalf of the Jews. In December 1944 he was posted as nuncio to Paris, where he strongly supported the movement of worker-priests, and in 1953 he was named a cardinal and Patriarch of Venice, where he remained until his election.

Once Pope, John gave a clear impression of a man in a hurry. On 26 January 1959, just three months after his election, *L'Osservatore Romano* reported that he was planning three important projects: a Diocesan Synod in Rome, an Ecumenical Council and a revision of the canon law. Of the three, the second was clearly by far the most ambitious; to many people it seemed curious that it had not been given an announcement of its own. In fact, the Pope was almost certainly testing the waters. His time in the Balkans had given him much experience of the Eastern Churches, and he was anxious to find out as discreetly as he could how they would view his proposal. If their reaction was favourable, he might broaden the Council to include them; otherwise it would be restricted to the Church of Rome.

The old guard at the Vatican was appalled. Pope Pius XII had been an icy autocrat: he and he alone gave the orders; the bishops, even the cardinals, existed merely to carry them out. Now here, suddenly, was a proposal to bring together all the world's bishops for free and uncontrolled discussions. Even the liberal Cardinal Montini, Archbishop of Milan and future Pope Paul VI, believed that the new pope was 'stirring up a hornet's nest'. But John was determined. The days of papal dictatorship were over. Henceforth the Church would be a collegiate body, with Pope and bishops sharing responsibility between them. No longer could it turn its face away from the modern age. *Aggiornamento* – that was the new watchword – the bringing up to date of both its organisation and its teaching. It was time, said the Pope, to throw open the windows of the Church and let in some fresh air.

There was inevitably a vast amount of preliminary work to be done before the projected Council could take place. The diocesan synod – surprisingly, the first in papal history – was held at the Lateran in January 1960; but the Second Vatican Council itself (it was in fact the Twenty-First Ecumenical Council of the Roman Catholic Church) did not open until nearly two years later, on 11 October 1962. The opening session in St Peter's was attended by 2,540 delegates, mostly bishops and superiors of religious orders, making it by far the largest gathering of any council in Church history. Almost half were non-European; 250 were African, with roughly the same number from Asia, while Latin America sent 600. Seventeen Orthodox and Protestant Churches were represented by observers. In his inaugural address the Pope radiated optimism:

> We feel we must disagree with those prophets of gloom, who are always foretelling disaster, as though the end of the world were at hand . . .
> The Church should never depart from the sacred patrimony of truth received from the Fathers. But at the same time she must ever look to the present, to the new conditions and new forms of life introduced into the modern world, which have opened new avenues . . . For this reason, the Church has not watched inertly the marvellous progress of the discoveries of human genius . . .
> The Council now beginning rises in the Church like daybreak, a forerunner of most splendid light. It is now only dawn. And already at this first announcement of the rising day, how much sweetness fills our heart. Everything here breathes sanctity and arouses great joy. Let us contemplate the stars . . .

Less than a year later, on 3 June 1963 and after the shortest pontificate for two centuries, Pope John died of cancer. The Council had been his idea and very largely his creation, and although most of its final decisions were the work of others – above all his successor – it was from first to last imbued with his spirit. In five short years he had opened up the Church to the twentieth century. He had reached out to the other Christian Churches, and particularly to the Jews, to whom he always showed a special affection. As Apostolic Delegate in Turkey during the Second World War he had saved the lives of several thousand Jewish children from Romania and Bulgaria, providing them with blank baptismal certificates; and within a year of his election he did what Pius XII had always refused to consider: he deleted the phrase *pro perfidis Judaeis* (faithless Jews) from the Good Friday liturgy. One day when he was driving through Rome he happened to pass a synagogue just as all the worshippers were leaving; he stopped his car to talk to them and bless them. No wonder, on the night before his death, that Rome's Chief Rabbi went, with many of the Jewish faithful, to pray in St Peter's.

Until his appointment as Archbishop of Milan in 1954, Giovanni Battista Montini had spent virtually his whole working life in the papal Secretariat. Son of a prosperous lawyer and parliamentary deputy, already in 1937 at the age of forty he had been appointed assistant to Cardinal Pacelli, then Secretary of State, at whose side he was to remain for the next seventeen years. In 1953 he had declined a cardinal's hat, knowing that this would remove him from his unique position of power; but it seems likely that soon after this his influence anyway began to decline. As a relative liberal, he almost certainly antagonised the reactionary old guard, including Pius himself, who began to want him out of the way; and he had no delusions that by his appointment to Milan he was not in fact being kicked upstairs. It was a further mark of disfavour that – despite strong and repeated representations from the Milanese themselves – membership of the Sacred College continued to be withheld from him; and without a red hat he was obviously not qualified to be elected, as many would otherwise have expected, as the next pope.

It is a characteristic of dictators (and Pius XII was a dictator if anyone was) to give little or no thought to their successors. Perhaps it was an aspect of Pius's autocratic instincts – 'après moi le déluge', he is said to have murmured – that he seems to have distrusted his cardinals and taken curiously little interest in them. In nineteen years he held just two consistories, and when he died the Sacred College, whose full complement had been set by Sixtus V at seventy, had only fifty-one members, half of whom were well over eighty years old. All this had been immediately rectified by Pope John on his accession. At his first consistory – when Archbishop Montini at last received his red hat – he abolished Pope Sixtus's maximum, and by 1962 the College numbered no fewer than eighty-seven.

Of these cardinals, eighty assembled on the evening of 19 June for the Conclave. Montini was the favourite, but was nevertheless elected only on the fifth ballot, taking the name of Paul VI (1963–78); he wanted, he said, to reach out to the modern Gentiles. Few pontiffs have accepted the Triple Crown with greater or more genuine reluctance. Now sixty-five, he knew – no one better – what it meant to be Pope: not just the responsibility, but the aching personal loneliness. He knew too that he had just a hundred days before the second session of the Council began. The first, in which he had played a significant part, had not been an unqualified success: there had been several angry clashes of ideas, and several more of personalities. But this had been inevitable, for never in papal history had there been such outspokenness, such total freedom of expression: in the words of Thomas Roberts, formerly Archbishop of Bombay, the children of God had been able to slide down the banisters in the house of the Lord.

It was only with the second session that the Council got into its stride, proving itself to be the most revolutionary Christian phenomenon since the Reformation. It contradicted Pius XII's pronouncements on almost every main issue: ecumenism, liturgical reform, communism, freedom of religion and, above all, Judaism. The key document was *Lumen Gentium*, the Decree on the Church. Pius would have hated it – especially the section that took care not to identify the Roman Catholic Church with the Church of Christ. The latter, it maintained, simply 'subsisted' within it, 'although many elements of sanctification and of truth are found outside its visible structure'. This meant effectively that it could coexist equally with other Churches: Catholicism no longer claimed the monopoly on divine truth. Elsewhere, the Decree undermined the whole concept of papal autocracy by emphasising the importance of the bishops, and indeed of the laity. The Church is described as a pilgrim Church, the faithful as a pilgrim people.

Of the several other Decrees approved by the Council, the Decree on the Liturgy transformed Roman Catholic worship, establishing the principle of greater participation in the Mass by the laity, introducing the vernacular in place of Latin and requiring that the celebrant should face the congregation rather than the altar. The Decree on Ecumenism made the quest for religious unity central to the Church's work. The Decree on Religious Liberty (primarily an American initiative) declared that freedom of worship was a fundamental element of human dignity. The Decree on Other Religions (*Nostra Aetate*) – vehemently opposed by the still anti-Semitic Curia – was of particular importance in defining the Church's attitude to the Jews:

> True, the Jewish authorities and those who followed their lead pressed for the death of Christ; yet what occurred in His passion cannot be charged against all the Jews without distinction then alive, nor against the Jews of today. Although the Church is the new people of God, the Jews should not be presented as rejected or accursed by God, as if this

followed from the Holy Scriptures. All should see to it, then, that in catechetical work or in the preaching of the word of God they do not teach anything that does not conform to the truth of the Gospel and the spirit of Christ. Furthermore, in her rejection of every persecution against any man, the Church, mindful of the patrimony she shares with the Jews and moved not by political reasons but by the Gospel's spiritual love, decries hatred, persecutions and displays of anti-Semitism, directed against the Jews at any time and by anyone.

The Council continued for just over three years, being finally closed by Pope Paul on 8 December 1965. From the first preparations until the end, its success had been very largely due to him. The opposition of the old guard had continued throughout, and it is unlikely that Pope John, even had he lived, could have forced most of the measures through. Paul, by contrast, who had spent his whole working life in the Vatican bureaucracy, possessed the knowledge and experience to steer the Council with a firm and confident hand. He dealt with the old guard by imposing on all bishops compulsory retirement at the age of seventy-five. An exception was made only for the Pope in his capacity of Bishop of Rome. Cardinals would be obliged to retire from the Curia at eighty, after which they would no longer be permitted to participate in papal conclaves – the only privilege to which their rank entitled them. On the other hand, the size of the Sacred College was drastically increased, with the appointment of many new cardinals from the Third World; henceforth Italians would never again enjoy an absolute majority.

The Church had been transformed to the point of unrecognisability. For many Catholics, it had at last moved with the times. For many others, it had destroyed itself. Congregations, even in old strongholds like Spain and Sicily, fell away. Priests tore off their collars, and several Orders of nuns put away their old habits and dressed more like air hostesses. Particularly among the older generation, the disappearance of the familiar and beloved Latin proved hard to accept; to some it was even heart-breaking. Apart from its intrinsic beauty, Latin had served as a lingua franca; in every country of the world, the Mass had been identical, and thus immediately familiar. Now – just at the moment when civil aviation was opening up and people were travelling more than ever before – the faithful were all too often obliged to hear it in languages of which they understood not a word.

It was Paul's task to hold all these conflicting elements together.

This he managed, on the whole, successfully, though he was unable to prevent the breakaway traditionalist Archbishop Marcel Lefebvre from founding his 'Society of St Pius X', which firmly upheld the old order together with the full Tridentine Mass. Paul drove the Council forward and ensured that there was no backsliding when it was over; but in other respects he remained staunchly conservative. On the question of priestly celibacy he refused to budge; while the stand he took on birth control greatly damaged his reputation.

Perhaps unwisely, he had considered this subject too hot a potato for the Council; instead he had entrusted it to a special commission of theologians, doctors, scientists and – somewhat surprisingly – married couples. This commission recommended that the Church's traditional teaching should be modified to allow artificial contraception, at least in certain circumstances; and it was generally expected that the Pope would accept the recommendation, which had already been endorsed by the majority of a panel of bishops. Alas, he did nothing of the sort: his consequent encyclical *Humanae Vitae* of 1968 simply reconfirmed the old Vatican line. It caused much disappointment and, in many cases, disgust. Particularly in pullulating South America, hundreds of priests resigned; hundreds more continued to encourage contraception among their flock, just as they always had.

Paul should perhaps have visited South America himself; he certainly could have done, for he was the first pope to travel on a grand scale – seeing it, indeed, as part of his pastoral duty. In 1963 he addressed the United Nations in New York; in 1964 the International Eucharistic Congress in Bombay. That year also saw him in Jerusalem, where he and the Ecumenical Patriarch Athenagoras took what seemed to be the first step in the ending of the Great Schism, which had split the Eastern and Western Churches from 1054.[1] In 1967 he was the first pope since the Ottoman conquest to visit Istanbul, where he made the embarrassing mistake of falling on his knees on entering St Sophia – giving the hardline Islamists the opportunity of accusing him of attempting to convert the building back into a Christian church.[2] In 1969, for the World Council of Churches – where his presence would have been unthinkable before Vatican II – he was in, of all places, Geneva; in that same year he went to Uganda, thus becoming the first pontiff ever to set foot on the African continent; and in 1970 he visited

---

[1] See Chapter VIII.
[2] It had served as a mosque throughout the Ottoman period, but had been declared a secular museum by Kemal Atatürk in 1935.

the Philippines (where he narrowly escaped assassination) and Australia.

By this time, however, he was giving several of his closest associates cause for concern. His responsibilities were becoming too much for him; he was a deeply unhappy man. The loneliness of his position, his increasing unpopularity – especially after *Humanae Vitae* – the increasing tensions within the Church as the full consequences of Vatican II slowly became apparent, the increase in international terrorism and the Italian 'Red Brigades' all took their toll and increased his depression. In 1974 there were even rumours of his possible resignation; and in 1978 the kidnapping and subsequent murder of his close friend, the Christian Democrat politician Aldo Moro (at whose funeral he presided) was a blow from which he never properly recovered. He died that same year – of acute cystitis, culminating in a massive heart attack – in his summer palace of Castel Gandolfo. It was on the evening of Sunday, 6 August, the Feast of the Transfiguration.

Cardinal Albino Luciani was elected Pope on the fourth ballot, on the first and last day of the conclave of 26 August 1978. He was of poor, working-class background from near Belluno, his father passing much of his working life as a seasonal worker – bricklayer and electrician – in Switzerland. Albino had been Bishop of Vittorio Veneto, and subsequently for nine years Patriarch of Venice; he was, however, little known outside Italy, and it was a matter of considerable surprise that the 111 voting cardinals (of whom only twenty-seven were Italian) should have chosen him so quickly. The English cardinal Basil Hume had an explanation: 'Seldom have I had such an experience of the presence of God . . . I am not one for whom the dictates of the Holy Spirit are self-evident. I'm slightly hard-boiled on that . . . But for me he was God's candidate.'

Paul VI had, as we have seen, accepted the papacy only with extreme reluctance; his successor felt much the same. After the penultimate ballot, when he was well in the lead and within seven votes of the papacy, he was heard to murmur, 'No, please no . . .' Many of his closest associates thought he might well refuse; but slowly and sadly he nodded his head. He took the name of John Paul I (1973) – the first double-barrelled name in papal history. In his first speech to the people of Rome he explained why:

> Pope John had wanted to consecrate me with his own hands here in the basilica of St Peter's. Then, though unworthy, I succeeded him in the cathedral of St Mark – in that Venice that is still filled with the spirit of Pope

John ... On the other hand, Pope Paul not only made me a cardinal, but some months before that, in St Mark's Square, he made me blush in front of 20,000 people, because he took off his stole and placed it on my shoulders. Never was my face so red ... And so I took the name 'John Paul'.

Be sure of this. I do not have the wisdom of heart of Pope John. I do not have the preparation and culture of Pope Paul. But I now stand in their place. I will seek to serve the Church and hope that you will help me with your prayers.

This informal, familiar tone set the seal on John Paul's papacy. No pope had ever been more approachable; no pope ever had such a warm and captivating smile – a smile that reached out to everyone he met. Pomposity he detested. It was of course inseparable from his position, but he reduced it to a minimum. He was, for example, the first pope to refuse a coronation; there were no more triple crowns, no more gestatorial chairs in which he would be carried shoulder-high through the crowds, no more swaying ostrich feathers, no more of the royal 'We'. He longed to take the Church back to its origins, to the humility and simplicity, the honesty and poverty of Jesus Christ himself.

But how was it to be done? First of all, there was the Curia to contend with. He had no enemies in it – indeed, at the time of his election he had no enemies at all. But his refusal to be crowned with all the usual trappings had horrified the traditionalists, and his decision that the extra month's salary normally paid on the election of a new pope should be cut by half had not increased his popularity. He soon found, too, that the Vatican was a hotbed of petty hatreds, rivalries and jealousies. 'I hear nothing but malice, directed against everything and everyone,' he complained. 'Also, I have noticed two things that appear to be in very short supply: honesty and a good cup of coffee.'

In such an atmosphere it was inevitable that he would be misinterpreted and misrepresented. L'Osservatore Romano, for example, in a special edition published within hours of his election, reported that he was among the first of the bishops to circulate the encyclical Humanae Vitae, 'and to insist that its teaching was beyond question'. This was completely untrue. It was well known that in 1968, as Bishop of Vittorio Veneto, he had submitted a confidential report to his predecessor as Patriarch of Venice, recommending that the recently developed contraceptive pill should be permitted by the Church; and that this report, having been approved by his fellow-bishops, was submitted to Paul VI. As we know, Paul rejected it; but John Paul had not changed his opinion. In 1978 he had been invited to speak at an International Congress in Milan to celebrate the tenth anniversary of *Humanae Vitae*, but had refused to go. Within days of his election he agreed to receive the American Congressman James Scheuer, who headed a House Select Committee on Population. 'To my mind,' he had remarked to the Secretary of State, Cardinal Villot, 'we cannot leave the situation as it currently stands.'

Had he lived his full term, this quiet, gentle, smiling man might well have achieved a revolution in the Church – a revolution even more dramatic and profound than that created by Pope John's Second Vatican Council. But he did not live. Shortly before 5.30 a.m. on Friday, 29 September 1978 he was found dead in his bed. He had been Pope for just thirty-three days – the shortest reign since that of Leo XI in 1605.

Was John Paul I murdered? Certainly, there were reasons to believe so. For a man of sixty-seven he was in excellent health; there was no post-mortem or autopsy; the Curia obviously panicked, and was caught out in any number of small lies as to the manner of his death and the finding of his body; and if, as was widely believed, he was on the point of exposing a major financial scandal in which the Vatican Bank and its director, Archbishop Paul Marcinkus, were deeply implicated, there were at least three international criminals – one of whom, Roberto Calvi of the Banco Ambrosiano, was later found hanging under Blackfriars Bridge in London – who would have gone to any lengths to prevent him from doing so. The Vatican, moreover, is an easy place for murder. It is an independent state with no police force of its own; the Italian police can enter only if invited – which they were not.

The arguments for and against the conspiracy theory are long and complicated. To set them out here would mean devoting twenty or thirty pages to a pope who reigned for only a month, and would hopelessly unbalance a book which is already overlong. Anyone who would like to study them – and they are well worth studying – should read two books: *In God's Name* by David Yallop (in favour of the theory) and *A Thief in the Night* by John Cornwell (against it). They can then decide for themselves.[1]

* * *

[1] Having for many years been convinced that the Pope was indeed murdered, I have now reread the evidence on both sides and have changed my mind. The murderer – if there was one – must somehow have gained admittance to the papal apartments in the middle of the night. Unless one or both of the papal secretaries (or one or more of the small team of nuns who did the cooking and cleaning) were implicated in the plot – which I find hard to believe – I do not see how he could have managed to do so.

It was remarkable that the first-ever Polish pope and the first non-Italian pope to be elected since Hadrian VI in 1522, should have been elected on only the second day of voting, gaining 103 of the 109 votes cast; but Karol Wojtyła was a remarkable man. Still only fifty-eight, he was a published poet and playwright, an accomplished skier and mountaineer, and was fluent in six (some say ten) languages. He had studied at the University of Cracow, but after the German invasion of Poland on 1 September 1939 the university was closed down. He then took several labourer's jobs – including one in a quarry – and is said to have had a relationship with a local girl before deciding on the priesthood at the comparatively late age of twenty-two. Thereafter he rose fast. After just three years as a parish priest he returned to the university to study philosophy and to lecture on social ethics. He was nominated bishop at the early age of thirty-eight, and five years later Paul VI appointed him Archbishop of Cracow.

Two days after his election as John Paul II (1978–2005), in his first important speech as Pope, he emphasised his international role as head of the universal Church. 'From now on,' he said, 'the particular nature of our country of origin is of little importance.' It was of course nothing of the kind. Poland, where he had lived for the first fifty-eight years of his life, remained his spiritual home. It coloured all his policies, all his decisions, all his public pronouncements. During his pontificate he went back there on no fewer than nine occasions – far more than to any other country. He remembered all too clearly the Warsaw Rising, and the Holocaust. On 'Black Sunday', 6 August 1944, the Gestapo had rounded up 8,000 young Polish men in Cracow; Wojtyła had escaped by hiding in a basement while the Germans searched upstairs. After the war he endured nearly half a century of communism, and from 1980, when the communist monolith began to crack, he gave every encouragement to the Polish Solidarity movement and its leader, Lech Wałęsa, to whom he may well have secretly channelled funds through Archbishop Marcinkus and the Vatican Bank. As Mikhail Gorbachev once remarked, 'The collapse of the iron curtain would have been impossible without John Paul II'.

In the late afternoon of 13 May 1981, while the Pope was being driven round St Peter's Square in his Popemobile during a general audience, a Turkish gunman named Ali Agca fired three shots at him at almost point-blank range. John Paul was rushed to the Gemelli Hospital. Agca was immediately arrested, later telling the examining magistrate that he was a 'nationalist atheist' who hated both the

Catholic Church and American and Russian imperialism. He added that he had hoped to kill the Pope during his visit to Turkey in November 1979, but that his intended victim had then been too well protected. In Rome he was an open target. Agca's paymasters (if any) were never revealed, though the Bulgarian government came under heavy suspicion. On his recovery John Paul announced that he had forgiven his would-be assassin; in 1983 he visited him in prison and something approaching friendship developed between them. In later years the Pope also received Agca's mother and brother in audience.

After five hours of surgery and the loss of three-quarters of his blood, his convalescence was long: it was not until October that he was completely restored to health. But by 1982 – having by now become something of a media superstar – he was able to resume his harrowing travel schedule, making four or five major journeys a year across the world. By the end of his twenty-six-year pontificate he had chalked up a total of 104 foreign journeys to 129 countries. In May-June 1982 (despite the Falklands War, which very nearly caused a cancellation) he came on a six-day visit to Britain, the first ever by a reigning pope, during which he preached in Canterbury Cathedral. In March 2000 he was in Israel: what, one wonders, would Pius XII have thought?[1] In 2001, in Damascus, he became the first pope ever to pray in a mosque. His one regret was that he never managed to get to Russia.

In other respects, however, John Paul II can now be seen to have been closer in thought to Pius XII than he was to John XXIII. And perhaps it was not entirely surprising. For virtually his entire adult life until he came to Rome, the Polish Church had its back to the wall, struggling – first against the Germans, then against the Russians – for its very survival. Wojtyła had fought for that Church as it was, not as it might be; and on becoming Pope at fifty-eight, he was too old to change. His fourteen encyclicals reveal him if anything as a reactionary, doggedly reasserting the old Catholic teachings on euthanasia, abortion, the ordination of women, homosexuality and same-sex marriage. Those who had looked to his predecessor for a major change of policy on birth control – permitting the use of condoms, if only to prevent the spread of HIV – knew all too well that from John Paul II they could expect nothing of the kind. Where he surprised everybody was in his berserk canonisations of everything

---

[1] He would at least have been relieved that, even at the Yad Vashem Holocaust Memorial, John Paul made no apologies for past silences.

in sight: quite apart from the 1,340 men and women whom he beatified (the first step to sainthood) he canonised no fewer than 483 new saints, more than had been made in the previous five centuries.

Towards the end of his pontificate John Paul was a firm opponent of the Iraq War. In his 2003 State of the World address he made his views abundantly clear: 'No to war!', he declared. 'War is *not* always inevitable, but it *is* always a defeat for humanity.' Later he is quoted as pointing out that 'Wars do not in general resolve the problems for which they are fought, and therefore ultimately prove futile.' But by this time he was failing fast. In 1991 there had appeared the first signs of Parkinson's disease, though the Vatican characteristically kept it secret for twelve years, admitting it only in 2003, by which time his speech was noticeably slurred and he was confined to a wheelchair. He died on the evening of Saturday, 2 April 2005, forty-six days short of his eighty-fifth birthday. The Requiem Mass that was said for him six days later was attended by well over four million people, almost certainly the largest single Christian pilgrimage in history.

The funeral service for John Paul II was conducted by Cardinal Joseph Ratzinger, at that time Prefect of the Congregation for the Doctrine of the Faith – formerly known as the Holy Office, and before that as the Holy Inquisition. There his principal duty was to ensure that those teaching in Catholic institutions kept within the strict doctrines laid down by Rome. Despite his reputation as 'God's rottweiler', Ratzinger was in fact of a mild and gentle disposition and was generally considered the favourite for the succession; and although favourites have often been passed over by the conclaves, no one was surprised when, at the fifth ballot, he was duly elected, the seventh German pope, but the first since the eleventh century.

For the highly intelligent theologian that he undoubtedly is, Benedict XVI (2005–) has not, at the time of writing, proved himself as surefooted as one might have hoped. In little more than two years he managed seriously to offend three important religious groups: first the Muslims, then the Jews and finally the Protestant Churches. The first faux pas occurred in a lecture that he gave less than eighteen months after his accession, in his old university of Regensburg on 12 September 2006. 'Show me,' he said, 'just what Mohammed introduced that was new, and there you will find things only evil and inhuman, such as his command to spread by the sword the faith that he preached.'

It subsequently appeared that the Pope had merely been quoting

– rather than endorsing – the alleged words of the Byzantine Emperor Manuel II Palaeologus in 1391; unfortunately he failed to make this clear at the time. There were widespread protests all over the Muslim world, and on the West Bank two Christian churches were fire-bombed. Later the Pope made a handsome apology, which he repeated at a specially convened reception for twenty high-ranking Muslim diplomats at Castel Gandolfo. Two months later he paid an official visit to Turkey. There were hostile demonstrations at Istanbul airport, and special security measures had to be taken for his protection; but he prayed in the Blue Mosque, and the visit was accounted a fair success.

He also needlessly antagonised the Protestants. A papal declaration issued on 11 July 2007 stated:

> It is nevertheless difficult to see how the title of 'Church' could possibly be attributed to [Protestant communities], given that they do not accept the theological notion of the Church in the Catholic sense and that they lack elements considered essential to the Catholic Church.

This time there was a howl of protest. The President of the Italian Federation of Evangelical Churches described the declaration as 'a huge step backwards', while his French equivalent gave a sinister warning of 'external repercussions' – though no one was quite sure what he meant.

Shortly beforehand Benedict had turned his attention to the Jews, many of whom already felt a sense of outrage at the Church's apparent insistence on canonising Pope Pius XII. Although Benedict has given no grounds for accusations of personal anti-Semitism, his decision on 7 July 2007 to permit once again the Tridentine Mass – which includes a prayer that asks God to lift the veil, so that the Jews 'may be delivered from their darkness' – was not well received in Jewish circles. Still less popular was the subsequent lifting of excommunication on the four breakaway bishops from Archbishop Lefebvre's 'Society of St Pius X', among whom was Bishop Richard Williamson, notorious for his continued denial of the Holocaust.[1]

These were all deliberate actions, which could – and should – have been avoided. But the far greater storm in which Benedict soon found himself engulfed was not of his own making. This storm broke

---

[1] A visit to Israel in May 2009, during which Benedict naturally followed John Paul II's example with a visit to the Yad Vashem memorial, did much to mend fences.

first in Ireland, with horrific revelations of widespread child abuse, and frequently of gratuitous physical violence, in Catholic schools and orphanages. Almost as reprehensible was the instinctive cover-up by the Church, which had tended to transfer those responsible to another parish rather than risk unpleasant publicity by defrocking them on the spot. The Pope could have earned a reputation for swift, decisive action by instantly removing the Irish Primate, Cardinal Sean Brady, after he admitted being involved in this cover-up during the 1970s; but at the time of writing Brady remains in his position. Meanwhile the scandal over clerical paedophilia has spread across Europe and the United States. True, in March 2010 the Pope wrote a letter addressed to the Catholics of Ireland, apologising for the 'sinful and criminal' abuses that had been going on for several decades. Here again, one wonders why he limited his apology to Ireland – with the result that Catholics in Austria, the Netherlands, Switzerland, Italy and above all Germany inevitably feel that what happened in their countries is of less concern to him. Benedict's reactions have been too little, too late; and the storm shows no sign of abating.

It is now well over half a century since progressive Catholics have longed to see their Church bring itself into the modern age. With the accession of every succeeding pontiff they have raised their hopes that some progress might be made on the leading issues of the day: on homosexuality, on contraception, on the ordination of women priests. And each time they have been disappointed. Sometimes, indeed, the Church seems to take a step backwards: as recently as 15 July 2010 it elevated the ordination of women to the status of 'grave delict' – making it one of the most serious crimes in canon law and effectively putting it on the same level as child abuse.[1]

And so although Benedict's visit to Great Britain in September 2010 was – contrary to many expectations – a remarkable success, the present pontificate has got off to a distinctly shaky start. The Anglican hierarchy was hard pressed to hide its indignation at his recent offer to welcome into the Catholic priesthood those married members of the Protestant clergy who were leaving their own Church in protest against the ordination of women bishops. But the pontificate is still unfinished, and we can as yet draw no final conclusions. All that can be said is

---

[1] *The Times*, Friday, 15 July 2010. It is only fair to add that in subsequent issues the charge was indignantly rebutted by Catholic apologists.

that Pope Benedict will prove better than many of his predecessors, worse than others; and that after nearly 2,000 years, and despite the atmosphere of agnosticism that prevails in much of the world today, the Roman Catholic Church – with its two billion members, representing as it does half of all Christians and about one-sixth of the global population – is, despite everything, flourishing as perhaps it has never flourished before. If he could see it now, St Peter would be proud indeed.

Bibliography

ABOUT, E., *La question romaine*, Paris, 1859

ALAND, K., *A History of Christianity*, tr. J.L. Schaaf, 2 vols, Philadelphia, 1985

ASTON, N., *Religion and Revolution in France*, London, 2000

AVELING, J.C.H., *The Jesuits*, London, 1981

BARING-GOULD, S., *Curious Myths of the Middle Ages*, London, 1897

BARRACLOUGH, G., *The Medieval Papacy*, London, 1968

BEDE, *Ecclesiastical History of England*, tr. and ed. A.M. Sellar, London, 1907

BIGG, C., *The Church's Task under the Roman Empire*, Oxford, 1905

BLAKISTON, N (ed.), *The Roman Question: Extracts from the Despatches of Odo Russell from Rome, 1858–1870*, London, 1962

BOCCACCIO, G., *Concerning Famous Women*, tr. G.A. Guarino, London, 1964

BOUREAU, A., *The Myth of Pope Joan*, tr. L.G. Cochrane, Chicago, 2001

BRADFORD, S., *Cesare Borgia: His Life and Times*, London, 1976

BURCHARD, J., *At the Court of the Borgias*, tr. G. Parker, London, 1963

BURY, J.B., *History of the Later Roman Empire from Arcadius to Irene*, 2 vols, London, 1889

Cambridge Medieval History, 8 vols, Cambridge, 1911–36

Cambridge Modern History, 12 vols, Cambridge, 1902–10

CARRINGTON, P., *The Early Christian Church*, 2 vols, Cambridge, 1957

CHADWICK, O., *Britain and the Vatican during the Second World War*, Cambridge, 1986

CHAMBERLIN, E.R., *The Bad Popes*, London, 1970

CHEETHAM, N., *Keepers of the Keys: The Pope in History*, London, 1982

CLARKE, C.P.S., *A Short History of the Christian Church*, London, 1929

CLEMENT, ST, *The Epistles of St Clement of Rome and St Ignatius of Antioch*, tr. and ed. J.A. Kleist, London, 1946

COLLINS, P., *Papal Power*, London, 1997

COOPER, A.D., *Talleyrand*, London, 1932

CORNWELL, J., *Hitler's Pope: The Secret History of Pius XII*, London, 1999

CORNWELL, R., *God's Banker: An Account of the Life and Death of Roberto Calvi*, London, 1984

CREIGHTON, M., *History of the Papacy during the Period of the Reformation*, 6 vols, London, 1903–7

CULLMAN, O., *Peter: Disciple – Apostle – Martyr*, London, 1953

Dictionnaire d'histoire et de géographie ecclésiastiques, ed. A. Baudrillart, Paris, in progress

Dictionnaire de théologie catholique, ed. A. Vacant and E. Mangenot, 9 vols in 15, Paris, 1926–50

DÖLLINGER, J.J.I., *Fables Respecting the Popes of the Middle Ages*, tr. A. Plummer, London, 1871

DUDDEN, F.H., *Gregory the Great: His Place in History and Thought*, 2 vols, London, 1905

DUFFY, E., *Saints and Sinners: A History of the Popes*, New Haven, 1997

EGGENBERGER, D., *A Dictionary of Battles*, London, 1967

Enciclopedia Italiana, 36 vols. Rome 1925–36

EUSEBIUS, BISHOP OF CAESAREA, *Ecclesiastical History*, tr. C.F. Crusé, London, 1894

FALCONI, C., *The Silence of Pius XII*, tr. B. Wall, London, 1970

FRIEDLÄNDER, S., *Pius XII and the Third Reich*, tr. C. Fullman, London, 1966

GASCOIGNE, B., *The Christians*, London, 1977

GIBBON, E., *The History of the Decline and Fall of the Roman Empire*, ed. J.B. Bury, 7 vols, London, 1896

GILLEY, S., *Newman and His Age*, London, 1990

GREELEY, A., *The Making of the Popes*, London, 1979

GREGOROVIOUS, F., *History of the City of Rome in the Middle Ages*, London, 1895

GREGORY, BISHOP OF TOURS, *The History of the Franks*, tr. O.M. Dalton, 2 vols, Oxford, 1927

GRISAR, H., *History of Rome and the Popes in the Middle Ages*, London, 1911–12

GUICCIARDINI, F., *The History of Italy*, ed. and tr. S. Alexander, New York, 1969

HALE, J.R., *The Civilisation of Europe in the Renaissance*, London, 1993

HALES, E.E.Y., *Pio Nono*, London, 1954

——*Pope John and His Revolution*, London, 1965

HEBBLETHWAITE, P., *John XXIII, Pope of the Council*, London, 1984

——*Paul VI: The First Modern Pope*, London, 1993

——*The Year of the Three Popes*, London, 1978

HOOK, J., *The Sack of Rome*, London, 1972

HUGHES, P., *Pope Pius the Eleventh*, London, 1937

JAMESON, MRS A., *Sacred and Legendary Art*, 2 vols, London, 1896

JOHNSON, M., *The Borgias*, London, 1981

JOHNSON, P., *A History of Christianity*, London, 1976

JONES, A.H.M., *The Later Roman Empire, 284–602: A Social, Economic and Administrative Survey*, 3 vols, Oxford, 1964

KANTOROWICZ, E., *Frederick the Second*, tr. E.O. Lorimer, London, 1931

KATZ, R., *Black Sabbath: A Journey through a Crime against Humanity*, London, 1969

KÜNG, H., *The Catholic Church*, London and New York, 2001

LACEY, R., *The Life and Times of Henry VIII*, London, 1972

LE ROY LADURIE, E., *Montaillou: Cathars and Catholics in a French Village, 1294–1324*, tr. Barbara Bray, London, 1978

LEVILLAIN, P., *Dictionnaire historique de la papauté*, Paris, 1994

LEWY, G., *The Catholic Church and Nazi Germany*, New York, 1964

LIUDPRAND, BISHOP OF CREMONA, *Works*, tr. F.A. Wright, London, 1930

LOWE, J., *Saint Peter*, Oxford, 1956

MACNUTT, F.A., *A Papal Chamberlain*, London, 1936

MALLETT, M., *The Borgias: The Rise and Fall of a Renaissance Dynasty*, London, 1969

MANN, H.K., *Lives of the Popes in the Early Middle Ages*, London, 1902

MARTINES, L., *April Blood: Florence and the Plot against the Medici*, London, 2003

MASSON, G., *The Companion Guide to Rome*, London, 1965

——*Frederick II of Hohenstaufen: A Life*, London, 1957

MAUROIS, A., *A History of France*, tr. H.L. Binsse and G. Hopkins, London, 1960

MIGNE, J.P. *Patrologia Latina*, 587

MOLLAT, G., *The Popes at Avignon*, London, 1963

MOORHEAD, J., *Gregory the Great*, London, 2005

MULLINS, E., *Avignon of the Popes: City of Exiles*, Oxford, 2007

New Catholic Encyclopedia, Washington, DC, 1967–

New Encyclopaedia Britannica, 15th edn, 32 vols, Chicago, 1998

NOEL, G., *The Renaissance Popes*, London, 2006

NORWICH, J. J., *Byzantium: The Early Centuries*, London, 1988; *The Apogee*, 1991; *The Decline and Fall*, 1995

——*The Normans in the South*, London, 1967

——*The Kingdom in the Sun*, London, 1970

——*Venice: The Greatness and the Fall*, London, 1981

ORIGO, I., *The Merchant of Prato: Francesco di Marco Datini*, London, 1957

Oxford Dictionary of Popes, ed. J.N.D. Kelly, Oxford, 1986

PARDOE, R. AND D., *The Female Pope: The Mystery of Pope Joan: The First Complete Documentation of the Facts behind the Legend*, Wellingborough, 1988

PASTOR, L. VON, *History of the Popes from the Close of the Middle Ages*, 40 vols, London, 1891–1953

PETRARCH, F., *Petrarch at Vaucluse: Letters in Verse and Prose*, tr. E.H. Wilkins, Chicago, 1968

PIUS II, POPE, *Memoirs of a Renaissance Pope: The Commentaries of Pius II*, tr. F.A. Gragg, London, 1960

PLATINA, B., *The Lives of the Popes*, ed. and tr. W. Benham, London, 1888

POLLARD, J.F., *The Unknown Pope: Benedict XV (1914–1922) and the Pursuit of Peace*, London, 1999

——*The Vatican and Italian Fascism, 1929–32: A Study in Conflict*, Cambridge, 1985

POPE-HENNESSY, J., *Fra Angelico*, London, 1952

POWELL, J.M. (ed.), *Innocent III*, Washington, DC, 1994

RANKE, L. VON, *History of the Popes in the 16th and 17th Centuries*, London, 1847

RENOUARD, Y., *The Avignon Papacy*, London, 1970

RHODES, A., *The Vatican in the Age of the Dictators, 1922–45*, London, 1973

RHOIDIS, E., *Pope Joan, a Romantic Biography*, tr. L. Durrell, London, 1954

RICHARDS, J., *The Popes and the Papacy in the Early Middle Ages*, London, 1979

ROYAL, R., *The Pope's Army: 500 years of the Papal Swiss Guard*, New York, 2006

RUNCIMAN, S., *The Eastern Schism*, Oxford, 1955

——*History of the Crusades*, 3 vols, Cambridge, 1951–4

RUSTICI, C.M., *The Afterlife of Pope Joan: Deploying the Popess Legend in Early Modern England*, Ann Arbor, 2006

SELWYN, E.G., *The First Epistle of St Peter*, London, 1946

SPANHEIM, F., *Histoire de la Papesse Joanno*, tr. J. Lenfant, 2 vols, The Hague, 1720

STANFORD, P., *The She-Pope: A Quest for the Truth behind the Mystery of Pope Joan*, London, 1998

THOMAS, G. AND MORGAN-WITTS, M., *Pontiff*, London, 1984

TILLMANN, H., *Pope Innocent III*, tr. W. Sax, Amsterdam, 1980

TOYNBEE, J.M.C. and WARD PERKINS, J., *The Shrine of St Peter and the Vatican Excavations*, London, 1956

TREASE, G., *The Condottieri: Soldiers of Fortune*, London, 1970

TUCHMAN, B., *The March of Folly: From Troy to Vietnam*, New York, 1984

ULLMANA, W., *The Growth of Papal Government in the Middle Ages*, London, 1962

——*The Origins of the Great Schism*, London, 1948

——*A Short History of the Papacy in the Middle Ages*, London, 1972

ZAMOYSKI, A., *The Polish Way*, London, 1987

ZIEGLER, P., *The Black Death*, London, 1969

List of popes and antipopes

Antipopes are given in italics. Dates of popes in the first two centuries are approximate; all concluding dates represent the end of the papal reign, rather than that of the pope's death or deposition/retirement.

PAPAL NAME	ORIGINAL NAME	PAPAL DATES
I St Peter		
Peter	Simon/Symeon	?–c.64
Linus		67–76
Anacletus		76–88
Clement I		88–97
Evaristus		97–105
II Defenders of the City		
Alexander I		105–15
Sixtus I		115–25
Telesphorus		125–36
Hyginus		136–40
Pius I		140–55
Anicetus		155–66
Soter		166–75
Eleutherius		175–89
Victor I		189–99
Zephyrinus		199–217
Callistus I		217–22
Hippolytus (antipope)		*217–35*
Urban I		222–30
Pontian		230–5
Anterus		235–6
Fabian		236–50
Cornelius		251–3
Novatian (antipope)		*251*
Lucius		253–4
Stephen I		254–7

Vigilius	537–55
Pelagius I	556–61
John III	561–74

IV Gregory the Great

Benedict I	575–9
Pelagius II	579–90
Gregory I (the Great)	590–604
Sabinian	604–6
Boniface III	607
Boniface IV	608–15
Deusdedit I (Adeodatus I)	615–18
Boniface V	619–25
Honorius I	625–38
Severinus	640
John IV	640–2
Theodore I	642–9

V Leo III and Charlemagne

Martin I	649–53
Eugenius I	654–7
Vitalian	657–72
Adeodatus II	672–6
Donus	676–8
Agatho	678–81
Leo II	682–3
Benedict II	684–5
John V	685–6
Conon	686–7
Sergius I	687–701
Theodore (antipope)	687
Paschal (antipope)	687
John VI	701–5
John VII	705–7
Sisinnius	708
Constantine	708–15
Gregory II	715–31
Gregory III	731–41
Zachary	741–52
Stephen II	752–7
Paul I	757–67
Constantine II (antipope)	767–8
Philip (antipope)	768

Stephen III	768–72
Hadrian I	772–95
Leo III	795–816
Stephen IV	816–17
Paschal I	817–24
Eugenius II	824–7
Valentine	827
Gregory IV	827–44
John (antipope)	*844*
Sergius II	844–7
Leo IV	847–55

VI Pope Joan

[Joan	?855–7]
Benedict III	855–8
Anastasius (antipope)	*855*

VII Nicholas I and the Pornocracy

Nicholas I (the Great)	858–67
Hadrian II	867–72
John VIII	872–82
Marinus I	882–4
Hadrian III	884–5
Stephen V	885–91
Formosus	891–6
Boniface VI	896
Stephen VI	896–7
Romanus	897
Theodore II	897
John IX	898–900
Benedict IV	900–3
Leo V	903
Christopher (antipope)	*903–4*
Sergius III	904–11
Anastasius III	911–13
Lando	913–14
John X	914–28
Leo VI	928
Stephen VII	928–31
John XI	931–5
Leo VII	936–9
Stephen VIII	939–42
Marinus II	942–6

Agapetus II		946–55
John XII		955–64
Leo VIII		963–5

VIII Schism

Benedict V		964
John XIII		965–72
Benedict VI		973–4
Boniface VII (antipope)		974, 984–5
Benedict VII		974–83
John XIV	Peter Canepanova	983–4
John XV	John Crescentius	985–96
Gregory V	Bruno of Carinthia	996–9
John XVI (antipope)	*John Philagathos*	*997–8*
Sylvester II	Gerbert of Aurillac	999–1003
John XVII	John Sicco	1003
John XVIII	John Fasanus	1003–9
Sergius IV	Pietro Buccaporca	1009–12
Gregory VI (antipope)		*1012*
Benedict VIII	Theophylact II of Tusculum	1012–24
John XIX	Romanus of Tusculum	1024–32
Benedict IX	Theophylact III of Tusculum	1032–45, 1047–8
Sylvester III	John of Sabina	1045
Gregory VI	John Gratian	1045–6
Clement II	Suidger of Bamberg	1046–7
Damasus II	Poppo of Brixen	1048
Leo IX	Bruno of Egisheim	1049–54

IX Gregory VII and the Normans

Victor II	Gebhard of Dollnstein-Hirschberg	1055–7
Stephen IX	Frederick of Lorraine	1057–8
Benedict X (antipope)	*John Mincius*	*1058–9*
Nicholas II	Gérard of Lorraine	1058–61
Alexander II	Anselm of Baggio	1061–73
Honorius II (antipope)	*Peter Cadalus*	*1061–4*
Gregory VII	Hildebrand	1073–85

X Innocent and Anacletus

Clement III (antipope)	*Guibert of Ravenna*	*1080, 1084–1100*
Victor III	Desiderius of Monte Cassino	1086–7
Urban II	Odo of Lagery	1088–99
Paschal II	Rainerius of Bieda	1099–1118
Theodoric (antipope)		*1100–1*

Albert (Aleric) (antipope)		*1101–2*
Sylvester IV (antipope)	*Maginulf*	*1105–11*
Gelasius II	John of Gaeta	1118–9
Gregory VIII (antipope)	*Maurice Burdanus*	*1118–21*
Calixtus II	Guido of Burgundy	1119–24
Honorius II	Lambert Scannabecchi	1124–30
Celestine II (antipope)	*Teobaldo*	*1124*
Innocent II	Gregorio Papareschi	1130–43
Anacletus II (antipope)	*Pietro Pierleoni*	*1130–8*
Victor IV (antipope)	*Gregorio Conti*	*1138*

XI The English Pope

Celestine II	Guido di Castello	1143–4
Lucius II	Gherardo Caccianemici	1144–5
Eugenius III	Bernardo Pignatelli	1145–53
Anastasius IV	Conrad of Rome	1153–4
Hadrian IV	Nicholas Breakspear	1154–9

XII Alexander III and Frederick Barbarossa

Alexander III	Orlando Bandinelli	1159–81
Victor IV (antipope)	*Ottaviano of Monticelli*	*1159–64*
Paschal III (antipope)	*Guido of Crema*	*1164–8*
Callistus III (antipope)	*Giovanni of Struma*	*1168–78*
Innocent III (antipope)	*Lando of Sezze*	*1179–80*
Lucius III	Ubaldo Allucingoli	1181–5
Urban III	Umberto Crivelli	1185–7
Gregory VIII	Alberto di Morra	1187
Clement III	Paulo Scolari	1187–91
Celestine III	Giacinto Boboni	1191–8

XIII Innocent III

Innocent III	Lotario di Segni	1198–1216

XIV The End of the Hohenstaufen

Honorius III	Cencio Savelli	1216–27
Gregory IX	Ugolino of Ostia	1227–41
Celestine IV	Goffredo da Castiglione	1241
Innocent IV	Sinibaldo dei Fieschi	1243–54
Alexander VI	Rainaldo dei Conti di Segni	1254–61
Urban IV	Jacques Pantaléon	1261–4
Clement IV	Guy Foulques	1265–8
Gregory X	Tedaldo Visconti	1271–6
Innocent V	Pierre of Tarantaise	1276

Hadrian V	Ottobono Fieschi	1276
John XXI	Pedro Juliano	1276-7
Nicholas III	Giovanni Gaetano Orsini	1277-80
Martin IV	Simon de Brie	1281-5
Honorius IV	Giacomo Savelli	1285-7
Nicholas IV	Girolamo Masci	1288-92
Celestine V	Pietro del Morrone	1294
Boniface VIII	Benedetto Caetani	1294-1303

XV Avignon

Benedict XI	Niccolo Boccasino	1303-4
Clement V	Bertrand de Got	1305-14
John XXII	Jacques Duèse	1316-34
Nicholas V (antipope)	*Pietro Rainalducci*	*1328-30*
Benedict XII	Jacques Fournier	1334-42
Clement VI	Pierre Roger	1342-52
Innocent VI	Etienne Aubert	1352-62
Urban V	Guillaume de Grimoard	1362-70
Gregory XI	Pierre-Roger de Beaufort	1370-8

XVI Laetentur Coeli!

Urban VI	Bartolomeo Prignano	1378-89
Clement VII (antipope)	*Robert of Geneva*	*1378-94*
Boniface IX	Pietro Tomacelli	1389-1404
Benedict XIII (antipope)	*Pedro de Luna*	*1394-1417*
Innocent VII	Cosimo Gentile dei Migliorati	1404-6
Gregory XII	Angelo Correr	1406-15
Alexander V (antipope)	*Pietro Philarghi*	*1409-10*
John XXIII (antipope)	*Baldassare Cossa*	*1410-15*
Martin V	Oddone Colonna	1417-31
Clement VIII (antipope)	*Gil Sanchez Munoz*	*1423-9*
Benedict XIV (antipope)	*Bernard Garier*	*1425-?*
Eugenius IV	Gabriele Condulmer	1431-47
Felix V (antipope)	*Amadeus VIII of Savoy*	*1439-49*

XVII The Renaissance

Nicholas V	Tommaso Parentucelli	1447-55
Calixtus III	Alfonso de Borja (Borgia)	1455-8
Pius II	Aeneas Silvius Piccolomini	1458-64
Paul II	Pietro Barbo	1464-71
Sixtus IV	Francesco della Rovere	1471-84
Innocent VIII	Giambattistata Cibo	1484-92

XVIII The Monsters

Alexander VI	Rodrigo Borgia	1492–1503
Pius III	Francesco Todeschini-Piccolomini	1503
Julius II	Giuliano della Rovere	1503–13

XIX The Medici Pair

Leo X	Giovanni de' Medici	1513–21
Hadrian VI	Adrian Florensz Dedal	1522–3
Clement VII	Giulio de' Medici	1523–34

XX The Counter-Reformation

Paul III	Alessandro Farnese	1534–49
Julius III	Giovanni Maria Ciocchi del Monte	1550–5
Marcellus II	Marcello Cervini	1555
Paul IV	Giampietro Carafa	1555–9
Pius IV	Giovanni Angelo Medici	1559–65
Pius V	Michele Ghislieri	1566–72
Gregory XIII	Ugo Boncompagni	1572–85
Sixtus V	Felice Peretti	1585–90
Urban VII	Giambattista Castagna	1590
Gregory XIV	Nicolo Sfondrati	1590–1
Innocent IX	Giovanni Antonio Fachinetti	1591
Clement VIII	Ippolito Aldobrandini	1592–1605

XXI Baroque Rome

Leo XI	Alessandro de' Medici	1605
Paul V	Camillo Borghese	1605–21
Gregory XV	Alessandro Ludovisi	1621–3
Urban VIII	Maffeo Barberini	1623–44
Innocent X	Giambattista Pamfili	1644–55
Alexander VII	Fabio Chigi	1655–67
Clement IX	Giulio Rospigliosi	1667–9
Clement X	Emilio Altieri	1670–6
Innocent XI	Benedetto Odescalchi	1676–89
Alexander VIII	Pietro Ottoboni	1689–91
Innocent XII	Antonio Pignatelli	1691–1700

XXII The Age of Reason

Clement XI	Gian Francesco Albani	1700–21
Innocent XIII	Michelangelo de' Conti	1721–4
Benedict XIII	Pietro Francesco Orsini-Gravina	1724–30
Clement XII	Lorenzo Corsini	1730–40
Benedict XIV	Prospero Lorenzo Lambertini	1740–58

XXIII The Jesuits and the Revolution

Clement XIII	Carlo della Torre Rezzonico	1758–69
Clement XIV	Lorenzo Ganganelli	1769–74
Pius VI	Giovanni Angelo Braschi	1775–99

XXIV Progress and Reaction

Pius VII	Barnaba Chiaramonti	1800–23
Leo XII	Annibale Sermattei della Genga	1823–9
Pius VIII	Francesco Saverio Castiglione	1829–30
Gregory XVI	Bartolomeo Albreto Cappellari	1831–46

XXV Pio Nono

Pius IX	Giovanni Maria Mastai-Ferretti	1846–78

XXVI Leo XIII and the First World War

Leo XIII	Gioacchino Vincenzo Pecci	1878–1903
Pius X	Giuseppe Sarto	1903–14
Benedict XV	Giacomo della Chiesa	1914–22

XXVII Pius XI and Pius XII

Pius XI	Achille Ratti	1922–39
Pius XII	Eugenio Pacelli	1939–58

XXVIII Vatican II and After

John XXIII	Angelo Giuseppe Roncalli	1958–63
Paul VI	Giovanni Battista Montini	1963–78
John Paul I	Albino Luciani	1978
John Paul II	Karol Wojtyla	1978–2005
Benedict XVI	Joseph Ratzinger	2005–

Index

Visconti, Filippo Maria, Duke of
Milan 231
Visconti, Duchess Valentina 257
Visconti family 210, 217
Visigoths 19, 43
Vitelleschi, Giovanni 231
Viterbo 185, 187 *and n*, 210,
214, 224, 265, 300
Vitiges, King of the Goths 27
Voltaire 352, 354, 364*n*
Mahomet 352*n*
Volturno, battle of the (1860)
394, 395
Vulgate, the 18, 315

Wałęsa, Lech 447
Walpole, Horace 352
War of the Austrian Succession
(1740–48) 347, 349
War of the Spanish Succession
(1701–14) 340
Weizsäcker, Baron Ernst von
431–2
Wenceslas, King of Bohemia 226
White Mountain, battle of
(1620) 323
Wilhelm II, Kaiser 424
William I (the Conqueror), of
England 104
William I, of the Netherlands
380
William I (the Bad), of Sicily
143, 144, 145, 146–7, 151,
157, 160*n*
William II (William Rufus), of
England 115
William II (the Good), of Sicily
159, 160, 161
William III (William of Orange),
of England 332

William X, Duke of Aquitaine
124
Williamson, Bishop Richard
450
Winchelsey, Robert, Archbishop
of Canterbury 196
Winckelmann, Johann Joachim
352
Wolsey, Cardinal Thomas 287
women priests, ordination of
448, 451
World Council of Churches
(1969) 443
World War, First 411, 412–13,
424–5, 427
World War, Second 419, 426–7,
428–34, 438, 439
Worms
Concordat of (1122) 118–19
General Council (1076) 106–7
Wotton, Sir Henry 318
Wycliffe, John 226

Yad Vashem Holocaust
Memorial, papal visits to
448*n*, 450*n*
Yallop, David: *In God's Name*
446
Yolande de Brienne, Queen of
Jerusalem 175, 176, 178,
184

Zachary, Pope (741–52) 50, 51,
65
Zachary (prelate) 70–71
Zara (Dalmatia) 166
Zebedee 1
Zeno, Byzantine Emperor 25
Ziani, Sebastiano, Doge of
Venice 156, 157